WE, THE ALIEN

WE, THE ALIEN

AN INTRODUCTION TO CULTURAL ANTHROPOLOGY

Paul Bohannan

Consulting Editor: Martha C. Ward

WAVELAND

PRESS, INC.

Long Grove, Illinois

For information about this book, contact:
Waveland Press, Inc.
4180 IL Route 83, Suite 101
Long Grove, IL 60047-9580
(847) 634-0081
info@waveland.com
www.waveland.com

to

LISA

We, The Alien

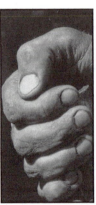

Contents

Preface

Textbooks are a difficult literary form. The author of a textbook is writing for two audiences: students and professors. It's something like children's books. Children don't buy books—adults buy books to give to children; the challenge, therefore, is to write a book that adults will buy and that children will like. College students do indeed buy textbooks, but they *don't* select them—professors do. The task is to cover what the professor thinks students should know, in a way congenial to the professor, at the same time that students find it interesting and worthwhile.

Biographies follow a life; good nonfiction follows an argument; novels follow a story. But a textbook must have the temerity to outline a whole discipline; that outline must be constantly recreated as the discipline grows and as research emphases change. A textbook should be original without being quirky or idiosyncratic.

The basic job of a textbook is not only to include the right stuff, but to get it in the right order—an order that makes repetition unnecessary, and that makes the subject grow from idea to idea. You have to be a generalist even to contemplate writing an introductory text, and genuine generalists are fairly rare birds. However, the introductory textbook is the major forum for synthesizing anthropological ideas. That may be a pity, but it's true.

Like a dramatist or a composer, a textbook writer knows that an "interpreter" is necessary—the professor who stands between the writer and the intended audience. The book must give the professor plenty of room to expand, to disagree, to personalize, to start arguments—to do things with the material that the author never even thought about. This is something like the difference between a novel and a play. A novelist is in direct contact with his reader, but a playwright has to write so that actors can make the contact. The actor's contribution is a vital part of the whole.

Right here, I cast a challenge: at the beginning of each chapter, you will find, stated as clearly as I can state them, my values and the premises that underlie my arguments. Disagree with these premises if you can! But remember, your disagreement must be based on facts and reasoning that can stand up to the possibility of disproof, not on some unexamined cultural prejudice or on the kind of "common sense" that is neither common nor sensible. If you can't do that, then you have either to deal with the premises as given or drop out.

The title of this book—*We, the Alien*—needs explaining. Students, like everybody else, need to realize that they too have a culture. Of the many strange cultures of the world, ours may be among the strangest—at least, we might as well get used to the fact that the world is full of people who think so. When I first began this book several years ago, I used "We, the Alien" as a heading to set off examples from our own society. But the idea of "seeing ourselves as others see us" became increasingly important as I wrote. It finally became the title of the book as well as the heading for examples from American culture. The other items set off in the text, marked "They Said It," are quotations from authors who have made a point so well that I cannot make the same point without diminishing it.

The captions below the photos, figures and other illustrations are arranged in such a way that, read in succession, they form a summary of the chapter. They are meant to assist you in reviewing. You may be able to pass the tests on the captions—but don't try it because you'll get only a C at best.

Professors don't need as much encouragement to disagree with the text as most students do. I request not only that they follow the same procedures as I outlined above but also that they write to me to correct my errors or to provide better examples.

The Teacher's Manual that accompanies this textbook gives information as up-to-date as we can get it about films to illuminate each chapter, and where to order them. The Manual also contains a large bank of sample examination questions. Good examinations are an integral part of the learning experience but creating them takes time. Teachers who have to teach four courses (some places even more), do research, perform university service and community service—then shop and cook and help their children with their homework and mow the lawn and fix the car when they get home—need all the help they can get. However, we have not created the kind of examinations that can be ripped out, xeroxed, and "administered." The collaboration between author and teacher means that the professor's input into the quiz and exam questions is vital.

Finally, remember that anthropology is fun because it stretches your imagination and gives you new insights about yourself and the weird way your culture (whatever it is) does things. In that way, it gives you a base for broadening your life and savoring your experience.

Enjoy!

What you perceive depends on your vantage point. Changing your vantage point expands perception.
The most dangerous assumption: to presume that you already understand.

WE, THE ALIEN

PEOPLE

I

People are good at communicating meanings and abstract ideas. They have also taken an ability to use tools to a high plane. This talent for tools and meaning is the basis of culture; it separates us from other animals. Human beings share some of the social principles—principles on which their society is organized—with many other creatures of the animal kingdom. But people have added complex social customs as well as complex meanings.

Anthropology is about people—their tools and their meanings. Its value to you is that it allows you, by learning how other people do things, to broaden your own choices and options.

People have to learn culture. Although the capacity to learn is inborn, what is actually learned always results from what is in their environment.

Cultural anthropologists are people too—but they bring to the humanity they share with every other living person a conviction that there are many good ways to solve the problems and to enjoy the rewards of living. Each of those ways can be enriched if we learn some other ways to compare it with. We spend all of our lives learning culture. Anthropologists make a special attempt to learn other people's culture so that their own becomes constantly more meaningful.

Books to Change Your Life   *Martha C. Ward*

Students like you often fall in love with anthropology and ask us what else you can read. Alternatively, you may have a term paper to do and want some ideas and references. To give you some help we have included a list of possible readings at the beginning of each major section of this textbook. These lists are just a tiny portion of the many wonderful books available to you. Consider them an appetizer selection before the main courses. Your anthropology professor may disagree with our selection and give you a list of books he or she believes are equally exciting and important. You may have found books in the bookstore or library that suit you even better. Meanwhile, good reading!

Anderson, Barbara Gallatin

1990 *First Fieldwork: The Misadventures of an Anthropologist*. Prospect Heights, IL: Waveland Press, Inc. This is a readable and funny confession about the author's first experience in doing enthnography. It's more exciting to start reading about anthropology when you select an "ethnography without tears."

Auel, Jean M.

1980 *The Clan of the Cave Bear*. New York: Crown Publishers (Random House).
1982 *The Valley of the Horses*. New York: Crown Publishers (Random House).
1985 *The Mammoth Hunters*. New York: Crown Publishers (Random House).
1990 *Plains of Passage*. New York: Crown Publishers (Random House).

Yes, these are all bestselling novels. Many anthropologists read them; most enjoy them; some anthropologists recommend them to others. A few of us even wish we had written them. You will learn a lot about the problems of making culture, social organization, technology, ritual, animals, plants and the survival of our species in the long-distant past. Be warned: a few anthropologists will disapprove of these books being on this list at all, and no anthropologist believes that sex in the Old Stone Age was as thrilling as this!

Bowen, Elenore Smith (Laura Bohannan)

1954 *Return to Laughter: An Anthropological Novel* (with Foreword by David Riesmann). New York: Harper & Bros. Reissued 1964 by Doubleday & Co., Inc., New York. This novel, written under a pseudonym by Laura Bohannan, at one time married to the author of this textbook, is about the Tiv although that tribal name is never mentioned. Many generations of anthropology students first learned about the delights and dilemmas of fieldwork from this book.

Goodall, Jane

1988 *In the Shadow of Man, Revised Edition*. Boston: Houghton Mifflin Co. The pioneering fieldwork of Jane Goodall is one of the great adventures of modern science. Her style of presenting the culture and society of chimps, our nearest living relatives, has entertained millions as well as revolutionizing anthropology. The lives of Flo, David Graybeard and other chimpanzees of the Gombe National Park in Tanzania have engrossed readers of three decades. Goodall has also written extensively for *National Geographic* over the years. She has written prize-winning children's books. The scientific summary of the first twenty-five years of her work is to be found in *The Chimpanzees of Gombe: Patterns of Behavior*, Cambridge, MA: Belknap Press, 1986.

Powdermaker, Hortense

1966 *Stranger and Friend: The Way of an Anthropologist*. New York: W.W. Norton & Co., Inc. Powdermaker was one of the first to write a good book about her four fieldwork jobs. It is straightforward, honest, and engaging. This is the way it really was for a hard-working and original anthropologist who became one of the really great people of all time.

Ward, Martha C.

1989 *Nest in the Wind: Adventures in Anthropology on a Tropical Island*. Prospect Heights, IL: Waveland Press, Inc. This personal story about fieldwork on a Pacific island is described by its author as a shameless attempt to seduce students into the romance and excitement of doing anthropology. From culture shock and dead pigs to pregnancy and giant yams, you can see how research really gets done.

Anthropology, Culture and Society

1

PROPOSITIONS AND PREMISES

- Human beings are primate mammals who have, in the course of evolution, adopted culture as their major means of adaptation.

- Human beings have "culturized" all their behavior, which sets them apart from other animals.

- There are thus two general categories of culture:

    culturized animal behavior: concepts such as kinship and power—now so thoroughly culturized that they are scarcely recognizable as "animal"

    pure culture: concepts such as thought and meaning—which have little or nothing to do with animal behavior

- Culture is (with minor exceptions for the protoculture of chimps and probably other animals) a human prerogative. Where you draw the line between culture and learned behavior is purely a matter of anthropological decision. Human society, on the other hand, is *not* a human prerogative. Human beings share some basic organizational principles with nonhuman societies. Humans, using culture, have also added new organizational principles.

3

As a young man, I discovered anthropology with a sense of relief—I could see almost instantly that if I became an anthropologist, I would give up fewer of the things I wanted to do in my life than would have been true for any other career. I still think that is the case. I wanted to travel and to write. I wanted to learn foreign languages so I could find out how other peoples live. I wanted to be sure that I experienced everything—I wanted it all. But I also wanted a secure job in which I could control at least some of my own time and my own destiny. Anthropology has given me those things.

Anthropology has also given me some other things which I hadn't bargained for. They may be even more important:

- Anthropology demands that a person constantly reassess what he or she stands for.
- Anthropology provides a firm foundation to stand on as we look critically at our own **society** and at global society. Looking critically does not mean carping or finding fault— it means looking at events and trends from a broader point of view and seeing what works and what doesn't. Anthropology offers a basis for forming ideas and for understanding political and social processes, both in history and at the present time.
- Anthropology trains observers as well as active participants.
- Anthropology encourages us to question every value we hold. I now hold my values because of my own thought-out conviction, not because I just stumbled into them or because I learned them from my parents (although some are the ones I learned from my parents).

Anthropology frees you. Indeed, it sometimes forces freedom upon you even when you'd rather not have it. One of the great privileges of living is liberating oneself from comfortably routine—but limiting—behavior.

The word anthropology is derived from the Greek words meaning "the study (logos) of human beings (anthropos)." As you begin this cultural anthropology course, you should have some idea about what anthropologists do, about what students of anthropology can be expected to learn, and why the undertaking is worthwhile.

WHAT ANTHROPOLOGISTS THINK AND DO

Learning

Cultural anthropologists must first learn some basics about human beings if they are going to study them. We begin with physical aspects—the study of human biology.

Anthropologists must also learn something about the process of learning. We evolve continually and adapt to newly gained information. One major aspect of human evolution is language; we must understand what language has done for us.

Two of the most important aspects of human life are the use of tools and the search for meaning in life. Anthro-

pologists study both and ask questions such as: Why is there such a great range of variation in tools used by various peoples? Why do some cultures choose one set of meanings to explain people's actions and intentions while other cultures choose another?

Anthropologists not only have to learn strange tools and new meanings, but they must also realize that their prior knowledge may interfere with new learning about other ways to do things or to think about meanings. We must examine the context of any action or any idea. The importance of context is an essential message of anthropology.

Anthropology will make you question your deepest values. But remember, anthropologists are not missionaries trying to make converts to any specific belief. The point is not necessarily to change your views, but rather to listen to other people's views. You can then look clearly at your own views from somebody else's perspective. Your views probably appear as wrong-headed, even silly, to others as theirs do to you. To them, you are the alien.

Questioning your own views is not a dangerous process. *Not* questioning your own views and values from time to time may be a very dangerous business.

Fieldwork

After exploring these basic issues, cultural anthropologists then proceed to the most exciting learning experience they (or anybody else) can have: they go to the field. The "field" may be anywhere in the world where you can find a group

1-1. *Anthropology gives one a place to stand, other than one's own culture, while one learns and examines what it means to be human. Your own culture does not— cannot—provide an adequate guide to understand the culture of other people. Anthropology tries to provide that guide—a guidebook to the human condition. Here anthropologist Alice Beck Kehoe was asked by Aymara women of Bolivia to help them celebrate planting seed potatoes in their new fields. They supplied the Aymara woman's outfit for her.*

of people whose lives are very different from your own. While anthropologists often prefer to go to distant places and to learn new languages, you can find "foreign" ways of living by going around any city block or taking a drive in the country, no matter where you are. In the field, an anthropologist learns a new language, even if it is a dialect of his or her own. As you begin to use the new language and to adjust your behavior to these different people, something interesting happens. Because you are living by a new set of rules while in the field, you become another kind of person. While it can be exciting, it can also be deeply threatening to see what kind of person you become in a strange society. You become an alien. However, you can walk away from the alienness—you can go home again. The field offers the best way to find out about yourself and about both the freedoms your culture gives you and the restrictions it puts on you.

The first rule for doing anthropological fieldwork is that you take your cues for what is significant from the people whom you are studying. You find out what they think is important. It does not mean that you give up your own views, but rather that you set them aside while you examine theirs.

You have to give up most of your comforts and learn to enjoy new ones. That may be difficult. A few people can't manage it. To be an anthropologist means several things—some serious, some trivial. First of all, you should be able to eat almost anything that the people you are studying eat. If you are too squeamish, you miss a lot—and your new peers will see you as somebody who really isn't willing or able to go all the way in learning their ways and values.

In the field you learn the tools and the meanings of the new culture—what they value. By keeping close track of your own emotional reactions, you learn a lot about your own values that you might not have recognized until they were challenged. Anthropologists are convinced that you cannot truly understand your own values until they have been tested by fire. Fieldwork provides the fire.

In 1950, I was doing fieldwork among the Tiv of central Nigeria. I had houses built in a Tiv compound of about eighty people; various other compounds, some of them smaller, were scattered around the countryside among the farms. Tiv assistants (not interpreters, for they knew little English) helped me with my work.

One evening, one of those assistants came back from having his bath in the local river—we all bathed in the streams. He poked his head into my hut to tell me he had returned. I asked what had happened. He replied, "Not much. A man drowned."

I instantly sprang to attention. "What? Drowned?"

"You know that place in the river where the bottom drops off? Well, he was a stranger. He stepped off that ledge and he couldn't swim."

"Didn't anybody save him? Didn't *you* try to save him?" (I knew him to be a strong swimmer.)

The reply was devastating: "He wasn't mine."

I understood well enough what he meant: Tiv go out of the way to do services for kinfolk, but not for just anybody. I found myself hating him and his values because I had been brought up to think that a human life is a human life, no matter whose it is. I thought—and still think—it would have cost him very little to rescue that stranger.

A few weeks later, when I was talking to that same assistant about Tiv families, I mentioned that I had not seen my mother for almost five years. He looked at me in horror. "You mean you do not go home to help your mother?" I tried to tell him that we wrote letters, that we were in touch every week or so, that she did not need my help. My explanations did no good. He was as outraged by my values as I was by his. After thinking about it off and on for years, I still think mine are better. He undoubtedly still thinks his are better.

While studying Tiv religion, I had an opportunity to become a diviner. Among the Tiv, a diviner is a person who has drunk medicines and learned to use some ritual equipment so that he can understand causes and forces that are hidden from ordinary people. To become a diviner, I underwent a ritual initiation. There were invocations and chants. I had to drink several different medicines made from roots and leaves. At the climax, my teacher sacrificed a chicken—he held the body of the chicken and cut its throat while I held its head. I still remember the sensation that the chicken was swallowing as its neck muscles contracted. My teacher then quickly cut out the heart of the chicken and fed it—still beating—to me. I swallowed it whole. The life force in the chicken heart was meant to activate all the medicines I previously swallowed. I don't think this process made me clairvoyant, but I do think it made me a better anthropologist. I had experienced a ritual in which the Tiv put great store; I learned in a new and personal way what the life force meant to them. It's meaning for me was thus vastly enriched.

Since anthropologists can never learn everything about the people they study, how do they know when their fieldwork is finished? It has been suggested that once the people you are studying can understand three out of four of the jokes you make in their language, you can come home. If you have taken good notes, you have enough data for several books.

Ethnography

Now comes the hard part. Once you have done your fieldwork, you have to communicate what you have learned so that people in your own culture can understand it. Keep in mind that you are telling your friends and readers what is important to the people you were studying.

The field-working anthropologist's writing is called an **ethnography**. The first decision is what topic to write about first—what will be the most important and basic part of the ethnography? Let us say it is the economy. You now should learn as much about economics and the economy of your own culture as you learned about the economy in your field study. You have to be sure that specialists in your own culture do not misunderstand you, even if they disagree. There may also be some good ideas in your own economy that will

illuminate what you learned in the field—but remember that ideas and terms used to explain institutions in one's own society will not necessarily translate directly to the field economy. The danger is that you will warp the field ideas to fit into Western economics—they *may* fit, but they also may not!

You must, in other words, translate what you know about the field into English. It is a treacherous task for the same reason that translating poetry is treacherous. The words in the two languages may cover similar territory, but the overlap is probably never precise. The two languages almost surely will differ so that literal translation is not possible.

Life After the Field

The modes of working that you develop in fieldwork are habit forming. You will keep right on observing carefully when you get home. The more you participate, the more opportunity you have to observe. All this observation doesn't mean that you can understand other people or other institutions just by observing, but it does mean that you can put your judgment on hold while you give yourself a chance to understand what you observe.

Your own culture thus becomes your guide but not your limitation. You have learned that it is not merely others who are the alien. We are ourselves the alien. Slowly we will come to the realization that *nobody* is alien. We are all human—nothing is really alien to us unless we limit ourselves enough to make it so. Limitations create aliens.

The Anthropological Attitude

Once you have studied anthropology, you can never again look at the world from one single point of view. You are no longer a "monocult"—my adaptation from monoglot, who is a person who speaks only one language. A monocult always sees the world and his or her experience from a single standpoint. The richness of that experience is never fully understood and cherished if there is nothing with which to compare it. Knowing two or more cultures—even just knowing that there are many cultures—provides you with

◄1-2. The anthropological attitude gives us a sort of binocular vision: we see simultaneously from the point of view of our own culture and the point of view of the culture of the people we are observing. We can also see from the point of view of several cultures at once. People in all cultures cook—but this Nigerian woman prepares food very differently from the Italian American grandmother who is making pasta. Everybody who wears clothes has to keep them clean, but the Tarahumara woman (in north central Mexico) has a very different washday experience from the old woman in the Portuguese village as they both do the family wash.

something like binocular vision. You will have two sets of lenses through which to view yourself and your culture. The foreground stands out; the background becomes clear, and the enrichment is stunning. You realize that living with only one culture, one way of doing things, is a prison. When you expand your perspective, some of the walls of your cultural prison will disappear.

Anthropology is the best way I know to make people more wholly human. It reveals what a privilege it is—and how much fun it is—to be human.

THE FOUR BASIC FIELDS OF ANTHROPOLOGY

There are four major components of anthropology. Each focuses on a different aspect of the human being.

Physical Anthropology or Biological Anthropology

As we mentioned earlier, anthropologists are concerned with the human animal. To understand that dimension, we have to know something about animals. The subfield of anthropology concerned with the biological dimension is **physical anthropology** or **biological anthropology**. Many physical anthropologists work in medical schools. Other physical anthropologists are geneticists. Understanding human genetics has generally replaced the earlier concern of physical anthropologists with races. Population genetics of human beings is also an important specialization. Still other biological anthropologists study the behavior of non-human **primates** such as monkeys and apes. A thorough understanding of closely related species can help us grasp the evolution of all primates, including human beings.

Cultural Anthropology

The focus of **cultural anthropology** is not on the human animal but on two important characteristics of the human animal: tools and meaning. Although chimpanzees and perhaps other animals use crude tools, humankind has turned toolmaking into a specialty. A tool is something that is manufactured in order to create or to achieve something else. Tools may be contrivances like hoes, screwdrivers, or machines. But tools may also be ideas. And, importantly, tools may be social devices and inventions like governments, specialized social groups to achieve economic production or religious enlightenment, or many other organizations for specific purposes.

Meaning has to do with intention or purpose. A look into any dictionary should convince you that "tool" and "meaning" are words that are so basic as to be almost impossible to define. Human beings create words and other symbols to assign meaning. They use myths and theories to organize it. Tools and meaning are absolutely basic to the study of cultural anthropology and we shall come back to them again and again.

1-3. Anthropology is divided into four main branches.

◄ Archaeology is concerned with the prehistory of both human beings and their culture. The nature of archaeological data means that, although some tools can be discovered, meaning must be implied.

Linguistics studies human speech and other forms of communication. It implies comparisons with the communication systems of other species, hence is interested both in signs and in symbol systems.

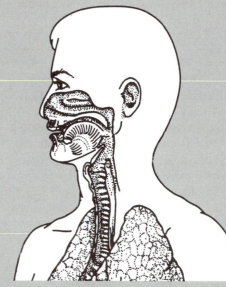

Physical anthropology or biological anthropology studies the physical aspects of the human body. It implies comparisons across species, especially other species of primates such as the chimpanzee shown here. Its major theoretical orientation is biological evolution.

Cultural anthropology studies human culture. Culture is ►
both the ideas held by people and the manifestation of those ideas in act and artifact. In other words, culture includes tools (including social tools) and meanings.

Linguistics

Language is the most important vehicle by which human beings create, understand and communicate meaning. All animals, including human beings, communicate by non-linguistic means. But human beings also speak. Language underlies human communication. It gives communication entire ranges of meaning that cannot be reached without it.

The study of language flourished in many different academic areas, primarily philosophy departments, English departments, and foreign language departments. Anthropological linguists, at first, were primarily interested in unwritten languages, particularly non-Indo-European languages. In the early part of the twentieth century, the most significant developments in **linguistics** came from anthropology departments. Since about 1950, linguistics has declared itself to be an independent discipline, although it also remains a subfield of anthropology. Today, most linguistics departments as well as large anthropology departments have anthropological linguists. Language is a vital and important part of culture because it is the means by which people communicate about their culture. It is important, especially to cultural anthropologists, because grammar (the regularities of a language) and phonetics (the selection of particular sounds and their production) are well studied and provide a model for organizing other aspects of culture.

Archaeology

Archaeology is the study by cultural anthropologists of the material remains of past cultures. Their work is restricted to only half the culture—although the tools and their context are there to be studied, the meaning must be inferred for civilizations with no written record of history. Archaeologists study artifacts that people made and used, but they have at best only deductions about what those people thought or said or believed. Archaeologists use many of the natural sciences such as geology, biology, hydrology, the study of pollens, and others to recreate as authentically as possible the lives and environment of earlier peoples. Archaeologists also use written records if they are available.

Some archaeologists study the material culture of *living* peoples so that they can understand better the relationship between people and the things they make that will leave traces of their having lived in a place. To oversimplify, archaeologists specialize in tools and the history of toolmaking (and, of course, in the history of the evolution of the animal) much as linguists specialize in meaning.

Most cultural anthropologists spend more time with problems of meaning than they do with tools, although those who work in museums and a few others become experts in tools and their use. Meaning, which is largely hidden from archaeologists, is the essence of cultural anthropology. Cultural anthropologists have the immense advantage that they can go ask about meanings—but unfortunately they can ask only their contemporaries.

Cultural anthropology can be done with historical data as well as it can be done with ethnographic data gathered by a fieldworker—well, almost as well. Historical studies have to be done with whatever data were recorded or are archaeologically available. The ethnographic fieldworker can go out and question people about puzzling situations.

THE DYNAMICS OF CULTURAL ANTHROPOLOGY

Anthropology can make a difference in the world around us in one of two ways. It helps us to find ways to understand the *current* culture and to make it work better. The second way is to design innovative culture that will supersede current ideas—*new* culture that will change the context, including people's attitudes about cultural change.

These two ways of making a difference are equally important. The first is called practicing anthropology. It asks how we can use our present knowledge to alleviate or solve current problems. The second is far more visionary—enough so that it can be called visionary anthropology. It asks how culture can be purposefully changed in order to improve the quality of life and of the environment.

The two forms run into one another and may, of course, be carried out by the same people. The difference is in the context. The context of practicing anthropology tends to be set; it presents immediate problems that need prompt answers. The context of visionary anthropology is the scholarly study room, the library, the conference, the planning session. The major problem in transferring the ideas of visionary anthropology into practicing anthropology is the standard problem encountered by new theory: will people accept new proposals or reject them because they don't fit accepted practices?

Practicing anthropology was in its early days called applied anthropology. A practicing anthropologist works in industry, government or international agencies; practicing anthropologists distinguish themselves from academic anthropologists who make their livings by teaching. Practicing anthropology necessarily starts with the tasks that people already understand and need done. However, people do not always know that anthropology has answers for their problems. There are few if any specialties in which anthropologists are the only practitioners. Moreover, academic anthropologists have in the past been so successful in defining themselves as students of exotic, even primitive, people that many outsiders do not know that practicing anthropologists can apply the same skills that they developed in the field to industry and government.

Visionary anthropology, on the other hand, questions the existing culture in search for new forms that can be used or adapted. We know, for example, that if the Greek city states could have solved their problems by means other than destructive war, they might not have perished. We know, further, that tyrannical dictatorships perish because their

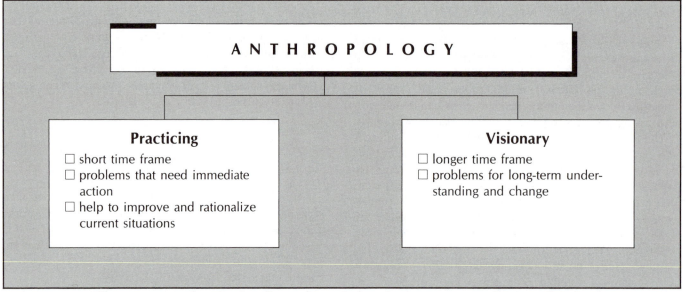

ANTHROPOLOGY

Practicing
☐ short time frame
☐ problems that need immediate action
☐ help to improve and rationalize current situations

Visionary
☐ longer time frame
☐ problems for long-term understanding and change

1-4. There are two modes of anthropology. The applied mode, practicing anthropology, is involved with current cultures and helping people utilize their current resources and beliefs to greater effect. The visionary mode, visionary anthropology, is involved with understanding human differences across a wide palette, and with criticizing long-term culture, policy, and beliefs in such a way that culture can be improved. Some anthropologists do both, and many anthropologists go from one to the other.

leaders (like three-year-olds) push the boundaries of what they can get away with until somebody overthrows them.

Practicing anthropologists must accept the rules as they are now defined. If change is to come, it must come slowly. These anthropologists accept most of the premises of the culture within which they work because they are team players; other members of the team cannot change their basic ideas or ingrained ways of doing things merely because an anthropologist asks.

Visionaries seek to identify the underlying aspects of our culture that prevent adequate solutions to far-reaching problems which may be invisible to the common person. They search beyond the recognized rules and question the ideas that support present arrangements. Sometimes the first task is to establish just what those ideas are so that they can be adequately questioned. Visionary anthropologists recompute the logic of a cultural situation, asking what would happen if other ideas were to be introduced and accepted.

Administrators need anthropology and the other social sciences in order to analyze the problems that they face daily in the course of doing their jobs. Such specialties as development anthropology and educational anthropology create programs for reeducating administrators about answers that the culture already provides. In short, some problems have to be dealt with immediately whether we know how to solve them or not. That is the practicing anthropologist's kind of problem. They necessarily deal in short-term solutions and problems because action cannot wait. Nevertheless, they may find solutions that actually change and improve the culture.

The visionaries, on the other hand, are concerned with the implications of long-term change. They are convinced

that we cannot allow ourselves merely to drift into the future. Visionaries need anthropology so that they can question everything, including their own motives and their own premises. They must separate, as thoroughly as they can, the tasks to be accomplished from the current methods under which the society and the culture are operating. They assume that the social problems that plague us are so burdened with economic and moral investments from the past as to make change impossibly expensive or that we have never created adequate culture to solve our problems.

Why Study Cultural Anthropology?

There are at least three good reasons to study cultural anthropology. The first is to discover the many different ways to lead a good life. Examining those many ways helps us clarify our own ideas. Anthropology helps us envision human beings in the sweep of space and time.

But there is an arresting second reason. Anthropology throws into relief what we are by teaching us about what we are not. Learning other cultures throws our own culture into relief, just as learning another language teaches us things we didn't know about our own language and the way of thought it imposes. Learning about other cultures not only makes us better human specimens, it makes us better citizens.

The third reason, however, may be the most compelling of all. Anthropology gives us a place to stand as we examine the new cultural and social situation that is emerging all around us. This point is especially important today when culture is changing so fast. We are in persistent danger of shrugging off new ideas and new organizations simply because we lull ourselves into thinking that they are variations of

1-5. *Just as life imparts new qualities to inert matter, so culture imparts new qualities to living matter. When the qualities of the throughput system (taking in fuel, eliminating waste) and of reproduction are added to matter, a whole new realm appears. In the same way, when tools and meaning are added to life, a whole new realm appears.*

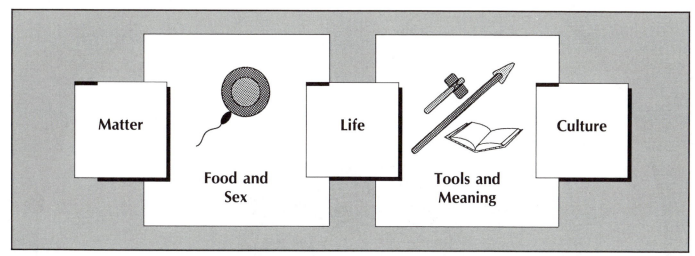

old ones. This is, as we shall see below, particularly true of social inventions. The seeds of tragedy lurk in the fact that people understand the present from the point of view of an imperfectly understood past. In fact, understanding the full implications of new culture may be the major challenge of our age.

Anthropology makes it possible for you to understand the world better. With that understanding, you will enjoy it more.

HOW CULTURE CHANGES MATTER AND LIFE

People are made of living matter. Their bodies follow the rules of chemistry and physics. Everything in the universe is made of matter.

Until life is added, matter is inert. Life gives matter many qualities that are not present in nonliving matter. Human bodies also follow the rules of biology.

But human beings also have something else: culture. It is our purpose to understand culture, to grasp the way it enriches and adds to chemistry and physics and biology without changing those basic contributions. Culture, as we shall see, is what makes human animals human.

Matter and Life

The dividing line between living things like trees and non-living things like rock is easy to see in ordinary circumstances. It is nevertheless difficult to draw the line cleanly. Viruses, for example, are inert substances until they get inside a living cell, whereupon they take on some of the qualities of living things. The special characteristics of living things—all of them vital characteristics of our humanity—are easy to grasp, and all are important to human culture.

- *Living things are feedback systems.* They sense the

environment, which they experience as stimuli. Living things can, within their limitations, respond or adapt to those stimuli.

- *Living things are throughput systems.* They absorb substances from the environment, turn parts of them into usable energy, and expel the rest back into the environment. In other words, living things have metabolisms.

- *Living things involve movement.* Movement may be fairly limited—sap mounts the stems of plants; flowers open and close. Sponges cannot move their bodies from one place to another but can circulate sea water within themselves in order to extract nutriments from it. At the other extreme, the amount of movement may be extensive, as in the migration of caribou or birds or the globe-trotting (even the beginnings of space-faring) that goes on among human beings.

- *Living things undergo processes of growth.* Animals and plants all follow a course from conception to birth to youth to maturity to death.

- *Living things are capable of reproduction.* Reproduction may take place sexually or asexually (bacteria reproduce asexually, plants such as geraniums can grow from slips; a few female lizards are capable of asexual reproduction, basically creating clones of themselves).

Culture

Culture imparts new qualities to living things just as life imparts new qualities to material things. Culture is traditionally defined as "that complex whole which includes knowledge, belief, art, law, morals, custom, and any other capability acquired by man as a member of society" (Tylor 1871). This old and respected definition is full of subtleties. In the first place, culture is a complex whole—one part is intimately related to all other parts. We shall see dramatically

Culture is a prosthetic device in the sense that it is an extension of biological capabilities.

Culture is the medium of personhood and also the medium of social relationships.

Culture in an interlinked web of symbols.

Only part of culture is conscious.

Culture is a device for channeling and limiting human choices.

Culture must be in two places at once; it must be in people's minds, and it must exist in the environment, either as act (including spoken statements) or artifact.

1-6a. Characteristics of Culture.

in Chapter 14 the ways in which culture can collapse when some parts are destroyed.

In the second place, culture is "acquired," which is to say learned. Human beings have an inborn capacity for *learning* culture. Culture is not inherited; it does not enter the genes, which are the carriers of biological information. Culture is *what* we learn, as distinguished from our ability to learn. Chapter 2 is about learning culture.

Culture is used by persons as members of society; indeed, culture is the very substance of human society. Culture can be divided into many parts—"knowledge, belief, art, law,

morals, custom." The list could, of course, be much more detailed. Chapters 3 through 12 of this book study some of those cultural components.

Culture is also a device for channeling choice so that the experiences of one person can be made useful to neighbors and descendants. The young of many species are instructed by their elders about how to use their bodies and the environment. However, culture provides a store of information that is external to any animal. Any individual person can draw on it by learning about it. A cultured animal faced with a choice has already learned enough culture to know,

¹Culture is a complex whole. One part is related to every other.

²Culture is learned. The capacity to acquire culture is genetic. The subject matter of culture itself is not genetic—it must be learned by each person.

³Culture depends on an underlying social matrix if it is to continue or to be used at all.

1-6b. *The original definition of culture published in 1871 is still serviceable if we add some characteristics discovered later: "that complex whole¹ which includes knowledge, belief, art, law, morals, custom and any other capability acquired by man² as a member of society.³"*

before any action is taken, the probable results of each of the options.

Culture allows the creature to extend its capacities and to do things that its body cannot do without assistance. Culture allows persons to do things that their biological equipment alone will not permit them to do. Chimpanzees are not genetically equipped to get termites out of mounds, although all of them like to eat termites. They can, however, make primitive tools—termite-fishing sticks—and use them to fish out the termites. Like any tool, the specially-peeled stick is a cultural extension of the chimpanzee that uses it. Such cultural extensions, involving choice and a knowledge of design, seem to be rare in the nonhuman world. They are wildly prolific among human beings—people could not keep warm or get their food without cultural extensions of their bodies.

Culture gives human beings an immense capacity for choice that allows many different satisfactory solutions to the challenges of living. Those choices, once made, become the basis of cultural knowledge. Culture can thus be seen as a storehouse of choices made over long periods of time. It allows people to ascertain before they act that some types of choices are suitable in specific circumstances; certain kinds of behavior work because they get expected results or because they are acceptable to others. Cultured creatures not only learn from others—many animals can do that—but they build on the experience of others. Culture is thus a means of standardizing choices and of sharing successful results of choices made by others in the past. It is a storehouse for maintaining records of successful—and unsuccessful—choices.

Thus, you can see that culture is at least as hard to define as life, and for the same reasons. Yet, some characteristics of culture and of creatures who are sustained by it can be sorted out and studied:

- *Culture is learned.* As people mature, they acquire ready-made cultural ways of looking at their own experiences and at the environment. This is far more complex than merely learning to interact with the environment. For example, when young crows learn to fly, they must judge which tree branches will support their weight. Watching them learn to sit on a telephone wire is instructive. Although they learn to do it, their brains are not developed to the point where it can occur to them to ask how to do it, let alone whether they *should* do it. Chimpanzees learn to make termite-fishing twigs from their mothers. Human babies learn to speak; they even learn to go to school to learn how to learn. The difference may seem small, but it is immense.

- *Every human activity is culturized.* Human beings do a lot of things that other animals do. However, *all* human behavior, no matter how much a part of our inherited genes it may be, carries an overload. It is evaluated for good or bad, right or wrong—both by the individual person and by everybody in his or her presence. This evaluation of our behavior grows out of cultural convictions and multi-generational experience about efficiency, appropriateness or moral suitability. Behavior that carries a cultural overload can be called culturized behavior.

Even those activities that human beings share with other

animals are culturized. Behavior is seen through filters of meaning and ideas about right and wrong, sensible and crazy. For example, people everywhere have cultural attitudes toward their own alimentary systems. Because we are throughput systems, we have to eat, but we eat only some of the edible products that our environment provides. What is culturally defined as decent food? People's attitudes about certain foods, which are always cultural as well as personal, color their entire perception of eating. We cannot just eat without our attitudes—even after we have learned to consider some of them unduly restricting. Our culture gets inside us as we learn to survive.

Where and when should elimination occur? Most people of the world eat publicly and eliminate privately. But the Jukun of Nigeria traditionally required their nobility to eat privately because they were taught that eating is a human weakness, and nobles must not appear weak. The U.S. Army turns elimination into a public act, and some recruits have difficulty adjusting to that.

Our attitudes toward our own reproductive systems are beset by our cultural ideas. Where, when, with whom, and under what conditions is sex suitable? Our sexual acts are shot through with the values we learned when we learned about sex itself.

We can, however, consciously change our attitudes and evaluations of the culture involved in our animal activity. It is one of the advantages of culture that it can be changed, as inborn characteristics cannot—or at least cannot until science gets far enough along to show us how to do it. Culture is, for that reason as well as others, highly adaptive.

- *Culture is the medium of our individuality and personhood.* It is a medium in the same sense that paint is the medium of a picture. You can express your Self only with the culture that is available and acceptable to you. Thus, culture lies at the basis of personality. A human personality cannot be expressed without culture.

- *Culture is the medium of human social relationships.* A human social relationship cannot be carried out without culture. The shared culture may be minimal. Culture that is not shared may lead to misunderstanding. But culture is always there.

- *Culture can be seen as a series of symbols.* A symbol is a sound, an act, or a thing to which people assign meaning. The meaning is not a part of the thing itself. The act of swallowing, for example, is expressed by a different word in different languages. The specific words are all symbols; each is in itself irrelevant to the meaning. The capacity for using symbols is at the basis of all language. All human emotions carry symbols of meaning. Animals can be frightened, but they do not have attitudes about fear that lead to symbolic ideas such as bravery or cowardice. Human emotions, thus, carry an overload of meaning that can be manipulated. Symbols are everywhere. There are religious symbols, political symbols, gender symbols. All

All human activity is culturized— all kinds of behavior that we share with other animals is accompanied by attitudes about how and when that behavior should be performed. It is impossible for normal people to behave without cultural evaluations. Such culturization of behavior is what makes human beings distinctively human.

1-7.

are cultural symbols.

- *Only parts of our culture are conscious.* Large segments of any culture are out of awareness. Edward T. Hall (1966) showed how we learn the approved distances at which to place ourselves from other people as we interact with them, although we are not aware that we know it. French people stand closer together than Americans, and Arabs stand closer than either. When the distances are not "right," we become uncomfortable. We become aware that people of other cultures stand in the "wrong" place when we are confronted with behavior that differs from our own. There are other elements in our out-of-awareness culture that affect our conduct. This dimension of culture has only begun to be studied.

- *Culture, to be culture, must be simultaneously in somebody's head and in the environment.* In somebody's head, it is meaning—what the old French social scientists called representations. In the outside world, it takes the form of behavior and tools. Tools are artifacts and are more or less permanent; behavior is largely ephemeral. If any item is not in both places, it is not culture. Transferring culture from inside the head to the outside world is behavior. Transferring culture from the outside world to our minds is learning.

HOW CULTURE CHANGES SOCIETY

Human beings are classified by biologists into the various categories summarized in 1-8. Because the earliest surviving classification (called taxonomy) was done by the Swedish scientist Linneaus, they are usually called Linnean classifications, although many changes have been introduced since his time.

Homo sapiens is the scientific name for living human beings — 1-8 shows that those names represent our genus and species. We are the only surviving species of our genus. As we get to more general classifications, we find more and more creatures to which we are related, ever more distantly. For cultural anthropologists, the most important categories are the Family of Hominidae because we are the only members of it to have a full-blown culture. Other members of the Family may exhibit rudimentary culture, but *Homo sapiens* is the only member to have taken culture and run with it, as it were. The Primate Order is also important. It includes all of the monkeys and apes but excludes all the other animals. We can learn a great deal about ourselves, particularly our bodies and our social structure, by careful study of the other members of the Primate Order.

The Class of Mammals is important to anthropologists because, as mammals, human beings are born alive and immature. They are fed at the breasts of their mothers — at least until culture finds another way. They have a lot to learn as they grow up. Not only do human beings have to grow up physically, but they have to grow up culturally. The relationship with the mother is extremely important to the successful growth of all mammals because the mother is the most important teacher in early life. Human beings also learn immense amounts of culture, including their language, from their mothers without even knowing they are learning it.

In spite of all the differences culture makes, apes and humankind share considerable body structure and many genes. Some peoples recognize their kinship with other primates; others do not. The Idoma of Nigeria, for example, eat monkeys. Their neighbors, the Tiv, find the practice shockingly akin to cannibalism.

An animal, in pursuing a successful life, has to do several tasks well enough. The most important of these tasks are: get sufficient food, escape predators, court, mate, rear the offspring. If the animal does all those things successfully, he or she survives, and the species also survives.

Society in the animal world has evolved because it increases the animals' capacity to carry out necessary tasks. Society involves one animal changing its behavior in response to another animal. Those animals can be human beings as well as any other kind of creature.

Society is a structure of relationships between individual persons or between the social groups and the persons who form them. The way such relationships fit together into a system is called the social structure. It is in the realm of social structure that comparison between human beings and the other primates is most instructive. People use some of the

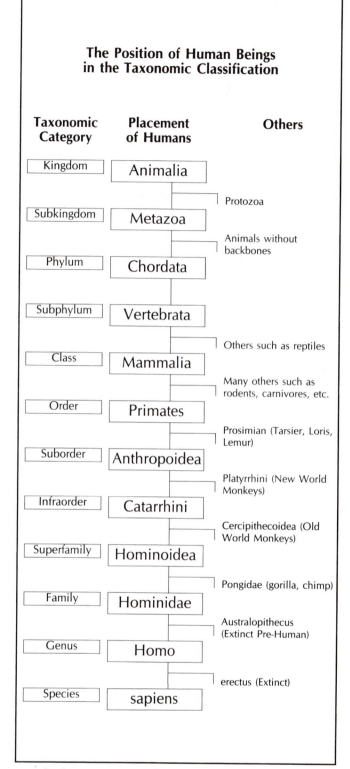

The Position of Human Beings in the Taxonomic Classification

Taxonomic Category	Placement of Humans	Others
Kingdom	Animalia	
Subkingdom	Metazoa	Protozoa
Phylum	Chordata	Animals without backbones
Subphylum	Vertebrata	
Class	Mammalia	Others such as reptiles
Order	Primates	Many others such as rodents, carnivores, etc.
Suborder	Anthropoidea	Prosimian (Tarsier, Loris, Lemur)
Infraorder	Catarrhini	Platyrrhini (New World Monkeys)
Superfamily	Hominoidea	Cercipithecoidea (Old World Monkeys)
Family	Hominidae	Pongidae (gorilla, chimp)
Genus	Homo	Australopithecus (Extinct Pre-Human)
Species	sapiens	erectus (Extinct)

1-8. At every stage, we share some qualities with "others." Among the most striking are the qualities we share with other primates, other mammals, and other vertebrates. This chart was built to show the position of human beings. That is hard to do without making it look as if evolution had built "up" to human beings. The same kind of chart could be made for making the chart build toward porcupines or oysters.

1-9. A successful animal life demands the following achievements: acquiring sufficient food; escaping predators; courting and finding a mate; reproducing; and rearing the young. To these achievements, human beings add: learning to speak and use culture; and making a contribution to culture — producing and reproducing culture as well as (or rather than) reproducing the species.

same mechanisms of social organization as do other animals but have added many additional mechanisms unique to human beings. Looking at the similarities and differences shows that human beings, using culture, have indeed been successful in using social tools to survive.

People have culturized their society in the same way they have culturized their animal behavior. The particular way in which relationships are carried out is subject to a constant cultural overload. Different peoples, faced with different goals and different environments, have culturized society in different ways. Animals choose whether or not to associate with one another. While human beings do that too, people may also choose to change the cultural forms that their societies are to take. They can think about and alter the social structure rather than merely participate or withdraw.

The way in which people have culturized animal behavior and the ways they have culturized society are an important part of what cultural anthropology is about.

Primate Society

Human beings and apes share at least four basic principles

on which their societies are built. Indeed, all mammals share these principles. Societies of wolves, prairie dogs, and antelopes show interesting differences from, but even more interesting similarities to, primate society.

(1) *The Principle of Dominance (Hierarchy).*
  "I can lick you."
  "Okay. You can lick me."

All animals struggle to find and keep a place in the environment from which they can get what they need to survive. That struggle takes two main forms: territoriality and dominance. Some primates stake out territories from which they exclude other members of their own species, thus insuring adequate resources for their own survival. Territoriality among human beings permeates many more subtle social principles. Dominance hierarchies are structures of dyadic relationships in which one animal is recognized as more powerful than the other. The admission by the weaker animal that another is stronger cements the relationship. The relationship can now proceed peacefully. Dominance relationships can then be chained—the dominant animal in one relationship may be the subordinate one in another. They can be worked into complex social structures that continue to exist over time. Dominance is always based on the recognized power of individual animals. Once the hierarchy is established, there is no need for continual fighting to maintain the peace.

(2) *The Principle of Kinship.*
"No matter how much I hate you, you've got my genes, so I love you."

Almost all mammals and birds recognize their own individual young. They protect those young against predators and against other members of their own species. Only by doing so will their genes survive. The principle of kinship, built on the parent-child relationships, may also involve long-term relationships between parents and their young. Although the parents are probably not kinfolk of one another (although in human societies, they may well be), both are kinfolk of the young animals. They therefore have common interests.

(3) *The Principle of Specialization of Tasks.*
"You can depend on me to do what I can do if I can depend on you to do what you can do."

This principle is also found in most vertebrate species, including all mammals. Its most common form is the separation of male tasks from female tasks, then fitting the two together in such a way that the sexes need one another for more purposes than merely reproductive ones. Culture has allowed human beings to question whether specific tasks are most suitably carried out by males or females rather than blindly follow previously established patterns; nevertheless it has not as yet allowed us (and it may never), to make gender differences disappear.

Tasks may also be specialized by age so that young and old depend on one another. Human beings, in culturizing this principle, have also come to specialize tasks by inclination and talent, by training, by social rank, and by many other criteria.

(4) *The Principle of Cooperation.*
"I'll help you as long as it is worth my while."

This principle means that a number of animals or people working together toward a common goal can often reach that goal whereas individuals cannot do it alone. Although individual animals can usually win more by not cooperating with one another—that is, the animal that cooperates can be easily cheated by one that does not cooperate—cheaters usually will be excluded from coalitions and from special benefits. Animals that meet only once seldom cooperate. Animals that are repeatedly in contact with one another can win more by cooperating with one another. Cooperation develops from predictable long-term social structure: the association allows the creatures to trust one another sufficiently that they will sometimes cooperate to achieve common goals (Axelrod and Hamilton 1981).

Our understanding of primate society was revolutionized by the new discipline of sociobiology that came of age in the 1970s. Sociobiology made the important points (1) that behavior can be treated as an artifact and (2) that it is associated with individual animals. A species cannot behave. Only its members, the individual animals, can do that.

Another idea emerged at about the same time. The basic building block of life is what is called the "selfish gene" (Dawkins 1976). In its urge for self-preservation, the gene "uses" organisms as the vehicles for its long-term survival. In order to survive, an animal must act in such a way as to pass its genes to the next generation. Thus will the genes, and therefore the species, survive. An animal's ability to leave offspring is called personal fitness. The greater the number of reproducing offspring, the greater the fitness of the animal.

1-10. Society is prior to cultural achievement: human beings were social before they were cultured.

The behavior of any individual animal, further, is determined by a series of strategies. There are three such strategies (Dunbar 1988). The following terms are my adaptations:

Heritage. This strategy emerged in the course of evolution. The descendants of animals who "chose" particular behavior strategies, either consciously or not, survived. The information resulting from their choices is likely to be encoded in the present animal's genes and show up as capabilities and limitations shared by all members of the species. Because these "choices" from the past are encoded genetically, the individual animal has no control over them.

Fate. Experiences imposed by the environment as an individual grows up leave a biological residue. If an animal grew up in a time of famine, it suffered because the environment didn't provide enough food. It made no cognitively aware choice but was affected by fate. Could our parent(s) provide adequate food at critical stages of growth? Were our mothers constantly tense and insecure because of the threats and aggression of other members of the group? The early experience of individual animals has an immense impact on their later ability to survive and breed.

Free choice. The third kind of strategy becomes more important as we depend more and more on culture and as we have a choice. Decisions are actively made by the animal itself, in more or less full awareness of the options. Among primates, this kind of "choice" is often, but certainly not always, made cognitively. The baboon, for example, assesses its options and chooses those that best serve its purposes. Cats do that too within a more limited scope. So, presumably, within their limitations, do all other creatures.

Human Society

Human beings, in the course of evolution, emerged bearing specialized versions of these primate social characteristics. However, human beings also added a number of new and unique principles. Culture gives people additional expectations, which lead them to use society for new purposes.

For human beings, then, the requirement for long-term survival of the species is not merely passing along genes to a new generation of animals. It is passing along genes-and-culture to a new generation. Not only does the species have to be carried on, but also the culture has to be carried on. The genes do indeed have to survive. But the culture also must survive. Human genes without human culture cannot create the species. We would not be human without culture.

The presence of culture reduces the individual person's need for offspring—there is an alternative route for contributing to the future of the species. Human beings who do not have children are not considered failures for that reason. Einstein is important for his cultural achievements in physics, not for his offspring. Johann Sebastian Bach's children are remembered not because they were fertile children of a fertile father but because several of them were talented musicians who took music lessons from their father. Parents provide the genes; teachers (including parents, of course) provide the culture. A person can make a contribution to culture that enriches all lives in the next generation. Descendants are not the only proof that one has indeed lived.

Human beings, thus, add a number of additional tasks to the list of basic animal tasks. They must learn their cultures, practice their cultures, and teach the cultures to the new generation. In the process of doing these things over many millennia, human beings have created new principles of social relationship—purely human and not shared by other animals.

(5) *The Principle of Contract.*
   "Let's make a deal."

The principle of contract implies not just cooperation, but more: it is an enforceable agreement in which two parties, either individuals or groups, agree that one party will provide a specific good or specific service in return for a complementary good or service supplied by the other.

The larger a society gets, the more likely it is that the realm of contract will expand. In small and culturally simple communities, it is not necessary to specify as many aspects of a contract as it is in large-scale complex societies. That is especially true in societies that are small enough that they can be dominated by kinship.

Contract assumes a legal system that can and will require people to fulfill their contracts.

(6) *The Principle of Role.*
   "It isn't really me who is doing this to you."

This principle has had a profound effect on the course of human history. People began to differentiate between a **role** in an organization and the person who fills it. It is this principle that is described in the old statement, "The king is dead; long live the king." The idea appeared that rights and obligations in an organization (say a school) were attached to roles, not to the people who played those roles. Your teacher has both the right and the obligation to test you and to grade your work. That right comes from the fact that the college is organized as it is and you have voluntarily come to college. Without the role, the teacher has no authority but would have to depend on personal characteristics.

(7) *The Principle of Ranking.*
   "I'm simply better than you, and for the following reasons. . . ."

This principle underlies the human tendency to derive complex systems of social position from criteria other than personal power. People rank roles—as a result, kings outrank commoners. They rank jobs so that managers outrank workers. They rank culture traits so that people who use fine china may outrank those who use crockery.

(8) *The Principle of Property.*
   "That one's mine. The only rights you have in it are the rights I give you."

This principle involves the institution of slavery. It has a prominent place in the history of all societies that are today considered civilized. Today remnants of it are found in a few of the world's societies.

Insofar as property consists of material objects, we do not need a principle of social relationship. People own property; they use it but do not interact with it in the social sense. To sell one's labor on the market is a matter of contract, which is very different from slavery.

(9) *The Cost-Benefit Principle.*
   "I'll buy it from you or do it for you if the price isn't too high."

Numerous individual decisions, made by many different persons each for his or her own good and independently of one another, have a cumulative effect. The market is the best understood manifestation of this principle. Individual decisions about health practices and reproduction affect the distribution of human populations. Marriage and divorce rates—individuals marrying and divorcing to adjust their personal costs and benefits—have an immense impact on family. Cumulative individual decisions based upon cost-benefit directly affect society.

(10) *The Principle of Networking.*
   "Get your friends to give me a hand."

Networking involves groups built on a common interest. A **network** is one of the basic social forms; societies have used this form for years as a means of communicating and sharing. However, using the network to supplement or replace

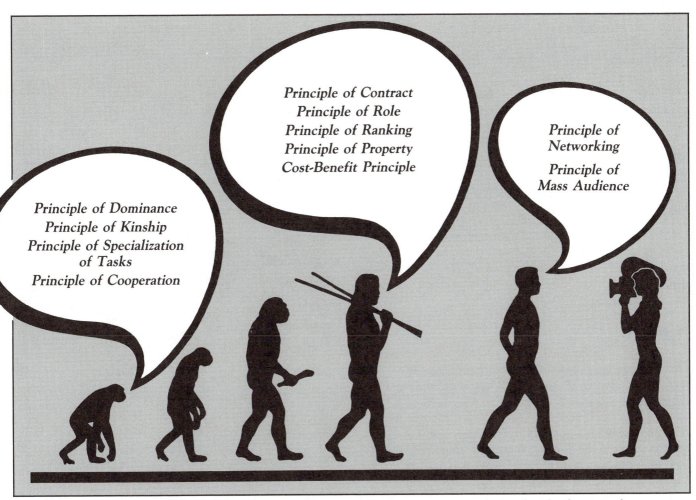

1-11. *There are at least eleven basic principles of social organization; some are shared with other animals, some seem to be distinctly human.*

organized social groups has taken on new importance in the last two or three decades. If you need a new job, you network—tell your friends to tell their friends. Networking is important in the modern world where a person can become isolated; it scarcely exists in small-scale societies.

(11) *The Principle of Mass Audience.*
"I saw it on television. . . ."

Audiences existed long before printing presses, but they were face-to-face audiences. The mass audience began with the printing press and the spread of literacy. However, the power of mass audience came into its own with radio and positively exploded with television. It is one of the most important social principles in the modern world.

An individual, whether human or other primate, must coordinate its activities with other members of its species in order to carry out the life tasks of finding food and safety, mating and raising young. To do that successfully means that the animal must take the behavior of other animals into account when making choices about its own behavior. In other words, the animals enter into social relationships which provide a basis for a systematic structure of society. And

society is a survival mechanism; most but not quite all animal species exhibit it.

Social Relations

Behaving takes time. For example, it takes time for baboons to eat, to go from one feeding ground to the next, and to prepare their sleeping quarters for the night. It takes time to do what you have to do to make social relations worthwhile. The more time and effort you put into the relationship, the less time there is for other activities. Hence, in the long run the rewards of social relations must equal or exceed their cost. Sociality can never be allowed to press too far into eating time, traveling time from one source of food to another, sleeping time, child-care time.

It has been known for decades (Wilson and Wilson 1954) that if you increase the number of people with whom an individual person interacts, or increase the number of contexts of interaction, then the nature of that individual's interactions will have to change because of the enlargement. The person no longer has the same amount of time and energy to put into the relationships that occupied him or

Anthropology, Culture and Society

her earlier. When colonial society or global society impinges on the individual who has lived all his life in a small-scale society, that individual's focus has to change. He or she no longer has as much time to spend on relationships in the small-scale society. That means that, willy-nilly, the relationships that used to enjoy leisurely association are now given short shrift.

Any animal that is overburdened trying to achieve the optimal conditions for maximal fitness, including time to rest, is at a disadvantage when it comes to reproduction. Animals will abandon social relationships that take so much time as to eclipse other necessary activities. Human beings are, obviously, in the same spot.

When the price one pays is larger than the rewards one gets from an association, the animal is, using the cost-benefit principle, likely to cut off the association. This general principle would seem to be as true for human beings as for any other species.

The Europeans who first encountered the Tiv about 1909 found that they were living, for their own protection, in large stockaded villages of several hundred people. By 1949, with the general peace brought by the British colonial power, the Tiv had spread out evenly over the land into compounds containing from ten to eighty-five people. Since protection was no longer an issue, the personal cost of living in larger groups was experienced as too high and they moved into smaller ones.

Just so, the number of Americans living alone rose steeply in the 1960s, 1970s, and 1980s. As more and more goods and services came onto the market, and as sexual mores changed, the price that individual persons had traditionally been paying for reciprocal services and sex began to seem too high. The result is that they "moved out" and lived alone.

WE, THE ALIEN

Human beings, however, are intensely social animals. We shall see in Chapter 13 that as the size of the human social group increased, new culture, including social culture, was invented in order to keep the group from falling to pieces. Today, although all of us also participate in small groups, the entire world is a single society. As a result, the number of social principles is at an all-time high, and the amount of time we spend on sociality is immense.

Social Forms

Although it is possible to make heavy sledding of it, the fundamental tenet of society, human or animal, is really very simple.* Just as the basic unit of behavior is the person behaving, the basic unit of society is two persons adjusting to one another.

There are three major forms found in any social structure: the network, the category, and the group. Social principles discussed earlier underlie the social form.

Dyads and Networks. The basic unit of both social group and social network is the **dyad**, which is a relationship between two behaving persons. Although each person is the *behaving* unit that is a member of society, the dyad is the basic *social* unit. Every stable dyad (like every person) has

1-12. *Two human beings (or two groups of human beings) may form a dyadic relationship. Person A takes person B's acts and wishes into consideration when he or she acts; Person B does the same for person A. The person is the basic actor and decider. But the dyad of two interacting parties is the basic social unit. As you can see from the photograph, one person, without another, is not a social unit. Chains of such dyads (each of the persons in a dyad is part of many other dyads) form networks. Clusters of dyads form groups.*

---

* This section is written from the standpoint of human beings, but many of the principles apply to societies of other animals as well.

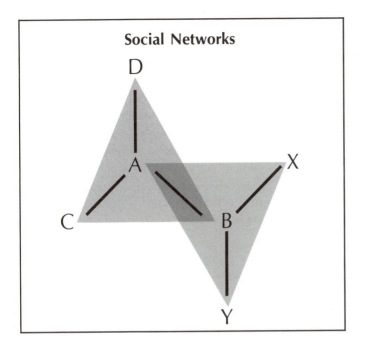

Social Networks

D

A

X

C

B

Y

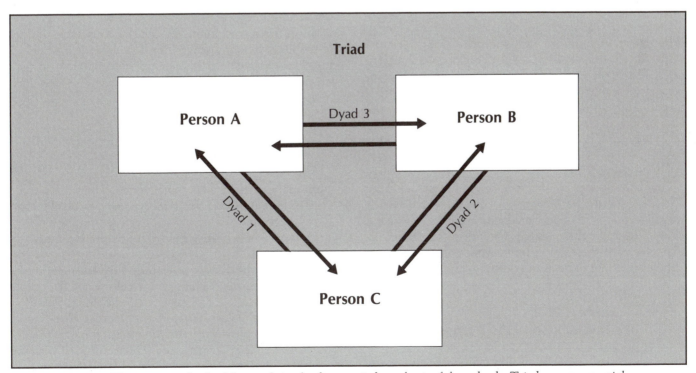

Triad

Person A ——Dyad 3—→ **Person B**

Dyad 1

Dyad 2

Person C

1-14. The presence of a third human being leads to a triad, made up of three dyads. Triads are an essential feature of human groups.

1-13. Networks of social relationships, cultural categories into which people may be classified, and groups into which they may be organized, are to be distinguished: A has direct relations with B, C and D; these latter three are indirectly linked with one another because they all know A. B has direct links with X and Y, who therefore have indirect links with one another as well as with A. If B introduces A and Y, that creates a direct link, and they may even become friends and may help each other in many ways.

Networking is using the network to forward one's ends. If D needs help in finding a new job, say, he may talk to A. A then talks about D's need to several of his friends, including B, who tells his friends—and it just happens that X has heard of a new job that might be suitable. The information gets back to D, who applies and gets the job. D and X may never have met.

its own culture (most but not quite all of which is shared by many other persons and dyads).

A social network is a number of interlinked dyads. The linkages occur when one person is involved with more than one other person. If A is linked with B and is also linked to C and D, then C is indirectly linked to B and D by virtue of their common relationship with A (see 1-13). The network exists because many persons are in chained relationships with one another. Networking, as we saw earlier, is using the network for specific social ends. Networks are present even when networking is not a common social principle.

A network is a web. Networks are involved in kinship systems or trading systems—even if those involved do not use the principle of networking. In many of the networks of modern society, however, networking may be the only principle that keeps people connected to one another.

The units in a dyad can be individual persons; they can also be social groups. An international treaty or trade agreement between two countries is a dyad. So is a feud or a contract. Social dyads are marked by the fact that the two individuals profit from their association with one another. The dyad will disintegrate when they cease to be valuable to one another, when the costs to one or both animals greatly exceed the rewards, or when the dyad is seriously beset by envy.

Problems that arise in the dyad are solved either by separation of the two parties (thus destroying the dyad) or by importing a third party and imbedding the simple dyad in a triad.

Triads and Groups. A **triad** is formed when three animals all have relationships with one another. That is, A and B have a relationship, B and C have one, and C and A have one. The triad is composed, thus, of three dyads. Larger groups can then be made by linking dyads and triads into larger units. The number of principles does not necessarily increase just because the size of the unit does.

Social triads have a built-in weakness that arises because one member may envy another's relationship with the third, thus creating a situation of jealousy. Jealousy may cause one animal to withdraw from the field or two animals to gang up on the third. In the triad, each of the dyads within it is "refereed" by the third party. Such refereeing may sometimes be a strength. For example, in the NATO-USSR-China triad of mutual distrust during the Cold War, each monitored the relationship between the other two. Larger social groups are concatenations of dyads and triads, such as The West, the Communist World —and the "Third" World. And so is the smallest and most fundamental triad: mother, father— and baby.

Categories. A social category is of a different order. It is not based on dyads, but rather on the classification and cultural evaluation of persons on the basis of their characteristics. Thus, a social category is a cultural device for lumping persons together. Males and females are each a category of people. They do not necessarily form groups or networks, although gender may be used as a criterion for admission to some groups. The "races" are, as we shall see in Chapter 9, social categories. The old and the young may be seen as social categories.

These distinctions are simple once you master them. But if we confuse categories with groups, or either with networks, we will have trouble understanding the societies that we live in as well as those that we study. Understanding the culture that makes all these social forms work is more complex, although it is not difficult. The distinctions made here are vital to the rest of this book.

CONCLUDING THOUGHTS

Learning about somebody or something completely different allows us to compare ourselves with what we are not. Learning what you are not helps to define what you are. Throughout this book, therefore, we shall do three sets of comparisons.

- We shall compare other species to our own—this process is particularly useful in understanding both the nature of culture and how human beings have culturized their animal behavior and parts of their social structure.

- We shall compare other cultures to our own culture. This process allows us to understand the historical peculiarity of our own ways of perceiving the world we live in.

- We shall compare the experiences of other people to our own experiences. This helps us to grasp the importance of our own learning and our own social position.

We can also learn a great deal about culture and about ourselves by inventing cultures that have never existed at all. This text contains no "cultures of the imagination," but they are to be found in *Discovering the Alien,* the accompanying workbook. As we invent cultures, we necessarily throw our own characteristics into both cultural relief and biological relief. We can choose aspects of our own or some other culture, then postulate cultures of the imagination in which such characteristics are lacking. Such an exercise requires that we examine everything that is connected with the characteristic on which we have focused. We have to ask what else must be changed as we change the one characteristic. For example, in order to understand the way in which gender is intermixed with all cultural aspects, we can postulate cultures of the imagination in which gender is lacking, then discover that sex and family and many other dimensions of our lives will also have to be changed.

We can make up a culture in which there is no strife, no warfare. In the process, we can begin to understand why war exists in our own culture. We can, by using such cultures of the imagination, discover just how difficult it would be to create permanent peace among humankind.

BUZZWORDS

anthropology the study of humankind. The word was derived from the Greek words for the study (logos) of human beings (anthropos). It was used before the year 1600 in philosophy and history, but got its present meaning only in about 1870.

archaeology the study of prehistorical or historical culture by examining the remains of that culture and the people who lived it.

cultural anthropology starts from the fact that human beings are tool-using animals who assign meaning to their acts as well as to their bodies. It concerns itself with the toolkits and meanings that peoples have developed.

culture the capacity to use tools and symbols.

dyad a group of two.

ethnography the study of a single people and their culture.

linguistics begins with the human capacity to speak, considers the biology of the vocal apparatus as well as speech, language, and the history and development of languages.

network a meshing of dyadic social relationships, of which the nodes are individual persons or social groups. Networks form because every person (or group) is involved in many relationships with people who often are not in relationships with one another. Information travels rapidly along networks; individual persons can use them for support.

physical anthropology or **biological anthropology** starts from the biological basis of human beings. It concerns itself with the anatomy and physiology of the human species, with the biology and behavior of those species of apes and monkeys most closely related to human beings, and with the impact of culture on human biology.

primate an order of mammals that contains monkeys, apes, and human beings.

role a part to be played by an individual human being. Roles are marked by rights and obligations, by expected activities, and the moral dimension for judging those activities. Roles are interlinked with one another—one role helps to define others. Persons play roles but are not to be confused with their roles.

society a group of people in interaction who see themselves as a unit, differentiated from other similar units.

triad a group or set of three, especially of persons or things. A triad contains three dyads.

Learning Culture

2

PROPOSITIONS AND PREMISES

- All culture is learned (experience is one form of learning). Every individual absorbs some aspects of one or more cultures. Both learning and experiencing are lifelong activities, but what we learn, and perhaps how we learn, changes as we grow up and grow older.

- Because each person learns culture, there is at least some idiosyncrasy in the culture of each of us. The greater the differences in cultural environment and experience between any two persons or groups, the greater the degree of idiosyncrasy. However, because we grow up experiencing in the company of others, much of our culture is shared, especially language.

- Anthropological fieldworkers learn what are, for them, alien cultures as a major part of their professional activity. Methods for learning new cultures as an adult can be learned. Anthropologists have developed, and are still developing, such methods.

- People who have learned two very different cultures have the advantage of bicultural vision; like binocular vision, bicultural vision allows people to see in depth: that is, they know that there are several ways to understand and utilize any situation.

In the course of evolution, our ancestors developed the ability to speak. They learned to invent tools and to use culture. Those abilities are genetic—each of us is born ready to learn to use language and culture. We are evolutionarily so well prepared that from the moment of birth, and perhaps before, we start to learn everything we are exposed to.

A deep irony is involved in our learning language and culture. The very fact of growing up and learning a culture makes us human. Without the culture we cannot be fully human. BUT—the fact that we learn one culture makes it difficult, sometimes even impossible, to learn any other culture in the intimate, natural way that we know the first one. The very process that makes us human also makes us provincial.

We human beings are genetically programmed to learn the culture in our environment. But learning "our" culture, ironically enough, estranges us from other cultures.

2-1.

HOW WE LEARN OUR OWN CULTURE

Human beings begin learning in the first minutes after birth; we continue learning until death. In the process of learning culture, we regard the particular version that we learn—our own culture—as part of the natural world. We cannot see, hear or feel anything without simultaneously sensing the cultural dimensions.

This fact can be described as a social trap. That is to say, culture ultimately becomes a destructive force in our lives

at the same time that it solves our immediate problems. By our language and culture we are bonded with our own group, and (here is the trap) we are estranged from others.

Today, the need for the many peoples in the world to get along with one another makes it imperative that we move beyond the narrow cultural dimensions of any one group. Not only do we have to learn our own culture as we grow up (in order to grow up at all) but we must then actively seek to learn that our own culture provides only one way of being cultured and being human. There are other ways that work just as well.

A few of us have two "native" cultures—perhaps one for home life and another for school or work life. Others of us learn a second culture when we are older children. Many people, when they are adult, move into strange societies and learn those new cultures. Some of these adult learners are refugees who have escaped tyranny with no more than their lives; others go to new countries to improve their life chances. Still others want to do business in foreign lands.

When we learn cultures other than our mother-culture, especially when we learn them as adults, the process is more conscious. When we are young, we learn our own specific culture without being aware of the process. It seems as natural as any other part of our environment. But as we learn new cultures when we are older, we are acutely conscious both of the act of learning and the unfamiliarity of what we are learning. The act of learning is no longer merely a matter of development of our brains and bodies—it has become a conscious process. What we are learning is not merely a part of our environment (although it remains that)—it is an alternative to what we first learned. The fact that we know two alternatives will mark us forever.

This chapter is about both types of learning. First, we will examine how people learn their own cultures; we will take a person through the life course, looking at how he or she learns the mother-culture as part of growing and living. Then, in the second part of the chapter, we will switch our focus to examine how adults learn foreign cultures—our specific focal point will be how anthropologists learn.

The basis of our personalities is genetic, and thus chemical. All parents learn quickly that their child has inborn personality characteristics that they had not anticipated. These innate traits, however, are guided and influenced by the culture we learn. One of my most profound experiences when I worked among the Tiv was my acquaintance with a Tiv woman whose inborn characteristics were astonishingly similar to those of my own mother. She did not look like my mother; she did not act like my mother. However, the way she laughed was like my mother. The way she turned her head was like my mother. The way she interacted with other people—the particular combination of good humor, patience, sincere care and an uncompromising demand for what she considered to be considerate and correct behavior—that too was like my mother. I realize, of course, that much of this similarity may have existed in my eyes only. But if that woman had grown up in my mother's culture or if my mother had grown up in hers, they would have been noticeably alike to most observers. I do not know whether those qualities were inborn. But with a change of culture, the two would have been almost interchangeable. Thus I learned firsthand that all human beings are siblings divided by culture.

Early in the twentieth century, the stimulus-response model dominated thinking about learning—indeed, thinking about all behavior. The basic premise was this: a stimulus external to an animal "causes" it to behave. The simple formulation was "stimulus leads to behavior" (see 2-2). It is correct—as far as it goes.

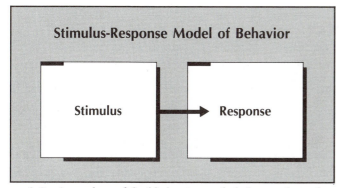

Stimulus-Response Model of Behavior

2-2. An early model of behavior made behavior depend entirely on response to outside stimulus.

However, this so-called stimulus-response model turns the behaving animal into a passive receptor. It leaves out learning. It also leaves out the purposes or intentions of the behaving animal. It further assumes what we know to be untrue: that all stimuli felt by the person or animal come from outside. Critics of the stimulus-response model pointed out that there was a feeling, thinking, learning organism

between the stimulus and the response. Both the perceiving organism and the environment that supplies major parts of the stimuli are important factors missing from the stimulus-response model (see 2-3).

Feedback

It was not until the 1960s and 1970s that a further complication of the model was introduced. A book called *Behavior: The Control of Perception* (Powers 1973) proposed the idea that an animal organism is a feedback mechanism that works like a thermostat. The basic premise is that the purpose of any behavior is to affect and to control the stimulus. Animals, including human animals, act to bring stimulus into line with what they, consciously or unconsciously, want to perceive—by no means all of our wants are purposeful; some are the result of the workings of our bodies. Our behavior, then, may—but it may not—have an impact on the actual physical environment.

But how do we know what we want to perceive? What is right? All feedback mechanisms—the simplest is the thermostat on a furnace—need a comparator (see 2-4). For example, every thermostat is set so that within a limited range of stimulus, no response is called for. That is, because the stimulus is "right," everything is allowed to continue doing exactly what it is already doing. When the stimulus exceeds or falls below that limit, however, a signal is sent that something should happen. With that signal of "too much" or "too little," the thermostat or the animal does something to bring the stimulus back into the preset sphere.

Comparator. The basic setting of any animal's comparator is genetic. As a result of evolution, the creature is born to know when some stimuli are right. Particular responses to particular stimuli have, through the evolutionary ages,

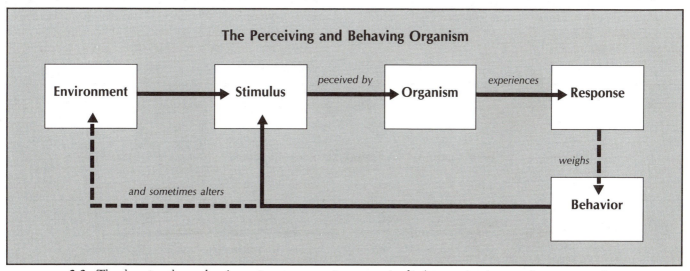

The Perceiving and Behaving Organism

Environment → **Stimulus** —*peceived by*→ **Organism** —*experiences*→ **Response** —*weighs*→ **Behavior**

and sometimes alters

2-3. The chart is to be read: An environment contains many stimuli. An organism in an environment perceives an event; the perception is a stimulus. The perceiving organism experiences a response—it registers the event. It may or may not behave. The behavior will have an effect on the stimulus and may alter it considerably. It may in fact, alter the environment as well.

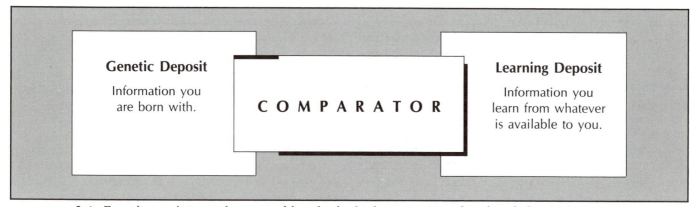

2-4. *Every human being is characterized by a bank of information (everything boxed above). An immense amount of that information is inherited information. We seldom, if ever, are aware of it. It is carried in the genes and is here called the genetic deposit. People also add more information by learning from experience. That is called the learning deposit. Both types of information, when they are commingled, feed into the comparator. The comparator is the brain, working with all the information (of both types) available to it. It is this comparator that tells us what is comfortable—what is "right."*

allowed the creature's ancestors to survive. When a response is inborn instead of learned, it is a *genetic deposit* which we can characterize as opening an individual creature's account at the information bank.

Human beings add another dimension to the comparator—learned, cultural rightness. Behavior not only alters what the person perceives, but it has an extremely important second result. The person learns through trial and error, or by instruction, *how* to behave to bring the stimulus to an acceptable state. He or she thus "knows" something beyond the genetic. For better or for worse, we learn from experience. Thus, behavior not only affects the stimulus, it also leaves a residue in the behaving organism. That residue may change the standards of the comparator. We can characterize this as the *learning deposit* in the creature's information bank.

Genetic information and learned information, once deposited, become operationally inseparable. In terms used by savings banks about funds from several sources, the genetic deposit and the learning deposit are "commingled." These processes are summarized in 2-4.

The most interesting aspect of all this is the flow. Most (not all) stimuli originate in the environment—the rest originate in the workings of the body, coming to us as pain or emotion. An external stimulus is perceived by means of an "acceptor system"—sense organs like the ears, eyes and skin. Reactions to that stimulus flow through the comparator, where they are weighed against all the combined genetic and experiential information in the bank (2-5). Any response, thus, leads simultaneously to more experiential information in the bank and to behavior that changes the stimulus. Such processes start at conception and end with death.

Thus, the total information available to the perceiving creature is set by the genes on the one hand and by personal experience on the other. Our experience, enlarged by the range of possible options, is in fact limited by the choices we have made. Each time the stimulus is perceived, it is compared with the information internalized by decisions and actions from earlier experiences. The creature either repeats the action it learned earlier or, if the results were unsatisfactory, makes a specific effort not to repeat it. In

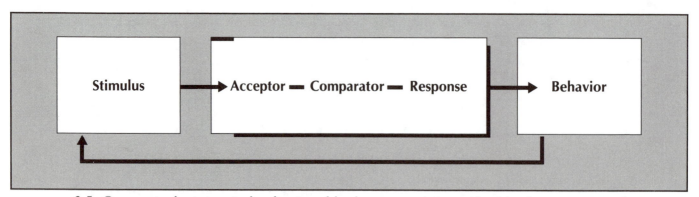

2-5. *Once a stimulus is perceived and registered by the acceptor, it is considered by the comparator and a response occurs. Behavior may or may not occur. If it does occur, it will change either the stimulus or the comparator or both. Both response and behavior (including the decision not to behave overtly) leave a residue in the experience information account.*

making these choices, the individual internalizes culture as an effective part of the information about dealing with the environment.

At least two variables add complications to the way people learn culture. First of all, the behaving organism is genetically programmed to grow and to age. Growth changes the genetic standards of the comparator. Thus, the genetic dimensions of the comparator do not reflect the same standards for behavior at all stages of the life course. The experience dimension is also changed each day as we grow older, learn more, and take on new social tasks. It is the nature of human experience that it is constantly reevaluated in light of changes in the environment and of later experiences. Our past experiences obviously do not change. What happened, happened. But our evaluation of those experiences can change several times a day. Reassessing our experience is a normal dimension of growth and maturation.

Schemata. Second, the learning person has to learn categories in which to put the information that is learned. If we could not make such categories—learning theorists in cognitive anthropology and the other cognitive sciences call them **schemata** (singular, schema)—it would be impossible to organize all the information that we learn. We would soon be swamped with information overload. Although some of the schemata are universal among human beings and some may even be peculiar to one individual, most are culturally shared—not by all human beings but by those who share the same culture. Schemata are "conceptual abstractions that mediate between stimuli received by the sense organs and behavioral responses" (Casson 1983). The term schemata puts what we have previously called the comparator into the plural.

To understand the term schema, think about the grammar of your native language. No baby learning any language knows that grammar exists. We have to be taught about it. Yet, grammar is an indispensable part of expressing one's thought. In accordance with the grammars of our languages, we divide meaning into units that are recognizable by others who speak the same language. We then put the units into the "right" (that is, grammatical) order as we speak. We can transform the units in accordance with a set of grammatical rules—that is, we can change tenses, make plurals, and adjust verb endings or adjective forms. The categories of grammar shape not only our speech but our thoughts. We may not always think in words, but to express ourselves in language we must have words and grammar. When we communicate, we must do so within the schemata of the grammar of some language.

2-6. Information in each person's data bank is arranged in patterns called schemata. New information is filed into this same filing system, which is provided by the genetic (biological) and learned (cultural) schemata.

Some aspects of grammar are common to all languages, presumably reflecting proclivities of the human brain. All languages have nouns and verbs. But many other aspects are not universal. In the Tiv language, the words for color are verbs instead of adjectives—Tiv do not say that something is red, but that it reds. The information can be translated, but the feeling is far different because the schemata are different. Schemata such as grammar are laid down in the comparator and become a permanent part of the way we experience the world and communicate about it.

Thus, what we learn is no mere copy of external reality. The schemata by which we organize experiences as we perceive them and as we act actually *create* our own reality. We can only grasp what the framework allows us to understand. To perceive a different reality would require an alternative framework.

Grammar is only one of the many schemata. At a less abstract level, there is a schema (or, if one adds more detail, many schemata) for acquiring and using the furnishings in our homes—we know what to sit on, what to pull up to, where to put our feet. There is a schema for going to the movies or watching television, for reading or studying, for writing a book. A schema is "a data structure for representing the generic concepts stored in the memory" (Casson 1983 quoting Rumelhart). The schemata of foreign languages we learn as adults may never be fully internalized, and thus we may never speak them quite as natives do.

Another way of saying all this is that we perceive—that is, our senses work. When the perceptions go into the comparator, they are sorted into the categories that are parts of the schemata. The contents of those categories are interrelated by the principles that are manifested in the schemata. We therefore "understand" what we see in terms of the schemata already in the comparator (or, on rare occasions, we add to or subtract from the schemata). A "thought" therefore is a schematically organized perception.

The schemata in the comparator work to file what we perceive into patterns we already know. Schemata are thus not just structures but also are processes. When we sense new information, we go through the process of fitting it into our accustomed patterns of perceiving and behaving. Sometimes the schemata constrain what we perceive so as not to upset the pattern—they sometimes keep us from recognizing reality if that reality does not fit our schemata. As we shall see later in the chapter, this constraint is what must be carefully monitored in fieldwork. In order to control it, we must become aware of our schemata so that we *know* we are using them and how we are using them.

JOURNEY THROUGH A LIFE

Within a few hours of birth, the human child adjusts his or her movements to the rhythms of adult speech (Condor and Sander 1974). Analyzing sound films frame by frame, psychologists and pediatricians found that the body movements of the baby and the rhythm of the emphases in

(2) he or she must learn it in accordance with the demands made by other people in the environment; even at a very early age different demands may be made based on gender or on class, for example; and (3) there are some things that adults will not allow the child to learn.

Interaction

The child learns to interact with one person at a time. The first intense and prolonged social relationship usually occurs with the mother. But soon the child is also actively relating to father, to siblings, to other kinfolk, perhaps to the dog (if the dog is part of the household as it is in the United States) or with the cattle (if the cattle are part of the community as they are in some areas of East Africa).

As the child interacts with others, he or she is learning a sex identity. By the age of about one year, a child knows

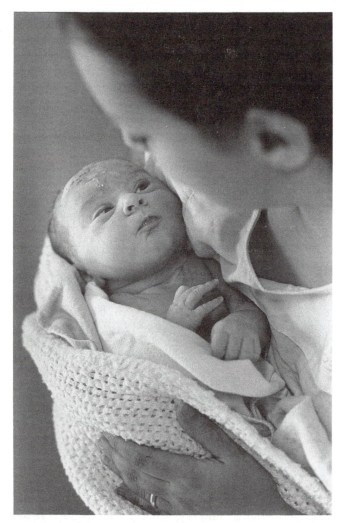

2-7. Within a few minutes of birth, a child adjusts its body rhythms to the rhythms of the language spoken around her or him. Babies can see well—this little girl is only about a minute old.

adult speech coincide. Moreover, these scientists discovered that the correlation was true for all cultures. When the experimenters used several languages, the newborn's movements changed whenever the language changed. When the adults spoke a different language, the infant adapted to the rhythm of the new language.

Culture thus influences us from the moment we are born. Our very first body movements are associated with the language of our parents and our neighbors. This first cultural stimulus marks us for life.

A young animal, human or any other, must be stimulated by its environment. Only when the young are stimulated do they grow and prosper. Capacities are developed through responses to environmental stimuli. Stimulation is as vital to growth as adequate nutrition. Human infants die if they are not stimulated. No stimulus—no behavior.

Three limiting conditions affect the culture we learn: (1) a child (or an adult) can learn only what the cultural environment provides, no matter what the genetic capacity;

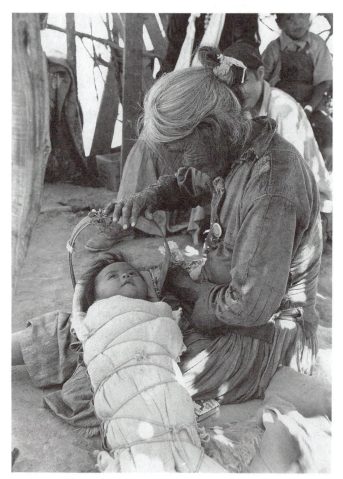

2-8. Young children need stimulus in order to learn. People and cultural things provide the stimulus. Indeed, all people need stimulus at all stages of their lives, but very early childhood and old age are the points at which a lack is most apparent. There has long been a dispute—never settled—about whether tight swaddling, like that of this Navajo child on a cradle board, inhibits some kinds of physical development as well as about how or whether it affects the adult personality.

which sex he or she is. Most people have no difficulty accepting the fact that they are the sex they are. However, as we shall see in Chapter 3, all people have some difficulty, and some have a very considerable difficulty, in accepting the gender limitations associated with their sex.

As the child grows and learns to speak, the schemata in the child's comparator develop. The perception and expression of color is a traditional example. All human languages make the same fundamental distinctions: they have words for black and white—that is, dark color and light color. Most, but not all, add a word for red. Other colors, if they are coded in language, always follow in a specific order (Berlin and Kay 1969). That much would appear to result from the inborn perceiving apparatus of human beings. Tiv have a word for black (which includes blue), for white (which includes all light colors, even light blue), and for red (which includes yellow and orange). Their capacity to distinguish color is as sharp as anyone else's, but in order to express in language the other distinctions they perceive and care to make, they resort to metaphor: grass-colored or sky-colored. We do the same thing in English: the words orange, lavender, cerise—all are metaphors. Thus, the boundaries between color words exhibit a cultural dimension added to the physical perception.

Other schemata appear early. Anthropologists have paid most attention to the schemata underlying kinship terms (Lounsbury 1964), classification of body parts (Werner et al. 1986) or of plants (Berlin, Breedlove and Raven 1974). All contain a fascinating combination of the genetic and the cultural.

Choices

In the process of learning and adapting, a child makes the choices that ultimately create the person he or she becomes. There is no way that the child's choices can be controlled by someone else. The choices may be circumscribed by what the culture provides or by demanding individuals like parents, teachers or political leaders. But the child himself or herself makes the choices from among the available options.

The genetic endowment and the culture, taken together, set the parameters of choices, both conscious and unconscious. Faced with the options, the actual choice is what builds the person. When a child, for the first time, makes

Ethnocentrism is a natural result of human learning and of cultural stigmata. However, if we are to live in and run the global society into which we have evolved, we have to overcome that ethnocentrism. Anthropology is a good device for teaching people how to overcome ethnocentrism.

The choices people actually make from among possible choices determine what they become.

2-9.

a choice about how to solve a problem, and it works, then the child knows "how to do that." Knowing how to do something is of monumental significance for future behavior: the next time such a situation comes along, the child repeats the successful action. A barrier has been passed. To do it any other way means either that something has to be unlearned or that the child must begin to make further choices among several ways previously learned. We are marked by our choices, and thus by the cultural options we have chosen.

To sum up, in infancy and early childhood, the genetic capacities of the person are impacted by culture. The result is immense variation in people, far beyond their genetic differences. The cultural component becomes more and more dominant as the person gets older, makes more choices, has more experience. You are what you learn and what you do.

In every society, people recognize one or more ideal types of person. They may exert every effort to turn infants into one or another of those ideal types.

 Americans pay a lot of lip service to allowing children to develop in accordance with their own capacities. Yet, behind that lip service, a lot of pressure is applied to turn the kids into good little Americans. One of the most unusual aspects of American child rearing is that children learn very early that they are supposed to be independent and autonomous. I know a Dutch woman who saw an American mother who was having trouble with her two-year-old. When the mother said, "Well, make up your mind!", the Dutch woman was incensed—it was her premise that no child of that age should be allowed to, much less encouraged to, make up his or her own mind.

Other tenets of American culture are that children should be protected from death, that they should not learn about sex too young, and that there are many subjects simply unsuitable for children. Because some adults see at least some aspects of these subjects as shameful or as burdens, they say that they do not want to burden the child.

WE, THE ALIEN

Mobility

Once a child can walk, both the geographical sphere and the cultural sphere widen. Relationships with everybody and everything in the environment change. The people around the child step in to limit movement, sometimes by quite stringent means. In industrial societies, children have to be kept out of the way of automobiles; in technically simple societies, children have to be taught to avoid the open fire.

The most urgent task for two- or three-year-olds is learning the social skills that allow them to participate in social groups made up of three people or three parties—the triads we discussed in Chapter 1. The child learns that people with whom he or she interacts have social relationships with one another and that those relationships sometimes exclude the child. The child must learn the trust and patience required to wait, alone, until these important people resume interaction with him or her. The dyad and the triad are the basic social forms everywhere. We learn them before we are six.

Although they have been acquiring culture from the time of birth, children of five or six become aware that they must actively learn specific culture. All of us continue to pick up the way things are done—people of the modern world pick up a lot of culture from television—but we also turn to specific content of lessons in and out of school. "Acquired culture" is what we pick up in the processes of everyday living. "Learned culture" is what we purposefully set out to master.

"Learned Culture"

In most cultures today, a child becomes aware of peers at about the same time they are all required to attend school. Schools, and the education systems of which they are a part, primarily serve the needs of society. Only secondarily do they try to serve any special needs of the children. All schools are built to educate the young, and perhaps adults as well, in the ways of the culture. But that also means to indoctrinate. In school, the child learns not only academic subjects but also approved attitudes and behavior.

Schools, even simple ones, are complicated social systems. They have complex and specialized cultures. The more complex the cultural lessons that have to be taught, the more complex the social system of the school is likely to become. The social complexity may be a stumbling block in learning lessons.

Children today are expected to learn to read and write. Literacy involves transferring stimuli from one sense receptor channel to another. The fundamentally aural phenomenon of language must be reexperienced as a visual phenomenon. Some children have difficulty with this shift.

Becoming Adult

At puberty, the culture we must learn changes dramatically. Puberty is the set of physical changes that occur as a person reaches adulthood. Adolescence, on the other hand, is a culturally defined social status as well as a state of mind that begins at or before puberty and may go on long after physical maturity.

Most adolescents are physically adult but are socially and culturally unpracticed. Many societies mark the move from childhood to adulthood with a ritual or ceremony, as we shall see in Chapter 11. American adolescents, lacking initiation, find themselves in a sort of social limbo. The culture they learn or make up while in that limbo sometimes seems so attractive that they are reluctant to abandon it when they get older. Yet adulthood is the most rewarded status in all societies.

The view has long prevailed in the Western world that both character and social development are complete at the end of adolescence. That idea was so prevailing, in fact, that the study of the personal development of adults was scarcely deemed worthy of scientific effort. Adult problems were considered to be neuroses or personal inadequacies instead of problems of normal development. We have come at last to see that idea as an error.

As one moves from adolescence to adulthood, the pressures of bodily growth subside but the pressures of one's cultural environment leap into even greater prominence. People must, in the novice phase of adulthood (Levinson 1978), begin to find their own pathway through life. Most will want to build a career, find a mate, and learn about marriage and starting a family. The culture puts its stamp on all those activities.

 In the United States, young people of both sexes are asked to separate from their families of origin and reintegrate themselves into what is called a family of their own. They must alter their relationships with their parents so that their own autonomy is assured.

After our break from our parents' authority, we then reestablish a new kind of relationship with our parents. The cultural goal is relationships that are loving and warm but which have no authority dimension or, ultimately, an inverted authority dimension.

Many cultures make demands of this sort on only one sex. In many societies in Africa, it is the women who must break with their parental homes and join their husbands' homes. They must adapt to the authority of a mother-in-law or a senior wife or both. And men must live their lives under the authority of their fathers as long as the father lives. It is true that the nature of the father's authority is changed and attenuated, but it is there. I have heard Africans say that so-and-so is unlucky because, when he is sixty, his old father is still alive. The implication is that, as long as the father lives, the son cannot fully become his own man.

American culture makes us free of these requirements. Americans do not have to "suffer" (in their terms) living with their mothers-in-law or waiting until the death of their fathers to become fully adult. The down-side of this arrangement is, of course, that they are sometimes lonely and without social support.

WE, THE ALIEN

The first half of life is built around a biological program: you grow up, go through puberty, and become an adult. During the second half of life, the biological dimension continues but diminishes in importance until the onset of old age. The study of the mature years, like that of young adulthood, is seriously neglected.

American culture, in spite of the fact that it tries to convince us that it is a youth-oriented culture, nevertheless gives most of the advantages and rewards to the middle-aged. American educational systems, health care system, and many services are inadequate both for the young and the very old—but more nearly adequate for people of middle age.

Parenting

Parenthood most often begins when one is in early adulthood. Like marriage, parenthood confers a status that, in most societies, is highly valued. The parent observes the child traversing the same life-space as the parent traveled; the roles are now reversed. The parent is learning to teach culture as well as continuing to learn it. Just as the healthy infant thrives on good parenting, so the healthy parent arrives at a new level of personal satisfaction as the child thrives. Being a parent gives you a view of the life course—and hence of your culture—from two places at once. If culture in the outside world is changing rapidly, the difference between the generations may become painful or even incomprehensible to the parent.

Grandparenting is a superb arena for reviewing the life course—and culture. As you watch your grandchildren growing up, and as you identify with them, you have an opportunity to view a third trip through the life course. The similarities—and differences—between your own experiences, those of your children, and those of the grandchildren offer an excellent means of tracing both genetic and cultural influences. Grandparents also have a ringside seat for the interplay between the two younger generations.

Essential Selves

The biology of aging is not yet well understood. We do know that aging is genetically triggered. In the early 1960s, it was discovered that our cells themselves go through a process of aging. After a certain number of generations, they die. Aging seems to result from the inability of cells to replicate indefinitely without some loss of their capacity to function. Aging is genetically encoded in the cell.

The older person's capacity to function is absolutely dependent on the twin pillars of good health and cultural support.

With interesting work and a degree of self-direction, intellectual functioning improves in old age. However, some societies—especially those who live at the edge of subsistence—were simply not equipped to deal with members who had outlived their capacity to make direct contributions of food and work. In traditional Eskimo societies of the 1800s,

Learning to be old is a difficult cultural lesson in American society. It involves giving up a lot of culture and a lot of activities. Our language does not even have adequate words to describe older people who are healthy, active and creative. We fall back on calling them "young at heart," and tell them they don't look their age. Being healthy, active and creative has no biological correlation with youth—our culture makes the correlation because it hasn't as yet created other means for thinking about and expressing these ideas.

WE, THE ALIEN

old people were sometimes abandoned to die when they could no longer keep up. Records of several hunting and gathering societies tell of such abandoning of the very old. Some even report that the people were callous about abandoning them—perhaps, but what feelings might that callousness have covered? We don't know.

2-10. We learn our mother-culture as we grow up. All our lives we continue learning more parts of it—learning culture is a lifelong process. If we do not drop out, the learning process continues—dropping out is refusing the challenge to learn anything new.

Even in our own society, the lives of old people may be subject to severe stimulus deprivation; old people who are healthy and get enough stimulus, do not deteriorate mentally. Stimulus is as important to the very old as it is to the very young.

In the early twentieth century, almost everyone defined aging in terms of decline rather than in terms of development. That is an error like defining mental disease as a moral flaw in the patient. In the 1960s, doctors and biologists began to realize that mental impairment is not a natural condition of old age. Senility is a product either of disease or of stimulus deprivation.

All of us reinterpret our lives at many stages, but old age seems to work best if we can organize a full review of our lives. An honest review involves coming to terms with both our accomplishments and our shortcomings without denial and without falling back on old defenses. It is the time to organize one's autobiography—an acceptable view of oneself, and one's culture.

One of the first signs that young Americans have reached adulthood is that at age twelve, they are required to pay adult prices to the movies and they are no longer eligible for a child's portion at a restaurant. One of the first signs to older Americans that they are senior citizens is that they receive a discount at some movies and reduced senior prices/portions are available at some restaurants.

WE, THE ALIEN

The differences among persons are more stark in old age than is true for any earlier life stage. As gerontologist Robert Kastenbaum puts it in his lectures, "Life experience particularizes us." Old people have become their essential selves. At the earliest ages of life, genetic endowment was paramount; in middle life, cultural dimensions are most prominent. But with old age, it is the person that shows—one's character and the culture it has encapsulated. *This* is what we are. It was our genes and our culture that have made us so.

ETHNOCENTRISM

The same processes through which we learn culture, which makes us persons and allows us to share ideas, also make us ethnocentric. **Ethnocentrism** is an anthropological term that has made it into the dictionaries. It is an attitude that regards one's own group or culture as superior and is contemptuous of other groups and cultures. Every group looks down on

2-11. We can also learn foreign languages and cultures as we grow older, but once we are adult, learning other cultures becomes a conscious process. Not only do we learn, but we realize that we are learning alternative ways of doing what we already know one way to do. These Americans are trying to learn Philippine dance steps at an outdoor exhibition in San Francisco.

others, although how it does so may vary culturally.

Ethnocentrism comes in three forms. The simplest form occurs when a person naively assumes that the premises underlying culture are the same everywhere. During my field-work among the Tiv, I spent a morning questioning an old man about the political organization of his society. After a couple of hours, he said, "I have now told you everything. You know all that I know. Now you must tell me how your country is governed." I took a deep breath and began with what was a true statement at the time, "We have an immensely big country that is divided into forty-eight segments that we call states."

The old man interrupted. "You skipped some generations," he said with total certainty. That is not a nonsequitur in his culture. The political organization of his society, and therefore his view of political organizations in general, is based on a cultural model that holds that (1) each geographical segment of his country is occupied by the descendants of one man and (2) the ancestor of the next adjacent segment was his brother. To describe the next level of organization, the Tiv refer to all people who live in the two adjacent segments as descended from brothers with a common ancestor. So it goes, with ever larger groups, for seventeen to twenty generations. The map of the entire countryside is thus coordinated with a single genealogy that includes a million people. Knowing that premise, you can understand why the old man said, "You skipped some generations" when I jumped from one to forty-eight. All of us on some occasions are probably guilty of this kind of simple ethnocentrism—indeed some humanist scholars call it "naive realism."

A more complex kind of ethnocentrism arises when

people know very well that cultural differences exist but rather than trying to understand the other culture and to see the common humanity through the differences, they brand the other culture as incorrect at best, perhaps immoral, maybe even inferior, and at worst downright evil (LeVine and Campbell 1972). A liberal education can be viewed as a running battle with ethnocentric ideas. The more we learn, the better we understand the provincialism in our premises and the attitudes that grow from them.

The most complex form of ethnocentrism—and the first step in moving beyond it—involves the realization that other peoples are also ethnocentric. They think their way is good and true for exactly the same reason that we believe in ours. They think the way we do things is really weird. From their point of view, they are right—we are the aliens.

I was coming home on a streetcar late one August afternoon from the play-ground where I taught during some summer vacations while I was a college student. White and Negro men who had obviously been digging and . . . working in the sun boarded the car. They were all dirty and sweaty. . . . A white woman standing by me complained about the smell of the Negroes; they did smell. I wondered about the white workers and moved next to them; they smelled, too. The blue cotton uniform which I wore as a playground teacher was wet with perspiration from my strenuous day. I then became aware that I smelled. [It] was a discovery.

Hortense Powdermaker (1966)

THEY SAID IT

FIELDWORK: HOW WE LEARN OTHER CULTURES

All ethnographic facts have two components: (1) what some people themselves did or said or meant, and (2) what some fieldworker (or historian) made of it. There is no such thing as an unobserved ethnographic fact. Therefore, the personal qualities and observational skill of the observer are central.

Alien and Friend

Anthropologists are different from travelers or immigrants. Alien status is an essential point to be used, not just an inconvenience to be overcome. Travel to distant lands, or down the street, is for the specific purpose of not only learning but also understanding another culture—ideally, understanding it just as the natives themselves understand it. Whereas

Learning Culture

immigrants adapt their ways to become more like their new neighbors, anthropological fieldworkers must keep a foot in both cultures—their own and the one they are studying. We ourselves become the bridge across which information flows from one culture to the other.

When anthropologists go to the field, they necessarily take their own version of their native culture. They also take special anthropological training. The training includes ways of using the self in observing alien cultures in order to understand how the people themselves view the culture. Sometimes both the anthropologist's native culture and the training must be overcome. While those two elements can be beneficial in understanding new behavior, they can also act as blinders.

In the ritualized anthropological process known as participant observation, we lived for one year (on boiled eel and other delicacies from the sea) in a thatched two-story cottage (available because no fisherman would live in it) warmed by a single pot-bellied stove through a winter that froze the open sea and locked all sailing vessels in the long twilight of the subarctic.

Most fieldwork, I suspect, begins badly. More charitably I should perhaps state that my record in establishing field rapport is far from emulable. During our first month in Taarnby I was inadequate in everything I did. As a matter of fact, just plain inadequacy was a level of performance to which I aspired.

Barbara Gallatin Anderson (1990)

THEY SAID IT

Anthropologists are themselves the instruments for studying other people. Although they can achieve a certain objectivity through training and practice, they cannot become a machine or a camera. An anthropologist cannot keep his or her personality out of the work. This human instrument is a product of biological and cultural conditioning, just like the people studied, but the content of the anthropologist's conditioning is different.

Ethnography

Ethnography involves two stages. The first is fieldwork. In the field you must learn to understand the subject culture. That involves two simultaneous understandings: you must know why you see it as you do—that is, you make some of your own schemata conscious—and you must be able to communicate with the people you are studying, in their own language, so that you can, at least to some degree, also under-

stand why they see it as they see it—a process that means internalizing *their* schemata.

In the second stage, you must help others overcome ethnocentrism—you must describe the "native" version of reality in English or some other language of analysis, using your knowledge of your discipline and taking the reader's culture into account so that the reader's culture will not get in the way of his or her understanding.

This task—writing ethnography—involves translating what you have learned from the people you have studied into what is, for them and for the data, a foreign language. Carrying out this task demands more than the study of a subject people. It also demands careful study of similar aspects of one's own culture in order to achieve the kind of stereoscopic vision that brings *both* cultures into focus.

2-12. Anthropologists struggle to overcome ethnocentrism, both their own and that of their readers. They translate what they have learned in the field into the language and schemata that can be understood by readers and students— but they do it by explaining the schemata of the people they studied.

Preparation for the Field

In the early days of anthropology, the desire to do fieldwork was fueled by the fact that nothing was known about many existing peoples. In the late 1930s, as more anthropologists went to the field, that began to change. With more information available, the fieldworker had to isolate a more specific problem to be investigated. Anthropologists today almost without exception go to the field with elaborate plans to garner specific types of information about specific areas of life of the people they study.

The goal is both to fill in blanks in the ethnographic map or the history of a people and to make contributions to anthropological theory. If a fieldworker specializes too narrowly and does not cut a broad enough cultural swath, he or she misses the ways in which the topics of special interest fit into the whole context of the culture. A good example of how to do it right is found in the work of Nancy Levine, whose studies of family life in the Himalayas we shall review in Chapter 4. She set out to gather specific information on polyandry, the system in which one woman marries a group of brothers. Her work is a model of the ideal balance between selecting and analyzing a problem and reporting its context.

Before you go to the field, you must study everything that has been written or filmed about the people you propose to study, as well as their neighbors. Be forewarned, however, that the situation you find will differ from what earlier ethnographers reported. There are two reasons for the difference. First, cultures change rapidly with time. And

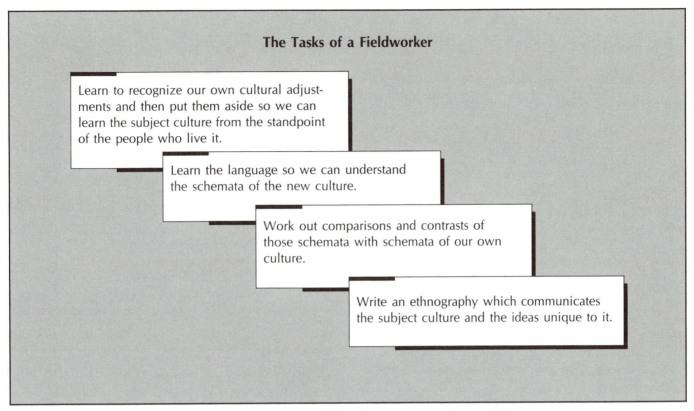

The Tasks of a Fieldworker

Learn to recognize our own cultural adjustments and then put them aside so we can learn the subject culture from the standpoint of the people who live it.

Learn the language so we can understand the schemata of the new culture.

Work out comparisons and contrasts of those schemata with schemata of our own culture.

Write an ethnography which communicates the subject culture and the ideas unique to it.

2-13. The above shows a common pattern to follow when we learn cultures which are foreign to us.

second, the ideas you bring with you will be somewhat different from those of your predecessors. For example, Rupert East, who translated *Akiga's Story* (Akiga, 1939), a book by a Tiv in his own language about his own people, said specifically that the Tiv had an ancestral cult. During my fieldwork, I looked in vain for that ancestral cult. Finally a young man who had traveled widely in Nigeria and was home for a visit told me, "You are asking questions as if we were Igbo." His statement made me consider for the first time that perhaps the Tiv did *not* have an ancestral cult, rather than making the uncharitable and, as it turned out, false assumption that they were holding out on me. When I went back to *Akiga's Story* I discovered that it was not Akiga who said anything about an ancestral cult; Rupert East, the translator, said it in his otherwise useful notes. The Tiv have all the components of an ancestral cult, but they do not organize the components in that way.

Fieldwork in Small-scale Societies

The major technique of modern fieldwork is called **participant observation**. The fieldworker lives with the people he or she has chosen to study, participates in their lives to whatever extent they allow, and takes notes on what happens. Before one can do that, however, basic necessities must be arranged.

A fieldworker first needs a place to live. The great ethnographer Bronislaw Malinowski pitched a tent a few paces from the center of the village of Kiriwina on the Trobriand Islands

off the coast of New Guinea when he worked there in the 1920s. He could see almost everything that was going on in the public places of the village; conversely, the villagers could see him and almost everything he did. Evans-Pritchard, a British ethnographer who worked in Africa in the 1930s, lived in an empty Nuer hut. In 1949, in the south part of Tivland, I had huts built by the local people, and I paid them

2-14. Fieldworkers must live close to the people they study. This photograph shows Bronislaw Malinowski's tent in a village in the Trobriand Islands in the early 1920s, with Malinowski himself standing beside it.

Learning Culture

for the materials and for the work. My compound within the compound of an important man in the area of MbaDuku was composed of a sleeping hut with a large veranda where I could work, a sleeping hut for the cook, a kitchen hut, and a big reception hut (like the other reception huts of the area) where people could come to sit and talk. Fieldworkers today may rent houses or rooms; some move in with families. The only real requirement is that your residence not be cut off from the people you study. You don't finish a day's work and "go home." Fieldwork is a twenty-four-hour-a-day undertaking.

Some fieldworkers are willing to rough it more than others. Whatever your own preferences, the people you are studying will also have some ideas about where—and how—you are going to live. Listening to their opinions is an important first step in successful fieldwork.

Another major concern is deciding how to spend your time. Running a household, securing supplies, and cooking could steal valuable time from the observation of other activities. Time budgets work for anthropologists in exactly the same way as they do for anyone else; time spent on one task means less time for another. Fieldworkers often need someone to help with routine chores. In Africa in the 1940s and 1950s, anthropologists hired local people to market, cook, wash clothes, and sweep the compound. The earliest close relationships developed during fieldwork are usually with the people who work for and, ultimately, with the fieldworker.

2-15. Fieldworkers must be able to eat almost anything. (They don't have to like it, but it helps.)

One of the requirements of fieldworking anthropologists is that they be able to eat almost anything. Many anthropologists in the early part of this century, especially those who worked among Native North Americans and Africans, did their own hunting and helped supply meat to the village. In most places today, fieldworkers buy their food in the local market. If you go to the market yourself, it will be time-consuming and you will probably pay several times as much as your cook would. During my stay in Africa, cooks saved me at least as much as I paid them. At any rate, it is the fieldworker's business to find out what foods are available, how they are grown or gathered, and how they are prepared. You will either eat what the locals eat (perhaps prepared a little differently) or will be faced with importing food, which may be difficult and expensive. It is no accident that experienced fieldworkers have published several anthropological cookbooks of field-tested recipes from all over the world.

Many anthropologists take their spouses with them on field expeditions, but for the single fieldworker sexual relations should be considered carefully. A lot of advice is exchanged among fieldworkers concerning this topic. Several points are critical. First of all, if you do engage in sexual relations with someone from the native culture, do not use that experience as the basis for writing about native sexual practices. In the second place, you should think about all the implications of your behavior. What will be the expectations of the sexual partner? Or his or her kinfolk? Of the community? What have you started that may not have a comfortable ending? Although many fieldworkers, both male and female, have carried out successful affairs in the field, the usual advice has been, and still is, don't try it. If you do, you increase the complexity of your position in the society. You cease to be what Hortense Powdermaker called "stranger and friend"; instead, you become quasi-kinsperson who either lives up to the intensified cultural expectations—or doesn't, and has to suffer the consequences.

Fieldworkers need emotional support in the field as much as they do anywhere else. A letter from a colleague or a supervisor can be a great respite. However, for sheer human companionship, for people to reassure you that you exist because they recognize that you are there and listen to what you say, you have to fall back on the people of the community you are studying.

This was my first night in Lesu alone. I sat on the veranda of my thatch-roofed two-room house in the early evening. I felt uncertain and scared, not of anything in particular but just of being alone in a native village. I asked myself, 'What am I doing here, all alone and at the edge of the world?' . . . Sitting on my veranda, presumably ready to begin work, yet in a panic[,] I asked myself again, why am I here alone? . . . I must have been mad. . . . I would go home on the next boat. . . . [Then] visitors arrived. Ongus, the *luluai* [chief appointed by the Australian colonial government], with his wife Pulong, and their adolescent daughter Batu. . . . They presented me with a baked taro. . . . Ongus and his daughter spoke pidgin English. As we talked, Ongus gave me some words of the native language which I wrote down. . . . He also told me a little about himself. . . . At the end of a few hours he said that he would soon call all the people together so that I could explain to them what I planned to do. He mentioned that they were very curious. . . . When they were leaving, Ongus said that I should 'sing out' if I needed anything and he would come immediately. Their house was directly opposite mine.

I was no longer alone. I had friends. I went to bed and fell asleep almost immediately. . . . Several years later I learned that a definition of panic is a state of unrelatedness.

Hortense Powdermaker (1966)

THEY SAID IT

It helps if the people allow you to make friends without joining factions. In some communities this proves difficult because friendships with members of one group may identify you with that group, which may mean that you are shunned or even reviled by members of some other groups. If that happens to you, you can get only a very partial view of the culture. Being aware of the possible difficulty is usually enough to allow you to avoid the trap.

There are a number of jobs that require concerted effort with all aspects of one's personality: teaching, parenting, being a psychotherapist. Fieldwork is such a job. You are yourself the tool or instrument through which you discover a new culture. Therefore, the better you know the quirks and limitations of your instrument, the better your field research. What is called for is to be honest with yourself. That is easy to say but difficult to do. Our defense mechanisms are so good that we often confuse what we want to be with what we really are.

One of the best ways to sharpen your research skills is to acknowledge and then to analyze the moral and physical discomforts you experience in the field. Almost all field-workers are emotionally uncomfortable from time to time (Malinowski 1967; Cesara 1982). That discomfort provides the best raw material for insights. If you are emotionally uncomfortable—that is if you irrationally hate the people you came to study, are plagued by homesickness, or are depressed—you have to figure out why. Conversely, you may sometimes need to decide why you are not emotionally uncomfortable in the field! The results can lead to important insights about both the people you are studying and yourself.

2-16. Anthropologists must figure out what makes them uncomfortable in the field, then question that part of their own culture and experience which creates the discomfort. That process is the best way to reveal their own schemata, which were probably unconscious until they were exposed by the discomfort.

Taking care of basic needs is one way that a fieldworker participates in daily life. Once those needs are satisfied, the participant observation should take a new turn. You must join the people in their activities so that you can get the culture into your mind and muscles. It is learning-through-doing. Such participation is necessarily limited by the degree to which the people will allow it. More often, however, the major limitations are in the fieldworker. In these early days of your fieldwork, you can make dictionaries or word-lists of the language. You can make censuses of the community if nobody objects. You can learn technical processes and you can collect some folk tales to assist in learning the language. Even the best and most thorough participant observation will move you only to the point where you can say "Some people do and some don't" about any subject. To get beyond

that point, you have to turn to other methods.

Interviewing soon becomes an integral part of your participant observation process—you are the participant who asks all those strange questions. At first, the interviews must be open-ended and informal—that is, you will learn what the people do and say among themselves rather than seeking answers to specific questions. As the fieldwork proceeds, issues will emerge clearly from the informal exchanges. You may want to zero in on those issues that you don't fully understand. You will need precise information when you return home to inform your colleagues about the culture. You can now begin to do closed-ended interviews—interviews that follow a specific structure instead of casual associations. You can also ask people to answer a questionnaire. But remember that building a good questionnaire is a highly skilled occupation; most questionnaires are unconsciously designed only to confirm what people think they already know or what they want to hear.

Perhaps most important of all is what can be called accidental fieldwork. It occurs when you are not trying to "do fieldwork" at all but are merely in search of human companionship. On evenings when nothing much was happening, I would wander out into the larger compound just to talk to other people who were sitting in front of their houses enjoying the breeze. I did not take a notebook. I wasn't consciously doing fieldwork; I was looking for company. Only later did I realize that some of the most rewarding fieldwork of my entire stay came in these sessions when I was nobody but me, going out to find people I liked, to yatter with my friends. When that happens, the information is likely to come almost as if by magic—and you know you are doing something right.

You will be accepted, one way or another, on the basis of your personality. If you are nit-picking, guarded and selfish, you will be accepted as a miser. If you are open and joking, you will be accepted as a joker. If you are genuinely helpful—and especially if you really listen—you will be accepted as a "good guy." Acceptance is quite different from finding your role in the community. Ultimately, the people will decide your role. You certainly will not be able to plan what your role will be before you go. Like all social relationships, fieldwork is a two-way street.

One person can never know what another feels or thinks. However, one person can know, with a greater or lesser degree of understanding, what another person says or does. We necessarily run the messages we receive from others through our own perceptual apparatus, as was diagrammed in 2-5. The process is likely to introduce some differences from the original message. Fieldwork is a constant struggle to refine one's own schemata so that the distortion is reduced.

Observation has been scientized in recent years with the development of a number of specific techniques. **Ethnoscience** is a set of methods, based on linguistic schemata, for understanding the criteria by which people make linguistic or other distinctions. Discourse analysis is an organized way for examining what people mean when they say what they say.

Learning Culture

Participant observation objectives:

☐ Find a place to live with which you and the people you are studying are both comfortable.

☐ Learn the language well enough that they can understand what you say and you can understand what they say to each other. Only in this way can an ethnographer come to grips with the schemata of the people whose culture he or she is studying.

☐ Find your major companionships and friendships among the people you are studying. Attend as many happenings or events as possible. Hang out! Work along side. Be there!

You then may wish to add:

☐ Specific linguistic research into the schemata of the people.

☐ Censuses or other records of who is present.

☐ Interviews on specific topics.

In more complex cultures you may add:

☐ Survey research with questionnaires.

☐ Other projects using methods more commonly employed by political scientists and sociologists.

2-17. *Primary Field Methods.*

A month after the curing ceremonies, I paid my last visit to Sohn Alpet.... As always, he had something to tell me. ''I am going to die and we must say good-bye.''

My capacity for denial is immense, and no one had ever spoken to me like this. ''Oh no, Nahnid, don't say that. We haven't tried everything to cure you. You won't die. You can't die....''

He persisted, ''Karapei, be calm. How many times have I told you not to wave your arms around, raise your voice, and reveal your feelings? ... I have had a good, long life and die surrounded by my family. You will have to learn to say good-bye to those who are dying and grieving well for them is a gift of the spirit few are granted. This is the last thing I can teach you.''

I cried, tried other avenues of defense, and finally relented to listen as I had on so many less painful occasions.... We laughed and joked. We talked about death. He was right; I had much to learn. And then we said good-bye.

Martha C. Ward (1989)

THEY SAID IT

One must be careful, however, that one does not use scientific methods as a buffer against the very kinds of discomfort that lead to learning. Achieving insight into other cultures can be an intense and confrontive personal experience. Sometimes it is painful (Devereaux 1968).

Fieldwork is a highly emotional undertaking. Good fieldworkers often use their emotions as guides for inquiry. They find that much of their best data comes from exploring the situations that produce emotions in them. The emotions are not the data. The data come from discovery of the reasons behind the emotional reactions. The stimulus is the original emotional reaction; the behavior is the intellectual analysis that results from the comparator weighing the input based on all the genetic and learned experience available.

Fieldwork in Complex Modern Societies

Working in complex societies imposes different conditions on the fieldworker. Much (but by no means all) fieldwork carried out by practicing anthropologists today is done in large-scale complex cultures.

I know, for example, an anthropologist whose assignment was to analyze why so few American customers came to a shopping mall owned by a Japanese firm located in the United States. By hanging out in the mall and doing participant observation, the anthropologist discovered many things about American preferences. When Americans go shopping, they like to browse. They want to sit, to talk, to have plenty of opportunity to look at the products without being approached by a clerk, although they want a clerk handy when they need one. Clerks had been trained by the Japanese owners to approach customers immediately. The anthropologist urged the owners to create a browsing environment and to train their clerks in the American way. Business immediately picked up. Obviously this particular fieldwork experience did not involve selecting a place to live, resolving the question of shopping/cooking, or learning a language.

My own field research among aging men living in center city hotels in San Diego taught me a lot. I lived in the hotels only for a few weeks, although two of my colleagues (there were four fieldworkers involved in this study) lived there for months at a time and one even took a job as hotel clerk (Eckert 1980). Their observations about what happened at night or on holidays proved, once again, that in order to be close to people you must live where they live. We could begin formal interviews at an earlier stage than we would have if we had not already known the language. The four of us soon began to zero in on the precise information we needed; we used questionnaires to elicit much of it. These methods work in our society because Americans expect social scientists to do this type of investigation and are ready for the inquiries (Bohannan 1981).

2-18. The processes of learning and reporting other cultures make the anthropologist realize that our own culture is only one more way to lead a good-enough human life. It is alien to everyone except ourselves. The photograph shows anthropologist Laura Nader in rural southern Mexico.

CONCLUDING THOUGHTS

An anthropologist who does fieldwork learns culture twice. We can apply the same principles to our own journey through life—to participate actively in that journey as opposed to passively absorbing whatever comes our way. We can begin by looking carefully at what goes on around us. What is that person telling me? What in my own training and experience makes it difficult for me to understand what is going on? You begin to see all around you the interplay of culture and character, of differentness, of discourse. You see with a new awareness. "Fieldwork," once you become familiar with it, becomes a way of life, a sort of sixth sense that broadens you as you respond to any environment, familiar or strange. Ultimately, you are never out of the field, no matter where you go.

BUZZWORDS

ethnocentrism the emotional attitude, whether conscious or unconscious, that regards one's own group and its culture as the measure by which all others should be judged.

ethnoscience a technique of field research that helps uncover how the native people in a culture view the organization of their ideas and activities.

participant observation a research technique in which the anthropologist participates in the activities of the people being studied, as far as they will allow. The anthropologist also takes careful notes and makes preliminary analyses that are checked out with the people for correction.

schemata (singular, schema) conceptual categories, often abstract, for understanding and interrelating what we perceive with what we already know, and for making organized sense of what is in our minds. Schemata are something like a filing system—they give us a place to put new ideas and make it possible to interconnect and find the many different parts of our culture.

KINSHIP

II

The most fundamental of all social relationships are the relationships of kinship. Kinship has both a biological and a cultural meaning. The biological meaning is concerned with shared genes, and the cultural meaning is concerned with cooperation, education, and inheritance. The biological and the cultural dimensions of kinship are intertwined and complex. Their relationship poses some of the toughest questions in anthropology. Kinship involves reproduction, thus sex, and therefore, among human beings at least, gender. It involves parenthood. It involves sisterhood, brotherhood and trust.

The human family is the most fundamental of all human social institutions. It can provide everything that a person needs except a mate—and more inclusive kinship systems can do even that. Small, technologically simple social groups of human beings need no further institutions beyond the family and the group of families. As society becomes more complex and culture is more highly developed, specialized social organizations take over some of the basic activities that were previously family functions. In almost every social context, sex and the family remain at the core of human concerns.

Books to Change Your Life   *Martha C. Ward*

Fernea, Elizabeth Warnock
1965 *Guests of the Sheik: An Ethnography of an Iraqi Village*. New York: Doubleday & Co., Inc.
1975 *A Street in Marrakech: A Personal View of Urban Women in Morocco*. New York: Doubleday & Co.,
      Inc. Reissued 1988 by Waveland Press, Inc., Prospect Heights, IL.
1991 *Nubian Ethnographies* (with Robert A. Fernea and Aleya Rouchdy). Prospect Heights, IL: Waveland Press, Inc.
      All of Fernea's books enter the unknown and private world of veiled women, devout Muslims and Middle
      Eastern households. From hostility to trust, she shows lives most Westerners will never see.

Hart, C.W.M., Arnold Pilling, and Jane Goodale
1988 *The Tiwi of North Australia, Third Edition*. New York: Holt, Rinehart and Winston, Inc.   Three
      anthropologists who have worked there at different times cover the wheeling and dealing around marriage
      contracts and modern consumer goods (among many other problems). This new cooperative synthesis
      brings these important people into a new incarnation.

Herdt, Gilbert H.
1986 *The Sambia: Ritual and Gender in New Guinea*. New York: Holt, Rinehart and Winston, Inc.   What can
      the ritualized homosexuality among young boys tell us about our own rituals and about formation of
      gender identity in our own society? You will read this avidly—that question may not occur to you until
      after you finish the book because you will be too busy to ask it on the way through.

Malinowski, Bronislaw Kasper
1929 *The Sexual Life of Savages in North-Western Melanesia*. London: Routledge & Kegan Paul. Reissued 1987
      by Beacon Press, Boston.   Malinowski wrote fine, clear English, although it was not his native language.
      Anything he wrote is worth reading. This book is so good you will not want to skip directly to the steamy
      parts. Like all of Malinowski's books, this one contains very important—and very early—insights into
      what anthropologists have learned and how they have learned it. You may also want to try Malinowski's
      Argonauts of the Western Pacific (1922), which is about the economic system of the Trobriand Islands, or
      *Coral Gardens and Their Magic: A Study of the Methods of Tilling the Soil and of Agricultural Rites in
      the Trobriand Islands, Vols. I and II* (London: Allen & Unwin, 1935; reissued 1965 by Indiana University
      Press, Bloomington), which is about agriculture, language, and magic.

Mead, Margaret
1930 *Growing Up in New Guinea: A Comparative Study of Primitive Education*. New York: William Morrow
      and Co.   Here is one of Mead's most widely read and copied studies. It was, and is, an important source
      about growing up. If this were a movie, the ads would say "So you thought your parents were weird!—
      peek in on the Manus." There is even a sequel called *New Lives for Old* (1956) about what happened to
      the children Mead studied when they had grown up.

Mead, Margaret
1935 *Sex and Temperament in Three Primitive Societies*. New York: Dell. Reissued 1971 by William Morrow
      and Co., New York.   A society where men are maternal; a society where foreplay means biting off
      eyebrows and a society where women are practical businessmen. This book is one of the masterpieces in
      the study of sex roles. Whether you believe them or not, Mead's examples of men and women in
      comparative cultures will haunt your thoughts and shift your perspectives.

Murphy, Yolanda and Robert F. Murphy
1985 *Women of the Forest, Second Edition*. New York: Columbia University Press.   An acute and fascinating
      battle of the sexes is going on deep in the Amazon rain forest. Why are the men obsessed with flutes?
      What are the women doing behind their backs? What does all this show us about how we ourselves live?

Turnbull, Colin M.
1961 *The Forest People* (with Foreword by Harry L. Shapiro). New York: Simon & Schuster.   This account of
      the lives of the gentle Mbuti pygmy hunters and gatherers has been popular for decades—for the very
      good reason that it is good ethnography and absolutely absorbing to read. The pygmies' capacity to make
      life feel good and simple makes you root for their survival.

Turnbull, Colin M.
1972 *The Mountain People*. New York: Simon & Schuster.
      The nasty habits of the Ik and their disregard for human life and civility made Turnbull ill. This book,
      and the Ik themselves, are fascinating for the same reason that horror movies are.

Weiner, Annette
1988 *The Trobrianders of Papua New Guinea*. New York: Holt, Rinehart and Winston, Inc.   After you have
      read Malinowski's justly famous books, you will want to turn to this one to find out what happens next to
      the Trobriand Islanders.

Men and Women, Sex and Babies

3

PROPOSITIONS AND PREMISES

- Because human beings are mammals, each individual is either male or female. Many characteristics besides reproduction derive from that fact.

- The sex drive is "culturized" among all human beings so that the resulting cultural practices, and especially evaluations of them, vary.

- Gender is any cultural way of assigning prerogatives and tasks to one sex or the other and of understanding and institutionalizing the similarities and differences between male and female. Gender is a cultural matter that may or may not be associated with biology.

- Sex identity is different from, and is recognized earlier (about the end of the first year) than, gender identity (about the fourth or even fifth year).

- Women are the "back-up gender" everywhere—they do the jobs that are not otherwise done.

- Sexism (which might better be called genderism) involves the introduction of a power system to disadvantage one sex or the other, usually women.

Reproduction, from the standpoint of the species, is the most vital goal for any animal; the survival of the species depends upon the production of new generations. For human beings, a second goal is added. For humanity to survive, culture must survive. For culture to survive, it must constantly be renewed, reinvented, and taught to new generations. The human species depends on culture as the primary means of adapting to changing environmental situations—the primary strategy for survival. Thus, for human beings, cultural contributions to the next generation may be as important as genetic contributions.

Among all mammals, the contribution of the female to reproduction takes far more time and effort than does the contribution of the male. Not only does a baby develop within the female's body, but it may also be nourished at her breasts for months or even years. A mammalian male can father literally dozens or even hundreds of offspring while a female is occupied with only one. These facts color the lives and reproductive strategies of human females and males just as much as they do those of any other mammals. These facts also color the *cultural* strategies of the two sexes, although anthropologists are only beginning to examine cultural strategies.

The disparity in the amount of time and energy required

3-2. *This picture shows an Indian mother in Bolivia. All mammalian females, including human females, invest more time and energy in the next generation than do males. Carrying, bearing, and nursing a child require far more time than begetting that same child. During the period of nursing, a female (almost always the mother) becomes the primary teacher of culture to the young. Once the child is weaned, males may (but may not) become more important in the education of the young.*

3-1. *Reproduction is, for all nonhuman animals, the ultimate goal of life. Successful reproduction requires success in food seeking, in surviving environmental dangers, and in rearing the young to adulthood.*

for reproduction, in complex cultures at least, may cause conflict. The consequences of reproduction are different for females and males. Men and women have similar goals in wanting to structure a meaningful life, but genetic constraints may sometimes interfere with their plans.

There are at least two aspects of **reproduction** (see 3-3). One is **procreation**—the biological processes of conceiving and bearing the next generation. The other is nurturing the young until they reach an adult state so they can, in their turn, reproduce. Among human beings, that means **enculturation** (providing the situation in which the young person can acquire culture). Because a baby learns culture from the

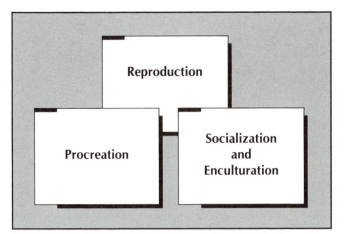

3-3. *There are two dimensions of successful reproduction: the sexual act (biological process) by which the young are conceived and born, and the care and enculturation of the young.*

moment of birth, early cultural lessons primarily come from women, usually from mothers. In both biological and cultural processes, the female is usually responsible for the young for longer periods of time than is the male. The role of women in reproduction is central. It is so central that males in some societies, particularly in South America and New Guinea, have tried to usurp, at least symbolically, the female role in reproduction. We shall examine these attempts later in this chapter.

There are issues of vital importance to every human group which can be culturized in different ways. We will explore: (1) cultural variation in attitudes toward sexuality, (2) cultural ideas about the contributions of the two sexes to reproduction, (3) nonreproductive sexual activities, and (4) sexism (the relationship between gender and power).

3-4. *Among human beings, a second goal is just as important as biological reproduction: assuring the survival of culture and its adjustment and change. Human beings are not human without culture. Teachers (including parents) are to the survival of culture what parents are to the survival of genes.*

3-5. *Sexuality, child rearing practices, and education are the essential underpinning of reproductive success among human beings. If all of them are successful, both genes and culture survive and prosper. Henry Moore,* Family Group, *(1948-49).*

SEXUALITY

Sexuality has an immense capacity for integrating society — and just as immense a capacity for disrupting it. The fact that almost everybody does it does not mean that they (or we) know a great deal about it. It is similar to the fact that you don't have to understand the principles of the internal combustion engine to be able to drive a car. The topic of sexuality is so culturally overloaded that it is very difficult for anybody to think clearly about it.

A beginning step in the complex task of understanding sexuality is to distinguish four distinct but related facets of the subject.

- **Sex** is *genetically determined*. It is about the biological differences between males and females. It is not sufficiently distinguished, in our culture, from either gender or sexuality.
- **Sexuality** is *behavior* involving the organs that determine sex.
- **Gender** is about *social roles* — the cultural assignment of personal qualities and activities for each sex.
- **Reproduction** includes both procreation and bringing the offspring to successful adulthood. The future of both the species and the culture are thus assured.

Men and Women, Sex and Babies

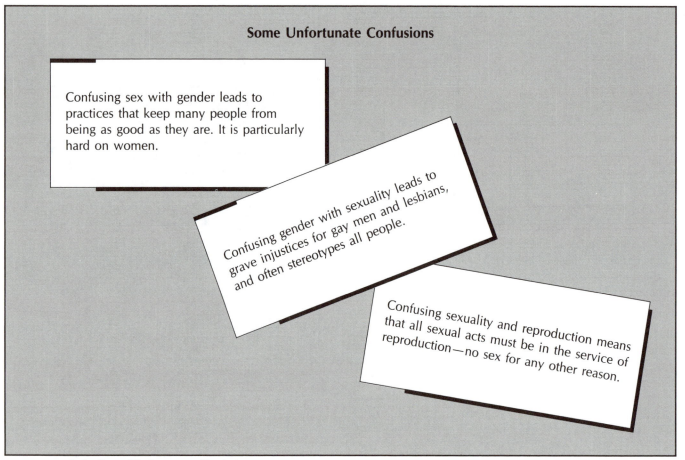

Some Unfortunate Confusions

Confusing sex with gender leads to practices that keep many people from being as good as they are. It is particularly hard on women.

Confusing gender with sexuality leads to grave injustices for gay men and lesbians, and often stereotypes all people.

Confusing sexuality and reproduction means that all sexual acts must be in the service of reproduction—no sex for any other reason.

3-6. Some Unfortunate Confusions.

Distinguishing among these topics is the first requirement for clarifying our thinking. First, (biological) *sex* is to be distinguished from (cultural) *gender*; Westerners have long been uncertain about this topic, in part because we have not sufficiently taken into consideration that sex is only one of many criteria in any definition of gender.

Next, *sex* (what you are) is also to be distinguished from *sexuality* (what you do). Sexuality includes both your opinions about what you do and the opinions of other people.

Gender is also to be distinguished from *sexuality*. Any culture's idea of gender both limits and directs the possible sexual behavior males and females will choose in their sexual relations.

Further, *sexuality* must be distinguished from *procreation*—the creation of offspring—and from *reproduction*, which includes procreation *and* cultural ways of assuring a qualified new generation. Sexual intercourse—penetration of a penis into a vagina—is the only technique of sexuality that can result in procreation. For this reason, it has been the overwhelmingly privileged expression of sexuality in law, custom, and religion. It is certainly not, however, the only common expression of sexuality. For the individual, sexuality affects such matters as formation and maintenance of a good self-image and many aspects of behavior related to issues of power or the lack of it, as we shall discuss below.

Anthropologists who are interested in *reproduction* study a wide range of behavior. Sexuality and procreation form part of the range of reproductive behavior; other aspects include householding and the protection and enculturation of the young.

Attitudes Toward Sexuality

Among human beings, sexuality is not only about reproduction but also about love, kinship, power, guilt, joy, fun and good times, sadness and bad times, and attitudes toward the self and others. Sexuality is thoroughly culturized. There is, in fact, no nonculturized way for human beings to express or act out their sexuality. Sexuality is a series of structured activities—the structure and the behavior have to be learned. Sexuality may "come naturally," but no sexual acts can be performed nonculturally. Like all culture, it has to be learned—and may vary immensely from one place to another. In some places, people learn that it is normal to have sex three or more times a day. In other places, sexual activity is a rare occurrence. In some places, people are taught that in order to be potent, young men must first experience sexuality with older men. The actual sexual deeds that human beings can perform may be limited, but the way in which people can view those deeds and give preference to some over others does not seem to be.

Sexuality-Positive and Sexuality-Negative Cultures

Some societies take a negative view of sexuality while others take a positive view. A society has not yet been found in which there is never any anxiety about sexuality. Some societies are described as permissive, others as strict or controlling, but those distinctions are so oversimplified as to be almost unusable. Every society controls sexuality in the sense that none grants legitimacy to every possible sexual act. Our own has traditionally been what is usually called a sex-negative culture (to maintain the distinctions made above, sexuality-negative would be the correct, although admittedly clumsy, term). At the height of the negative phase, sexuality was to be expressed only in the service of procreation, and the association of the two was deemed "unfortunate." In other words, some self-appointed moralists considered it distasteful that sexuality was linked with the creation of offspring. During the twentieth century, American attitudes began to soften, and control was loosened. It is a matter of definition whether we are still a sexuality-negative culture.

Euro-American ideas about the nature of women changed completely between the seventeenth and the nineteenth centuries. The seventeenth century characterization as "the lusty sex" was slowly revised. By the nineteenth century, new attitudes assigned women the role of the passionless sex. In the same period, male sexuality was perceived as a danger to the man's health. Masturbation was condemned and said to lead to insanity; "excessive" sexuality was said to weaken the man and ultimately to kill him.

Clearly sexuality is more freely expressed in some societies than in others. The most restrictive society that has been reported in the literature is a community called Inis Beag (not its real name) in the islands west of Ireland (studied for a total of eighteen months between 1958 and 1966). The population at that time was about 350, distributed among four villages with a total of seventy-one cottages. Men were more socially active. Women left their cottages only to go to church, funerals and wakes, or to make an occasional call on relatives. The islanders lacked sexual knowledge and never talked about sex. They said that after marriage, "nature takes its course," and added that hence there was no need for sex education. These Irish islanders told the ethnographers that men were more libidinous than women; one woman said that "Men can wait a long time for 'it,' but we can wait a lot longer." Women said that sex was a duty to be endured. Female orgasm was apparently unknown. Men said intercourse was debilitating, and they stayed away from it before doing any job that would take strength.

The sexes were separated in almost all activities, even in church. Males told the ethnographers that they did not masturbate because they would be required to confess it to the priest. The report says that premarital coitus is unknown. Nudity is abhorred; indeed, they never learn to swim because they would have to undress. Infants are bathed every week; everybody else washes faces, necks, lower arms, hands, lower

3-7. All societies control people's sexuality—nowhere are all possible sexual acts approved or condoned. Attitudes toward sexuality can be arranged on a continuum between repressive and permissive. The first picture is an Israeli woman sunbathing in the Dead Sea. The second picture are Israeli women of the puritan quarter of Meir Shearim, where they are often segregated, in Jerusalem. Both pictures were taken in 1988.

Men and Women, Sex and Babies

legs, and feet—that's all. They change clothes in absolute privacy (under the bedclothes if privacy can be had no other way) and sleep in their underwear. Urination and defecation are done in secret. There is no dirty joke tradition. When they dance, the sexes never touch.

The ethnographers collected several explanations for this massive sexual repression. The historical explanations emphasize that when the Irish adopted Christianity very early, they particularly adhered to the sexuality-negative doctrine favored by St. Paul. The psychological explanations focus on the idea that Irish mothers, who were the cornerstone of the family, were nevertheless domineering, which led to anxiety in all men toward all women. Neither explanation is totally convincing.

This repression was anchored by (1) religious customs, including the idea, true or not, that some priests had informants in the community so that they could punish wrongdoers who did not confess, and (2) fear of gossip. People tried to avoid being gossiped about by giving nobody anything to say. All were constantly on guard against compromising situations. This fear of gossip was the major limitation on the activities of women: "If I went for a walk, they'd wonder why I wasn't home tending my chores" (Messenger 1971). (We should remember that the ethnography of Inis Beag in the 1950s does not represent all, or perhaps any significant proportion of, Irish culture in the 1990s.)

At the other extreme is another famous example—the Trobriand Islands of New Guinea, where youngsters are allowed complete sexual freedom until the time they marry. Young men entertain their girlfriends in the so-called bachelor's house with the knowledge and approval of the older generation (Malinowski 1929).

Attitudes about sex are so complex that one soon comes to realize that societies cannot be classified by anything so simplistic as whether they take a positive or negative view of sexuality. At first glance, the Mehinaku people of central Brazil seem to fit the label sexuality-positive. In one small Mehinaku village, there were twenty sexually active men and seventeen sexually active women. Only three of the women and none of the men were *not* active in extramarital affairs. One woman had had affairs with fourteen of the men; four women had had five affairs. One man had had ten affairs, and the average for the men was 4.4. Those extramarital affairs seldom provoked confrontations. Despite all this sexual contact, however, the Mehinaku suffer considerable anxiety about sexuality. Mehinaku divide their society into male and female worlds, kept separate by the men's fear of sexual pollution and by their anxiety that sexuality could make them ill, stunt their growth, and weaken their skill as wrestlers. Worst of all, it might attract dangerous spirits and limit their capacity to hunt and fish (Gregor 1985).

People in different societies discriminate differently about just which acts are permitted and which are restricted (Broude 1981). Classifying societies as merely positive or negative is too simplistic. One thing is certain: there is no society without an elaborate pattern of what forms of sexuality are permitted and what are restricted. The differences lie in just what and how much is permitted or restricted.

Cultural Ideas About Menstruation

The so-called sexual revolution has given us considerable freedom in talking about some aspects of reproduction. However, menstruation is still a taboo topic for many Americans. Although it is an integral physical part of procreation, its most interesting aspects are cultural. Many societies mark menstruation with special treatment of women. In fact, one study found that only fourteen out of seventy-one tribal cultures did *not* have menstrual taboos (Gregor 1985, citing Stephens).

In Inis Beag, both menstruation (for which the islanders have no explanation) and menopause (which they also cannot explain but which, they said, could create madness) build anxiety because nobody understands why these physical functions occur. Young women are absolutely unprepared. Men are said to know nothing about it. In Mehinaku, everybody knows about it, even the children, but menstruating women are nevertheless secluded—the reported purpose of the seclusion is to protect men, medicines, and sacred symbols from pollution.

Many cultures, like the Mehinaku, claim that menstrual fluids harm males, or that they also harm the crops, the gods, or the sacred emblems of the group. Women may be isolated from men during the period of menstruation and often go through purification after each period. Recent research reveals, however, that seclusion during menstruation often works in women's favor, giving them a much needed rest from the hard work they do the rest of the time and offering special opportunities for socializing with other women (Buckley and Gottlieb 1988).

There are a few societies in the world, particularly in New Guinea, in which men are made either symbolically or artificially to menstruate. Most do this by inserting some instrument into the urethra to make the penis bleed. In many of these same societies, the men also perform ceremonies of giving birth symbolically. The reason they give is that such practices make men more important in the reproductive process.

Although in many societies women are isolated during menstruation, in others they are not. Among Tiv, I have heard men say to women during their periods, "You dripped." The women then use their big toes to cover the dripped menstrual fluid with dust. The attitude toward sexual intercourse during a woman's period also varies vastly. Tiv say it is okay to have intercourse with women during their periods, whereas in some other societies to do so is said to be the equivalent of inviting disaster and death.

Menstruation is an area in which today's Americans are not entirely free and natural. Most men, and no inconsiderable number of women, know almost nothing about how the process works, and what is achieved by it.

REPRODUCTION

All peoples have ideas and beliefs about the processes of conception and prenatal growth—ideas that significantly affect their behavior and the life experiences of their children. Beliefs about conception range from the claim of the Trobriand Islanders and some Australian aborigines in the early 1900s that males had nothing whatever to do with the process, to the notion held by the Hua of New Guinea that the child is made from the coagulation of semen and menstrual fluid (and that the more semen infused during early pregnancy, the better the child will grow), to the belief in some Islamic and central African countries that the female merely provides a bag into which the seed of the completed child is deposited.

Study of the doctrine of procreation held by the members of any society reveals not only what they believe but also their behavioral expectations—how they think they should deal with one another during the process. Those expectations affect both the way they make love and the way they make laws about the rights of women. People often sum up these doctrines in mythical, pseudoscientific, or scientific terms. Both myth and science reflect people's deepest attitudes toward life as well as the sum total of their knowledge about children—both before and after birth.

As mentioned earlier, the Hua believe that children are made from the mixing of semen and menstrual fluid. They believe that after birth the children are nourished by a combination of breast milk, blood obtained from parents' veins and fed to the child, sweat and body oils rubbed on the child's skin, and food (Meigs 1984). These beliefs mirror the fundamental Hua notion that the body is an empty vessel which grows, reproduces, becomes ill, and ages specifically as a result of substances put into and taken out of it. Their belief is very different from the American idea that the body is separate from the world and full of organs that act internally to accomplish physical functions. (It is not that the Hua don't recognize the existence of internal organs. Rather, the Hua see the function of the organs as less important than the constant exchanges going on between the body and the outside world.)

We should remember that only recently did modern medicine discover the scientific facts about procreation. Although people had beliefs about the function of the male in procreation millennia ago, their discussions of the topic were totally prescientific until the invention of the microscope. Among the classical Greeks, two viewpoints were held. The "preformation" view was that everything in the embryo was formed simultaneously, that tiny limbs and a head were present from the first. The Roman poet Seneca said that all bodily characteristics and personality were to be found from the earliest moment. Medieval beliefs in such *homunculi* (tiny preformed human beings said to be present in semen) led to enormous complications in the marriage laws and the laws for dealing with adultery, especially the adultery of wives.

The other viewpoint was the "epigenetic" position;

3-8. Each culture has a set of beliefs (the doctrine of procreation) about the physiology of reproduction. Our own society has many popular doctrines of procreation that co-exist with the scientific ones. Many cultures also have policies about procreation. This photograph shows a Chinese propaganda poster for the policy allowing each Chinese couple to have only one child.

Aristotle favored this explanation. He posited a set of successive differentiations similar to what we recognize today as critical phases of fetal development, each impossible until the one before it had been completed.

Both these points of view obviously presage scientific information, but they were the ones that Westerners wavered between until very recently. Today we know that genes provide the building blocks proposed by the preformationists and that genes also control the successive differentiations posited by Aristotle and his followers.

With the development of the microscope in the middle 1600s, the existence of sperm was discovered in semen. Anton van Leeuwenhoek, the earliest microscopist, claimed at first to be able to see the head of a homunculus and a complete tiny body in each sperm. As microscopes improved, Leeuwenhoek and his students later made accurate drawings of the sperm of several animals.

In the late 1800s, the human egg was discovered through

the microscope. Only with the development of the science of genetics in the twentieth century did the processes of inheritance of physical characteristics come to be scientifically understood.

Anthropologists of the nineteenth and early twentieth centuries were fascinated by the idea that some peoples might not know about the relationship between sexuality and pregnancy. Those were also the days when "scientific" and "true" were considered synonyms. Not to know about paternity seemed to be about as "wrong" and as primitive as it was possible to get.

Although there had been early reports of peoples who did not know about paternity, Bronislaw Malinowski's field research in the Trobriand Islands just after World War I provided relatively reliable information for the first time. The true complexity of the problem of trying to understand what other peoples "know" began to emerge. Earlier reports were not valid because many of the fieldworkers did not speak the language of the people they studied well enough to understand the metaphors and allusions used by informants. Thus, the anthropologists could not accurately report what the natives "knew." Even though Malinowski spoke the Trobriand language fluently, he was influenced by earlier studies. However, the information he provided ushered in a new era in which fundamental ideas about conception and fetal growth are inextricably linked to the cultural definition of human nature.

Anthropologists still argue about whether the traditional Trobrianders "knew" about physical conception. Certainly they noted the relationship between menstrual blood and pregnancy but seemed to have no specific doctrine about it. They told Malinowski that a baby's body is built from the physical substances contributed by the mother alone and that the father made no physical contribution to the body of the child (Malinowski 1929). They, like the Hua, believed that the mother reinforced her own substance in the child through nursing. Malinowski correlated these notions directly with the Trobriand principle of matrilineal descent—that is, they inherited property, office, rank, and magic from their mother—actually from her brother, who was her closest male kinsman. The Trobrianders believed that only the mother was involved in procreation, because that belief validated their established principles of social organization. At least they said they believed it. When pressed by Malinowski on the issue of paternity, or teased by neighboring Dobuans, they showed signs of intense embarrassment, giving the impression that they were "trying to maintain unquestioningly a stand in which they had to believe" (Lee 1950).

Forty years after Malinowski's fieldwork, descendants of the Trobriand Islanders he studied told anthropologist Annette Weiner that they knew the scientific facts about conception and that the old-timers who believed that men had nothing to do with conception were all dead. However, Weiner (1976) also found that they fell back on the old beliefs whenever it was convenient. Women would claim that magic made them pregnant when they did not wish to confess to

adultery—a claim that nobody disputed. The scientific truth had a place, but the mythical truth had quite another, honored, place. The question is whether that was their position all along.

Most Americans claim that conception is "caused" by sexual intercourse. That description is not precise since women do not become pregnant every time they have intercourse. The accurate explanation, of course, is the scientific one—conception is caused by the union of sperm and egg. Yet few Americans can explain the ovulation cycle or other details of the process.

Although its canons of proof are far more rigorous, a scientific explanation is still a set of cultural beliefs that can be studied by the ethnographic method. Many people in Western society maintain nonscientific ideas even when they know the science, because mythic social truth is as important to them as factual scientific truth (and is often more emotionally and spiritually fulfilling).

WE, THE ALIEN

Some of the other peoples who were reported not to understand the function of the male in procreation counted descent through males, where it would seem to be more difficult to explain the fatherless child than among the matrilineal Trobrianders. Some Australian groups cited mythical connections between the religious substances associated with the father and child. Indeed, in some parts of Australia, a person was said to be descended from the mother and the religious entity called a totem, which was associated with the father.

The Aranda of Australia call any piece of ceremonial equipment that is deemed sacred a *tjurunga*. They also say that one's "other body" survives and is reborn in a *tjurunga*. Aranda explain that during the daily gathering of food a woman may feel a sudden pain in her abdomen. She focuses her awareness of her pregnancy on that event. She shows her husband the exact location where the pain occurred. He, with the help of the old men, recalls the oral history of their group. They remember an ancestor of the woman's husband who was associated with the spot. The people thereupon say that the ancestor caused the pregnancy—either he entered her body himself to be reincarnated, or he threw a *tjurunga* in such a way that it entered her body. The life-giving properties come from the ancestor and the *tjurunga*, not the husband. The child is therefore "descended" directly from that ancestor.

For example, a man named Urbala and his wife Kaltia lived in an area in which there is a large rock (Strehlow 1947).

Myth had it that one of Urbala's ancestors had lived in this place and when he died was turned into that rock. One night, the ancestor came forth from the rock and visited Urbala's camp—Urbala dreamed his visit very clearly. When Urbala went hunting the next morning, his dead (and invisible) ancestor went with him. As they returned that night from a successful hunt, the wife Kaltia saw the two of them at a distance, but the ancestor vanished when they got closer and Urbala was alone. When Kaltia ate a piece of meat from the hunt, she became ill. When Kaltia went past the rock the next day, she saw a man with a white decorated band around his forehead. The man carried a hunting stick and a *tjurunga*. He threw the *tjurunga* at Kaltia, who felt a pain in her belly. When she went home and told her husband of this experience, they both knew that she had conceived a child.

Attitudes About Men and Reproduction

An old joke in the Navy—now considered unenlightened and sexist—tells of the sailor who asked for a week's leave because his wife was having a baby. His commanding officer denied his request, "It is my understanding that the husband is necessary at the laying of the keel, but not at the launching." Although men are important in rearing children—what we called socialization and enculturation in 3-2—their contribution to the biological dimension of reproduction is far less obvious and time-consuming than the contribution of women.

Men in some societies try to "prove" that they as well as—or instead of—women make babies. In many places there are ritual or other means to enhance the importance of men in the reproductive process. As we saw earlier, some New Guinea men try to simulate menstruation by making their penises bleed. Among the Mehinaku, men's bodies are said to transform certain foods into semen and other kinds into feces. The semen-producing foods, specifically the starchy staple, manioc, are those grown by women. The food that men themselves produce—meat and fish—are said to form feces. Men brew special medicines that are ritually fed to pubescent boys in order to assure that the boys will produce semen. People in parts of New Guinea believe that men not only have an active part in impregnating a woman but that they are also responsible for turning boys into men with semen, a belief we will learn more about when we discuss homosexuality below.

The custom of involving the father more directly in reproduction—and giving him more credit for what his wife is doing—is called the **couvade**. In the view of some women, the couvade is a way in which men try to impose themselves into the processes of pregnancy and giving birth, where they have no natural function. In some forms of couvade, the father must observe all the food taboos that the mother must observe; if he does not, the child will be harmed. In other

3-9. *Men of some societies keep some of the taboos of their pregnant wives; in other places, they horn in on or even usurp the importance of the woman's role in reproduction. The couvade is the most widespread of these institutions. In this photograph, middle-class American men are attending a childbirth class with their wives.*

Men and Women, Sex and Babies

places, the father takes to his bed when his wife gives birth and sometimes is secluded and pampered far more than she is. Among the Wogeo, on an island off the coast of New Guinea, men with pregnant wives say that they suffer from morning sickness as much as the women do; they tire easily and have to avoid strenuous activity like hunting and fighting.

In the United States over the last twenty-five years, we have been developing our own unique institution that has overtones of couvade. Modern males often accompany their pregnant wives on visits to the obstetrician's office, attend six weeks of childbirth education classes with them, report experiencing backaches and stomach upsets during the pregnancy, support their wives physically and emotionally through labor, and are present at the birth. Fathers sometimes cut the umbilical cord and are often the first to hold the newborn. We emphasize that the men are there to support the women—but it still gives them a place in procreation they did not have earlier.

WE, THE ALIEN

Although fathers in many societies are excluded from the birth processes themselves, many men tell loving stories about the intense feelings they had at the birth of their children. Their importance comes into its own in rearing children—men are important as parents.

NONREPRODUCTIVE SEXUALITY

Sex for Fun

Sexuality is of importance in far more contexts than procreation. The Mehinaku Indians of Brazil have a saying, "Good fish gets dull, but sex is always fun" (Gregor 1985). Many peoples of the world—probably most—would agree with them. People sometimes want their sexuality not to result in procreation. For millennia they have practiced barrier methods of contraception—methods that place a physical obstruction such as cervical shields or condoms in the path of the semen so that it cannot impregnate the woman. They have put lemon juice and vinegar into the vagina; they have used cervical plugs of cocaine leaves; they

---

3-10. People everywhere want their sexuality to be fertile when they want babies and sterile when they don't.

---

have tried sponges. Many used rhythm methods; many others used nonintercourse modes of sexuality. Abortion, infanticide and praying a lot have all had long histories.

Both nonmarital and marital sex in our society can be specifically divorced from procreation, although it often is not. In spite of the fact that many methods of contraception were known from ancient times, there was formerly much religious and political prejudice against them in the United States (in many states it was illegal to sell contraceptives); they were used widely only after World War II. The increased availability of contraceptives was one important factor leading to the freedom and "permissiveness" that our culture saw in the years following 1960.

Homosexuality

Many peoples of the world do not have a specific word for what Westerners call homosexuality. Indeed, the word came into use in English only in the late 1800s. Opinions about homosexuality tend to be formed by the cultural interrelations among the variables with which we began this chapter:

- Sex: According to our original definition, people are biologically either male or female.
- Procreation: If sexuality is culturally limited to procreation, homosexuality will be construed as anomalous because no procreation can occur.
- The tasks of "reproduction" that lie beyond procreation—rearing children to be viable adults—do not exclude homosexual people. If the distinction between procreation and reproduction is not made, this point will not make sense.
- Sexuality: Since gender is the cultural assignment of activities based on biological sex, when a culture strongly assumes that sexuality (behavior involving the organs that determine sex) and cultural gender must absolutely overlap, the stage is set for persecution of homosexual acts and the denigration of people who perform them. Such acts blur the boundaries between gender categories and thus present a threat to the established social order.
- Gender: Homosexuals are masculine or feminine to the same degree that heterosexuals are except for sexual preference. That is, they can exhibit the same characteristics assigned by the culture to males and females in all nonsexual areas.

It would seem thus that insofar as homosexuality is a problem, it is a problem in gender definition. In Mombasa, as we shall see, gender is determined by sex alone. In the United States, gender is in part determined by sexuality. Because we tend to think in binary terms (which means that if you are not one thing you must be its opposite) we lack any available third option. Some Native American groups provided a special category, which anthropologists traditionly call by the French term *berdache*, for homosexual men who chose to take up female gender roles (Williams 1986).

3-11. Attitudes toward homosexuality vary widely, in association with the way sex, sexuality, gender and reproduction are visualized and institutionalized. Historically, Euro-American societies have confused sexuality and gender and hence persecuted people who perform homosexual acts, particularly males. Since the 1960s, most Americans have become more tolerant. Other societies are far more permissive; some (especially in New Guinea) have used what we would consider homosexuality to insure what they consider the masculinization of boys. The first photograph is of a gay man in his fifties with his mother who was eighty-eight at the time the picture was taken, in a parade in New York, going past Stonewall, the site of one of the earliest struggles for gay rights. Interesting things in the second picture are the presence of police and the church in the background.

Mombasa is a traditionally Arab city on the east coast of Africa. About 10 percent of its inhabitants are homosexual, but because people switch back and forth between homosexual and heterosexual lifestyles, somewhat more than that have, at one point or another, lived as homosexuals (Shepherd 1987). In Mombasa, sex alone determines gender. People can live part of their lives as what Westerners would call homosexuals, but neither their sex nor their gender is sacrificed or even linked with that fact. Gender is not the basic consideration for determining social status; rank serves that function.

Either a man or a woman in Mombasa can establish a homosexual relationship that improves his or her economic and social position. Male homosexual couples often consist of a poor younger man and a rich older one. The younger, poorer man is almost always the passive partner, but his social position derives no more from that passivity than does his gender. It derives from his social rank, computed by a combination of wealth, Arab ancestry and Muslim piety. Rank is the primary consideration when marriages are arranged, when loyalties are determined, and when it is decided "who runs the errands, and who sits and waits" (Shepherd 1987).

Many Mombasa boys have homosexual experiences beginning when they are about twelve years old. Most of them

proceed into heterosexual adventures, then marry. But some of these young men prostitute themselves homosexually and make a lot of money before they marry; a few never marry. Men living as homosexuals prefer to spend most of their time in one another's company, but they never live together.

Mombasa lesbians are women who may be single, married, divorced or widowed. The women form groups that meet regularly, sometimes with expensive and elaborate entertainment. These circles are made up of older wealthy women and their poorer, usually younger lovers. The younger women chose these relationships at least in part because they could not find a man who could provide the same degree of security and luxury.

Women in Mombasa society marry when they are very young. The marriages are arranged, and they have little or no choice in the matter. Since a married woman's property is always and necessarily administered by her husband, a woman who has property and wants to run it herself must be either divorced or widowed. Divorced is better because then her husband's brothers have no claims. If she were to remarry, she would lose control to the new husband. If she does not want to live alone, she may set up a lesbian relationship. Unlike the men, the women often live together.

In Mombasa society, a large number of dependents makes you an esteemed person. Since some of these women have

Men and Women, Sex and Babies

large numbers of dependents, they are admired by both women and men. In short, some people make homosexual choices in order to have what they define as the better things of life. It is recognized in Mombasa society that homosexual unions provide a way to improve one's economic situation. It is usually thought of as a patron-client relationship with a sexual dimension.

The buccaneers of the sixteenth and seventeenth centuries in the Caribbean provide an example of a primarily single-sex society. There is no record of any female serving as a crew member on a pirate ship. Most pirates rejected heterosexuality even when in ports where prostitutes were available. Captured women were seldom used sexually, but rather were held for ransom. Very few accounts of rape appear in the records. The pirates lived in a situation in which heterosexuality was not the norm: they had either chosen or been kidnapped into a life which abhorred both social rules and women.

Some of the pirates preferred boys, most of them kidnapped as companions. The captured boys had to learn the skills of seamanship and would be taught by a single sailor. The supervising sailor became very attached to his boy and they would eat and sleep together. The experienced sailor would protect the youngster from other crewman and give the boy a share of the loot.

The institution of *matelotage*, a linking of a buccaneer with another male in a relationship with clearly homosexual characteristics, was widespread. The *matelot* was a servant, most often a man who had sold his services for a specific number of years; occasionally the *matelot* was purchased as a slave. The two inherited property from one another, and sometimes formally co-owned property. There are written records of such co-ownership.

An excellent illustration of *matelotage* is the history of the well-known pirate LeGolif. When he married one of the women imported into Tortuga by a Spanish governor (about 1665) his *matelot*, Pulverin, was upset. Subsequently, Pulverin claimed his right to share all of LeGolif's property, including the wife. However, Pulverin did not want to share LeGolif with a woman. Returning from a raid, LeGolif sent Pulverin ashore to notify the wife that they had returned. Pulverin caught her in bed with another man, killed both her and her lover and disappeared. LeGolif went into deep mourning—not for the wife but for the *matelot* (Burg 1983).

In New Guinea, homosexuality has taken on meanings that go far beyond the mere idea of sexual preference that we discuss in our own society. Although we know little about female homosexuality in New Guinea, we do know that male homosexuality is a complex phenomenon associated with turning boys into men, with economic exchange and prestige, and with ritually reinforcing and restructuring the social world.

While Western cultures also require that boys undergo a disconnection from their mothers as part of establishing their masculine gender, the New Guinea experience is much more extreme. Some New Guinea peoples believe that boys must be detached from the influence not only of their mothers but of all femaleness. Males cannot become "men" until that break occurs. A few New Guinea groups have also premised that men will not naturally grow and develop to the point of producing semen. Rather, it is up to older men to implant the semen so that the boys will eventually be able to produce their own from that seed. This means that men are, to a degree, responsible for the growth of boys into men (and, in a metaphorical sense, have reproductive powers analogous to those of women).

The issue becomes more complex when, in some New Guinea societies, this homosexuality is combined with marriage based on sister exchange. A wife's younger brother becomes the husband's junior partner for whom he is personally responsible. At some stages of his life, the husband has sexual relations both with his wife to give her children and with her younger brother to give him the semen that will bring him to full adulthood.

Another idea found in New Guinea is the characterization of semen as a gift. In some of these societies, it is (or was) the ultimate gift that could be bestowed. Because reproduction was the greatest goal, the gift of semen represented a gift of spiritual essence from an ancestor (Schwimmer 1984). The practice of ritual homosexuality discussed earlier overlapped this area of ritual gift giving. Trading of culturally declared "valuables" made men into what the literature calls "big men." When the missionaries and Australian government officials began a campaign against this practice, a substitute was found for the gift of semen. Soon, marriage by exchange of gifts or bridewealth was taking place. The important idea is that both heterosexuality and homosexuality can be endowed with meanings that have little or nothing to do with procreation (Herdt 1984; Lindenbaum 1987).

GENDER

Biological differences between "male" and "female"—sex—are determined at the time of conception and depend on whether or not an X or a Y chromosome is present in the genetic inheritance of the individual. The differences between **masculinity** and **femininity** are cultural. Gender is about roles and attributes that are assigned to one sex or the other. One's gender is formed and exhibited every day anew. In many areas of the world, it is set into a cultural environment in which the traditional associations between sex and gender have been challenged and are changing.

It is perfectly possible—in fact, it is common—to be glad one is female but incensed and irate about what are perceived as limitations in the gender roles that are culturally ascribed to women. It is just as possible, but perhaps not so common, to be glad one is male but to resent the cultural requirements of masculinity—especially the need to be aggressive. Each of us has a sex identity and a gender identity. When the two do not fit neatly together as our cultural precepts say they ought, we may have problems of stress; we may find ourselves

3-12. Unlike the differences between male and female, which are biological, the differences between masculine and feminine are cultural. Because nonreproductive tasks are assigned to females or to males on a cultural basis, the assignment can be altered without biological consideration.

enraged and turn that rage either onto ourselves or onto society.

Even experts sometimes confuse sex and gender. Nobody has yet figured out scientifically just how being feminine relates to being female or how being masculine relates to being male. Traditionally it was assumed that certain cultural roles are assigned to one of the sexes because that sex is "naturally" designed to carry out those roles. However, most complex modern culture can be used by one sex just as well as by the other—and that goes for everything from backhoes to baby bottles. Cultural complexity complicates the issue of gender.

As stated above, we have not yet satisfactorily figured out where sex stops and gender starts. By and large, people solve this problem by artificial definitions. Some claim that sex differences include differences in behavior. If we do that, we must then define which bits of behavior are masculine and which are feminine, and we will be contradicted by somebody who has different views on the subject. This approach boils down to "biology is fate," even if the "fate" is hotly contested. Other people maintain that the only differences between male capacities and female capacities are their activities in procreation—that in all other ways they are equal, even identical. Both these positions beg most of the questions. Even stating the questions clearly enough to begin answering them is a difficult task.

In exactly the same way that we become ethnocentric as

we learn culture, we also become gendercentric. In American hospitals, babies are provided with identification bracelets when they are first born. The color of the bracelet is different for boys and girls. When nurses in hospital maternity wards talk to girl babies, they raise the pitch of their voices—as much as a third higher than when they talk to boys. Careful studies show that nurses actually handle boy babies with larger gestures than they do girls, and postulate that such a difference provides boys the experience of greater motion. Everybody, unconsciously, treats members of one sex in a different way than they treat members of the other.

3-13. We become gendercentric for the same reasons we become ethnocentric: all of us have to struggle to learn ways and attitudes that are not part of our own experience.

Therefore, just as ethnocentrism is natural but has to be overcome in the interests of global society, so gendercentrism is natural but has to be overcome. Gendercentrism is based on (1) our experiences of being male and female and our reactions to the way people deal with us, and (2) what we are taught and how, given the social positions and situations to which we are assigned. Males not understanding females or vice versa would seem to be a matter of gender experience,

Men and Women, Sex and Babies

not a matter of their sex (but this statement may be challenged—it has to be refined and studied).

People have opinions, most of them intuitive and experiential, about gender. We learn very early to say "Men are such and such" or "Women do so and so" and then pattern our perceptions of men and women on those stereotypes. Although these stereotypical opinions are often wrong, they are nonetheless powerful.

Masculinity and Femininity

One of the best ways to begin the process of distinguishing sex from gender is to realize that each of us has to make two adjustments. We have to adjust to being the sex we are. And we also have to adjust to being the gender we are. The two are not the same thing.

Sex identity involves knowing what sex we are and making peace with that fact. Before eighteen months of age, as we noted in Chapter 2, a child knows whether she is a girl or he is a boy. Before that time, what some pediatricians call "the sex of assignment" can be changed without undue

difficulty for the child (although parents may have so much difficulty with it that the child has little chance of adjusting). We have many case histories of hormone abnormalities, some children born with questionable external genitalia, and still others of chromosomal abnormalities. In such cases, the ascribed sex of the child must be decided, usually by medical doctors. We also have some cases of medical malpractice such as botched circumcision—the situation is sometimes "corrected" by hormone therapy and surgery. That is, a child born unequivocally male can, following the surgical error, be turned into a sort of female. Although these studies are controversial and often questioned, it would appear that a child can grow up to be a functioning member of whichever sex to which he or she is assigned (Gregor 1985; Money and Ehrhardt 1972). In short, most people have little difficulty with sex identity—with being the sex they are.

However, *all* people have at least some difficulty with gender identity. Gender identity has to do with the social position and cultural tasks that a person is assigned on the basis of sex. It involves personality characteristics that are thought to be either masculine or feminine. Thus, in adjusting

3-14. Sex identity means that each of us makes peace with being the sex we are. Gender identity means that we have to make peace with not being the gender we are not. That is, we have to come to terms with cultural restrictions on our gender. The restrictions are almost everywhere more burdensome for women than for men—which does not mean that men do not sometimes have a considerable burden.

Chapter Three

to their gender, all people are faced with repressing more or fewer aspects of their personalities in order to fit the cultural pattern. Gender identity is formed later in life than sex identity—it is well on the way to being formed in the fourth and fifth year of life, but (unlike sex identity) it has to be reviewed and reinforced throughout life.

Every person is called upon to repress whatever she finds in herself or he finds in himself that is culturally defined as an attribute of the other gender. In some societies, initiation ceremonies for boys are aimed specifically at stamping out all identification with the feminine. Yet Confucius long ago, and Freud much more recently, discovered that there are attributes of both the feminine and the masculine in all of us. That does *not* necessarily mean, as some experts would have it, that there are attributes of the male and the female in all of us. The question depends in part on whether one includes behavior and special talents in one's definition of male and female, or limits that definition to physiology.

Repression of the qualities of the opposite sex is rarely accomplished completely and unequivocally. The guilt over this inability may leave scars, and the personal cost may be overwhelming. However, because that personal cost has usually been shoved into the unconscious to avoid pain, we may not even recognize the original behavior we were trying to erase.

In most societies, and in almost every historical epoch, cultural assumptions about what is masculine and what is feminine were rarely questioned. In our own society, however, this question has now become central to many economic and political issues, as well as to family and kinship issues. The qualities that are culturally assigned to the two genders are strenuously questioned today. We have to deal with that fact, even if we find the results confusing.

Gender and Social Role

In all societies, gender is a primary criterion for assigning social roles. Two things are unmistakable: first of all, procreative and reproductive roles of the two sexes are different (the latter may or may not be successfully altered in the future); second, most assignment of economic, political and religious roles have a gender component that may well change with cultural needs and demands.

The bare-bones basics are simple: women are the mothers. The evidence from human societies is overwhelming that mothers will care for their own children—and will do it at great sacrifice if there is nobody else to help them with the job. Who else cares for children? It depends in large part on the ideas of the culture and on the household pattern.

3-15. The correlation between female and feminine or between male and masculine is cultural. It can be altered if people are willing to change their convictions.

In cultures in which the husband-wife relationship forms the basis of the household, the father of the children may pitch in. In many places, it is the mother's mother or other of the mother's kin. The father's mother or other father's kin help in some places. Older children, usually but not always siblings of the child, may be called into service. In some earlier societies, slaves sometimes cared for babies, even acting as wet nurses. In today's world, some of these services are available by contract. Individuals can be hired if there is a market; if there is money to be made, specialized institutions sell such services as diapers, prepared baby food, child care in preschools, kindergartens, and schools.

Until quite recent times, the fact that women bear the children meant that they also had to nurse them. Before the invention of the baby bottle and the general distribution of contraceptives, women were constantly strapped with childbearing and nursing. They were thus handicapped in trying to do anything else unless they gave up sex and family life. The rare exception, like the French novelist Georges Sand or German pianist Clara Schumann (who nevertheless bore seven children), can be found here and there in history.

Men are the fathers. Fathering involves support—not just material support—for the mother and the children. It also involves educating the young. We can ask whether fathers can do what mothers usually do if mothers do not or cannot. Given the culture of baby bottles, prepared baby food and diaper services, men can attend the needs of babies. In the absence of such culture, it is questionable whether they *can* do it, let alone whether they will do it. Although some nonhuman primate males protect the young and sometimes play with them, none can care for unweaned young.

Child rearing everywhere adjusts to the kind of work that women do. One of the victories of feminist anthropology in the 1980s was to make us understand that child rearing is *not* based directly on biology but rather on cultural interpretations of biology. There are no biologically prior criteria for assignment of gender characteristics or tasks (Collier and Yanagisako 1987).

Gender distinctions have often been resented, more verbally by women than by men but sometimes by men as well. That resentment was seen by most men and many women as foolish or neurotic until comparatively recently. People thought—and many still hold—that gender differences are an integral part of sex differences. Yet, women cannot cook better than men, men cannot shoot straighter than women. Women are probably not more sensitive than men, but they have been taught to use their sensitivity overtly. Men are not more rational than women, despite being told that they are from earliest age.

Within our own culture, males as a group perform better on some tests (mathematics, getting from one place to another), while females as a group perform better on other tests (verbal skills of speaking and writing; explaining in words how they got from one place to another) (Maccoby and Jacklin 1974, but see Nielsen 1990). We do not know whether these differences are genetically acquired or whether they are culturally taught and learned, but we do know that if the culture is organized to take advantage of everybody's specific talents, that question is irrelevant.

We shall discuss gender division of labor in detail in Chapter 6. Here we will note that the more technologically developed the culture, the less important the sex of the person who uses that culture, especially for acts that must be overtly learned. It is true that men are stronger than women; they can lift and move forty pounds at a time, and do it all day without undue fatigue. Women can do the same thing with about thirty pounds, and women have more endurance than men. But few in today's developed culture have to do such repeated lifting when we have elevators and forklifts. We know that in many preliterate societies women carry far heavier loads than men (and get exhausted) because carrying is culturally defined as women's work. What is "fair" in any division of labor? Why isn't culture organized in such a way as to take advantage of everybody's talents?

Women everywhere are what might be called the back-up gender. That is to say, when nobody else does some job, the women do it. In many cases this position may be thrust on them by cultural fiat. Yet many women do it "because it has to be done and nobody else is doing it." Women today are working seriously at overcoming this dimension of their training and at changing cultural attitudes to a more positive image for themselves.

Women have always worked. Many (perhaps most) women have little choice about wage labor—they have to do it to help support the family. When men cannot do what they have to do, women back them up. Even when they work at agricultural pursuits or waitressing or law or changing sheets in a hotel, women as mothers and wives still have to go home and work that second shift. The situation is analogous to the family as the general back-up institution. When no other institution does some job, the family does it because it has to be done. Obviously, we do not know whether that is natural. But, until the field research is in, that would seem to be the way it is.

Sex, Gender and Power

The sex drive in both males and females is fired by androgens, the so-called male sex hormones. The aggressive drive in both sexes is fired by adrenaline; the androgens increase the pressures of adrenaline. The connection between sex and power is therefore a fundamental one. Sometimes sex and power are even confused with one another. Gendercentrism thrives on such confusion.

Both sexes may find power in their sexuality. For some women, in some circumstances, getting a man into her bed gives the elated feeling of great power. Mata Hari, a famous German spy during World War I, forwarded her career this way. Gender may also be used as a power ploy. I once, at a conference, saw a courtly and elderly southern lawyer begin to state his disagreement with a young woman lawyer by saying, "I hate to disagree with a charming lady, but . . ."

The young woman broke in: "Let the record show I intend to use every advantage I've got." The courtly southern gentleman did not voice his disagreement.

Men often experience sexual success as power. Sometimes, some men even confuse sex with aggression. Rape is far more often a matter of power than it is of sexuality. For many men some of the time, and for a few disturbed men all the time, gaining power seems to be the major point of sexuality. Male sexual violence against women stems from this kind of confusion about sex and power.

3-16. Because of cultural restrictions on one gender or the other, access to power is likely to be unequal between the two sexes. Because women are heavily invested in reproduction, they sometimes willingly restrict their activities in exchange for security.

Powerful people, whether male or female, usually have a wide choice of sex partners and allowable sexual practices. They may use sex to increase their power. The powerless can sometimes use sex as a device for gaining at least some power.

SEXISM

Sexism is about this confusion of sexuality, gender, and power. Like racism, it is a kind of prejudice that leads to gross inequality. Gendercentrism is at least as powerful as ethnocentrism. Because the two sexes experience some aspects of the world differently, and because the order of events in the life course of men and women is different, each sex may assume that their own views and particularly their own timing of events in the life course are natural and right. In order to understand the differences in viewpoint of males and females that result both from sex and from gender, special efforts must be made. One of the victories of the feminist movement is bringing the ideas about gender into the open, along with ideas about family violence and discrimination in the workplace.

3-17. Sexism is the practice of unsuitably discriminating against one sex (usually women) on the basis of mislinkage of sex and gender rather than on the basis of ability. Women of different cultures, however, may not agree about what is unsuitable, or even about what is discrimination. American women tend to think that Arab women are subject to serious discrimination. Arab women claim that their situation is far better than that of women in the United States.

CONCLUDING THOUGHTS

We are living in the midst of great change in the cultural definition of sexual practices, reproductive practices, family structures, and gender roles. Such changes are showing anthropologists that gender issues are relevant in all contexts. In fact, gender is a component in all the remaining chapters in this book. (If I have failed to discuss it, you yourself can correct my omission.) Both sexes can, if we rid ourselves of gender stereotypes and arrange our culture beneficially, apply all of our capacities to both the family job and to the job of developing and maintaining the nonfamilial parts of the culture. *All* the brains and talent of the species can be applied to the total cultural mission instead of insisting that tasks be compartmentalized, thus wasting a lot of brains and talent simply because of the cultural definition of gender.

Marriage and Family

4

PROPOSITIONS AND PREMISES

■ Marriage is (with a supple enough definition) a human universal. Marriage is a process with a beginning, a middle, and an end. It has traditionally been defined on the basis of sexual and residence rights. A more pliable definition deals with positioning the offspring in a kinship system.

■ The family is the human version of one of the two most basic social arrangements: creating, tending and training the next generation, thus leading to the survival of the genes of the species. (The other basic social arrangement is the hierarchy.)

■ Because human beings have culturized all their behavior, maintaining and improving the culture is as important as maintaining the genes. Thus, teaching (which is a part of parenting) is a fundamental human need.

■ Humans share with other animals many of the attributes of the family, but not all: the human family is unique.

■ Most human beings, most of the time, center their reproduction in the family.

■ The human family depends on good mothering (which is true of all mammals), on good fathering (which is not true of most other mammals), and on the support of mother and father either by other kinfolk or by specialized institutions.

■ Human families can take care of everything people need in the absence of specialized institutions. The family is, thus, the chief "back-up institution" everywhere.

■ Parenting is the single most important task that any adult animal, including human beings, carries out.

Marriage is a peculiarly human way of looking at and organizing mating. It blends sex, sexuality, gender, procreation, and reproduction and is connected with many other social and cultural institutions. Marriage often provides a way of linking separate segments of a society together, thus serving political ends. In many places, it is intimately related to the production and distribution of goods, as well as to the inheritance of material wealth, and hence serves economic ends.

Marriage is, among other definitions, a cultural device by which a society recognizes the bonding between a man and a woman to make their children legitimate. The children are thus recognized by a full set of kinfolk on both their mother's and their father's side.

4-1. Marriage brings sex, sexuality, reproduction, and gender together in a single institution. This young family is from Moscow.

Americans, when they examine marriage cross-culturally, have to overcome some of their own culture-specific views. First of all, they should recognize that marriage in many societies is as much about subsistence, property, and power as it is about partnership—indeed, in only a comparatively few societies is marriage considered a partnership in the sense that it is in our own. Americans should also be aware that they are unusual in basing marriage on romantic love. Even if romantic love is recognized in other societies, it may not be the only, or even the best, basis of marriage. Marriage in many societies is viewed as an important stage in the process of becoming fully adult.

The **family** is a kinship group. The fundamental unit of the family is a woman and her children (which can be called a **matricentric family**). All human societies, at least ideally, postulate a husband/father (whereupon it becomes what is generally called a **nuclear family**). The word family is elastic—it may be stretched to other kinfolk in almost any direction (making what anthropologists call an **extended family**). Importantly, it is unlike every other kinship group because it includes not only people who share genealogical descent but also some (seldom all) of those related by marriage.

MARRIAGE

Marriage is a chain of many events in the long processes of our personal and social growth. Five links of that chain will be examined here. Each link is associated with ideas and customs that answer a particular question.

Link/Question 1: How do women and men find one another? The field of eligible candidates for marriage in any given society is defined by rules governing incest prohibition (which forbid sexual intercourse between people who stand in certain kinship relationships with one another) and **exogamy** (which are rules that forbid marriage within a specified social group). We will examine ways in which women and men find one another. We will look at some cultures that mandate specific individuals to be the spouse, at others in which marriages are arranged by parents or other kinfolk, matchmakers or other third parties, and finally at cultures in which the principal parties to the marriage are themselves responsible for finding one another.

Link/Question 2: How are weddings performed? That is, what actions confer the status of married spouses? Weddings usually are events, whereas marriages are chains of events. Weddings show many cultural variations—ritual, legal, exchange of goods, contract. The most common practice is to establish a ritual or legal or economic event which is the socially recognized demarcation prior to which the marriage process can be merely abandoned but after which a divorce must occur.

Link/Question 3: What are the cultural and personal expectations of the spouses of each other, as well as of other kinfolk, and how do the expectations vary during the life course? Again, the answer to this question is a long process of growth, not an event. This aspect of marriage is the least well reported in the ethnographic and historical record and has been given new relevance and importance by feminist anthropologists in the 1970s and 1980s. Our new understandings of it demand fuller treatment than the other stages.

Link/Question 4: How do marriages end? All marriages do end, either in the death of one of the partners, or by divorce. But people of some cultures claim that death does not end a marriage.

Link/Question 5: What happens to the survivors after the marriage has ended? What are the practices for dealing with widows and widowers? With divorced women and men?

These five links—the stages of marriage—can be seen as a developmental trajectory as in 4-2.

4-2. *Marriage is a human universal—all societies recognize it. Every individual marriage goes through some version of the same action chain. (1) The partners must be selected, by themselves or by others. (2) A socially sanctioned act declares the bond. (3) A personal relationship grows between the spouses (as well as relationships with the spouses' kinfolk). (4) All marriages end, either by the death of one of the spouses or by divorce. (5) Survivors of marriage are in the social position of widow (widower) or divorcee.*

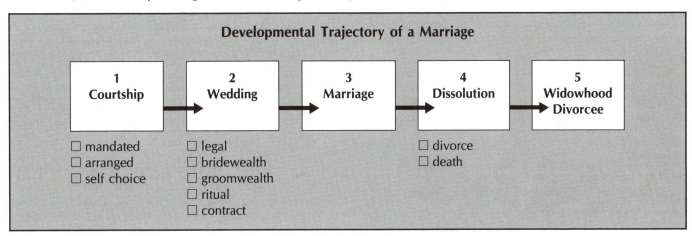

Developmental Trajectory of a Marriage

1 Courtship	2 Wedding	3 Marriage	4 Dissolution	5 Widowhood Divorcee
☐ mandated ☐ arranged ☐ self choice	☐ legal ☐ bridewealth ☐ groomwealth ☐ ritual ☐ contract		☐ divorce ☐ death	

Finding a Partner

All societies prohibit sexuality within the nuclear family except between husband and wife. Most extend this incest taboo to include siblings of the parents—to those we call aunts and uncles in English. Many extend it to include first cousins, and some extend it far beyond that point. Tiv, for example, consider sexual relations with anyone with whom you share one grandparent to be incestuous.

Many animals have social devices that prohibit inbreeding of close kin. These devices are advantageous because close interbreeding sometimes produces less viable offspring than does breeding with those more distantly related.

Exogamy, on the other hand, has to do not just with sex but also with many other dimensions of marriage: an exogamic group is one in which one member of the group cannot marry another. Exogamy may or may not be directly associated with incest prohibition, and it usually works to

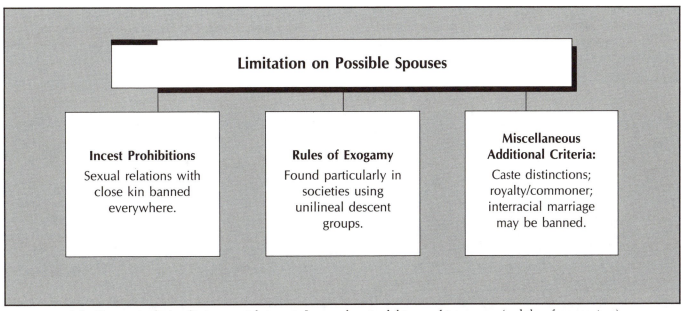

Limitation on Possible Spouses

Incest Prohibitions
Sexual relations with close kin banned everywhere.

Rules of Exogamy
Found particularly in societies using unilineal descent groups.

Miscellaneous Additional Criteria:
Caste distinctions; royalty/commoner; interracial marriage may be banned.

4-3. *Two main devices limit potential spouses. Incest taboos prohibit sexual intercourse (and therefore marriage) between close kinspersons. Almost all societies ban sexuality between members of a nuclear family—the exceptions are three known royal houses (Ancient Egypt, Polynesia, Inca). Rules of exogamy deny a person the privilege of marrying within a specific kin group of which one is a member. Some cultures may have other regulations, based on caste, race, or other considerations prohibiting some marriages.*

Marriage and Family

encourage both the biological and economic exchange between groups.

A few societies find no place at all for unmarried people. Therefore, like the Tiwi of Australia, they betroth infants and remarry widows and widowers instantly.

Some people have their culturally approved partners determined for them by the kinship system or the religious system. Many societies prefer that people marry a specific cousin.

Many peoples have marriages arranged by parents, by fortune tellers, or by special functionaries, with little or no input from the marriage partners themselves. Although Westerners may find it hard to believe, such marriages usually

4-4. American modes of courtship and marriage are highly individualized and seem totally alien to most peoples of the world. Americans select their own spouses. In many cultures, marriages are arranged. This picture shows a group of Basseri men preparing a marriage contract.

work well. The expectations of spouses in those societies are less demanding, and often no attempt at intimacy between the spouses is made or even condoned.

Still other societies say that they arrange marriages when in fact they merely formalize marriages already agreed upon by the bride and groom. Therefore the boundaries are hazy between marriages arranged by parents or by specialists and those that are arranged between the marrying partners themselves. Many young people, in many cultures, will not marry a person whom their parents dislike—although in our own culture, some may marry a person specifically because their parents disapprove. Selecting one's own spouse is the form that young people in most societies say they prefer. Despite the stated preference, some do not exercise this freedom even when given the opportunity.

One disadvantage of making one's own selection is that people sometimes seem to select a spouse who will shore up their weak points. If the spouse fails to do this, the marriage is in trouble. However, it may also be in trouble if it succeeds so well that the weak points disappear—when that happens, the original need has evaporated. The spouse's other characteristics emerge in importance. These newly salient characteristics may not be required or even liked. People who choose their own spouses are faced with many problems—most of them masked by some idea such as romantic love.

There are several aspects to a **courtship**. Some cultures ignore one or more of them, and different cultures arrange them in different time sequences. The aspects are: (1) getting acquainted and/or falling in love, (2) the first sexual intercourse, (3) setting up a household, (4) a wedding. These events may be arranged in any preferred order (see 4-5). The preferred order in the America of the 1950s was: 1, then 4, after which 2 and 3 were more or less simultaneous. However, the 1960s changed American practices and preferences. The sequence became, at the extreme, 2, 1 (if

The Order of Events in Establishing a Marriage				
Event	U.S. before 1950	U.S. during 1960s	Traditional India	Trobriands
1. Getting acquainted and/or falling in love	First	Second	Fourth	Second
2. First sexual intercourse	Fourth	First	Third	First
3. Setting up a household	Third	Third (?)	Second	Fourth
4. Wedding	Second	Fourth (?)	First	Third

4-5. Several events must occur in order for a marriage to be established. We have selected four of those events and show that the order is variable, depending on cultural conviction and values.

Chapter Four

it happened at all), 3, 4 (if it happened at all). In parts of traditional India, the order was 4, 3, 2, 1.

Societies differ in what they prefer and demand in these matters—and most of them differ from one historical period to the next. In the Trobriand Islands, the preferred order is 2, 1, 4, 3. We saw in Chapter 3 that Trobriand adolescents had considerable sexual freedom. They were, for many anthropological generations, the classic example of a people who granted young men and women premarital freedom. It was, however, a great relief to our intellectual ancestors of the 1930s and 1940s that the Trobrianders settled down when they married. When a Trobriand couple decide to marry, they leave the bachelor hut and move into the hut of the groom's parents while a long series of gift exchanges occurs. At the time of the next harvest, they move into their own house.

While in the bachelor's hut, their primary interest is sex. After the marriage when living with the groom's parents, the young couple focuses primarily on the change in their relationships with almost everybody in the community; sex is no longer the primary interest. They behave with great circumspection while they are in the parents' house. Although the bride and bridegroom sleep on the same bunk, the Trobrianders told Malinowski that the early days after the wedding were days of abstinence. Nobody took off his or her clothes during this period because of the shame caused by sexual behavior when the senior generation was present.

When they move into their own hut, they usually sleep together early in the marriage but have separate beds later. Malinowski found that getting information about the sexual behavior of married people was very difficult, although he easily got information about premarital sexual behavior. Husband and wife must never hear one another discussing sex; they must not even hold onto one another for support as they walk along the path. Other than this prohibition on touching in public, they were relaxed together and appeared to be good friends.

Weddings: Events That Confirm Marital Status

In most societies, the wedding serves as the point in the marriage process before which a courtship or negotiation can be broken off and after which the marriage must be ended by divorce. A wedding can take many forms. In our society, a legal action is required which may or may not be accompanied by a religious ceremony. In other societies, ritual alone may be used. Marriage may be carried out by exchange of wealth or it may be done by contract, either between the parties themselves or between their families. In some European countries there may be two weddings: a small one to take care of the legal demands and a large public one to celebrate the ritual. Living together for a certain number of years may be legally defined as marriage, as it is in some American states (often called "common-law marriage" although true common-law marriage is a contract between the spouses).

4-6. *Marriage is a cultural device for socially approving the bond between a woman and a man that makes their children legitimate. A legitimate child is one who has a full complement of kinfolk on both father's and mother's side. In some societies (including American society until World War II) legitimacy is considered important; in many societies it affects rights to inherit property. This wedding picture was taken in San Jeronimo, Cuzco, Peru, in 1973. This sort of picture can be duplicated from family albums in many parts of the world.*

The form which requires special attention is the exchange of goods. Gifts may be exchanged at weddings in many societies, including our own, but those gifts are not what actually create the wedding. **Bridewealth** is a payment that does constitute a wedding, or an important part of it. In some societies, particularly in Africa, specific goods pass from the groom's family to the bride's family creating a bond between the two kinship groups, and hence between the couple. In many places bridewealth is said to repay the bride's family for rearing her, then losing her. The web of contract that results from bridewealth may be a stabilizing factor not only of the marriage but of the relationships between in-laws throughout the society; it is bridewealth that makes the children unequivocal members of their fathers' groups. In the early days of ethnography, bridewealth was confused with purchase of the bride, which most people who practice it deny vociferously. The bridewealth is payment for specific rights in the wife, most notably rights to her childbearing capacity and to her domestic labor. These rights in the wife are always reciprocated by obligations from the husband which can, of course, be seen as the rights of the wife in her husband.

Groomwealth is found in a few societies in which the groom's family receive payments from the bride's family. Neither bridewealth nor groomwealth are to be confused with the **dowry**, which is a gift of property that accompanies the bride and is intended to be used for her support. In a few societies, the property of the dowry may be declared to belong to the bride and she may have primary responsibility for its administration, but in most places control of a woman's dowry passes to her husband.

What Spouses Do

Because what spouses do for one another is so important in our own society, it is astonishing that there is so little record of these activities for other societies. The American institutions of family therapy and marital therapy, and many discussion groups and support groups focus on the subject of whether one is behaving adequately as a spouse, whether the spouse is behaving well, and what to do about it to make marriage ''happy.''

4-8. *All marriages begin with some cultural sign (usually a wedding) that follows a process of self-selection of partners or else their selection by a third party. They then proceed through a set of developmental stages linked to age, the achievement of the partners, the age and development of children. They all end, either with the death of one spouse or by divorce. The wedding is often an elaborate ritual, with costume and feasting, as you can see with this Moro couple in the Philippines.*

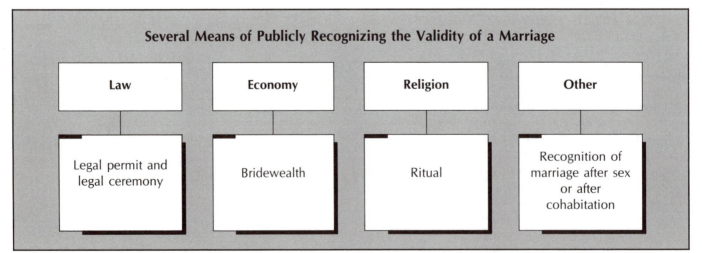

Several Means of Publicly Recognizing the Validity of a Marriage

Law	Economy	Religion	Other
Legal permit and legal ceremony	Bridewealth	Ritual	Recognition of marriage after sex or after cohabitation

4-7. *Marriages can be validated by several means. In our society, we recognize legal validation: a license, a legal ceremony, witnesses, a certificate proving the wedding occurred. Some people, particularly in Europe and Latin America, also have both a legal ceremony and a religious ritual marking the marriage before God. Among many peoples of traditional Africa, bridewealth is the most common method—certain rights in a woman are acquired by her husband and his social group by paying her father and his social group. Eskimo claim that sexual relations—even clandestine ones—cement a marriage.*

Americans more or less invented the idea that marriages should be "happy." Obviously, all people, everywhere, prefer that spouses be congenial, but the fact that Americans have so much choice—including the choice of a spouse—means that their concern with the behavior and "satisfactoriness" of spouses becomes dominant—Americans invest much more in spouses than they do in other kinfolk. Spouses are primary to, and sometimes even responsible for, our well-being. American spouses must "communicate" well with one another, so that they can "cooperate" and "support" one another. These words indicate a set of ideas that never occur to people who live in technologically simpler cultures.

In most societies, the rules of marriage are simple and rigid. A Tiv woman, for example, must keep her house neat, tend her farms, cook for her husband at least once a day, and take her turn sleeping with him. The husband must keep the wife clothed, must prepare adequate farmland for her, and must consult a diviner if she becomes ill.

Tiv spouses sometimes become friends, but they are not really expected to do so—and it isn't necessary. The success of a marriage to Tiv is determined by lack of fuss, by plenty of children, hard-work, good nature. They find laughable any suggestion that any one person is singularly qualified to be the spouse of another specific person.

In short, Americans have not only made marriage more central to their lives, they have complicated it vastly.

WE, THE ALIEN

How Marriages End

All marriages end, either by death or by divorce. It is important to note, however, that ending a marriage does not end the family. We often talk about "broken families," but a minute's thought will convince you that although the family no longer forms a household (and in our society, that can be a grave difficulty), the kinship relations among other family members are not broken, either by death or by divorce. The only thing broken is the marriage.

What Happens to the Survivors?

The answer to this question depends on cultural norms and how the marriage ended.

Widowhood. When death ends a marriage the surviving spouse must make personal adjustments and learn to fit into society in new ways. I once met a Texas woman on an excursion boat that followed the Rhine from the Netherlands to Switzerland. She told me that she was a recent widow, and that she had decided to come to Europe (she pronounced it "Yurp" as one syllable) "to find out if I should remember him or forget him." American society in the 1980s had six times as many widows as widowers. Most widowers remarry. Whether widows remarry is correlated with their age: those who are still in their childbearing years usually do. The Texas woman (about sixty-five years old) had been thrust by the death of her husband into a number of unfamiliar circumstances, like most widows in our society.

The way societies treat (or treated) widowhood varies all the way from the Tiwi in Australia, who remarry the widow at the time of her husband's funeral, to the *sutee* practices of some castes of traditional India, who in earlier times insisted that the widow be burned to death on the funeral pyre of her dead husband. The ruling groups in parts of traditional Fiji strangled a dead man's widows. Such extreme solutions are rare. Most societies merely demand that widows adjust and give them more or less—usually less—help. In most societies, widows are allowed to remarry, but in other societies (particularly in earlier historical times) they were not. For example, in the fifteenth century a Korean ruler went so far as to declare that the legitimate children of a widow would be made illegitmate by her remarriage (Koo 1987). In others, like the Nandi of Kenya, the widow cannot remarry but does have her own property which she administers for herself; she may take lovers if she wishes; any future children would be considered the children of her dead husband (Oboler 1986).

In societies like our own where the household is based on the husband-wife relationship, the adjustment to widowhood is severe. The widow's primary companion is absent, and her household is short-handed. In other groups, like the Muslims in Turkey, men and women occupy such different social worlds and have so little to do with one another that the adjustment is, socially at least, quite simple (Heisel 1987).

Everywhere there are cultural expectations about the response of widows to their husbands' deaths. In Iran, the assumption is that the widow will be emotionally overwhelmed and unable to cope with the real world. Ceremonies immediately after the death of an Iranian spouse can be quite elaborate. The funeral is usually held the same day or the day after death occurs since there are no embalming practices. Then, for six days, the widow and the family receive visits of consolation. On the seventh day, another visit is paid to the cemetery where another ritual is performed. Then from the eighth to the fortieth day, the widow and some other relatives return the calls that were paid to them during the first seven days. After that, the widow is more or less ignored (Touba 1987).

In order to adjust, a widowed person needs four kinds of support: economic support, help in getting the daily work done, help in establishing a new set of roles or adapting old ones, and an emotional support system (Lopata 1987). In kinship-based societies, rights in the widow may be inherited

Marriage and Family

by one of the kinfolk of the dead husband. In others, the widow is taken care of by her children, usually by her sons, although in our own society it is most commonly daughters who care for widowed mothers. In modern Western societies, social security, pensions, and life insurance help with financial support. In many cases, no one helps with the housework; few people—perhaps none—help the widow make personal adjustments in order to reenter society in her new, unmarried role.

 Life insurance was designed to meet the contingencies of widows and orphans.

Insurance is a very old institution—the code of Hammurabi mentions a form of insurance. Burial societies, in which the members make contributions to pay for the burial expenses of other members, are at least as old as the ancient Greeks, and are common throughout the world. Life insurance, however, is more recent. The first American life insurance company was The Presbyterian Ministers' Fund, formed in 1759. It still exists. Life insurance grew slowly through the first half of the 1800s. Moral systems had to be adjusted to the new situation because life insurance was at first seen as placing a value on a human life, and some lives would be declared, by insurers, to be more valuable than others. After the illogic of that situation was worked out (adjusting to new situations always takes time), the life insurance industry began to grow in the second half of the nineteenth century. Today life insurance provides a degree of financial security for at least the middle class in the United States; most middle-class families have bought it.

WE, THE ALIEN

In some societies, the husband's kinfolk assist a widow by assigning her to one special man among those kinfolk. He is called the *levir* (the Latin word for younger brother), and the institution is known as the **levirate**. The ways in which the levirate is organized vary. The role of the levir may go all the way from his more or less ignoring the widow at one extreme to his turning her into a wife (the only distinction being that the children she bears are filiated to her dead husband, not to the levir). Luo women of Kenya, for example, select a levir from among the dead husband's kin; levirs say that they help the widows, but most widows do not agree. The only responsibility of the levir, the widows say, is to provide them with further children who will be members of her late husband's lineage (Potash 1986).

The levirate is found in the Old Testament. The story of the Book of Ruth relates how Ruth accompanied her mother-in-law back to her husband's group where she was rejected

4-9. Widows must be dealt with by every society. Widowers are less common and seem not to call for such elaborate institutions, in part probably because widowers' rights are not put into question because their status never depended on the status of their spouses. Widows in many societies are victims of ageism and sexism.

by one levir and then accepted by another. The Book of Genesis (Chapter 38) tells the story of Onan who became the levir of his brother's widow, Tamar. Since Onan did not wish to father children who would be considered his brother's children, he "spilled his seed on the ground" every time he had relations with Tamar. Tamar, in order to bear further legitimate children, masqueraded as a harlot and trapped Onan's (and her deceased husband's) father into impregnating her. In memory of these events, humorist Dorothy Parker named her pet canary Onan because he spilled his seed on the ground.

The Tiv practiced a modified form of the levirate when I worked among them in the 1950s. The choice to take a levir or to leave the household and marry elsewhere lies with the widow. If she leaves, part of the bridewealth must be repaid. Further, she has to give up her children because they have rights only in their father's community and will not accompany her if they are over five years old or so. If, on the other hand, she remarries one of her dead husband's kinfolk, she does not have to leave her farms, and she continues residence in a compound in which her sons have full rights and from which her daughters will be married. The widow has a right, in Tiv custom, to enter into sexual relationships with any or all of the men who might inherit her. Then, in a public ceremony a year after the death of the husband, she is asked to select her next husband from among the men she has been involved with. It is a hilariously good time for Tiv. The widow names one man to be her new husband. If she has already borne a son, he will be her levir; if she has not, he will be her husband. The man is bound to accept, usually only too eagerly, especially if she is young and has not borne a son. In that case, her future children will be formally as well as biologically his children. He is teased unmercifully about his sexual prowess and how good he is with women. All the other eligible men also come in for a ribbing because they were not chosen and, by inference, must not be as pleasing to women in general.

In many societies, including Western society, widows are often the victims of sexism and ageism. It is thus difficult to tell how much difficulty arises from their role as widows and how much arises because of their age and sex.

Widowers have not been much studied—perhaps because most remarry (and in some societies may already have other wives), but also because they are not expected to be able to take care of themselves, as widows are, and hence are not perceived as a problem.

Divorce

Divorce occurs in most societies, but not in all, even though marriages do indeed collapse everywhere. In a few of the world's societies, divorce is made impossible either for religious or other reasons. The Roman Catholic church, for example, holds that marriage is a sacrament that cannot be undone (although Catholics do divorce—indeed, in some places, the Catholic rate of divorce is higher than either the Protestant or the Jewish rates).

The Nandi of East Africa make divorce almost impossible once children are born. If a Nandi woman refuses to live with her husband and forms another relationship, the new household is not regarded as a marital household. Thus, lack of divorce does not imply that the couple continues to live together but only that they are still married.

Even in societies where divorce does occur, it would seem that not all of the things that were done at the time of the wedding are undone at the time of divorce. No divorce custom in any society can break the kinship-like relationship between the couple after a child is born. As co-parents of a child, the ex-husband and ex-wife share kinship descendants. Some divorcees in our own society are uncomfortable

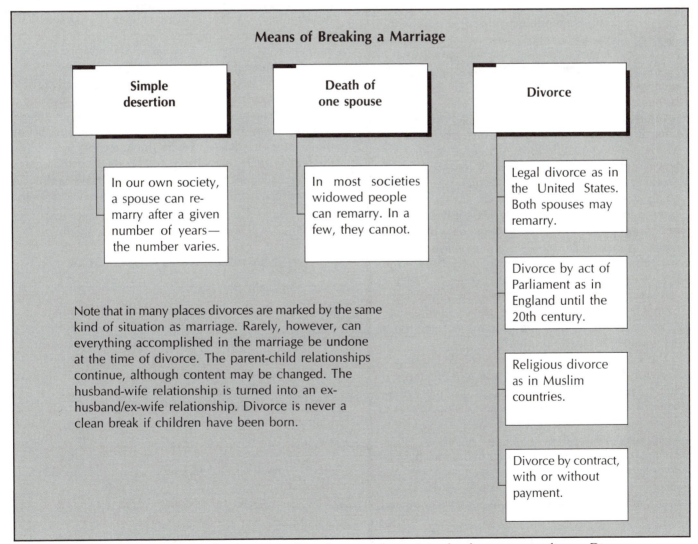

Means of Breaking a Marriage

Simple desertion

In our own society, a spouse can remarry after a given number of years—the number varies.

Death of one spouse

In most societies widowed people can remarry. In a few, they cannot.

Divorce

Legal divorce as in the United States. Both spouses may remarry.

Divorce by act of Parliament as in England until the 20th century.

Religious divorce as in Muslim countries.

Divorce by contract, with or without payment.

Note that in many places divorces are marked by the same kind of situation as marriage. Rarely, however, can everything accomplished in the marriage be undone at the time of divorce. The parent-child relationships continue, although content may be changed. The husband-wife relationship is turned into an ex-husband/ex-wife relationship. Divorce is never a clean break if children have been born.

4-10. Although marriages break up everywhere, there are a few societies that do not recognize divorce. Divorce may be achieved by legal or ritual means, economic payments, or simple desertion. If children were born to the marriage, divorce does not erase all the bonds established during the marriage.

because we create divorces legally but (except for the Mormon and Jewish religions) have no way of undoing the religious rituals that made the marriage. (The institution of annulment of a marriage is limited to a few Western societies. It promotes a legal fiction that a valid marriage did not in fact take place.)

Divorce is more complicated than widowhood in all societies, because ex-spouses have to be dealt with. The traditional Eskimo offer a particularly clear example of just how complicated the situation can become. Eskimo marriage is a matter of setting up a residence. There is no ritual or legal act, and no bridewealth. The Eskimo remain attached to every person with whom they have had sexual relationships. An equivalent of divorce involves moving to separate households. However, they are still husband and wife. When they remarry, they remain husband and wife, and the new spouses become co-spouses of the old ones. That factor is important because any descendants of any two people who call one another spouse are forbidden to have sexual relations. A young man is forbidden to be involved sexually with the daughters of any woman with whom his father had a sexual relationship, no matter how fleeting (Burch 1970).

Among the Muslim Kanuri of Nigeria, divorce approaches 100 percent of marriages. In six areas from which samples are available, from 66-99 percent of completed marriages were ended by divorce rather than death. Indeed, over half of Kanuri marriages end in divorce within four years (Cohen 1963). Being divorced is attractive to Kanuri women, who marry between the ages of twelve and sixteen, because the role provides them with freedom that they cannot get any other way. However, if a woman leaves her husband and his household, her children remain behind. This factor is ameliorated by the fact that children are passed around from household to household, living in many different places even if their parents are not divorced. Another primary factor is important—Kanuri women pass out of the marriageable population at menopause. A menopausal woman, considering herself unmarriageable, is likely to return to the household of her son or sons. Thus, the society does not fall to pieces because of such high divorce rates. The primary reason is that the household has a firm foundation.

As we have seen, the impact of divorce is directly related to household form. In societies in which the household is based on a parent-child relationship, the impact of divorce is fairly benign; the households remain as they were before the divorce. In societies where the household is based on the husband-wife relationship and breaks up at the time of divorce, the impact can be devastating, especially to children who lose their homes when their parents' household collapses.

FAMILIES AND HOUSEHOLDS

It is species-specific human behavior to arrange parenting, which is the protection and instruction of the young, in a situation that we call the family. The family is universal among human beings, but it takes many forms. Families in different cultures do not always look like our own, and they may have very different problems. The meaning of the word family will expand as we discuss it.

The family is the primary determinant of a person's fate. It provides the psychological tone, the earliest cultural environment; it is the primary criterion for establishing a young person's social position. The family, built as it is on shared genes, is also the repository of shared cultural details and shared trust.

The family can do, and does, everything that society requires that is not done by some other social group. On the basis of its broad capabilities and its comparatively few members, it is the general back-up institution. That means that the family steps in at every crisis; it is there whenever other institutions fail.

The Puritan founders were at odds with the Church of England about divorce. England did not recognize any divorce except that granted by the legislature until well into the twentieth century. The Puritans, however, were convinced that it was one's duty to love the spouse, and if you couldn't carry out that obligation, it was your duty to divorce that spouse and find one you could love. As a result, the institution of judicial divorce was more or less invented in Massachusetts about 1630. The divorce rate has been going up ever since the first judicial divorce was granted in Plymouth Colony. By 1804 it had reached one in a hundred in Connecticut, the only place for which we have data. Ministers and moralists began preaching the same kind of sermons about social ruin that were still heard in the 1960s. As life expectancy increased (from forty-nine to seventy-six during the twentieth century) and as age at marriage decreased (it was over twenty-eight for men in 1900), the rise in the divorce rate sped up.

The expectations of longer-living people became higher as the standard of living rose in the United States. The divorce rate continued to rise until today one of every two or three marriages (depending on which indexes you use) end in divorce. These factors taken together have had a profound impact on American households. There is no indication that the divorce rate will come down; we seem as of this writing to be in a stable period in which it is not rising, but we have been in stable periods before and the rise has, so far, always returned.

WE, THE ALIEN

The family is the most efficient of all human institutions—efficient in the sense that so few people can accomplish so much. Indeed, the human family can do everything except provide a mate. It can even do that if you extend the intermarrying group the right way. It is an organizational miracle.

Specific families may, of course, not work very well. A few may even do their members more harm than good. But for the most part, the family provides basic shelter (in every sense of that word) and gives each person a trusted group of people. The growth of social culture arises when nonfamilial groups are added to carry out specialized functions formerly carried out within the family. It is something like chipping flint to make specialized tools, leaving the core as a generalized tool.

Family-like Arrangements of Animals

The word family is often used to describe mating pairs and their offspring in other species. That usage is either fable as in Goldilocks and the Three Bears or else it is grossly anthropocentric. For us to see other animals as the image of ourselves is dangerous; it blocks us from learning what they are and what they do. All mammals, of course, have what animal breeders call sires (male parents) and dams (female parents). But the mere presence of sires, dams and offspring does not make a family in the human sense. In all cases, the human family performs many basic tasks that are simply not found in the rest of the animal kingdom. Other mammalian species do put some, but never all; of the family components together. Such activities provide a good place to begin our exploration of family and its evolution.

Baboons. Baboons are found in Africa and live in bands. A **band** moves across the countryside as a group from one food source to another. There is much variation among the species of baboons. One of the most common patterns contains several males and a somewhat larger number of females. This skewed sex ratio occurs because the females become adult at an earlier age than males and because, unlike females, baboon males (of most species) leave their natal bands. They may or may not join peripheral groups of other males. To join another band means hanging around the edges of a new group until they are known. They then fight to win a position in the hierarchy of the males who are already in the new group. During this period, when they do not have a social group for protection, they are in great danger from predators.

Female baboons remain in their natal bands, providing a stable core and depending on their female relatives. They form dominance hierarchies that remain stable over long periods of time. A daughter takes a place in the hierarchy just below her mother but above her elder sister. High-ranking females get more support and less aggression than do low-ranking ones. Most of their social interactions occur with close maternal kin.

Most baboon bands contain several males who are unre-

4-11. Although all animals have sires and dams and all mammals (and many others, such as birds) need parental care, human beings have organized parenthood and marriage into an institution of the family. The family is marked by being set into a more inclusive kinship system. Baboons (shown here) or chimps recognize mothers and siblings, but not fathers or husbands. Gibbons are monogamous, but when the young grow up, ties with the parents are broken—there is nothing resembling an extended family or a kinship system.

lated to one another. They arrange themselves in dominance hierarchies, separate from but interfaced with the female hierarchies. Male-male relationships are sometimes aggressive, especially during periods when changes are being made in the dominance order, but males also form cooperating alliance groups. The dominance hierarchy depends on the size and fighting ability of the males. There may be long periods of time without fighting if the hierarchy is uncontested.

Mating is affected by female choice and by the dominance rank of the male. Particular males and females often create close bonds with each other; sometimes these bonds are described as friendships. Male friends protect their female friends from other males. Such a male is usually, but not always, the favorite mate of the female friend. Females can have as many male friends as they choose. While the young are reared by their mothers, the adult males sometimes play with the young, and they are instrumental in protecting the whole group.

Gibbons. Gibbons live in the tropical forests of southeast Asia. They are monogamous and highly territorial. Their average territory is about eighty acres, which the monogamous pair covers every few days, moving through the tree tops in the quest for food. Both members of the pair defend their territory by singing loudly at dawn. The pair may be accompanied by an infant up to two years old, a juvenile from two to four, or an adolescent from four to six. As the young become older, they are forced more and more to the periphery of their parents' territory. More and more hostility

Marriage and Family

between the generations emerges, most especially with the parent of same sex. Mother-daughter aggression can be especially bitter. The result of their territoriality is that young gibbons have no same-age playmates. The generational hostility results in a system with no grandparents, aunts, uncles or cousins.

When gibbon parents evict their near-adult young, the latter must find a mate and a territory. Sometimes a young female, and occasionally a young male, will replace a dead or ailing mate in a pair. Commonly, the young find one another in their wanderings and then carve out a territory by fighting. The mortality rate for young gibbons is apparently high.

Male and female are absolutely equal; they look just alike; no tasks except the procreative are specialized by sex. The males may spend more time playing with the young than do the females, although the females spend more time carrying them.

Although at first glance the gibbon pair with their young may look like a human family, they specifically do not show some of the most vital characteristics that make human families human. The human family is set into an extended kinship network. Kinship lasts and is recognized throughout life, so that the kinship links form a basis for extended social grouping. Neither gibbons nor baboons do any such thing. When gibbon young reach adulthood, both sexes are expelled from the parental territory to find their own mates and their own territories.

Human Families and Households

The family is a peculiarly human way of arranging the building blocks: adult women, children, and adult men. It is a structure of elegance and efficiency. Different convictions about the nature of parenting, kinship, sex and marriage, production of economic goods, and sharing—all of these forces pull the family into different shapes.

There are two primary questions. First, on what cultural grounds are women, men and children actually conjoined into families? Second, where does the family live and how?

The weakest link in any human family system is the link between the mated pair. There is no absolute necessity for the adult men and women to be joined together at all. In some family circumstances in many cultures, the males are extraneous and irrelevant, although the degree to which they are made to feel so differs. Almost everywhere, however, the conscious and purposeful assignment of **paternity** gives some adult male the position of husband and father. Paternity is important and desirable almost everywhere. In some specific circumstances, of course, some men may seek to avoid the social demands of paternity, especially if it has more legal or economic liabilities than it has advantages. But there is no society in which the close connection between a woman and her children is not central. By and large, the male is more detachable than the female.

The second major question is: where does the family live? Because people are material, they have to *be* some place.

4-12. The relationship between mother and child is the cornerstone of all human families as well as all mammalian family-like arrangements. This Tiv mother took her twins to market as she sold peanuts and sorghum. Human recognition of paternity has altered the basic primate patterns by giving the husband/father special roles in child care—Wape fathers in New Guinea tend babies on many occasions. Although paternity is actively sought by most men in most societies at least some of the time, the husband/father remains the most loosely tied member of the family; his responsibilities and rights vary widely from culture to culture.

Chapter Four

They need a safe place to sleep and to protect themselves from enemies and from the pressures of the environment. Just as some other animals have dens and nests, human beings have households. Our household gives each of us a place to be, indeed to *belong*, usually with other people.

The household itself, being material, also has to be some place. Just as animals have herds, colonies, and the like, human beings have families set into bands or some more complex type of community.

The geographical or spatial aspects of household and community are the infrastructure to which human culture adds an immense amount of variety. Community and household both vary because of what is added. They also vary with the way they are run. Households are formed as people live out their convictions about who should reside with whom and what they should do for one another. The density of households in a community is determined by cultural response to environment.

The differences between family and household are vital. It is little short of astounding how many books, even modern ones, define the family as a man, a woman, and their children—and then add a rider, who live together. The problems in such a definition should be obvious. The family is a matter of kinship. That means that its members recognize an association with one another on the basis of shared biological descent. Ascription of biological descent (whatever the facts) is important, even when it is denied, as in the Trobriand Islands.

The **household**, on the other hand, is a matter of spatial arrangement. Its members are bound to one another on the basis of shared residence. The family is a kinship group, defined by the kinship (putative or real) of its members. The household is a domestic residential group whose members may or may not constitute a family. Because we so often confuse them—even the U.S. Bureau of the Census confuses them—we shall develop the two ideas as they interlink in order to keep them straight. Because there are two criteria, there is room for four classes, as 4-13 illustrates.

The problem can be put into researchable terms: in any specific society, what is the correlation between kinship groups and household groups? The proportion worldwide of families whose members live together is high, but it is *not* 100 percent. Defining families by linking them to households is faulty procedure. The terms are not interchangeable.

In our own society, the majority of households are usually occupied by families; thus, confusion of household and family is easy to understand. The differences are clearer in some other cultures. Among the traditional Ashanti, for example, spouses did not live together. Both lived in households made up of members of their natal families. Children always live with their mothers—as we shall see in the next chapter, Ashanti society is called matrilineal because of the special values they place on descent from the mother.

Households can, of course, exist when there is no kinship relationship at all—many American college students set up such households, as do young men who live in bachelor's

Family and Household	
Households both kinship and residence	**Dorms** residence without kinship
Extended families that do not live together kinship without residence	**Clubs and associations** neither kinship nor residence

4-13. A family is a group of people united by kinship links or other links culturally considered to be their functional equivalent. A household is a group of people living in the same house, compound, or community. The fact that in most places families live in households should not allow us to blur this important distinction, because households may be made up of nonkinfolk, and the specific kinfolk who may be present varies widely.

houses in some traditional societies.

Rather than search for a theory of households (as Netting, Wilk and Arnould 1984 did) we are going to look briefly at a few of the questions we can ask about households:

- Who is in the household? Why? Who has legal rights to be in the household and who is there for other reasons? How does this correlate with sex and age? Who would like to be someplace else? If so, why?

- What does each member do? How does this correlate with the age and sex of the person?

- What is the power structure within the household? The authority structure? What is the reason that people assign for the authority?

- What is the household division of labor in production processes? Consumption processes?

- Who sleeps where? Who eats where? Who cooks for whom?

Residence. The earliest way that anthropologists attacked these problems was to inquire about the place of residence of a newly married pair. The first accepted method of classifying their residence was to consider where they established a household vis-a-vis their parents. The term **patrilocal** was applied if they lived with the husband's parents and **matrilocal** if they lived with the wife's.

Several uncoordinated attacks on this oversimplification emerged in the 1940s. The first suggestion was that the terms matrilocal and patrilocal be abandoned and replaced with **uxorilocal** (wife's locality) and **virilocal** (husband's locality) (Adam 1948). However, because these terms don't distinguish between residence with the husband's father or with some other kinsman on the husband's side, both sets of terms continue to be used.

4-14. *A newly-married pair may move in with the parents of one or the other, with some other kinfolk, or may establish an independent household. The Hopi, shown here, are matrilocal, which means that the newly-married pair move into the household of the bride. Anthropologists have created an elaborate terminology for classifying the household arrangements that result from these decisions.*

The distinction between (A) a new household in the area of the parents of one spouse and (B) entrance of the married pair into an already existing household was also noted, and a new principle enunciated. **Unilocal** residence means that the married pair moves into an already existing household of one spouse or the other (Titiev 1943). You can then talk about unilocal-matrilocal. If unilocal-patrilocal residence, for example, is consistently practiced, the result is the formation of local communities containing a man, his sons, grandsons, and so on, together with their respective wives and unmarried daughters. Thus, residence patterns may affect small-scale communities in a way comparable to the way they affect households.

Still other terms were invented: **bilocal** if there was a choice; **neolocal** if the pair established a new household; **avunculocal** if they moved to the groom's mother's brother (Murdock 1949). Obviously, there were still some situations that could not be fitted into this kind of terminology, especially cases in which the couple lives with one group until a child is born, then moves somewhere else until something else happens, and then moves again. These classifications fail to cover some of the recognized types of households in our own society—especially the mother-child households common in American cities.

I prefer a simpler method, based on the question: what dyadic relationship is the fundamental one in the household? Middle-class Americans usually build households on the husband-wife relationship. If that relationship falters, the household breaks down. Tiv base households on the father-son relationship; if those two quarrel or part, the household breaks down. Iroquois and Hopi base households on the mother-daughter relationship. I have found no society in which the norm is to build the household around a mother-son relationship. Households based on the father-daughter relationship are rare and apparently in all cases associated with the institution of **groom service**, in which a man spends a considerable period of time working for his father-in-law before he has earned permission to take his wife to some other household.

Residences in Western civilization are most often based on the husband-wife relationship. In any disagreement between a spouse and an in-law, a person is expected to support the spouse. A middle-class child grows up in a household in which the parents are in league, trying to present a united front. There probably are no other adults present in the house-hold. Most Americans frown on three-generational households, even when they have had pleasant experiences in them. It is considered a grave difficulty to have to "move in with" the parents of either spouse. Having aged parents in one's home is often done but it is also often uncomfortable.

In such a household, if anything destroys the husband-wife relationship, that "household" falls to pieces, and two new ones are set up—one around each ex-spouse. It is difficult to know just how many of the problems children experience when their parents divorce have to do with the disappearance of their households. If the parents are in separate house-holds, "which one is mine?" The marital household puts an immense burden on marriage—the pressure to "stay together for the sake of the children."

Many American households today, however, have only one parent in them—usually the mother. Some households are step-family households. Households that differ from what we still consider to be the norm now outnumber those with mother, children and father, that conform to the norm.

WE, THE ALIEN

The Tiv are virilocal and usually patrilocal, which is a complicated way of saying that all wives move to their husbands' households, called compounds. About 83 percent of the time, that compound is with the husband's father's lineage area. In the United States, the domestic situation at marriage is seen as a new couple establishing a new home. The Tiv see the people of a permanent compound losing daughters and, in their terms, "acquiring a wife."

The interfering wife is as deadly in a Tiv household as an

interfering in-law is deadly to an American middle-class household. The cause is the same: there is an interloper who is causing difficulty in the cornerstone relationship. A Tiv woman acquires an undisputed place in her husband's household only as the mother of his sons.

Marriage does not significantly alter a father-son household other than providing a means for it to grow. Neither does divorce. In our society, marital difficulty and divorce threaten the household and split it into two households. In Tiv society, strife between father and son threatens the household. If the son moves out or is thrown out, he will have to establish a new household. Some of his brothers may

join him. The Tiv say the compound is "spoiled" if it splits, whereas we say "broken" to describe a household after divorce.

The power situation in a father-son household like that of the Tiv is the balance of power between fathers and adult sons, and subordinately among brothers and half brothers. The power situation in a marriage-based household like that of the Americans is the balance of rights and duties between husband and wife, and subordinately between parents and children. In the husband-wife household, the sibling relationship is the one of least structural importance; in the father-son household, the marital relationship is of minimal

---

The Strengths and Problems of Households Based on Different Kinship Relationships

Household based on	Strengths	Difficulties	Who Causes Trouble?
Husband-wife relationship[1]	☐ Mobility ☐ Privacy	☐ No varied role models for children ☐ Collapses if marriage fails ☐ Isolated—too much privacy[3] ☐ Understaffed	In-laws[4]
Father-son relationship[2]	☐ Permanence	☐ No privacy ☐ Collapses if father and son disagree ☐ Sexual competition between father and son or between brothers ☐ Women peripheral	Any wife who drives a wedge between brothers or father-son
Mother-daughter relationship	☐ Permanence ☐ Perhaps the most stable overall	☐ No privacy ☐ Collapses if daughter leaves ☐ Men peripheral	Adult males (stepfather)
What kind do you live in?	— FILL IN THE BLANKS —		

[1]If this relationship is multiple, it is almost never the basis for the household.
[2]These relationships may be multiple.
[3]Does too much privacy allow opportunity for physical, sexual and emotional abuse?
[4]It is not only people who cause trouble: money, religion, and sex are other factors.

4-15. Households based on the husband-wife relationship are understaffed; a child has no intimate role models except the parents; the most dangerous element is the breakup of the husband-wife relationship, in which case the household collapses, or the interfering in-law. Households based on the father-son relationship break up when father and son have a falling out; such households put women in a peripheral position in the household of their husbands. The most dangerous element is that a wife will cause hard feelings between her husband and his brothers or father. Households based on the mother-daughter relationship put men in the peripheral position—they must always move out, often back to their own mothers' households when they are widowed or divorced.

structural importance.

Until the late eighteenth century, the Iroquois—Native Americans of New York state—lived in long-houses that were mother-daughter based. Sisters and their married daughters all had rooms in a long-house, where their husbands joined them. Mother-daughter relationships form chains made up of a woman, her daughters, and the daughters' daughters. Mother-daughter links are far more efficient in household contexts than are father-son relationships because the group of women who must work together have been doing it all their lives. Thus, although the wife is somewhat peripheral in a father-son based household, the husband is extremely peripheral in a mother-daughter dominated household. Although men are of importance in specific situations, marriages are structurally almost irrelevant to the mother-daughter household. This obviously does not mean that marriages are emotionally or personally unimportant, but only that the household structure is neither created nor undone on the basis of them. Wallace (1970) has shown that Iroquois husband-fathers were lightly attached to the household, often forming hunting and war parties that were gone for months at a time. Households based on the mother-daughter relationship are so nearly complete that peripheral males, not intensely involved in any household, may form gangs or other antisocial groups.

Division of Domestic Labor. It is the household that fulfills people's most basic physical needs. It also provides most people with responsible work assignments. It is associated with shelter, so who builds the house? Who helps? Whose house is it?

Food provision is usually organized within the household. Who grows it or hunts it or pays for it? Who cooks it and who has a right to eat there? The household is usually a consumption unit and often is a production unit as well. Babies and the very old are members of the household. If they have to be tended, who tends them? There are so many variables of equal importance that classification of households into types verges on the impossible. Fortunately, that fact doesn't matter. However organized, households, like communities, are vital in every society.

Tasks within the household for the most part are divided on the basis of age and on sex. In some societies children can do many of the necessary tasks and are given regular chores. In societies like our own, children have to go to school. Their schedules are as filled as those of their parents. Yet many share the work of the household.

Families and Households of Plural Marriage

The size of the family household can be affected by several factors. The two most important are (1) the number of marriages of each adult male or female, but seldom both, can increase, and (2) the number of generations who live in the household can be increased. Both have powerful effects on the shape and working of family households.

Households based on a monogamous married pair are common almost everywhere. But they leave a serious problem of back-up for the adults involved. If one partner becomes ill or is incapable of some of the prescribed duties, the other partner must bear all the responsibility of running the household. The monogamous household is thus likely to be short-handed, at least from time to time. The children have only two adults for role models, instructors, or playmates. For people who grew up in larger households, this situation seems strained and empty. In the United States, intact monogamous households are still the moral norm but are no longer the statistical norm. Matricentric families, step families, and families of divorce, taken together, add up to considerably more households than do traditional monogamous family households.

Polygyny. **Polygyny** (literally, plural women in Greek) is the form of **polygamy** (plural marriage) in which several women, each with her young, are all attached to one male. Polygyny is still common in Africa and in the Muslim world. It was found among the nineteenth-century Mormons in Utah. The Old Testament offers many examples. Indeed, if one counts cultures or societies and looks at preferences, polygyny is the preferred form in far and away the largest number of societies.

4-16. Plural marriage—polygyny and polyandry—have important repercussions in the household. It creates relationships, and sometimes problems, between half-siblings. Households of plural marriage require overtly stated standards of the way co-wives or co-husbands should relate to one another. Neither polygyny nor polyandry much affects the number of children a woman bears.

Men often prefer polygyny because it is the best way to assure themselves the greatest number of children (having a large number of children is desirable in many non-Western societies and may be considered the only way to make a contribution to society). Households based on polygyny need precise, sometimes rigid, rules if they are to succeed. Polygyny works best where more wives and children increase the wealth of the husband/father, whether that wealth be in land holdings and prestige or in some other form. For women, polygyny offers fewer rewards than for men, but there are some: they are more likely to marry a rich and successful man if they are willing to share him, their children are likely to be heirs to greater amounts of property and higher honors, and they can benefit from the shared labor and companionship of their co-wives. Although jealousy may be a problem, most polygynous women can overcome sexual jealousy more successfully than they can tolerate real or imagined slights to their children.

Polygyny is most tenacious in societies in which economic rights in women can be acquired by men. In Western society, men no longer have rights to their wives' property, nor do they have unequivocal rights over their wives' earnings. The number of men who could afford more than one wife would be small. If wives are economically self-sufficient, or if they produce more than they cost, then polygyny is sensible from a man's point of view. The issue is not so clear for women— indeed, if women are economically independent, they don't need a man at all.

Households of polygynous families work best when the relationships between the wives are culturally defined in detail. The behavior expected of a good co-wife is governed by a set of rules that establish the norm of the relationship. If a woman lives up to those rules, she is a good co-wife. Whether she likes her husband's other wives is unimportant. However, if she does not live up to the rules, she is not a good co-wife.

The cultural definition of the relationship between co-wives varies widely from one society to another. In some societies, there is an institutionalized relationship of hostility. In others there is one of cooperation and friendliness. Among Tiv, for example, a good co-wife takes over all her co-wife's duties, including farming and sometimes even cooking, during the last month or two of the latter's pregnancy. She acts as assistant to the midwife when the child is born and helps to care for her co-wife for a few days or even weeks after the confinement. To have any sort of overt difficulty with a co-wife is not only in the worst possible taste, it cuts off the major source of cooperation. Only if one's co-wife does not live up to the required patterns is one forgiven for fighting and arguing with her—not because she is a co-wife but because she is a bad co-wife.

Westerners with whom one discusses polygyny almost always assume that sexual jealously would make such a relationship difficult. Co-wives are, as a matter of fact, usually jealous of one another unless they have a good husband. Yet, a man who treats all his wives equally—or at least equitably in whatever respects are considered important by them—is considered a good husband by all his wives. In polygynous societies women usually want co-wives in order to lighten their own workloads. In traditional Africa, no nursing mother wanted to become pregnant again until her child is weaned. Children are nursed as long as three years. These women took no chances; they made sure that they would not get pregnant by abstaining from all sexual relations, with husbands or anyone else. Under such circumstances, most women preferred that there be another wife or two in the compound so that husbands would stay home and help with their share of the chores instead of running around the countryside looking for sex.

I have known African women (and many others are reported in the literature) who made the initial arrangements for a congenial young woman and brought her home to be their husband's new wife because they wanted the companionship and help of a good co-wife. Most polygynous peoples think it is a good idea for a man's wives to check out a new wife before she is brought into the group of co-

4-17. *Polygyny allows one man to father greater numbers of children than does monogamy. This successful but obstreperous young Tiv, in 1950, is surrounded by his three wives. About a month after the photograph was taken, the three wives talked it over and decided to leave him. The three of them left together, taking all their property; two of them also carried their young children, leaving him "sitting alone in the bush."*

wives. Men see this as evidence that the wives are forming a congenial group. Many women will not stay with husbands they like if they cannot get along with co-wives. If a woman likes her co-wives, she may put up with a lot from her husband.

Kitchens are probably harder to share than husbands. In most African societies, each wife has her own hut or rooms, and each has her own kitchen. Each cooks separately, which is especially important after she has children. The husband either divides his mealtimes among his wives, or more commonly eats a little of the food from each of his wives, sharing the rest with any children who may happen to be nearby. Thus, each wife has a sphere of her own. She can reduce the co-wife relationship to a formal one if it becomes necessary. Co-wives who are not congenial can stay out of one another's way if they prefer.

Polygyny must not be viewed as multiple **monogamy**. The relationships of spouses are quite different in the two systems.

The polygynist husband has to be an effective personnel manager. He is outnumbered if the wives decide to act in concert! Some men in polygynous societies anticipate the polygynous state with dread. But as one African elder put it, the only sure way to gain trusted followers is to beget them. Given that philosophy, polygyny becomes an essential mark of the successful man.

The problem of assuring peace and stability among co-wives in polygynous households is a common concern in all polygynous societies. Some have instituted **sororal polygyny** in which a man marries two or more sisters under the assumption that women who are already related to one another will make better co-wives than those who are not. For every society which has found sororal polygyny a workable approach, there is another that expresses shock that anyone could let the possibilities of conflict inherent in the co-wife relationship affect the amity of sisters.

Polygyny does not mean that there are more women than men in the society, but rather that more women are married than men. Given approximately equal numbers of men and women, if women marry when they are fifteen and men when they are twenty-five, there are obviously many more marriageable women than marriageable men.

The complexity of the polygynous family household arises even more from relationships among half-siblings than it does from relationships among co-wives. Differences between half-siblings often create the cleavages that result in the break-up of such households. Although most women can get along well enough with their co-wives, the task becomes considerably greater when their children begin to fight. A child, even a grown child, sides with full-siblings against his or her half-siblings. A woman sides with her children against the children of her co-wives. This struggle may become intense, especially when they involve large inheritances. Precise rules of inheritance and ranking of the children, by age or by social status of the mother or some other means, may ameliorate the struggle. However, rules and ranking do not eliminate the conflict. Sometimes the household will split from the stress. When that happens, the struggle intensifies. Who gets the most fertile piece of land? Who gets father's best shotgun? Who gets the second-best bed?

Thus, the polygynous family contains special seeds of the dissolution of any household based on it. The fact that sons have different mothers, and hence different sets of kin on the mother's side, tends to push them apart. Think about it: what would a soap opera script look like in a culture that practices the kind of multiple marriages we have been talking about? What relationships would be central to the story line? What special difficulties would emerge? Who would be the villain? The heroine? What would you have to do to win? Win what?

Every society that prefers polygynous households must overcome two problems: (1) how do you assure that co-wives get along? and (2) how do you regulate the behavior of half-siblings? The most successful instances are those in which the content of both sets of relationships is clearly stated so that only a minimum of options is left to be worked out on a personal basis.

Polyandry and Why It Is Rare. When several adult males are attached to one-female-and-her-young, the result is called **polyandry** (plural males in Greek). This system of marriage has been found in Tibet and other parts of central Asia, and a few other places, but it is rare. Even more rarely are polygyny and polyandry conjoined—a practice (called group marriage in the nineteenth century) that is occasionally found in North India and Tibet.

Our understanding of polyandry took leaps forward during the late 1970s and the 1980s because two things had happened. First, the insights provided by sociobiology made polyandry understandable for the first time. In most recorded cases of polyandry, the husbands are brothers; the children of each increases the genetic fitness of all. Second, several ethnographers have finally done the kind of intensive fieldwork necessary to understand polyandry as it is understood by the people who practice it.

Until we had this research, the perception of polyandry had been clouded by "lurking assumptions" (premises that are not conscious but nevertheless affect your reasoning) that men would not share women because they would not be willing to give up sole rights in a wife's sexuality. That idea lingered from the patriarchal assumption that the only way to be assured of the legitimacy of a man's children was to control the wife's sexual activity. Second, because paternity was and is impossible to determine in polyandry, it was said to deprive men of children. The idea of paternity is indeed important to men, even (the new literature assures us) those who are involved in polyandrous marriages.

In most places where polyandry occurs, the co-husbands already are bound together by strong relationships. Although most commonly they are brothers, cases are reported in which business or trading partners share a wife. Therefore, the tie between co-husbands is intensified, and perhaps controlled, by their prior relationships. Several authors (this discussion concentrates on Levine [1988]) discovered that these Tibetan men who shared wives with their brothers were not primarily concerned with sex or even with children. Rather, the principal motivation was to avoid subdividing their land. They live in an economically marginal area in which land is scarce. Subdivision of the family farms among the sons would result in each son's inheriting such a small piece of land that he could not sustain a family. If the brothers share a wife, only one set of children will have to live on the inheritance. One could almost call polyandry a form of birth control, for a woman will bear approximately the same number of children whether she is married to one man or several.

In the community of Tibetan Nepalese studied by Nancy Levine, if there are more than three brothers, or if one of the brothers is totally out of sympathy with their joint wife, there is a tendency for the brothers, as a group, to take an additional wife. This step adds all the problems of polygyny to the problems of polyandry. In an attempt to combat the

4-18. *Polyandry requires some device for attributing paternity to one of the husbands—one of several reasons for the fact that polyandry is rare is that paternity is a great problem. The husbands are brothers in most known polyandrous societies. This polyandrous Tibetan family in Nepal is made up of, from left to right, the eldest husband; the joint wife with the youngest child, a girl; the eldest girl with her brother, the only son; and the youngest of the three husbands. The second husband was away from home when the photo was taken.*

divisiveness of polygyny, the second wife is also shared by all the brothers. To do otherwise means the establishment of two separate families—and that will result in the partition of the household and its lands, thereby impoverishing the entire group. In a few of the families Levine studied, they did otherwise, and poverty did indeed ensue.

From a Tibetan woman's point of view, the children of her co-wives are mere competitors. They are not her kin at all. This is of course true in all polygyny, but has special effects here because a woman is not related to her co-wife's children. To avoid the negative impact of co-wives who resent each other, the brothers think it best to marry their wife's sister, whose children *would* be related to the first wife. Then the children of different mothers do not have different mothers' kinfolk. Thus, they have added sororal polygyny (the wives are sisters) to fraternal polyandry (the husbands are brothers).

In Levine's group of Tibetan Nepalese, the wife announced which of the brothers was the father of each of her children. One of the earlier examples of polyandry was a study of the Toda of southern India (Rivers 1904), who assigned all the children to the eldest brother until a ritual was performed to change the assignment of paternity to the next brother. Assignment of paternity, whether by the wife or by a ritual, created a special relationship between that child and the man, although each husband was considered father to them all.

Yet, every man wanted a child, preferably a son, attributed to him. In any case, the brothers in the polyandrous family were seen as socially identical—as members of a unitary group-of-brothers. Therefore, every child increased both the genetic and cultural fitness of every male.

A polyandrous wife divides her time equitably, but not equally, among her husbands. The husbands may be involved in love affairs in the community or might be gone on trading trips for long periods of time. In a society in which men are the chief breadwinners, and in which it is difficult to make a living, having several cooperating men in the household is one way to ensure greater prosperity for all household members.

Households of Divorce and Remarriage

As we have seen, divorce and remarriage make comparatively little difference in households built on the father-son or the mother-daughter relationships. However, any society that bases its households on the husband-wife relationship must make immense adjustments to high rates of divorce and remarriage. In the Western world at the end of the twentieth century, and particularly in the United States, the statistically dominant family household is no longer built around

Marriage and Family

monogamous marriage and the nuclear family. Rather, we have households built on many forms of family, some of which are complicated, most of which are understaffed. There is a regrettable tendency not to deal with these many forms of household as part of a long-term cultural change but rather to consider them to be the result of impoverished morals or of social disorganization. We do not yet know how to deal with these new household forms. We especially do not know enough techniques for preserving family when it is not associated with household. We have a lot to learn.

The new situation of understaffed households is not caused by the divorce rate alone. There has also been a dramatic rise in the number of one-person households. In Puritan New England it was against the law to live alone; unmarried people either lived with kin or as boarders in the households of a married couple. By the middle of the twentieth century, it had become the norm for many people to live alone or to form a temporary household with friends of the same sex between the time they finished their education and the time they themselves established a monogamous household.

Households of Unmarried Parents—Usually Mother-centered Households. The position of women has changed enough that there are now many women in our society who are self-supporting or on public assistance and do not need a man to provide support for their families. The rate of what used to be called "illegitimate births" in the United States has skyrocketed. Although this situation is sometimes called a sign of family breakdown, it is better regarded as a sign of family change. Households of divorce are also sometimes mother-centered, but they should not be confused with the households of never-married parents because they usually are perceived differently by society.

One-parent Households of Divorce. American households break up at the time of divorce. If there are children, they live with their mother about 90 percent of the time. The household and the marriage have broken up, but the family remains. The parents are as much parents of their children

as they ever were. That means that the family is now living in two households: a one-person household (usually the husband/father) and a household containing a woman and her children. One-parent households are seriously understaffed. There is a shameful connection between this type of household and poverty because our society has not yet figured out how to finance such households.

Households made up of fathers and their children are no longer as rare as they were a few years ago. Beginning in the 1960s, the assumption that children should go with their mothers, no matter what other considerations might be relevant, was successfully questioned. Today some 10 percent of children of divorce live in households with their fathers and siblings. The position of the male in American society has indeed been changing. Fathers who do not have custody of their children, who visit them either on weekends or even more rarely, may have difficulty in fulfilling their role as father. For some this causes considerable pain. Some give up trying to father their children because there is pain and hassle in the relationship with the ex-spouse. We have not yet found adequate solutions to the household problems brought about by our new family forms.

Families and Households of Remarriage. When a divorced man or woman remarries, they are likely to bring their children into households that contain **stepfamilies.**

 In the United States, many men move out of the households of their own children when they divorce. They then move into the households of new wives who have given birth to somebody else's children whom the new husband will now help rear.

WE, THE ALIEN

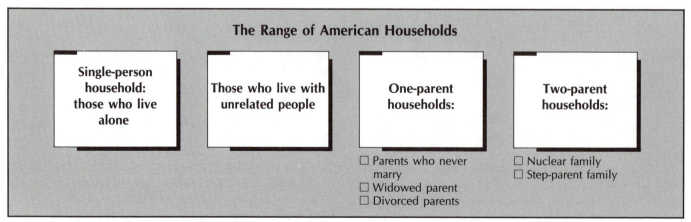

The Range of American Households

Single-person household: those who live alone	Those who live with unrelated people	One-parent households:	Two-parent households:
		☐ Parents who never marry ☐ Widowed parent ☐ Divorced parents	☐ Nuclear family ☐ Step-parent family

4-19. In the United States we have many household forms, based on many different expressions of family: people living alone, parents who have never married (most are mothers, but there are a few fathers who are rearing children), nuclear families, single-parent households of divorce, and stepfamilies.

The household of remarriage is a complex form, especially after divorce. Americans as a society have not yet mastered it. Where the household of the nuclear family contains at most eight types of relationships, households of remarriage can lead to twenty-two: stepparent-stepchild relationships have been added, and the former spouses of the parents (who are the other parents of the children) have some say and, in many cases, make financial contributions to the household. The children have to learn to adjust to both father and stepfather, mother and stepmother, each with his or her own prerogatives and parenting style. As the children go back and forth between such households, stepmothers and stepfathers must also adjust to each other, and their differing values may clash. Children can adjust to this situation readily enough—if the adults can spell out what the rules and the goals are.

All these difficulties would disappear if we could change our mode of forming households. If all women, for example, were to continue to live with their sisters and mothers—and if the women of those households had adequate means for supporting themselves—the problems of the stepfamily household would disappear. However, such households would seriously cut down on the social mobility of their members and would make the problem of peripheral males worse than it already is. It would present many other problems that Americans would have even more difficulty handling.

CONCLUDING THOUGHTS

In summary, the family is species-specific behavior for human beings and would seem to be unique to them, although some components are found in other species. Marriage is a cultural universal. Marriages have to be formed, have to endure, and have to end. Households, usually but not always based on family, including marriage, form basic social groups everywhere. Sometimes the only one. Family and household, both of which may occur in several forms, are the core human organizations and their values permeate every culture.

BUZZWORDS

This chapter and the next contain far more technical terms than any other chapters. It is not possible to discuss these matters without the terms. These terms were, by and large, made up by anthropologists so that they could make the kind of distinctions that allow us to get differences in family life firmly into our heads. No other subject in anthropology requires so many made-up terms and distinctions. The words appear in several categories on the next page.

General Buzzwords

band a group of families who live together. In most bands, the families are related by kinship, and in most there is also a hierarchy among the males.

divorce the undoing of a marriage. It may be done by legal, financial, religious or other means. After a divorce, the marriage no longer exists but is acknowledged once to have existed. It differs from *annulment* which creates a fiction that the marriage never existed in the first place.

household a group of people who live together in a single dwelling or group of dwellings that is considered a unit by the members of the household and their neighbors in other households.

paternity fatherhood. The term is complex. A *sire* is the biological dimension of father; fathers of race horses and other animals are called sires. Paternity is social ascription of fatherhood; it may or may not be the same as the biological paternity.

Words Pertaining to the Process of Finding a Spouse

bridewealth the amount paid by the groom's kinfolk for rights in a bride—they may include rights to her labor, sexual rights, and rights to filiate her children to the groom's kinship group.

courtship an old-fashioned word that means what men do to "win" their brides. When the word was first used, women were not supposed to do anything except resist. Today anthropologists use the word for the traditional ways in which women and men find each other.

dowry the property that a woman brings with her at the time of marriage. If the property remains hers, it is called a dot (pronounced doh).

exogamy the practice forbidding two members of the same kinship group (or, occasionally, some other group) to marry one another. Its opposite is *endogamy*, the practice that requires that people marry within the kinship group.

groom service the work that a man must do for his wife's father before he may claim her as his wife.

groomwealth the amount paid by the bride's family in exchange for rights in the groom. Although it is rare, it has been found.

levirate the institution in which a man is responsible for the wife or wives of his dead brother (or, occasionally, the wives of his father except for his own mother) or other kinfolk. This resembles inheritance of widows except that subsequent children are filiated to the dead husband. In inheritance of widows, subsequent children are filiated to the living heir.

Words Pertaining to Where a Newly Married Couple Lives

avunculocal the couple lives with the groom's mother's brother. This may occur only in matrilineal societies.

bilocal the couple lives with the parents of either the bride or the groom.

matrilocal the couple lives with the parents of the bride.

neolocal the couple establishes a home of their own and does not live with either parent.

patrilocal the couple lives with the parents of the groom.

unilocal the couple not only lives with the parents of one or the other, but also lives in the same actual house as the parents.

uxorilocal the couple lives with the parents of the wife. Originally coined to take the place of matrilocal, but both are in common use.

virilocal the couple lives with the parents of the groom. Originally coined to take the place of the term patrilocal, but both are used.

Words Pertaining to the Number of Spouses

monogamy one husband and one wife

polyandry several husbands and one wife

polygamy plural marriage; both polyandry and polygyny are types of polygamy.

polygyny one husband and several wives

sororal polygyny (sometimes called the sororate) polygyny in which a man marries two or more sisters.

Words Pertaining to the Type of Family

extended family a family that includes three or more generations and includes all members of the family back to a single couple (or, in cases of polygyny, a single male), and extends along all lines.

family a woman and her children; most commonly at least one adult male is added. Most commonly that male is the woman's husband, and ideally the father of her children.

matricentric family a woman and her children.

nuclear family a woman and her children plus her husband. The children were presumably begotten by the husband. In the United States and most other countries, the fact that the children were begotten by someone other than the husband must be determined by a court in order for the husband not to be considered the legal father of the children.

stepfamily a family in which one of a married pair is parent to the children, but the other spouse is not the parent of the children. Obviously, both spouses may bring children into a stepfamily; children may be born to the stepfamily—whereupon, their nuclear family lies within the stepfamily.

Kinship and Community

5

PROPOSITIONS AND PREMISES

- A kinship system is a cultural arrangement of the biological facts of parenting and sexual reproduction (other aspects of sex may or may not be relevant to the kinship system depending on the views held in different cultures).

- Three categories of kin are useful for comparative purposes: relations of (1) descent (lineal kinship), of (2) shared descent (collateral kinship), and of (3) affinity (marriage).

- Kinship terminology is a central schema in every culture—it provides a system of role tags to call up specific behavior, and it creates a ready analogy to describe relationships among many kinds of things.

- Kinship groups other than families are formed by excluding some classes of kinfolk and then increasing the range at which the remaining classes are recognized.

- Lineal descent groups are important in many horticultural and herding societies and may occur in other types. Such groups can serve as governments, economic organizations, and religious congregations.

- Most societies have mechanisms for adoption and may have many other institutions based on fictive kinship.

- Community has two elements: settlements and interest groups. In traditional societies, the two go together. In modern technological cultures, they may be separated.

- The most vital focus of both kinship and community is producing and educating the next generation. Good parenting insures both the survival of the species and the continuation and development of culture.

To understand any society, it is essential to understand kinship. Kinship—the culturized understanding of genetic relatedness among people—undergirds many institutions everywhere. Kinship provides cultural ways of viewing the biological facts of reproduction, of attenuating them, extending them, and making them serve far-flung interests of society. Kinship is important in all societies because it provides a built-in basis for trust.

In small-scale societies, kinship is usually the dominant social principle—it can be used to do almost anything in a small population. In such societies, kinship underlies political and economic institutions. It is the underpinning of many religious activities.

At the other end of the scale, societies that use advanced technologies may grow so large that the kinship principle cannot provide an adequate basis for all social organization. Once the social division of labor separates people by interest and experience, organizations based on kinship become inept if they try to do political and economic jobs. Specialized institutions based on other organizing principles are created to do such tasks. Kinship plays a more restricted role in modern developed societies, but it is still of vital importance—think about what you would do without your own kinship network.

In between the very small societies and the very large ones are societies that use kinship principles as a device for creating groups to do some of those specialized nonfamilial jobs. Terms such as lineages and clans are used to describe groups structured on kinship principles. While such societies have specialized institutions, those institutions use an altered form of the kinship principle. That is, all such institutions are formed by systematically excluding some types of kinfolk and giving special assignments to those that remain.

5-1. *The study of kinship concerns the culturized understanding of the genetic relatedness among people. It does indeed involve biological relatedness. But biological relatedness is the same the whole world over; therefore, it is not of much social interest. The interesting point is that the cultural explanations of that relatedness can be given many forms and serve many social purposes. The photograph is of a Hutterite family taken in Washington state in 1987.*

for you and what you should do for them.

Here we shall focus on three points: (1) the three different kinds of kinship links, (2) the way the terms for kinfolk are used to solicit expected behavior, and (3) how some (but never all) of the kinship links are used to form groups that are assigned specific social tasks beyond the realm of biological relatedness and family.

Three Kinds of Kinship

To help us grasp the complexity of human kinship, 5-3 illustrates three **generations** of relationships which will help us distinguish lineal kinship, collateral kinship, and affines.

Lineal Kinship. Looking at 5-3, we can make some valuable distinctions. First of all, there is a distinction between kinship derived from direct descent and that derived from shared descent. Each of us is a direct descendant of our parents and our grandparents. We are or will be direct ascendants of our children and grandchildren. These kinfolk to whom we are related by direct descent and ascent are called *lineal kin*—they form lines of descent. In 5-3, persons *A*, *2* and *a* have direct or lineal kinship links. So do *B*, *3* and *c*. Thus, our lineal kin are those to whom we trace our kinship only through "begats," as in Genesis (which means that the senior kinfolk is male) or "conceiveds" (which means that the senior one is female).

A further distinction among lineal kin can be made on

Students will find the next section of this chapter to be more technical than any other in the book. Some teachers think it is not necessary to study the technicalities of kinship; others think this is the heartland of anthropology. If your teacher tells you to skip the technical parts, go from here to the section marked "Fictive Kinship" on page 98. If you are going to major in anthropology, you might want to read the whole chapter. I honestly believe that the description of this important subject is presented more clearly here than in most other sources.

KINSHIP

Kinship involves biological relatedness. However, the culturized meaning of relatedness is far more concerned with ideas and values that are associated, either actually or fictitiously, with biological links than it is with the biology itself. All people have ideas about what kinfolk should do

> Among many species, kinfolk cooperate and protect one another.

> Kinship is fundamental to mammalian child-rearing arrangements.

> Human beings extend kinship to create specialized institutions. They do this by utilizing kinship amity and cooperation to cement groups that do specialized economic, religious, and political jobs.

5-2.

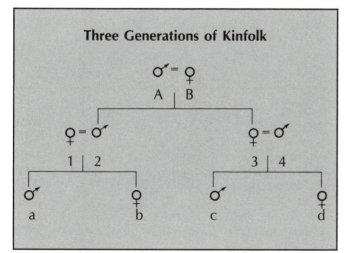

Three Generations of Kinfolk

5-3. Anthropologists—and most of the world's peoples— make several important distinctions on the basis of kinship criteria: (a) lineal kin (who are descended from one another, such as persons A-2-a or B-3-d in the diagram), (b) collateral kin (who share descent from common ancestors, but are not descended from one another such as 2-3 or 3-a-b in the diagram), and (c) affines (who are linked via marriage—A-B or 3-4 in the diagram).

the basis of the sex of the senior member of a lineal link. If the older member is male, the link is an **agnatic** lineal link; if female, the link is **uterine**. This distinction is important because many societies use it when offices or property pass from one generation to the next, and others use it as a criterion for membership when they organize specialized kinship groups.

Some descent links can form chains. Because a woman can be both daughter and mother, mother-daughter relationships form a chain that grows as each daughter herself becomes a mother of daughters. In 5-3, the chain is *B-3-d*. Such chains are, as we shall see, separated out and given special meaning or attention in many societies. Anthropologists call them either **matrilineal** chains or uterine chains. Matrilineal chains are common in the animal kingdom. Primates like chimpanzees and rhesus monkeys have based important dimensions of their social organization on such chains.

Father-son relationships can be made to chain the same way, and can be called **patrilineal** or agnatic chains. Patrilineal chains do not occur among other primates.

When the sex of parent and child are not the same, chains do not result. Mother-son links or father-daughter links, no matter how important, do not chain because the son cannot

Kinship and Community

become a mother or the daughter a father. Therefore *B-2-b* in 5-3 is not a chain.

Matrilineal groups form around matrilineal chains. The groups (not the chains) contain a woman's sons, but not the sons' children. Similarly, patrilineal groups contain daughters, but not daughters' children.

Collateral Kinship. We share descent with quite another group of kinfolk. They are those people who are descended from the same ancestors as we are, but who are neither our direct ascendants or descendants. Our siblings, our aunts and uncles and our cousins share descent with us from common ancestors, but are not descended from one another. People with whom we share descent are called our **collateral** kin. In 5-3, *a* and *c* have shared kinship, as do *2* and *3* or *a* and *b*. The difference between lineal and collateral kinfolk is given great importance in some societies.

Affines. A further distinction is that between biological kinfolk and those we call in-laws in everyday English, but whom genealogists and anthropologists call **affines**. Your affines are all those kinfolk to whom you trace your relationship through a marriage link. Your spouse, your parents' siblings' spouses, and your own spouse's lineal or collateral kinfolk are your affines. The kinfolk of your children, who are related to them through their other parent, are your affines. In 5-3, person *1* is an affine of everyone on the chart except her descendants, *a* and *b*. The only other possible exception is person *4*, who is married to Person 1's husband's sister. Because there are two marriage links, some systems do and others do not count them as affines. Although, as we say in American English, they are "not related," affines nevertheless occupy a vital place in every kinship system.

If you master the above distinctions, most discussions of kinship groups will be clear.

Kinship Terms

Kinship terms are role tags. They imply specific kinds of role behavior and are sometimes used to call up that behavior.

Me, Uncle Sol + Mel   Me, Dad, Mom + Mel

5-4. Kinship terms are language tags for referring to and addressing kinfolk. Each tag lumps some kinfolk together and separates them from all the others.

Such kinship behavior is, in many situations, far more important than the biological facts.

Kinship terms form what we called a schema in Chapter 2. A kinship system is also a set of categories into which various kinfolk can be filed. Words like mother and father imply certain kinds of behavior. So do words like uncle or cousin or grandmother. All the people in the category are expected to comply with a core of expected behavior—and often to add personal dimensions as well.

Terminological Distinctions. The schemata for classifying meanings of kinship terms differ from one language to another. Although multilingual people from ancient times knew about the differences, the significance of the variation was grasped only in the late nineteenth century. Lewis H. Morgan, a prosperous lawyer from upper New York state, studied Native Americans. He got interested in kinship terms while he was working among the Iroquois and Ojibwa Indians. He discovered in these two unrelated languages more or less identical ways of classifying kinfolk—ways that were far different from the way kinfolk were described in English or Latin or any other language he knew. Morgan was excited by his discovery. He began to collect terminologies from hundreds of languages by sending out questionnaires to colonial administrative officers, missionaries, and travelers in faraway places. He requested that they fill out his questionnaires, which he carefully set up in purely descriptive terms such as "mother's brother" rather than the schema of ordinary English in which terms like "uncle" refer to several kinfolk that other languages could classify in different ways. The English word uncle, for example, does not translate into Iroquois.

Morgan organized vast quantities of data and published a book in 1871 that remains a classic (*Systems of Consanguinity and Affinity of the Human Family*). His main point was that some kinship terms, and by extension, some terminological systems, are descriptive whereas others are classificatory. A descriptive system uses only primary terms such as father, mother, son, daughter, husband, wife, so that a grandparent is called mother's father, an aunt is father's sister.

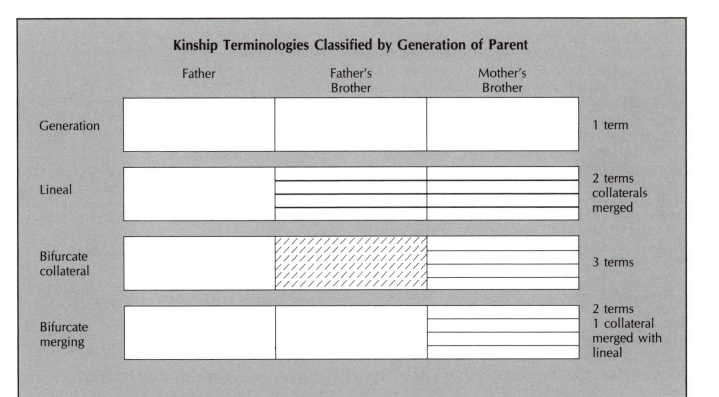

5-5. *Each kinship term implies certain kinds of behavior. The collection of categories is thus a schema of great importance. One basic mode of classification of kinship terms is by the closest kin in the generation just older than ego. (Ego is the person who is using the terms, that is, the "my" of "my father.") Generational schema call father, father's brother and mother's brother all by the same term. Lineal systems separate lineal kin (father) from collateral terms (uncle—both father's brother and mother's brother), but call both collaterals by the same term. Bifurcate collateral separates the two collaterals from one another as well as from the lineal kinsman and so has three terms. Bifurcate merging merges the father's brother with the father as a single term, but calls the mother's brother by a different term. That means that father and father's brother are expected to do much the same thing for the individual, although the father may be recognized as closer and more dependable.*

Thus, all other kin are described by piling up the primary terms. The Scandinavian languages use such descriptive terms to a far greater extent than any other European language.

A **classificatory** system, on the other hand, is one that depends on a quite different schema. In such a system, what are several different types of kinfolk by descriptive criteria are lumped into a single terminological category. "Uncle" is such a term, because it categorizes mother's brother, father's brother, mother's sister's husband, and father's sister's husband. In our system, the behavior expected of one uncle is much the same as that for another kind of uncle.

However, this was not the type of grouping that Morgan was interested in. His major discovery was that kind of "classificatory" which grouped some of the collateral kin with lineal kin. Thus, in a "classificatory system" such as Iroquois, the father and the father's brother were called by the same term.

English terms always carefully distinguish lineal from collateral kin. However, in some terminologies, considerations of generation and shared descent override or displace distinctions between lineal and collateral in the creation of terms. In such a system, my father and all his male siblings (and, in a few cases, female ones as well) and his agnatic cousins are called by the same term. Now note, I did *not* say that the father's siblings are called "father." This seemingly pedantic point underlies what is still a major source of misunderstanding in kinship terminologies: faulty translation. The English word "father" recognizes three principles of classification: generation, sex and descent. The Iroquois word *hanih* recognizes generation and sex but does not distinguish descent from collaterality. Therefore, to translate *hanih* as "father" is an inadequate translation. It is worth noting, however, that people who use such systems say that the term, when used for distant kinfolk, is more or less a metaphor for the closest relative in the category.

Actually, there are four logical ways to create terminological distinctions among the male relatives of the next senior generation (see 5-5). The same kind of chart could be built for female relatives of the next senior generation.

This kind of analysis can also be carried out with the terms for siblings and cousins (see 5-6). All cousins may be called by a single term, either differentiated from siblings (as in English—called an Eskimo system) or not differentiated from them (called a Hawaiian system).

Some systems of kinship terminologies treat the various cousins very differently. The first distinction they make is between **cross cousins** and **parallel cousins**. Your cousin is a parallel cousin if your fathers are brothers or your mothers are sisters. Your cousin is a cross cousin if the two of you are offspring of opposite sex siblings. 5-6 shows that the Iroquois system calls parallel cousins by the same terms as brothers and sisters, but has a different term for cross cousins. The Crow system does the same thing, but instead of having a special word for cross cousin, they merge the cross cousins with other matrilineal kinfolk.

Systems of Kinship Terminology Computed by Cousins in Ego's Generation

	Br	Si	FaBr's So	FaBr's Da	FaSi's So	FaSi's Da	MoBr's So	MoBr's Da	MoSi's So	MoSi's Da
Eskimo	Br	Si	Co	Co	Co	Co	Co	Co	Co	Co
Hawaiian	Br	Si	Br	Si	Br	Si	Br	Si	Br	Si
Iroquois	Br	Si	Br	Si	Co	Co	Co	Co	Br	Si
Crow	Br	Si	Br	Si	Fa	FaSi	So	Da	Br	Si
Omaha	Br	Si	Br	Si	Neph	Niece	MoBr	Mo	Br	Si

5-6. In one's own generation, we can call all cousins by the same term as we do in English (although this schema was named "Eskimo" by anthropologists), implying that one cousin is much like another. We can call all cousins by the same terms we use for brother and sister (Hawaiian), which has very different implications for behavior than if we distinguish terminologically between cousins and siblings. We can call parallel cousins (offspring of same sex siblings) "brother" and "sister" but call cross cousins (offspring of opposite-sex siblings) "cousin" as in the Iroquois system. Both Crow and Omaha systems merge parallel cousins with brother and sister, but separate cross cousins in different ways. The behavior patterns mesh closely with lineage or clan memberships.

Linking Terms with Behavior. Now remember, kinship terms call up behavior. In societies that use different terms for parallel and cross cousins, the behavior of the two types of cousins is very different. As we shall see, the Crow system of terminology (which calls mother and mother's sister by the same term) goes with kinship groups based on matrilineal ties; the Omaha system goes with patrilineal groups.

Anthropologists have, over the years, spent a lot of effort on the analysis of kinship terminology. The single most important point is that it is unwise to work on kinship terminologies in translation—it is almost impossible to translate kinship terms.

Two examples are enough to show both how different cultures can, in their kinship terminology, emphasize quite different cultural points about the common biological base and to convince us that working in translation is treacherous.

Like most systems of kinship terminology, the Ashanti system is simple and logical, but only when it is viewed from the right vantage point. First of all, there are five primary terms for uterine kinfolk. One means "uterine kinperson of my own generation" (*nua*). This can be full brother, full sister, or any uterine cousin of my own generation, no matter the age or how distant. There is another word meaning "female uterine kinperson of the ascending generation" (*ena*); it

5-7. *The system of kinship terminology used by the Ashanti of Ghana is simple if we remember that they recognize one kind of behavior from members of their matrilineal (that is, uterine) kinfolk, but quite a different kind of behavior from their father's matriline. This photograph was taken in 1983.*

includes the mother, mother's sisters, mother's mother's sisters' daughters, and so on. There is another term meaning "male uterine kin of the ascending generation (*wofa*)," which includes the mother's brother, the mother's mother's sisters' sons, and so on. There is a word meaning "uterine kin of the descending generation" (*ba*). This term can be used *only* by women because, obviously, no male has uterine descendants. Males use another term (*wofase*) to apply to all uterine descendants of anyone they call *ena*. This, then, makes five terms for uterine kinfolk.

There are, next, two further words for the father's uterine kinfolk—one for males (*agya*), which includes the father, and one for females (*sewa*). There is another word (*nana*) that has two primary referents; it is, first, all persons to whom one is related lineally in alternate generations (grandparent, grandchild), and second, all uterine kinfolk in alternate

generations. There is a word (*ntoro*) used to describe the relationship of agnation, but it is not applied to specific agnates beyond saying "We are of the same *ntoro*."

There is one word (*akonta*) that means "affine of my own generation" and is applied to all save the spouse; there are special terms for husband and wife. All other Ashanti kinship terms are modifications of these basic ones. Obviously, it is simple because we have found the correct framework for viewing it: the merging of uterine kin by generations.

The Tiv system is even simpler than the Ashanti. Tiv have one term (*ityo*) that means "agnatic kinsperson." They have another (*igba*) that means "mother's agnatic kin." These terms, seldom used in address, do not recognize age, generation, or sex differences.

The chief terminological distinction Tiv make is between lineal and collateral kinfolk. All male ascendants are called by the same term (*ter*). The word is applied alike to father, father's father, and so on, as well as to mother's father, mother's mother's father, and so on. The word can be translated "male ancestor." There is another, equivalent word (*ngo*) for "female ancestor," which includes the mother, both grandmothers, all the great grandmothers, and so on. All collaterals with whom one shares a female ancestor in any line may be called "child (*wan*) of my mother" (*wanngo*). All collaterals with whom I share a male ancestor may be called "child of my father" (*wanter*). One's descendants are all called "child"; this term may be extended to those collaterals who are descended from kinfolk of one's own or junior generations, and (male speaking) it can be extended to any woman who is one's agnate. Tiv have another term, difficult because it is unique as far as I am aware, that means "someone to whom I am related through two routes" (*wangban*): full-siblings, double cousins, and other more distant kinfolk to whom I can trace relationship by two routes. My *wangban* is both my *wango* and my *wanter*. These, with the words for husband and wife (which are the generic terms for male and female—man and woman), and a single word for affine (which literally means "outside") complete the classification. Tiv say that a man's long-term wife who has borne children becomes his *wangban*. That is to say that the man and wife are related through their children. Thus, Tiv classify kin into very broad categories whose main purpose is to separate one's juniors from one's contemporaries and seniors, and secondly, to separate those of one's seniors who are lineal kin from those who are collateral kin.

The fact that kinship terms are behavioral tags was vividly illustrated to me during my fieldwork among the Tiv. I have been addressed by every kinship term suitable for a male, depending on what the speaker wanted me to do. If they called me "my father," they wanted me to give them something. If they called me "my child," they wanted to correct my grammar or my behavior. If someone called me "child of my mother," it was to indicate that I was closer to that individual than I was to somebody else. I was even told that the Tiv and the Americans have one mother, but the English have a different mother—that meant that I

5-8. *The Tiv system is simple if we remember that their primary concern is to distinguish lineal from collateral kinfolk. This photograph is of a man (seated) with his senior wife (standing just to his right). The two women kneeling are also his wives. Two sons are with him—the eldest son and his three wives (the three women on the left-hand side of the photograph), and a second son (half brother of the first) almost hidden behind his wife. The mothers of both sons are either divorced or dead.*

understood the ways of Tiv better than any Englishman they had met.

KINSHIP GROUPS

We have already noted that in very small societies, family and kinship provide the basis of all groups, whereas in very large societies (and in some not so large) kinship is limited to families. In the large societies, special-purpose groups are formed, using other social principles. However, many societies, especially medium-sized ones, have found ways to use specialized groups that are based on kinship.

Kinship groups are formally organized groups of people that contain some but not all of the kinfolk to whom a person is related. They are to be distinguished from families because kinship groups almost never contain affines and the family

5-9. *The schemata that emerge from different modes of reckoning kinship terms are often interlinked with religious, economic or other schemata.*

always does. The traditional Chinese practice in which a woman breaks off the relationship with her own family and lineage, becoming a member of her husband's kinship group as well as of his family, may be considered an exception. The severance of the relationship with her own kin is a step that few of the world's people take. In most societies, a wife remains a member of her own family and kinship groups and is to that degree a stranger in her husband's kinship groups for all that she is an essential member of the family.

Specialized kinship groups are formed by limiting just which categories of kinfolk can be included in them. Almost all of these specialized kinship groups exclude affines (their presence is a mark of the family) and hence can be called **consanguine** kinship groups (Latin for "with blood"—a "blood relative" is common English, but it is a misnomer because it is genes rather than "blood" that creates the relationship).

The problem becomes: whom do you leave out and whom do you put in when you create a special-purpose kinship group? It is theoretically possible to cut out either lineal kinfolk or collaterals and then create groups from those who are left. However, a moment's reflection shows that a group made of no one except lineal kinfolk would of necessity be very small and would be limited to one member of each generation. Such a group couldn't achieve much; it would have no point. A collateral group, on the other hand, would be one in which all lineal links are outlawed and thus would contain only siblings, cousins, aunts and uncles. Such collateral groups do appear as the core of residence groups among the traditional Nyakyusa of southern Tanzania and perhaps in a few other places, but they are rare largely because few have ever found a use for them.

Omnilateral Groups

Probably the best-known example of the collateral kinship group is the Anglo-Saxon group known as the **sib**. In computing my sib, I am the central point. I share my sib with my full brothers and sisters (or double cousins—that is, our fathers are brothers *and* our mothers are sisters). They and no others share *all* of my sib-mates. My half brothers share only half of my sib (unless, of course, the parents we do not share are full siblings).

To the Anglo-Saxons, one's sib contained all cognates computed to specific degrees (Radcliffe-Brown 1950). The father and mother were called kinfolk of the head. The full brothers and sisters were neck kinfolk. First cousins are in the shoulders, second cousins in the elbows, third cousins in the wrists. The next lot of kinfolk—fourth, fifth, and sixth cousins—at the joints of the fingers. Finally come the fingernails at which stand seventh cousins or "nail brothers." The term is still used in German, *Nagelbruder*, to mean distant kinfolk. The original Anglo-Saxon sib included sixth cousins but did not include the nail kinfolk. The computation went from self through all lines, through both men and women.

Another way of viewing the sib was to divide it into several concentric circles: a person's innermost circle included his father and mother, his brother and sister, and his son and daughter—the 'six limbs of the sib.' Another circle was that recognized as the 'relatives within the elbow'—that is, all my kinfolk through second cousins (all the descendants of my eight great-grandparents). The entire sib, which went through sixth cousins, included all the descendants of my 64 great-great-great-great grandparents.

The Anglo-Saxons appear to have assigned different functions to different circles of kin. One circle included all

those with whom marriage was forbidden. It is difficult among the Anglo-Saxon tribes to determine just exactly which kinfolk such a circle included—even when the Teutonic and Welsh records say that the limitation was carried out to the fifth degree, there is some dispute about whether they meant to include third cousins or fifth cousins. The lack of clarity comes in part from the state of the records.

The sib was occasionally called into action and performed as an organization. Although group action was rare, it did occur: at marriage, and when a man killed another man or was killed. There is more information concerning the implication of sibs in blood money (paid to a person's kinfolk by the kinfolk of the killer) than in any other context. If you killed a person, all of the members of your sib, to the sixth degree, contributed a share of the blood money to give to the sib of the victim. The various kinfolk contributed according to the distance of their relationship. When the sum was made up and handed over to the sib of the dead person, it was thereupon divided out again more or less on the same principles as those on which it was collected: the closest kinfolk got most, and the more distant members of the sib, further out in the circles or down the joints of the arm, increasingly less.

 In those parts of the United States in which kinship is recognized beyond the confines of the grandfamily, it is almost always figured in much the same way the sib was computed, with the notable difference that groups were not formed. In parts of the American South, notably Virginia, and in a few New England cultural enclaves, "quartering" is still important. A quartering is a statement delineating in all lines the ancestors of a given individual. When computing kinship for the purposes of suitability for marriage or for any other purpose, it is traced from the contemporary ego back in all lines, and then insofar as it is relevant down again to contemporaries.

It must be remembered, however, that First Families of Virginia and Boston Brahmins (a category of people who trace their ancestry to earliest colonial times), for all that kindred and quartering are of great importance, never call all the kindred into an active, social unit. Therefore, they have nothing resembling the sib in all its details. It is not possible for a Virginian, say, to get all of the people to whom he traces a socially important kinship link to form a group on his behalf. Indeed, there is no social situation in which it is desirable for them to do so. One's kinship position ratifies one's social position, but one's kinfolk as an organized group do not defend it.

WE, THE ALIEN

The **cognatic** kinship group—one that recognizes all kin, like the sib—is rare.

Agnatic or Uterine Lineal Groups. Far more common is to form groups based either on agnatic relationships or else uterine relationships. That means that a group of people who trace their kinship to one another only through males or only through females are used to form special-purpose groups. As noted earlier, anthropologists call those groups that are related through males agnatic groups or sometimes patrilineal groups. If they are related through females they are called uterine groups or sometimes matrilineal groups. These groups contain a relatively small percentage of one's kinfolk. However, they can be used to organize far larger societies than families can organize. Families extended to the same degree would contain too many people.

Position of Ego. The structure of a kinship group that includes only agnates or only uterine kinfolk can take two forms. The basic distinction is whether the pivotal person of the group (what anthropologists call the **ego**) is a long-departed ancestor or is a living contemporary. Citing the descendants of an ancestor or ancestress puts the emphasis within the group on lineality; a group that puts the emphasis on living people and pays little attention to the genealogy of descent puts the emphasis on collaterality. Because there are two criteria, we can create a four-square table, (see 5-10).

Cognatic kinship groups include all the descendants of an ancestor or ancestress (the **omnilineal** descent group) or else they include all the kinfolk, on all sides, of a contemporary ego, limited only by degree of kinship (an **omnilateral** group) like the sib discussed above.

Omnilineal Descent Groups. This is a cognatic group computed from an ancestral ego. Goodenough (1955), who was among the first to recognize this group, called it an "unlimited descent group." The criteria for limiting such groups are nonkinship criteria. Goodenough found three descent groups in the Gilbert Islands in the Pacific, none of them unilineal. (1) The *ooi* is the unlimited descent group (that is, all the descendants) of any single person. All are eligible to inherit land and position from their founder. After a few generations, that is a lot of people. In the same way, every living person is a member of many *ooi*—one for each ancestor—so comparatively few people take up land and position in any single *ooi*. When the members of an *ooi* were limited by including only those who had actually inherited land and certain seats in the community meeting house, that group was called a *bwoti*. The *kainga* are all those members of the *ooi* who form a local residential group. The primary criterion for all three groups is descent, but secondary criteria of a nonkinship nature limit those groups to practical sizes for specific purposes.

Exclusive Kinship Groups. The most commonly recognized kinship criterion for limiting consanguine groups is the sex of the parent in parent-child relationships. Mother-child links may be considered by the people to be of a different

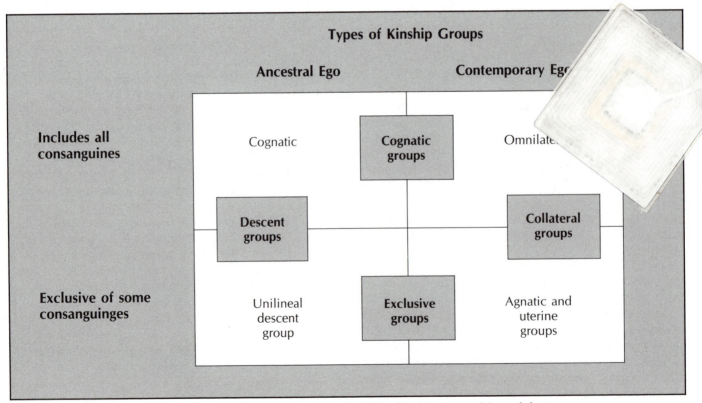

5-10. *Anthropologists have used many criteria for classifying kinship groups. Most of the important ones are summarized in this figure.*

nature from father-child links; either may be used to the exclusion of the other for creating viable and important social groups.

The link of a father to his children is called an agnatic descent link; that of a mother to her children is a uterine descent link. Either can be formed into chains: the father's father's father is a secondary agnatic kinsman; so is the father's brother's son's child. In exactly the same way, the mother's mother's mother or the mother's sister's child is uterine kin. However, the mother's father is neither a uterine nor an agnatic kinsman because there is a combination of one agnatic and one uterine link. A male, obviously, has no uterine descendants, a female no agnatic descendants.

Unilineal Descent Groups. The word descent has several meanings. Biological descent commonly forms a cultural basis on which jural descent is based. **Jural descent**—the inheritance of rights and duties—includes both inheritance of property and **succession** to social positions. It is one mechanism to determine how rank and property are handed from one generation to the next.

Obviously, there is no need whatever for biological and jural descent to overlap. That I am my father's son is biological descent. That I am his heir is jural descent. However, my father's heir may be his brother, and I may be the heir of my mother's brother. Biological descent and jural descent are phenomena in different spheres but may sometimes be brought together in the way people look at the association of biology and society.

Any group of agnates or of uterine kinfolk will, if they trace their ascendants far enough, reach a single ancestor or ancestress. There is, thus, an element of biological descent in every agnatic or uterine group, but it may or may not be jurally recognized. Conversely, the agnatic or uterine descendants of a given ancestor are obviously collaterals, so that such groups also have an element of collaterality. Some cultures emphasize the descent aspect in their image of the group; others, the aspect of collaterality.

A unilineal descent group is, then, a group of agnatic *or* uterine kinfolk based on an ancestral ego—a group in which descent is considered by members to be the essential point. If the genealogical links are known, such groups of kinfolk are called **lineages**. The agnatic lineage is called patrilineal; the uterine lineage matrilineal. The line back to the founding ancestor from any contemporary member is through a line of fathers or a line of mothers.

In patrilineal lineages, physical descent is paralleled by or

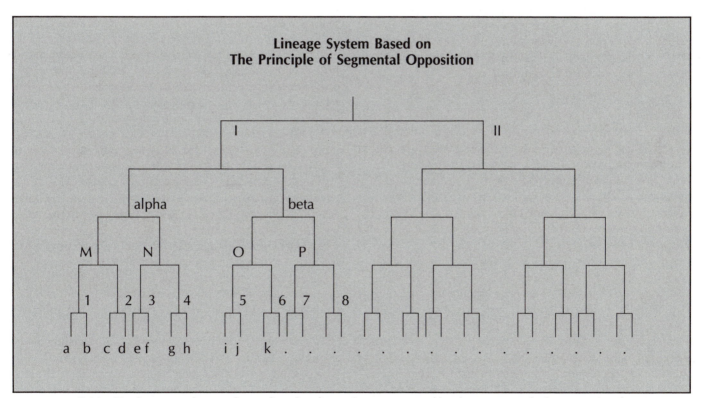

**Lineage System Based on
The Principle of Segmental Opposition**

5-11. *Kinship principles may be used as the idiom of organization of kinship groups—the lineage principle is one of the best recorded and analyzed. Some kinship categories may be isolated and used as a basis for forming specialized kinship groups. The most commonly isolated categories are the agnatic links (leading to patrilineal groups) and the uterine links (leading to matrilineal groups). Especially in Africa, lineages are nested into a lineage system that works on the principle of segmental opposition: that is, lineages (of whatever depth) descended from brothers vie with one another in some matters but join with one another to vie with members of lineages descended from agnates further removed from them in the genealogy.*

closely associated with jural descent. A European woman could, in some historical eras, commit adultery with impunity only when she was pregnant by her husband, because that is the only time, in European folk evaluation of reproduction, that she could not possibly conceive a child in adultery. In short, in societies with patrilineal descent, the "blood tie" between a man and his son is extremely important in assigning the legal right of that son to take over his father's offices and wealth. It also was used to justify stringent measures of social control over the bodies and behavior of women, some of which we still argue today.

In matrilineal lineages, however, biological descent and jural descent are always distinct. The biological line runs from mother to child. But since men are the primary holders of property and status in all societies, including matrilineal societies, the jural descent runs from a man to his closest uterine kinsman in the junior generation—his sister's son. The jural line of descent in matrilineal societies might be called "avunculineal" because it goes from mother's brother to sister's son. Only when the lines of jural descent are confused with those of biological descent does matriliny appear difficult to understand.

Lineage Systems. Lineages may stem from ancestors who were related to one another. They can therefore be linked, as groups, to one another using kinship. Such systems of linked lineages are called **lineage systems**. At least two principles are known on which lineages can be linked into systems: the principle of **segmental opposition** and the principle of succession to an office.

The Principle of Segmental Opposition. Political theorists have long known this principle—they have usually called it the balance of power. The principle, in agnatic kinship groups, is simple: it is a projection of the idea that my brother and I are antagonistic to each other only as long as there is no person more distantly related to us who is antagonistic to both of us. This principle is summed up in a famous Middle Eastern proverb: I against my brothers; my brothers and I against my cousins; my [patrilineal] cousins, my brothers and I against the world.

5-11 illustrates the point. Let us say that *a* on the chart is a group of agnates descended from a common grandfather; *b* is the group of descendants of the grandfather's brother. Both *a* and *b*, however, are all male descendants of 1, the great grandfather. In a conflict and other political action, *a* stands against *b* unless 2 gets into the fight. In that case, *a* and *b* ignore their differences and form group 1. This situation continues until N enters the picture, whereupon 1 and 2 bury their differences and become group M, as opposed to group N. Groups N and M join as group alpha against group beta. This process can be carried on for as many generations as it takes to include all of the members of the most inclusive lineage.

In a group of this sort, which is carefully structured internally, the same principle which separates the subgroups at one level, joins them at another level. This creates an

economical form of social organization and is widespread in Africa and in some places in Melanesia. The variants range from the Tikopia, a Polynesian outlier in Melanesia, to the Nuer in Africa; from the Tallensi to the Bedouin Arabs.

The Principle of Succession to an Office. This second form of lineage organization centers around a specific piece of property, usually an office like that of chief. It is also built around a dominant descent line, with various other lines tying in at various points in the genealogy. In such a system of unilineal descent groups, the dominant line is continually sloughing off collateral lineages. The entire descent group is organized in terms of the kingship, as can be seen in 5-12. There, C is the person or group that is directly descended from the king, via a line of kings. At each generation, there may be one or several collateral lineages. The principle of segmental opposition cannot work here because the presence of the indivisible office renders equality among the lines impossible. Rather, the tie is found in the relationship of each collateral lineage to the main line at the point in the genealogy at which it branches off. In the lineage system of segmental opposition all the branches, at every level, are equal, as 5-11 shows. In the lineage system of succession to an office, one lineage is senior in wealth, status, and rank, while the others hook into the main line of descent.

Double Descent

Many societies, such as our own, recognize neither agnatic nor uterine lineages. Some societies recognize one or the other. A few recognize both. These latter, in which both matrilineal and patrilineal lineages are recognized, are called **double descent** or double unilineal descent.

Anthropologists recognized the existence of double unilineal systems about 1940, although indications of them go back several decades. The first adequate treatment was an analysis of the Yako of eastern Nigeria (Forde 1964). Here patrilineal groups are recognized primarily as political units and units of landholding. Matrilineal groups are the units within which inheritance of movable property takes place. These matrilineal groups also provide a set of priests for shrines to the founding ancestresses. The priests act as an organized check on the political activities of the officeholders determined by membership in patrilineal groups. A neat balance is worked out between the two sets of unilineal descent groups.

In societies in which one line—say the patrilineal—is strongly institutionalized, the primary descent group with which a person is associated will be his own patrilineal lineage. However, it usually happens that a person's *mother's* patrilineage is also of great importance, particularly for men. Thus, Tiv men, for example, have an inalienable right to a farm in the area of their patrilineage. However, they cannot be turned away from the area of their mother's patrilineage; their mothers' brothers are likely to give them a farm on a temporary basis. Such association may be extended to the patrilineal descent groups of his two grandmothers. These

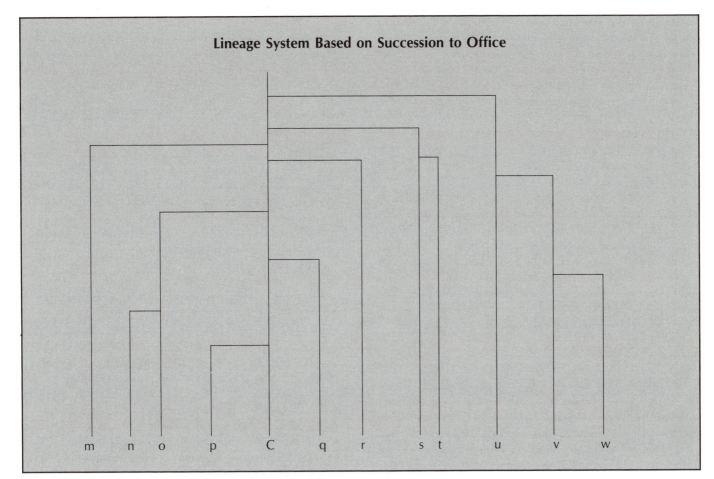

Lineage System Based on Succession to Office

m n o p C q r s t u v w

5-12. When an indivisible piece of property, such as an office that carries with it the right to rule (called "the crown" in European history) is introduced into a lineage system the equality among lineages is overridden. The lineage that inherits the crown, or other piece of property, outranks the other lineages. This type of lineage system, also called a ramage system, is found in many parts of the world.

patrilineal descent groups to which one is associated through uterine ties are not matrilineal descent groups. A Tiv's agnatic lineage is his *ityo*. His mother's agnatic lineage is his *igba*. Such a situation is not double descent; rather, every person is associated by different kinship links to several agnatic lineages.

Agnatic or Uterine Collateral Groups

The people of agnatic or uterine groups may see themselves in terms of collaterality instead of descent. Many agnatic or uterine groups claim to be ignorant of even the name of their founding ancestor, let alone the genealogical links between the ancestor and themselves. Some Native American societies exhibit this characteristic. In the past, such groups have been analyzed more or less as if they were the same thing as unilineal descent groups. We here call them agnatic or uterine collateral groups. The agnatic or uterine group may be made up of all the living agnates (only those people to whom relationship can be counted by agnatic links alone) or all uterine kin, with nobody worrying much about the ancestor. When the genealogy is not known or is not of vital

5-13. Clans are agnatic or uterine collateral groups — the people of the clan know that they are related through males or through females, but they don't pay much attention to the genealogy that would document the fact. Clans are often religious groups, have governing powers, and may be important economically, particularly in sharing.

importance, such a group is most often called a **clan.**

It should be remembered that words like lineage and clan — as well as words such as gens, sib, and many others — are just words. Not only that, they are words in English. Using them to gloss, let alone translate, the words of another language may be tricky. A lot of anthropological argument has been wasted on this point. The fact is that the language of the people being studied almost surely has a word for each kin-based group, and those words are subject to the same analysis we did of kinship terms above.

A few other words for kinship groups may be encountered

in the literature. The word **moiety** is used when the descent groups of a society are divided into two: each half is a moiety. This type of social organization is important in parts of Melanesia and Australia and is found among some traditional Native American people. In most societies with moieties, a person must marry somebody from the opposite moiety. In some, a corpse from one moiety must be buried by the other. A **phratry** is a group of clans that act together but do not presuppose a kinship relationship (or, if they do, that kinship relationship is secondary to other reasons for their associating).

Kinship groups work as organizational tools because kinship facilitates trust. Kinship groups, therefore, play special parts in the political, religious and economic domains of life, as we will investigate in later chapters. Kinship, although grounded in biological reproduction, plays itself out in far wider spheres of trust, cooperation, love, and sacrifice. As individual units of kinship, we each can serve many organizational purposes, from establishing sexual liaisons to building dynasties, monarchies and nations.

Fictive Kinship

Not all kinship is based on biological relatedness. There are three types of nonbiological kinship that are very different from one another. (1) Adoption is the practice in many societies of taking an unrelated child into a family and giving him or her a position in the kinship structure identical with what the child would have had if born to that position. (2) Ritual kinship—usually called godparenthood in English—is especially common in Latin America where it is called *compadrazgo* and creates kin-like networks of friends and neighbors among whom no biological relationship exists. (3) Kinship can also be an effective metaphor—relationships among many different people (or even animals or things) can be expressed in kinship terms when no biological kinship exists.

5-14. Special-purpose kinship groups may be further defined and limited by nonkinship criteria (such as land ownership) as well as by kinship criteria.

Adoption. **Adoption** is a means of creating a legal fiction: an adopted child is taken by parents as their own. Adoption creates a kinship tie by means other than birth. The adopted child has the entire legal position of a natural child. He or she is a full-fledged member of the family as well as of all kinship groups. Societies differ in the degree to which the adopted child retains legal ties with the natural parents. Adoption differs from **fosterage**, which means that people raise other people's children but do not alter the legal position of those children.

We can see adoption as a triad of possible relationships,

as is shown in 5-15. There is a relationship between the adoptive parents and the child. There may be a relationship between the child and the natural parents. There may also be a relationship between the adoptive parents and the natural parents.

Americans adopt children by a legal process. Adults can adopt children of any age, but adopting an infant is said to be most desirable because the child can then grow up learning the particular cultural ways of his or her family. Americans today would like to adopt more children than are available. They therefore sometimes adopt children from other countries.

In the years just after World War II, adoption agencies in the United States advised adoptive parents not to tell children they were adopted. The parents were to forget that the child was adopted, and the child would never know. That policy has changed; adoption agencies now advise parents that the child should know from the earliest time that he or she is adopted. Some adopted children search out their natural parents, which they can legally do after they reach the age of eighteen. The usual explanation for doing so is to discover any medical history that would be relevant for the child. Some adoptive parents cooperate with their children in the search for natural parents. Finding the natural parents seldom or never weakens the bond between a child and his or her adoptive parents.

WE, THE ALIEN

Adoption of a son to be heir by a family that has no children or has only daughters was once common in both China and Japan. The societies of Oceania have sophisticated adoption processes. Indeed, those societies share children the same way they share food, residence, land, labor, political support and money (Marshall 1976).

Fosterage was common in New England in colonial days. People at that time said that parents were inclined to be too lenient with their own children, so they sent boys of about twelve into apprenticeships with other families so that they could learn a trade, and they sent girls to be fostered in other families. They then brought other people's children into their own homes to be reared and, for boys, taught a trade.

Compadrazgo. The Roman Catholic church, and many other churches, recognize ritual kinship between a child and his or her godparents, who are important officiants in the ritual of baptism. Some societies, notably those of the Mediterranean region and of Latin America, have created involved patterns of cooperation and assistance, not only

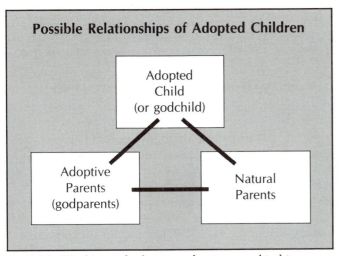

Possible Relationships of Adopted Children

Adopted
Child
(or godchild)

Adoptive
Parents
(godparents)

Natural
Parents

5-15. Kinship can be fictitious: that is to say, kinship may be extended to nonkinfolk. Adoption is widespread, although its forms and uses vary. Godparenthood is widely used in some societies (godparents may occupy a place in the chart similar to adoptive parents, which makes the chart useful in studying compadrazgo). *Adoption and godparenthood both have the effect of enlarging the scope of the kinship system. Kinship systems may be created when no biological relationship, or even any fiction of biological relationship, exists. Women's prisons provide a vivid example.*

Common ancestor

5-16. Kinship charts can be kept for many animals. In this chart, we see some of the relationships among the fourteen species of Darwin's finches on the Galapagos Islands. Kinship may also be used as a metaphor. Tiv say that the three varieties of beans they commonly use are brothers, but one species had a different mother from the other two. Such a kinship idiom is widely used almost everywhere to express nearness or distance among people, plants and objects.

between the child and the godparents, but between the natural parents and the godparents. Obviously, this is another triadic parenting situation, explainable by 5-15, although ritual kinship replaces the adoptive parents in the figure.

The Metaphoric Use of Kinship. Kinship also provides an impressive metaphor. Sometimes kinship terms are applied to plants. The Tiv, like many rural Americans, use kinship terms to discuss the relationships of plants or animals to one another. Just as my grandfather taught me when I was a child that the song sparrow is a cousin of the English sparrow, and that dewberries are cousins of blackberries, my Tiv informants taught me that the three species of beans that they grow are all brothers. They add that two species had the same mother, but the third had a different mother. It is their standard metaphor for indicating distance or closeness in the relationships of living things. A botanist told me that the Tiv are right in that two of the beans are genetically more closely related than either is to the third.

People of many societies use kinship terms to extend kinship amity and a feeling of closeness to people with whom no biological kinship exists. American middle-class people sometimes teach children to call the parents' close friends by their first name but to add "uncle" or "aunt" to assure a combination of familiarity and respect. Corporations sometimes talk of themselves as "the ABC family" or claim to be "one big happy family" because the use of the term

"family" implies the closeness and permanence that are felt to be lacking in purely contractual relationships. Africans are apt to say of anyone who had performed a major service for them, "He is my father and my mother."

Perhaps the most dramatic example is one found in institutional living in which kinship appears in the total absence of biological relationships. Nunneries, for example, have built-in kinship referents in their formal organization: God the Father, Mother Superior, Sister Mary Mercy and Sister Mary Bartholomew. Monasteries are only a little less dependent on kinship nomenclature: they have fathers and brothers—even "Our Lady" the mother is there at least in iconic form.

It has long been known that women in prison form mock families as a means for creating a self-reassuring in-group and for tolerating, or at least living in, the system. An early study by Rose Giallombardo (1966) reports the family systems formed by the women in an American federal prison for female offenders. In that prison, the kinship system centered around homosexual alliances. I believe that may be a function of this particular prison; it would seem that in state prisons, with more stable populations, they form around fictive mother-daughter relationships.

The homosexual relationships were analogized to marriages. Each inmate also had several kinship relationships, all entered into by common agreement: there were mother-daughter relationships, father-son relationships, brother-brother, sister-sister, brother-sister, and uncle and aunt, nephew or niece relationships. The relationships were clustered into what the inmates called families, usually built around either a couple or a mother. They worked like the families that exist in the outside world with two important exceptions. First, male roles were played by women who assumed them for this purpose alone. Giallombardo found that of 639 inmates in the prison, 215 played male roles. They were "studs" in prison terminology. There were 336 "femmes," prisoners who played female roles. The rest, she said, were not classified. Stud and femme (pronounced "fem") were the terms most often found for participants in long-term homosexual relationships. Second, the roles in the prison pseudofamilies did not cluster as they do in the outside world. In a prison family, my sister may not be my brother's sister. My uncle will almost surely not be my sister's uncle. The resulting pseudofamilies are important sharing units and create trustworthy, stable small groups in an otherwise anonymous or hostile environment.

The **pseudofamily** system and pseudokinship relationships spread out from each individual. The inmates do recognize affinal relationships in the families, but seem not to give them any substantial content. There are specific terms used by the inmates for changing gender roles. When an inmate does that, she retains her quasi-kinship relationships; sometimes they do and sometimes they do not change their gender identities in all the relationships.

The inmates analogize their kinship roles sufficiently to the outside norms that they follow incest prohibitions and claim to be shocked by incest. Giallombardo found one uncle-niece relationship that was transformed into a stud-femme relationship; it was disapproved by all. However, stud-femme relationships can be transformed into brother-sister relationships at the time of what they call divorce, and nobody is shocked.

Although there are references in literature to weddings in American male prisons (Thomas 1967), and although homosexuality is a commonplace there, the main studies of men's prisons in North America have found no quasi-kinship or family organization at all comparable to those in women's prisons. Male groups, rather, are founded on principles of dominance and submission. I have been told of one example of wives in a male prison in East Africa but the person who told me about it did not know whether they were set into pseudofamilies. The fact that pseudofamilies are not reported for male prisons does not necessarily mean that they are absent in all of them, although I believe they are absent in American prisons.

Such pseudofamilies have also been found in a Chinese factory. Young women who left their families to become factory workers and live in dormitories formed family groups. Although no homosexuality was reported, the kin-like relationships, clustered into families, were affected by Chinese family structure just as the American prison pseudofamilies were affected by American family structure. The metaphoric creation of a small, protecting group was very important.

COMMUNITY, SETTLEMENT AND INTEREST GROUPS

Human beings build dwellings (houses, tents, or windscreens) in the same sense that birds build nests—for shelter and for defining family space. They also build communities of like-minded people to help one another. Children grow up in households and communities in which they learn culture—techniques and values—as an integral part of growing up. Adults stay in communities for the companionship of people whose ideas and actions reinforce their own ideas and actions, for safety, for shared labor and subsistence, and for the pleasures of sociality.

Households seldom stand alone. Members of a number of clustered households within more or less specifically recognized boundaries may consider themselves linked. They may have a lot of ideas in common and regard themselves as people of the same sort, different from those in the next settlement. They cooperate with one another in preserving life and health; they speak the same language, worship the same gods, and eat the same kind of food.

Such a group of households is usually called a **community.** Just as family and household have to be kept separate, so the community is composed of components that must be kept conceptually separate so that we can see the ways they can be interconnected.

Community is best understood in terms of a simple formula:

Community = Settlement + Interest Group

Settlement is a geographer's term for a group of buildings and the people living in them. Interest group is a fairly new term to describe people who come together because they share one or more specific interests. In the industrial and post-industrial world, the members of an interest group often have only one common interest. In small-scale societies, the interest groups are more broadly based and the members have many interests in common. In those societies, settlement and interest group tend to be made up of the same people, many of whom may be kinfolk. This kind of community is the kith in the term "kith and kin." The industrial world loses this kind of community, based on the combination of settlement and interests.

The settlement and interest group that make up a community can be compared to the household and family that make up what Americans call a home. 5-18 shows the way in which the two sets of ideas are analogous. The household is a component of the settlement. But the ideas and the sentiments that move the people who live in those houses come from family values just as the ideas that move people who live in communities come from their common interest groups (some of which do indeed run or care for the community).

5-17. A community has two vital components: it is a settlement plus an interest group. Settlements change with the way people within them utilize their environment to make a living and they way they govern themselves. Interest groups change by the complexity of division of labor and the kind and number of choices that members must make. As a result, the community is a readily changing type of organization. The community on the left is in Philadelphia. That on the right is a Kickapoo community in northern Mexico. The people lived in these wigwams for six months of the year, then removed the mats from the walls to take them to their summer homes, leaving the frameworks standing.

In the present-day developed world, interest groups and settlements have become separated, just as family and household are becoming separated. People go about their work, which is likely to be away from the settlement, and they follow their own interests, turning the maintenance and policy of the settlement over to hired specialists. Yet, we still have settlements; we will always have them because people will always live near one another. Interest groups, however, have changed. The connection between interest groups and settlements has been largely severed. Given our mobility and the widespread choices that we can make in modern culture, each of us is likely to be a part of several interest groups, none of which is associated with a local settlement. Most people, in fact, do not involve themselves in local politics; many do not even know their neighbors—a condition unheard of in earlier communities.

Nevertheless, both household and community demand upkeep and maintenance. Order must be kept in both household and settlement. Therefore law, professionally administered, is a dimension of the modern settlement, analogous to the sanctioned way of doing things in the household that is very like unwritten law. The moral persuasion that underlies the law comes from the moral demands of the

Home and Community	
Family Held together by common genes.	**Interest Group** Held together by common ideas.
Household A house and the people in it.	**Settlement** A collection of houses.

5-18. Just as all households (spatial groups) are not necessarily comprised of families (kinship groups), people with a great deal in common (interest groups) may form settlements (a spatial group). However, many interest groups do not have spatial expression in this way. People involved in many interest groups may travel from one geographical area to the next in order to participate in them.

Kinship and Community

common interest group or the family.

Settlements are not very well studied in anthropology. The ethnographic sources may be adequate, but the synthesis and theorizing have yet to be done. We do, however, have a number of good ethnographies that are called community studies because they deal with segments of larger societies. One of the primary problems examined in such studies is how the community, made up of a settlement and interlaced interest groups, links into the larger society. Here is a place in which there is a lot of room for further anthropological contributions.

PARENTHOOD: THE FOCUS OF KINSHIP AND COMMUNITY

The quality of the next generation depends more on **parenting** than on any other single item. The family and the community are the context of parenting. It makes very little difference to the future of the species, as a species, which particular individual has sex with whom. Because almost all human genes are good enough, it makes very little biological difference who mates with whom (except in cases of incest, as we saw in the last chapter). Who marries whom and under what conditions makes immense social difference, but (again, except for incest) little biological difference. The issue of parenting, however, is of central importance. So are the families and communities in which children are reared.

Among animals that have effective ways of protecting their young from predators, the young are born at an early stage of development. That is true, for example, for all the cats and many canines, but it is not true for cattle, horses or deer. The young of those species can walk and move about effec-

tively within a few hours of birth. Human beings have an effective set of ways—culture—for protecting the young. And indeed, human young are born at an earlier stage in their development than is true for most other animals. To care for children demands not only the concern and work of parents, but the support of community.

Not only are parents our caretakers in most societies, but they, and especially our mothers, are our first teachers. We get not only genes but also our earliest culture from them. And, just as important, we get at least some of our emotional parameters from them. Good parenting is almost as rewarding to the parents as it is to the children.

There are good and bad chimpanzee mothers. The young of good chimp mothers make more efficient adults than do the offspring of not-so-good mothers (Goodall 1986). Chimps who had good mothers become good mothers. That is also true for human beings. Human mothering is learned behavior. One of the reasons that fieldworkers could even make such observations is that modern Westerners have become very sensitive to the quality of parenting through the discoveries of psychoanalysis and developmental psychology.

However, we must not confuse mothering with an over-simplification like maternal instinct. Mothering means caring for the bearers of one's own genes; human mothering also means caring for the bearers of one's own culture.

Good fathering underwrites good mothering as one of the sources of people's emotional make-up. Anthropologist Francis Deng (1986) tells us vividly that his father, Deng Majok, a Dinka of the southern Sudan who was one of the most powerful chiefs during the British colonial period, was convinced that his father did not love him. Deng Majok's mother had been the first woman to be engaged to Deng Majok's father but had refused to go through with the

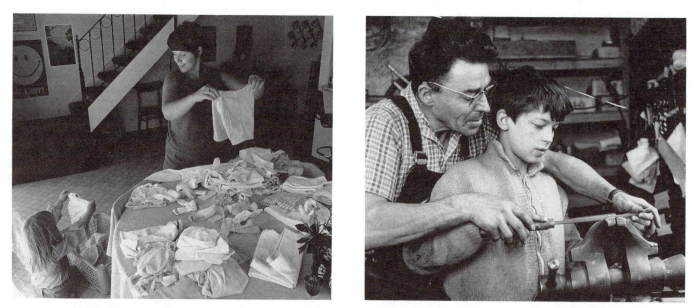

5-19. *Parenting the next generation—assuring its survival and education—is an essential human activity. To do it well requires support from the kinship system (however it may be organized) and the community (whatever forms it takes).*

Chapter Five

102

marriage. The father thereupon married another woman, who became his senior wife. When Deng Majok's mother fell ill, the cause was diagnosed as her turning him down, so she consented to marry him, but now was the second wife. Deng Majok felt all his life that his father disliked his mother for having refused to be the first wife, and therefore disliked her son. He thought his father preferred the less able son by the first wife. Deng Majok was especially hurt when his father kept comparing his leadership abilities to his mother's stubbornness. Deng Majok's conviction drove him to prove his superiority over both his half brother and even his father. He worked harder, made more influential connections, and had a bigger family than either. But with all that, he was never convinced of people's regard for him or loyalty to him.

Deng Majok may or may not have been an even greater man if his father had loved him and preferred him. The point to be made is that most people spend their lives living their cultures in a way set by their response to the way they were parented. That is neither a good nor a bad thing; it is a fact— a fact that brings to attention the importance of parenting.

In developed societies today, people may be having fewer children but they are demanding what pediatricians call "quality children." To get quality children not only means good health practices, but it also demands quality parenting.

CONCLUDING THOUGHTS

Nothing is more important for the future of the species, and ipso facto, of our culture, than is good parenting. Most people learn, in the course of their adult lives, that their parents were either good parents or, more commonly, what psychiatrists call good-enough parents. Most people try to be good parents themselves. To do so, they need the back-up of a larger network—whether kinship or interest groups. A community of interests can provide support. In the United States today, that support is not as unstinting as it should be. Given all the new culture, parenting is at a crisis point.

BUZZWORDS

As was the case in the last chapter, anthropologists have had to be clever and busy in order to understand and classify all the ways that people throughout the world look at their kinfolk. These terms are, for the most part, based on the ordinary language, but have been given special meanings by anthropologists so that the many ways of being a kinsman could be made clear in English. The words appear in several categories on the next two pages.

General Buzzwords

adoption the practice of granting a person, most often a child, a legal kinship position which, by biological descent, is not accurate.

classificatory anthropological term for the practice of categorizing several types of kinfolk under a single term—especially if the resultant categories include both lineal and nonlineal kin.

ego means "I" in Latin. However, in anthropological studies of kinship it refers to the person on whom a genealogy centers. The ego may be a living individual, with ascendants, descendants, and collaterals showing, or it may be an ancestral figure from whom many persons are descended.

fictive fictional. Fictive kinship is any use of kinship terms or practices applied to persons who are not biologically related.

fosterage rearing or bringing up a child. The word applies to one's own children, to adoptive children, and to children who are taken in for rearing in "foster" homes.

generation all the people born during a fairly short period of time. Parents and children are of different generations—indeed, lineal kinfolk are necessarily of different generations.

parenting the acts involved in rearing children, giving them sufficient education, physical and moral support to allow them to grow into adults.

pseudofamily people who link together and act as if they were a family when, in fact, there is no biological or no legal association among them.

segmental opposition a principle in which two equivalent social units that are contrasted to one another, or even in conflict, necessarily join forces when contrasted to yet another, more inclusive, group.

settlement a group of dwellings in an area.

sib In Old English, this word meant "kinsperson." In modern American English, it is sometimes used as an abbreviation for "sibling." The *group* called a sib is made up by counting all kinfolk of a contemporary ego, in any line, to the sixth level (or some other level, depending on the culture). Unfortunately, the word was also used by some anthropologists in the 1940s to mean an agnatic lineal descent group (the corresponding uterine descent group was called a "clan," also a misnomer).

Words Pertaining to Groups

clan a descent group, either agnatic or uterine, whose members do not postulate a known and exact genealogy of descent from the common ancestor or ancestress.

community traditionally, a group of people held together by two specific bonds: the bond of common locality and the bond of shared interest. In the Industrial Age, the word is often applied to a group of people who share a common interest, regardless of their residence.

double descent both the matrilineal group and the patrilineal group are recognized, but are assigned different purposes.

lineage a group of people who share descent *either* matrilineally *or* patrilineally from a common ancestor to whom the genealogy of all members is claimed to be known.

lineage system a hierarchal system of lineages. That is to say, lineages descended from brothers are joined because all are descended from those brothers' father.

moiety each of two comparable groups. The word is especially useful if the entire society is divided into two sections.

phratry a word of many meanings, but usually implying a group of clans that are associated by nonkinship means.

Words Pertaining to Descent

agnatic pertaining to the male. A parent-child relationship is agnatic if the parent is male.

jural descent the descent of property titles whether or not it follows biological descent.

matriliny/matrilineal descended through a series of uterine relationships.

omnilineal related in any line—a combination of matrilineal and patrilineal links.

patriliny/patrilineal descended through a series of agnatic relationships.

succession inheritance or other type of acquisition of rights to office or roles. Succession is to be distinguished from inheritance, which applies to property. One succeeds to the kingship but inherits one's parents' property.

uterine pertaining to the female. A parent-child relationship is uterine if the parent is female.

Words Pertaining to Relatedness Other Than Descent

affine a person to whom one is related through marriage.

cognatic inclusive of all kin, either descendents of one person or computed from a contemporary person.

collateral a person with whom one shares ascendant kin, but from whom one is not descended.

consanguine literally "common blood" in Latin. Used to refer to all kinfolk except affines.

cross cousin offspring of opposite sex siblings are cross cousins.

omnilateral literally "all sides." It means including kinfolk in all directions.

parallel cousin offspring of same sex siblings are parallel cousins.

POWER

III

Power is, next to kinship and family, the most dominant social force in our lives. Power is the capacity to alter something in the environment or the behavior of another person. Personal power can be transformed into power invested in roles and hierarchies. Power in social relationships implies inequality.

Power can also be used antisocially, for selfish personal purposes. It can be wielded in the name of destructive ideologies as readily as for enhancing and protecting the community. Power is required to create the economic necessities of life—but powerful people can corner the economy and use it for their own selfish ends. Standing up for one's rights takes power—and so does settling disputes that arise among kinfolk and neighbors—but power can also be used to strip people of any rights. Protecting the group from invaders takes power—but powerful people can use that same power to create tyranny. Economic success and political security both contain within them the seeds of inequality that may in some places grow into monsters.

Obviously, we must wield power to guard against its misuse. It permeates human culture. Because power is a two-edged sword, we are never finished dealing with it. This part of the book deals specifically with economic and political power, but power is all around us.

Books to Change Your Life   *Martha C. Ward*

Balikci, Asen

1970   *The Netsilik Eskimo*. New York: Doubleday & Co., Inc. Reissued 1989 by Waveland Press, Inc., Prospect Heights, IL.   A full anthropological life is incomplete without Eskimos. There are many classic works about life on the Arctic ice, but this one includes their history, an ethnography of survival under hostile conditions and an update about the traumas of what we loosely call "contact and modernization." This book is linked to the famous PBS television series, so you may already have images of the Netsilik in your imagination.

Benedict, Ruth

1946   *The Chrysanthemum and the Sword: Patterns of Japanese Culture*. Boston: Houghton Mifflin Co.   This is a slightly rewritten version of what was originally a guide for those making policy for the U.S. Occupation Forces in Japan at the end of World War II. It remains the ultimate book for understanding many of the subtleties of Japanese culture.

Chagnon, Napoleon A.

1983   *The Yanomamö: The Fierce People, Third Edition*. New York: Holt, Rinehart and Winston, Inc.   This book has a major cult following among anthropologists. Students are fascinated by this exotic South American Indian tribe with their strange habits of finding mates, taking drugs, fighting each other, and living in a hostile jungle. Timothy Asch and Chagnon have produced good movies about the Yanomamö too. They are good source material about social organization, warfare, and marriage alliances.

Fortune, Reo F.

1932   *Sorcerers of Dobu: The Social Anthropology of the Dobu Islanders of the Western Pacific* (with Introduction by Bronislaw Malinowski). New York: E.P. Dutton & Co. Reissued 1989 by Waveland Press, Inc., Prospect Heights, IL.   Here is the time-honored account [by one of Margaret Mead's ex-husbands] about all the paranoid fantasies, fears and frights as sorcerers bewitch and cast spells on a tropical island in Melanesia.

Lewis, Oscar

1959   *Five Families: Mexican Case Studies in the Culture of Poverty*. New York: Basic Books, Inc.   The simple and riveting style of this book, as it explores the lives of five families in Mexico, set up an immense opposition within anthropology. Some say it is unbelievably good; others undescribably bad. Today most anthropologists would not agree with this author's idea of the culture of poverty, but there are pockets of opinion that still think it is a key to living in the modern world.

Malinowski, Bronislaw Kasper

1922   *Argonauts of the Western Pacific: An Account of Native Enterprise and Adventures in the Archipelagoes of Melanesian New Guinea* (with Preface by Sir James George Frazer). New York: E.P. Dutton & Co. Reissued 1984 by Waveland Press, Inc., Prospect Heights, IL.   This book can be considered the "founding document" of economic anthropology, and remains the best one to read. Trade, life and meaning in the Trobriand Islands are explained by one of the all-time great anthropologists of the world.

Wolf, Eric R.

1959   *Sons of the Shaking Earth*. Chicago: University of Chicago Press.   This prize-winning ethnohistoric classic is set in Mexico and Guatemala. You cannot beat volcanoes, Indians, Spaniards, rebellions and the sweep of opposing cultures for exciting reading.

Bread and Work

6

PROPOSITIONS AND PREMISES

- All people (like all other animals) must utilize the products of their environment in order to survive.

- People can live anywhere in the universe if they have adequate culture in order to derive their requirements from the environment. Resources + culture + work = standard of living.

- Human individuals and human societies are both elements in a total ecological picture. However, culture can vastly speed up the rate of ecological change.

- Most human societies today do not merely gather food and other requirements, they actively produce it. Their technology and ecological situation determine which raw materials are "resources."

- Production and distribution of the necessities of life make up the economy.

- Economic anthropology is the systematic study of production and distribution of the necessities of life (plus the culturally defined niceties of life).

- Wealth is power: the translation from economic power to social power is quite different in simple economies than in complex capitalist or socialist economies.

- Gender is a fundamental determinant of division of work. Therefore, division of work is one of the major indicators of gender status. Both the kind of work and the status associated with gender vary with basic modes of production.

Human beings, like other animals, must get the biological necessities of life from the **environment** in which they live. They must also exploit the environment for the raw materials needed to develop and to maintain culture. That situation demands that anthropologists consider two topics: (1) the way people organize their activities for producing and distributing the necessities and luxuries of life, and (2) the way they regard the environment and its capacity to continue providing the necessary raw materials.

6-1. *Human beings can live anywhere in the universe if they have adequate resources and adequate culture for working those resources. Eskimo adaptation to the Arctic is one of the most dramatic. This picture was taken in Arctic Canada about 1918.*

RESOURCES

People can live anywhere in the universe—all known environments on Earth, including the deep sea and much of deep space—if the resources they need are there, if they have the culture to survive and to turn those resources into usable products, and if they work hard enough.

Resources + Culture + Work = Standard of Living

Materials are not resources unless people can use them. The coal in Pennsylvania was not a resource for the Native Americans who lived there, yet latter-day Euro-Americans based the early stages of an entire industrial system on it. The seed-bearing grasses of the Great Basin of Utah, Nevada, and Idaho are not resources to the Americans who live there today, yet they once dominated the way of life of the Shoshone and Paiute peoples. The Nuer of the southern Sudan lived in an area rich in wild game which they, being a herding people, did not exploit; therefore, wild animals were not for them an important resource. For other peoples with other technologies and other cultural goals, the game might be a resource or even the staff of life.

People in our culture—just like those in any other—use only a few of the resources their environment provides.

Concentration of use on those few resources upsets the balance of the environment.

American food derives from astonishingly few species of animals and plants. We eat beef, pork, and occasionally lamb. We eat some fish—more than in the past—as well as chicken, turkey, duck, and a few geese. Antelope is good red meat, but we do nothing to insure a supply of it; yet, antelopes would harvest the Great Plains with far greater efficiency than cattle. We could domesticate antelope, but given our ideas of private ownership, they would have to be penned. Because antelopes can jump higher than any fence that is "economically feasible," we tell ourselves ranching antelope is not feasible.

Modern industrial people use only a few grains—wheat, oats, rye, barley, corn, and few others. Our starchy tubers are limited to potatoes and sweet potatoes (some varieties of which we call yams). Large Indonesian yams are more nutritious than either and are used widely in the Pacific and in Africa, but not in the United States.

The oil in Oklahoma and Texas was not an important resource until the invention of the automobile. Today oil is so vital to running all industrial economies that we dislike even experimenting with what we call "alternative fuels" in spite of the fact that we know that petroleum is not a renewable resource.

WE, THE ALIENS

Culture identifies the items in our environment that are resources and the ones that are not. American culture is improvident—probably most cultures are. But should we let the petroleum run out before we alter our ways? We are, culturally, not only shortsighted—we are culturally hesitant as far as our food and some basic resources are concerned.

WORK

Most people of the world work. Even many of those who "don't need the money" work in order to give their lives meaning. The basic meaning of work seems to be what people do in order to use resources or to turn them into products that will allow those people to survive and prosper. Hunting, gathering, farming, cooking, caring for the children, manufacturing, providing skilled services—all are work.

The work that has to be done in any society is always divided up among the members of that society; in simple hunting and gathering societies, the primary division of work is between women and men. Most such societies also exhibit

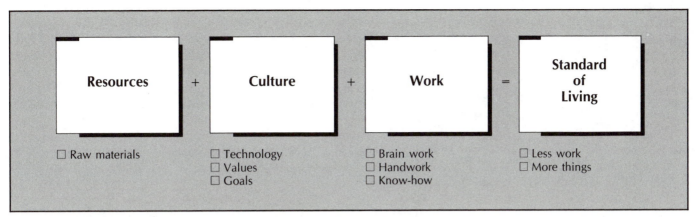

6-2. *Without culture, resources are meaningless. Work is the activity which utilizes resources and culture. The three combine to equal standard of living.*

some difference of work according to age. Children are not expected to work until they reach a certain age, which varies widely. What they are expected to do later varies with what is needed, with the child's capacity, and with the other social demands on the child's time. Old people seldom work as hard physically as young adults, but some elders may do work that is considered of even greater importance. African men do hard physical labor when they are young, but by the time they are middle-aged, they settle disputes, run households, and perform religious ceremonies.

As culture grew more complex and new resources were utilized, the division of work moved to new spheres. Full-time specialists developed; there are now thousands of different jobs to be done in our complex modern society.

Another aspect of division of labor is that whenever work is divided, new organization must be added to maintain a relationship among the people doing different jobs. Commerce and government both provide such organization. So, often, do kinship groups or church-based groups. Therefore, as work becomes more varied, social organization must grow. If the division of labor is to lead to greater production and security rather than to disaster, the social structure must take ever greater control of many dimensions of life—and that means more specialized social institutions to do specific jobs.

Industrial people's views of work may not be unique, but they are unusual. In our thought, work has many opposites: play, idleness, fun, leisure—even pleasure. People of industrialized societies sometimes assume that work is painful and play is pleasurable. Of course, if they think about it, they know that sometimes they enjoy their work, and some kinds of play turn out to be painful or a terrible bore. The pleasure-pain dichotomy is nevertheless sometimes confused with the play-work dichotomy.

Many peoples of the world, on the other hand, contrast work with laziness. They see work as an integrative activity: a person performs his work with the assurance that somebody else will perform complementary work. They understand that their own work demands complementary work on the part of the people they live with and depend on. The efforts of all people are required for the integration of society. In short,

because the organization is complementary to the division of labor, one's particular place in the organization comes to be valued as much as or more than the work itself.

The activities of artists, priests, farmers, professional ball players are all work—no matter how much "fun" is involved. Their products and acts are all reciprocated in some form. Yet, industrialized people are likely to draw a distinction between "productive work" and other work. Productive work is required to furnish the basic economic products—without them, we would perish. Nonproductive work merely provides the decorations; we would not perish if that work were not performed (although important parts of our culture *would* perish). It is a distinction that sells the value of culture short. There are times when the distinction is made for a compelling reason. During World War II, for example, the **economy** of the United States was altered to turn all possible activity into production for the war effort. The goals of the country were completely changed until the war ended.

In industrial society, particularly capitalist society, we divide work into three types and value them differently. (1) The work that is rewarded with money, in the **market**, is considered to be the highest form. We also recognize (2) work that leads directly to our own subsistence. Most tribal peoples either downplay or are not familiar with paid work; they depend on the second kind of work. Today subsistence work is too often confused with some housework: cooking and child care are the most common. Yet a third kind of work (3) is required to maintain ourselves and our households. Today that is the rest of housework: cleaning the house, washing and ironing clothes, washing the car, mowing the lawn. Although most of us do some of this third kind of work, it is nevertheless disdained. This attitude is responsible for a large part of the misconceptions which women confront today. Historically women's work was made up of subsistence and maintenance work which, as described above, did not have the same meaning as it does in our society. Now, women are in paying jobs (type-1 work) everywhere, but we still haven't been able to escape completely the idea that much maintenance and subsistence are considered to be women's work.

Bread and Work

6-3. Work is a mechanism for turning resources (including human resources) into forms or organizations that enhance the possibility of survival and increase the pleasures in life. One of the basic characteristics of society (including many animal societies) is the division of labor—measuring out who will do which work, then organizing the people who do the various jobs into an entity. Sex and age are the primordial bases for dividing the work. This Tiv woman is brewing beer for an important meeting that will be held in her husband's reception hut; women do all the cooking except cooking the meat of sacrifices, which is men's work. Girls begin to help their mothers and learn cooking skills when they are about six or seven years old. The second photograph shows a man planting seed yams in the top of mounts with a small hand-held hoe. Weaving baskets and cloth is boys' work. As culture becomes more complex, individual tasks become more specialized so that labor may be divided on the basis of training, aptitude, inheritance and other criteria.

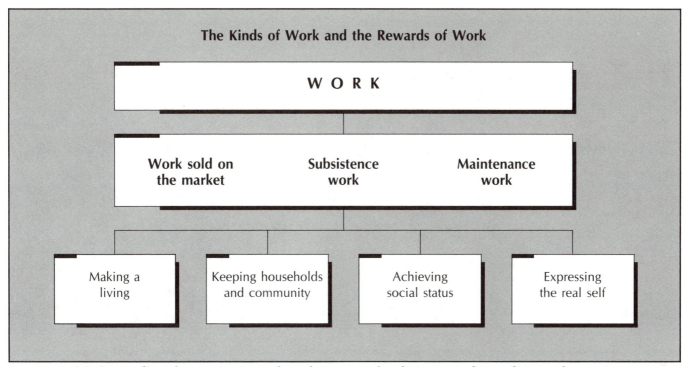

The Kinds of Work and the Rewards of Work

WORK

Work sold on the market   Subsistence work   Maintenance work

Making a living   Keeping households and community   Achieving social status   Expressing the real self

6-4. In preindustrial societies, most work is subsistence work—that is required in producing and processing the necessities of life for self and for family. Skills of specialists like potters or weavers may be exchanged, perhaps by means of free market. Maintenance work is required to keep clean, get rid of detritus, keep everything in neat-enough order (by whatever standards the community applies). People may work for four purposes: to make a living, to keep households and community clean, to achieve social status, and to express one's own capacities and interests.

The idea of work in our society has also been blurred by the economists' idea of labor. Western economics has, indeed, turned work into "labor" that can be evaluated and compared with other items that are bought and sold (have a market price), such as land, groceries, automobiles, or money itself. Economists deal only with type-1 work—that which enters the market and therefore goes into processes of production and distribution. The other two kinds of work—work for subsistence and maintenance, in short, the work done in the household whether by women or by men—are not compensated with money. Hence they are not "labor" when the economists compute the gross national product, no matter how difficult the tasks may be or how exhausting they are for people (including economists).

Maintenance work, unless it is sold on the market by janitors, gardeners, or cleaning companies, is usually not part of our national income. Yet a housewife's work, if it were sold on the market as labor, would bring from $6-$10 an hour (for cleaning the floors or dusting) up to $50 or more an hour (for gourmet cooking). No one denies that domestic activities are work. No one denies that they are productive. However, they do not enter the market system or any other system of distribution, they thus are not "labor" to economic theory.

In our society today, another dimension has been added to work; it has become a factor in our personality. We try to find the kind of paying work that will allow us to enjoy ourselves—indeed, to express our "real selves." Even hard work, if it allows an expression of some valued quality within one's self, is said not to be "really work" because it offers purpose and fulfillment.

Thus, in today's world, work is what we do to (1) make a living, (2) keep our households and communities running, (3) achieve social status, and (4) express ourselves. The third of these defining characteristics was added at the time of the agricultural revolution; the fourth is being added today, even as you read this book.

Subsistence

The kind of work that people of different societies do varies with the way they use the environment to make a living. It also varies with the purposes they bring to the work and with the cultural toolkit they use to do it.

Hunting and Gathering. People who depend on gathering and hunting for their **subsistence**, and who do it with a simple toolkit, are dependent on the immediately usable products that the environment provides. They may store the food they gather or they may cook it (which some anthropologists, particularly in France, regard as one of the great human accomplishments). Fundamentally, however, they are foragers or food *gatherers*, depending on resources that need minimal

6-5. *Hunting and gathering societies divide the labor equitably between the sexes, and the resulting status of the two sexes is approximate equality. These pictures show !Kung men talking over a successful hunt and a !Kung woman using a digging stick to gather roots as she also tends her child.*

further work to make them usable.

Hunting and gathering as a mode of getting one's subsistence does not mean that the culture is "poor." Indeed, hunters and gatherers in a generous environment probably have a better—and certainly a less hard-working—life than do people who subsist by herding or by **agriculture**. They are at the mercy only of weather and disease or any natural catastrophes that affect the plants and animals they utilize.

Societies that depended on hunting and gathering were still fairly common as late as the early twentieth century. Almost all of the **indigenous** people of Australia were hunters and gatherers. The western half of North America was, a little earlier than that, the preserve of people who gained the major part of their livings by hunting and gathering. The Northwest Coast depended on fishing and berries, the California Indians on acorns (which had to be treated to be edible), the Indians of the Great Basin of Nevada and Utah on grass, seeds and game. Plains Indian culture depended primarily on buffalo and on wild plants as the basis of subsistence. In Africa the hunters and gatherers ranged from the Pygmies of the Ituri Forest to the San (so-called Bushmen) of the Kalahari Desert. Many South American Indians depended on hunting, though in many areas they also grew manioc.

Although the number of societies that subsisted from hunting and gathering was large, the number of *people* involved in each of those societies was small. No environment can support very many people on the basis of its wildlife and its wild plants. One of the major exceptions is the area from Puget Sound northward along the Pacific coast of North America. The fantastically plentiful wildlife in this area supported a large Indian population. Hunting, gathering, and fishing were easily accomplished because of the abundant supply of salmon in the river, other fish in the ocean, and deer, berries and roots in the woods. Most of the rest of the world, however, could support communities of at most a few hundred people. People in harsh environments—the Eskimos in the Arctic or the San of the Kalahari Desert or the peoples of the great deserts of Australia and North America—were limited in number.

Probably the most important single feature about a hunting and gathering society is that the economy of the society and the economy of the domestic group are largely undifferentiated from one another. In every society, there is a basic household or domestic unit in which food and other items of primary consumption are prepared. In hunting and gathering societies—and in a few others—the basic consumption unit, which is the domestic group, is also the production unit. The San production unit is the entire village, perhaps half a dozen families.

Hunters and gatherers all developed plans for sharing whatever resources they had with other members of the community. Sharing, and particularly reciprocal gift giving, became part of the cement of such communities.

The sole division of labor in hunting and gathering societies was between women and men. In most places, the women predominantly gathered wild food, perhaps also hunting small animals that could be killed with the digging sticks they took with them to gather roots. Men mainly hunted, but if they found good food, they would also gather it and bring it back to camp. Other work, such as building windscreens or bringing water were assigned primarily to one sex or the other. There was seemingly little difficulty in one helping with or even doing the work of the other. Everybody's work linked her or him directly to the group as a whole. There was almost no differentiation of rank to set one person apart from other members of the group—no social stratification. The two genders were separated, but the work of one was not valued more highly than the work of the other.

Hunting and gathering as a technology supported comparatively few people on any piece of land, but it did offer a healthy, environmentally sensible, and secure lifestyle. It provided more leisure and was more environmentally sound than farming or industrial labor. People of modern industrial societies have the idea that living with a daily necessity to forage for subsistence would be chancy—that disaster would always be around the corner. According to most experts on these societies life was secure and there was leisure to enjoy it.

Herding or Pastoralism. Throughout the world there are peoples whose basic technique for using the environment is to domesticate and keep animals rather than hunt them. The animals may be reindeer, as among the Saami of northernmost Scandanavia (formerly called Lapps) or the Northern Siberians; they may be goats in Morocco and along the northern edges of the Sahara; they may be the cattle of the Near East and much of Africa; they may be the camels that are found in Arabia and the Sahara; they may be horses as was the case in the Great Plains area of North America (although the horse was brought in by Spanish colonists); they may be pigs as in Melanesia; and in South America there are herds of llama.

6-6. In herding societies, most work with the animals was defined as men's work. These are Maasai from southern Kenya. In such societies, the importance of female tasks is reduced and the status of women is likely to be reduced with it.

The division of labor in herding societies puts more emphasis on men's work. In almost all herding societies, the major care of the herds is defined as men's work—indeed, men probably discovered herding as an extension of hunting, just as we shall note below that women probably were the first agriculturalists as an extension of their gathering. Boys are usually the herdsmen. Less commonly girls and even, occasionally, women may do the herding if there are no boys present and the men are busy. Caring for the herd is primarily a male job. If the members of the society depend on milk to any degree, women may do the major part of the dairying, but in some societies men do that too. The position of women in these groups is probably lower than in any other. In pastoral societies, women play a minimal role in subsistence work (unlike foraging societies, in which they provide over half). Thus their contributions are not perceived as vital to the existence of the society. In addition, if warfare is a central issue, the major task of the women may be raising sons for the fighting forces.

The number of people who can live solely off their herds is, of course, very much smaller than the number of people who carry on some herding activities while depending primarily on farming. However, it is not negligible. Whereas the insecurities of hunting people focus around scarcity of game, the insecurities of herders are bound up with the welfare of their beasts. Damage from an animal disease (such as rinderpest among cattle) may leave a whole society in a tenuous condition for years.

Herding usually allows greater density of population than does hunting and gathering. It also, however, requires that people move about so that their animals can have adequate water and pasturage. Therefore, most herding peoples are either nomadic or transhumant (see below).

Nomads follow the demands of their animals for pasture and water; they move in careful response to those needs. They do not, however, just "wander." Even if they wanted to wander at random, other people who live around them would not allow them to do so. Rather, they have definite routes along which they proceed, and they go over the same routes in a sort of circle again and again. They may take shortcuts in the route, and they may take some areas in a different order on one occasion than on another. However, the nomad "route" is a known one, requiring three or four years—up to as many as fifty—to complete.

Nomadism enforces certain limitations on material possessions. Nomads must live either in movable houses like the skin tipis of the Plains Indians, the camel hair tents of the Bedouin Arabs, or in rude and hastily constructed shelters that are made anew at each campsite and abandoned when camp is moved.

Transhumance differs from nomadism in that the cycle of movement is an annual one and follows the seasons, rather than a longer one requiring several years. Some Saami are transhumant, moving their reindeer herds between coastal areas where they can provide food in the wintertime and the mountain recesses where the pasturage is best in summer.

Bread and Work

Alpine herders often take cattle to the high mountains in the summer, then bring them back into the valleys in winter. Many Pakistani and Indian peoples move their herds to the mountains in the summer and back in the winter. The cattle-herding peoples of the upper Nile are almost all transhumant. During the wet season they live in villages with fixed huts and herd their cattle in nearby areas on the higher hummocks, which are not flooded by the annual rise of the Nile River. Then, as the dry season arrives and the water recedes, they are forced to take their cattle farther away, sometimes to live in cattle camps at some distance from their permanent villages in smaller (but, in a few specific situations, larger) groups than the villages themselves provide. This annual movement between village and cattle camp is the most striking characteristic of transhumant societies just as temporary, movable shelters are characteristic of nomads.

The society reflected in the first five books of the Bible was a pastoral society. Its values and patriarchal structure are clearly expressed there.

Herding people throughout the world are said to be of a noble and independent frame of mind. Without exception, they are said to scorn settled life and agricultural pursuits even when they, or at least the women, engage in limited agriculture. It is probably safe to say that herding peoples have had a more difficult time than others adjusting to life in a modern world on the fringes of an industrial economy. Certainly they have held out longest against it.

Horticulture or Gardening. **Horticulture** involves gardening with hand tools such as the digging stick and the hoe. It was probably the earliest form of agriculture. A large variety of crops can be grown by horticultural techniques. Grains such as corn, millet and sorghum, and roots like manioc, taro, yams, or potatoes are the staple foods of horticulturalists.

Gardening allows a much more dense population than does either foraging or herding. Indeed, it allows the population to become sedentary to a degree, but only to a degree, because most peoples who subsist by gardening do not have adequate technology to maintain the fertility of the soil if it is used year after year. Therefore, they must move their gardens every year or every few years to allow the old gardens to lie fallow, thus fertility will be restored by natural means. Despite the necessity of moving gardens, horticulture does reduce the distance that people move when compared with herding.

Garden horticulture, if it is to be successful, requires techniques that alter the environment. Land must be cleared of grass and bush, and trees must be removed or at least thinned out. Horticulture also entails several insecurities for those people who practice it. Irregularities of weather and infestations of destructive insects and birds can create hunger for an entire year. Horticultural peoples are usually dependent for their food on the crops they themselves produce, with only a minimum amount of exchange and trading.

Without exception, people who practice horticulture work hard. In most places the men do the heaviest work and the dangerous work such as felling trees. In many places, horticultural activities such as planting, weeding, and

6-7. With hoe horticulture, men do the heaviest work. These men are making mounds on which yams and many side crops will be planted. In such societies, the importance of women's work is extended—almost everywhere they do all but the heaviest work in the fields. The importance of women's heavy responsibility for producing subsistence is usually covered over because men do the initial heavy work and because they are owners of the fields and of the tools of production.

harvesting are carried out by women.

Tiv are horticulturalists. Every year the men do the backbreaking work of piling the thin soil into mounds in which yams (as much as two and a half feet long) can grow. Both women and men then plant yams at the top of the mounds, and manioc toward the base; women then plant vegetables and greens around the sides of the mounds. At the end of the growing season, women harvest the yams and carry them on their heads to the compounds—these loads of yams may weigh as much as eighty pounds. To complete the picture, the women might also have babies strapped to their backs. In the second year, the men level the mounds and plant guinea corn—that is culturally defined as a man's crop, and men take care of harvesting it; women use mortars to pound the grain and then separate the chaff. In the third year, men plant sesame, a cash crop. Tiv themselves use sesame for a spice and condiment and as a source of cooking oil, but most of it is sold to the European market (oil is extracted from the seeds to be sold; the leftover substance, called cake, becomes feed for race horses). The fields are then allowed to lie fallow for several years.

Women are extremely important in all horticultural

societies. Women were probably the first farmers, combining it with the gathering they continued to do. To this day, women still dominate the production of food in many horticultural societies in Africa, southern Asia, the Pacific Islands and the jungle areas of South America.

Plow Agriculture. The invention of the plow was undoubtedly one of the most important points of change in the history of humankind, for it combined horticulture with the effective use of animals as a new source of energy to acquire the necessities of life.

When agriculture becomes more efficient and more complicated through the use of the plow, irrigation and fertilizer, the size of the population that can be supported in a comparatively small space may become very large. When that happens, not only do the institutions that provide social organization grow apace, but the gender differentiation of labor takes another turn. In most agrarian societies, men do more and more of the farmwork. Indeed, more labor is required in plow agriculture than in horticulture. When draft animals are used, the care of these animals and the work done by them are usually (not always) in the male realm. Many agrarian tasks take greater strength than do those of horticulture, and even in horticulture men do the tasks that require the greatest strength.

In such circumstances, women become dependent on men for their subsistence as they never were in foraging societies or in horticultural ones. As the importance of women's work for subsistence declines, so does their status. Institutions like *purdah* emerged—women, no longer necessary in the fields, were secluded in their households and were not allowed to go outside without the permission of their fathers or, later, of their husbands. Women's work, in such circumstances, was in the home. This can, all too frequently, translate into a women's "place" is in the home.

The position of women in plow agriculture may become so disadvantageous that they are purposefully turned into decoration. In China, beginning about 1000 B.C., the feet of upper-class women were bound so that movement was extremely difficult. Work was impossible. Having a wife with

6-8. *With plow agriculture, and its use of animals in the farming processes, the male realm expanded. Males usually did the plowing and heavy farm work. As a result, the importance of women to the production and survival processes became less important. If women are relegated solely to domestic chores and reproduction, their position suffers because such work is not valued as highly as the work of direct production of food. Even in those conditions, however, women sometimes did the hard work of plowing. Indeed, as in this picture taken in the United States in the late nineteenth century or early twentieth century, men, women, and children were all set to plowing.*

bound feet indicated to the world that the husband was wealthy enough not to need the labor of his wife.

Plow agriculture also reduces the hazards, or at least substitutes a new set of hazards, in the regularity of the supply of necessary products. Agricultural work is seasonal. In the off-season, other types of production can be carried out. New and sometimes more complex industries can be developed in agricultural situations than in horticultural or certainly in herding situations.

Factory Industrialism. Factory **industrialism** which emerged after thousands of years of agricultural production, assumes a form of energy beyond that of human beings and their domesticated animals. It is traditional to date the beginning of the Industrial Revolution from the invention of the modern steam engine in 1769 (although the idea behind the steam engine can be traced back as early as A.D. 60).

Monumental changes occurred in human social life with the Industrial Revolution. Two of the most important were the centralization of the workplace and completely new forms in the sexual division of labor. In all societies before industrial society, most work occurred either in the home or close to the home. The Industrial Revolution separated the workplace from the home and neighborhood. Two spheres resulted; the home and the workplace became quite distinct.

Industrial production implies some other things: the most important is the extensive use of machines. Machines need to be operated, and they need to be built and repaired. Industrial production also alters the hierarchal structure of agricultural society. There are now people who work for money, having only a paycheck to mark their relationship

6-9. *The position of women in industrial societies was equivocal. They were the first factory workers, but many of them were soon relegated to "their place in the home," which meant that they lost sources of income. In this 1889 photograph, French women are working in a mine, sifting and shoveling coal.*

with the machines they use and the products they make. Industrial production, further, gives rise to different settlement patterns, new kinds of communities, and new sets of values.

Lower-class women and children were the first to go into new factories—especially into textile mills which were among the first factories. In these early days of factories, factory work was considered demeaning for men. Factory work was quite different from the agrarian situation in which men did the work of the fields and women the work of the household, including processing the crops or feeding all of the laborers who were called in for assistance. The new situation of factory work brought in money. Men soon saw that nobody was at home to mind the younger children and that money was to be made in factories. "It was not women working, but women going out to work, that conflicted with male interests" (Nielsen 1990).

When men entered the factories, they tried to establish that women's place was at home. By no means all the women left the factories, but it nevertheless soon became the norm in Western society to say that men were to work for wages and women were to work in the home. Put another way, that means that men's work was production work while women's work was primarily maintenance work. Theoretically, husband and wife were a partnership and the money was for both of them, as was the maintenance work; practically, it didn't always work out that way.

During the nineteenth century, a new idea emerged about what being a woman meant. When it was discovered that literally nobody was doing the jobs of child care, those jobs were overtly defined as women's work. Although women had always been responsible for child rearing, the cultural emphasis and the definitive descriptions were new. The idea grew that minding children should be a mother's first consideration. Women were soon broken into two groups: upper- and middle-class white women were said to be moral and pure creatures who had to be protected from the rough demands of manufacturing and commerce. Acquisition of social graces soon followed—indeed, the social history of the piano reflects closely the need for "ladies" to acquire social graces (Loesser 1954). At the same time, a second group of women—poor women—worked in the factories or in household service and were never defined as moral, pure, or worthy of protection.

Nobody saw that, within the span of about a century, the definition of women's work and the ideals of femininity had changed out of recognition. From being able, hard-working people, one group of women became delicate creatures who should be protected—but if they were poor or nonwhite, the new definitions did not apply.

During this period, the newly organized labor unions specifically and openly excluded women. The idea grew that industrial jobs were men's work and that men had to support their families (another new idea). Therefore, any woman who took a job on the market was thereby depriving some man of that same job. The idea was extended (not always with truth) that since women did not have to support families as men did, they would receive lower wages. Many desperate women took the lower wages as better than no income at all. Labor legislation generally reinforced these concepts. The overt goal was to assure that men could support their families; women were either left out of, or disadvantaged by, labor legislation. Those who had to work were, thus, forced into low-paying jobs.

The efficacy of factory industrialism and the society and economy that can be based on it, including the industrialization of agriculture, is reflected in the small portion of the population engaged in producing basic foodstuffs. That is much different from hunting and gathering, herding, and horticultural societies, in which the major effort of almost all of the people goes into the acquisition of food. With agriculture, the number may be reduced. With factory industrialism, the percentage of people engaged in producing primary food crops may be reduced to less than 10 percent of the population. In the United States, the percentage is far less.

Factory industrialism is, in one sense at least, the logical opposite of hunting and gathering societies. In hunting and gathering societies there is minimal separation of domestic and community economy. In factory industrialism, the domestic economy and the economy of the community are institutionally separated. The household remains the major consuming unit, but it is no longer a basic production unit. Production is carried out by new social groups (of which business firms are representative) that are based on the principle and ethic of contract rather than on the principle and ethic of kinship. The household, or consuming unit, and the workplace, firm or producing unit are linked by two means: (1) individuals play roles both in the household (where a man is husband/father/breadwinner) and in the workplace (where he is an executive or a workman), and (2) material items and overwhelmingly powerful ideas such as money provide the means for the movement of goods both from producer to consumer and from one producer to the next. Such a description fits all developed societies.

The Service Society. In a process that began after World War II and has speeded up since about 1965, fewer and fewer people of the developed world are employed in factories and in industrial production. The number is falling just as the number of people employed in primary agricultural jobs fell when the economy came to be based on industrial production—today many of the industrial as well as the agricultural jobs are being assigned to the Third World.

6-10. In a service society like our own (especially in the presence of adequate contraception), women can achieve equality with men in the workplace, although that equality is not yet complete. They still do more of the subsistence work and maintenance work than men.

The people who used to work in factories have been shunted into the so-called service arena. They are performing services instead of making goods. At the same time, many **entrepreneurs** moved into services businesses—they could make more money and did not have the heavy expenses of large inventories or costly equipment.

The most difficult demand of service industries is that people who perform the services should smile and project the idea that they are enjoying themselves, even when they feel awful. No matter how the customer or the client behaves, the person providing the service must be pleasant. They must appear to have a lot of energy, no matter how tired they are. Some must pretend that their clients are their friends. It is a special burden added to those that were inherited from the industrial era. One might say that workers in industrial society wear out whereas workers in service society burn out.

6-11 shows the six basic modes of subsistence accompanied by different types of community. It also highlights the fact that individuals are vastly affected by the subsistence form in two main areas of their lives: what they eat and the way they spend their time and energy.

ECOLOGY AND ECOLOGICAL AWARENESS

People—like all other animals—use the environment to obtain what they need. Like all animals, they make an impact on the environment. Porcupines can kill all the pine trees in an environment. But humankind, using culture, can absolutely ravage an environment.

Ecology is the study of the interrelationships, in any given geographical area, of all the animal and plant populations—including, of course, human beings. It is concerned with the way plants and animals live together in space and how each species takes certain elements out of the natural environment and puts other elements back into it.

The science of ecology came of age in the middle nineteenth century and formed one of the foundations of Darwin's biological studies. Indeed, his ecological studies are still among the most informative we have. He recorded every weed that came up on a piece of cleared ground three feet by two feet in dimension (Darwin 1859). During the season, 357 plants sprouted in those six square feet. Of that number, 295 were destroyed as seedlings, most of them by insects and slugs. In another experiment on a piece of mown turf three by four feet, Darwin found that twenty species of plant germinated. Nine of those species perished merely because all the others were allowed to grow freely.

Many anthropologists study the interrelationships of environment and culture. Human beings use culture to bend the environment to their own needs. That fact soon becomes a potent force in the particular ecology of the environment. Attitudes toward the environment are important, but they may not actually determine the outcome of cultural action. For example, some Westerners have the illusion that they control the environment technologically, just as some other

Bread and Work

Economic and Community Organization		Work (including Division of Labor)	Diet	Insecurities
Hunting and gathering	Band	W - Gathering M - Hunting	☐ Roots ☐ Seeds ☐ Leaves ☐ Meat	☐ Disappearance of game ☐ Drought ☐ Natural catastrophes
Herding	Band	M - Herding W - Gathering, gardens?	☐ Milk ☐ Meat	☐ Livestock diseases
Horticulture	Village	Extensive division of labor by sex	☐ Roots ☐ Grains	☐ Drought ☐ Irregular rainfall
Agriculture	Village	M - Heavy work W - Constant work	☐ Roots ☐ Grains ☐ Fruits ☐ Vegetables	☐ Drought ☐ Plant disease
Factory Industrialism	City	☐ Same, but men get better jobs ☐ Some women do maintenance work and are "supported" by their husbands	What the market provides	☐ Loss of job ☐ Damage to the environment
Service Society	Megalopolis	☐ Men and women theoretically the same ☐ Specialization	☐ Junk food ☐ Medically-approved diets	☐ Loss of job ☐ Human burnout

6-11. Correlation of Work, Food and Insecurities Examined From the Standpoint of Economic Organization.

peoples such as the traditional Hopi or the Australian aborigines have the idea that they control it ritually. Although the "control" is illusory, nevertheless culture—including both technology and ritual—creates great complexity in the ecological balance.

Change in the environment can occur in one of two ways: matter can be removed from it, and matter can be put into it. Material could be taken out and not replaced, or materials that are put into it may make it unusable by some animal and plant forms. In either case, the environment may be ruined.

Agricultural and commercial production today are ruining the environment in many areas of the world. Although our civilization is doing it more efficiently than any other on record, it is not the first time the environment has been ruined. Many millennia ago, hunters and gatherers of large

mammals ruined the environment. Changes in weather conditions contributed to the demise of some of the mammals, but successful hunting led the number of hunters to multiply. The result was overhunting, which reduced the supply of large mammals and added to the stress caused by climatic change. The combined effect of overhunting and long-term climate change meant that people had either to invent agriculture or perish.

Agriculture, too, systematically ruins environments if it is not controlled. The so-called slash-and-burn method of agriculture is especially destructive. People clear the growth of an unused patch of land—growth which has been developing for aeons by the simple principle that plants and animals finding adequate nutriment to live and reproduce will survive. The slash-and-burn farmers then plant their root crops or grain crops, using up whatever nutrients are in the soil. When that patch is exhausted, they move and clear another. The land may never be the same.

The ravaged countryside in eighteenth- and nineteenth-century Europe and Asia produced a flood of migrants to the United States. Combined carelessness about the environment and overpopulation led to a ruinous end of the peasant way of life. Herding peoples can also ravage the environment—herding too many sheep and goats in the Mediterranean Middle East or North Africa can ruin long-term stock raising in the interest of short-term gains. Indeed, if industrialism had not developed when it did, the human species might have perished from its abuse of the environment.

Human beings, with the help of industrial culture, are again in the process of ruining the environment. We have reversed the method of destruction, however. Our environment today suffers not only from what we take out of it but even more from the materials we put into it. Air, water, and atomic pollution have made many parts of the world uninhabitable (even though some people continue to live in them and suffer the consequences).

Thus, we are doing a better job of ruining the environment than was ever done before. Never has culture been so efficient; therefore, never have the results been so devastating. Fortunately, enough people are aware of the importance of the environment that perhaps we can (1) restore the materials we remove, (2) develop new culture that will utilize other aspects of the environment, thereby reducing the load on the part we already use, and (3) find other ways of disposing of waste other than merely "throwing it away" (where is a safe "away" to throw it?).

Until recently the peoples of Europe and America saw the environment as an available resource to be exploited for their own comfort. Not only did they take out whatever they needed, they often took out much they didn't need. They gave no thought to the many foreign elements dumped in the environment that destroy its usability for other animals or plants, and ultimately for human beings themselves. The industrialized communist and capitalist systems have proved to be equally damaging to the environment. As commercial fertilizers and industrial practices are introduced into the Third World, the environment suffers even more. Air quality is reduced; pure water becomes almost unobtainable.

The irony is that short-term industrial successes lead to population increase, which increases pressure on the environment. Few environments in the world today are unaffected by human culture. The impact of human beings and their culture is carried even into the wilderness on the wind and in the rain.

Use your own experience: how has environmental change and pollution affected your life? How often are you aware of it? What would the world be like if the pollution were not there? If the changes going on could be altered or reversed? How might we go about it?

In the 1970s, the destruction of the environment was extended to space and to the moon. Venus and Mars both

6-12. *Ecology concerns the way all plant and animal species interact as they use the environment. Culture increases human capacity both to take things out of the environment and to put things back into it. The environment has been ravaged many times in human history because of what was taken out of it. In our own day, the more serious problem is what we are putting into it, whether it be automobile exhaust, nuclear disaster like that at Chernobyl which laid a whole area of Ukraine to waste in April of 1986, or the oil spill in Alaska that did immense damage to wildlife both in the sea and on the shore in 1989.*

have manifestations of human culture from Terra on their surfaces. The moon has several earth-made pieces of culture, sent there or taken there to accomplish specific tasks. The very space around the Earth has become a floating junkyard. And this is only the beginning.

The task of ecological anthropology is to discover what kinds of damage to the environment are created by different kinds of culture. Some anthropologists, as a result of those discoveries, may choose to become activists.

ECONOMY

Every economy involves the production, distribution and consumption of goods and services. The way these activities are accomplished has immense impact on other aspects of culture. Making a living, and the way people organize themselves to do it, is called the economy. The main task of economic anthropology is to explain how production and distribution of necessary goods are organized in the absence of a market system or of central government control.

When members of capitalist economies (Americans, Western Europeans, or Japanese) examine different economic systems ranging from industrialized communist countries to technologically simpler cultures—they must recognize and guard against preconceived notions. They are frequently taught to be proud of their capitalistic society long before they are taught what it actually means.

The American economy, as well as that of Europe and Japan, is based on the free market, which is a special form of the cost/benefit principle. Marketplaces, in which small amounts of food and other goods are exchanged, are found in many parts of the world. But in market economies, labor can be bought and sold; so can land—so can organizational skill, risk taking, and even money itself. All those items enter into the same market as the products of agriculture and industry enter. Unless we comprehend the central position of the market in our own society, we cannot understand either communist countries or simple economies based on considerations other than the market.

The science of economics is also centered on the idea of markets. Communist economy, in contrast, banished the market principle and was based on government control of production and distribution, a form of what we shall later call redistribution.

WE, THE ALIEN

6-13. *Land, labor, entrepreneurial risk, and capital are called the factors of production. In Western economy— this photo shows Dan Manzo, who owns his highstall at Pike Place Market in Seattle—each factor enters the market and has a price (rent, work for wages, profit, and interest). In economies not organized by the market principle, the factors are different—land may be merely the right to use the site one occupies; labor may be no more than work that one does to get the job done and interlink with other members of the community. Entrepreneurial risk does not exist outside a market economy; the word capital in a non-market economy may be only a metaphor.*

The Factors of Production

Economics recognizes four important elements called the factors of production: labor, land, the kind of risk taking called entrepreneurship, and capital. If production is to take place at all, these factors have to be present in some form. They vary from one culture to another, and hence need special explanation when we discuss simpler societies.

Labor. As we saw above, any work that is paid for is called labor in modern capitalist society. Subsistence work and maintenance work do not qualify as "labor" unless wages are paid. In most societies of the world, especially historical societies and simple societies, such distinctions were not drawn. Work was seldom paid for with money or anything like it—work was, instead, what one did to survive and to maintain one's position in society.

Land. In capitalist society, land can be bought and sold. In most earlier or simpler societies, that is not the case— indeed, such an idea would be absurd. The word "land" means at least two things. In the first place, it means a site— people's homes and workplaces identify them with the geography. But, second, land is a source of resources. Nobody can produce anything without access to those parts of the environment—the site and resources. When land and its resources enter the market, people can own them; if somebody else then wants to use them, they have to pay rent for the site or buy the resources. Parts of the environment are rich in resources; others are valuable in that they are close to large populations. The land produces the subsistence that keeps people alive at the same time that it is the milieu in which they live and work. For these reasons, membership in a local group, family or nation is often defined to include rights to exploit certain pieces of land.

Our first purpose here is to see how the association between people and land can be institutionalized in the absence of a market system. Again, it is best to look at our own system first so that it doesn't blind us to other systems.

 Westerners have, for some centuries now, viewed the world as a sphere covered with a grid. The grid can be manipulated in scale from the size of the earth itself down to the size of a classroom globe. It can even be reduced to two dimensions and represented on a piece of paper. The next step is to take up a position on the earth, and then, using an instrument called a sextant (invented in 1723), locate this position vis-a-vis the stars, whose positions relative to the earth are fixed. The position is then given an arbitrary but culturally accepted numerical label on the grid.

The piece of land is then further marked off by lines extending from the point checked with the sextant, by use of another instrument called a transit, and by precise measurement. In this way, it is possible to make lines on maps that do not correlate with any terrestrial landmarks but that will nevertheless outlast such landmarks. Land is specifically *not* defined by earthly landmarks such as streams and hills, except as those landmarks have first been located astrally—rivers readily change courses.

We Westerners have thus taken a seafarer's map and, with the aid of precision instruments, applied it to the measurement and delineation of the land. These measured pieces of land become, for purposes of legal and economic activity, precise, identifiable things that can be held and transferred in the market system.

Thus, in our culture, land—whatever else it may be—is a measurable entity divisible into thing-like "parcels" by means of the mathematical and technical processes of surveying and cartography. We live on some of these parcels, produce food on others, and build factories and roads on still others.

WE, THE ALIEN

In other societies there are other kinds of maps and other kinds of rights. The Tiv see geography in the same image as they see their lineage system. We saw in Chapter 5 how a group of agnates descended from a single ancestor is located spatially beside another group descended from his brother. When these two lineages form an inclusive lineage, their combined territories form a spatial unit (see 6-14). This process continues genealogically for several generations until all Tiv are included in the genealogy; it continues geographically until the entirety of Tivland is seen as a single area inhabited by people with a genealogical connection. Tiv name streams and hills. Otherwise, their only place names are the names of lineages.

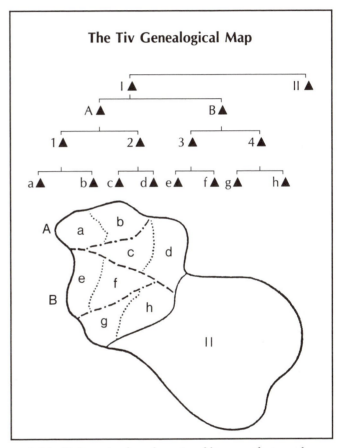

6-14. *Rights to land can be assigned by many devices other than ownership, which is the Western means of assigning them. Tiv have rights to a farm in the area occupied by their agnatic lineage. Farms are used for no more than three years, after which people move to new farm sites while the land resuscitates. After that period, rights in specific farms lapse. Rights to a farm in the correct genealogical position, however, does not lapse.*

The genealogical map of the Tiv moves around on the surface of the earth. The map is the genealogy—association with specific pieces of ground is of only brief duration. Every man, as an agnatic right, and every woman, as a wife, has precise rights to a farm during the time it is cultivated. But when that farm is allowed to return to fallow after two or three years, the rights to that specific piece lapse. But rights in the genealogical map and rights to some farm or other never lapse. A man's wife *always* has rights to a farm in the space claimed by her husband. As a result, the genealogical map responds to the demands of many individual farmers as their needs change from year to year. Whereas the Western map is rigid and precise, the Tiv map is constantly changing both in reference to genealogy and in its correlation with the earth.

The horticultural Plateau Tonga of Zambia (Colson 1948, 1951, 1954, 1958) see land in yet a different way. Their map is a series of points, each representing a rain shrine, where people make offerings to the spirits to call attention to their needs. Rain shrines are either natural features that have been made sacred by ritual or specially built small huts. A rain shrine never changes geographical location, although it may and probably will be forgotten after a generation or so. In former times, if a man's family lived within the area associated with a rain shrine, he was required to participate in the ritual surrounding it. Rain-shrine neighborhoods were the basic territorial grouping. There were usually from four to six villages in a rain-shrine area. People changed villages frequently, creating constant movement from one village to another. Concomitantly, but over a longer time span, the villages themselves changed locations.

Residence in a village carried with it rights to clear farms in the vicinity. Every man selected his own site and, with the help of his wives and family, worked it. Once he had cleared it, he had rights there until he abandoned the site or moved to another village. Farms of members of different villages could be intermixed.

To discuss "ownership" of land, in our sense, about Tiv or Tonga land usage is to misrepresent it. They cannot sell land because they do not own it, any more than we can own and sell air. Yet both peoples have access to the land and the resources that they need. To introduce ownership into those societies is to destroy them by making meaningless the rights people already have. To remove our kind of "ownership" from our own culture would totally destroy it.

Ingenuity and Risk Taking. Two important kinds of ingenuity are maximization and entrepreneurial activity. **Maximization** is the notion that an ordinary person, given the opportunity and not held back by cultural ideas or social pressures, will work to improve his or her lot. Entrepreneurial activity is management skill, including technical "know-how"; it is also the daring required to risk one's energy, work, and money to produce goods or services profitably for the market. In market societies, if entrepreneurs are successful, they get rich. Nonmarket societies have no place for this kind of individual risk taking. Among peasant farmers, everyone takes risks in order to make a living. Among herdsmen or hunters, sharing is far better insurance against disaster than any specialized risks could ever provide, no matter how successful. In communist countries, only the government takes risks.

Capital. Capital is the money or property that a person or a company uses to carry on a business. Outside a capitalistic system—certainly beyond an industrial system—the idea of capital is metaphorical. It is possible, of course, to say that a peasant's tools and animals are capital, or that a huntsman's bow or a gatherer's digging stick is capital. But calling them that doesn't help us understand them.

In Western style **capitalism**, capital implies general-purpose money. Money is one of the great simplifying inventions of all time. It has three uses:

- It is a means for evaluating many different kinds of goods on a common scale.

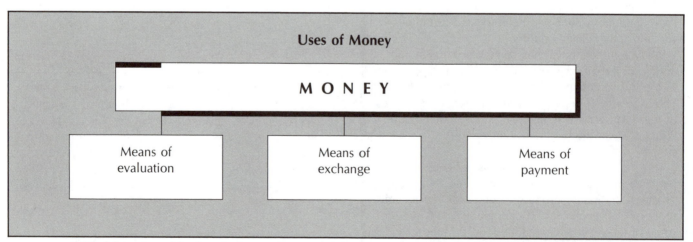

6-15. *Money is used for three fundamental purposes: it is a means of evaluation so that the value of different types of goods can be instantly compared; it is a means of exchange because people can use it to buy items without the inconveniences of barter; and it is a means of payment—any economic indebtedness, however acquired, can be paid by means of money. When all three purposes are represented by a single currency, the result is general-purpose money. When only one or two of the purposes are present, it is called special-purpose money.*

- Money is also a means of exchange—it allows you to sell what you have (including your labor) and buy what you want. Barter, which is the direct exchange of goods without the intervention of money, is far more difficult than money trade. You must find somebody who has what you want and needs what you have.
- Money is a means of payment—no matter how a debt was contracted, it can be paid in money.

Any item that demonstrates all three of these characteristics can be called general-purpose money. Some items can be used (like brass rods among the Tiv which we shall examine below) for only some purposes or in only some spheres, and are hence special-purpose money. We shall see below what people do in the absence of general-purpose money.

Money itself, in capitalist societies, enters the market and becomes a tool—you have to pay interest or dividends in order to use somebody else's money. Money, in societies like ours, is the means of acquiring and financing all the other factors of production. Like land, capital can be owned. In Western society, land, capital, and money enter the market. In many societies, such a market does not exist.

Allocation of Goods and Services

How are goods circulated and allocated in noncapitalist societies? There are four basic modes of allocation (Polanyi 1957): householding, reciprocity, redistribution, and market. We shall investigate them in that order.

Householding. When the members of a household produce their own subsistence, where there is minimal

6-16. Householding is a system in which members of a household produce the major part of their own subsistence. It may be supplemented by other sources of goods or income.

dependence on trade for food or other necessities, the result is called **householding**. Householding may be supplemented by trade, which may be done according to the market principle, but that trade is not central, and usually not even necessary, for the survival and prosperity of the group. American agricultural pioneers were householders: they produced their own shelter, fuel, and food. If they could sell something on the market, they could buy sugar and coffee—but they didn't need them to survive.

Then, in the early days of factory industrialism, piecework was sometimes done at home for pay, by members of the household. The term householding is usually extended to include that kind of work. Today, with hookups and computers, much work is done from offices in the home. It is a matter of choice whether we call that householding; if we do, we must note that the market principle has totally invaded householding.

Reciprocity. **Reciprocity** involves exchange of goods between people who are already associated with one another, most often by ties of kinship or community. Sometimes contracts to trade are made with strangers; the reciprocity of such arrangements may constitute a bond that can be used for political purposes. Among some South American tribal groups like the Yanomamö, people create peace by establishing economic ties of reciprocity. Below, we will examine some examples of reciprocity in the Trobriand Islands.

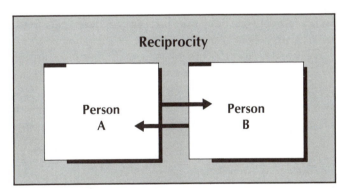

6-17. Reciprocity occurs when two persons already in an established relationship with one another, exchange gifts. Major segments of an economy may be controlled by conventional gift giving.

Redistribution. **Redistribution** is a systematic movement of wealth toward an administrative center and its reallocation by authorities. Modern tax institutions redistribute wealth in society. So do institutions in which the followers of the head of a band or compound put some (or occasionally all) of their subsistence into a common store, which is then redistributed under the chief or one of his officials.

The Marketplace and the Market Principle. Market exchange is the exchange of goods at prices determined by

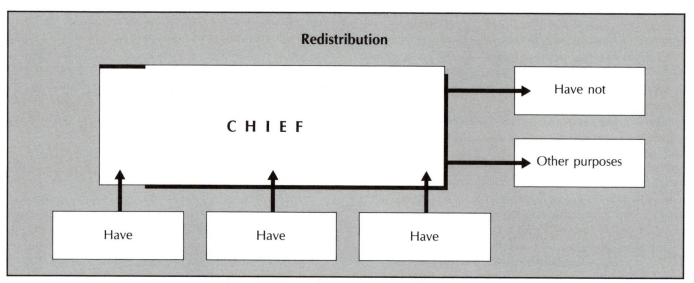

6-18. *Redistribution is a method of removing wealth from the people. The wealth is redistributed either to those who do not have it or, more commonly, to other purposes such as the expenses of government. At least theoretically, the public benefits from the redistribution.*

the law of supply and demand. If goods are available, the price will reflect how much people want them. Great demand usually means a higher price; little demand usually means a much lower price. No demand means out of business. Its essence is free and casual contract—that is, people are free to make contracts with anyone they choose. The **market principle** is to be distinguished from the presence or absence of marketplaces, which are present in many societies where they affect daily life only little, because one of the other forms of allocation is central.

Only in a society in which there is an enforceable contract law can the market principle gain great predominance. Supply and demand are probably present in all cases of exchange, and probably in most cases price is determined by the market mechanism. However, if householding or redistribution is the dominant mode, the mere presence of a marketplace does not mean that the market principle is very important in peoples' lives.

Every empirical economy exhibits at least one of the four principles of distribution; most economies exhibit two; many, like our own, are characterized by all of them.

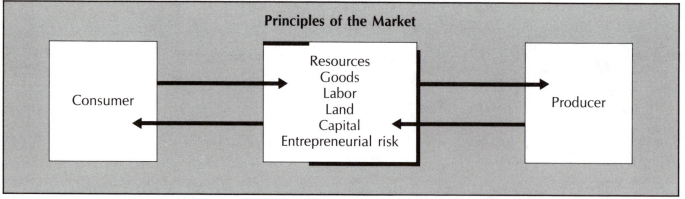

6-19. *All resources, goods, labor, land, capital and entrepreneurial risk enter the same market. The entire system is mediated by money. The consumer buys all needed supplies on the market and sells labor on the same market. Selling on the market provides money for the producer to buy, on the market, all necessary resources to create a product which is sold on the market. Goods are then returned to the consumer, via the market mechanism; the consumer is also either a laborer or owner of land or capital which is sold on the market and provides an income. In brief, all transactions are determined by the market mechanism, and all goods (including the factors of production) enter into the market. Money provides the mechanism by which a market moves resources, goods and services among consumers and producers.*

In spite of the fact that the American economy is uncompromisingly based on the market mechanism—if the market were to disappear, American society would collapse—there are small areas in our lives that are subject to all three of the other principles.

A large and important sector of American economy is controlled by redistribution—taxes and fines are the most prominent examples. Taxes are a form of redistribution in which our money moves into the center (county, state or federal) and certain benefits then derive from that center. Charities to which we give contributions also redistribute the wealth they garner to benefit those for whom the money was given.

There is also a small corner of the American economy dominated by the principle of reciprocity in the form of gift exchange. The fact that Americans buy on the market most of the gifts they exchange does not mean that there is not a nonmarket aspect to the allocation involved in the actual giving. In fact, we are highly critical, even indignant, of the person who overtly computes the market value of reciprocal gifts, although we probably all do it covertly.

Many people in fully developed economies exhibit some aspects of householding: they grow gardens and orchards, preserving and storing food for the winter— these household gardens often make significant contributions to their food store.

In the American economy, householding, redistribution and reciprocity as principles of distribution are peripheral, whereas the market principle is central. In other societies, some other principle may be central, and the market, if it is present at all, is peripheral.

WE, THE ALIEN

Nonmarket Economies

In the absence of general market principles, elaborate economies can grow up. Here we will examine only three of them: spheres of exchange, *kula*, and potlatch.

The four principles of exchange are not limited to subsistence goods or even luxury goods or tools. Prestige is a cultural creation that can be regarded as a scarce good. People can work, struggle, connive and sacrifice to garner prestige. Prestige can be the basis of elaborate economic institutions that have startlingly little to do with subsistence. Modern capitalism, based on money, is fairly obvious in its handling of prestige, which is at least in part associated with the amount of money that is owned or controlled. Some pre-

monetary economies create far more subtle and complex economic institutions around their ideas of prestige.

Spheres of Exchange. Exchangeable goods may be ranked into two or more mutually exclusive spheres, each marked by different moral values. At the time Tiv came under colonial control in the early part of the twentieth century, they recognized three of these morally separate spheres. The lowest ranked was linked with subsistence; Tiv bartered subsistence goods on the basis of market prices. The second sphere was related to prestige, for which they have a specific word (*shagba*). This sphere included slaves, cattle, ritual offices, a type of white cloth known as *tugudu*, some medicines, and metal rods. Within this sphere, brass rods were used as money, in the sense that prices were quoted in terms of rods. The third, and supreme, sphere of Tiv exchange was rights in wives. In the best of all situations,

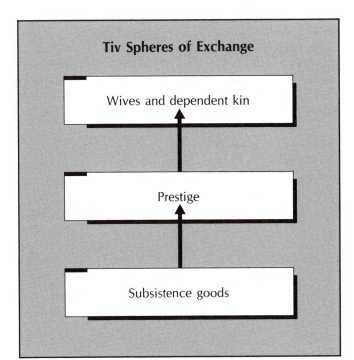

Tiv Spheres of Exchange

Wives and dependent kin

Prestige

Subsistence goods

6-20. Subsistence goods are traded among Tiv either by barter or for a price determined by the market principle. They do something more or less equivalent to our investing by trying to convert subsistence goods into prestige goods. According to their values, the two are not merely tradeable. However, in desperation, a person may dispose of prestige items (particularly brass rods) in exchange for subsistence goods. Traditional Tiv marriage was based on exchange of sisters. Since Tiv also "follow their hearts" by marrying whom they please, this exchange was an elaborate bookkeeping exercise among kinship groups. When "exchanges" could not be worked out, Tiv married by "accumulating a wife," which meant they managed to pay bridewealth from prestige goods. The sign of success among traditional Tiv was to have many wives and many dependent kin: in other words, to convert subsistence into prestige and both into wives.

Bread and Work

Tiv exchanged sisters for wives. But anything as simple as direct exchange seldom happened; therefore, other ways of getting a wife were more usual. Tiv could "accumulate a wife" by making sufficient payments of prestige goods, especially brass rods, over a long period of time. They could also marry women from other tribal groups, often for bridewealth paid in brass rods or some other item in the prestige category. Wives acquired in this way did not have the same prestige as those acquired by exchange. Kinship was a higher value than prestige, which was itself a higher value than mere subsistence.

The goal of a Tiv "investor" was to convert as much subsistence as possible into prestige goods (usually possible only during bad years when desperate men were willing to give up brass rods for food) and as many prestige goods as possible into wives and the resulting kinship links.

When general-purpose money entered Tivland with the British colonial administration, it was first used for redistribution—tax paid to the colonial government. It soon took hold in the market sphere of subsistence as a replacement for barter. Not many years later, when the colonial administration outlawed exchange marriage, money also came to be used as bridewealth. Money thus permeated all the spheres. One could now sell foodstuffs for money to be exchanged for a wife. Since, in a polygynous society, the demand for wives is unlimited, the price of bridewealth rose staggeringly.

Kula. The economy of the Trobriand Islands is complex; its analysis has become a favorite anthropological pastime (Malinowski 1922; Weiner 1976). All the forms of exchange are present, but their particular organization is of great interest. Trobriand economy includes reciprocity (called *wasi*) in which people from inland villages who have no place to fish bring yams to people in shore villages, who don't have enough farmland. Their gift of yams indemnifies the shore people to make a return gift of fish. This "fish and chips exchange" is not carried out on the basis of supply and demand, although a rough equivalency is achieved. Rather, a bundle of yams of standard size (by Trobriand definition) is exchanged for a string of fish, also of standard size: so many yams for so many fish, with little attention to the supply of either yams or fish. The exchanges take place between specific villages. The yams are then widely distributed, again by reciprocity, among the shore villages, as are the fish in the inland villages. It is important because the exchange, although it is between traditional partners, is always begun by the "seller" who indemnifies the "buyer," not the buyer who seeks something like credit from the seller.

The other side of this redistribution system is that the people send yams as tribute to their chiefs, who put the yams in storehouses to be used as a source of food for festivals and for entertainment for the very villagers who provided the yams in the first place.

Of greater interest is the kind of reciprocity known as *kula*. *Kula* is important for two reasons: (1) it is an excellent example of how prestige can be defined by people so that

it is in short supply; it can then be treated as a scarce good the same as any other good of which supplies are limited; (2) exchange of prestige items is the basis of a system of ranking having little or nothing to do with subsistence.

Kula exchange takes place when adult men, in search of prestige, form permanent trading relationships with men in other villages. They indemnify their partners with "valuables," not with useful or edible items. In this formalized exchange, there are two types of valuables—armbands made from large shells, and necklaces made from small shells. The "*kula* ring" traverses a number of islands with a

6-21. Kula *exchange is a system of garnering prestige by giving special prestige goods to trading partners. One type of prestige goods moves clockwise around a large ring, while the other type of goods moves counterclockwise. This photograph shows a* Kula *armshell.*

circumference of several hundred miles. The armbands move around the ring one way; the necklaces in the other. As they move, they collect a patina of myth and legend. The individual valuables are named and become famous. The point is to get your partner to give you one of his valuables instead of giving it to one of his other partners. One does not keep the valuable; rather one garners prestige by having had it and having given it away in a grand ritual gesture.

Production of Trobriand wealth is an elaborate choreography of work and exchange done by both men and women (although only men do *kula*). Exchanges of both subsistence and prestige items are woven together into an elaborate system that lies at the core of Trobriand life.

Potlatch. In the midst of the plenty provided by the lush Northwest Coast of North America, the basic form of subsistence economy was householding. However, people created artificial scarcities in prestige and rank, and then built some of the most compelling parts of their culture on those artificial scarcities. Although the potlatch in one form or another was general in the area, the best documented of the potlatches are those of the Kwakiutl (another classic people in the anthropological literature) who lived on the eastern shore of Vancouver Island.

The potlatch is one version of a "giveaway"—an elaborate game for turning goods and effort into prestige—indeed, into glory. The Kwakiutl were divided into twenty-five village groups; they recognized a hierarchy of offices, each marked by titles, crests, and ceremonial privileges. A potlatch (the word is from the Chinook language and means gift) is a ceremonial occasion on which a person who occupies a named prestigious office gives gifts to his rival. With ostentation and considerable bragging, the rival was openly dared to do anything half so theatrical. The potlatch was,

6-22. The potlatch is representative of the economies that are based on prestige garnered by giving away valuables rather than by accumulating goods. Potlatch valuables never include subsistence goods. Although large quantities of subsistence goods may be expended in the course of a potlatch, they are not part of the potlatch. This photograph, taken about 1895, shows the people and some of the goods involved in a potlatch among the Tlingit, a people of the southern peninsula of Alaska.

Bread and Work

seen economically, a conversion of one category of goods into a higher category. In one category were blankets, made either from animal skins or from pounded and woven cedar bark. For example, a man who wanted to pass his potlatch office on to his son would convince other members of his tribe to give the son blankets. The young man would then publicly give the blankets to others of his tribe who had to return them with 100 percent interest, from which the young man repaid, with interest, those who had originally set him up. Soon the young man accumulated several hundred blankets. He and his father then gave a potlatch, during which the youngster gave all those blankets away. The rival to whom he gave them had to repay them, again with 100 percent interest.

The number of blankets soon becomes astronomical. The mounting debts were often not paid in blankets themselves—rather, the Kwakiutl had an elaborate system of conversion among economic spheres. The highest value was assigned to "coppers." These sheets of pounded copper, about two and a half feet long, were named; their history and value were publicly known. When a copper was given in payment of a blanket debt, its value in blankets was thereby determined—but the real value was now in the prestige sphere. Having a famous copper to give away, then giving it away with adequate flourish and ceremony, turned the blankets into glory, symbolized by the copper. Again, the 100 percent interest reemerged. The value of the coppers skyrocketed. The system was played out when an office holder, scorning his rivals, destroyed a copper by breaking it into pieces or throwing it into the sea. With that gesture, both blankets and coppers had been turned into pure prestige. The "investor" strategy was to get as many blankets as possible, convert them into coppers, and then achieve unassailable prestige by destroying a copper. The element of contest and competition was high—a good player could humiliate his rivals or be humiliated just as fast. In short, the items defined as wealth were spent on prestige rather than on subsistence.

CONCLUDING THOUGHTS

The market principle is the only one so far discovered that can successfully run a complex and elaborate industrial economy. That does not mean, however, that societies that are dominated by the market principle do not have problems. Here we shall note only two: market capitalism requires a permanent underclass if it is to continue to work. Capitalism will not work without an underclass to provide workers to carry out the production of goods and services. A widget factory needs someone to make the widgets. If everyone strives to own the factory and no one is willing to work in the factory, capitalism collapses. It is also marked by the insecurities of unemployment. Capitalism will not work without unemployment as a balance wheel for growth. Supply and demand regulate success and failure. Factories that produce goods no longer desired by the public will fail. Growth is curbed, but the workers in that factory lose their jobs.

Socialism is government ownership of the means of production. Production decisions are made by the government rather than by the dictates of the market principle. Socialism began as an attempt to do away with unemployment and the insecurity that it brings, as well as to ameliorate the privilege of class. Some small countries such as Sweden have introduced a modified socialism that does not completely discard the market principle; it seems to work. The Swedish welfare state seems to have been successful in countering unemployment and class privileges. It is *very* expensive in terms of taxation—it is doubtful that Americans would pay as much tax as Swedes without a major revolt. The demise of communism that became apparent in 1989 provides excellent examples of what happens when the basis of an economy is changed radically. Poland, the Baltic States, the part of Germany which had been East Germany and the Soviet Union have all experienced prices skyrocketing and vast unemployment. The eventual results may depend, in part, upon culture. The Poles understand market economy; the Russians have never, at any time of their history, experienced a market economy. Germany is now reunited. Do sufficient remnants of shared culture remain to facilitate finding solutions to problems?

As we watch history unfold in Eastern Europe, we better examine our own society. How do we get the economic advantages of capitalism at the same time that we find solutions to the problems that capitalism creates? The need for creative social invention never ends.

BUZZWORDS

agriculture the science or art of cultivating the soil. However, anthropologists give additional meanings to the term. In contrast with horticulture, agriculture means growing crops with the aid of the plow.

capitalism an economic system in which land and resources as well as labor, risk, and even money itself are controlled by the market mechanism of supply and demand. Another way to put it is that work, resources, land, managerial skill and risk taking have all been turned into commodities, which means that they can be evaluated in terms of money.

ecology the science that studies the ways in which all living things adapt to one another and to the nonliving part of their environment.

economy a system for managing the production, distribution, and consumption of goods and services.

entrepreneur the person who organizes and manages a business or industrial enterprise, who takes the risk of not making a profit, and who gets the profit when there is one.

environment all of the surrounding conditions and influences that affect living organisms. All of the physical and cultural context into which any specific cultural act is set and by which it is evaluated.

horticulture growing crops by methods of gardening. No plow is used in horticulture.

householding the economic practice by which a household produces everything, or almost everything, that it consumes. Little exchange or trade enters in.

indigenous originating in the region of the country or of the world in which it is presently found.

industrialism a system of social and economic organization in which goods are mass produced by groups of large organizations, called industries; especially such a system in which the interests of such large industries prevail in political and economic life.

market two fundamental meanings must not be confused: market exchange is the exchange of goods or services solely on the basis of price determined by supply and demand. Marketplace is a location where goods are bought and sold. Marketplaces may occur in the absence of market exchange.

market principle the situation in which the free play of supply and demand create the price of any commodity.

It is to be distinguished from the marketplace, which is the location where buyers and sellers meet. In capitalist systems, manufactured goods, produce, labor, capital, land and entrepreneurship all enter the same market.

maximization getting the greatest possible benefit from any social or economic transaction.

reciprocity a type of economy in which services and goods are exchanged between people because of their rank or their relationship. Market principle is not involved. Obviously, reciprocity can be affected by moral values that may demand that specific people help one another regardless of whether the reciprocal service is of equal value.

redistribution a type of economy in which goods and services flow into a central point (such as a chiefship or, in the case of taxes, a government), from which other goods and services are handed out to other persons. No reciprocity or market mechanism need be involved.

subsistence whatever it is—particularly food—that must be supplied with great regularity in order for life to continue.

Conflict
and Order

7

PROPOSITIONS AND PREMISES

- The allocation and use of social power stands beside kinship as one of the two fundamental social characteristics. The survival of any species or any human culture depends on both of these factors.

- Power is based on aggression and in the inherent conflict to which it sometimes (not always) gives rise. We are *not* talking about anything so simplistic as whether human beings are "naturally aggressive," but rather about what individuals must do to acquire the wherewithal to survive.

- Hierarchy is a widespread social principle (among many genera and orders, not human beings alone) for countering aggression and managing conflict.

- Every culture provides more or less successful ways of managing conflict. The history of culture shows continual development in managing conflict ranging from self-help to courts.

- The major way of managing conflict is a counteraction by certain persons or institutions when any act occurs that breaches behavioral norms. If the counteraction is successful, a correction is reached so that predictable social relations can proceed.

- Some political systems have a single power base; we have called them unicentric. Others, called bicentric or multicentric, have two or more power bases. The latter require cooperation by the two or more power bases if they are to be successful. Some political systems (like those of the Western democracies) use both systems in order first to discover all ideas and viewpoints, then to create a consensus about the actual course of events to be followed.

A social relationship is a situation in which two people each change their behavior in recognition of the other. Each has the power to adapt behavior to further the relationship or to break that relationship. Some people allow themselves to be walked all over by others because they do not choose to exercise the power they have, especially their power to leave a relationship. Such people see the other person (or, sometimes, law or custom) imposing such restricting conditions that they have no choice, sometimes not even the choice of leaving. You are trapped when the price of exercising your power is so high that you are unwilling or unable to pay that price, and so must continue in a humiliating or even damaging situation.

7-1. A social relationship exists when two people each change their behavior because of the presence of the other. Power is the capacity of one person in the relationship to direct the behavior of the other person (or to work change on a material object).

If a person's power is recognized by others (or, more shakily, by law or custom) as a right, that person can be said to have authority. Authority may inhere in individual people. In very small-scale societies, that is usually the case. In large-scale societies, there may be charismatic individuals who accrue a great deal of power, but that power is more likely to inhere in roles, especially those called offices. The person who plays the role has the authority, by popular recognition of the

---

7-2. There is a power structure, and often an authority structure, in all enduring social groups. Domination of one person over others can be achieved by using one's power to raise the price of the second person's using his or her power so high that the second person becomes submissive. Some submissive people do not exert any power at all. But sometimes such a submissive person may exert all his or her power at once—break out of the submission and even kill.

7-3. Authority implies general recognition by a group that power legitimately lies with a given person or in a known role, usually called an office. Power can legitimately be exerted by the person who occupies the authoritative role or office. Martin Luther King, Jr., shown here, held no office and had no political authority. He nevertheless had a lot of power.

office, to exercise as much power as that role allows.

There is a power structure in all social groups. Families have power structures within them. The power system within the traditional patriarchal family centered on the senior male (called the *paterfamilias* by the Romans). The power that senior women held within such families was often superficially denied, even though it might have been the most important factor in holding the family together. There is power in firms, in communities, in states, in churches.

AGGRESSION

Power derives from aggression or its threat. The word aggression, in American English, carries the value judgment "bad," in part because we tend to confuse its several meanings. War, unprovoked attack, hostility, starting fights—all can be labelled aggression, and all have negative connotations. Most dictionaries never get to the ethologists' (those who study behavior of animals) or the psychoanalysts' views of aggression. In those disciplines, aggression is a technical, scientific term that carries no value judgments. We sorely need, in English, a set of commonly recognized words that make the following distinctions clearly.

Aggressive Drive

Aggression is a drive that can be compared to the sex drive, but appears to be more complex. It is fired by the hormone adrenalin, produced in the adrenal gland just above the kidneys. That drive allows individual animals, including human beings, to assert themselves sufficiently in social and ecological conditions to get whatever resources they need to survive. Although aggression is the term used by all ethologists, the general public needs a word other than "aggression" for this drive. I shall compromise and call it the aggressive drive.

Agonistic Behavior

Agonistic behavior results from the biological, aggressive drive. It can take two very different paths of expression. Antagonistic behavior is the path that provokes hostility, dissension, and strife. The aggressive drive can be expressed in many kinds of behavior that are not antagonistic: bravery, studying or working hard, ambition, efforts to make the law work better for the good of humankind, or good business practice. We will call this type of behavior (the second path) assertive. Confusion results if we use the same terms to describe both antagonistic and assertive bahavior.

Conflict

Conflict may result from an antagonistic display of aggression, but conflict and aggression are not identical. The difficulty in the word aggression arises again because we compete with other members of our own species, especially when vital resources are scarce. You might recoil from this basic truth, but an individual must strive against others in order to get enough resources to survive. Such competitive assertion often takes the form of threat and sometimes results in actual conflict. It is interesting that the term "assertive" has gained a more positive, separate meaning from the everyday meaning of aggression. Americans even take classes in assertiveness training so they can learn to stand up for themselves against the "aggression" of others.

To sum up, our day-to-day vocabulary does not adequately distinguish between the aggressive drive (which is biological), antagonistic behavior (which is a matter of dominance and combativeness), assertiveness (which is knowing how to get what you need without becoming antisocial) and conflict (which is agonistic social action that, among human beings, is evaluated and culturized).

7-5. Uncontrolled conflict will destroy any social fabric. Because conflict involves more or less aggressive behavior (at very least, strong assertiveness) on the part of two people, its control is a social task. The social trick is to allow pro-social use of the aggressive drive, to instill sufficient personal control, and nurture good enough cultural institutions to control conflict.

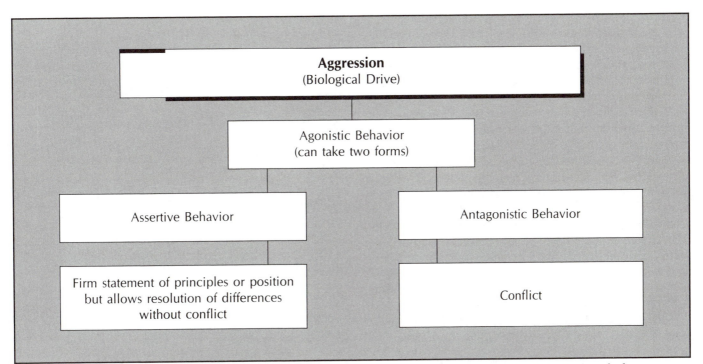

7-4. Aggression is a complex idea—actually, it is a combination of several ideas that should be distinguished: the aggressive drive is a biological factor associated with adrenaline and other hormones, which we all have. Agonistic behavior—whether assertive or antagonistic—is often called aggression. Agonism involves contesting or bullying, but it can be controlled on personal or cultural demand. In our society, assertiveness (being assertive takes aggressive drive) is socially acceptable whereas antagonistic behavior is not. Conflict is also sometimes called aggression. Conflict is a social action in that it requires two people—an aggressor and a victim.

Although conflict is not to be found in all vertebrate species, and certainly not in all situations, the aggressive drive is found in all individuals who survive. Inadequate aggressive drive means that some animals cannot stand up for their rights against others. In situations of abundance, those animals may survive, but in situations of scarce resources, they perish. This idea underlies not only the major premises of evolutionary theory, but also our understanding of the place of conflict and order in society.

Order

The task for any animal species, then, is to allow behavior based on the aggressive drive that leads to success both of individuals and ultimately of the species, yet also to control the conflict that may arise from antagonism and competition so that the conflict itself does not result in the species' destruction.

Order, in short, must be brought out of conflict. Order is not, however, the opposite of conflict. The opposite of conflict is a state of harmony in which there is no conflict. The opposite of order is chaos. Harmony may involve co-operation or it may, on the other hand, involve internalizing one's feelings and not allowing any strife to break out.

Obviously, neither chaos nor harmony will ever last for long. People will search for the security of organization within any situation they consider chaotic, and there will always be differences of opinion about how things should be organized. Utopia will never be achieved. It would mean a permanent absence of conflict. As we have seen, conflict is a component of life.

We must therefore conclude that order is organization to overcome conflict—the necessary ingredient to reconcile competing interests and to allow society to thrive. There are two social systems that nonhuman species have worked out for achieving this end: territoriality and hierarchy.

Some animals use a system of territoriality to control conflict. The animal stakes out a piece of geography to which ethologists assign the technical term territory. The territory has sufficient resources to fulfill the animal's needs as well as the needs of its mate and offspring. The animal then proceeds to defend this territory against all comers, especially those of its own species or of other species that use the same resources. If resources are scarce, the nonaggressive or the weak are either driven from their territories or try to survive in peripheral and inadequate territories, and so perish. It is not a pretty picture by standards of human morality.

Human territoriality is culturized animal behavior (Ardrey 1966; Fox and Tiger 1971). It has in fact been culturized into ideas of ownership, privacy, trespass, and the like. We all sometimes feel the emotions of territoriality: first the discomfort and then the rage when somebody invades our space without being invited (Hall 1966). People whose houses have been burgled are sometimes more upset by the violation of what they thought was safe private space than they are about the loss of property.

The other mode by which animals control and deal with conflict (which is intertwined with the aggression needed to survive) is hierarchy. Hierarchy is a ranking in accordance with the degree of power of the adult animals in a group. The animal at the top of the hierarchy is said to be dominant over all the others. The second is dominant over all but the highest, and so on. When it comes to protecting themselves and assuring their own survival, human beings are much more likely to use the principle of hierarchy—also highly culturized, of course, into notions of authority and legitimacy—than they are to use territoriality.

Seldom does any species use both territoriality and hierarchy to an equal extent. Among the primates, for example, howler monkeys and gibbons are territorial; hierarchy is rarely used. Only when the territory is threatened does conflict erupt. In contrast, baboons and, to a lesser degree, chimpanzees use hierarchy as their primary mechanism, although both are sometimes territorial.

Position in a hierarchy may come from fighting for the position—the animal that can lick everybody else is on top, and is called the "alpha male." However, the recognition of the hierarchy by all its members can be reduced to a set of signs so that the animals can interact without overt conflict. The ritual of these signs is that the higher-ranking animal may make a threat gesture. The lower-ranking then responds with a gesture of submission. Often the lower-ranking animal makes the submission gesture even if the higher-ranking one makes no threat. In some species, the females also form hierarchies, which may or may not be interlinked with the hierarchy of males.

The following story was told to an American anthropologist by a man in his thirties: "When I was fourteen, we moved, and I suddenly found myself attending a new junior high in a tougher part of town. Within the first two weeks of school I found myself challenged by a series of guys. At first they came from my own freshman class, but after I had defeated them all in fistfights, I faced a new series of challenges from the best fighters of the sophomore and then junior classes. One by one, I beat them all. Then I went home and told my mother that we had better move immediately or I would be dead come Monday morning, because the next challenger in the pecking order was the senior they called 'The Hulk.' We packed that night."

WE, THE ALIEN

When an animal stays out of the territory of another, or chooses to admit that another outranks his or her position

7-6. *The primordial social mechanisms for controlling conflict are territoriality and hierarchy. Both are found among many animal species but rarely exist together in any highly developed form. Gibbons are territorial. This white-chested gibbon is protecting his territory; human territoriality has been culturized into ownership and trespassing rights. Baboons are hierarchal; human hierarchy has been turned into prohibitions, authority structures, and bureaucracy.*

NO
FISHING
SWIMMING
PICNICKING
OR LOITERING
POLICE ORDER

NO
PARKING
OR
STANDING

7-7. Successfully controlled conflict is called peace. The interplay of conflict and peace are an essential part of any political system. Maintaining order is part of the political task. Said another way: management of conflict is one of the most important parts of the political process. In this picture, representatives of the Fox and Sauk tribes discuss peace with officials of the Department of the Interior in 1867.

in a hierarchy, such behavior leads to social stability. Such controlled conflict can be called peace. Peace is *not* the opposite of conflict; rather it is a state of affairs in which conflict between groups is adequately controlled. As we pursue peace studies, we must be sure that we understand we are *managing* conflict rather than trying to ban it. Peace is a dynamic and, so far, a tenuous and temporary state that arises when conflict is well managed; if it is ever made more permanent, the social and cultural outcomes will be immensely complex. We do not yet know much about the characteristics or extent of that complexity.

When conflict and peace are culturized by human beings, we can call the resulting situation a political system. Human political systems add many concepts about such things as justice and equality, and they almost surely are interlinked with doctrines that explain a people's ideas about the nature of God. The human political system, like its animal counterparts, is a system of power relationships whose purpose is to keep peace within the community (whatever the compo-

sition of the community) and to protect the community against invaders.

This chapter is about conflict and order. In a complex society, the establishment and maintenance of order are almost always defined as part of the political job. The rest of the political jobs have to do with governing and will be dealt with in the next chapter.

THE COMPLEXITY OF CONFLICT

Like aggression, the idea of conflict is complex. However, it is easier to understand than aggression because its complexity arises from several contexts rather than from several meanings (related but nevertheless different).

A conflict is a struggle between two opposing forces. In social conflict, those forces may be individual animals or people, opposing clans, generations, churches, or nations. In ideological conflict, the opposing forces may be ideas; and in psychological conflict, they may be pressures that arise from moral contradictions. A conflict always implies two forces or two points of view. When there are more than two people or points of view in the total field, the tendency to create two sides reasserts itself as two of the parties bury their conflict long enough to gang up on a third. That repressed conflict will almost surely re-erupt when the third party has been eliminated.

Thus, a conflict takes the form of a struggle, a quarrel or a fight. Among human beings, physical conflict breaks out under two conditions: (1) when at least one of the two sides *wants* to fight, or (2) when the culture is not adequately developed to allow a solution by any means *except* fighting.

Like an athletic contest, a good fight can make its participants—particularly the winners—feel good. For the winners, it is reassurance: "I am great, and I have proved it." There are physical outputs, in the form of hormones, involved with fighting and especially with winning. Those hormones, apparently, trigger endorphins in the brain which we experience as feelings of well-being or elation. When good feelings are underwritten by cultural values that grant prestige to the people who win fights, then those in search of a rush or of superiority may systematically start fights. The world is full of warrior cultures and of self-proclaimed warriors.

Warrior Cultures

In the second half of the nineteenth century, Native Americans of the Great Plains exhibited warrior cultures. Perhaps the most warrior-like were the Comanches (Wallace and Hoebel 1952). They were a fierce people who held that the greatest of all honors was to be a successful hunter, raider, and warrior. At puberty or soon after, the young men began the religious search for personal power. That search had to be carried out alone. For four days they were alone in the wilderness. They ate nothing and drank no water during that period. Power, which Comanche called *puha*, came from supernatural sources in the form of visions which were hallucinatory experiences or dreams, aided and induced by hunger, thirst, lack of sleep, and purgatives. Among some other Plains tribes, but not among the Comanche, self-inflicted wounds were thought to assist in the power quest.

By the time a young man returned to camp, he almost always had experienced his vision. He knew the symbolic source of his power and his place in nature. He was ready for the buffalo hunt, then the warpath. If he was successful, his reputation as a distinguished warrior grew. Warriors were highly influential, but there was no formal government for them to serve. They themselves made up the power structure of the society. The Comanche were formidable enemies in their fighting, both against other Native Americans and against the EuroAmericans and AfroAmericans who were pushing into their territories.

Self-proclaimed Warriors

Self-proclaimed warriors exist in modern society. Fighting gangs in the inner cities of the United States are warrior cultures (Keiser 1969). The members achieve their reputations by fighting, even killing; they do not consider themselves bound by the legal system of the larger society.

There are even warrior-like professions in which perfectly law-abiding practitioners are ranked by daring deeds that go into their records. These are usually dangerous and physically demanding professions like fire fighting, high altitude construction, or repairing the lines that carry electrical power. Firemen, policemen, ambulance drivers, and many others collect tales of their daring; these stories are repeated by both the person who did the daring deed and by their friends and supporters; sometimes such become almost cult heroes.

Always the warrior is an individual—perhaps, but not necessarily, at odds with the system. Comanche warriors were themselves the heart of the system. The most noble acts of warriors are marked by winning conflicts and by physical bravery. The ultimate expectations in physical conflict and warrior society are simple, perhaps the simplest in any social relationship: kill or be killed.

However, only half the people who fight can be winners. Losing exacts a high cost. Losing leads to hormonal, psychological, and social responses that lead to depression rather than elation. Therefore, the human animal, always culturally clever, often searches for ways to gain a favorable outcome without the risk of losing a fight.

The central problem, however, remains: people do have conflicting views about conflict; some extol it, some deplore it. People do have conflicting rights in things or in each other; they do have psychological reactions of rage and hatred. Potential conflict always lurks just under the surface of the most genteel drawing rooms, the best-run board rooms, even the most civil of parliaments.

MANAGING CONFLICT

Techniques and social institutions for managing conflict are vital to every social system. With the help of culture, human social systems have created political solutions beyond fight or flight to deal with conflict. The legal system and its forerunners are one example. Another is distancing the self from conflict and then denying that it even exists.

Management of conflict is thus a major responsibility of political organizations. There are two mechanisms by which specific conflict can be resolved. First, within an organization, internal conflict can be resolved by law. Law is based on moralities that are widely accepted, which may or may not be associated with religion. These consensual moralities are the backbone of all legal systems; when people discard those moralities, the other dimensions of legal systems have great difficulty maintaining order. Law may further call upon power or its threats by recognizing and using deterrence and punishment like police and prisons. Second, external conflict between two organizations, particularly states, can be controlled by diplomacy. The threat of force—warfare—is

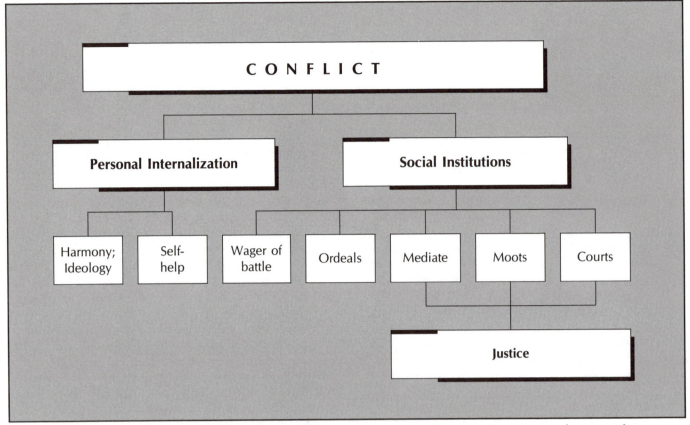

7-8. *First, conflict can be dealt with by self-help or it can be internalized into the person, in the name of harmony. People can behave so that no conflict ever appears in their behavior. The psychological cost is high. Second, social institutions can be invented or developed so that conflict can be controlled without outlawing all assertive behavior. Some, but not all, of these social institutions may have something to do with what we call justice. A worthy goal is to create institutions that will assure justice for all people.*

always close to the surface in diplomatic discussions.

Some peoples control conflict by a plea to a concept of social harmony. Indians of Middle America as well as the Pueblo peoples of the American Southwest prize harmony far more than warriorhood. Prizing harmony does not mean that such peoples do not fight for their rights, but rather that they consider other means more productive; they certainly do not grant the warrior prestige or social prominence.

One of the most interesting studies of a group attempting to achieve harmony is about a community of Baptists near Atlanta, Georgia that its ethnographer calls Hopewell. These devout Baptists not only define aggressive behavior as outside their community, they also reject political solutions. Their ideology precludes using the American court system or any other system in which there is a winner and loser. They "define conflict out of existence" (Greenhouse 1986). They hold that by their refusal to participate in conflict, they are reaffirming their faith in God and in the system of harmony He created. Hopewell Baptists measure their own inner strength by their capacity to transcend conflict. They say that all conflict arises from the self-interest of individuals. They make it a point to avoid all people and all situations that are marked by the self-interest of others. Within their

own community, they have verbal remedies to prevent disagreements from escalating into conflicts. People are controlled by gossip, by joking with one another yet vigorously implying correct action through the humor, by prayer, and by what the ethnographer calls dueling with scripture—quoting the Bible to one another to justify their own beliefs and actions. By definition, no one can win such a duel with scripture because no part of the Bible is false.

Hopewell Baptists do not see God's will as a legal code, as, for example, Muslims specifically do. They see it rather as a system of knowledge. However, because no one can know the entire system, a person must have faith in God that His plan is good. Thus, good behavior does not follow rules but rather accepts "a system of facts and reasons, which my faith makes available" (Greenhouse 1986). By definition, anyone who chooses not to accept God's plan will make mistakes in judgment. Conflict, in this view, is not a dimension of human relationships, but rather an aberration of some people who do not follow God's plan. They see the larger society outside their own community as driven by self-interest which they consider the opposite of the Christian way of achieving God's kingdom. All conflict, they say, flows from this self-interest among non-Baptists, which is dangerous and corrupting.

Conflict, in the theory of these Baptists, has three elements: (1) it is a rejection of God, (2) it comes from association with outsiders, and (3) it is a specific quality of the self-interest of some people who are thus to be avoided. Such an idea of harmony makes authority unnecessary. Harmony is associated with purity. It involves silencing disputes and so denying the presence of disagreement and conflict. As the ethnographer sums it up, "Salvation is contingent on acknowledging one's own spiritual and perhaps physical frailty. The liberation is as large as the burden" (Greenhouse 1986).

The Zapotec Indians of the Mexican state of Oaxaca (Nader 1990) established a political rather than religious mode for maintaining harmony. Instead of eschewing litigation, they have enshrined it as the mode par excellence of achieving harmony in their social relationships. The people of the Zapotec village of Talea say that every dispute that is brought to the courts should be heard. The court is made up entirely of lay people from the village; its officials are unpaid citizens who donate their time for a specific period to do the tasks that all consider necessary to keep the village running.

One theme that recurs in all of the cases that come before this court is that a balance must be achieved between the principal parties of the case. They see theirs as a peaceful town, and the court officials take seriously the charge of keeping it that way. The village court officials are likely to give long harangues on harmony and the importance of living up to one's obligations in order to maintain harmony. In cases involving property, the officials are more interested in the relationship between the disputants than they are in the disputed property.

The Zapotec aim of adjudication is to "rectify the situation by achieving or reinstating a balance between the parties

7-9. The Zapotec courts use control of conflict for the stated purpose of achieving social harmony. These Zapotec are waiting in the outside corridor of the court.

involved in a dispute" (Nader 1969). That idea was prevalent during much of the Spanish colonial regime in Mexico. Spanish custom in the 1500s and 1600s was heavily weighted toward conciliation as a means of settling disputes, and these ideas were imported with Spanish government and religion. Similarly, the Zapotec have been missionized for 400 years. The missionaries, like the Hopewell Baptists, set forth values of harmony as the Christian imperative. In many instances the missionaries actually ran courts themselves either in the absence of government courts or in competition with them.

This mode of achieving harmony by confrontation and adversarial action achieves the same kind of peaceful results that the Hopewell Baptists achieve, but by totally different means. It is overt and social instead of covert and psychological. The basic value would seem to be, "Get it all up front so that the community can deal with it." Both methods may lead to justice or injustice. In one, the price is social uproar; in the other, the cost is psychological repression.

The goals of the Zapotec judges are to arrive at a written or verbal agreement between the parties to the conflict. That does not mean that the agreement is a compromise, but only that both have concurred in the judgment and will conduct their future actions in accordance with it. Balance and harmony have been restored in the village.

The Basis of Legal Institutions

Although the forms of legal institutions vary widely from one society to the next, there is a series of three typical actions that mark a situation as legal (Bohannan 1957). 7-12 illustrates this idea.

First, there is an overt act that is a breach of **norm.** Somebody breaks the law or goes against custom. Norm here means, obviously, what people ought to do. A norm may be a law, custom, or ethical precept; it may be morals or manners. The norm itself is not a social act but a cultural guide to action. Acts can be either in accord with or not in accord with norms; the norm may be interpreted differently by different people. Breaches of the norm, however, are always social acts.

The second characteristic action in a legal situation follows breach of norm. Sometimes when norms are broken by what we call deviant social acts, nothing happens even if these acts are considered wrong. In such cases, the legal institutions are not working. It is the follow-up on such a breach that creates the legal situation. In every society, reactions against some breaches of norms set off a chain reaction. These reactions can be called **counteractions.** In our own society, counteractions are the concerted activities of the police, of courts, of lawyers, of other agencies of law enforcement. In other words, the counteraction occurs as a deliberate attempt to counter the original breach of the norm, to "right" the wrong.

Finally, there is a third set of activities that follow the counteraction. These activities can be labelled **correction.** Correction is a good word to express the meaning here because it contains an ambiguity composed of two meanings, each of which represents a type of final action in the chain. Correction, in the first instance, means to make somebody reperform the original action in accordance with the norm. Thus, for example, when a man does something that is counter to the norm, his action makes another whole set of institutions swing into action. As a result, the man is made to perform the original action again, this time in accordance with the norm. I know a Tiv, Gbawase, who was sent by another, Oryongo, to pay a sum of money that Oryongo owed his father-in-law. Gbawase, however, spent the money on something else. When Oryongo brought Gbawase before the court, the court members made Gbawase sell a goat and deliver the correct sum to Oryongo's father-in-law as he should have done in the first place. Among Tiv, the original breach is often forgotten or ignored, or at least forgiven, and the fiction is created that he did it right in the first place.

The other meaning of the word correction comes into play in those examples in which someone performs an act like homicide that cannot be undone. Correction, in this second sense, means that another act is performed which, by retaliation or punishment, corrects the initial breach. Thus, correction means either a return to the *status quo ante* or else the establishment of a new *status quo* from which life in accordance with the norms can again proceed.

If a social act that breaches a norm leads to effective counteraction by a political group, and if the counteraction is followed by some form of correction that allows the processes of society to continue more or less intact, then the situation can be said to represent a legal institution.

Law

Law in a developed legal system is a sophisticated device that is marked by several additional criteria. (1) The law takes some of the customs within a culture out of their original context and reformulates them as a guide for management of conflict. (2) Law has a set of specialized institutions that are charged with creating the reformulations (legislatures) or else of managing their application (courts). (3) Law has a set of known sanctions or punishments—corrections that are meant to deter people from breaching the norms in the first place.

Many ideas or artifacts may have two contexts in a culture. They are likely to have different meanings and different uses in each context. Law and religion are the two areas of life that are most likely to draw ideas from other realms of social life, changing the meanings somewhat in the new context. This act can be called recontexting. It means that an idea taken from one part or context of the culture is specifically edited, then inserted in a different context within the same culture. Myth, for example, has an important place in ritual, but the ideas that underlie the myth also have an important place in politics and perhaps in economics. Law is an even more vivid example. The sources of law are to be found in the customs of other institutions of society and in the ideas

7-10. *Law is a situation in which some (never all) of the norms of society are recontexted so as to form guidelines for controlling conflict. This photograph shows a 1981 pretrial hearing of Kenneth Bianchi, the Hillside strangler of Los Angeles. He was brought to trial and found guilty of many murders. This trial showed conclusively how complicated and involved the social organization behind law can become in a complex society.*

and values that underlie those institutions. Comparatively little law arises in a purely legal context. The commercial code of our own law, for example, is a restatement of part of what people generally agree is moral business practice. Some parts of that practice are edited and recontexted into the code. The new context is the specialized institution—usually courts in the legal example—by which people can insure that others carry out their business according to the code. Thus, the same ideas have a context in the institutions of business and also, somewhat edited, in context of the courts.

 In certain reaches of our own culture, killing is not wrong, or at least not illegal. When the agent of homicide is the state—that is, when the homicide is an execution ordered by officers of the state—the law does not label it a crime. Some people may, of course, label it immoral and work to abolish capital punishment. Killing in warfare may be considered immoral, but it carries no counteraction.

WE, THE ALIEN

The comparative study of crime is a seriously underdeveloped field that cries out for cross-cultural comparison to reinforce the sociological studies comparing crime rates in recordkeeping societies.

We can compare the acts that different cultures have branded as crime. Some acts are, in some circumstances, universally declared to be wrong in that they incite counteraction and correction. Yet, the context of the acts is of great importance. Although all peoples find some killing wrong, we must hastily add that contexts for such wrongful killing vary enormously.

7-11. *Crime and social problems are the price any society pays for living as its people in fact live. Reducing crime means a change in lifestyle for all people, not just those who are defined as criminal.*

In other societies, homicide in the course of headhunting or human sacrifice in the course of religious ritual are not considered wrong. Indeed, great honors may be bestowed on killers or victims in those situations. Other homicides, no matter how wrong, are not subject to counteraction. For instance, the crime of fratricide (killing a sibling) is probably considered wrong everywhere. However, societies that lack specialized police and court systems have no way of exercising counteraction. Killing the perpetrator makes the kinfolk of the original victim lose yet another kinsman. Fratricide is mentioned several times in the Old Testament—and, although killing one's brothers is an act repugnant to God, the killer is not otherwise punished. In the absence of a court system, there is no punishment that would not compound the loss.

It would also be good to know, in societies at all levels of development, just what circumstances people are reacting to when they commit crimes. Again, the most vivid cases involve homicide. The circumstances in which homicide is committed vary from one culture to another. In a study carried out in seven African tribal groups in the 1950s, it was discovered that Africa exhibited a low incidence of homicide, a very large proportion of which involved killing kinfolk (Bohannan 1960). Americans, on the other hand, give relatively little of their time to any kinship groups except for the nuclear family; therefore, comparatively few American crimes are committed against kinfolk other than those in the nuclear family. Wives and husbands are overwhelmingly the favorite victims.

The African study found, however, that people in different societies did not kill the same kinfolk—wives and full brothers were the only victims to appear in all the samples. Some tribes killed their father's brothers with regularity, others not at all; some tribes killed mothers with startling frequency, others rarely or never.

Crime is a good indicator of where the tensions in a society are to be found. It is likely that if the juvenile and adult criminals in the Western world were able to reach the point of prosperity, status, and satisfaction that is deemed a suitable goal for human endeavor, and reach it by noncriminal means, most would not employ criminal means. The ends that most criminals seek are goals that are approved and valued by society. However, there are some criminals in our society and probably in most others who commit crimes precisely because their goal is to commit a crime. Again, a comparative study is needed. If we knew just what crimes are committed in just what ways, we would know a lot more about the tensions in culture than we know now. We might even be able to alter some of the conditions for the better if we were willing to pay the price that such changes would demand.

 Americans know right now a very great deal about the situations that lead to crime in the United States. However, altering those situations is so expensive and would lead to changes in so many other aspects of the culture (perhaps putting some of our personal freedoms in danger) that most Americans are unwilling to pay that price, so the crime rate continues to be what it is.

WE, THE ALIEN

Some societies—like our own—play host to riots from time to time and in certain situations. Political riots are not exactly common, but are scarcely uncommon, in the United States. Riots may accompany street demonstrations; they and the looting that often goes with them usually accompany natural disasters. Riots in prisons recur regularly. Almost without exception, riots are displaced rage and do not deal directly with whatever forces created the tension that led to the riots.

RESOLVING CONFLICT

The steps required to achieve an efficient and predictable legal system can be examined from historical accounts as well as from ethnographic accounts. There are several ways of determining or defining norms so that people know just what norm has been breached or what inadequate behavior actually occurred, and what makes it inadequate. Counteractions take a number of forms, just as there are a number of possible institutions of correction. 7-12 shows some of the types of action that may constitute each step.

Some of these legal or legal-like institutions will be described here in a rational order, not in any historical order. Some have been superseded in our society but others are still practiced today.

Self-help

Every legal system, including our own, gives us at least some leeway in helping ourselves when our rights are contravened. However, the more developed the legal system, the more circumscribed the rights of self-help. In societies that lack police systems, self-help is likely to be highly developed.

One of the best recorded examples of a society that lacked specialized institutions for dealing with disputes was the Nuer of the Sudan in the 1930s (Evans-Pritchard 1940). The Nuer were, in those days, a society without either law or government in the sense we know them. That does not mean there was no order, but rather that there was no designated institution for maintaining order. The Nuer relied on self-help in order to protect their rights.

In the 1930s, the Nuer were prone to fighting. Many of them had scars and marks from clubs or spears. They fought in disputes about cattle, over damage that their animals did to the crops of others, over supposed slights or cruelties to their children, over adultery, over dry season watering holes, over pasturage, or over objects that were borrowed without

7-13. *Some societies, such as the traditional Nuer, have few institutionalized ways of settling disputes other than conflict between the principals to the dispute. You can tell this picture was posed—look at the smile on the man on the right—but it nevertheless shows the spears and the gestures of fighting.*

permission. Nuer fought if they considered themselves insulted. There was no authority to whom people could go instead of fighting. Therefore, "a man's courage is his only immediate protection against aggression" (Evans-Pritchard 1940). Children were encouraged by their elders to settle their disputes by fighting; being a good fighter was the equivalent of being a virtuous man. Nuer boys used spiked

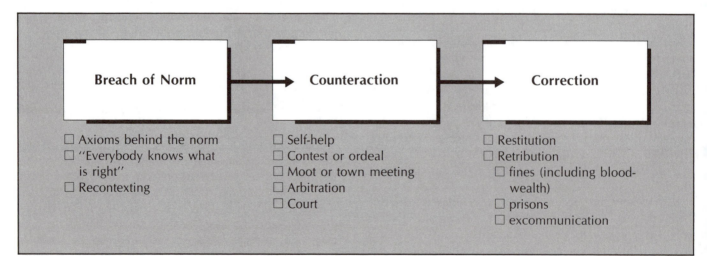

7-12. *There are many ways in which norms are recontexted into a legal or jural sphere. There are also several forms that both counteraction and correction can take.*

bracelets when they fought. Adult men fought with clubs within their lineage groups and with spears when they fought outsiders. Sometimes people got killed. When that happened, the result was a feud because there were no other institutions to hand down a solution to the problem.

A few years later, the British Administration of what was then called the Anglo-Egyptian Sudan established courts among the Nuer, who apparently welcomed them; certainly some of their representatives worked hard to create a body of law that could be applied by these courts (Howell 1954).

Another example of self-help as the only possible counteraction was found among the Eskimo of the late nineteenth and early twentieth centuries. Individuals were the sole source of reparation if rights were violated. There was no political power to invoke to redress a wrong. Qijuk's wife died (Hoebel 1954). Being without a wife in Eskimo societies is serious because the division of labor between men and women is very precise—it takes two people to run a household. When Qijuk looked around for another wife, his eye lit on a woman married to Kinger in a neighboring settlement. Qijuk and his brothers went to get the woman. When they arrived, Kinger was out hunting. Qijuk moved in with Kinger's wife (we have no information on what she thought about this situation). When Kinger came home, Qijuk told him to be off. Everyone agreed that right was on Kinger's side. So he did the only thing he could do: he killed Qijuk. Kinger's friends came to help and killed one of the brothers; the other brother got away.

That ended the matter. The wronged man had used self-help to correct the situation. He had his wife back and the lawbreaker was punished. This situation could have led to feud but did not because Qijuk's surviving brother did not feel strong enough to risk it, so he never sought revenge for his brothers.

Ordeal

Ordeals were an important part of the judicial processes of the Middle Ages in Europe and have been reported from many other parts of the world. The ordeal was a way of dealing with cases that could not be rationally decided by human agencies; the decision making was handed over to God. If ordeals were ordered by the court, the people involved in the case, whether plaintiff, defendant or witness, had to undergo them, although in some situations people could buy off the other party to the case or could employ another person to take the ordeal for him. The premise was that God would not allow an innocent person to be harmed.

The major ordeals were those by water and by fire. They were used throughout Europe "from Spain to Constantinople, and from Scandinavia to Naples" (Lea 1878). For example, in Anglo-Saxon England, the trial by fire involved the accused's carrying a red-hot piece of iron weighing one pound for nine feet. Such ordeals were always held on Wednesday. On the preceding Monday and Tuesday, the accused was fed only bread and water; the hand was washed and not allowed

to touch anything. After the ordeal, the hand was wrapped until Saturday, when it was unbandaged in the presence of accuser and judges. Guilt or innocence were determined by the degree to which the hand had been burned.

In the triple ordeal, the iron weighed three pounds, but that at first was reserved "for incendiaries and 'morth-slayers' [secret murderers], for counterfeiting, and for plotting against the king's life" (Lea 1878). After about 1300 the efficacy of this procedure fell into doubt as it was considered that Satan as well as God had the power to bring people through the ordeal unharmed—one of the ideas that bolstered the Inquisition.

7-14. *The ordeal as a legal device is found in many societies. Here is an example of the "dunking stool" used to try witches in the ordeal by water in Europe as well as in the American colonies in the 1600s and early 1700s.*

As late as 1960, I saw an ordeal used in a case in upcountry Liberia. That dispute was about whether or not a lorry driver had been cheated by his small-boy (which means a junior assistant). The driver said he had given the small-boy money for purchases. There was no evidence whatever except that the money was missing and the conflicting statements of the two involved. Obviously this was a situation for what, in Liberia, was called a "sassywood man." Sassywood is the poisonous bark of an African tree which was administered to people by some African courts in the eighteenth and nineteenth centuries. People charged with crimes were required to drink an infusion of it. If they vomited, they were innocent; if they did not, they were guilty and usually died.

This sassywood man, a distinguished elder in a purple shirt and a pair of khaki shorts, did not use the poison tree. Rather, he sat on the ground with a small fire burning in front of him. A foot from the fire was a black pot of what was called medicine in English, the lingua franca of Liberia. Into the fire he thrust the eighteen-inch blade of a West African matchet—a long single-edged knife something like the East Asian machete. He took some medicine from his pot and rubbed it on his own lower leg. He then took the matchet from the fire and, moving it slowly up and down, touched it to the medicine on his leg. A dull blue smoke rose.

The sassywood man then announced that he was ready. He called the small-boy to step forward. The young man was about sixteen and obviously frightened. The sassywood man placed the youngster's right foot between the pot and the fire. He swabbed medicine on the youth's lower leg, just as he had on his own. Then he reached calmly toward the fire and, with all deliberation, withdrew the gleaming matchet, moving it toward the youth's leg. When the knife was within an inch, the young man jerked his leg away and cowered backward.

"Ah-haaah!" cried the crowd.

The sassywood man demanded stillness. Again he brought the young man's foot back into position. Again he swabbed; again he moved the hot matchet slowly toward the leg; again the young man jerked away. The small-boy was thus "obviously" guilty. The judges, made up of a chief and elders, told the small-boy to repay twice the amount of money the lorry driver claimed he had stolen.

It is quite evident that ordeals have little to do with what we in the West call "justice." They do, however, solve cases. Once the ordeal has taken place, there is no longer a dispute. Life can continue.

Games and the Wager of Battle

One of the ways of "managing" violence is to reduce its range, and then to make the solution of the part stand as the solution for the whole. Traditional Eskimo often used song contests to settle disputes. A successful song contest demanded an audience and was sometimes done at festivals as part of the entertainment. The person whose songs were most heartily applauded was the winner. Some song duels in Greenland were carried on for years because people thought them a lot of fun. Elsewhere, they seem to have been settled within a single season. In some cases, the entire household joined in singing the songs. When the context was decided, the dispute was declared to be at an end, and the former disputants lived together in peace. The song duel of the Eskimos was sometimes accompanied by headbutting, in which the disputants knocked their foreheads together until one of them cried a halt, thus declaring himself the loser (Hoebel 1954).

Contests that amounted to little more than controlled fighting were found among the Eskimo and also in the so-called trial by battle, or wager of battle, in Medieval Europe. There the accused and the accuser fought, at the order of the court and under the supervision of the judges, under closely controlled conditions. The winner of the fight was the winner in the dispute on the premise that God's might lay with the innocent (Lea 1878).

The ordeal by battle was an accepted mode of solving disputes throughout most of Europe, well into the thirteenth century. Such a trial was, for the most part, considered to be conclusive. "He who had duly sunk under water, walked

7-15. *The wager of battle was a medieval custom in which either the principals to a dispute, or champions who stood in for them for a fee, fought one another under carefully controlled conditions. One of the most interesting is the wager of battle between a man and a woman. The man was placed in a pit up to his waist and armed with a club; the woman was on the surface and was armed with a stone wrapped in a piece of cloth. Whoever won the fight won the dispute.*

unharmed among the burning shares, or withdrawn an unblistered hand from a caldron of legal temperature stood forth among his fellows as innocent. So, even now, the verdict of twelve fools or knaves in a jury box may discharge any criminal, against the plainest dictates of common sense" (Lea 1878).

Mediation

Mediation occurs when an individual, or a group of people, stands between the disputants in a conflict, in an effort to help them understand one another's viewpoints and to reach agreement. The mediator has no authority and, usually, no special power except the power of persuasion. Mediation works when both sides want their conflict resolved and when neither of them really wants to fight. However, if the conflict itself is of value, or if they really do want to fight, mediation will not work because no one has any authority to enforce any decision.

The most famous mediator in legal anthropology is the leopard-skin chief of the Nuer. As we have seen, the Nuer in the 1930s had no specialized legal institutions. The leopard-skin chief was a religious figure, not a political one. His only power was to threaten to lay a curse if the disputants became willful and uncooperative. One or both parties to a dispute approached the leopard-skin chief to mediate between them.

of the arbiter. Although arbitration may be marked by witnesses and by the presence of a judge (the arbiter), there is no political (legal) authority behind an arbitration. In developed legal systems such as our own, the principals in a dispute may agree to conform to "binding" arbitration. In that case, they have agreed to a form of contract and the legal system would enforce those results.

Moots

The moot is a kind of town meeting. It is a gathering of neighbors and peers who come together to settle disputes that have arisen within the community. The Tiv call such action "repairing the land." Disputes, once repaired, leave the land and the people in it again at peace. The moot is not a court. Courts are specialized institutions; the moot is an aspect of the community.

The word moot is derived from the Old Norse word for a meeting. In the history of northwestern Europe, it applies to an assembly of the people who have come together—often outdoors, under a tree—to discuss local political affairs and to hear disputes. They have been traced throughout most of Western Europe north of the Alps and Pyrenees. The moots of Iceland were first called "mot-things" and later shortened to "things." Iceland was occupied by a number of small Norse kingdoms. At stated times of the year the king convened all the adult male residents to meet to settle

7-16. *The leopard-skin chief among the Nuer is an institutionalized means by which people save face: they call in a leopard-skin chief, who insists that they do the right thing, as the community agrees on that right way to behave.*

He had no authority; all he could do was to urge the disputing parties to compromise and to make suggestions about how each of them could, at least to some degree, win a point. His compromises were made in the interests of peace for the entire community.

Arbitration

Arbitration—settlement of a dispute by persons chosen by the people disputing—adds another layer to mediation. The two parties in conflict agree to abide by the decision

7-17. *The moot is like a town meeting: all the important people (or in some places, only the important men) meet to hammer out a resolution of a dispute. This photograph of a Tiv moot was taken in 1950. They are hearing a dispute that concerned a lot of people; everybody in the neighborhood came to hear what the principals had to say.*

Conflict and Order

matters of concern to them all (Gomme 1880). With time, the Icelandic thing became the world's first parliament. A couple of centuries later, it was an English moot that challenged King John and made him sign the Magna Carta.

The Tiv of Nigeria used moots in their precontact culture; moots were still common in the early 1950s to hear disputes that were not suitable to bring before the courts that had been established by the British colonial administration (Bohannan 1957). Moots are still found in many parts of West Africa.

Courts

Courts are specialized political institutions that deal with law and with the conflicts, disputes and breakdowns in social order that are brought before them. Courts, in the fully developed sense, cannot exist without the authority to see that their decisions are carried out, which means the presence of a state organization. The development of courts and legal systems took place as part of the growth of the state, which will be considered in the next chapter.

Africa had many courts because indigenous states were highly developed there. The best described is probably that of the Lozi of central Africa, studied in the early 1940s (Gluckman 1955, 1965). The king occupied a central position, although he usually did not attend court and did not participate when he did, for the king was a court of appeal. Each Lozi court had three different sets of councilors, each called a mat because these people were expected to sit on mats. Each mat had several positions, and the people

7-18. A court is an especially appointed arm of the state to hear and settle disputes. This is a Lozi court, in what is today Zambia in southern Africa, as it appeared in the 1940s.

holding those positions sat in that precise location. The most powerful group was that group of officials who sat to the right of the king's position. The senior member of this group was head of the court. On the left side of the king sat another set of officials; they too were powerful because they occupied not only important offices in the kingdom but also offices within the household of the king. Opposite this group of officials-of-the-left was a mat occupied by members of the royal family.

The litigants sat before the judges, each surrounded by witnesses. The plaintiff first stated his case. He was not interrupted but was allowed to finish, with all the detail he deemed necessary. The defendant then stated his case in the same way. They were followed by statements by the witnesses. The members of the court, assisted by anyone present, then cross-examined by asking specific questions or by getting two principals or witnesses to discuss their contradictions. When this process was finished, the most junior official on the right mat gave the first judgment. It was followed by the judgment of the most junior official on the left. Each judge, in order of juniority, gave a judgment. The last judgment was handed down by the most senior official on the mat-to-the-right who was the head of the court. That was the judgment that went to the king for review and, unless the king ordered further investigation, it was the judgment that stuck. Obviously the opinions of representatives of the entire community had been heard.

ORDER IN POLITICAL SYSTEMS

Traditional lore in anthropology holds that a political system has two major tasks. The first is the preservation and restoration of order in society; protection of that society from external foes is the second.

Both these tasks center around the quality and effectiveness of the cultural institutions for controlling disputes. At one extreme, a culture may be so impoverished (or so regulated) that no disputes whatsoever are allowed to surface. Such a system is a dictatorship. Dictatorships occur when the people in power prohibit disputing, or perhaps even discussion, in order to maintain their own power. The short step across the boundary between discussion and disputing is so difficult to define, let alone control, that discussion may be forbidden in order to assure that no uncontrollable disputes occur. Dictatorships are thus likely to quash all discussion in the name of maintaining order. Such societies eschew institutions for resolving disputes in favor of power mechanisms for disallowing disputes (and, hence, curtailing possibly subversive discussions).

At the other extreme, people in a society that has no mechanisms for either settling disputes or preventing them must fall back on self-help. The size of any social group that depends on self-help as its primary means of dispute settlement is probably severely limited. As such a society gets larger, it will come closer and closer to chaos unless it finds an organized means of conflict resolution.

Chapter Seven

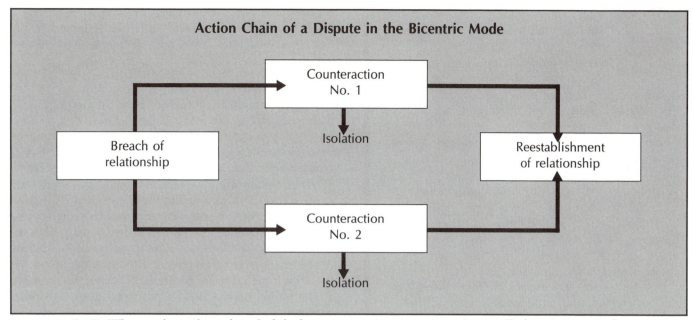

Action Chain of a Dispute in the Bicentric Mode

Breach of relationship

Counteraction No. 1

Isolation

Counteraction No. 2

Isolation

Reestablishment of relationship

7-19. *When a relationship is breached, both parties may institute a counteraction. Each party may see the situation in a different light. In that case, both parties must work to reestablish the relationship, or else they remain isolated from one another.*

Ideally, institutions for resolving conflict are those that allow a society (1) to leave room for discussion, including disputes, so that all sides of a problem can be heard (and, hence, rationality and orderly cultural growth have at least a chance to emerge and survive), and (2) to create and maintain a means for establishing consensus and making decisions stick so that orderly and predictable life can continue.

Discussion and, hence, dispute settlement lie at the heart of the political process. The genius of a good-enough polity is allowing discussion and dispute to take place so that better solutions can emerge, at the same time that there is enough control to allow orderly and predictable life to proceed.

Life in every political system is, thus, a struggle between control and chaos. Different polities draw the boundary in different places and have different ideologies about where the line should be drawn. Some have efficient institutions to allow, control and profit from disputes. Others do not.

Political Modes of Operation

There are two kinds of political action, or, better, two ways in which a political system can work. The first occurs when the system presents itself as a single entity—a powerful monolith. All the power in the system is organized around one center. This can be called the **unicentric** mode. The second occurs when the polity divides into two or more subordinate entities between which discussions, and sometimes disputes, are allowed. That is the **multicentric** mode. The most common form of multicentric mode, and surely the one most familiar to Americans, is the **bicentric** mode. The unicentric and multicentric modes are frequently intertwined.

The action chain in the bicentric mode is illustrated in 7-19. In the bicentric mode, the breach which sets off the chain is subject to more than one interpretation. If the two interpretations are not discussed, serious disputes may arise. Both sides may take what they consider to be a counteraction to set things right, by their different definitions of right. The result will be either isolation if one or both sides withdraws, or else a clash if both sides stand their ground. In that situation, the "correction," if it occurs, is reestablishment of

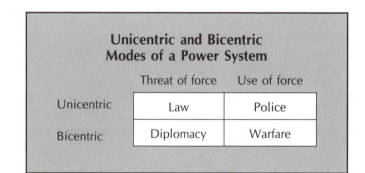

Unicentric and Bicentric Modes of a Power System

	Threat of force	Use of force
Unicentric	Law	Police
Bicentric	Diplomacy	Warfare

7-20. *A unicentric political system is one that presents a united front in all contexts. It may be a dictatorship or a one-party state. A multicentric system is a political entity with two or more centers that may be in controlled conflict, such as the multi-party states of modern-day democracies. The trick in running a democracy is alternating the unicentric and bicentric modes of a single system. International dealings are always done in a bicentric mode, although some actions by the United Nations resemble the unicentric mode.*

Conflict and Order

The American political system makes extensive use of both unicentric and bicentric modes. It allows the people of the country, or their representatives, to divide into two or more parties. Discussions between the members of the parties, often bordering on disputes, clarify issues. Then, by process of voting, the unicentric mode of the system is reasserted. In that way, some of the issues are decided. In the same way, checks and balances are created within the governing system by the extension of the bicentric mode to the discussion about laws and policy. Once votes have been taken and the law has been passed, however, the unicentric mode reasserts itself. The executive system, including the police system and the courts, then swings into action.

One-party states like the Soviet Union before 1989 did not allow the bicentric mode to emerge at all. The result was that both ideas for changing policy and any individual difference of opinion had to be hidden behind veils of secrecy. Similarly, during 1989, a student movement in China was violently suppressed by the Communist government. In demonstrating for democracy, the students were in fact asking that the boundaries between the unicentric and the bicentric modes of their system be altered. Either because China had no experience or knowledge of institutions for running a society with built-in dispute, or precisely because the leaders feared the results of allowing disputes, that student movement was defined as an "uprising," the army was called in, and the movement was totally crushed.

The moral is simple: a political system cannot run a democracy if it does not have the institutions for dealing with the bicentric mode. Even a democracy must constantly guard the boundaries between the unicentric and the bicentric modes of its polity: between power and discussion, ultimately between justice and tyranny.

WE, THE ALIEN

the relationship, either on the same old basis or on a new basis. Governments like those of Italy and France, with many political parties, adjust the unicentric mode to a multicentric mode (not just to two as Americans do).

Interweaving unicentric and bicentric or multicentric systems leads to one of the most intricate patterns that anthropologists have found in comparing political systems.

The use of force is interestingly different in unicentric and bicentric political modes, as shown in 7-20. Within a unicentric mode, law is the principal sanction and the police

are used to "keep order." In a bicentric mode, discussion—often international diplomacy—is central; if discussion fails, two forces (which may be armies) each struggle to establish and preserve their idea of what order should be.

Communication. For the bicentric mode to operate, the two factions must be allowed to state their positions. As mentioned earlier, the Soviet Union before 1989 put all the power in a single entity in order to maintain unicentric processes at all levels throughout the system. The Soviet Union was technically composed of fifteen republics. Before 1989, communication (expression of opinion, dissent, and so on) was strictly controlled by the government. The multicentric or bicentric modes were effectively eliminated. The bicentric and multicentric modes emerged when *perestroika* (restructuring) allowed communication to surface, and six of the fifteen republics petitioned to leave the union. At the same time, *glasnost* (openness) changed the way the Soviet Union approached its communication with other nations.

Dual Organization. Some societies, like Tewa Pueblo in New Mexico, use the bicentric mode—usually called dual organization—at all levels almost to the point that there are no persons or bodies with authority. The Tewa divide the year and all of nature into summer and winter. They have two sets of officials, one for winter and one for summer. Maleness and hunting are associated with winter; femaleness with summer. The ritual calendar is divided between the two; political action is done by constantly hearing from the two sides, each with its own duties that demand cooperation from the other.

7-21. Dual organization is one way to turn all situations into a bicentric mode so that no individual has uncontested or uncontrolled authority.

Sovereignty. The state, as we shall see in the next chapter, is a unicentric system (it may, as modern democracies do, allow bicentric modes of action within it, but many states do not). A state may be made up of a complex of relationships, social groups, or subcultures, but its citizens all subscribe to it. Everybody understands that it is a single system that, like a successful marriage, contains something resembling a two-party system.

Most states also define themselves as sovereign systems. That means that there is no larger political group with whom they will join—the sovereign state considers itself the ultimate political power within its geographical area. However, most sovereign states are involved with other sovereign states. Political systems involving two or more sovereign states are, because of the idea of sovereignty, limited to bicentric modes of operation. Like the situation described in 7-19, each

7-22. *When two sides coexist, they may fight. Warrior cultures sometimes focus on personal aggrandizement in the course of fights for specific purposes. Warfare in which the warrior element is minimal demands a highly complex political system. Here is a sculpture of American Indian warriors fighting cavalrymen from the U.S. Army. In Vietnam, a lot of American men did battle but did not really consider themselves primarily warriors.*

works out its own cultural interpretation of the relationship between the two sovereign states. Thus, because of the two sovereignties, international relationships are regulated through diplomacy and warfare.

Diplomacy

In diplomacy, the problems behind a dispute can sometimes be reduced to problems of translation. The first task of diplomacy is to translate one cultural idiom into another while simultaneously stating the case for one's own cultural values so strongly as to win the day. Diplomacy can, obviously, break down if translations fail to lead to common understanding (or to what has been called a working misunderstanding) or if the very success of the translation makes it apparent that the goals of the two power systems are totally incompatible. As is the case with simple social relationships, such incompatibility can be countered in two ways: avoidance and the use of force.

Diplomacy has been scurrilously called "the art of saying nothing" or "the art of lying" because the language must be understated or obscure. Diplomatic discussion must be noninflammatory and must also overcome mere talk meant only to gain time or to cover misdeeds. If a basis of common understanding is not established, diplomats sometimes "talk past one another" without knowing it. The subtleties of diplomatic communication are frequently lost when the information is fed back into the vernacular of either culture. Therefore, even if the diplomats of two countries understand one another, there is no assurance that those harmonious results will survive the translation back to the people of one or both countries.

International law is the name given when two separate powers (individuals, groups or states) use legal concepts in the bicentric mode. As when people seek mediation or the Nuer attend to a leopard-skin chief, when two sovereign states want to cooperate, they can do so through diplomacy and negotiation. Treaties may result. Threat of **war**, which is a culturally complex form of self-help, is the ultimate sanction. There is no "outside" institution with the power to enforce the mutually agreed-upon order between two sovereignties. The United Nations was created to fill that capacity, but it has no means of enforcing its resolutions unless member nations willingly cooperate in deterring a rebel member(s) as did many countries in the 1991 war against Iraq.

When diplomacy fails, either isolation or warfare takes over. Isolation, by definition, does not need to maintain communication channels. In fact, isolation deliberately seeks the closing of such channels. In today's world, warring parties need to communicate with one another. People—particularly women—who have kinfolk on both sides are often the go-betweens in warfare between small-scale societies. In warfare between nations, neutral countries are vital links in the chain—if Switzerland and Sweden did not exist, they would have to be invented.

CONCLUDING THOUGHTS

Conflict, as we have seen, is everywhere; it permeates our whole lives. If it is not adequately controlled, it is a far-reaching problem. Techniques for control of conflict are to be found in legal and governmental institutions that allow both for discussion and sufficient power to manage disputes. When such institutions are lacking—particularly institutions to deal with bicentric situations (argument) within the unicentric political system—consensus cannot be reached. Lack of such institutions was one of the causes of the decline

Conflict and Order

of the ancient Greek city-states. Today's institutions for use and control of power are almost as tenuous. One can watch their struggles and their weaknesses almost every night on the television news. Seeking the balance between conflict and order is a never-ending process.

BUZZWORDS

aggression a threat of attack by one animal toward another. Aggression is, in ethology, anthropology and psychoanalysis, the response to adrenaline which makes it possible for a creature to press its own demands in order to survive. In ordinary language it means the first step toward a conflict and is often confused with conflict.

agonistic behavior the aggression-based behavior among animals that can be assertive or antagonistic.

bicentric a political situation or system in which there are two centers of power. The creative tension between the legislative branch and the executive branch in the American government is a case in point. All disputes and all international agreements are bicentric.

conflict a disagreement, dispute, quarrel, struggle, or fight between two parties. If more parties are involved, they almost always form two sides.

counteraction any action taken at the time a norm is broken. The purpose is to counter the original breach.

correction the result of a successful counteraction—either the original breach of norm is erased by correct behavior or else a price is levied for the incorrect behavior.

law a body of rules recognized by a community as binding on its members. Each law must be a guideline for settling disputes or governing conduct. Although rules are found in all societies, law is usually not highly developed in the absence of a state.

multicentric describes a legal system or situation in which there are several power structures, none subject to the sovereignty of any others.

norm a standard for behavior within a certain group—what it is agreed that people *should* do, a pattern for behavior to be followed. It is often erroneously confused with "average" behavior—that is, what most people do.

order the state of social activity in which everything is predictable because it is done in accordance with law and custom.

unicentric a legal system in which all power is concentrated in one person, one institution or one government. There is no control or no check on the power of that person or group.

war a highly organized armed conflict between two highly organized sides.

Getting Control

PROPOSITIONS AND PREMISES

- Government and state should not be confused: absence of the state does not imply absence of government.

- The core government tasks are conflict management and intergroup ("international") relations.

- Families can run government (Navajo). So can ceremonial groups (Hopi), lineages (Tiv, Nuer), and ramages. In some parts of New Guinea, the government jobs are done by big men, people whose leadership is built on personal qualities but not associated by their position in any group.

- The state is a cultural invention—a social tool—that allows a role structure to supersede or reinforce the hierarchy of individuals for purposes of managing conflict and protecting the group from enemies or predators. (As we have seen, in the absence of a state, the political needs of the group are met by family, kinship groups, religious groups or powerful individuals.)

- The state is perhaps ten thousand years old. The nation-state (cultural coordination of the "nation," which we have come to call the localized ethnic group, and the state) is only a few hundred years old.

- Bureaucracy grew up as an integral part of the state. The definition is a hierarchy of roles. As such, bureaucracy is also used by other kinds of institutions.

- Modern governments have assumed tasks beyond the basic political ones: welfare, control of the market, education, and many more.

We live in a political age, in the same sense that the Medieval Period was a theological age. In the Middle Ages, all moral questions were referred to God, either directly or in the guise of His minions on Earth. Today, all social problems that are not thrust either on the family or on the schools are handed to the government. Problems concerned with the emerging global society or the trenchant problems of the economy are all defined as government problems.

We Americans, like the people of other industrial societies, are used to having a powerful, highly specialized governing institution called the **state**. For that reason, we have trouble understanding what life is like without that powerful state. Indeed, the sheer magnitude of the state as a social force

8-1. *Government and state are not the same thing. The state (represented here by a view of the Kremlin in Moscow) is a specialized institution of government; government can be carried out many other ways.*

makes it difficult to think creatively about governments. What we sense as the power and impersonality of the governing state makes it difficult to introduce constructive changes.

Government should not be confused with the state. There was government long before there were states. Government

A community of people—a *society*—runs its affairs within an agreed-upon form, a *government*. Just as the established scientific paradigm provides for "normal science," so the government and prevailing social customs provide for the normal transactions of a society. *Politics* is the exercise of power within this consensus.

Marilyn Ferguson (1980)

THEY SAID IT

is any set of social processes for doing the basic political jobs. There are two core responsibilities: settling disputes and keeping the domestic peace on the one hand, and maintaining integrity of the social group against outside invaders on the other—domestic issues and international relations. We shall see as this chapter unfolds that some governments, especially centralized states, often add other jobs to these basic political ones.

The state, on the other hand, is a specialized institution that emerges to carry out the government jobs when the social groups get so big that people can no longer govern themselves using kinship groups, religious congregations, and community. The state commonly emerges in periods of rapid population growth or dramatic cultural change. The state makes it possible for large-scale society to exist, even prosper. The state is, as you read this, undergoing startling changes, again in a period of staggering cultural growth that accompanies population expansion.

8-2. There are two basic government jobs: settling disputes and maintaining the integrity of the social group against outside invaders. Many other jobs are added in some states. Addition of too many tasks may make the institution of the state unwieldy.

Government may become unwieldy when social problems far removed from the core tasks are dumped on the state. It becomes more evident every day that in a complex postindustrial society, the state is overburdened. Just as the family in its present context may have difficulty accomplishing all the jobs assigned to it, so the state may not be capable of carrying out all the duties thrust upon it. Just as the market mechanism has difficulty addressing problems of the immorality of inequality, so the state mechanism struggles with the burden of a welfare system or impending ecological disaster.

As we proceed with this chapter, we must remember that today we may need new kinds of social institutions to deal with the problems of today's global society—not to replace the old ones but to supplement them (a point that will be expanded in Chapter 15).

STATELESS SOCIETIES

Societies that lack states have so many different mechanisms for doing the government jobs that no term for them has ever been found except "stateless societies." What they all have in common is that hierarchy is not permanently institutionalized. For that reason, they are sometimes called "egalitarian." Hierarchies, in most such societies, are allowed to form and are used only when they are needed for specific purposes. Once that purpose is achieved (or attempting to

8-3. Stateless societies may found government functions on extended families as among the traditional Navajo. Navajo families were matrilineally based—that is, based on relationships among women. Here a group of Navajo women are weaving outside a traditional hogan, the Navajo house.

achieve it is rejected) the hierarchy dissipates. What are political matters like in such stateless societies? How is order maintained?

Families as Government

Navajo divide the world into two kinds of people: kinfolk related to one another by *k'e*, which means friendliness and peacefulness, and those who are related on the basis of reciprocity exchange. Traditionally, Navajo lived—and many still do—in small residence groups built around a woman and her daughters. This matrilineal arrangement was reinforced at marriage, when the most common residence site for the newly married pair was in the home of the wife's mother. There was, traditionally, no clearly defined group larger than the residence group (Witherspoon 1975).

Navajos are adamant that every person has a right to speak for herself or himself. They hope that other people will act in predictable and good ways, but they do not require it. Coercion is deplored, no matter how or for what purpose it is used. Nobody ever, under any circumstances, has a right to impose his or her decision on the group or on any individual. Unanimity is the only basis for collective action that Navajo traditionally recognized. Leadership is a personal quality based on ability and the requirements of the moment. Traditionally, the Navajo had no form of government

separate from their family and community system, which did the tasks that governments do. When the Navajo were settled on their reservation in the late nineteenth century, loosely defined groups under a local headman were formed to deal with outsiders, particularly the United States government. The headman, representing the various groups, signed peace treaties. By the early twentieth century, recognized local groups had developed around trading centers, schools, missions. In 1923, a Tribal Council was formed, and Navajo territory was divided into more than one hundred chapters, brought together into eighteen districts. The Navajo felt the need for this Tribal Council because somebody had to sign oil leases. The functions of the Tribal Council have expanded since then as a result of Navajo participation in American culture. Centralization of power in the Tribal Council has resulted in the growth of nationalism among Navajo in the second half of the twentieth century—indeed, a Navajo state within the United States has even been suggested.

Ceremonial Groups as Government

Leadership may take the form of religious conviction and power, which may also be intermeshed with kinship roles within clans. It is still, however, largely a set of personal qualities.

Hopi, for example, is a small society of Native Americans

Getting Control

who have lived for many centuries in what is now the northeast part of Arizona, surrounded by Navajo. Although Hopi society had been bigger in ancient days, it had been reduced to some 3,500 people by about 1950. Since then, the population has again grown larger. Hopiland was and is a land of villages. Each village is politically independent. Previously, no traditional organization existed to tie the villages together. They acted in concert only when attacked from the outside. Alliances disappeared when the external threat disappeared. The Bureau of Indian Affairs organized a Tribal Council; Hopi now consider it an essential device in dealing with that Bureau, in their conflict with the neighboring Navajo over land rights, and as a device through which all Hopi as a unit can make contracts and agreements with people in the outside world.

8-4. *Stateless governments may be based on ceremonial groups as among the traditional Hopi.*

Members of a Hopi village are divided into a number of matrilineal clans (Eggan 1950). A person is a member of his or her mother's clan but is also closely associated with the matriclans of the father and of the mother's father. Hopi assign each child a ceremonial father who is responsible for the child's passage through the initiation ceremonies. The child is said to become a kinsman of the clan of the ceremonial father. Moreover, if a child becomes ill, he or she may be "given" to a doctor, which means that the child also becomes a kinsman of the doctor's matrilineal clan. Affines are also important kinfolk. Thus, multiple uses of kinship attach a person to many different people and qualify him or her for membership in many groups. Since kinship ties these large numbers of people together, it also provides a way of dealing with disputes and with village policy.

The Hopi household is based on matrilocal residence. As a result, each village has a permanent core of matrilineally related women. The women of a household look to their husbands and fathers to provide the economic mainstay of the household, but to their brothers and sons to carry out the necessary ritual.

The clan, a small group of matrilineal relatives, is also the most important feature of Hopi social organization—it is the basic ritual unit because all the important ceremonies are controlled by, and are the major responsibility of, a clan or group of clans. Although most clans are found in several villages, each village has its own calendar of important rituals, and each clan has an important part to play in the rituals.

The clans are totemic, in the sense that each clan is associated with a number of animals or manifestations of nature, and is named for one of the members of that category. Some (not all) clans use a metaphor of descent from the clan animal. All of nature is classified into categories, and the different clans are put into that same set of categories. Each clan thus ends up with a special association with certain animals. The clan animals are sometimes represented by masks owned by the clans, kept by the clan's senior woman, and used in some ceremonies.

Hopi have, besides clans, an elaborate set of ceremonial organizations. Among others, they are (1) the Kachina cult (Kachinas are spirits associated both with clans and with elements of nature), (2) men's societies responsible for the ritual initiation of the young into full adult membership of Hopi society and for the winter solstice ceremony, as well as some other ceremonies, and (3) societies concerned with rain, war, clowning and curing.

Each village has a ceremonial cycle. Ceremonies follow a calendar, somewhat different in each village. The welfare of all the people—and indeed, of the whole world—is said to depend on the adequate performance of the ceremonies. Social organization is thus closely aligned with ecology. Each ceremony is owned and controlled by a single clan, whose eldest members are in charge of the ritual for that ceremony. However, the ceremony is *performed* by members of one of the societies. Membership in the societies cuts across all clans. The Kachina cult is the only tribal-wide association; it (like the men's society) is important in the initiation of young people and also in the ancestral cult—ancestors return annually in the course of the ceremonies. They are impersonated—that is to say, their presence is given reality—by masked dancers.

In such a complex social context, the basic governing jobs

can get done in the process of carrying out other business. The Hopi are a relatively small society who, until modern times, had no need for a tribal government.

Lineages as Government

In Chapter 5, we discussed lineage systems based on the principle of segmental opposition and how they work in a kinship context. When we discussed moots in Chapter 7, we saw that lineage systems could be central to the process of resolving disputes and noted that the Tiv use them as a political device to reach and maintain internal harmony. Here we want to concentrate on how lineage systems are used politically to control warfare.

8-5 Stateless governments may utilize a lineage system based on the Principle of Segmental Opposition to control and avert warfare, as among the Tiv.

The lineage system coincides neatly with a general rule of self-interest: if two people I know are fighting, I may join the one who is most closely related to me in the lineage system; if one of them is closely associated, I do not have the option of staying out of it, but must join his side. In the simplest case of the patrilineal lineages discussed briefly in Chapter 6, if my full brother and my paternal half brother are in an argument, I must support my full brother. If that same paternal half brother is in an argument with our father's brother's son, I must join my half brother. At that level he and I are, as the Tiv say, "one person." If, however, a son of the son of my father's father's brother starts a dispute, then I must join my father's brother against him, because I am more closely related to him both in kinship and in the lineage system. In other words, I join the members of my own lineage at whatever point the lineages of the two combatants fork. Together we fight enemies from another lineage, although at a more inclusive level, we are also related to the people we are fighting. If still another enemy appears who is more distantly related to both of us than we are to each other, then all of us who have been fighting one another must join to fight against the outsider. The only time when all the Tiv might join one another against an enemy is when that enemy is non-Tiv. The principle was illustrated in 5-11 and 6-15.

By the same principle, if I am equally related to two men who are disputing or fighting, I obviously have to stay out of it. The only exception comes when one of the two is closely related to me through my mother. If I allow kinship to override lineage membership and assist my matrilateral kinfolk, I must realize that I have acted on my own, against the principle of segmental opposition. The action was all mine. None of my lineage mates will help me if I get in trouble.

Obviously, the lineage system is an effective mode of performing the tasks of government in the absence of a state. The lineage system controls both the judicial process—by providing the basis for settlement of disputes—and warfare—by limiting and defining the range of adversaries. There is no need for the special institution of the state. The only thing lacking is a permanent set of representatives vis-a-vis outsiders.

Leadership is always personal within a lineage system. There can be no positions of authority to which any sort of right can inhere. If there were, the principle of equality that underlies segmental opposition would be negated.

Thus, in the lineage system, leadership amounts to surveying the opinions of those in your lineage and then expressing them verbally. When you have agreed on a course of action, you can then actually lead its execution. Again, because there is no aspect of role for this leadership, it cannot be institutionalized. For example, when the British colonial government set out to rule the Tiv, they insisted on appointing "recognized chiefs" because they could not figure out any other way to "organize" the people. Although the "recognized chiefs" could have been excellent representatives of their groups vis-a-vis all outsiders, they were helpless to try to resolve disputes within the groups. To do that, they had to call in the elders of the disputing groups. From the Tiv point of view, any government chief was a member of one of the subgroups within the lineage, and hence was by definition biased. In short, all disputes were settled by bicentric means. Some of these appointed chiefs tried to use the force that the colonial government provided them to settle disputes within the group. They were instantly branded tyrants—and the whole group turned against them.

Ramages as Government

Lineages turn into **ramages** with the introduction of any symbol or property that creates a difference in kind, subordinating some lineages to others. When inequality of lineages is introduced into a lineage structure, the result is a ramage, a word that refers to the pattern formed by the branches of a tree. The presence of a symbolic piece of property like "the crown" in European history creates a basic inequality. 8-6 illustrates how a ramage system works.

Introducing inequality into a lineage system opens the road toward state organization. The inequality is, at one level, part of the process of institutionalization of power. One cannot have division of power without inequality, which may spread to some of the many forms discussed in Chapter 7.

Big Men as Government

The institution called the **big man**, which performs some of the tasks of government in Melanesia, is a particular adaptation of charismatic leadership. It is built on personal leadership but usually lacks any association with a descent group and is not based on lineage or ramage. Any inequality

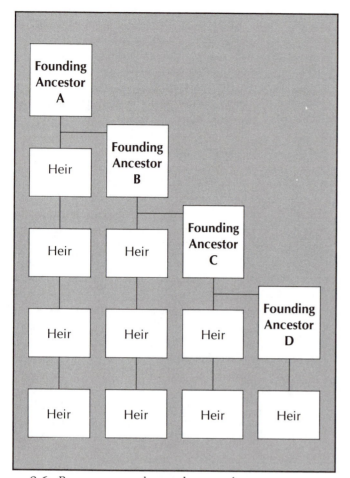

8-6. *Ramages may be used to perform government functions—indeed, a ramage system is well on the way toward chiefship. Here, power extends to only one descendant of the original founder (A), represented in the left column. Every other ramage descended from the original founder must create new heritable symbols—ramages B, C and D were later, and therefore junior, to ramage A. Each ramage has its own symbol of succession (adapted from Service 1975).*

that emerges does not coalesce into a system of roles. The societies that have big men are not structured around any idea of authority, although power may indeed inhere in the big men.

The typical society in western Melanesia is based on kinship groups that are also residential; each lives in a small village; each village is much like the others. Economically, the people of the village make their own decisions and are, to a great extent, self-sufficient, although some trade in foodstuffs may occur and trade in prestige items may be central to the interests of the men. The segments formed by these villages are not integrated into a greater polity.

A Melanesian big man never makes a move that is not designed to constitute "a competitive and invidious comparison with others" (Sahlins 1963). He stands out from other men by his own efforts. His power is personal power—there

is no office for him to occupy. His status comes because he is able to attract a set of loyal followers. His followers are not a stratum of society. Nobody occupies a special role that supersedes an individual. Rather, they form factions.

In some Melanesian languages, the big man is called the centerman. The term centerman is particularly appropriate because he becomes a point for redistribution of goods and services. His followers—seldom more than eighty people—are attached to him like satellites. There are several such centermen with their satellites in the totality of any of these particular societies. Within the faction that he leads, the Melanesian big man has some power—but outside that group, he has only prestige. He may make compacts or deals with other big men, but the result is a bicentric system at best (that is, two or more segments, each under a big man); the groups involved are still very small.

8-7. *Big men—charismatic leaders characteristic of many Melanesian societies—may perform the central roles of government. They have no authority, only personal power maintained by talent, trade and generosity.*

Because of the social fragmentation inherent in this system, both warfare and ceremonial are kept small-scale. Melanesian politics is, by and large, the "creation of followership" (Sahlins 1963) by such big men. To get followers, they must demonstrate admirable qualities such as being a master trader, especially of prestige goods. They must also treat their followers with generosity, be good gardeners, or brave war leaders. In some societies, "great men" are respected and followed because of the latter qualities alone; in other societies, the major qualification is the mastery of trade (Godelier 1986).

To be a successful trader and especially to display the great generosity that earns the loyalty of followers, a man must amass enough wealth—vegetable food, pigs, shell money. These goods are then redistributed, most often at feasts and ceremonies benefitting his followers and their families. Trade in prestige goods with other big men creates allies for himself and his faction.

However, successful big men run into a trap. Gifts have to be returned. The obligation to return gifts can keep people under a long-term bond to the original giver. As this kind of gift giving and return continues and grows, it soon comes to resemble the economic mode of allocation called redistribution (see Chapter 6). If the society begins to depend on such redistribution, the need for a person or persons at the center is acute. A big man's renown grows as the size of his faction grows. However, authority is fragmented by the same social principles that create it. As the faction grows, the big man must strain off more and more wealth to maintain his external reputation and his trade with other big men. The rewards to the faction members thus are decreased. Extortion from the faction becomes necessary if the big man is to retain, let alone expand, his external position. That is the social trap—at some time or another, the faction will rebel.

The number of people who can be controlled by a big man structure is small. It also contains within it the seeds of its own destruction. Although it carries out some of the tasks of government, the social trap prohibits its development into larger government forms. As long as people continue to behave in accordance with the principles of the big man, there will be a long line of rising and falling big men. They have reached a "developmental plateau" (Sahlins 1963).

The personal power of big men is absolutely dependent on continued successes in trade or war and generous gift giving. While the success lasts, the big man is a sort of government based on a combination of pecking order hierarchy reflecting his reputation and generosity and cooperation from others in the form of gift exchange and protecting the group (Service 1975).

The big man is an active, personal leader whose success arises from his own qualities. There are struggles for reputation, but the victor does not represent the kind of leadership we ascribe to government, for the leadership does not devolve to others. The attributes of the big men are not embodied in a role that can be passed to other people.

 Judging by the success of movies, TV programs, newscasts, and books about big men, Americans are fascinated by this type of power. All three parts of *The Godfather* have been immense popular successes, and there have been numerous other dramas based on the big men of the mafia. Other crime lords like the leaders of Colombian drug cartels and gangs are also built on big man principles.

WE, THE ALIENS

What all stateless societies have in common is that power is not permanently associated with any roles. Leadership is, as a result, a matter of individual personality and capacity. When a situation requires leaders, one may emerge (but, of course, may not). When the situation changes and a leader is no longer immediately required, the temporary leader fades into the background. He may emerge again in a new emergency, but he may not—somebody else may emerge the next time. No one occupies any role that implies inherent power. We might see this situation as egalitarianism (Service 1975). However, stateless societies are egalitarian only in the sense that there is no broadly recognized basis for allocating power other than personal capacity. Allocating powers requires status definition—rank or something like it.

CENTRALIZED LEADERSHIP

Specialized institutions of government are marked by several characteristics. Such institutions, first of all, involve a new principle of social organization: role, specifically as role is marked by a recognized office. Leadership that inheres in offices involves the leaders in different activities from leadership based on personal capacity alone. At least some of the struggle for prominence and leadership goes into getting the offices. The criteria of success are the achievements that result when an officeholder carries out the responsibilities of the office.

Allowing power to inhere in offices gives one individual access to legitimate power in many situations. That fact is considered dangerous by many of the world's peoples. Those who traditionally lived in stateless societies are especially adamant about the danger. When I worked among the Tiv in the late days of the British colonial period, they insisted that the British idea of giving legitimate power to chiefs was dangerous. They were right.

Assigning power to roles and distributing power among a system of role-players, gives each role-player rights and capacities to use that power widely. At least two results emerge. First of all, inequality permeates the entire social

8-8. *When specialized institutions of government appear, a new kind of leadership emerges: leadership that is based on authority deriving from an office. Such leadership has several advantages over charisma alone: the office can be held by a succession of persons, thereby creating stability through time; the office can be made part of a permanent structure of offices, thereby providing leadership for a far larger population than individual charisma allows.*

system. Power itself is the greatest marker of status among human beings. Assigning power by roles creates inequality. There is no way to avoid such inequality and still concentrate power in some roles. Second, when power is assigned to people occupying specific roles, the danger of tyranny is always present. Tyranny—the arbitrary or oppressive use of power—is an ever-present danger in all hierarchical organizations.

If the particular social design of the hierarchy assumes overarching importance, whether in government or in other walks of life, powerful roles must be checked by power in other roles. In order for such a system to work well, a balance must be struck among the powers. When such a balance is not achieved, tyranny runs rampant. Tyrants may be dictators, prime ministers, or a shift foreman in a factory.

Chapter Eight

160

8-9. *Tyranny—the arbitrary or oppressive use of power—is a danger when power is associated with office. Big men cannot become tyrants—their followers would simply leave them or ignore them. When power is institutionalized in offices, the danger of tyranny is present.*

Cherokee Peace Chiefs and War Chiefs

Some Native American groups had peace chiefs and war chiefs, thus separating the political task of maintaining internal harmony and the task of protecting the group from outside marauders into two sets of roles. This scheme had

8-10. *Cherokee and some other Native American societies separated the two primary political functions and assigned each to a different set of offices. The Cherokee, as a result, had two sets of chiefs, usually called the peace chiefs and the war chiefs. This photograph was taken in 1869, after the Cherokee were moved to Oklahoma.*

the advantage that no individual could accumulate enough power to become a tyrant. One center of power balanced the other. We noted Comanche examples in the last chapter.

In the early 1700s, the Cherokee occupied the valleys on both sides of the Great Smokey Mountains. They lived in thirty or forty villages, each containing about four hundred people. Each village had a priest-chief called the white chief who assured that internal affairs were stable. Each also had a red chief in charge of warfare. The two basic political tasks were thus kept organizationally separate. There was, however, no formal system for dealing with relations between the villages. Intermarriage led to kinship connections among them; seven clans were widely spread among all the villages. Affinal relations and dealings among clansmen kept communications open. There was no specialized institution of government, but there was usually no fighting between the villages.

In the early 1700s, the incoming British and French were disputing and fighting over control of the Carolinas. Both made allies among the Native Americans. The Cherokee joined the English colonists in the struggle against France and also against those Native American tribes who had allied themselves with the French. Cherokee warriors, however, sometimes stole from the settler villages or from colonial traders. The Carolinians did not understand how the Cherokee were organized. Thus, if they wanted reprisal or revenge against the particular Cherokee who had robbed or attacked them, they considered any Cherokee at fault. The Cherokee were thus driven to reorganize as a group in order to keep their young warriors from committing such crimes against the Carolina colonials. The first statelike organization was based on the red council—the chiefs who dealt with war.

It was a European who suggested to the Cherokee that they choose a single ruler. They elected a war chief named Moytoy as their "emperor." Moytoy died about ten years later and was succeeded by his son, still associated with the war-organization. The war chief, besides controlling the Cherokee braves, began to deal with the Carolina officials. By 1758, the war chief organization had been superseded by a structure of village councils, the council of the whole headed by a "wise man."

The South Carolinians continued to encroach on Cherokee territory and offered to buy what is now Kentucky. The old chiefs accepted, but younger Cherokee refused to accept that decision. At this time, the British-French struggle gave way to the battles between British loyalists and American revolutionaries (the American Revolution). The loyalists armed willing young Cherokee warriors, encouraging them to attack American revolutionaries along the frontier. The revolutionaries, still not able to distinguish one Cherokee from another, attacked the entire people. The young warriors fled to the south and established a new group that came to be called the Chicamauga. The young warriors had represented the red, or war, leadership. The older men were part of the white priest-chiefs. Seldom have authority and force been organized in such a way that it was possible to

see the difference so clearly (Service 1975; Gearing 1962).

Polynesian Chiefdoms

Polynesian local groups are kinship based much as Melanesian groups are. However, unlike the Melanesian groups, they assign power to roles, then rank the roles and, ipso facto, the groups. The ranked groups are integrated into larger units on the basis of a pyramidal hierarchy of roles. The type of leadership that is found in this hierarchy is far different from the Melanesian big man's struggle for personal power.

Unlike Melanesian big men, Polynesian chiefs are officially set apart from other people; they do not constantly have to prove their superior position by their daily actions. The characteristics that a Melanesian big man has to strive to acquire are handed to a Polynesian chief by reason of position. He or she (some Polynesian rulers were women) has inherited a right to the roles. Thus, Polynesian chiefs have a *right* to call on their subjects for produce and for labor. They do not have to obligate their followers as Melanesians did. The followers are obligated by citizenship—the rules of the social structure. Because he or she could call on status loyalties rather than personal loyalties, the Polynesian chief could build temples, support fine arts and crafts, and could finance ceremonies, large social works, and warfare on a far larger scale than was possible in Melanesia. The chief's powers to redistribute goods in large quantities were far greater than those of the Melanesian counterpart.

When Polynesia was discovered by Europeans, the usual social organization was a chiefship based on ramage. All the people were descended from a common ancestral couple, who were associated with the gods. The senior lineage in the ramage occupied the chiefship—the chief was said to be the firstborn son descended from a line of firstborn sons. As such, the firstborn always inherited the religious or mystical power of the original ancestors and the gods from whom they descended; hence his or her person was sacred. This ranking system was underwritten by ideas of **mana** and **tabu** (often spelled taboo). Mana was the emanation of supernatural power to the chiefs that was dangerous to commoners. Tabu (which in English now means anything that is traditionally banned, especially if it has a moral dimension) was a set of religious prohibitions against getting too close to the chiefs. Tabu prevented commoners from getting too much mana; if people followed the tabu, they would not be damaged by the chief's mana, his power. These customs served to maintain social distance between the chiefs and the commoners.

The chief, as mentioned above, was important in redistribution of goods. Commoners not only produced enough for their own subsistence but also enough to pay tribute to the chief. The chief's household and court lived from that surplus but also redistributed parts of it to the people. The social trap, however, is evident: Polynesian chiefs sometimes extorted too much from the commoners. When that happened, the people would remove their support of

8-11. *Chiefs, especially hereditary chiefs like those of Polynesia, are set aside from common people by reason of their inherited status. The social trap in chiefship (as well as with the offices in many bureaucracies) is that wealth extracted legitimately from the people for running the government may readily topple over into tyrannical aggrandizement of the chief and his kinfolk. This photograph is a coronation ceremony of a chief of Rarotonga, some time during the colonial period.*

the chief, and the chiefdoms would fall apart into smaller chiefdoms. Thereupon, each chief of these smaller chiefdoms began anew his struggle to enlarge his following at the expense of the others.

The Polynesian form of chiefship or monarchy was thus limited by its own built-in social trap—a "short circuit" created by "an overload on the relations between leaders and their people" (Sahlins 1960). Unlike the difficulties faced by Melanesian big men, the most common difficulty of the Polynesian chief was that more and more of the goods and services that the monarch extracted from the population had to go to glorify the monarch and to set him and his family apart from the general population. When the pressure became too great, the only way open to the people was to turn to the lesser chiefs and rebel against the monarch. Rebellions were not organized to change the system, but rather to find a better chief in the current system.

On the big island of Hawaii, where the precontact population reached a hundred thousand people, there was sometimes a single kingdom which would periodically break apart into several kingdoms. The regular rise and fall of kings kept pace with the pressures that individual kings, for their own aggrandizement, put on their people.

Most disputes in Polynesia were resolved by lineage action within the ramage organization. The chief interfered only if feud seemed inevitable. Peaceful succession to office was solved, insofar as it was, by the religious mandate to the people in power. Polynesian chiefships were **theocracies** maintained by custom and by codes of etiquette. Chiefdoms differ from states, which add a structure to administer force and to maintain their rule. Polynesia generally did not have a structure which utilized force (Service 1975).

When the Europeans arrived, only Hawaii, Tahiti and Tonga used the hierarchal organization as a form of defense against the European steamroller. European influence combined with the considerable ability of these three hierarchies transformed Hawaii, Tahiti and Tonga into states when they began to use public law, taxes, and a new hierarchy of ministers and bureaucrats.

In many places, role-based power systems emerged as priesthoods. Priests, who are said to be able to control relationships with the divine, can expand into solving what our society considers secular problems. Most modern democracies have strict rules about separating the two kinds of power, and we are meticulous about keeping church and state in separate realms. Secular and religious problems in many cultures, however, are not thought of as separate. In such circumstances, religious leadership and political leadership are not differentiated. Power is power.

What anthropologists usually call "chiefdoms" show centralized leadership. When chiefdoms exist, they seem to be theocratic—that is, submission to the chief's authority is a religious submission. The chieftains' centralized leadership may encompass the economy—or at least may manipulate economic factors to gain or maintain power. Chiefdoms differ from states in that they have no formal, legal apparatus for exercising repression by force. Force that backs up authority is a stigma of the state (Service 1975).

Ancient Egypt

Ancient Egypt is one of the earliest states for which we have both archaeological and written records (Frankfort 1948) describing religious and political organization. Egyptian culture was based on the idea that human life extends deep into the natural world. The political king of Egypt (called the Pharaoh) became a representative of the connection between human beings and the earth. Festivals marked the annual harvest and the annual rise of the Nile. Among the ancient Egyptians, state and religion were one. One festival celebrating this relationship marked the resurrection of the god Osiris.

The Egyptian pattern of leadership, based on religious doctrine and a festival calendar, became part of a priesthood. No distinction was made between priest and ruler. The Pharaoh was considered divine—an idea that goes back as

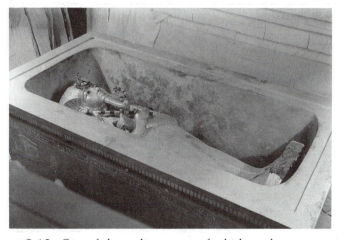

8-12. One of the earliest states of which we have any record is that of Ancient Egypt. Egyptian kingship was based on religion, and the Pharaoh was considered divine. The link between government and religion is a common one— one that modern Americans try hard to prevent. Egyptian kings, called Pharaohs, were embalmed and buried with great treasures.

far as the very first Egyptian records. Pharaoh's task was "to maintain an established order (of which justice is an essential element) against the onslaught of the powers of chaos" (Frankfort 1948). The first Pharaoh, Menes, was enshrouded in religious doctrine: "There is a mystic communion between father and son at the moment of succession, a unity and continuity of divine power which suggests a stream in which the individual rulers come and go like waves" (Frankfort 1948).

As the new form of state evolved, difficulties and traps emerged with it. Some chiefs would conquer others, and the balance of power would constantly shift among many chiefs. Unfortunately, we have little further detail. Few administrative documents remain of early Egypt.

THE STATE

The state is a specialized institution that does the basic political jobs. It usually takes on other jobs as well. Just as the principle of role was added to social structure when chiefship emerged, so bureaucracy and its approved use of force are added when the state emerges. These two elements—centralized leadership and bureaucracy—are the

---

8-13. The state is a specialized institution for doing the basic political jobs.

---

major markers of the state. The gravest social trap is that when the state institutionalizes force, the members of the bureaucracy may overstep the legitimate bounds of power and use it selfishly.

Bureaucracy

The word **bureaucracy** literally means "desk power." It was made up in the 1700s from the French word for desk (bureau) and the Greek word for power (the "cracy" of democracy or autocracy). By the nineteenth century the word had become pejorative. Its tortuous procedures had become infamous; the highhanded ways of bureaucratic officials became legendary. That pejorative meaning still clings to the term. Bureaucracy is a derisive term in our society.

The technical meaning of bureaucracy is instructive. A bureaucracy is a hierarchy of roles or offices which are marked by overt levels of authority and responsibility. The offices form a system in that the occupants of these offices must work together. This kind of interlinking makes the entire system work. These offices are assumed by individuals— indeed, politics in a complex bureaucracy may center around what people have to do to get and keep the positions. When an incumbent dies or retires, another person moves in. The office, however, and the system of which it is a part, continue to function.

8-14. *Bureaucracy is the framework of state political organization. It is a hierarchy of offices; holders of those offices perform intermeshed jobs, which means that a large society can be administered by impersonal standards.*

Bureaucracies, thus, all show specific characteristics:

- They are systems of authority relations among recognized officials. Authority is inherent in the relations between the positions.
- Each office is characterized by defined rights and duties. The assigned duties of the office are public information.
- There is strict separation of office and incumbent (called a bureaucrat). For a person to acquire an office, he or she must demonstrate technical training or experience (or in some places just have important kinship connections). Bureaucrats are reimbursed with salaries. Attending to their offices is considered to be a full-time occupation.

A Bantu Bureaucracy. Africa was traditionally the home not only of some of the most successful stateless governments, but also of many complex states. The Soga are a Bantu group who live on the northern shores of Lake Victoria in Uganda.

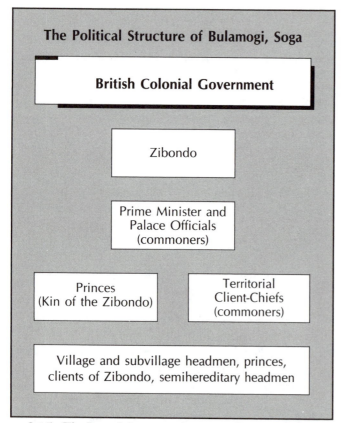

The Political Structure of Bulamogi, Soga

British Colonial Government

Zibondo

Prime Minister and Palace Officials (commoners)

Princes (Kin of the Zibondo)

Territorial Client-Chiefs (commoners)

Village and subvillage headmen, princes, clients of Zibondo, semihereditary headmen

8-15. *The Prime Minister and various officials, including some princes, the client-chiefs and the village headmen, create a bureaucracy through which the Zibondo can govern the Soga people.*

Their traditional political organization was a complex mesh of several institutions and principles: patrilineal kinship, ascribed rank, and **patron-client** relationships. Using bureaucracy and kingship, they conjoined these institutions into several Soga states (Fallers 1965).

Soga are organized into patrilineal clans. The members of a clan claim common descent from the ancestor whose name they take but cannot trace the steps of that descent. Clan members are widely dispersed; the patrilineal clan is never a localized unit. Lineages are recognized within these clans. A Soga lineage is made up of clan members who can trace agnatic ancestry, through a known genealogy, to one of the descendants of the clan ancestor. The lineages do not form a lineage system in the sense that the Tiv used a lineage system for government. The senior males of each lineage form a council, which becomes an important level in the bureaucracy. Because the religion is based on ancestor worship, the lineage also is a religious group.

Lineages and clans are not all considered to be equal. The royal clan is ranked above the others; its members are said to have an inborn fitness to rule. A royal clan (there is one for each Soga kingdom) is like any other clan in that it has a council of elders to resolve disputes and other problems that arise within the clan. It differs from other clans, however, in that its affairs extend to include all of the people and business of other clans in the kingdom. This authority, and the ancestors of the royal clan, form the basic outline on which the state is erected. The ruler has authority not only over members of his own clan, but over everybody in the area, whatever his or her clan. The ancestors of the royal clan are, for religious purposes, ancestors of all the citizens of the state.

Any male member of the royal clan may become a ruler. In actual practice, the immediate sons and brothers of rulers have more power than do clansmen related more distantly to a recent ruler. Rank, thus, is found even within the royal clan, although it is not as marked as the rank differences between the royal clan and the commoners.

A ruler's assistants and staff are not chosen from among his clan brothers. All clan brothers have a right to rule; therefore, any of them—even those who appear most trustworthy—are possible usurpers. For this reason, no ruler could ever trust that his clansmen would not rise up to overthrow him in order to become ruler. Within the royal clan, the state has poisoned kinship as a basis for trust. In that situation, the ruler turns to nonroyal clans for his bureaucratic assistants. He binds trusted commoners to him by giving them authority as ministers. Although the commoners could never become rulers, they could become powerful bureaucrats. Their power is reflected in their personal relationship with the ruler—indeed, it derives from the personal grace of the ruler. The ruler is the patron; the minister is the client. That power base is sometimes cemented when the ruler marries a clan sister of a minister, or when he gives one of his sisters or daughters to the commoner minister as a wife. Because the authority of the commoner is dependent on his personal relationship with the ruler, the commoner can be counted on to be fully loyal at all times. These powerful commoners are also called client-chiefs.

The most powerful of the client-chiefs was the prime minister. His position called on him to run the palace household. In that role, he had full control over who was granted audience with the ruler and who was not. Other client-chiefs were assigned to different parts of the kingdom, each put in charge of a series of villages. The clan of the client-chief was responsible for and to that entire series of villages, just as the clan of the ruler was responsible to the entire kingdom. The client-chief's lineage held sway over the lineages who reported to him. Thus, the villages were organized like the state: a clan system and a client system conjoined to form the government.

The ruler of one of the larger Soga states, Bulamogi, bore the title Zibondo. The Zibondo's staff was made up of his clients who held bureaucratic jobs and thus controlled the entire organization of the state. These client-chiefs had an important voice in the selection of the next Zibondo. The more support from such commoner client-chiefs a young member of the royal clan could command, the more likely he was to be selected as the next Zibondo.

At one time, three princes of the Zibondo's clan ruled princedoms under the Zibondo and were subordinate to him. These princedoms were states-within-the-state. However, the princes were difficult to deal with and were never to be trusted. They often refused to obey the Zibondo; on occasion they made pacts with groups outside the kingdom to overthrow him. These princes, like the Zibando himself, had prime ministers and staffs of officials bound to them by clientage. In this way, princedoms could be inserted into a bureaucratic hierarchy to create something like an empire. However, the situation rarely lasted very long. One of the princes would conquer the others, throw them out of office, and insert his own commoner ministers.

This hierarchal arrangement could be used to form ever bigger units. When the Europeans appeared in Uganda, several Soga rulers were themselves clients of the ruler of the Baganda, the largest state in the area. From the standpoint of the Baganda ruler, the Soga chiefs were client-chiefs. The British colonial government, indeed, fitted like a cap on the top of the system, being just an additional stratum; most of the kings were retained in their offices—as they saw it, client-chiefs to the British.

Protection against tyranny was built into the system. Tyrannical rulers were overthrown when one of their clan-mates got enough support; they were also said to be punished by the ancestors whom their tyranny had misrepresented.

Why Bureaucracies Fail. Several social traps may cause bureaucracies to fail. At least three basic difficulties or temptations for officeholders can lead to failure:

- The bureaucracy may become so rigid that it can no longer adapt to change—in fact, it may not work at all.
- The bureaucrats may become incompetent, in which case the bureaucracy does not perform the tasks it was designed to do. Nothing gets done and the state collapses.
- Individual interests of bureaucrats may conflict with the aims and tasks assigned to the bureaucracy. If, in this situation of contradiction between official duties and personal interest, a bureaucrat leans too far toward personal interests, the mesh of responsibilities in the system fails to link up. If very many bureaucrats succumb to the temptations of self-interest, the whole bureaucracy loses its capacity to administer the government or aid the people.

The Nation-State

In early Europe, kings were often called "the King of the Jutes" or "the King of the Franks." The territory of the kingdom was stressed less than the ethnicity of the subjects.

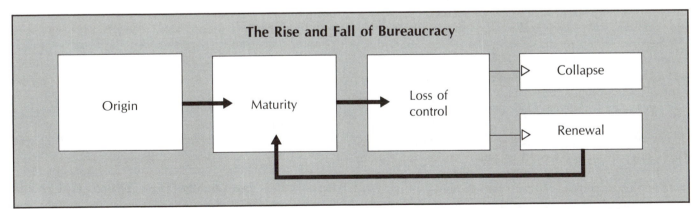

The Rise and Fall of Bureaucracy

Origin → Maturity → Loss of control → Collapse / Renewal

8-16. Bureaucracies are originally created from personal followings. They grow to maturity as they are fully developed into accepted systems of roles. However, a bureaucracy may lose control of its primary tasks. The usual reasons are that it (1) becomes inefficient, (2) becomes so rigid that it cannot respond to the needs of the people to be governed, and (3) becomes nepotistic or so self-interested that it selfishly looks only for its own continuation and aggrandizement. Such situations may lead to its collapse. However, able leaders or bureaucrats may be able to put it back on course so that it returns to a state of maturity and efficiency.

The idea that the state should be associated with both a specific ethnicity and with a specific territory may be traced to earlier origins, but it flourished among the Portuguese in the fourteenth century. The idea logically leads to the idea that the state should be associated not only with government but that it should be the representative of a particular **ethnic** group—a group which should occupy and control its own territory and whose members should be the only people with full rights within the territory. The idea that the ethnic group (replete with its own mystical cultural identity) is the natural unit of government is the basic idea that underlies the nation-state. That idea has been the plague of Europe ever since it arose. After Portugal, the idea was taken up next in Holland, Britain and France—it is still spreading. The greatest philosophical development of the idea occurred in Germany, where it intertwined with the ideas of the movement called German romanticism. The Germans thought of the *Volk* (folk) as something like a huge descent group with common ancestry, a common culture, and a common language. It is much like the American idea of an ethnic group—with the addition that the group was, or ideally should be, defined by the geographical boundaries of their country. The desirability of this correspondence between ethnic group and state was central to the peace process at the end of World War I—an unspoken premise that guided the redrawing of the map of Europe.

The primacy of this idea became evident to me when, in the summer of 1966, I spent some time in the Tirol. The Tirolese people told me (I certainly would never have thought to ask) that the greatest villain of this century was Woodrow Wilson because he (actually, of course, it was the peace conference) split the Tirolean people among Switzerland, Italy, Austria, and Liechtenstein instead of providing them with their own nation-state. In the early 1990s, we saw this struggle among the Baltic peoples—Lithuania, Estonia and Latvia—as they tried to break away from the dominion of the Soviet Union. The Palestinians are now divided among Israel, Jordan and other Near Eastern countries and seek to establish a "homeland." We see it in India and in Yugoslavia.

When the nation in the sense of the ethnic group (the word nation comes from the Latin word meaning "to be born") is conjoined with the state, the nation-state can approach the strength of the family in demanding loyalties and commanding hatreds. "Outsiders" are often reviled and excluded from positions of power. "Insiders" strive for "self-determination," insisting that the leading members of the bureaucracy be chosen from their ranks. In this way, both personal identity and ethnocentrism are tied to the nation-state and often confounded with patriotism.

From the global perspective, the nation-state is both an unattainable and undesirable imaginative construct. Among modern countries today, there are few states whose people are a single ethnic group: I can think of only Iceland and Japan (whose few tiny minorities—the largest is the Korean—are rigidly denied most rights). Most states are dazzlingly multiethnic and multicultural. In the United States, literally

8-17. The nation is a group of people held together by a common culture, a common language and a mythology and/or history; a nation resembles an ethnic group. A state, on the other hand, is a social organization that is specifically an instrument of government. In modern English, the two words (nation and state) have become so confused that we sometimes use the term nation to mean state. When several nations are found in one state, or when the two terms are confused, a social trap is created: all people who are citizens of the state may not be members of the nation. Hence, in some situations, they may be considered outsiders or second-rate citizens.

hundreds of ethnic groups (there are over eighty in the central valley of California) interact. Except in cases of social exclusion (legal exclusion is now against the law), they do not form territorial groups; a fact for which we should be grateful. Moreover, with a few exceptions, the ancestors of most modern Americans came to this country because they wanted to come; today the ancestors of future generations of Americans are still coming.

The situation is quite different in Canada where the French of Quebec are trying to acquire "self-determination." It is also different in the USSR, which is an empire formed by conquest. (The British, French, and Dutch also formed empires at about the same time, but those realms broke up in the late 1940s and 1950s.) In the USSR, many ethnic groups were subjugated first by the tsarist regime and later by the Soviets, who organized the Union of Soviet Socialist Republics. The aim of the central state was to transform ethnic loyalty into citizenship loyalty to the state. To help in the process, they allowed people to maintain their ethnic identity only by museums of folklore and costumes. In the late 1980s and early 1990s when the communist system of economy and government collapsed, these ethnic groups, regarding themselves as nations, reemerged and sought to establish independent nation-states.

The association of the state with the kind of ethnic group called a nation would seem to be one of the great social traps of modern times. Just as the United States is an amalgam of ethnicities, so are most other modern states. Not all of Quebec is French. Within the Soviet Union, none of the substates is occupied solely by a single ethnic group. Do you extradite anyone who is not "ethnic"? On what basis do you make the determination? There is no way, in most cases, for the ethnic group and the state to be correlated without mass movements of peoples, loss of property and life, and unimaginable agonies of displacement of peoples and of culture.

Problems of States

Generations of scholars have studied the state by inquiring into its origin. Some have claimed that states are formed as a result of expansion of one people against another—the conquest theory of the state. Although not the universal origin, many states formed by conquest can be found. Others have claimed that the state develops to "overcome the disincentives against social cooperation in groups largely composed of nonkin or even of distant kin" (Masters 1989). The author of that quotation cites the fact that many animals cooperate with their kin, but not with nonkin. The state is, in his view, a cultural mechanism by which cooperation can be achieved with nonkin. The state, seen this way, is a social solution to problems created by population growth or by changes of ecological niche. Many examples can be cited. Large-scale irrigation systems such as those on the Tigris-Euphrates rivers, the Nile, and the Yellow River in China demanded a coordinated labor supply. The bureaucratic state was the only institution that could provide it. Still other scholars claim that the state emerged in the interplay of not one but many causal elements.

8-18. The state can be seen as a mechanism for getting nonkin to cooperate with one another.

When a new level of organization emerges, the earlier ones are usually retained. People do not stop dealing with kin just because they start to deal with nonkin. Trade may cause wider communities to form, but the narrower ones are not abandoned. Kinship groups, production groups, and ethnic groups form segments within the larger unit; they may even be given representation in the bureaucracy. Leaders have to learn to use and manipulate these several levels, each run by different social principles.

Certainly, however, the state has some specific jobs that are not shared by other forms of government.

(1) *Loyalty.* How do you get people to be loyal to a bureaucracy? Lenin tried it in the USSR. Russians were already loyal to "Mother Russia"; some of them resented the fact that Russian culture was written off in favor of Soviet culture. Indeed, in 1990, they sought to re-establish Russia as an independent state, outside the Soviet Union. The Armenians, Lithuanians, and other groups retained loyalty to their "nations," and won independence, as we mentioned earlier. The attempt to replace loyalty to the ethnic group (the "nation" in the literal sense of nation) with loyalty to a bureaucratic state was eventually unsuccessful in the Soviet Union. In the United States, the two groups—ethnic group and state—have been coordinated so that each is acceptable in a different realm of cultural life. So far there has been no serious attempt by an ethnic group to secede from the United States.

(2) *Force.* A lot of thought has gone into the idea of force as the primary requisite of state government. But the need for force surely is an admission that authority has failed.

Nevertheless, most scholars since Machiavelli have thought it a necessary dimension of the state.

Since authority always demands obedience, it is commonly mistaken for some form of power or violence. Yet authority precludes the use of external means of coercion; where force is used, authority itself has failed. Authority, on the other hand, is incompatible with persuasion, which presupposes equality and works through a process of argumentation. . . .

Hannah Arendt (1961)

THEY SAID IT

Force has often been called the essential characteristic of the state. The force, or right to use force, was said to rest with the sovereign, an idea predominant in the time that Europe was ruled by royal families. Although the power of royalty has faded (royal families in Europe today do not rule even where they reign), the idea of maintaining sovereignty through force has endured.

(3) *Legitimacy* or authority has to do with the consent of the governed. That consent is not always well-informed, and it is not always beneficial for the very people who do the consenting. Legitimacy can be seen as the right given by many to a few individuals to exercise the roles of government (or some other roles). Authority inheres in the roles. Force is needed only when such consensual legitimacy wavers or is withdrawn. Stalinist USSR demonstrates the worst that can happen when an absolute ruler tries to remodel society in the absence of such consent. To achieve his objectives, he murdered millions of people (Conquest 1990).

The Tasks of Government

The primary tasks, as we have already seen, are maintenance of order and peace by assuring a rule of law and adequate defense—"maintenance of the social order within the community and of the community itself in defense against outsiders" (Service 1975).

The heartland of government, therefore, deals with problems of (1) territory, which we have solved with borders and border guards, (2) security, which is served by the law, by police systems, by diplomats, by the army, and (3) finances for paying for government activities. This latter includes the power to tax (or, in more primitive states, to demand labor and tribute payments).

Because specialized governments need funds to carry out their work, most have the authority to tax—they thus become the collection point of wealth for redistribution. Because of

8-19. *Force is often said to be an integral aspect of the state. The state, it is said by many traditional theorists, is the only institution that has the authority to use force to carry out its tasks. Nevertheless, states are actually required to use force only when no other way can be found to reach goals. Therefore, use of force can be looked at as a symptom of disease in the state, or inadequacy in a culture. In 1989, the Chinese government used force against demonstrators for democracy in Tiananmen Square in Beijing. After the government use of force, the Square was empty, guarded by soldiers.*

this fact, governments often take on many activities beyond the basic political ones of maintaining order and security. The definition of just which of these additional tasks are political changes rapidly as social problems change. In fact, this is one of the basic distinguishing features of large-scale bureaucratic governments today. Socialist governments (which include communist societies) claim that government has the prime responsibility for all economic matters; the so-called Free World says that government has only a limited place—or no place—in economic endeavors. There are similar arguments about religion and government, as we have seen.

We still, within our own government, recognize the primacy of law and war. When the U.S. government was founded, no mention was made of a cabinet, but the President was given express permission to consult with the heads of departments. Then in 1789, Congress set up three departments: the Departments of State, of War, and the Treasury. The founders also made arrangements for the appointment of an Attorney General. We might note that in these four officials, the core of any government is represented: relationships with outsiders, particularly other governments, were taken care of by the Departments of State and of War (which later became Defense); internal law and justice by the Attorney General; the management of government resources by the Department of the Treasury.

The other members of the cabinet have been added (and sometimes subtracted) as the special tasks of government have expanded.

WE, THE ALIEN

At the time of the Spanish Conquest of the New World, the church was the only institution besides the government that controlled large supplies of wealth. Because the church had full commitments within its own realm (which had expanded in much the same way the realm of the government had expanded), the government was the only organization that could pay for overseas voyages for discovery or trade. Today the government and the corporation are the only institutions that command large amounts of money. However, even governments do not have enough money—just as there are tasks that the Spanish kingdom could not adequately pay for, so there are important tasks like clean air and welfare and foreign aid that present governments cannot adequately pay for.

Modern governments have taken on tasks such as welfare that in previous days were performed by families or other kinship groups, or else not performed at all. The degree to which this responsibility is legitimately a problem of the state (which was not originally designed to do it and may not do it well) is an open question. But one thing is certain: no other institution has appeared that can solve such problems.

Social security, or caring for the aged, is a problem that emerged in catastrophic proportions in the early part of the twentieth century. Governments were the only institutions able to handle it financially. Social security is, in the United States, not part of the welfare system. But as life expectancy expands (it was less than fifty years in 1900 and is now over seventy-six years), there seems to be no other organization to shoulder the responsibility.

8-20. The tasks assigned to the modern state have increased far beyond the basic political tasks simply because we do not have any other institutions to do them: education, housing, energy, and welfare, social security, unemployment insurance, and health insurance. Just as the family cannot handle government tasks in a large-scale society, so we must ask whether the state can actually handle well many of the tasks we now require of it. And, if not, what kind of institution can we create that will handle these problems?

Unemployment insurance is another part of the welfare system that the government has assumed: unemployment is a chronic condition in capitalist societies. Your answer to whether the federal government should be involved in it may depend on whether you are a Democrat or a Republican. But in either case, it is not part of the original political problems. The responsibilities of the state grow apace.

The United States Government now gives cabinet status to many departments and agencies that lie beyond the basic government tasks that were recognized in the earliest days of the nation. As of 1990, these agencies were: (1) Labor, (2) Agriculture, (3) Commerce, (4) Health, (5) Education, (6) Housing, (7) Veterans' Affairs, (8) Energy, (9) Interior, and (10) Transportation. At one time, the postal service merited cabinet status. Many other modern states have departments of communication that rank the equivalent of cabinet status.

The United States government is also asked to solve the drug problem, economic problems like the banking fiascos, and social problems like poverty and homelessness because these problems are immense and no other institutions have the resources or the mandate to deal with them.

WE, THE ALIEN

The problem that current generations face is whether the government is an adequate institution to do all these jobs. If we answer in the negative, we have to create other social means of doing them, or else allow them to go undone.

CONCLUDING THOUGHTS

Modern-day pressures are out of line with our primate heritage, with our foraging heritage, and with our horticultural and agricultural heritage. With this realization, a new naturalism seems to be emerging. It is based on respect for human individual and cultural differences, on duties of virtue entailed by social obligation, and with a concern for human justice (Masters 1989).

We do not yet know, of course, what changes will be made in the nature of states within the next few decades, but all the evidence points to the idea that the kind of changes that have been made in the past are preliminaries to even more important changes that are now in process. We do know, however, that even as we study this topic, new modes of government and new patterns of dealing with power are emerging all around us. We shall return to these topics in Chapter 15.

BUZZWORDS

big man a leader whose entire power comes from his or her personal characteristics and charisma.

bureaucracy a hierarchal structure of roles to administer power within a government or a firm.

ethnic having to do with a particular group of people who share a cultural tradition.

government the social organization responsible for settling disputes, maintaining order, and protecting society from external aggressors. Modern governments are loaded with many additional functions.

mana a Polynesian word for the sacredness said to be characteristic of chiefs, and dangerous to commoners. (Not to be confused with manna, which the book of Exodus tells us was the food supplied to the Israelites in the wilderness.)

patron-client a nonkinship relationship in which the low-ranking client depends for his welfare and social position on the high-ranking patron. The patron can count on the complete loyalty of the client.

ramage a type of organization which branches from a single point, parts of which then branch again.

state a political organization based on a hierarchy of roles. The hierarchy forms the basis for a bureaucracy.

tabu (often spelled taboo) a Polynesian word for an element so sacred as to be harmful to those not of sufficient rank to deal with it. Taken over into English, it means something that is forbidden—usually having a flavor of sinfulness rather than mere illegality.

theocracy a government in which God, or several gods, are recognized as the supreme rulers, and in which divine laws are taken as laws of the state.

Born Equal?

PROPOSITIONS AND PREMISES

■ The bases for claiming superiority may change with geography and with time, but the tendency to elevate oneself at the expense of others is a human universal. It takes a lot of training for people to learn that others have an equal right to think themselves superior.

■ People categorize many things in order to clarify and simplify thinking. In the process, they may rate roles, social groups, social categories, or items of material culture to arrive at a system of rank or inequality.

■ If the categories which are ranked come to be regarded as part of the natural real world instead of as cultural inventions, social and political problems result.

■ Some people or groups may be defined as pariahs, which is to say that they have been forced outside the system of ranking.

■ Race is a *cultural* classification of individuals and/or categories based on selected overt physical differences. All such classifications are historically and culturally bound. The science of genetics has no need for such a classification.

■ Ethnicity is a *cultural* classification of categories or groups of people whose cultures differ from one another but who nevertheless are within the same social system.

■ Power, prestige, property and pleasure (the four Ps) are permanently in short supply—no matter how much there may be, it is never enough. The four are often traditionally lumped together—that is, those who have most of one also have most of the others—but they can be separated, and many people forego one in favor of another.

■ Prejudice is the use of criteria of rank to create or maintain differences in opportunity in distribution of the four Ps. Racism is prejudice deriving from cultural ranking of (and hence, unequal opportunities for) the races as perceived in the common culture. Sexism is prejudice derived from cultural perceptions of gender and resulting unequal opportunities for the two sexes.

As division of labor became more specialized and economic organization more complex in the course of history, inequalities among persons appeared. Inequality grew as governments and bureaucracies grew. All large and complex cultures, and many small ones, rank people, roles, and culture traits. All exhibit inequality. Because the American Declaration of Independence champions equality for all (belatedly including women and the people of all races in "all"), we are used to thinking of inequality as unjust. Nevertheless it is a basic feature of all complex societies. Inequality is evil only when it blocks opportunities. Caste systems, and many class systems, do indeed limit people's lives; so did medieval estate systems. So do many modern governments and some economic organizations. However, at the end of this chapter we shall look at some ideas about optional inequality—inequality that we can choose in order to increase our rewards rather than inequality that is forced on us and reduces rewards.

Male chimps and baboons exhibit what is called display behavior to create and exercise dominance over others. They strut, raise the hair on their bodies, assume fearsome postures, bare their teeth, shout, and shake the trees and bushes. Occasionally they fight one another in order to change their position in the dominance hierarchy. The resulting hierarchy, based on the individual strengths and tactics of each animal, assures social order within the band, at least until it is challenged again. Human beings have culturized such activities to achieve those same ends.

9-1. *Stratification involves the sorting of a population into categories, then ranking the categories hierarchically, extending different social privileges and rank to each category.*

In addition to hierarchies of individuals, cultural ranking systems establish power hierarchies of the sort commonly called social stratification. Until recently, people enslaved one another, leading to accepted institutions of servitude. They even threw some categories of people out of the recognized classifications of rank so that they had no rank at all, even though these outcastes may have held a vital place in the economic system. When this happens, pariah institutions—groups of people who are defined out of social existence—are created. Distinctions for imposing inequality can be made on the basis of occupation, wealth, race, ethnicity, gender, education, rank of the parents, and any number of other cultural markers.

The term stratification, commonly used by social scientists, carries an overload of meaning that may hide the principles by which ranking is actually achieved. Discussions of stratification too often use English words like class or caste so carelessly that no precise meaning attaches to them. For example, the word caste, when it is used to describe the

situation in India, has several essential components to its meaning. When the same word is then applied to situations in American society, only one or two of those components are emphasized—the others are absent in America. Thus the word caste quickly loses its power for denoting, let alone analyzing, both situations.

Our goal in this chapter is to go back to the defining characteristics themselves to discover how they cluster. We are looking for the bases on which inequality can be institutionalized so that we can compare those bases from one culture to another. We do this by a method called componential analysis. A component is any criterion that can be used to make distinctions. Any given component may be either present or absent; it may be given different weight according to different values about what is important. The cluster that results is what gives an institution its distinguishing characteristics.

RANKING

When we have a lot of information to keep straight, we put things and ideas into general categories, which we then name. If we could not put the details we know into categories, thinking could not proceed on a more general level. We would suffer from an overload of detail to the point that we could not think at all. However, the categories are linguistic and cultural, useful only in our organizing scheme. Difficulties pop up quickly if we ignore the artificial origins and regard those categories as part of nature. As we saw in Chapter 2, lending reality to schemata means that the categories and the words that describe them seem to be a part of the natural world. Actually, of course, they express cultural values. It is not necessarily the categorizations that create difficulties— it is failing to understand that the categories are cultural shortcuts for thinking and acting, not reflections of the natural order.

Institutions of rank arise when we first categorize people, roles, social groups, or cultural items, and then arrange the categories in a hierarchy from worst to best. They become culturally set when we presume that the members of some categories are naturally entitled to more rights and privileges than others. For example, people may classify their trading partners by saying "they worship false gods so we don't marry them." Enemies are always ranked by shortcomings which reflect the values of the opposing culture. Tiv, for example, say their enemies to the south eat dog, which among Tiv implies that they are cannibals. Emphasizing that difference justifies the Tiv belief in their own natural superiority. The practice of categorizing people or roles or social groups and then ranking them along some culturally determined good-to-bad axis often leads to gross injustice.

When social scientists think about rank, they have to beware of two kinds of traps. The first trap derives from ethnocentric terms, including social science theorizing itself if it is used ethnocentrically. Probably no institutions are more

9-2. Institutions of rank arise when people are classified into a hierarchy of opportunities. Classifying is a mode of human thought; but ranking the classes by social esteem or privilege leads to the social trap of not utilizing all human talent to the maximum.

likely to be confused with the practices of one's own culture than are institutions of rank. Class in Europe or the very different class system of the United States are all too often promoted to the position of analytical systems. Very few other societies show ranking systems precisely like either the European or the American ones.

The second trap arises from doctrinal moral convictions or from social science analyses to which one becomes a convert rather than a scientific observer. A doctrinal backdrop like conservatism or liberalism or Marxism may prove even more difficult to overcome than the ethnocentric terminology. We shall follow the anthropological method of examining the data before we make theories. We shall first look briefly at the caste system of preindependence India, then at the estate system of feudal Europe, and finally at the class system today in the United States, with glances at how it differs from the class systems of Europe.

Ranking Social Groups in India: A Caste System

Preindependence India was organized under a **caste** system. Indeed, Indian caste is so uniquely complex that experts disagree about the advisability of using the word for any other known system. A caste was a corporate group composed of extended families (the word "corporate" comes from the Latin word for body). Corporate groups were overtly recognized, and usually named, by the society in which they were found, and they contained a generally understood and approved organizational structure. The boundaries of a corporate group were defined. Everyone knew who was in it and who was not.

The Indian caste was an agglomeration of extended families interrelated by marriage and kinship. The caste, or its subcastes (Klass 1980), was endogamous, which means that people marry within their own group. There was very little intercaste marriage (there are a few examples in which women of one specific caste were expected to marry men of a specific higher caste, linking the two castes together by kinship, but that practice was not general). More commonly, if intercaste marriage occurred both spouses would be rejected by their castes and, in the process, lose their kinship associations. Only a few educated city people were willing to pay that price to escape the system.

The Indian word for the caste group was *jati*. It was circumscribed spatially. The *jati* had a head man and a council called a *panchayat*. Many caste names were found in many different parts of India, particularly the Brahmins who were the top-ranking caste everywhere. However, these scattered *jati* were not organizationally linked. A Brahmin from the South who went to the North could not become a member of the local Brahmin caste in North India; he was still associated with his own caste in the South.

Each *jati* in the Indian system had its own part of a total culture. Much of that culture, but not all, was shared with at least some other castes. Each caste also had its own ideas about the total culture. For such reasons, each *jati* was commonly called a subculture.

Most *jati* were marked by an occupation. Although many of the members of the caste did not follow that occupation, they nevertheless still carried the association. A caste also had a common set of religious observances and prohibitions which distinguished it from all the other castes. All the members of the *jati* had a similar standard of living and more or less comparable tastes.

The several castes in a locality were ranked in a systematic way, based on values inherent in Hinduism. Several of these *jati*, ranked hierarchically, lived in the same village. In addition to a *panchayat* for each caste, the village and the state also had *panchayats* to control the relationships and settle disputes between members of different castes. The caste *panchayat* controlled the difficulties and disputes only among its own members. The caste *panchayat* was the guardian of the rules of the caste, and it expelled or "outcasted" members who refused to live up to these rules. Being outcasted was

Born Equal?

9-3. *A caste system is a ranking of social groups. India was the home of an elaborate caste system, although that system was outlawed soon after India's independence from the British empire in 1947. Each Indian caste was a group of extended families who shared a status stated in terms of the values of Hindu religion. On the left is the Maharajah of Mysore, probably in the late 1800s; on the right is an Untouchable woman drying cow manure for fuel.*

a serious affair in traditional India. It meant that one did not belong to any group in a society in which belonging to a group was everything. One could not marry because the only available spouse was in the group from which one had been expelled. Outcasting cut one off from one's kinfolk, and hence there was no one to call for help or for company at the time of a funeral or a wedding (Isaacs 1972). The *panchayat* could readmit members whom they had outcasted if those members paid penalties and went through a set of purification rituals. To be out of touch with one's caste is still serious, although the caste system was legally abolished soon after India's independence in 1947; caste and kinship have not yet been adequately disentangled.

The caste system is thus a ranking of *jati* according to principles codified within Hindu religion. Every *jati* is associated with one of the four *varna* (since *varna* is translated as color, Westerners of the nineteenth century proposed absurd theories about racial purity on that basis alone). The four *varna* are associated with the four strata of society set forth

in the scripture, the Rig Veda. They are the Brahmins (priests and scholars), the Kshatriya (rulers and soldiers, which was not a closed group because anyone who seized power could be regarded as Kshatriya), the Vaisha (merchants), and the Shudra (peasants, laborers, and servants) (Srinivas 1962). The first three *varna* are called twice-born—an idiom of the Hindu religion implying full human status. The Untouchables, are, as we shall see when we discuss pariahs later in this chapter, outside the *varna* system. The top and the bottom castes of the system are clear, but ranking of the middle castes varies from area to area and from time to time.

From the Western point of view, the most important characteristic of a caste system is an epiphenomenon in the Indian caste system itself. Social mobility of individuals is all but impossible within the system. Yet, the system is not as inflexible as it appears—the unit of mobility, like the unit of organization, is the group itself. This group mobility is called "Sanskritization" (Srinivas 1962). A *jati* takes on the diet and the other cultural markers of the higher castes, and then lays claim to higher status. It may, over a period of two or three generations, be successful in its claims.

One of the most important developments in the caste system during colonial times was the vast increase in the social range in which caste considerations applied. In the precolonial days, when transport and communication facilities were limited, a caste was more or less restricted to a locality in order for its organization to work. However, as education and communication facilities improved, caste members could and did travel more widely. In the process, they communicated with members of similarly placed castes over a much wider area. The low-ranking castes, in particular, began to organize more widely. Associations of like-castes had branches all over India. There was even, in some cases, a central headquarters.

And so, caste in traditional India was a system of ranked, localized, endogamous corporate groups. Each group is marked by a different subculture. Most castes were associated with an occupation. Each had different degrees of purity in the Hindu religion depending on diet and on inherited status. The social extent of the caste was almost total—there was no aspect of life it did not influence. And—important for today's Americans, who should use this fact to examine some of their own ideas—social mobility within the system took several generations.

Rank in Medieval Europe: An Estate System

All European ideas about ranking of people and social groups reflect at least to some degree the **estate** system, which was the ranking system of feudal society of medieval Europe.

In feudal Europe, an estate was defined by rights and duties concerning land. There were three primary estates: (1) the landowners or nobility; (2) the **yeomanry**, who owed the nobility certain types of allegiance, including armed service, as well as an annual percentage of their crops or animals. In return they and their families received the protection of the lord and his army (of which they were a part), limited rights in land—sites for homes and farms and often serfs to help with the work—and some rights to their harvest. At the bottom were (3) the **serfs** who had rights to protection and some rights in the land to which they were assigned.

The feudal estate system has some components in common with the Indian caste system so that the two can be confused if the words within one system are allowed to slop over into descriptions of the other. They are quite different—the problem arises from the words that have in the past been used to describe them. For example, to ask "are serfs a caste?" is not a good question because there were nothing like serfs in India and no Indian caste (*jati*) in medieval Europe.

The differences between medieval European estates and Indian castes are manifold. Whereas a caste is, as we have seen, a structured and organized group, an estate is a category of people. People are not organized into formal groups by their estate ranking. Rather, they take their position from the fact that they share legal rights and obligations specifically different from the legal rights and obligations of people in other estates; the estates were not equal before the law.

Today we also sometimes confuse serfs with slaves because the serfs could not leave the land. Yet, we add, they were better off than slaves because they could not be sold. Again, such comparison is deceptive. By the criterion of individual mobility (which Americans are quick to invoke because it is primary in their own class system) the serfs were indeed similar to slaves. But serfs had nothing else in common with slaves, as we shall see when we study slaves. It was a fact that serfs could not leave the land—it was also a fact that yeomen and nobles could not leave the land. That factor was quite different in the Japanese feudal system in which samurai (yeomen of a sort) could move from one noble to another.

European estates, however, were not organized—either as a caste was organized or any other way. The nobility knew one another and intermarried and so cooperated on the basis of kinship. But they were not otherwise organized. The primary organization was the manor, which was economically a more or less self-sufficient local group. To operate a manor, people from each of the estates were necessary.

The basic idioms of organization in the feudal system were land tenure and land rights. The exceptions were urban craftsmen and traders, organized into guilds. One's rank applied in all situations. The social *category* was ranked—noblemen, yeoman, serf. There were scores of roles within each category. However, there was no group; there were no officers and no formally structured relationships. 9-5 shows in graphic form the differences between Indian castes and feudal estates, and the difference of each from modern class systems.

Ranking Culture Traits: The American System

Westerners, especially Americans, see lack of a kinship base in their **class** society as *opportunity* for the *individual* to *move* from one class to another—all the italicized words are important in the value system. Family interests and class interests often clash, whereas in India family and caste interests were always and necessarily the same.

In the American class system, the primary criterion of rank is material culture. The possessions a person has (including, but certainly not limited to wealth) and the culture traits (What kind of car? How do you speak English? How do you spend your leisure—beer and bowling or wine and tennis?) that he or she commands, practices, demonstrates or stands for are indicative of position in the class system.

9-4. The European estate system found in Medieval times in much, but certainly not all, of Europe, was a ranking of persons on the basis of their control over land and their control of other persons by a system of contracts and agreements to provide services.

Born Equal?

Components of Ranking

	Indian caste	Medieval estate	American class	Primate dominance hierarchy
Persons	+ +	+ –	+ –	+ + +
Roles	+ +	+ + +	+ +	–
Organized groups	+ + +	–	–	+ –
Culture traits	+ +	+ –	+ + +	–
Occupation	+ +	+ +	+ –	–
Subculture	+ +	+ –	+ –	–

+ + + Dominant criterion
+ + Criterion present and culturally important
+ – Criterion present but may be culturally unimportant
– Criterion absent

9-5. *The components of ranking are used differently in different systems of ranking. Students are encouraged to investigate the classifying characteristics given here and to communicate discrepancies to the author, in care of the publisher.*

Before 1925, social scientists took very little interest in the American system of stratification—indeed, our avowed adherence to equality even convinced some people that there was no stratification. In the 1930s, American social scientists realized not only that their society ranked people but also that the ranks were divided into strata, and the process could be readily studied. European ways of looking at class offered more difficulty than clarity for studying the American systems of rank. Much of Europe inherited the estate system from the Middle Ages. Europeans, even in those areas where aristocracy is gone and where serf-like conditions have long since ceased to exist, often still think in terms of aristocracy, landowning farmers, people involved in commerce, and the working classes, in that order.

The present-day concept of the American class system was invented—at the very least, codified—by anthropologist Lloyd Warner in the 1940s. Warner discovered that the middle class was huge, that its boundaries were fuzzy, and that it was readily divided into three strata, which he categorized into upper-middle, middle-middle and lower-middle. Each stratum exhibited quite different concatenations of culture. Because this conglomerate class called itself middle, there had to be an upper and a lower class. Warner then assumed that each of them could also be divided into three groups. Terms like upper-upper or middle-lower were invented. Further tripartition could be continued if there were any point in it—indeed, the whole might facetiously be called the principle of infinite tripartition.

Today it is hard to distinguish how analytically successful the Warner tripartitions may have been because they so quickly fed back into the general culture. The nine hierarchically arranged classes that he postulated became for a while part of the daily speech. Upper-middle class and lower-middle class are probably the two most commonly cited today. We tend to confuse the upper classes with the wealthy, to lump most of what the Europeans would call a working class into the lower-middle class, and then to use the idea of a lower class for the poverty stricken or the chronically unemployable.

9-6. *The present-day American class system is a ranking based primarily on the particular culture traits that people can own, use, and manipulate. It is associated with, but not entirely determined by, wealth. The photo on the left is a private home in suburban Chicago; the one on the right shows a rural home in the southern United States.*

American society was "born free" of the estate system, whereas European societies bear the marks of it to this day. Therefore, remnants of that system do not affect American perceptions of class. Six variables are usually considered when sociologists examine the American class system: 1. Prestige, 2. Occupation, 3. Possessions, 4. Interaction within a class, 5. Class consciousness, and 6. Values orientation. Only one of these, occupations, fits neatly with anything we have found in the Indian caste system or the feudal estate system. Prestige and occupation are computed differently in the several systems: whereas in caste or estate systems the rank determines the occupation and prestige, in the American class system prestige and occupation determine the rank.

WE, THE ALIEN

Today one constantly hears that upward social mobility within the middle class is not as easy as it used to be. Even some social scientists have assumed that the upward mobility typical of the post-World War II period was normal and that its change is a sign of deterioration. Another and probably more accurate way to see the same phenomenon is that the postwar period was an unusual time of great opportunity (the value word again) which has now passed.

Because different classes in the United States are composed of people who have both different occupational experiences and knowledge and different economic incomes and purchasing power, they obviously show different specific culture—what people today call different lifestyles. People following different lifestyles have different ideas of child rearing, dating, food choices, recreation, religion. Over forty years ago, it was discovered that sexual behavior varied with class as determined by occupation and income (Kinsey 1948). Voting behavior and many other areas of life also vary widely with class, determined by these two criteria. Criminologists discovered soon after (Sutherland 1960) that criminality is a culture that is learned and that, at least before television, it was differentially known to the classes.

Therefore, seen from an anthropological viewpoint, the American class system is a system of ranked culture traits. Insofar as a person shows these culture traits he or she can be classified. American culture is a melange of subcultures and lifestyles which are only roughly separable into ranked strata. Some anthropologists have even said that there is no American culture because there is no longer anything we all have in common—an overstatement, but one that nevertheless expresses the complexity of the situation.

A hierarchy of culture traits, and therefore of classes, leads to a ranking of the people who practice or demonstrate those traits. Although some traits can be seen as the prerogatives

of the wealthy, or of the upper-middle class or lower-middle class, nevertheless the American class system is malleable and responsive to the rush of culture change.

Classes in both the United States and Europe are sometimes seen as devices for filling social positions by economic criteria. We have noted something similar for castes, which also are subcultures within a cultural system. However, castes are organized, structured social groups marked by religious function and practice; religion and ritual provide the means of filling all the roles. The various estates of medieval Europe were a politico-legal means of filling the slots, and each resulting stratum had a different culture.

Primary Criteria in Various Ranking Systems

	Group membership	Position vis-a-vis land	Individual mobility
Indian	+	–	–
Medieval estate	–	+	–
American class	–	–	+

9-7. In the Indian caste system, the primary criterion was group membership, then groups were ranked. The criterion of land ownership was of relatively little importance, and mobility (what there was) resulted from the movement of social groups, not individuals. In the Medieval estate system, the primary criterion was one's position vis-a-vis the land. One was either an owner, or else had some rights that derived from the owner, or else worked it but had no rights in it. There was little or no individual mobility for anyone. In the American class system, people's own primary characteristic is individual mobility. Since land can be bought and sold, it follows the criterion of mobility.

Comparison with preindependence India highlights two important aspects of present-day United States culture. The first difference is that in India culture was ascribed, whereas in the United States (and to an increasing degree in post-independence India) it is selected and achieved by the person. If Americans want to change classes, they must first learn the culture of the group they are moving into. After that they can, with greater (especially if they change communities) or lesser ease, move into that class and be that class. Failure to learn the culture adequately before the move (or, sometimes, failure to abandon some aspects of an ethnic culture) leads to class anomalies such as the *nouveau riche*. The second difference is that the subcultures of caste India were unified into a single simplistic system—the key was religion. In the United States, on the other hand, there is no central key (although some people claim, over-simplistically, that money or race provide such a key).

9-8. *Karl Marx saw the class system of Europe as a ranking system of the positions that persons or groups or categories held in relation to the total system of production of goods and services.*

One can, thus, look at ranking as a series of necessary positions in a social system that must be filled and that there are several ways of getting people into those positions. One can do it by fiat or tradition; one can do it by market mechanisms or some other mechanism. The result can be seen as stratification or ranking.

SERVITUDE

A slave system has little in common with either a class system or a caste system, although both affect it profoundly. It is, rather, based on different assumptions and uses different principles of social organization. A slave relationship exists when one person has legal rights in another *if* the rights are not derived from kinship, citizenship, or contractual obligation (all three of which can also establish legal rights in another person). Because they are analogous to property, it is traditional to discuss slaves as chattels. Conversely, the rights of the slave in the master, although they may be few

and usually not honored, are likewise nonkinship, noncontractual, but nevertheless legal. They can be exercised against only one master and only by his recognized slave.

In the modern West, all our legal rights derive from the principles of kinship, citizenship, or contract. Because we do not recognize property rights in other people, we might mistakenly regard a slave population as the bottom tier of a stratification system. But slavery is far more complicated than that.

Slaves

Slaves are rare in hunting and gathering societies. No more than 3 percent of the recorded examples of hunters and gatherers had slaves. Those who did were groups like the Native Americans of the Northwest Coast who, while nominally gatherers and hunters, lived in an area so rich in food resources that they could form large local groups. The figure rises to 43 percent of societies that used advanced

9-9. *In a servile system, one person can have property rights in another. Slaves are persons who have been stripped of their kinship and citizenship ties and have then been attached to social groups by the mechanism of property ownership or something close to it. This stereograph, taken in South Carolina, shows women and children in front of a plantation cabin in the American South. It had to be posed because the exposure took a while. Note the young woman at the right who has a book.*

were often manumitted, the system itself was stable and considered part of the natural order. Indeed the classical Greek language was extraordinarily rich in words distinguishing various kinds of slaves (Finley 1960), and, except in the political arena, there were few activities in Greek society that were not sometimes performed by slaves. They could not hold office, but they were often policemen or prison attendants; they could not participate in judicial bodies, although they were often clerks or secretaries to those bodies. Their assigned tasks did not distinguish them from free persons, who did all of the same jobs, sometimes side by side with the slaves. The Greeks did not underline the slave status by defining which work was done by slaves, but rather by noting who profited from the work—the masters, not the slaves themselves.

Slaves performed a significant part of the agriculture and mining work in ancient Greece. The silver mines of Athens at one time had as many as thirty thousand slaves in them. Alongside their masters, slaves worked at handicrafts and manufacturing. There may have been as many a 100,000 slaves in Athens at the peak periods (Finley 1960); about 40 B.C., slaves made up about a third of the population. Rome was riddled with slavery. Slavery also appeared in India and in China.

At least four aspects of servile relationships can be examined as questions. (1) How does slavery impact the family

9-10. Every major civilization (with the possible exception of Japan) went through an historical period in which a major form of organization for production and for many other purposes was some form of slavery. This painting shows forced labor in Siberia in 1889—a practice that the Russian imperial government, and then the Soviet government, continued almost until our own day. Thousands of convicts died in the mines and camps of Siberia.

agriculture and shoots to a startling 78 percent of pastoral societies (Goody 1980).

The claim is often made that the world has never seen a major advanced civilization that did not pass through a period of slavery (although I cannot find such a period for Japan). Slave society is one of the theoretical stages of the Marxist analysis of the history of society. Slavery was a recognized institution by the time written records start. The earliest historical record of slavery—in Sumeria—was the earliest historical record of anything. Classical Greek civilization took slave labor absolutely for granted. At no time did the ancient Greeks question the institution. Although individual slaves

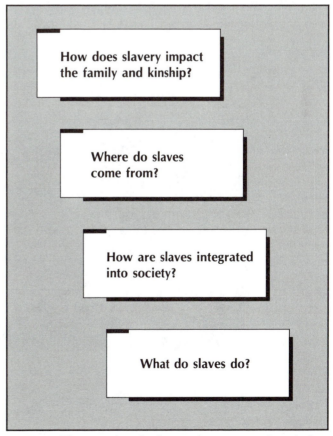

9-11. There are four fundamental questions to be asked about slavery systems.

How does slavery impact the family and kinship?

Where do slaves come from?

How are slaves integrated into society?

What do slaves do?

and kinship? (2) Where did slaves come from? People had to get slaves from somewhere without unduly unsettling their own society. (3) How were slaves integrated into society? Was the range of their servitude total or could it be limited? (4) What did slaves do?

Slavery is often masked by rank systems such as class or caste in the societies in which it occurs. Actually, it coexists with them. All slavery systems are marked by the values of the social structure of which they are a part.

Servile relationships are not merely *non*kinship as are relationships based on contract or those established by rank. They are, rather, actively antikinship inasmuch as a slave can have no kinfolk and may be connected into kinship groups not by kinship but by ownership criteria. The only evident kinship relationship of slaves was the mother-child (except as noted below). Even that relationship could be broken as soon as the child was adult. A good master in the American slave system was one who did not break up the nuclear families of his slaves for whim or profit, but he had a legal right to do so—and many did.

The primary source of slaves in most societies was capture in warfare or slave raids. In many societies, female captives were taken into their captors' groups as wives. Male captives were either killed or sacrificed outright or else attached as workers to existing families or domestic groups.

In some societies, a person, almost always a man, could be sold by his kinship group. Women of questionable character could usually be displaced through marriage, but men of questionable character had to be "unkinned." In much of traditional Africa, for example, the kinship group could agree to turn a man into a nonkinsman through the performance of a simple ritual. After the ritual, he had absolutely no rights. In societies in which the major determinant of position was kinship affiliation, he necessarily became either an exile, a hermit or a slave.

Some societies sell children, especially in hard times. Although this practice was widespread throughout the world, it grew to a vast enterprise in pre-Communist China, particularly southern China. Indeed, one authority states that "until the foundation of the People's Republic in 1949 China had one of the largest and most comprehensive markets for the exchange of human beings in the world" (Watson 1980).

The fate of these children was different for boys than for girls. Elite Chinese lineages, if they found themselves without heirs, could buy an heir. If the purchased boy actually inherited, he of course ceased to be a slave. Other males became slaves. Girls bought by elite families were either slaves who would eventually marry out, or else they became "little wives" or concubines. Chattel slavery in China was abolished in the last few years of Manchu rule (in the early part of the twentieth century) but continued illegally until the Communists came to power in 1949. A few slaves were still exchanged, in great secrecy, as late as 1980. The market in people was one of the institutions of ancient Chinese society that persisted until very recently.

Still another way to become a slave was to be born into the position. Laws concerning this matter differed widely in different societies. In China, the child of a slave woman or

9-12. *Slaves were often attached to households, including the households of high officials and rulers. They were attached by property-type legal bonds to the master. Female slaves could be used as concubines. Since slaves were not allowed to participate in kinship groups (other than the matricentric family), they got little support from kinfolk. Within their households or comparable small groups, slaves could achieve a very high status at the same time that their overall status in society remained low. This lithograph shows George Washington on his Virginia plantation, with slaves in the background. He disapproved of slavery, but did not free his slaves.*

a concubine was, if acknowledged by a free father, a legitimate child and was absolutely free. The child of a male slave, however, was a slave in perpetuity. In the American South, the position of the mother determined the status of her child—if she was a slave, the child was a slave. In some places (including the American South) the slave population was purposefully bred (sometimes with white men) to increase the number of slaves.

Complementary to the slave's kinlessness is his or her immediate legal dependence on the master. The male slave is his master's man in much the same sense that a son is his father's man. Female slaves occasionally enter the kinship system and thus have a somewhat different position. With a few exceptions, a slave cannot change masters, but he or she can be readily sold. For this reason, slaves were considered trustworthy—they had no place to go if they engaged in double-dealing with their masters. Slaves were more to be trusted than contractual partners, and certainly more to be trusted than employees!

In some societies, slaves often enjoyed very high status within the domestic group of their master or within the political group if their master was a chief or king. Greek and Roman slaves could rise to great heights of eminence and power within the families of their masters. Slaves, like other members of society, occupy two hierarchal positions: one within the overall social structure, the other within a smaller community of their master's family. Within the total social structure, the rank of a slave is low. Within limited structures, the slave's position may be very high. Thus, the range of inequality in slavery turns out to be similar to that found in institutions of rank.

Slavery everywhere reflects the rest of the social structure. One instructive case is India where slavery had to accommodate itself to the caste system. High caste slaveowners had to have ritually pure slaves for their households. This meant that those from the impure castes could only do agricultural work for rich landowners or corvée work for the government—for high caste persons to have physical contact with the impure castes would pollute them. Slaves from the higher castes, however, could be turned into domestic slaves. The problem of range of status thus took an interesting turn. A slave's ritual status was unaffected by being a slave. Domestic slaves were treated like members of the household; owners provided for them as long as they could work, took care of them when they were ill or old, and paid for their funerals. Although their status was low, their degree of security was high. Marriages could take place between free and slave as long as the caste memberships were right. When the British investigated the subject of slavery in India in the late eighteenth and early nineteenth centuries they came to the conclusion that its most important purpose was bestowing prestige. A family took its prestige from the number of its dependents, and slaves raised the number.

Africa was a home of slavery long before European traders became involved. Much African slavery was household slavery, but plantation slavery existed in a few areas of coastal West Africa. The trade of African slaves across the Sahara to Europe and from East African ports to the Arab countries and Persia was a long-standing operation. European traders extended this trade into one of the largest and most extensive slave systems the world has ever known. Africans were forcibly transported to South America, the Caribbean, and the Southern states of the United States. The latter experience is what most Americans understand about the subject of slavery.

Pawns

Pawns were almost as important as slaves in many places. The best examples come from Africa. During the time that I was working among the Tiv between 1949 and 1953, debtors sometimes sent a child to work for their lenders until such time as the debt was paid. The child never ceased to be a member of his or her kinship group, and never changed any allegiances. I know one case in which the original debt was paid with the bridewealth received for the pawn when she married.

9-13. Pawning is a social institution in which one can pledge one's self or one's dependents to work for another until a debt is repaid. It differs from slavery because it is temporary and because the pawn's original kinship ties are not broken. Clients are groups who have put themselves into permanent bondage to other groups, usually as a means of securing the use of adequate tools of production.

It was also possible, Tiv told me, for a man to put himself forward as a pawn, but it happened rarely. This kind of servile institution is unlike slavery because no one is ever unkinned. It is also unlike the indentured servants that were brought to the American colonies—indentured servants had signed contracts to work for a certain number of years in return for their passage and sometimes for being outfitted with farm tools and animals at the end of their period of **indenture**. Many Americans, both black and white, have ancestors who came to this country as bondsmen, or indentured servants, and successfully worked out their bonds.

Clientage

One other type of servitude should be mentioned: an entire social group may be servile to another social group. The usual term, taken from European feudalism, is clientage. One of the clearest examples comes from the Bedouin Arabs of Cyrenaica just after World War II. Some of the Bedouin kinship groups were "owners of the land" and considered themselves to be descendants of the prophet. Others had no pastureland or wells of their own and could not claim such descent. Those without resources became clients and attached themselves to the kinship groups descended from the prophet. In exchange for grazing rights and water, they offered specific service (Evans-Pritchard 1949).

An interesting case of clientage is reported from the Northwest Coast of North America in the early twentieth century. In this area, some clans had lost, or had never had, the boats and fishing tackle that were basic to the production of livelihood. They therefore attached themselves in quasi-permanent bondage to groups who did own the means of production in order to use those resources under certain fixed and limited circumstances.

PARIAHS

One further type of inequality must be considered, the **pariah**. Pariah is an Indian word for an unowned scavenger dog. It is applied, in analogy, to the Untouchables in India and to all outcastes. Pariahs are outsiders without being foreigners. They are neither part of an accepted rank system nor occupants of servile positions. In the ranking system, a pariah group is denied all the qualities that would make its members eligible for any rank at all. It thus appears to some outsiders that they are at the bottom of the system. From the point of view of the social system as a whole, however, the pariahs occupy an integral position because their activities are essential to the operation of the culture.

9-14. Pariahs are outcastes who are said not to be ranked at all, in whatever ranking system the society uses. They do society's dirty work; in fact, they are usually essential to the continued functioning of society.

The Eta of Japan were an especially interesting pariah group because racially and culturally they did not differ from other Japanese (DeVos and Wagatsuma 1967). They provided the butchers, tanners, and candlemakers for the entire society. Those jobs were considered polluting and dirty, in part because people who did them handled dead animals. Their only relationship with the in-group was an economic one. Aside from that, they were considered not to exist. Although the Eta now have been accorded full political rights, they nevertheless have not completely lost their pariah status.

The Untouchables of India can be seen as occupying a similar position: they did necessary jobs such as shoemaking, removing the carcasses of dead animals, and cleaning up the community. But their range of interaction with other members of the community was minimal. They did not have a *varna*, and, like the Eta, were defined as nonexistent.

Slaves are not pariahs. They are an element of the institutions of the societies in which they live. Pariahs are, by definition, kept outside the recognized major institutions of the social structure, in spite of their economic importance.

ATTITUDES THAT CREATE INEQUALITY

Although **race** and ethnicity ought, by rational criteria, to have no place in a chapter on inequality, they must be included because both are used to create inequality. Gender differences also lead to distinctions that can be interpreted as inequality, even though the criteria for judging gender inequality and its disabilities vary from one culture to another.

9-15. Race and ethnicity are often used as criteria for ranking. The two should not be confused. Ethnicity uses culture as a device for distinguishing people.

In many of the world's societies, social evaluations of differences in physical type, differences in the jobs assigned to one gender or the other, and differences in ethnic culture have been the basis for discrimination and prejudice as well as for ranking and even slavery.

Race and Racism

Four problems must be tackled here:

(1) Genetic, heritable differences found in various groups of human beings. At one time, this was considered the basis for a science; it no longer is.
(2) Cultural assessments of these differences. This problem is about stereotypes.
(3) Social groups and categories that use either the differences or the assessments or both as criteria of admission. Social inequality is the central issue here.
(4) Doctrines that seek to maintain or change the political status quo on the basis of these groups or categories. This type of action is racism.

Genetic physical differences among peoples exist. Social problems between classes and culture groups made up of some of these peoples exist. The correct question is: do race and racism provide a sensible way to connect the two? Every year the answer becomes a more resounding "No."

For decades physical anthropologists attempted, by more or less scientific methods, to classify the varieties of humankind into definite groups, the so-called races. They were wholly unable to agree on results until they arrived at a single proposition. Just as a variety of finches resulted from small interbreeding groups in the isolated Galapagos Islands, geographically isolated human groups may begin to diverge in physical type from other isolated groups. Because the total human population was not in touch with one another, smaller gene pools became specialized. When that degree of geographical isolation was reduced, the "separate" races began to mingle.

One of the real booboos—no more genteel word will do— made by our founding ancestors in physical anthropology was the premise that in the beginning there were "pure" races. As a poet once put it, the different races were different thoughts of God. They thought, mistakenly, that everybody who wasn't of a "pure" race must be a "mixture," and thus impure. The search for racial purity was on, but nobody ever found it.

Today, as geneticists approach the completion of the human gene map, the science of genetics has found no use for a criterion of race. Races are, in the present state of development of genetics at least, irrelevant. This leads to important social consequences: the validity of any system of classification depends utterly on the problem it was designed to solve. We know that there are genetic differences among geographical populations; those differences have an historical explanation. We know that some diseases, such as sickle-cell anemia and Tay-Sachs disease, are limited to some genetic populations. However, the only justification for any system of classification is that it simplifies the overwhelming complexity of reality in some useful way. The important question, therefore, is not "Do races exist?" but rather "What problem is the classification of races designed to solve?"

Race is a cultural classification designed to deal with social problems, not a scientific classification in genetics or any other subject. Even forensic anthropologists—physical anthropologists who, using the remains of deceased persons, determine sex, age, race and perhaps some other characteristics, usually for the courts—now say that race is a social identifying tag, and therefore important in identifying victims of crime within a culture-bound society, but that it does not provide the basis for a science of humankind (Sauer 1988). We can, if it is relevant to a suitable problem, define races and study them ethnographically or historically, but we cannot define them genetically. Therefore, we have to proceed to racism.

Racism is like religion: it must be evaluated "by its fruits, by its votaries, and by its ulterior purposes" (Benedict 1940). Racism was never a scourge in Greece or Rome, although those peoples noted the physical differences among populations in their art. In the Middle Ages the criterion for hatred of one group by another was religion, not race, and among some peoples that is still true. Racism in the West grew up after the years of European exploration that began about A.D. 1400.

When the Spanish and Portuguese came to the Caribbean and Brazil, they tried to enslave the Native Americans they encountered, who promptly died. They turned to Africa, since the Iberian peninsula (especially when it was part of the Arab world) traditionally had slaves, many of whom were African. The first Africans in the North American colonies were indentured servants, like many Europeans who came at the same time. In the late 1600s and early 1700s, masters began to abrogate their agreements with the Africans and kept them indentured even after they had worked out the terms of their original contracts.

Racism in Europe, on the other hand, grew out of conflict

9-16. *Race can be regarded as a cultural classification of people derived from accepted ways of observing and evaluating heritable physical characteristics. Race is not part of any recognized present-day science. Racism is a social practice of withholding civil and human rights from some people on the basis of race. Racism is still common throughout much of the world. In the United States freed slaves were, in the second half of the nineteenth century, systematically turned into a pariah group. Beginning with the Civil Rights movements of the 1950s, black Americans, joined by many white Americans, set out to get all laws based on race taken off the books. One of their early victories was the integration of buses. This picture, taken in 1956 in Alabama, shows blacks daring to sit in the front of the bus from which they were legally barred—the law said they had to stand in back. Their efforts have been successful. The laws have been removed, but the struggle for full equality continues.*

among the classes. Until well into the nineteenth century, "race" in Europe referred primarily to physical differences among so-called Aryan, Alpine, and Mediterranean "sub-races" (so to speak) of Caucasians rather than among the Caucasoid, Mongoloid, and Negroid "races." (In America race has always referred to the recognized "primary races"—white, black, brown, red, and yellow.)

Racism didn't get going full speed until the 1850s. DeGobineau's *Essay on the Inequality of the Human Races*, the sourcebook on racism, was published in the same decade as Darwin's *Origin of Species*. Racism became associated with nationalism only when DeGobineau's and Darwin's successors added the idea of the survival of the fittest to racist doctrine—an association that Darwin himself explicitly rejected. In the late nineteenth century, this position led physical anthropologists to perfect techniques for measuring people, especially their skulls, to determine their race. When

Born Equal?

anthropologist Ruth Benedict compared Nazi race policy with the Spanish Inquisition's policy on religion, she made the famous statement, "in order to understand race persecution, we do not need to investigate race; we need to investigate persecution. Persecution was an old, old story before racism was thought of" (Benedict 1940).

In North America the idea of race had been perverted so as to create a pariah situation for freed slaves when the institution of slavery was abolished. During the Nazi era, the idea of racial purity was perverted to turn the pariah status of the Jews into the horrors of genocide.

 The racist situation in the United States has often, and to little advantage, been analyzed as a caste system on the grounds that the categories created were endogamous, that movement among them was restricted, and that one ranked far higher than the others. In my opinion, to talk about Black and White castes in the United States may once have been instructive but is no longer valid. It is better to say that we once had a racially defined cultural category of slaves. When they were emancipated at the end of the Civil War, there was no category for them. Since most Whites were unwilling to share their own status with slaves, the Blacks were forced into the situation of pariahs. They fought hard to win the legal civil rights that were finally granted to them in *Brown vs. Board of Education* in the 1950s. Once the external legal rights were secured, Blacks could focus inward.

The "Black Is Beautiful" movement of the 1960s highlighted the ethnicity of blacks as a group within American culture. This transformation in cultural perception gave the Black middle class better opportunities. Unfortunately, vestiges of the earlier pariah status still haunt many Blacks today, despite both legal and social progress.

WE, THE ALIEN

Gender and Sexism

The most widespread inequality in the modern world is that based on gender. Some of it—like that associated with repayment for work and that associated with violence, is brutal. But some of it, as we shall see, is far more subtle. In Chapter 6, we investigated the way in which the cultural evolution of the division of labor came to be more and more biased against women, and the results and implications of that prejudice today. 9-17 summarizes the material we have covered on the ways that subsistence types, mode of residence,

sexual division of labor, control of resources and kinship groups, particularly descent group, all feed into determining status based on gender.

The fact that work everywhere is divided into men's work and women's work is probably not the source of the problem. The problem arises, rather, from the fact that the work of one sex, always men, is valued more highly than that of women. 9-18 reviews summarily the material on division of labor and inequality of the sexes. Another instance of the inequality between women and men in our society is that working women do a "second shift" (Hochschild 1989). That is to say, large numbers of women not only work full time at market-oriented jobs, for pay, but also have the child care and the maintenance work of the household to do when they get home. Combining work at a paid job and work around the house, women work an average fifteen hours a week more than men in the United States. That means an extra month of workdays a year. This fact emerges because so many men—and a lot of women—think that child care and housework are women's work. Even when men help, they seldom take full responsibility. They are also likely to whittle down their demands by redefining what has to be done. Women too whittle down what has to be done in the house by such redefinition, but apparently not as far. Differences of opinion between men and women about who should do what and what has to be done is a fertile source of marital difficulty.

The second shift is not just an American problem. Over 80 percent of Soviet women work outside the home and still do the second shift. As one expert put it, "the image of the working father is still largely missing, and with it the very issue of sharing" (Hochschild 1989).

Another obvious and overt issue involved with gender relations in Western, particularly American, society has become evident in recent years: women, like children, are victims of male violence. The problem has long existed and is only now receiving the attention it has long deserved. There have been many attempts to explain violent behavior of men toward women and children. The most compelling reason is that they can get away with violent behavior in the family that they could not get away with in any other social situation. In the words of one set of experts, "people hit family members because they can" (Gelles and Strauss 1988). Although all fifty American states have laws against child abuse and most have laws against spouse abuse, nevertheless both children and spouses (usually but not always wives) are often abused.

Americans, both men and women, are abusive toward their children. Spanking is said to work in the sense that the child will stop doing what the adult wants him or her to stop. The effect of long-term corporal punishment is not adequately studied. In Sweden, it is against the law to spank a child. The American response to that piece of information is, "What do they do to you if you break that law?" The answer is—nothing. But the law brought the situation to general awareness and Swedes today disapprove of corporal punishment.

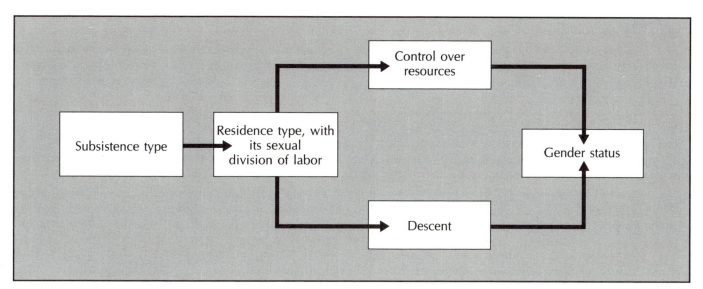

9-17. *Relationships among subsistence, gender, descent patterns, and division of labor (adapted from Nielsen 1990).*

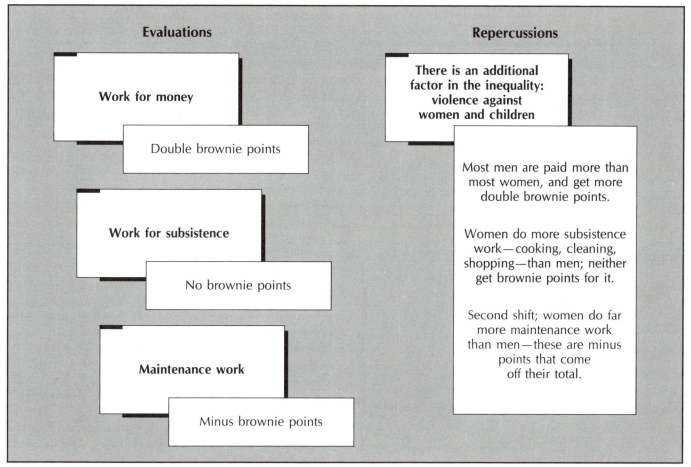

9-18. *Division of Labor and Equality of the Sexes.*

There is a tendency for Americans to see family violence as alien to themselves— as something other people do. "While people are quite willing to attribute violence to mentally disturbed, unbalanced people, they are unwilling to see the violent home as an outgrowth of the very structure of our society and family. . . . We tend to think of abusers as people other than us. . . . [that] victims are helpless, defenseless innocents" (Gelles and Strauss 1988). We invent myths to explain abuse—drunkenness is a common myth in spite of the fact that only 18 percent of the abusers tested were legally drunk. We tell ourselves, against all the evidence, that violence and love are incompatible. Yet we know that, like Siamese fighting fish, some human beings confuse sex and aggression. It would seem that, although family violence can occur at any level of society, it most commonly occurs when spouses cannot communicate with one another verbally and when one or both cannot live up to social and personal demands and responsibilities.

WE, THE ALIEN

Family violence in Western society is associated with the fact that Americans and Europeans live privately in houses often secluded from other members of society. Privacy hides the abusive behavior from others. The women's movement has fought to make the problem of family violence public. Whether family violence is increasing we do not know. We can be sure, however, that as long as it remains a public issue, the American family will be better off than it was when violence was hidden. Many of the aspects of inequality between the sexes are far more subtle. Here is one woman's statement of the problem as she perceived it:

In order for a female to be taken into the club, which is necessary in order to get cases and to get trained, you have to become a member. I decided that I would go along because I wanted to get where I wanted to be. I really wanted to be a neurosurgeon. I thought I could be a good neurosurgeon. Had I made an issue of some of the [sexist] things that were happening during the time that I was a resident, I wouldn't have gotten where I am.

Frances Conley (1991)

THEY SAID IT

9-19. Gender is today perceived as the most pervasive criterion used to maintain inequality. Sexism is the social practice of withholding esteem, remuneration, and civil rights from some persons on the basis of their sex. People of different cultures have vastly different ideas about the nature of female and male, not to mention masculinity and femininity—hence, different evaluations of gender, and different manifestations of sexism.

Cultural ideas about just what constitutes gender inequality differ. Many American women see the veils and restricted mobility of Arabic women and think themselves better off. Many Arabic women, on the other hand, look at the violence directed against American women and at the lack of ownership by American women of businesses that serve other women—and pronounce themselves better off.

Whereas most tribal peoples and many of those in foreign civilizations still see men and women living in different worlds, our avowed ideal of equality for all leads us to say that men and women should share the same basic rights. Although many inequalities still exist, they are coming under increasing scrutiny.

Ethnicity and Ethnocentrism

Ethnicity and race must not be confused. Ethnicity is about distinctions made on the basis of culture, whereas race concerns distinctions (albeit, cultural) made on the basis of inherited physical characteristics. They have one thing in common: both are ascribed on the basis of birth. Each of us is born into a family with a specific gene pool, and practicing a certain ethnic culture. If one is of mixed African and European parentage, as many Americans are, one is assigned a Black ethnic identity in the United States. Liberia, when it was founded by former slaves from America, went the other way. In Liberia to this day, if a person is of mixed parentage he or she is assigned a White identity. In the United States, people are assigned to ethnic groups primarily on the basis of their parents' ethnicity. Ann Landers's newspaper column included a letter from a woman saying she was Italian-American and her husband was Polish-American. The husband claimed their kids were Polish-American. She did not want her Italian heritage to be forgotten. She asked Landers whether it was true that the children were Polish-American. Ann Landers avoided the real issue by saying that the children were Americans.

Three main ideas are to be found in almost all definitions of an ethnic group or category: (1) real or ascribed common origins, (2) a sense of distinctiveness, and (3) the presence of at least one other ethnic category, because a single individual or group cannot be ethnic. To be an ethnic, you need somebody else to be ethnic in contrast to (Hicks in Hicks and Leis 1977).

Ethnics may or may not be organized into social groups. Rather, individuals are members of ethnically defined categories. Many systems for coordinating ethnic categories or groups have been reported. Among the most interesting are those reported for the Ottoman Empire of Turkey in which different ethnic groups had clear economic positions and even monopolies on some production; the modern day Soviet Union where most ethnic groups are associated with the governments of the member republics; the modern day United States where ethnic categories are not by and large geographically separated (although some segregated neighborhoods do exist).

9-20. *Systems of inequality that* limit *people's lives are ultimately self-defeating because people struggle to overthrow them at every opportunity. Slavery and Indian caste have both been outlawed. The criteria for class in capitalist societies seriously limits the lives of some people in matters like employment and adequate education. Some people say that capitalist systems are working toward "optional inequality" in which people choose their own limitations, but capitalism has yet to find mechanisms for equalizing opportunity and, hence, using all human capacities to the best advantage. These South Africans are reading a newspaper report of a clash between black miners and white police. As the headline reports, eleven of the miners were killed.*

In the United States, the culture of any ethnic group or category is not merely the culture inherited from their forebears. Although remnants of that ancestral culture may remain, the culture is created anew as its members face new contexts. It is the continuity of heritage and name that links people to their past history, not necessarily the performance of specific traditions. Their newly acquired characteristics mark them off from other groups as much as did the original culture. Thus, an American ethnic group is first and foremost an interest group. The groups and categories are in a constant state of flux. Indeed, they are created and recreated as their interests and their cultures change.

The boundaries between ethnic categories are at least as important as the cultural markers within them (Barth 1969). A boundary between such categories may be maintained for long periods, in spite of great changes in the cultures on either side of the boundary. The boundary may last through vast historical changes in the culture, or it may be cultural so that an individual can cross it by changing his or her behavior. For example, the definition of an "Indian" in American society is so vague that national and state commissions have been appointed to study the problem. Yet, long after cultural distinctions are gone, the boundary may be drawn—some people emphasize an Indian ancestor and may even label themselves "Native American" when they have never participated in the ways and customs that characterize today's Native American cultures. In another, more somber example, millions of educated Jews had been culturally assimilated into the nations of Europe. Then, as the 1930s progressed, the world learned to its horror that the bureaucracies of the National Socialist government in Germany defined the boundaries—and therefore the existence of the Jewish ethnic group—far more stringently than their self-definitions and lifestyles did.

 Americans have a strange and irrational system in that they claim that some citizens belong to ethnic groups but others do not. New England Yankees, California WASPs, and so-called Middle Americans are usually not called ethnics, even when they know what many of them call their nationalities. Americans thus use the word "American" to mean both a genus and one of its species. At the genus level, all citizens are Americans. At the species level, some are hyphenated Americans, while others are just plain Americans. An ethnic system that does not include everybody seems irrational and certainly is unlike the practice of most other peoples. In other societies, if anybody is ethnic, everybody is.

Another way to look at this is that all Americans live in a two-story culture. One level comprises the political and economic story—all Americans either have equal rights or are struggling to get them. The other level encompasses the home and community. Many Americans are struggling equally hard to maintain what they see as their cultural identities and to make the world safe for differences.

WE, THE ALIEN

Ethnicity and class cannot be reduced to one another any more than class and caste can be reduced to one another. India can be considered to have all three: class, caste and ethnicity. Class emerges among the Westernized or the educated groups, but is still vastly affected by ideas of caste. Each caste can be seen as an endogamous, bounded, cultural group resembling an ethnic group in that membership is by assignment.

Any person may have more than one ethnic identity, and may use them differently depending on context. "People often have a repertoire of ethnic attributes from which they can select the ones most suitable to a given situation" (Hicks in Hicks and Leis 1977). It is easiest to claim multiethnicity if you can be sure that your companions who validate one of your ethnicities do not overlap with those who validate another of your ethnicities (Nagata 1974).

Ethnicity and race have long been the focus of government policy in the United States, where they often mean minorities vs. the dominant groups.

The world has come a long way toward creating a society that is free of institutions of servitude. Separating the idea of a person's work from the person was a giant step. The job is not finished, especially for women, but the idea has become a commanding one. A worldwide attack has been launched against pariah institutions. Discrimination is illegal in Japan, India and the United States. The process of eliminating pariahism is not yet as far along as the process of eliminating slavery. It may be more difficult because there is no simple legal machinery for dealing with the remnants of it. The status has been abolished, but feelings and ingrained attitudes take longer to change. With vigilance, race may become irrelevant in more and more situations; we may be able to insure that fewer and fewer ethnicities are disadvantaged. Eventually, we may be able to equalize the cultural valuations of, and opportunities for, women and men.

We have not been able—and may never be able—to create a society that has no institutions of rank. Rank emerged with the earliest division of labor by specialty. No one has yet found a way to abolish rank in large-scale societies, but perhaps we are merely in a similar position to Aristotle who saw no way that slavery could be abolished. What we must do for now is to achieve a society in which there is justice and civil rights for all, even as rank persists. The goal of eliminating poverty is often confused with the goal of creating a rank-free society. The first is doable. The second probably is not.

BEYOND INEQUALITY?

Would it be possible, instead of trying to get rid of rank, to tame it so that we can maintain its social advantages but get rid of its injustices and disadvantages?

The four advantages that high rank bestow are power, prestige, property, and pleasure. We have referred to them as "the four Ps" (Van der Elst 1990). Modern American

9-21. *Some components of inequality:*
   Power
   Prestige
   Property
   Pleasure

society tends to lump the four Ps all together. People who have one usually have all the others. Movie stars or rock musicians have more property than the rest of us; they live in immense and beautiful homes, drive big cars, and wear expensive clothes. We like to think that they get more pleasures—fine food and drink, good sex, chances to travel widely. They have immense prestige—indeed, a professor cannot help noting that their ghost-written books sell whether the books are any good or not.

Yet, some Americans take a different attitude to the four Ps. They don't even want to "have it all." Artists, for example, frequently live lives that are rich in pleasure but poor in property. Most professors have little in the way of property, but they may enjoy their work to the point that they don't even notice what they lack. A few professors, over time, achieve as much power as Elvis Presley in changing people's ideas and altering their tastes.

The most harmful aspect of inequality is that many individual persons are not allowed to develop their talents fully. *That* is where the difficulty lies. Why can't we allow people to choose the ways they want to be unequal? Many people would elect security and a modest happiness. There are desirable qualities for which some people would be willing to sacrifice some or all of the four Ps. One is solitude. Solitude is a valued rarity in the modern world. Yet it is essential if one is to develop artistic talents, including writing.

CONCLUDING THOUGHTS

In a society with a just government and good economic opportunities, our struggles may not be so much against inequality as against systematic barriers to opportunity. We can learn to settle for not being *able* to do something. Not being *allowed* to try is the enemy. Perhaps the solution to the problem of rank is at hand. Perhaps institutions that allow us to choose—that sanction giving up ambitions to be high-ranking in return for other advantages—will help solve the problem. We are only beginning to examine the freedom that we might have if we could forget about rank.

BUZZWORDS

caste a hierarchy of social groups. The most typical example is the caste system of preindependence India. There, social groups were kinship groups and rank was based on principles of purity held by Hindus. Using the word in other contexts almost always results in oversimplification that blurs distinctions that could be made more effectively.

class a group of people who share cultural characteristics and have approximately the same rank in society.

estate one of the basic ranks in European feudal systems. (The word also has many other meanings, but this is the technical meaning of the term as used in this chapter.)

ethnicity identity with or membership in a particular cultural group all of whose members share language, beliefs, customs, values and identity.

indenture a contract by which one is bound to work for someone else. Thus, an indentured servant is one who has signed a contract to work for another until such time as the stipulations of the contract have been achieved.

pariah a person (in some cultures, the word is also applied to animals) who is despised and a social outcast.

pawn to leave property, or a dependent person, with another as security that a debt will be repaid.

race a category of plants or animals (including persons) who share common descent, as marked by common physical characteristics.

serf a person of the lowest rank in European feudal systems. These people were sometimes considered to be a part of the land; on those rare occasions when land was sold, the serfs passed to the new owner as part of the land. They are not to be confused with slaves.

slave a person who is the property of another.

yeoman in the European feudal system, an attendant in a noble household, or a person who has rights to land that are subordinate to those rights in the same land held by the lord.

MEANING
IV

There are two ways to approach the pursuit of happiness as well as to deal with the stresses of everyday life. One of these is narcotic. That means searching for ways to dull the mind so that it is momentarily stilled in its search for meaning. It can be done with drugs; it can be done with apathy.

The second way is creativity. This means to embrace the search for meaning: to find meaning and significance in the everyday works of nature and culture that surround us, then to shape that meaning into the life we must lead. Art, philosophy, science, religion—all are creative means of pursuing happiness, fighting boredom and nihilism, enhancing culture.

One's culture provides the basic rules from which creativity can take off—within which it can flourish. Without the rules of the cultural base, creativity has nothing to work with. But we are supplied only with the basic rules. After that, each person is on her or his own, either to accept the rules, or to bend them—with a few highly creative people, perhaps even to break them.

Within whatever limitations there are, you can either pursue meaning or you can drop out. The search for meaning is the most human of all human characteristics: the realm of pure culture.

Books to Change Your Life   *Martha C. Ward*

Benedict, Ruth

1934 *Patterns of Culture*. New York: New American Library. Reissued 1973 by Houghton Mifflin Co., Boston. This is one of the all-time classics in anthropology. It brings exotic cultures to life and makes you understand them from the inside out. Benedict's use of the philosophy of Nietzsche has been questioned by many. Never mind—you will find the examples illuminating.

Campbell, Joseph

1949 *The Hero with a Thousand Faces*. New York: Pantheon.

1959-1968 *The Masks of God, Vols. 1-4*. New York: Viking Press (Penguin USA).

1988 *The Power of Myth* (a book accompanying a TV series Campbell did with Bill Moyers; illustrated). New York: Doubleday & Co., Inc. Reissued 1991 by Anchor Books (non-illustrated), New York.

Great storytellers are honored in every society. Campbell uses modern media to recount ancient tales that give meaning and texture to human life. The fact that so many people read and quote Campbell demonstrates the power of story and myth to explain and answer the Big Questions.

Castaneda, Carlos

1971 *A Separate Reality*. New York: Simon & Schuster.

1971 *The Teachings of Don Juan*. Berkeley, CA: University of California Press.

1984 *The Fire Within*. New York: Simon & Schuster.

We have listed only three of these books—there are others; indeed, Casteneda has been a growth industry since the first book was published in 1968. A lot of anthropologists take a dim view of these books about an Indian shaman named Don Juan and his experiences with different consciousnesses. College students, however, find them un-put-downable and sometimes sneak around behind their professors' backs to read them. The big problem seems to be whether Don Juan exists or whether Casteneda made him up. It is our contention that it doesn't make much difference—the point is that people who read these books think about their own lives in a new and productive way.

Dozier, Edward P.

1970 *The Pueblo Indians of North America*. New York: Holt, Rinehart and Winston, Inc. Reissued 1983 by Waveland Press, Inc., Prospect Heights, IL. The author grew up in the Santa Clara Pueblo and held membership in it until his death. He was also an anthropologist who wrote beautifully about one of the most fascinating groups of people in the world. For thousands of years the Pueblo people have followed an elaborate artistic and ceremonial life in the oases of the dry Southwest. They did this in the face of bothersome neighbors like the Apache, the Navajo, the Spanish conquistadors, Catholic priests, American settlers and state bureaucrats.

Hall, Edward T.

1959 *The Silent Language*. New York: Doubleday & Co., Inc.

1966 *The Hidden Dimension*. New York: Doubleday & Co., Inc.

1976 *Beyond Culture*. New York: Doubleday & Co., Inc.

1983 *The Dance of Life*. New York: Doubleday & Co., Inc.

All of Edward T. Hall's books give us flashes of insight and recognition. "Yes—that is how the world really feels." He illuminates unspoken give-and-take of human relationships; his examples of how time, space, and rhythm operate have challenged a generation of readers, anthropologists and nonanthropologists alike.

Kluckhohn, Clyde

1944 *Navaho Witchcraft*. Papers of the Peabody Museum of American Archaeology and Ethnology 22, 2. Cambridge, MA: Harvard University Press. Reissued 1961 by Beacon Press, Boston. An "oldie-but-goodie," this book gives us deep understanding of the largest Indian group in the U.S. as well the processes of religion and worldviews.

Symbols
Language and Art

10

PROPOSITIONS AND PREMISES

- ■ Language is the primary means of culturizing communication. It turns sounds into symbols of meaning.

- ■ A symbol is anything to which some group of people assign arbitrary meaning. Symbols are essentials of culture and sharing symbols is one of the greatest bonds of culture.

- ■ People who speak the same language (or the same special dialect of a language) form a speech community. The community of people who share symbols (a speech community) leads to strong loyalties and ethnocentrism.

- ■ There are no "primitive" languages. All are highly developed structurally and can be used to carry any information known in the culture they accompany. Some languages do lack vocabulary that is needed in another culture. With contact, the vocabulary grows.

- ■ Play is activity that recontexts and redefines behavior, usually by increasing the number of rules and their stringency so that a person can compete or experiment within the new rules. (The new rules may allow for breaking the old rules.)

- ■ The goal of art is to reduce the scope of activity, to create and follow a set of rules, and then communicate an insight—a message—within the reduced framework.

- ■ Art is any number of ways of rearranging perception of the material and social worlds so that new views of "reality" can be tested and new appreciations of them projected.

- ■ Art may be (but may not be) aesthetically pleasing—that is, it gives us rewards either because it reaffirms the cultural pattern into which we are taught to arrange our perceptions, or else it gives us new and novel patterns into which to rearrange those perceptions.

Meaning is the most interesting aspect of human life—the essence of culturization. Everything to which we give meaning thereby goes beyond animal behavior. Meaning may be expressed in many ways: by signs, by language, and by all of the arts—dance, music, literature, poetry, painting and sculpture.

Meaning can be immensely, perhaps endlessly, elaborated. Meanings can be formed into doctrines. They provide the bases of morality and faith. People can speak and communicate about complex abstractions. They can make poems and theories, stories and hypotheses; they can play with ideas and venture boldly into the realm of the "what if."

A complex meaning lies behind every myth, ritual or dogma; every piece of art, literature or music; and every philosophy. Meaning may deal with the unknown. It may even deal with unknowables.

SYMBOLS AND COMMUNICATION

Understanding meaning involves grasping the fundamental importance of symbols and language. Speech and language are difficult to define because both are basic ideas that cannot be sensibly reduced to more basic terms without losing at least some of their essence. **Speech** is the use of language—any language that will be understood. To speak is to say words or talk; it also means to tell or to express. **Language**, on the other hand, has a specific reference: it is the speech (or writing) of a group of people who share a culture—an ethnic group. Speech is universal. Languages are parochial. Language and the capacity to use it allow us to think, to re-evaluate the past, to learn about many items we have never experienced, and to plan for the future. Language is the major vehicle for the culturization of communication.

Animal Communication

All mammals (and birds) communicate, but except for human beings their communications are about the here and now. Animal communications (except for human beings) are limited to the present tense and the immediate surroundings.

Apes. Apes do not have the physical equipment for speech. The anatomy and musculature of an ape's mouth and throat do not enable it to produce the kind of sounds that human beings regularly use for language. They do, however, have the intelligence. In the 1960s and later, chimpanzees were taught symbols for up to a hundred items. They learned to punch computer buttons to indicate what they wanted. Other chimpanzees were taught sign language and some of them became quite proficient in signing ideas. They seldom taught sign language to their young or to other apes, however. Although apes showed that they can, with human tutelage, use some parts of human language, human beings are the only primates to communicate by use of spoken language.

Dolphins. Dolphins are another species of large, intelligent mammals who almost surely have adequate intelligence to speak. It is even possible that they do talk. We aren't sure. Certainly, dolphins have a large vocabulary of sounds that they use to communicate information to one another (but, then, so do dogs). Dolphin vocabulary has been and is being intensively studied by human beings, but we have not yet broken the dolphin code.

10-1. Many animals communicate. Apes, dolphins, and dogs are all effective communicators. But animals communicate only about what is present—the here and the now. Human beings can add past, future, far away and "what if." Meaning pervades human life.

There may be a dolphin language, but we must also entertain the idea that there isn't. Look at it in comparison with the communications of dogs. A dog indicates rage and threat by making the hair on his neck and back stand on end. Dolphins have no hair. The dog, to indicate friendship and approachability, wags its tail. If dolphins wag their tails, they swim. Because dolphins adapted to the sea, the number of channels they can use for communication is limited. They cannot use visual channels because they cannot see very far or very clearly under water. They may use the channel of touch; perhaps even of smell. But most of their messages have been reduced to the aural channel—that is, to signals that can be heard. If dogs were to reduce all the information that they communicate into a single channel, they too would probably have as complex a system as do dolphins.

Dolphins, like dogs, can communicate with human beings. People attribute intelligence to dolphins in part because they are peaceful creatures and have befriended human beings. Although dolphins are undeniably intelligent, our wishful thinking (and sometimes faulty reasoning) may see what we seek to find rather than what actually exists.

Three facts become evident. (1) We have never thoroughly

or even adequately, broken an animal communication code, although we know quite a lot about communication among species as varied as bees and monkeys. (Bees can indicate precise direction and distance to sources of nectar for honey, but not much else.) (2) Some intelligent mammals can respond to human communications. (3) People use dolphins and other animals as symbols of something we value. These points don't help us very much to figure out human communication. We are, with human communication, reaching new territory—the distinctively human territory of formulating and communicating complex meaning that goes beyond danger signs, mating signs, and aggression signs.

Human Communication: The Power of Symbols

Most human messages are created and received in a medium of symbols. A symbol must be distinguished from a sign. A **sign** is anything that allows a person or an animal to infer the existence of something else. The tracks of an animal (or the odor of the animal, for a creature with a good enough sense of smell) are signs that the animal has been there.

10-2. Both animals and human beings use "signs" to communicate.

Animals—including people—employ signs. A **symbol**, on the other hand, is anything (either an utterance like a word or a material item like a flag) to which some group of people have assigned an arbitrary meaning that may have no connection with the thing itself (Bright 1968). Red and green traffic lights are symbols; so are the words "red" and "green." International road signs are symbols; so are the words "Stop," "Arrete," and "Alto."

Many scholars, because the idea of symbol "means" something very important, have an ineffable need to refine the definition. Yet, defining a symbol is like defining "meaning"

10-3. Symbols are shared cultural understandings about the meaning of certain words or items. There is no link between the symbol and its meaning other than the shared understandings. In this etching by Albrecht Dürer, called The Holy Trinity, *the Holy Ghost is represented by a dove above the Father and the Son.*

itself. The term "meaning" is so basic that defining it, which means describing it in more basic words, verges on the impossible. "Tool" is another of those words difficult to define—look in any dictionary to see how serious the problem is. The word symbol is that kind of word.

Learning language is intertwined with catching onto the idea of symbols. An extraordinary woman named Helen Keller was born deaf and blind. Her dedicated nurse and teacher, Anne Sullivan, left us an unparalleled record of how Helen began the process of learning language. The passage has often been quoted, but I can find no other that is so instructive about the intricate process of comprehending symbols. Helen was about five years old when this event occurred.

> We went to the pump, where I had Helen hold her cup under the opening while I pumped. As the cold water poured forth and filled the cup, I spelled out "water" by tapping on her free hand. The word, which followed so immediately upon the sensation of the cold water running

Symbols: Language and Art

10-4. *Children learn symbols early in life by using their sense perceptions of sight and sound and understanding the relationships between those perceptions and an external meaning. Helen Keller was born blind and deaf, but through the patience and skill of her teacher, Anne Sullivan, she discovered the idea of symbols later in her childhood and went on to write: "Smell is a potent wizard that transports us across a thousand miles and all our years. Even as I think of smells my nose is full of scents that awake sweet memories of summers gone and ripening grain fields far away."*

over her hand, seemed to puzzle her. Then she let the cup fall and stood as if she were rooted there. A completely new expression lighted her features. She spelled out the word "water" again and again. She knelt down and touched the earth and wanted to know its name, and she did the same for the pump and the nearby trellis. Then she turned around and inquired about my name. I spelled out "teacher" on her hand. At this moment, Helen's little sister's nurse brought her to the pump. Helen spelled out "baby" and got the meaning of her nurse. All the way back she was terribly excited and inquired after the name of everything she touched, so that in only a little over an hour, she had learned thirty words" (Sullivan in Keller 1904).

What Helen Keller learned at that moment was the principle of symbolization. She had made a discovery that most of us make long before we can realize what an immense discovery it is: the basic mode of human communication, the

symbolic meaning of words. The taps (equivalent to sounds for a nonhandicapped learner) that spelled out "w-a-t-e-r" stood for—meant—water. Her handicap had made her slow—so slow that her teacher was able to record the connection when it finally came. Keller fully connected with her culture when she understood the connection between the symbol and the sensation—and then used the symbol (representation) to communicate the sensation.

Symbols may be words. If you do not already know what a word in a foreign language—or, sometimes a word in your own language—means, it is merely a meaningless collection of sounds. You have to learn what it stands for.

Symbols may also be icons like a hieroglyph, or like the cartoons used by some computer programs to guide you through a series of choices, or the painting of a dove which represents the Holy Spirit to some Christians. Symbols may be natural phenomena given special meanings. An oak tree, for example, may be a symbol for strength; a palm may stand for warmth; a willow tree may stand for adaptability and capacity to bend with the wind.

Symbols can be complex because they can have several referents or several meanings. Take a complicated word-symbol: the word "honest" in Shakespeare's *Othello* is an excellent example. The word is used fifty-two times in the play (Empson 1951). With great artistry, Shakespeare swings his audience among a welter of meanings: honest means "*not telling lies*." It also means *faithful* to friends (even if one has to lie to do it), and *expressing one's emotions directly* (which implies lack of tact so that honest can mean both *tactful* and *tactless*). It means *genuine*, *frank*, *not hypocritical*. The list goes on. The poet's skill comes in building a picture of his characters that is complex because the word means so many things. The contradictions among the many meanings build rounded, very human characters. They also create the dramatic tension important to any play. As we shall see in the next chapter, a good myth has at least as many symbolic referents as a Shakespearean play. An abundance of meaning can be packed into fairly narrow confines.

Symbols enrich the perception we share with other animals. We can add agreed-upon meaning to signs so that they supersede being mere signs—they can become complex and abstract symbols. With both signs and symbols, communication can address increasingly complex issues. Creativity can flourish unfettered by the limitations of the concrete and the present.

Language. Language is a pervasive human symbol system. As we mentioned earlier, speech is present among all human beings. All human languages are complex sets of symbols by which people communicate, learn and express meaning.

There is no such thing as a "primitive" language. All languages have whatever words and grammar the people who speak them need to communicate and to use their culture. If new culture emerges, any language can change to accommodate it.

All languages are difficult for adults to learn. The degree of difficulty probably depends on how similar the grammar and syntax of the language being learned are to the language already spoken. The fact that it is easier for an adult speaker of English to learn French than it is to learn Chinese does not in itself make French an "easier" language than Chinese.

Gestures. Gestures are also vital symbols in human communication: gestures vary from culture to culture just as language varies from culture to culture. For example, when Tiv lift their right hands to their mouths, then in a series of waving gestures allow the hand slowly to fall toward their left, it adds the idea "completely" to whatever is being said.

Indeed, gestures vary with different sets of speakers of the same language. American, Australian, and British gestures show some differences in spite of the common language. When you cross the channel from England to the continent, you observe many sets of gestures that accompany different European languages. These symbols must be learned just as surely as the language symbols must be learned.

Even when the language and gestures have been mastered, it is difficult to discuss particular concepts without shared knowledge about culture. You can, to take an old example, translate Kant into Eskimo, but you may not be able to make an Eskimo understand it. If we learn the language, gestures and the culture which is responsible for the symbols, we can go far beyond everyday language and gesture to transcendent messages that are a mesh of symbols of symbols. All of us have experienced situations of high-context communication (Hall 1966) in which the proportion of shared verbal and nonverbal symbols and shared assumptions is so high that almost nothing need be actually said.

Intricacy of Symbols. Symbols are complex because they encompass so many meanings. They are powerful because they communicate all those meanings at once. Our thoughts and reactions can swing from one of those meanings to another without interruption. We don't stop to see that we

10-5. *Symbols may have many meanings. Flags are important symbols because they compress so many meanings into a single item. They represent the essence of the country however the particular peoples of that country may see their own essential characteristics. The 152 flags that fly at the United Nations headquarters in New York City express the "united" "nations."*

Symbols: Language and Art

have switched from emphasizing one aspect of a symbol's meaning to another. In fact, we might not even be aware that we have linked those meanings. The tone and mood of one meaning infests the other meanings, providing a reality in which one can move to a different plane within a single context.

The American flag is a good example of a complex symbol. The degree of its complexity became starkly clear in 1989 when the Supreme Court of the United States issued a decision that burning the flag was an expression of opinion and was therefore protected under the First Amendment to the Constitution which guarantees freedom of speech and expression.

Many Americans were outraged with that decision. To them the flag "stood for" the country. Burning the flag was therefore an act against the country—an act of treason. Yet other Americans, who treasured the First Amendment even more than they treasured the flag, said it was a correct decision.

The flag is not merely an emblem of the country; it is richer than that. It embodies our most heartfelt values and our deepest convictions—our view of what we stand for and who we are.

Those who accepted the decision analyzed the various levels of meaning of the flag. They reasoned that the flag was an important symbol, but even more important was one of the freedoms it symbolized—freedom of speech. Others found that type of analysis impossible. Questioning any part of the symbol, for them, threatened the whole system, First Amendment and all.

WE, THE ALIEN

We tend to think that a single symbol brings all its various meanings together as a single topic—the fact that it is a single symbol allows us to overlook the complexity. The symbol is powerful precisely *because* it makes the complexity seem simple—because it can link so many different contexts together. One meaning affects all the others. Art and religion thrive on this kind of linkage.

The purpose of ethnographic analysis is to expose the complexities of the symbols of the cultures being studied. That requires that we dissect and examine the strands of complex meaning. Only if the ethnographer succeeds in doing that can the reader understand the system of meaning underlying what the ethnographer describes.

Explanation. Meaning also involves explanation. Animals cannot explain. Explanation is culture that supersedes our animality.

To explain something is to tell somebody else how to do it. Even more important, it is to tell somebody else *why* to do it. With the "how," we are in the midst of technology and "correct" behavior. With the "why," we are in the midst of the network of meaning and values that hold a culture together.

People explain not just technological and social processes. They also explain their behavior—they give reasons, and perhaps excuses, for behaving as they do. People learn the explanations provided by their cultures. Sometimes those ready-made explanations are good enough—indeed, sometimes no other explanations will be accepted.

Many people dread change. But when the environment changes so much that old explanations no longer suffice, people will nevertheless modify their explanations or create new ones. The "new" explanations may be entirely new, or they may be a rearrangement of old ideas. New explanations can change our very lives because explanation lies at the foundation of every culture. Whenever the explanation changes, the culture has been changed just as much as when new tools are introduced.

LANGUAGE AND CULTURE

Language was an immense evolutionary step. We have an innate capacity for learning language. The fact that human children learn language so naturally and so constantly makes the process difficult to study and record.

Sound as Meaning

The most distinctive quality of speech is that everything is patterned in two ways at once: there is a system of sounds on the one hand, a system of meanings on the other. Although most speakers of any language never separate the two, they can be easily separated for purposes of study; that separation lies at the heart of linguistics, the study of language.

Of the myriad sounds that human vocal chords, tongue and lips can produce, every language selects only a small number of them, usually fewer than fifty. English uses only about forty sounds on which to build the entire language.

Phonemes. Each distinguishable sound that we physically produce is called a *phone*. A single sound that is actually selected for use in a language is called a **phoneme**. Phonemes are the smallest units of sound that are recognized by and have significance *only* for speakers of a specific language. Every phoneme is part of a phonemic system, which is the set of sounds that the speakers of any specific language have chosen to use from the myriad variety of sounds it is possible to make.

An "accent" occurs when a nonnative speaker utters the words of one language in the phonemes of another, so that listeners have to make adjustments to bring the strange sounds into line with the "right" sounds. Learning the phonemic system of a foreign language may, in the long run, be the most difficult part of learning a new language. German speakers, for example, have difficulty with the "th" sound in English; English speakers have difficulties with the uvular "r" in French—trying to pronounce *leur* or *brun* the way a Frenchman does can be daunting.

Learning to pronounce foreign languages with the proper phonemes can be fun. For example, English uses phonemes usually written "g" and "b." Each is an exploded sound— that is, the stream of breath is broken. For a "g," the breath is momentarily stopped by raising the back of the tongue to the roof of the mouth. For a "b," the breath is first stopped by the lips, then exploded from them. Many West African languages use both those phonemes, but also have an additional one: they explode the breath from both positions at once. The sound that comes out is usually written "gb." One of my best friends in Tivland was named Gbogboese. Go ahead and try it.

Morphemes. **Morphemes** are the smallest unit of *meaning*. Morphemes can be whole words or parts of words that either carry a meaning or affect the meaning of the word. For example, the word renew has two morphemes: *re* and *new*; bicycles has three: *bi, cycle,* and *s*. *Bi* means two, *cycle* means wheel, and *s* makes it plural. Morphemes may contain several phonemes. The difference is that the phoneme is about sound; the morpheme is about meaning.

The usual way to distinguish morphemes is by a method of altering one phoneme in a morpheme. If the meaning changes, then the two sounds are both morphemes. Hill and hell do not have the same meaning, nor do coal and goal. You can go through the entire language, looking at pairs of words in this way. The English language has approximately forty phonemes (the number varies a little with dialect and accent); the morphemes, too, are limited although their number is far greater than the number of phonemes. Morphemes are units that convey meaning; they are building blocks we put together to form words. They can be roots, prefixes and suffixes as in the bicycle example above. Meaning is the determining factor. For example, singer is composed of two morphemes—the root *sing* and the suffix *er* meaning one who. Finger, however is one morpheme. *Fing* has no meaning in English, thus the morpheme is finger.

The way phonemes and morphemes are strung together and organized is called **syntax**. In a language like English, word order is very important. Noam Chomsky, a linguist from the Massachusetts Institute of Technology, created an English sentence in the 1950s that became famous for demonstrating both the importance of word order and the fact that we need more than word order to make sense. "Colorless green ideas sleep furiously" is a perfectly good English sentence if we are concerned only with structure; unfortunately, it does not make sense. If you arrange those same words in any other order, then it not only doesn't make sense, but it is not a sentence. In Russian, word order is less important because the grammar is complex in other ways and speakers do not have to depend so fully on word order for the meaning to be evident.

Grammar. Grammar is an important part of language. All of us absorb correct grammar unconsciously as we learn our native language, although the irregular patterns, as mentioned below, may require specific learning. Grammar tells us which word order to use, which forms of verbs and adjectives to use to make our message intelligible. In Tiv and many other languages of the world, the tone of the syllables is an important part of syntax. The difference between "I don't go" and "I never go" in Tiv is a difference in the tone when pronouncing the word for go.

The study of language is based on this twofold structure of phonemes (sound) and morphemes (meaning) and the grammar which fits them together. If the rest of culture could be assessed in such simple terms, we would be fortunate— however, there is no unit in culturized behavior that is as specific as a phoneme. There is nothing as definitive in the interpretation of the meaning of culture as the morpheme.

Language Is Generative

The human brain appears to contain an inborn capacity to generate words and grammar from a few rules. When children learn to speak English, they are apt to say runned on the principle that you add *ed* to form a past tense. They must learn the exception: the past tense of run is ran. Children, from a very early age, can make up sentences that they never heard before (and perhaps nobody else ever heard) that follow the rules of grammar and other kinds of rules for generating language-messages. If that is the case (and, the only thing left in doubt is the precise extent to which it is the case), then all languages share the principles of organization, and the number of those principles may be fairly small. This universal grammar is, as the child learns, the basic structure over which the specifics of the grammar of a given language are superimposed. The universal set of rules is called deep structure, while the overlaid set of grammatical rules is called surface structure.

Symbols: Language and Art

10-8. *Language is generative. That means that the human brain is organized to follow patterns. Individual people including young children, can use the patterns to generate sentences and meanings that have never before been uttered, but which are nevertheless understandable.*

Language Communities

One of the most important bases for the solidarity and uniqueness of a social group is that the members share a common language. Nobody has to translate! Indeed, sharing common language may be the ineradicable distinction on which people fall back: we, who speak intelligibly—and they, who do not.

Sharing a language creates a vital social link between individuals. It creates community. A language community may be large or small; it may be based on an entire language or on a limited vocabulary. Ethnic peoples like the Lithuanians are held together in part by their language—and the distaste they feel at having to use another language (Russian) in many of their daily activities. When India achieved independence in the late 1940s, "language wars" broke out to determine which languages would be made official languages and which would be relegated to only domestic use. Gangs in American inner cities have special vocabularies that bind them together and separate them from others who do not know those particular words or use them the way the gang members do. The Catholic church has a large, specialized vocabulary that only believers understand—it marks them off from others—as well as a special liturgical

language (Latin), which separates most of the members from the clergy.

Speech communities may include regional dialects so that a particular way of speaking the mother tongue is marked by the dialect of the area in which one learned it. A Tennessee dialect or a Maine dialect is distinguishable anywhere, even though people from Maine and Tennessee communicate with one another without difficulty.

10-10. *Speech communities can form among some subgroup of users of a single language: among age-mates, among people who share the same training or job specialties; among gangs, lodges, or religions. They have special vocabularies that mark them off from all other people who speak their language. Some families have family vocabularies that separate them, even from (or perhaps especially from) their in-laws.*

10-9. *People who use the same language form a natural community because communication with one another is simple and appears to have no obstacles to be overcome. In an individual's perception, people who speak the same language are set off from all others who need an interpreter to "make sense." The resultant language community is the core unit of ethnocentrism.*

Language is a vital dimension of every culture. Language establishes a perceptual screen that exists between the natural world and any human perception of it. Language is thus an important mechanism for turning perception into culture. Edward Sapir once wrote: "The 'real world' is to a large extent unconsciously built up on the language habits of the group. No two languages are ever sufficiently similar to be considered as representing the same social reality. The worlds in which different societies live are distinct worlds, not merely the same world with different labels attached" (Sapir, quoted in Bright 1968).

One of Sapir's students, Benjamin Lee Whorf, took that idea even further. He held that language patterns and cultural norms influence one another directly. He claimed that the nature of any particular language limited—indeed, dictated—the way people perceive reality. His particular example was the Hopi language. The tenses of verbs in Hopi are very different from the tenses in English (so, of course, are tenses in Russian). The question still debated today is whether that means that Hopi speakers perceive the world differently than do English speakers. What is undeniable is that people tend to interpret their experiences in terms of the categories provided in their native languages. These categories thereupon exercise great influence on their perception and on their behavior.

Language and Power

Skill in using language is closely allied with power because people who speak well or write well have at their fingertips the capacity of manipulating meaning. Control of meaning may be the ultimate power.

Being able to communicate clearly in language—both spoken and written—and being able to listen and understand someone else who can do so, is one of the essentials of successful living in complex civilizations, and probably in any other culture. Language *is* power.

Our whole lives are spent in the midst of symbols. In the process of providing us with meaning, culture also becomes a screen between people and what they perceive. Our perception of the physical universe comes to us through this symbolic screen of meaning. The hunger for meaning added to basic animal curiosity makes people search far beyond the physical universe. To use language at all *demands* that we assign meaning. We use symbols to make the world more meaningful and to communicate that meaning. Theology is about meaning. Science is an organized mode of increasing and operationalizing meaning. Discovery and expression of meaning are the basis of every kind of art.

ART AND CULTURE

Art as a way of using symbols is generally not as well studied or as highly regarded by anthropologists as is language.

 Investigating art presents a particular problem: Americans passionately embrace ideas about what is art (and what isn't)—but there is almost no agreement on the subject. Among the many anthropologists who read this book in manuscript, there was far more disagreement about this section than about any other—and none of those who disagreed with me agreed with one another. Americans not only hold passionate opinions about art—they hold passionately personal opinions. That is an ethnographic fact that needs explaining. The following, therefore, is my passionate position on the subject. Your culture gives you carte blanche to hold some other opinion. The important point is to think clearly about your opinions and know how to defend them. If challenging my opinions leads to examining your own, that is a rewarding result. Art is a perfect foil for reflecting the wealth of skills culture gives us.

WE, THE ALIEN

If you are fully to understand the meanings within a culture, you have to understand its art. Art is human skill specifically applied toward drawing, painting, sculpture, architecture, poetry, music, dance and perhaps a number of other activities. Both the skill and the results are called art. The purpose of art is to communicate ideas and emotions. Some special quality within an art object carries a message—perhaps an unconscious message—from artist to observer. The elusive question is: what constitutes that quality?

There is no such thing as a primitive language. All languages can be stretched to communicate whatever the speakers need to say.

10-11.

Doodling and Decorating

People doodle. A doodle is something you draw or something you whittle or a paper you fold like an origami—anything you make while thinking of something else. Doodling would appear to have no purpose and no message. Indeed, its lack of meaning is part of its definition as a doodle. In various locales around the world, I have observed people from many cultures doodling. Their doodles, while culture-bound, nevertheless have no overt message to communicate (although a psychiatrist might attribute the result to something from the unconscious of the doodler). Most doodles are merely thrown away, although a few doodles by famous men and women are collected and acquire a market value. The market value occurs solely from their association with the people who doodled, not from the artistic merit within the doodles. President Kennedy's doodles are more elaborate than those of President Eisenhower—and, for whatever reason, also bring a higher price. Doodles are not art, but they may be one of the foundations of art.

10-12. Here is one of President Kennedy's doodles. Doodles are one of the precursors of art—and, perhaps, of thought.

Many peoples of the world—probably most—decorate the items around them. We Americans decorate Christmas trees by hanging baubles on them; we decorate a room by hanging colorful printed paper on its walls; we decorate people by hanging medals on them. Potters decorate their wares by painting or incising designs. Many craftsmen decorate the useful items they produce—carved house posts and knife handles in West Africa, elaborate carvings on furniture in Mexico, canoe paddles in traditional Polynesia, transfer patterns or decals on cabinet doors in middle-class Swedish (and sometimes American) kitchens. The purpose of decoration is to make things more visible, more noticeable (Langer 1953). The message of the decoration is the decorator's desire to add force, stimulus, and individuality—to communicate through channels other than language and gesture.

People may also decorate themselves with jewelry. They decorate their bodies with paint, whether cosmetics or war paint. Cosmetics can convey a sexual message, a conscious intent to mirror a commonly approved standard, or to exhibit the uniqueness of one's personality. War paint is used to

inspire fear. The communication of fear succeeds, in part, because the enemy knows that the very act of applying the paint made those warriors think of themselves symbolically as fearless. People in many cultures tattoo colorful designs on their skin to enhance their identity, to send political messages, or to turn themselves into walking decorations (Rubin 1988—take the time to find this book in the library; the color photographs of tattooing are interesting and revealing).

10-13. Many peoples of the world sculpt their flesh. This photograph of a Tiv drummer shows the six lumps around the eyes, a style of scarification that was popular in the 1930s, so that they marked middle-aged men in 1950. Younger men had quite different types of scars.

Some peoples of the world actually sculpt human flesh, creating decoration by means of scarification. Tiv men, when I lived with them in the early 1950s, were still making elaborate scars on their faces. Some of these scars were made by putting a hook through the skin, lifting it up and slicing it off with a razor. Charcoal was then rubbed into the wound so that it would heal as a keloid, a raised scar. Other facial scars were created by making intricate designs of small incisions, then rubbing blue dye into them. Women wore scars on their backs and legs. Tiv women's bellies are also elaborately scarred (Bohannan 1956; Keil 1979). The purpose was, as they explained, to make themselves "glow"; that is, to make themselves more individual and more attractive.

Adding the Message

The decorations on Pueblo Indian pottery had precise meanings to their makers and users; they also had meaning in Pueblo religion and in daily life. Some decorated items were ritual objects for religious or other rites. People decorate ritual objects or sacred places just as they decorate other objects and for the same reason: to enhance their stimulus value. Decoration, under these circumstances, becomes too flimsy a word. When decorations on ritual objects acquire symbolic meaning, the objects thereupon become icons standing for ideas—sometimes very powerful ideas. It is crucial to recognize this progression. Icons are symbols conveying specific messages. An important part of the message is in the decoration.

One of the messages of decorations may be trivial. Commercial art—that drawn for ads—is usually trivial, no matter how well it is executed. Yet how do you define "trivial" in a society in which we daily make many small decisions of little consequence—choosing one type of breakfast cereal or one type of toothpaste over the others? Does the art in a magazine ad or a TV commercial influence choice? Perhaps it does—it may even be the best thing about the products.

Messages in objects may be used for propaganda purposes; that is, they may be created to subserve the message. A primary example of this usage is political art. Most political movements generate art—posters, buttons, bumper stickers, hats, streamers and flags—to communicate their message and make it palatable. Much of Soviet music in the period

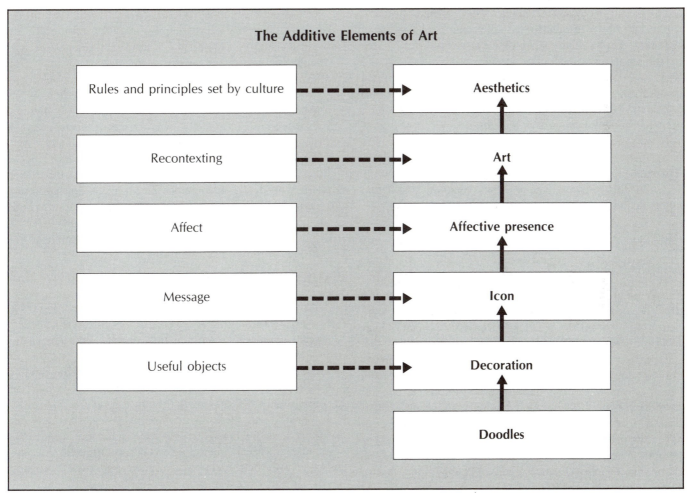

The Additive Elements of Art

Rules and principles set by culture ----> **Aesthetics**

Recontexting ----> **Art**

Affect ----> **Affective presence**

Message ----> **Icon**

Useful objects ----> **Decoration**

Doodles

10-14. Starting with doodles, if a useful object is decorated and the doodle becomes a recognized design, a new level has been reached. If a message is added, the piece becomes an icon. If sufficient artistry is added to call up affect, that is, to create an affecting presence in the piece, it can be considered art, although the appreciation of art involves recontexting from the piece itself to the idea of art. Finally, based on the idea of art and all the components in the progression, an aesthetics can be created.

The Progression can stop at any point on the way upward.

---- is to be read "becomes"
—— is to be read "exerts an influence on"

between World War II and the late 1980s was deliberately simplified so that peasants and political leaders could hum it. It existed primarily to communicate political messages. Like commercial art, propagandistic art is short-lived. When Eastern European countries established their independence from the Soviet Union in 1989, life-size statues of Lenin were torn down. The political message was no longer applicable. The citizens of the free nations wanted to destroy the message the statues symbolized.

Religious art is full of messages of piety, suffering, and/or winning out over great obstacles. The message in some African sculpture, once you learn to look at it, is that the ancestor represented has become a vital force; the ancestor has lost the characteristics that once made him human and has acquired those of a spirit that is part of the natural world. The messages in the types of art mentioned so far are overt.

The message communicated may also be the emotion and the insight of the artist. Human character can be captured by a sculptor, for example, so that each angle of the piece reveals a different aspect of personality. As you walk around the sculpture, you might first see a cruel and tyrannical person. Another angle might convey the impression of a person trying to mask cruelty by hiding behind a smile. Another angle might portray a frightened person trying to conquer the fear by presenting a domineering presence. Art with an overt message strives to avoid any such ambiguities. The messages in commercial, propaganda, and religious art seek a specific response. The messages communicated by the emotion and insight of the artist seek a reflective response.

Affect

The message in an icon does not by itself turn the object into art. That requires one more step. It must have an "affecting presence" (Armstrong 1971). That presence lies directly within the piece of art. It arouses emotion. One definition of art is "the creation of forms symbolic of human feeling" (Langer 1953).

This view of the "affecting presence" has done a tremendous service to the comparative study of art. The affecting presence is added to the messages. Decorations are icons if they have symbolic value and carry a message. If an icon also, by its presence, can stimulate a viewer at the level of affect, its cultural message fairly shouts! The message that makes the decorated object an icon may disappear from the piece with changes in cultural values or may not translate across cultures. But the affecting presence very often *can* cross cultural barriers and can even grow in intensity over time.

Aesthetics

Finally, two new principles may be added. The object, with its affecting presence, may be declared by the people of the culture to be art and put into a special category. When that happens, students such as art historians study the art work; philosophers develop a whole field of aesthetics around it.

We have little information on the ideas of other cultures that correspond to our ideas about art. In fact, we are not at all sure that art as a special realm is recognized in most societies. Keil (1979) found, after an exhaustive search, that the Tiv don't have a word for art and that they have no discoverable **aesthetic**. That does not mean that they are not affected by good carvings; rather, they don't formulate principles for judging the good from the bad. The message of Tiv carvings is not to be confused with what the Tiv people like or don't like. Any Tiv can tell you that the objects represent cosmic forces important in ritual situations or that they represent protection against witches—and then add in no uncertain terms which one is more pleasing apart from the symbolic meaning. Thus, the *idea* of art is a special cultural achievement of our own society (and of other societies such as those of India and China) rather than something that permeates all cultures.

In summary, people doodle. They doodle culturally. Doodles cease to be just doodles as purposive decoration becomes more important. Purposive decoration can "brighten" an object to the point that it becomes "an affecting presence." It may then be recognized as belonging to the special field of art. When the special field of art appears, then students of that field appear. The affecting presence may, but may not, lead to overt theories of art or aesthetics. We will say more about aesthetics later.

10-14 shows the progression of the qualities of art that we have discussed. Since it is not a cultural process, it has been written vertically. It must not be interpreted as evolution or history. Rather, it is a logical addition of elements to build up conceptualizations that lead to art. It is written in archaeological fashion with the most basic element at the bottom, working up as additions are made.

Music and Dance

Music, like decoration, exists almost everywhere. However, a word meaning "music" seems to be quite rare. The Tiv have many words for singing, flute playing, drumming—but no single word for music. Indeed, it may be true that no African language has a word that means what English speakers mean by music (Keil 1979), but what we would call music is nevertheless very important throughout Africa. Tiv songs are made by known composers; they are widely performed at dances, markets, celebrations, funerals. Composers' reputations usually do not spread beyond their local groups, but a few of them are known and their songs sung throughout the land of over a million people.

"There are many difficulties involved in the assumption that music is a symbol" (Langer 1953). The philosopher who said that, however, has also provided an answer: music may absorb everything that is combined with it. If you add words, they become part of the music. The symbolic message in the words can be immensely enhanced by the music. On the other hand, great music can carry even the silliest words, as many opera libretti, musical comedy scores or pop songs demonstrate. What is derisively called "mood music" can create a background sound that has a decided emotional

10-15. *Music plays an important part in the lives of many people. These Tiv are acting out part of a curing ritual. The drummer is an important part of the ritual. Spanish Gypsies (gitanos) are well-known for their flamenco music.*

10-16. *Most of the world's people dance. Dance is an exaggeration of ordinary movement; the tempo of the movement is altered. Such alterations allow emotional messages to be added to the movement.*

Dance affirms life, negates death and the evil aspect of *tsav* [witchcraft], demonstrates the enduring solidarity of the lineage and the strength, the discipline, the power of its young men and women who, in marriage across lineage and clan lines, will procreate and perpetuate the Tiv people. These themes underlie all dances and are stated explicitly in many of the most popular styles.

The men's dances . . . always display strength, speed, agility, and endurance, and often make a mockery of disease, witchcraft, and death. . . . *Ingiogh* . . . parodies 'dropsy,' [the wasting disease known as] kwashiorkor, madness, muscular dystrophy, and more; at a sign, a normal dance pattern is interrupted, and the dancers break from the line to distend their bellies grotesquely, take on idiotic grins, cross their eyes, and dangle or angle their arms, presenting a portrait gallery of total afflictions. At another signal, the situation returns abruptly to normal, the line moving, in a circle. . . . After some conventional circling, everyone gets the 'staggers,' and one dancer rolls over on his back, feet stiff in the air, dead. But he is quickly revived by his fellows. Now they dance their diseases in a line of bulging bellies, elbow thrusts, and shaking knees, facing out to the encircling audience."

Charles Keil (1979)

THEY SAID IT

Symbols: Language and Art

effect, even when the hearers are not particularly listening.

But not *everything* added to the music becomes part of the music: music in most movies, for example, is used to heighten the drama or lighten the comedy. It adds affect at another level. Yet the drama or the comedy does not become part of the music. In short, meaning in music may derive from its incorporated words, from the context in which it is considered suitable, or by the affect that its sounds produce in hearers.

Dancing is the central art of Tiv—and of much of the rest of Africa (Keil 1979). Except for some traditional dances that have to do with marriage, death and prestige, styles in Tiv dances change very rapidly. New dances are invented by individuals; some of them spread through the countryside, but most are forgotten in a few years. Tiv form dance groups that tour the country, performing in marketplaces. They are given food and money and, if they are really good, lots of prestige. These groups meet and practice diligently, sometimes for months, before they perform publicly. Dance groups are well organized—indeed, they "represent the highest degree of organizational complexity to be found in Tiv society" (Keil 1979).

Qualities of Art

Art is a unique combination of three elements: symbols, play and explanation.

- Any piece of art is a complex web of symbols. Graphic art can assign symbolic meaning to colors, shapes, and designs—almost anything. Musical art can assign emotional meaning to sounds and rhythms. Meaning can then be manipulated by manipulating the symbols.

- Art is a kind of play. No matter how serious the artist or the situation in which the art is used, it is still a form of play.

- Art is a form of explanation. It is a means of examining old ideas, creating new ideas, and critiquing all ideas. It is also one means of explaining how different ideas fit together.

Art may use thought or it may use the emotions as channels, or both at the same time. Art finds a way to make an explanatory web by allowing us to think and feel several things at once. In that way, we can see, sometimes in one illuminating moment, how everything fits together.

10-17. Art is a statement—a means of amalgamating meanings into powerful symbols. For that reason, studying the art of a culture is necessary to discover people's most profound values. The arts provide as much illumination about a culture as do the institutions of kinship and power. When art crosses cultures, as this painting of The Buffalo Hunt *by Charles M. Russell does, it tells you something about both cultures.*

10-18. *The goal of science is to tease apart many meanings and qualities so that each can be understood clearly. The goal of art is to create symbols and icons to form a complexity of meanings. Einstein, in a 1911 photo, is writing the equation for the density of the Milky Way. The Indian sculpture is from Kashmir.*

The special quality in art is easiest to see when we contrast it with science. The essence of science is dissecting complexity into parts and discovering the principles for combining the parts. The point of the scientific method is to *avoid* thinking of several things at once. The essence of art is, on the other hand, amalgamation of many meanings into one complex symbol.

An anthropologist's analysis of a piece of art or a myth is fundamentally different from the artist's creating it or a native's experiencing and using it. For anthropologists, the experience of the user of art is part of the data. What anthropologists do in order to explain a myth or a statue is to treat it scientifically—that is, to analyze it into its components and then discover how they combine to produce the artistic effect. If the analysis is successful, the anthropologist will be able to explain at least part of the meaning. Such a sciencelike understanding can be an experience as profound as any produced by the art itself, but it is based on different senses and different levels of awareness.

Art can also carry vital messages even when it is poorly executed. The artist's message can be that she or he does not want to send a message. That absence of message is in itself a powerful message. Andy Warhol's huge painting of a can of Campbell's Tomato Soup can mean either that there is no message or that much of our culture is trivial—or maybe some other things that you can add.

The trick in understanding art is the trick of looking for the complexity of the symbols, figuring out the many meanings and the way they illuminate one another.

Play and Art

Play may not be regarded as an art form by most people, but it is certainly an important dimension of art. The word play, like the word symbol, presents the difficulty that it has never been adequately defined. *The World Book Dictionary* gives seventeen basic meanings of play, only one of them obsolete. *The Oxford English Dictionary* fills eighteen finely-packed columns on the topic: six very large pages of very small type. Plainly, play is a topic that cannot be dismissed with a mere definition.

Symbols: Language and Art

Play is one way of taking ideas out of their original context, then using them in some other context. This recontexting quality of play—taking a small slice of life and putting it into a special situation—is the essence of creativity. Play gives us a way of getting ideas out of their original context so that they can be developed for themselves in a totally new context, free of the burdens and limitations of the context from which they stemmed. Play, thus, illuminates both the original context and the new one.

Playing a game like baseball means first accepting the rules of the game. Those rules define the game as a game, smaller in scope than real life. Within those rules, only the game matters; the rest of life has been shut out. Yet the game reflects some of our most important ideas about what real life is about. In the game, the goals are reduced to the achievable—if you are skillful enough, have good enough teammates, and follow the rules, you can reach the goal. The goal of all art is like that: you reduce the scope, create and follow a set of rules, then apply all your skill to putting across an insight—a message.

We not only play games, but both babies and adults also play with words. Children play house; from time to time in our lives, we play at love or at work. One way we play is by making art, and art can be about real life or about abstractions. I own an abstract painting by an anthropologist that is about eliciting structural principles from masses of details. She had a lot of fun painting it.

The scientific investigation of play began in the last part of the nineteenth century and was summarized neatly in a serious and boring book by Groos in 1898 which said firmly that play is a make-believe context in which the young can safely practice the skills that they will need in order to survive in the real world as adults. Recent studies of play among non-human primates have underscored Groos's insights. Among rhesus monkeys, most of the play among juveniles consists in play-chases and play-fights. In this play, the young monkeys learn how to bite without being bitten and how to evade their pursuers. Ultimately they will need these skills to see them through fights for rank and position and also to avoid danger, especially predators. Monkey play is, thus, aggressive. Male monkeys play far more than females; aggression in adult life is of far greater concern for males than for females (Symons 1978).

Among lions, however, by no means all of the animal's required adult behavior is practiced with play, and by no means all play involves skills that are useful in adult behavior. Lions use any of several signs to tell one another that their acts are to be taken as play. One may approach another with exaggerated bounds; like some other animals, notably dogs, they indicate readiness to play by lowering the front part of the body; they may roll on their backs; or nip at or push another lion. Like monkeys, they have a facial expression that ethologists call a "play face" that indicates the special context of play (Schaller 1972).

If the play is aggressive, where is the boundary between serious aggression and play-fighting? This is the precise question that drove Gregory Bateson, one of the most original of all anthropologists, to the zoo. He was in search of behavior that would indicate unquestionably that the animal understood that certain acts were a sign that behavior was to be understood differently in the present context than in other contexts. He found his answer in a gesture that many animals use that means "What I am about to do, I do in play." That gesture is a sign understood by other animals. The sign means

10-19 Play, like art, assigns restricted meanings to acts that are relevant only in the limited context of play. Both play and art are subject to far stricter rules than "real life." This photograph shows a group of Crow Indian women playing dice early in the twentieth century.

"These actions in which we now engage do not denote what those actions *for which they stand* would denote in other contexts." The playful nip denotes the bite, "but it does not denote what would be denoted by the bite" (Bateson 1972). In other words, the meanings of acts are different in play from what they would be in other contexts.

All this leaves us with an even more interesting question: what does play become when it is culturized? Human beings play not only for the sake of learning techniques for survival, but they also play at learning and manipulating culture. You can play house, play store, play king, play priest. You can even play God. Any part of the culture can be played with.

Play is one of the best ways to learn culture, for adults as well as for juveniles. Like art, play relies on restricted rules and stringently defined contexts. One reason television is such a powerful tool for education is that it changes the context of much culture from the big world and puts it in a small box. With TV, you can stand aside from life and watch it in condensed form. But because some of life is boring and without story, TV has to exaggerate the drama in life so it can constantly rev up the emotions in order to retain its audience.

A painter or playwright must be able to release ideas from his or her unconscious to use for creative purposes. To do that, he or she needs a safe place in which to play—to allow the experiences to be faced and understood and the vision to emerge without fear. This kind of creativity not only resembles play—it *is* a kind of play. What one is doing then goes beyond the ordinary. When this playlike context is gone, creativity vanishes. Play, or something like it, is an essential part of all art—indeed, of much learning. The artist must have a safe place to think "unthinkable" thoughts, and to express them so that people back in real life can expand their appreciation of the human condition. Artists are sometimes considered dangerous—they dare to question received ways, and they dare to play with the most serious subjects.

10-20. Political ideologies or religious theologies can be the underpinning of an artist's aesthetic. For some, it may make the idea of aesthetics irrelevant: it is the message they passionately care about. This mural of the great Mexican painter José Clemente Orozco is in the Baker Library of Dartmouth College; it is called Anglo-America *and* Hispanic-America.

10-21. *The overt aesthetic of an artist can become a screen between herself or himself and the art object. Even more crippling, the aesthetic of the consumer, especially when it is reinforced by critics, can become a screen between the art object and the viewer. The aesthetic of a performer may also come between the music or the drama and the listener.*

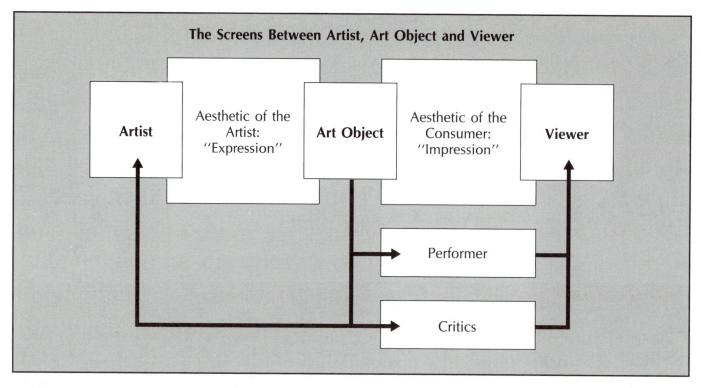

Explanation in Art

Art communicates feelings, insights, sensations, messages— a piece of art is a messenger with a message. These messages originate with the artist—some of them are conscious with the artist, some are not. (10-21 diagrams the process.) Art can be didactic and its message made very clear. The murals of Diego Rivera and José Clemente Orozco hammer home an earnest call for social justice. The message may be erotic, as in much sculpture from India, or it may speak of the peace of dead ancestors as in some West African sculpture.

The artist fuses technique and materials with messages. Such infusion of meaning is in part a matter of skill. Thus, some artists are more successful in reaching the audience than others. Since the message must be understood to be effective, the artist often puts into concrete form a message that is already sensed by the people.

The receiver of the messages of art experiences something quite different. The observer gets an impression from the object. He of she may or may not see a message in it. The question is: does the impression the audience gets (if it gets any message at all) resemble the message intended by the creativity of the artist? When I look at Diego Rivera's huge murals, do I "read" him correctly? When I see neurosis in Van Gogh's magnificent paintings (it shows up more when there are several of his paintings hanging together in a gallery), is the neurosis in him or in me or both?

At least two screens stand in the way of full communication in a medium as subtle as art. The first is positioned between the artist and his or her work. It can be understood as a creative aesthetic. It may be shared by everybody in the culture, or it may be more or less individual.

Most artists do not verbalize their own aesthetic. Indeed, many do not even know that they have an aesthetic. As we noted earlier, most African carvers know what a carving should look like and they know what they want to achieve, but they do not turn their ideas into an explicit aesthetic. One German anthropologist tried to get them to do so (Himmelheber 1960). He met with complete misunderstanding—largely because his premises were totally ethnocentric. He went to the Ivory Coast to study the sculpture of the Baule and other peoples. In the course of his studies, he tried to get information about the aesthetic of the sculptors. When he questioned them, the sculptors could not grasp what he was after. One of his questions was "When you are doing sculpture, do you feel any joy of creation?" All denied it; some vehemently denied it. Reading the report, there is no way to know for sure what the sculptors thought the question meant. One wonders what replies the anthropologist would have gathered if he had asked German or American sculptors the same question.

At the opposite extreme, twentieth-century artists— sculptor Jacob Epstein was an example—may be highly verbal. He meticulously made his aesthetic overt. He could

10-22. *It never occurs to many artists to make their aesthetic principles overt or try to express them in language. The art object itself is sufficient explanation — indeed, the only explanation. This Baule carving from the Ivory Coast in West Africa is magnificent but Baule artists do not talk about the aesthetic principles they use or what they are trying to achieve.*

10-23. *Some artists, like the sculptor Jacob Epstein, intellectualize their aesthetic and make it wholly available, in language, to admirers, critics, and the general public. This* Madonna and Child *of Epstein hangs above the entrance to a convent in London. At the time it was unveiled in the early 1950s, Epstein was very vocal in the press about the reason for each line in it.*

say in words what he wanted to achieve in sculpture; he talked in detail about the means by which he set about getting the effect he wanted.

In sum, some artists simply follow a cultural aesthetic, much of which is unconscious. Others make their aesthetic screen overt, trying to expand it or change it. Some cultures encourage the overt aesthetic; others never think about it.

The screen between the art object and the audience is even more complex. There are four main elements in that screen.

Symbols: Language and Art

First, an observer may narrow the field of art far more than the artists themselves. Audiences may have such rigid definitions about what art is that they instantly dismiss anything that does not conform to their definition. For example, an audience might define music as melody and harmony and, therefore, refuse to consider rap or twelve-tone a musical form. Some people have the prejudice (more common in the nineteenth century than today) that all art should be pretty. A piece may be nonrepresentational so that there is no likeness to any known object. Does that make it not art? I know some people who would rather claim imperiously that a painting or a sculpture is not "really" art than to look at it to see what, if anything, they can find there. They may, of course, be right—there may be nothing there. But we should be careful before we make such a claim—it may be our own limitations that keep us from seeing what is there.

Second, some art must be performed. Therefore the performer may intervene between the artist and the client. In music and drama, a performer must make an artistic input into somebody else's work of art to make it complete. The performers' or the director's abilities and egos may distort the original message; conversely, a good performer can create a worthwhile message where there would appear to be none, and a good director can find messages that the author did not even know were there.

Third, aesthetics in the modern industrial world has developed as a specialized field of study. The rest of us have been trained to think that we have to be educated about art before we can trust our impressions. Few of us have that special education. Therefore, the idea that a specialist is required to stand as a screen between us and the art object interferes with our even looking at, let alone seeing, what is there.

Art historians provide lots of information about the screen between artist and object. Art *critics*, on the other hand, mount a special guard over the screen between the art object and the observer. Too often we run to the critic to find out what we ought to see instead of looking for ourselves. We listen to the critic instead of to the art. We then see what the critics tell us to see, not what the artist tells us to see. In simpler societies, none of these screens are there. There is nothing but the art between the creator and the audience.

In modern capitalist societies, the market price of a piece of art mystically becomes its value. Thus, too often, critics take whatever messages are expressed in the art and turn them into manufactured aesthetics. The dealers put a price on it. Should we see art as an utterance, a stimulus, or an investment (Langer 1953)?

Finally, the viewer's own beliefs and values may form a screen that will lead to disapproval of the message. Art that is totally successful in technical terms alone, but conveys an unacceptable message, may be deemed pornographic. In the views of some, that makes it trash. But if the definition of pornography is that it stirs the sexual or aggressive appetites as well as the emotions, defining a piece of art as pornography may well indicate its success. Some people relegate some art to trash, no matter how well it is done, if they disapprove of the message. They may claim that no artist should be allowed to cross the boundaries of religious belief, for example. If a painting or sculpture makes a joke about a value highly prized in the culture, does that make it not art? Obviously, the boundaries that act as a screen between an art object and our perception of it are culturally drawn.

10-24. *Some art is bought to indicate "I have been there." The people who make such art, however, are often moved by far more aesthetic purposes. This Balinese sculptor is working with one of his chisels on the wood block resting in his lap. Note the carved door.*

When a piece of art crosses cultural boundaries, the expression of the artist and the impression of the receiver may be very different indeed. So-called tourist art, such as African carvings that are sold in airports, may have an inner meaning to the carver, yet the buyer may see in it only something that proves he or she has been there (Jules-Rosette 1984) or may even make it stand for ideas that the consumer wants to underline, but which the artist never heard of.

CONCLUDING THOUGHTS

The search by humans for meaning begins with language. Language allows us to communicate. Language is possible when we share the meanings of symbols; sharing symbols cements our relationship with others. The community of people who share symbols creates and solidifies their culture through communication.

Symbols lead us to another human need: the need for explanation. Culture is strengthened when we can explain not only how but why we do things. Discovery of meaning, explanation of the significance of that meaning, and

10-25. When explanations change—that is, when new ideas take over from old ones—the culture is changed as much or even more than it is changed by the introduction of new tools and work processes.

communication of both form the basis of all art. The arts can provide at least as much illumination about the way people view the world and the day-to-day course of their lives as do their kinship systems or their economy.

The purposes of art—and, as we shall see, of religion—can thus be described as the compounding and utilizing of complexities to provide deep satisfaction and a sense of purpose to individuals. Through recontexting, art reveals how the various pieces of the culture fit together. In the process, people are linked more securely to the culture, thereby reinforcing their sense of security in an insecure world. The purposes of social science are not to deny validity to any piece of art, but to understand through analysis how the art is considered to be valid. It takes courage and thought to allow art and aesthetics and criticism all to live in the same universe!

BUZZWORDS

aesthetic a philosophy or point of view about art and the way it is made. In the plural, aesthetics refers to a philosophy of the beautiful (as contrasted with the useful or the scientific).

language a specific example of a system of human speech that is shared by a group who also share other culture and values.

morpheme the minimal unit of meaning in a language.

phoneme the minimal unit of sound within a language.

sign a thing or action that directly conveys a meaning through an association with the object or idea indicated.

speech oral communication by means of language.

symbol a thing, sound or action that, by cultural agreement, indicates something else. Symbols are entirely cultural—that is, they are not based on a natural relationship between the symbol and the thing symbolized. The capacity to use symbols is the essential ingredient of living a cultured life.

syntax the patterns within a single language for arranging sounds, words or phrases in order to make sense.

Meaning
Creativity and Performance
11

PROPOSITIONS AND PREMISES

- People accept and renew culture by performing it and creating it—cultural creativity is a way of adapting to the environment.

- Questioning cultural premises and shifting ideas from one context to a new context are ways of being culturally creative.

- Most culture has been performed before. Most performances are reperformances.

- Stories underlie much cultural performance and creativity. They are repositories for people's deepest values.

- Myth is a device for bringing together in story, and often in performance, ideas about cosmology, the creation, the social structure, prehistory and history; it may also explain misfortune. Myth is untrue in the sense that the events did not actually happen as told in the story; it is, however, the epitome of truth in that it focuses and summarizes moral values.

- Ritual is a mechanism for acting out symbolized perceptions of the worldview, including the social structure. It is sometimes a reenactment of myth.

- Ritual may be satisfying because of the moral and aesthetic values it reaffirms.

215

People do not merely accept culture; they also perform it and create it. Culture is devised over and over again by individual people. If the old culture works well enough, the only reason people want to change it is their need for novelty. When the environment changes or old ideas are no longer useful as explanations, people become uncomfortable and tinker with their culture to make it more effective.

CULTURE AND CREATIVITY

Culture is the product of human creativity. Given the human brain and the capacity for detailed communication, cultural creativity has become the primary mode by which people adapt to the environment. Creativity is now prized for itself in some societies, including our own.

It has taken a long time for us to comprehend the simplicity of creativity. As we saw in 2-5, the learning processes are quite simple when we understand them from the standpoint of feedback theory. The idea of creativity is also simple if we look at it right, although achieving it may be very difficult.

Creativity involves at least two special qualities. Both are easy to state but perhaps not so easy to do. They are: (1) daring to question the standardized blueprint that your culture provides for how to do things (and that can be done effectively only by people who thoroughly understand their culture), and (2) lifting ideas from one context and transplanting them to another—an act which, in this book, we call recontexting.

Questioning the Blueprint

People perform the culture that they know. Those performances can be carried out on the basis of old ideas. If people do not question those ideas—if they do not challenge the received wisdom about how things *ought* to be done—they cannot change their culture. They can only repeat it.

In the late nineteenth and early twentieth centuries, almost nobody believed that the people they called savages could be creative. The ethnocentric assumption was that "savages" could not be creative because their technology was simple. It was also assumed that such cultures changed either very slowly or not at all. These cultures were called "stable." The assumption was that a stable culture underwent no change—we now know that we can have stability with change, something like the stable equilibrium in chemistry. There was even an idea called "the cake of custom" (cake in the sense of a hardened layer) that explained that falsehood. It claimed that unimaginative savages were kept by the weight of their traditions from ever changing anything.

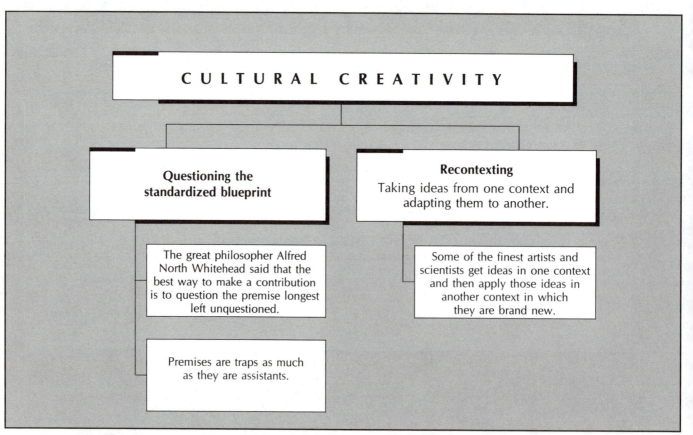

CULTURAL CREATIVITY

Questioning the standardized blueprint

The great philosopher Alfred North Whitehead said that the best way to make a contribution is to question the premise longest left unquestioned.

Premises are traps as much as they are assistants.

Recontexting
Taking ideas from one context and adapting them to another.

Some of the finest artists and scientists get ideas in one context and then apply those ideas in another context in which they are brand new.

11-1. There are two major avenues for cultural creativity: questioning (often unconsciously) the premises that underlie current ways of doing things, and recontexting—that is, transferring an idea to an arena in which it was never before examined.

11-2. When people cannot question the premises that underlie their reasoning they often fail to perceive what they see or hear; they may be led into social traps. Seventeenth-century misrepresentations of alien peoples by Europeans resulted in part because they could not question either the premise of the noble savage or the premise of the savage who had fallen from God's grace. This bronze head was made in Benin in West Africa during the seventeenth century, when Europe was having so much trouble seeing beyond the "savage."

Behind this idea lay two contradictory notions derived from philosophers of the seventeenth and eighteenth centuries. On the one hand was the idea that "primitive man" was a noble savage, healthy, moral, wise, and kind. On the other hand was the contradictory idea that primitive man was a debased creature who had fallen from God's grace. Both those ideas kept almost everybody from looking at the people they called savages to see who they in fact were. The idea of "savage" was in the premises, not in the data. It was the lens through which the early philosophers looked.

The world has, of course, seen many examples of cultures that appear to be relatively unchanged over many centuries. Yet, if there is a rule of cultural change and growth, it is

this: if human beings find their ways of doing things inadequate, they search for better ways to do them. If people are getting the results they want, they change nothing. If they are not getting the results they want, they seek other ways to accomplish their ends.

Most animals alter the environment they live in just by living there. Human beings make a point of altering the environment to fit what they see as their needs. People consciously create changes in their environment. They do it to make their lives easier and more assured. As we shall see as we proceed through the book, people create more and more changes in order to make the environment, as they experience it, more convenient or more beautiful or more meaningful.

11-3. Culture is a constantly evolving feedback between tools (including social tools) and meanings.

Culture can thus be seen as a constantly evolving mixture of tools and meanings. Tools allow us to be more efficient in altering our environments and therewith the stimuli we perceive. Meanings tell us why the environment, or some tool, or some action, or some idea is significant, efficient, beautiful—they also tell us that something doesn't work very well and has to be changed. Cultural life is a process not merely of using tools and meanings but of creatively improving whatever tools we find inadequate and reinterpreting the ideas we find unclear or limiting. Thus, the history of human culture is the history of human creativity in response to challenges from the physical and cultural environment.

Performing

Culture is created from time to time, but it is performed all the time. Once it is created, constant performance keeps the culture alive. Doing culture is a performance whether it is the industrial or business processes we do in work hours, or ritual, or preparing a meal. Culture can be stored in the form of artifacts and writings; it can be remembered in peoples' heads. But, to be living, vital culture, it has to be performed constantly.

Performance involves understanding our basic tools and meanings. It means summarizing experience so that it can guide future decisions. It means appreciating and acknowledging the importance of other people's experiences of pleasure and bitterness, betrayals and victories.

Shakespeare's phrase—all the world's a stage, and all the men and women merely players—is a useful metaphor even though we all know that it isn't so. Looking at the world as if it were a stage can be enlightening. The analogy of real life to drama has been a rewarding one for anthropology. In the 1930s, a great anthropologist named Ralph Linton elaborated the idea of "role" and helped move social science forward. Soon the word "actor" came to be standard parlance for the person who performs a role. In the 1950s, "presentation of self in everyday life" (Goffman 1959) extended the analogy between our everyday behavior and the performance of theatrical roles. In 1957, anthropologist Victor Turner used the term "sociodrama" to mean the kind of cultural processes illustrated in this book by flowcharts. Recently an anthropologically informed theater director has made still further analogies between theatrical performance and the cultural performance of our everyday lives (Schechner 1985).

Growing up and learning culture is learning to play our parts. We are given the scripts for these parts by the people around us. We learn the steps and skills of domestic and technological processes either from our parents and mentors or from educators and teachers. We learn manners. We perform the scripts more or less in accordance with the way we are expected to perform. We learn to say "thank you" if our culture thinks we should; we learn to eat with chopsticks or, even more difficult, with a fork; we learn to sleep in a bed (which may take more skill than you think—children often, some adults occasionally, fall out). We set silverware on the table one way if we are British and quite a different way if we are French—but we perform it repeatedly, day after day, meal after meal. Nineteenth-century American and European ladies learned to put on hats before going into a church. At the same time men were learning to take their hats off when going inside any building. We even have sex according to the rules of our culture; making love is a learned act. We also learn rules for breaking rules. Culture was there for you to learn, and it will be there (perhaps changed just a little) after you are gone. You are the performer—the actor. Every actor plays his own Hamlet—but Hamlet remains.

When we are growing up as children we learn parenting roles. Then, when we become parents, we perform one of those roles. We, of course, put our own stamp on all the roles we perform. We can change anything we opt to change. If we do not specifically decide to change something, we perform it the way we learned it when we were children. Fathering and mothering are complex roles. We learn both roles but ultimately perform only one of them. We know lots of roles we do not perform. We learn to perform at our jobs, to perform as citizens, as members of our congregations and of our families. You know the role of student, and how the teachers expect you to perform. You also know the role of professor, and you expect professors to perform at least well enough. Most of the behavior in most institutions is some combination of role behavior and technical behavior. Both are learned—both are performed.

Obviously, people don't always perform well. Sometimes people want to change the expectations of a role, so they change what they do when they perform it. Almost everybody ad libs occasionally. If they get away with it, their new way of doing things may even spread; other people may begin to perform the role that way.

A performance needs a performer and an audience. The

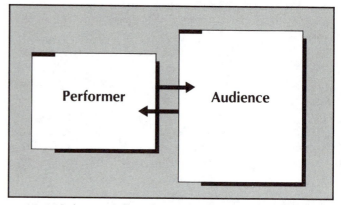

11-4. *Information flows between performer and audience. The audience may have considerable effect on the performance.*

performer and the audience both know that information passes between them, that a performance communicates a message. The message may be no more than "I am doing what is expected of me" or "I am great." The message may also have all sorts of political, artistic, scientific, or religious meaning. There may be a hidden message as well as an overt one. A performance can be about anything, and it can take place anywhere.

As we perform, we may begin to wonder "Which bits of what I am doing are the real me?" We may even ask, "Is there a 'real me' in there some place?" Schechner (1985) was fascinated by these questions as he watched a ritual the Yaqui Indians call the deer dance. The Indians perform the dance annually (near Tucson, Arizona) during their Easter celebration. The performance was riveting. The director asked himself: does putting on a deer mask turn the deer dancer into a deer as the Yaqui claim? His answer was: the dancer is not exactly himself, but he is not not-himself; he is not a deer, but he is not not-a-deer. He is some place in the middle. That middle is performance. We spend our lives in that middle.

Performing has an effect on the performer—maybe on the observers too, but certainly on the performer. To some degree we become what we perform, but we also continue not to be what we perform. By the time we are adult—and certainly by the time we are old—we are indelibly marked by our performances. We become ever more fully what we perform.

Behavior is made up, in part, of bits or "strips of behavior" (Schechner 1985) that have been performed by others before us. We put several of these strips together for each of our performances. The person and the prebehaved strips are brought together. Thus, we join ourselves irrevocably with other people whose strips intermesh with ours, as well as with those who once performed the same strips we are now performing. "Performance means: never for the first time. It means: from the second to the nth time. Performance is 'twice-behaved behavior'" (Schechner 1985).

It is also possible to bring new insights and new techniques into our performances—unlike the actor who plays Hamlet,

11-5. *Yaqui say that the dancer becomes the deer. We do not take that literally, but can see that the dancer represents the deer so that he is not not-the-deer. However, the dancer is also not not-himself.*

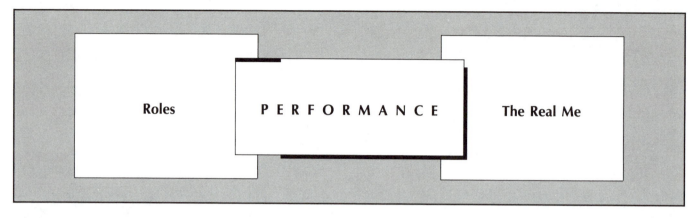

11-6. Performance stands between the role and the inner person. When you perform, the role is expressed and the inner person is also expressed. But as one performs better and better, both the role and the self become identified with the performance.

Roles   **P E R F O R M A N C E**   **The Real Me**

our performances may, just may, change the script. Our ideas may spread, may lead to questioning the old ways and premises of our culture.

Recontexting

Recontexting is a creative social process of duplicating meanings from one cultural context to another. In the new context, the old idea is wholly new and innovative. The duplication may not be precise, and almost certainly will not be complete. The new context almost always enforces reconsideration of the old meaning. We saw in the last chapter that recontexting the ideas of the real world into a world of play or of a game is a good way to learn, a good way to enjoy—and a good way to be creative. We also saw in Chapter 7 that recontexting morality and custom into a code of law is one of the vital points of justice and government.

STORIES

A culture is encapsulated in its stories. Stated in other terms, stories are creative expressions of essential aspects of culture. The creativity and fantasy expressed in stories help interpret established ideas. At the same time, stories (like riddles) serve to release the mind from some of its cultural strictures. You can think many thoughts in the form of stories that you cannot begin to think about in the realm of real life. Using stories, we can examine and question the basic premises of our culture, perhaps more effectively than any other way. We can recontext ideas into stories, either to underscore traditional values or to overthrow them with bold new cultural statements.

The art of the historian is the art of turning recorded past events into gripping stories. Religion is most often, and most convincingly, told with stories. Every person's life is a story—indeed, several stories. Whether they are epics, biographies, histories, scriptures or jokes, stories amuse and instruct us.

In the modern world, stories can be used as political propaganda.

Throughout most of history, stories have been told by word of mouth. They have also been cast into drama so that several people, each acting one of the characters, can tell the story in such a way that the storyteller becomes almost invisible.

11-7. Stories recontext familiar events. Like play, good stories offer relaxation, comfort, instruction. This photograph shows Leo Tolstoy, the great Russian novelist, storyteller and reformer, telling a story to his grandchildren.

With the introduction of writing about 3000 B.C., people began to write stories down. As printing and mass literacy became a reality, more and more people began to read stories from the written page. People, as they read, can picture the cultural background in their minds even more vividly than the most effective author can suggest. The reader, stimulated by a story whose problems and points he or she understands, is drawn in by her or his own capacity to imagine the situation. People who read well find this kind of participation in the story, indeed, in the storytelling, very rewarding.

In today's industrial world, the storyteller has left the marketplace or the fireside and gone into the television studio, often by way of the novelist's study. The fact that today a story can be copyrighted means that it can legally become the personal property of its author. The copyrighted story can be sold by its owner to the highest bidder; it can be rented, even syndicated. In some other societies, however, and in earlier days in our own, a story belonged to everybody.

Stories recontext the familiar events of living. When we tell stories, we set events over into a world of play, and then draw tight boundaries around them. Everything not in the story becomes momentarily irrelevant. It is like any other aspect of play: stories have rules that, as long as we follow them, allow us to shut out reality the very while we comment on reality and learn about it.

Successful storytellers must arrange the events in the story so that interest never flags. A good storyteller makes us lean forward, eager to know what happens next. The best novels are "page turners," which means that the reader continues reading compulsively just to see what will happen. Storytellers must create characters whom we can get to know, to hate or love, with whom we can identify or whom we want to destroy. Successful playwrights, especially when they write for television, always keep characters in action so that the next bit of the story dangles enticingly before us. The events that precede a commercial break must be powerful enough to keep us tuned in through commercials about breakfast foods and laxatives.

Storytelling is the art of summing up life, while at the same time making us see it from a new point of view. The storyteller must put the events of the story into an order that draws the listener further and further toward a conclusion: the ending.

At the ending of every successful story lurks a cultural premise. Virtue is rewarded. They lived happily ever after. Things are different since the war. They died tragically, but perhaps nobly. The villain, or somebody else who was far too clever for his or her own good, got his or her comeuppance. It may even be that there appears to be no ending—life goes on. The ending of every story is a cultural value, which is either reaffirmed, questioned, or both.

The most important forms of stories are: (1) tales (including folktales) that trace the adventures of characters who overcome obstacles or who otherwise have memorable experiences; tales often have overt morals that reinforce cultural convictions; (2) legends deal with important figures from the past, and their exploits; (3) aphorisms like proverbs, riddles, and maxims are very short stories that provide summaries of the lore about our culture; and (4) jokes turn stories into something to make us laugh—either because we are uncomfortable with the juxtaposition of ideas that we have never before associated, or because we have been in the same spot as the victim in the joke. We were embarrassed by those very things, but now we can laugh at ourselves by laughing at the people in the story. Some stories are told as poetry, which allows us to intensify and distill observation and emotion.

And, very importantly, myths are stories. Because of their great importance to ethnographic studies as clues to values and worldviews, we have given them a special place in this

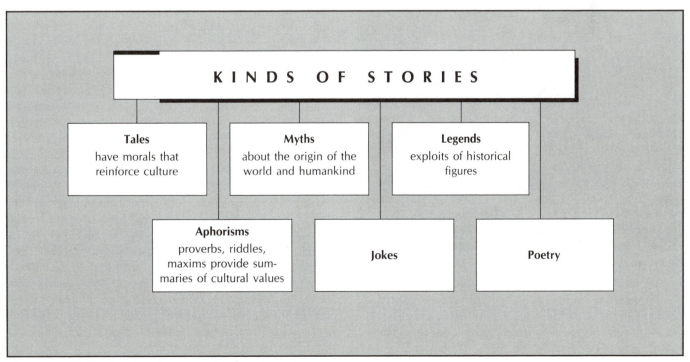

11-8. *A culture is encapsulated in its stories.*

chapter. They account for the origins of various plant and animal species, including human beings. They tell of the origins of the world and of geographical places in it. Myth is the great medium for getting everything in life to mesh with all the other aspects of life.

Tales

Tales are, most folklorists agree, nonreligious, nonhistorical stories, usually said to be fiction (but most of the peoples of the world do not make as strict a distinction on these points as do the folklorists). Folktales, like games, play with elemental themes and tensions so that they are simultaneously entertaining and instructive. Most end with a moral that expresses a cultural value. In its native habitat, a folktale is performed, either by a skilled storyteller or by a group of people who turn it into drama. In its original form, folklore is a vital set of stories, constantly recreated.

Folklore, as it is studied today, usually refers to knowledge that is transmitted orally in performance, although folklorists

11-9. Folktales are the basic texts that are embroidered by storytellers and dramatized to fit new conditions for performance. Their vitality arises from the telling or the dramatization, and from the cultural review or emphasis that moves people to be more loyal and better-behaving members of their own cultural groups. This masked dancer is from Bali.

have written illuminatingly on graffiti and those crafts that are learned by imitation and example. Most of the folklorists claim that anything that is mass produced or that is written down cannot be considered folklore.

The feeling—the entire point—of folklore is altered when a scholar writes the story down. When it is written down, it loses its performance value. The participation of a cooperative live audience disappears. Many folktales (like Cinderella or Hansel and Gretel) are ancient oral tales that were only written down after the invention of the printing press. Such stories are, to this day, far more effective when they are told or read aloud than when they are read silently.

Tiv women tell stories to their children and sometimes to their friends—but seldom to their co-wives' children for fear the entertainment in the stories could be viewed as trying to win the affection of those children away from their own mothers. The stories are short; the groups are small. Tiv men tell stories at evening gatherings to all who will listen, sometimes as many as two hundred people. When a group of that size gathers, usually two or three storytellers compete for the audience's attention. The better a person's stories, the more likely he is to get the audience's attention, and the more they encourage him to tell others.

Tiv storytellers use music, mime and dance to enhance their stories. They turn ordinary furniture, huge wooden mortars and pestles, cooking pots and gourd storage containers—anything that is handy—into props. They either make up their own songs or else a storyteller joins forces with a composer. The story then is acted out with exaggerated characters, often based on recognizable quirks of local people. Songs are interspersed. The songs demand a sung response from the audience. Therefore, the storyteller or composer must teach them their parts of the song. The storyteller then proceeds with his story and with his singing, signalling the audience to put in their part of the songs when it is relevant. The entire audience is thereupon singing the responses as it follows the story being performed.

Most of the stories are well-known to the audience, at least in bare-bones outline. They may be imaginative tales about the clever hare who sometimes is so clever that he outwits himself (this hare, by the way, is the great-great-ever so-great-grandfather of Brer Rabbit). Or about the monitor lizard and many other animal characters whose human characteristics make comments on the wits and witlessness of human actions. Some of the new versions are scurrilous, building on recent gossip. They always point to a moral about what good people should be doing. What we coyly call four-letter words in our language are three-letter words in Tiv, and there are no euphemisms. Sexual and scatological acts are discussed, even depicted, in great detail. They are hilarious. Everybody, including the ethnographer, thinks so. I have seen myself mercilessly lampooned—I have laughed and learned some of the things I did not do well enough to satisfy my friends, who wanted me to be a better Tiv than I ever was. I tried harder.

One simple story that Tiv use in many of their theatrical

evenings can be endlessly elaborated; its moral is one that means something quite different to Tiv men than to Tiv women, but when it is acted out with songs, it never ceases to delight Tiv of all ages. Once upon a time (or, as they put it, "long long ago, something befell") it was the custom that whenever a woman married, she gave her vulva to her husband. As he went around the countryside, he carried it with him, in his shoulder bag. In that way, every time he wished to use it, he had it handy. However, one thoughtless man once left his shoulder bag too near the fire. Everything in it, including his wife's vulva, was badly scorched. When he arrived home, his wife discovered the scorched and charred condition of her vulva. She became very angry and took it away from him. She refused ever again to allow him to carry it with him. And that is the reason that today every vulva is attached to a woman (which is the moral).

11-10. Great crowds of Tiv meet—usually just after dark, but sometimes, as here, in the late afternoon—to begin dramatizing folktales into performances in which song-makers and audience participate, in which new and original ways of looking at tradition and of laughing at troubles makes everybody relax.

When the tale is used as the basis of performance, it goes through many changes and elaborations, limited only to the imagination and directorial skill of the teller. The cast includes, at a minimum, the wife, the husband, and the vulva. The songs are bawdy. The situation in which the scorching happens is different in every performance. I have seen several—in one, the husband got drunk; in another he was chasing another woman; in still another he was called upon to act as a witness in settling a dispute between co-wives. In whatever form, the husband was always the one who grew careless and failed to appreciate the priceless treasure he carried. The various characterizations of the indignant wife (always played by a man) ran the entire gamut of emotions— all turned into comedy. The character of the vulva itself was sometimes coy, sometimes incisively angry, sometimes

pushing its own rights and feelings, sometimes sticking up for the wife, sometimes telling the husband to forget the wife for the moment.

Songs were made up for each of the characters. After every line of a song by each of the characters, the audience sang a response. Adventure could be piled on adventure. Taking the simple story, with its important moral, they made up funny and theatrical variations. The folktale was very much a live part of the culture. People reacted to it as they do to good theater everywhere: their basic values are underscored, they laugh or cry and relax, and go home feeling better.

Some Americans, especially women, find this tale offensive. They say that it denigrates women, turning them into sex objects. Some say that it tells you that men are the same the whole world over. Some have even told me that it cannot be true—that if I think Tiv women enjoy the story, I am wrong. Tiv women themselves say that the tale is a reaffirmation that they have to be considered as people. They are important in themselves—they are not, in today's feminist terms, merely sex objects. When an ethnographer discusses that story with Tiv men, they say that it means that men have to be responsive to the needs of women. In short, that is a story that can be used by any one of us to examine our attitudes and the premises that we each bring to enjoying or not enjoying a story. Every reader can find new meanings that might be attached to the story. That is what makes it important to Tiv: the meanings are constantly renewed as new ideas emerge. Most of all, it makes people laugh.

11-11. Stories, dramatizations, dances—all can be used to help maintain morale in the face of adversity. Tiv dramatize or dance diseases such as the deforming diseases mocked here, then overcome them by laughing at the dancers or the players.

In performed and danced satires, Tiv turn various diseases into characters who can be humiliated or dances in which they can be laughed at. Tiv life, like that of all peoples, is

Meaning: Creativity and Performance

beset by illnesses and disease. Yaws can disfigure one's legs and, in its later stages, twist the long bones into arcs. I have seen Tiv strap large flat gourds to their legs, cover them with mud or some other substance to make them look like scabs, then dance part of a story. Other Tiv find it hilarious. I have seen them put large gourds under their cloths to represent a scrotum swelled with elephantiasis. Keil reports (1979) one dance in which they put a soccer ball under the cloth, while other dancers kicked it, to the delight of all. Tiv make up stories and dances about the diseases that regularly afflict them, then laugh all the way through.

When American or European anthropologists first see and hear these stories performed, they get the queasy feeling that the Tiv are laughing at afflicted people. We Americans have been painstakingly taught not to laugh at people with disabilities or deformities. Tiv, however, do it all the time—but they are not laughing at the people themselves. They are using laughter to overcome their fear and horror of the diseases. It is the disease that is treated scurrilously, not the person who has it. The diseases and symptoms are depicted as characters that the courage and laughter of real people can overcome through ridicule.

All the tales that are told and often retold in new versions at these performances are hilarious or gripping in the performance context, with the audience responding to the songs. Tiv are masters of drawing out into long performances simple plots that, if written down, would be no more than a hundred words long. But writing them down takes all the juice out of them. Indeed, writing any folklore down may preserve the stories but cannot begin to preserve the performance.

 An American culture hero named George got a new hatchet as a present when he was about twelve years old. To try it out, he took a whack at a cherry tree. The hatchet, being a good one, so impressed the young man that he lost his sense of responsibility and cut the cherry tree all the way down. His father was very angry. But George, well-raised lad that he was, said "Father, I cannot tell a lie" and took his punishment for having done something bad. He, who became the father of his country, is now the model of honesty for all of his descendants.

This same young George, when he got a little bit older, threw a silver dollar across the widest part of the Rappohannock River. Some people say that the moral to this story is that he was very strong and could really throw straight; others say that he had not yet learned the value of a dollar.

WE, THE ALIEN

Legends

Legends are traditional stories told by people as if they were true. A legend is likely to be told about many different casts of characters and in many different places and times—the story remains the same, but the people to whom it allegedly happened may change. In southernmost Texas, in the lower Rio Grande Valley, Mexican-Americans keep many legends and stories from their Mexican heritage. Many of them deal with encounters with the dead, and many are said to have happened to acquaintances of those who tell the stories. For example, there is a story that "twenty years ago" a bride and groom on their way to their honeymoon had a car accident at a railroad crossing near Brownsville, Texas, and the bride was killed—still wearing her white wedding dress. Ever since, there have been reports of a young lady wearing a white wedding dress haunting that crossing between 11:30 at night and 2:00 in the morning (Glazer 1982).

Mexican-American truckdrivers in south Texas have a supply of stories about "road ghosts." In one of the most vivid ones, a truckdriver, late at night, found a barefooted nun beside the road asking for a ride. She was cold, so he gave her his jacket. As she requested, he took her to the house of a priest, next to a church. She asked him to go into the house, to ask for the priest. From the doorway, the truckdriver could see a photograph of the nun. He told the priest that the nun in the photograph had asked for a ride. The priest told him that the nun had been dead for twenty years and took the truckdriver to see her grave. On top of the grave lay the truckdriver's jacket.

Sometimes the figure of the devil appears in such stories. For example, a young woman defies her mother and goes to a dance; an attractive man appears and dances over and over with her. When it is discovered that this handsome man has one horse's hoof and one chicken foot instead of human feet, he—the devil—disappears, and the young woman collapses and dies.

A man who is a *mujeriego* (womanizer) may, according to the stories, approach a good-looking woman, making suggestions to her. When she looks directly at him, she has no face—only a skull. Invariably, this story goes, the man falls from shock (an ailment called *susto* in Mexico) and ultimately dies.

The story is often told, in many different versions, of the weeping woman who drowned her children for their own safety, but was told by God that she could not be forgiven until she found them. These stories are molded and remolded to make many moral points. Here is a simple form of the story of the weeping woman:

> There was a young girl that lived in Guanajuato. Her name was Luisa, and she was very pretty. One day, she fell in love with a young man of that town. They decided to live together for a while. The time went by and they had two sons. The young man got sick and died. Luisa felt lonely, and lost her senses. She threw her sons in the river called Rio Lerma and the

current took them. When she died God did not receive her. God wanted Luisa to take her sons with her, so, he sends her back to look for them. Luisa really does not know where her sons are. That is why Luisa cried wherever there is water because she's looking for her sons (Glazer 1982).

11-12. Mexican-Americans in Texas have huge supplies of folktales and legends. Like people everywhere, they change the qualities that the characters represent in order to make new points. In this artist's view, the Weeping Woman has the face of a horse. What might it mean?

The basic story—a woman who drowned her children and haunts waterways in search of them—has many elaborations. In some, the young husband falls in love with another woman and wants to leave the first wife and take his sons with him; the young mother drowns the boys to prevent it. In another version, the young husband's family threatens to disinherit him unless he leaves his beloved wife and children in order to make a socially suitable marriage. With a heavy heart he does so. Then, when the wife drowns their children, he leaves his new wife, takes the blame for what the first wife did, and they both go searching for the drowned children. One young man remembers that when he and his friends were growing up, they lived near a large canal. They built rafts to play

on top of the water. When their parents discovered what they were doing, they warned them not to do that again— the weeping woman, the children were warned, would come, think them her lost children, and carry them away.

Stories of this sort reinforce ideas of appropriate behavior—children shouldn't play near water, you shouldn't pick up hitchhikers, watch out for railroad tracks.

Riddles, Proverbs and Jokes

In addition to stories and tales, folklorists study riddles. They also examine the proverbs that adults drop into their conversation. Proverbs are highly concise phrases that sum up the values and ways that the culture should be performed in order to achieve prosperity, peace and enjoyment.

In simpler societies, such folklore as riddles, conundrums, and folktales are all performance forms. Poetry is another example of performance. In our own society, poets read their work aloud, often in small bookstores, sometimes in small rooms at universities. Some poets are better performers than others—it gives the illusion (and may be no more than that) that their poems are better. Reading poetry aloud—even if one is alone and reading to oneself—makes both the rhythm and the message more vibrant than when it is read silently.

Jokes may well be the stories most closely allied with specific cultures. Jokes are notoriously hard to translate—in part because they depend on specific words when no precise analog exists in another language. Jokes sometimes get into universal human characteristics, but more often they are take-offs of very specific cultural actions. When I first went to live in England many of the jokes were beyond me—I didn't know the cultural details or the allusions. It took me a couple of years to find out what was funny. In the same way, you don't really know any culture until you can understand the jokes and, if you are a joker, make jokes in that language and culture.

People in different cultures think quite different things are funny. They laugh at what seems, to the rest of the world, to be the most strange things! There is another grave problem: studying jokes is the surest way I know to turn them to dust. If you don't believe that, turn to Freud's theoretically important book, *Jokes and Their Relation to the Unconscious.* To analyze a joke is to misunderstand it (for all that the analysis may lead us to understand what jokes are used for and how they are created).

The uses of folklore are many. First of all, it is a source of amusement and fun. It is educational in the sense that cultural values are carefully highlighted in tales and riddles. Folklore, particularly proverbs, can be used as informal means for maintaining social control. Since many of the deepest values of the society are summed up in short aphorisms, a few words can convey the entire idea of the culturally approved behavior. Proverbs not only can express approval or disapproval, but they can minimize deviation from the culturally accepted norms. They can summarize succinctly the main points of the cultural charters. Jokes are powerful means of maintaining social control and punishing wrongdoers.

Myth

Myths, like any other stories, are performed in most societies, particularly those that are not yet literate. People make reference to myths in their daily lives—indeed, they may run their lives with the idioms and the meanings summarized in the myths. The only way that a nonliterate people can preserve and use their myths is by telling and performing them.

In order to gain a deeper understanding of the stories that are the charters for the cultures of the world, we will investigate four criteria for myth (Honko 1984). The (1) *content* of myths is concerned primarily with the events that stem from the beginning of time and are about the creation of nature and culture. In its (2) *form*, a myth is a story. The same story can be given form in ritual drama and in icons, sermons, and dance. The (3) *function* of the myth is to provide both an explanation and a blueprint for both social relationships and the relationship of humanity to the rest of nature. The (4) *context* in which the myth is used by the people is usually ritual, but it can be recontexted into many other dimensions of living.

Myths are usually stories about gods. Among the most vital of myths are accounts of the beginning of the world. Myths hold that deeds of the gods created nature and culture and the order which holds them together. The telling of such myths constantly reconfirms the values and norms of the people. They detail the behavior that people should try to imitate. They confirm the effectiveness of ritual.

The Tiv tell a short myth that explains how the world came to be. It is in many ways typical of African religious explanations, although it is starker than most because it postulates no spirits. In the beginning, the story goes, God (*Aondo*—the same word means sky and might well be translated as firmament) made the Earth and everything in it. As God made it, the world was good; it contained no evil. Evil entered the world with the secret intentions and greed of individual human beings, which are the sources of all evil.

Behind that stark simplicity lurk intense and difficult questions. The Tiv say that after Aondo made the world, he took no further interest in it; they never pray to God. They see him as an otiose God—that is, a distant and idle God, at leisure or rest. Although Aondo takes no interest in the world he made, he *knows* everything. Indeed, he may be the *only* one to know many things. Tiv do not allow their practical knowledge, which resembles science, to contradict their myth. They also do not project their personal troubles onto a divine plane. They require no devil or anything like a devil. The devil, they say, is in us all. They consider humankind—indeed, their kinfolk and neighbors—the source of evil as well as the source of support.

But Aondo did provide powers that evil people can use for evil purposes. The powers themselves are amoral; the evil motives of human beings can pervert them to selfish and evil ends. Therefore, not only evil, but also misfortune is caused by humankind. A whole attitude toward neighbors and kinfolk is reflected in such a myth.

How was the world made? The creation myth of the Judeo-Christian religions, in the first chapter of Genesis, tells us God did it in six days. The physicists say it happened in an instant. What was the origin of human beings? Genesis says God made us on the fifth day. The evolutionary biologists say we evolved through a process that took millions of years. How do we account for evil? Genesis lays the blame on a serpent. Psychologists find the seeds of evil behavior of adults in their childhood traumas and abuse. What are the roots of ill health? Medicine is hard at work to find out, but don't forget that astrology columns remain one of the most commonly consulted features of our daily newspapers.

Americans value freedom of thought and religion. A correlate is that we allow many orthodoxies and disallow few heterodoxies. Many components of many systems are to be found in different crannies of American culture. Many people, instead of or in addition to their recognized religions, create their own do-it-yourself belief systems out of these components.

WE, THE ALIEN

Anthropologists concerned with myth and ritual are faced not merely with determining what the symbols of a myth "mean," but also with ferreting out the core ideas of a culture and with showing how these many and perhaps disparate ideas fit together. People think and feel by means of the complexity of their myths, which they almost never analyze consciously.

The scholarly study of myth is replete with arguments and disagreements among erudite authorities. Many of the differences of opinion are based on definitions or translations of words. There is general agreement that myth must be differentiated from legend, and both from fictional stories. But making the distinctions is associated by many scholars with confusion about whether the people who tell the myths think they are true. What is a true story? Fiction contains many truths, but it isn't "true" in the sense that it actually happened. When my son was in the third grade, his teacher wrote on his report card that he had trouble distinguishing reality and make-believe. When I went for my regular interview with the teacher, I asked her what the difference was. She was nonplussed; I am sure that after I left she wrote in her records that he learned this confusion from his father. But who was confused? What *is* the difference? What does

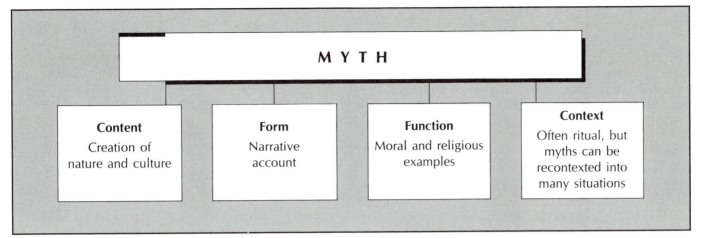

MYTH			
Content Creation of nature and culture	**Form** Narrative account	**Function** Moral and religious examples	**Context** Often ritual, but myths can be recontexted into many situations

11-13. The Criteria for Myth.

"true" mean? It can mean historically accurate (but how that is determined has puzzled historians for many years); it can mean valid from the standpoint of some criterion or other (but that means that the validity changes as the criterion changes). Tiv have two words for truth. One of them means what actually happened in the past. The other one is what you should say happened if you want to preserve amicable social relationships. Tiv think it unwise to tell the first kind of truth if it will not also serve the second. Whatever the historical truth, myths are true in the sense that they provide a set of premises for interpreting the world and judging the validity of the culture.

Our best chance of understanding the structure of mythical thought is to study cultures where myth is a 'living thing,' where it constitutes the very ground of the religious life; in other words, where myth, far from indicating a *fiction*, is considered to reveal the *truth par excellence*.

Mircea Eliade (1969), in Dundes (1984)

THEY SAID IT

The complex origin myths of the Dayaks of Borneo seem at the opposite extreme from the simple Tiv myth, although their message is the same kind of message. These Dayak myths form an elaborate poetic statement of Dayak cosmology, using highly imaginative symbols to account for both the principles of the cosmos and of human society (Scharer 1963; there is a good summary in Eliade 1984).

According to the Dayak myth, the cosmos began as an entity in the mouth of a coiled water snake. Then two mountains arose; from the clashing of the two mountains,

11-14. Mythology is studied not only by anthropologists, but also by folklorists, psychologists, historians and many others. Mircea Eliade was a highly original, and therefore controversial, student of myths. Although he was a philosopher by training, he made important contributions to the anthropological study of myth and religion.

Meaning: Creativity and Performance

cosmic reality began to emerge. The sun, the moon, clouds, hills—all sprang into being as a result of the conflict between the two mountains. The two supreme deities dwell on the two mountains—indeed, they and the mountains are the same. The deities eventually take human form: Mahatala and his wife Putir. In this human form, the two deities created two worlds, an upper world and an underworld, but there was still no middle world with people in it. In the next phase of creation, the deities take the form of birds—of two hornbills. Mahatala creates the tree of life in the center of everything that has been done so far. The two hornbills meet in the tree and begin to fight. The fight is so ferocious that the tree of life is severely damaged. Yet, from the tree and some moss that hung from the beak of the female hornbill, a young girl and a young man step forth. They are ancestors of all Dayaks. The two birds end by killing each other and destroying the tree of life in the process.

The deities have, in the course of that story, assumed several forms: cosmic and natural (as mountains), human-like (as Mahatala and Putir) and birdlike (the hornbills). Put another way, they represent the cosmos, nature, humanity, and animal life. All these forms are united in other symbols such as the water snake with which the story started.

Deep philosophical assumptions lurk within this story. For example, everything contains its opposite. The premises that underlie society are subtly hidden in the myth: the world was made in conflict between two polar principles; the conflict destroyed the tree of life; thus life springs from destruction, but again destroys itself.

Dayak ritual repeats these themes. They underlie Dayak thought. Even the marriage ceremony is a replay of the myth: the couple grasp a symbol of the tree of life, indicating that it can be destroyed by their violence toward one another. Girl's initiation ceremonies use the themes of the myth in

that the girls are separated from society and said to turn into the water snake; they are put into a room that is said to correspond to the primeval waters. In other words, they go back to the beginning. Then, to the accompaniment of complex rituals, they emerge as new persons, beginning new lives.

The Dayak creation myths form a framework for the most vital parts of their law. They dominate the rites that surround birth, initiation, marriage, death. Even gift giving and trade are all explained in terms of aspects of the myth. The whole of life is lived in terms of the myth.

The Aranda of Australia provide another well-documented example of how myth provides a blueprint for living. The Aranda say that the sky and the earth have existed for all of eternity. Supernatural beings have always lived in them. An emu-footed personage—the Great Father—lives in the sky with his emu-footed wives and children. Their land is perpetually green and filled with flowers and fruits. They are eternally young, the Great Father appearing no older than his children. And all of them are immortal, like the stars. Emu-foot did not make the Earth or humankind or any other part of the cosmos, and was never interested in events on Earth. He is a God more otiose even than the Tiv God, yet he is important to the Aranda.

During the dream time, the myths continue, formless masses of half-developed human babies filled the Earth. They could neither develop nor die because life and death were unknown. Life existed only below the Earth, where super-natural beings were sleeping. Then they awoke and broke through the surface of the Earth; the places where they emerged are still vibrant with their power. The Sun emerged in this way, flooding the world with light. Some emerged as animals; some as human beings. These creatures wandered the Earth and established all the geographical landmarks of

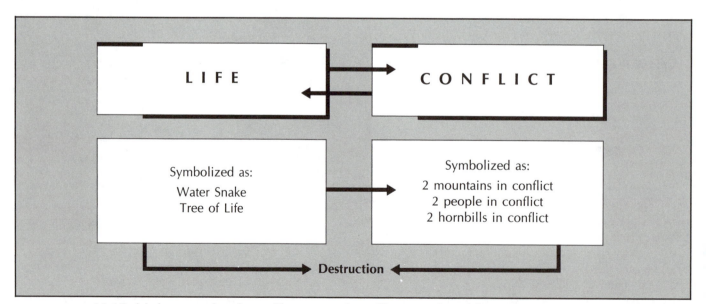

11-15. Myths encapsulate the worldview in a culture. Here are a few of the many meanings in the Dayak myth of origin. If you go to the original, you can find many other meanings, and perhaps diagram them.

11-16. Basic ideas about the nature of the cosmos are found in myth and often reenacted in ritual. The aboriginal people of Australia postulated—and still do—a dream time that is eternal; it is part of, yet separated from, the mundane world. Visions and ritual allow the two to touch and influence one another. This photograph was taken in the Northern Territories of Australia in 1911.

the land of the Aranda. They also gave form and life to the half-infants that already existed. The animals and the people are the totemic ancestors of today's Australian aborigines. Some of these ancestors became culture heroes, and the appearance of different cultural items and knowledge of their use is said to have been created by them. Because it was so much work, they sank into the ground in exhaustion. Rocks and trees and ritual objects are all that is left of them. However, they did not go back to the same state as before they emerged; they still watch over human beings. Every person is connected with one of the ancestors—a person is one of the many manifestations of that ancestor. It all weaves together.

Aranda ritual is a constant repetition of the activities of these totemic ancestors. As young Aranda men undergo initiation, they discover not only what happened in the dream time but that they themselves were there, a part of it all. The purpose of their initiation is to learn that they themselves are the heros of these myths.

Ritual

Ritual is the acting out, and therefore the renewal, of myth. A ritual is an enacted, performed, drama. It has a purpose, which is most commonly either curing a person who is ill,

commemorating an event in the life course of some individual or of the community, or recognizing the passage of the seasons. It may implore the spirits for needed sustenance; it may be giving thanks to God or the gods for a harvest or some other grace. But ritual is acted out—it is performance.

Much of ritual is of a religious nature, but by no means all of it. It was determined many decades ago that rituals follow precise patterns. One of the most precise patterns is that of the **rites of passage** (van Gennep [1908] 1960), as is illustrated in 11-17. A rite of passage is made up of three parts. The first part is a rite of separation—it removes the person from his current life status. Symbols of death are often used in rites of separation, as the person symbolically dies to his former identity, and is then free to enter an entirely new cultural realm. The middle stage is the transition ritual. Here the requirements and norms of everyday life do not hold. This situation is a threshold between the old and the new and is often considered a dangerous position. Then, in the third phase—the rites of incorporation—the person is reborn into a new cultural status or identity—an identity that the transition rites empowered him or her to assume.

Note that the Christian Easter ritual follows this pattern. Indeed, rituals of passage are found whenever an individual or a group is changing from one status to another: at birth, at initiation into adulthood, at marriage, even at death when

Meaning: Creativity and Performance

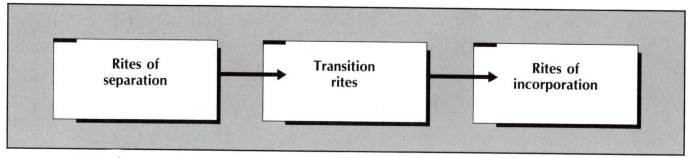

11-17. *Component Rituals of Rites of Passage.*

the dead person has to be separated from this world and incorporated into the next.

The individual is first separated from an existing status or an existing state of affairs (such as illness); he or she is put into a transitional world where none of the rules that have applied in the past any longer apply; he or she is then brought back into new roles and a new situation of health. This ritual recontexting is much like the recontexting of play, of art, and of law.

Rituals that do *not* follow the pattern of rites of passage have not been studied comparatively nearly as exhaustively as we could wish. Indeed, they seem to form a miscellaneous category whose primary characteristic is that they are not rites of passage. Foraging peoples perform rituals to assure the well-being of their game and the foods they gather. Horticulturalists perform rituals to assure fertility for their crops, and especially for favorable weather. Such rituals, obviously, follow the seasons and are sometimes called calendrical rituals—in some societies, religious rituals are performed in order to provide human cooperation in keeping the seasons on track.

The ritual acting out of myth implies the defence of the world order; by imitating sacred exemplars the world is prevented from being brought to chaos. The reenactment of a creative event, for example, the healing wrought by a god in the beginning of time, is the common aim of myth and ritual. In this way the event is transferred to the present and its result, i.e., the healing of a sick person, can be achieved once more here and now. In this way, too, the world order, which was created in the primeval era and which is reflected in myths, preserves its value as an exemplar and model for the people of today.

Lauri Honko, in Dundes (1984)

THEY SAID IT

We now have two points to consider carefully: that ritual accords with the major myths of the society, and that ritual follows a more or less precise program of occurrences.

Curing Ritual. The Isoma ritual of the Ndembu of Zambia is a typical and very well documented curing ritual. The Ndembu hold that when a person does not live up to obligations, the person may be "caught" by a shade or spirit of a neglected ancestor and afflicted by appropriate misfortune. In the case of a woman of childbearing age, the misfortune could be temporary barrenness. If an Ndembu woman does not get pregnant, or if her children abort or die soon after birth, her husband consults a diviner to determine the cause. (Diviners will be discussed at some length in Chapter 12.)

In one case, for example, a diviner revealed that matrilineal shades had "caught" the patient and had burdened her with infertility because she had "forgotten" them. Ndembu women live with the difficulty that their loyalties are divided between their matrilineal kin and their husbands. Maintaining both sets of obligations is difficult and takes a lot of time. The diviner also revealed that the shade had utilized either a bush-rat or the rodent known as an ant-bear to tie up the woman's fertility.

The patient's husband was next required to find a doctor to carry out the Isoma ritual, which is itself the remembrance. The rite is a typical rite of passage. In Ndembu terms, *Ilembi* separates the candidate from the profane world; *kunkunka* ("the grass hut") partially secludes her from daily life; *ku-tumbuka* is a festive dance celebrating the removal of the shade's curse, and the return of the celebrant to ordinary daily life.

The ritual is fraught with symbols. The articles used in the ritual, including each of the ingredients of the medicine, all have symbolic meanings. These articles are called by a word that means beacon or landmark; it also conveys the idea of order, as opposed to anything that is unstructured or chaotic. The ritual articles also connect the known world of everyday experience with the unknown realm of the shades.

The word *isoma* itself means "to slip out of place." The woman's children are said to "slip out of place" before they are born or even before they are conceived. Sometimes the woman's difficulty is accompanied by dreams, particularly dreams of Mwengi. Mwengi stands for the masculine principle, but it also thwarts female fertility.

11-18. Isoma ritual among the Mdembu of Zambia. This photograph shows treatment for a couple unable to bring up living children. Two holes are dug with a tunnel between them through which the couple passes. Here they are being washed in the hole designated for cold medicine.

The aim of the ritual, then, is to restore the woman's good standing with the deceased members of her own matrilineal kin group, to restructure the conjugal relations with her husband, and to make her get pregnant.

The rites are carried out at the hole of a rat or an ant-bear, near the source of the stream where a curse on the patient was said to have been uttered. The ritual scene is marked off by a ring of bent or broken branches. This ring separates the area of the ritual from the "formless milieu of the bush" (Turner 1957). At the site of the animal's burrow, a hole is dug, about four feet deep. Another hole, called the "new hole," is dug about four feet away. The hole at the burrow entrance is said to be hot; the new hole is cold. The hot hole is the "hole of death"; the new hole is the "hole of life." The two holes are then joined near the bottom by digging a tunnel big enough for one person to crawl through.

The priests who are charged with performing this ritual have collected medicines which are pounded together in a mortar, then soaked in water. The resulting liquid is divided. Half is heated over a fire made just beside the hot hole; the other half is poured cold into a calabash or other vessel and placed near the cool hole.

The patient and her husband must stand in the hole of life. She is given a white pullet to hold to represent purity and her coming children; a red cock representing her mystical misfortune or her suffering has been tied up and put beside the hole of death. Both the patient and the husband are sprinkled with cold medicines and then must crawl through the tunnel into the hole of death, where they are sprinkled with the hot medicines.

The patient and her husband pass back and forth through the tunnel between these two holes several times, each time symbolizing something different. Finally the red cock is beheaded, his blood poured on the fire that had been used to heat half the medicines, and the couple are again doused with both liquids. The other participants are singing songs from many important rituals, including the song for this one.

The difficulty has now been taken care of. The evil motive that had created the woman's barrenness has been countered. There is now no known reason she should not bear healthy children, which is considered the norm when there is no spiritual interference. The Isoma ritual is, of course, much more complex than the condensed version given here (Turner 1957).

In rituals such as the Isoma, everything is given a meaning, often based on physical qualities. These meanings may be assigned so that the physical quality represents the desired outcome. We are then in the realm of analogy. In the past such associations were called sympathetic magic, but in the opinion of most anthropologists today, calling it magic does not much help our understanding. Such a label might even allow us to dismiss the meanings without even seeking to understand them.

Life Course Rites of Passage. The Gisu live on the slopes of Mount Elgon on the border of Uganda and Kenya. The initiation of boys into men is the central concern of their ritual life; the climax of the ritual is circumcision. The Gisu say that initiation and circumcision make men of boys in the same way that first childbirth makes women of girls. The Gisu stress the development and testing of bravery and other male qualities that the initiation implies; initiation should turn them not merely into adult men but into full-fledged masculine males of the sort valued by the society.

The circumcision ritual is held soon after harvest when food is plentiful. Preparation for it takes several months. The young preinitiates visit the homes of their kinfolk, in groups, where they are given presents and encouragement. They wear headdresses made of colobus monkey fur and bells that are attached to their thighs; they also wear women's clothes and ornaments that have been given to them by their father's sisters (the symbolism of feminine things on which they will

Meaning: Creativity and Performance

turn their backs; the relationship between those feminine things and their own father is quite overt, but the Gisu do not make a point of it).

The psychological preparation is tended as carefully as the social dimension: the boys must develop the courage to stand absolutely still, with no visible expression, as the circumcision operation is performed. People realize how much courage and control that takes; the young men plan for it and steel themselves to bear the pain. As part of the preparation, the boys are expected to go through some difficulties with fortitude: Gisu say that they have to learn to be strong and tough, a quality they call *litima*; but they also have to learn to control the *litima* and to use it for social ends. The balance of toughness and control, which is a problem of masculinity in many societies, is carefully adjusted.

Three main rituals make up the rites. The first concerns the relations of the youths with their ancestors; it is a sacrifice with offerings of meat (the slaughtering of a bull) and beer so that the ancestors will protect them through the operation. The second ritual involves their relationships with senior members of their lineages; again a bull is sacrificed to the ancestors and the initiate is smeared with its chyme (the contents of the animal's first stomach—all cattle have two stomachs); one stated purpose of the rite is to assure that he will beget sons. The third rite deals with the land, and again involves contact with the ancestors.

11-19. *Myth and performance condense many meanings into a structure of meanings. The meaning of some items depends on similarity or association and, hence, has traditionally been called magic. Difficulty arises when we try to ascertain the extent to which people themselves recognize and value the structure of meaning. Is a structure valid if the anthropologist creates it with ideas he learned from the people, although the people themselves do not construct it?*

The actual circumcision ceremony takes place in small groups of boys—never more than four or five. The operators are strangers to the boys. Just inside the hut beside the place where the operation occurs, an older Gisu woman (who may be the mother of one of the boys) adopts the position taken in childbirth. Although Gisu say the reason is to give the young men strength, that practice also underscores the similarity that Gisu see between childbirth and the transition implied by circumcision. Both circumcision and childbirth are normal parts of adult life. The day ends with a feast, although the initiates cannot touch either the food or the beer. After the operation, the youths are secluded while their scars heal.

Two important distinctions in Gisu life are underscored by these rituals: between adults and children, and between masculine and feminine. Children, including uninitiated boys, are associated with women. The ritual underlines passage of the boys both to adulthood and to manhood. "Circumcision demonstrates the control which is necessary for the ideal man; it is self-control but fortified by ritual support provided by lineage superiors and kin" (LaFontaine 1988).

CONCLUDING THOUGHTS

Performance and story enrich the lives of people everywhere. Myth gives people a way of understanding the world, sanctions the institutions of society by giving them supernatural backup, and provides a text for ritual performance. Ritual is performed myth in action, its dominant ideas are brought into the here and now. Enormous reservoirs of cultural creativity reside in the power of the story, which enables us to imagine realities beyond myth, beyond performance—and so to create entirely new possibilities for the expansion of human potential.

Think for a minute about the rituals you yourself have been involved in. What kind of rituals have you attended? When, during your life course (or somebody else's) did they fall? What was the purpose, the content, the context? Sometimes the purpose of rituals is absolutely out front. Sometimes the purpose is covert or concealed. So, what happened? What was signified? Do you think that your classmates, your teacher, your family members might have different interpretations of what happened or what it meant?

BUZZWORDS

folklore   the traditional beliefs, myths, legends, stories and customs of a people.

rites of passage   rituals held either at specific junctures in the life course or else in the passage of the seasons, for curing or other purposes. A rite of passage is divided into three sections: the first in which a person is separated from his or her previous social position, a second in which the person is in touch with educational and/or mystical forces that provide new capacities, and third, the reentry into society in a new social position.

ritual   carrying out rites so that problems on the earthly plane can be solved symbolically and hence a step toward practical solution. Rituals may recur, hence the "problems" are not the essential point.

Creed
Religion and Ideology
12

PROPOSITIONS AND PREMISES

- ■ The worldview of any people is made up of its stories and theories about the origin and present working of the world, the place of people in it, and the causes and antidotes for misfortune.

- ■ Worldviews may contain gross contradictions without any diminution of their effectiveness as long as the contradictory elements do not appear in a single context.

- ■ Religion is, among other things, a recontexting (often a mythical restatement) of cultural ideas from other realms of living. Because that is so, religion is associated with ecological adaptation: hunters and gatherers show one sort of religious beliefs, peasants another, industrial and postindustrial societies still others.

- ■ People give information to the divine by means of prayer, invocation, and sacrifice. They get information through revelations, possession, divination, or drugs.

- ■ Religion depends on faith, for it has no rigorous canons of proof.

- ■ Science is also a mode of explaining the previously unknown. Its most important single characteristic is its canons of proof.

- ■ An ideology is a set of doctrines or assertions underlying a social or political movement. If held strongly, it resembles religion. Ideological premises can interfere with reaching viable conclusions (as, of course, can religious or scientific premises).

P eople explain everything—how tools work, how to behave toward each other, how to deal with the environment—even how to feel. They explain not only what they know but what they don't know—even what they can't know. There are three main sets of questions that are answered in some form everywhere.

(1) How were nature and the firmament created? What makes them continue to work?

(2) How did humanity come into being?
- What is the relationship of humanity to the rest of nature?
- How was human society created and how does it work?
- What am I and what am I doing here? How do *I* fit in with nature and society? How do *I* work?

(3) How did death and misfortune come into being? How do they work? How can we overcome them?

These are eternal questions. The answers that different peoples give are what anthropologists call a **worldview**.

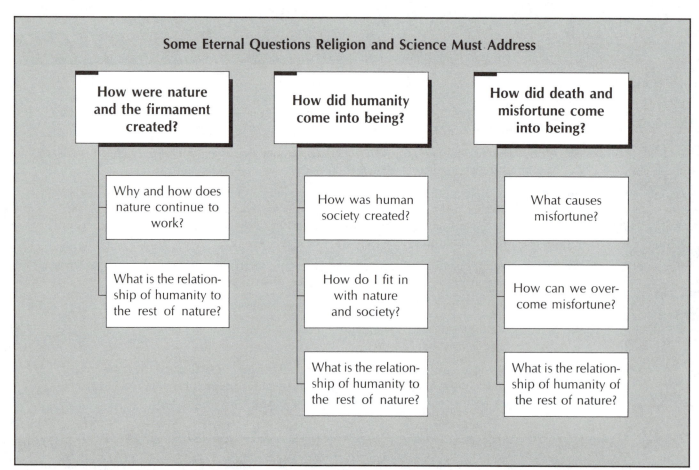

12-1. Eternal questions take many forms: Where did I come from? Why do people I love die? How can I live forever? Are bad people punished and good people rewarded? If not, why not? Whose idea was this? Why don't I have everything that everybody else has—good looks, plenty of money, charm, luck, health. What is the meaning of life? Is this on the test? Is everybody as nervous (or scared or angry or horny) as I am?

The worldview that any culture provides is often so deeply merged with the peoples' perceptions of the natural world that they never need to ask the eternal questions. Anthropologists, however, must explore the worldview to discover how any culture explains the natural world and peoples' place in it.

Religion and science both provide explanations to the eternal questions—not necessarily conflicting answers. Although the two differ in many ways, their difference is definitive in one way. In science the focus is on the questions. The quality of any science ultimately depends on the quality of its questions. The essence of science is to probe. Answers change with knowledge and information—and lead to new and better questions.

In the scientific process, and especially in the social sciences, the questions must themselves be questioned. Questioning the questions is sometimes very hard: we get the feeling that we have no secure place to stand. This insecurity, shaking our most basic assumptions, sometimes makes science seem dangerous. Science fails when the scientist's need for certainty becomes overpowering: when the will to believe overwhelms the need to find out and the will to question. Our insecurities then blunt our courage to question. We pull back from the questions. Governments or priesthoods—guardians of the established order—may even force us back as they did Galileo; the price of questioning may become unbearably high. It is hard to see that the price of not questioning is even higher. Rigid governmental or religious systems that systematically stultify curiosity and the need to know are on a road that inevitably leads to collapse.

The focus of religion, on the other hand, is on the answers to the eternal questions. Religion is the realm not of inquiry but of faith. To "have faith" in the answers means that curiosity must sometimes be stilled; inquiry must sometimes be rejected. Faith can supply immense psychological security and social predictability. Indeed, not to have to question is sometimes a great relief.

Both science and religion allow us to form pictures of our universe and our place in it. Such pictures become, in the long run, essential to our view of world and of self. Like all other peoples, Americans subscribe to both scientific explanations and religious explanations of the eternal questions. Indeed, many Americans combine both religious and scientific elements into their individual worldviews.

RELIGION

Some of the brainiest scholars from the mid-nineteenth century almost to the present day produced an immense

12-2. Science focuses on questions. Scientific inquiry demands a capacity to question basic assumptions.

12-3. Religion focuses on answers. Faith leads to the comfort of certainty.

Creed: Religion and Ideology

literature about the nature of what they called "primitive religion." At the time this material appeared, it was important—it allowed anthropologists to organize vast quantities of data. Today, however, we have come far enough to question the very theories that allowed such progress. Useful as they once were, they do not always stand up under the closer scrutiny we can give them today. Indeed, today they seem to be permeated with a basic error similar to the one that missionaries made when they first learned about "primitive" religions. The missionaries not only assumed that their own religion was the only correct one, they also assumed that the ideas underlying their own worldview—the ideas with which they looked at religion—were the only possible ones. Everything they saw was explained on the basis of their own worldview—we have earlier called that ethnocentrism. In some cases they said that the people they met had no religion or else that they worshiped the devil. (These remarks, by the way, should not be read to imply a wholesale criticism of missionaries, who during the colonial era were often the only people trying to build constructively for the future.) In short, early missionaries imported ethnocentric definitions of religion.

The scholars did something similar but more subtle. They created distinctions and definitions on the basis of one "primitive religion" and then imported *those* ideas rather than ideas from their own culture. In the new context, of course, the imported anthropological ideas may have been

just as foreign to the people being investigated, and just as far off the mark, as the missionaries' ethnocentric ideas.

To put it another way, words and concepts derived from one "primitive" religion were boosted into the realm of theory, then treated as if they were of the same order as discoveries in physics and hence true in all circumstances. This is specifically what social science should *not* do. Every culture, including what Western scholars would call the religion of the culture, must first be understood in terms of the people who live in and use it. Only then can we compare these various religions, adding explanations that come from anthropology or from our own culture. Only in that way can we see the comparisons as problems free of our premises and axioms.

When ideas are lifted out of the ethnography of one religion and made part of the premises for studying the next, it becomes all but impossible to understand the new worldview. In the new context, a concept derived from someplace else may cast far more shadow than light. It makes little difference whether the interloping idea is from the ethnographer's own religion or from some other.

Many of these scholars also asked questions about "primitive" religions they could not ask of their own religion (Geertz 1968)—they could question stranger gods but not their own. Those questions all too often had little to do with the religion they were studying. Hence, much of that literature is misleading and of almost no use in modern anthropological studies of belief systems.

Some scholars (Frazer 1922) dealt at great length with magic. Some of their classifications of different kinds of magic were useful—until the scholars thrust all examples into a box labeled magic—meaning something "they" believe and "we" don't. Other scholars (Durkheim 1912) postulated two spheres of life called the "sacred" and the "profane." That is, matters having to do with gods and the higher explanations were sacred; those having to do with everyday life were profane. Such a distinction is absolutely valid—in some religions. It is just as absolutely not valid in others.

In short, although they went about it differently, both early missionaries and early scholars sought rational explanations for what was to them unbelievable—then distanced themselves from what they could not believe. Their writings, fascinating as some of them are, provide a stumbling block to understanding the beliefs of exotic peoples (Evans-Pritchard 1965). Perhaps the most vivid example occurred in attempts to understand the religion of the Australian aborigines. The analysts took an American Indian word, totem, and applied it to the Australians; within a few years the study of **totemism** had become a growth industry in anthropology. Because it had little to do with what Australians themselves understood, it "set back understanding while appearing to advance it" (Stanner 1965).

The study of what used to be called "primitive religion" languished somewhat after about 1920, as anthropologists turned their fieldwork to easier topics. About 1960, the study of myth and ritual reemerged as a central ethnographic

Words like animism and totemism were made up by anthropologists to categorize religions that had no such words in their original languages. Distinctions between religion and magic were also made up by anthropologists for comparative purposes; most have no references in any culture except our own.

12-4.

concern. This time it was more successful. We now have good ethnographic accounts that explain religions precisely in their own terms. Building on that foundation, we should tackle the problem of religion in a wider perspective, taking care to avoid the ethnocentric, pseudoscientific mistakes of the past.

12-5. In many — perhaps most — cultures, religion is not separated out as a special area. Rather it is an integral part of life. It is thus advisable for anthropologists to search for the way people ask and answer the eternal questions instead of looking for "religion."

There is a related difficulty we have not discussed. Separating religion from the rest of culture sometimes throws a people's worldview into a wrong light for the simple reason that they themselves do not have a separate category for religion. To them, what we would call religion is not a special sphere of culture, but a perfectly natural part of everyday life. Both Western missionaries and scholars have tried to separate out beliefs and actions that they can put into a special category labelled religion.

Religion is better seen as an anthropological way of looking at how people search for meaning. Religious activity is also one basis for reinforcing groups of cooperating and like-

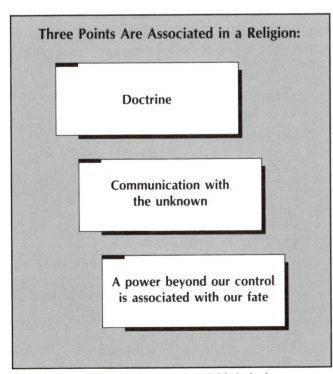

Three Points Are Associated in a Religion:

Doctrine

Communication with the unknown

A power beyond our control is associated with our fate

12-6. All religions have (1) a set of beliefs that act as doctrine, (2) devices for communicating with the unknown, and (3) the premise that some power beyond human control shapes our destinies.

minded people. It is, moreover, a means of establishing codes of good behavior and a device for providing comfort to people in adversity.

Religion is based on an association of (1) doctrine, usually explained in the form of stories, most often myth, (2) communication with the unknown, most commonly prayer, sacrifice, and ritual, and (3) feeling that a power beyond one's control is closely involved with one's fate.

Our approach to understanding religion will be to look at ways in which people give information to the powers that control the unknown and how they get information from those powers. We will try to remember in the course of these explanations that religion is a line of demarcation made by anthropologists — it may not be recognized at all by the people we are describing.

Communication with the Divine

In most religions, it is necessary to give information to God, the gods, or spirits so that attention is called to what people need. It is also necessary to learn what the powers want people to do. The usual means of communicating information to the higher spirits are prayer, invocation and sacrifice. The most common means of getting information are revelation, divination, possession, and drugs.

Putting Information into the System. The process of giving information to the gods or spirits usually follows three stages (the same general scheme as do rites of passage): First, there is an action to call the attention of the spirits to what is about to take place — an invocation is the term commonly used for an attention-gaining device.

Second, the message is declared — it is a prayer, or something like it, that may or may not be accompanied by sacrifice or some other gift to the gods. Prayers are words or thoughts directed toward whatever sacred power is recognized. Prayers may be sung or spoken — indeed, they may be silent. Many prayers contain praise of the god. Most prayers involve an entreaty. Prayers may be private or communal. They may be uttered by a priest or by the individual. When an individual prays, the prayer is almost always concerned with the well-being of the self or of some person close to the person who is praying. When a priest prays, he is more likely to pray for the entire community, though people often cannot distinguish between the individual good and the community good — one implies the other. Sometimes, of course, curses, oaths or vows take the form of prayer.

Third, the message is ended, and some action (the "Amen" or something like it) seals the deal, and then brings the people back into the everyday world. In other words, rites of separation, transition rites, and rites of reincorporation (see 12-1 and 12-7).

12-7 also shows that something else — the joining together and rededication of the social group — is happening at the same time. Such social reaffirmation is one of the most important things about most religious rituals or activities.

The religion of the Dinka of the Sudan presents one of

Creed: Religion and Ideology

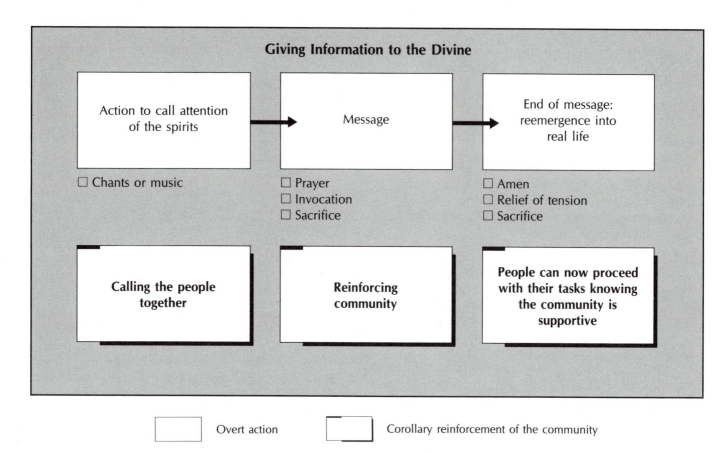

Giving Information to the Divine

| Action to call attention of the spirits | → | Message | → | End of message: reemergence into real life |

☐ Chants or music

☐ Prayer
☐ Invocation
☐ Sacrifice

☐ Amen
☐ Relief of tension
☐ Sacrifice

Calling the people together

Reinforcing community

People can now proceed with their tasks knowing the community is supportive

☐ Overt action   ☐ Corollary reinforcement of the community

12-7. Two things are going on at once. One is communication with the divine. The other is reinforcement of the community brought about by their sharing important ritual.

the clearest pictures of the three stages. Among the Dinka, an invocation is spoken by a priest; each phrase of it is repeated by the people who are gathered together (I hesitate to use the word congregation because that word, in English, implies a specialized group whose primary purpose is the religious one; among the Dinka and most other people studied by anthropologists, the group is a preexisting one, often a kinship group, and the people work together in many contexts to achieve many different purposes).

Spears are used in Dinka warfare and as symbols for truth and justice. Spears are made sacred by their contact with a sacrifice; some old spears are held in reverence because they were owned and used by ancestors. The spear stands for the idea of power and authority; the most powerful lines of descent are those with the most important spears. Animal sacrifice with spears is the core symbol of Dinka religion. In a prayer for someone who is ill, the priest picks up his spear, waving it in what would seem to be a threatening way, and begins the invocation:

> Priest: You of my father.
>
> Chorus: You of my father.
>
> Priest: I call upon you because my child is ill.
>
> Chorus: I call upon you because my child is ill.

Dinka seldom pray as individuals. Their masters of the

fishing spear have authority as priests. The invocation is followed by the prayer without a break:

> Priest: And I do not want words of sickness
>
> Chorus: And I do not want words of sickness. . . .

As the prayer continues, again each phrase is repeated:

> And you of my father, if you are called, then you will help me and join yourself with my words. And I did not speak [in the past] that my children should become ill . . . . And you my prayer, and you prayer of the distant past, prayer of my ancestors, you are spoken now. Meet together! It is that of my ancestor Guejok, it is not of the tongue only, it is that of Guejok, it is not of the tongue only'' (Lienhardt 1961).

Other prayers may also be uttered, again with repetitions by the attendees, by people who have a special interest in curing the person who is ill. In this particular ritual, the final element of the prayer contained the following:

> It is you divinities of my father that I call upon to come and help the child Akol Agany, that he may live. He is the child of your daughter, and if you abandon him to death, then all the Powers will mock at you [despise you]. And if you let him live, then you have helped the child of your daughter. And you of my father, I did not neglect you [treat you lightly] on the occasion

Chapter Twelve

in the past when my father died, it is not so, it is not true that I caused confusion in the descent group of my father.

Several things are to be noted: the person presenting the prayer is establishing his own good will—and his own lack of guilt for the sufferer's condition. The spirit is being constrained, almost threatened; peace within the lineage is an important value, stressed and restressed.

As the repetitions continue, a concentration of attention takes place. The most senior people speak or sing their prayers last, when the collective concentration has been achieved. They are all by that time "palpably members of a single undifferentiated body" focussing on a single common end. In this "climax of aggregation" (Lienhardt 1961), individual concerns are transcended by the speeches of the priests and the others concerned and are endorsed by all. The ritual thus prepares the sacrificial victim.

A sacrificial ox is killed when the concentration is at its height. "When sacrifice is made, the victim dies while the patient still lives, and his life, however weak, remains life in relation to the death of the victim. A Dinka sacrifice is in part, therefore, a drama of human survival" (Lienhardt 1961).

Misfortunes are listed and directed to "meet together on the back of the ox" (Lienhardt 1961). The people have exchanged the life of the sacrificial animal for the life of the person benefitted by the sacrifice. The references in the invocations to "that of the fathers" implies that in spite of the difficulties that beset human life, the people gathered are living and producing the next generation. They are winning over the odds. Quarrels weaken the human effort, and are neutralized by the sacrifice. Help is required to ensure human survival and prosperity—the ultimate religious purpose.

The tension that has mounted is suddenly released. The completed sacrifice puts the Dinka back into the real world. They butcher the carcass of the sacrificial ox and distribute its meat. The meaning transcends the rite. The sacrificial ox represents the unified gathering; division of its meat underscores their relationship with one another. Not only do we have the three stages of the ritual, we have a device for reinforcing and praising the community itself.

Dinka do not expect such a ritual sacrifice to work a magical cure. After the ceremony, they must wait to see the outcome. Divinity may refuse their request and their sacrifice. They also note that if the sick man's illness has not been properly identified, the sacrifice cannot work. Yet even if the sacrifice does not achieve its avowed purpose—the recovery of the patient—it succeeds because part of its reason is to create unanimity in the entire community. In that, it succeeds brilliantly. The community, in attending and participating in the sacrifice, has asserted its desire for the recovery of the patient, and thus has affirmed its own unity. Weakness—of both the individual and the social group—is dispelled and strength is asserted. The drama of life and death has been reenacted: a situation of death has been turned into a situation of life.

Americans do the same thing: invocations begin funerals; personal prayers often precede medical procedures. Holidays like Memorial Day are times of ritual that use religious invocation and prayer to bring us together.

Getting Information Out of the System. In modern Euro-America, religions are primarily religions of revelation. The major information was provided in the past and is thus already known. Judaism and Christianity are built on revelation; so is Islam. In some other parts of the world, however, no prior revelation is postulated. Practitioners of these latter religions must get information on a case by case basis—through modes such as divination, oracles, possession, or the altered mental states created by drugs.

We discussed oracles briefly in Chapter 7 when we talked about ordeals used as devices for shunting to God the questions that mere human beings could not answer. Oracles can be used to get answers to questions concerning misfortunes and illness as well as questions of culpability. Indeed, they can answer any questions to which there are no pragmatic, scientifically verifiable answers.

The Azande use a poison oracle which they call *benge* to make many sorts of decisions, even practical ones. *Benge* is a red powder made from a forest creeper. When it is mixed with water, the juice can be squeezed into the beaks of young chickens a few weeks old. Sometimes the chick dies. Just as often it doesn't. Some have spasms, others do not. From the behavior of the chicks, especially whether they live or die, the Azande read answers to questions that they asked the oracle. Azande consult the poison oracle not only about matters of their well-being, but also about their day-to-day problems. Indeed, the ethnographer E. E. Evans-Pritchard kept *benge* for both his own use and that of his neighbors. "We regulated our affairs in accordance with the oracles' decisions. I may remark that I found this as satisfactory a way of running my home and affairs as any other I know of. Among Azande it is the only satisfactory way of life because . . . it furnishes the only arguments by which they are wholly convinced and silenced" (Evans-Pritchard 1937).

When Azande suffer misfortune, they blame others—either mystical forces or other people. They consult oracles to determine what those forces are or who the people are. Witches can be caught by means of the oracle; so can adulterers. All a person need do is to place the names of people he suspects before the oracle and administer the poison to the chick.

American readers must remember that the Azande approach their oracles from the standpoint of faith, not the standpoint of science. Their culture does not encourage them to ask whether there is a provable relationship between the answer and the means they use to arrive at it. The relationship is best thought of as divine rather than scientific.

A group of American middle-class enthusiasts who call themselves EAN, which stands for "Everything and Nothing," believe the body has its own innate wisdom and can also act as a conduit for higher spiritual wisdom. They use muscle testing to answer questions. Muscle testing is a stylized way of "listening to the body." To explain how it works to others, they hold an arm straight out. Then, somebody says "two plus two equals four" and pushes firmly down on the outstretched arm. It stays in position. When they say "two plus two equals five" the arm goes weak because of the untruth of the statement, and a slight push on the arm will push it down. The EAN use such muscle testing to answer many questions: should I meditate now? Is it okay to eat a little junk food today? Should I marry Fred? The result of the muscle test removes any doubt—they abide by it, and they see the connection as divine.

WE, THE ALIEN

The Tiv told me in the early 1950s that misfortune is caused by others—usually by other people they call "those with *tsav*" who are something like witches. *Tsav* is a substance that is said to grow on the hearts of some people. Tiv held postmortem examinations on most corpses except the very young and the very old as part of the funeral ceremony. They had to discover whether the deceased had *tsav* on his heart. If there was no *tsav*, then that person had been killed by somebody with *tsav*; if there was *tsav* on the heart of the deceased, he or she was responsible not only for his or her own death but for other unexplained deaths as well. Good *tsav*, Tiv explain, is an essential factor for all leaders and for all persons of skill. Their *tsav* is small in size. However, if the *tsav* is large and jagged, and especially if it is many-colored—the worst is the *tsav* that grows claws—they say that the deceased was a selfish person who cultivated his or her *tsav* by eating human flesh. That is metaphorical language for people who claw their way to success by doing harm to others. *Tsav* looked to me like arterial or veinous blood-filled sacs in the tissues that surround the heart. I have never been able to get any doctor to say what the sacs were without first seeing them.

When Tiv suffer ill fortune, they go to a diviner who consults his oracles in order to find answers to several questions: which of the mystical forces called *akombo* was used to bring about such misfortune? (It is assumed that *akombo* are used primarily by people with evil *tsav*.) If the *akombo* is neutralized ritually—the Tiv call this "repairing" the *akombo*—no further damage can be done.

The diviners tell Tiv which *akombo* should be repaired.

When these rites are carried out, and the *akombo* thus neutralized, the medicines given to the patient will work. If the source of the matter was correctly diagnosed, the patient will recover or the misfortune will go away. Sometimes, however, it is necessary to discover the witch so that the person who has released the *akombo* can be made to desist. This procedure of discovering the witch may be done by diviners, but is more commonly undertaken by moots (Bohannan 1957).

12-8. The Tiv diviner in this 1950 photograph is setting up his equipment in order to get unknown information by using his ritually charged apparatus. He will first use the horns, with the small metal tubes attached at their top, to summon the sources of information. He will then put questions and throw the chains. There will be four of them when he finally gets set up. The chains are made of pods, connected by snake bones strung between them. If the pod falls with the open side up, the answer to the question is "a good thing." If the open convex side is up, it is "a bad thing."

In sum, all three groups (the Azande, the Tiv, and the New Age members of EAN) have found **divination** to be a useful mode of getting information from supernatural forces—information not obtainable any other way.

Possession by spirits is another mode of acquiring information from the supernatural. **Vodou** (commonly spelled voodoo) is a religion that West African slaves of Haiti based on ideas they brought with them from West Africa. In the new context, the old ideas were mixed with Christianity. Vodou suffered various persecutions by the Catholic church and by different political administrations, including an American occupation from 1910 to 1935. When tourism

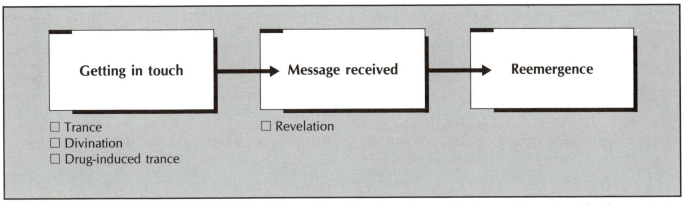

| Getting in touch | Message received | Reemergence |

□ Trance
□ Divination
□ Drug-induced trance

□ Revelation

12-9. As is the case when people give information to the divine, the community may be reinforced by the actions they take to get information from the divine.

began to thrive, vodou changed again. Some of its practitioners turned it into paid entertainment for the tourists. The commercialization added to previous misconceptions. Tourists spread the false idea that vodou deals only with black magic, fear, and mystical horror.

The basic assumption in vodou is that the everyday world is populated with spirits called *loa* who manifest themselves by entering and possessing people. Through such possession, there is constant and easy communication between the people and the spirits. A spirit is said to "ride" the person it possesses, who is called the horse of the spirit. Spirits usually ride only cult members, most often the priests and priestesses of the cults. When the priests and priestesses are ridden by spirits, they are said to have second sight, to have "knowledge"—meaning supernatural insights. People become priests at the demand of the spirits. However, since many of the priests seem well off or even rich compared with the rest of the population, it may be noted that "faith, ambition, love of power and sheer cupidity are all inextricably mixed" (Metraux 1959). Most members of the priesthood have gone through training of several months or even years. The gift of clairvoyance is the most desired of all insights; it is the climax of the training. Comparatively few of the priests reach this stage.

Vodou adherents say that trance occurs when a *loa* spirit moves into an individual. There are good spirits and bad spirits—gentle people who get along with everybody are usually possessed by the good spirits; bad spirits associate with their own type—people who are given to temper and often are not well liked.

Possessed people shake and stagger, make jerky movements, sometimes violent ones. This opening phase, during which they appear to lose control of the body, usually does not last very long. Suddenly they are in full trance. People who are possessed are surrounded by others who form what today might be called a support group. If the frenzy of the spirit makes its horse stagger, there are people there to catch her or him. If the possessed person writhes on the floor, people keep them from damaging themselves or others. The

12-10. Possession is a common way of getting information from the divine. Haitian culture has a particularly highly developed set of cults that center around possession. Although this picture of a possessed Haitian woman was taken in Brooklyn, it is absolutely typical of Haitian possession.

Creed: Religion and Ideology

"helpers" try to protect the clothing of the possessed person; if a woman is writhing on the floor, other women keep her clothing well below her knees. When this phase wears off, the "horse" takes on the recognizable characteristics of the spirit who is riding him. Under possession, they prophesy, give advice, and threaten sinners.

Signs of fatigue usually indicate that a trance is ending. A person who emerges from trance remembers nothing about what happened. Indeed, it was not himself or herself who was acting—it was the god or the spirit. Possession may last from a few seconds to several hours; stories are told of its lasting several days.

Trance most often occurs in the course of religious ceremonies—even family worship, when the different members of the family are more or less cast as specific spirits, the same spirit always riding the same person. In public ceremonies, the *loa* most often possess the priests and the people who are paying for the ceremonies; however, any member of the congregation or the audience may become possessed. Certain drumming rhythms seem to promote possession, although the drummers do not become possessed.

Possession sometimes occurs in daily life. People facing an especially difficult task may seek to be possessed, explaining that they need spiritual help to go through that difficult task. Trance can also be used to get out of an unpleasant situation. Since the possessed individual is not responsible for his or her own actions, whatever happens while in a state of trance is culturally accepted as the actions of the spirit.

Haiti is one of the poorest nations in the Caribbean. Vodou religion brings a strong measure of stability into Haitian society; possession gives Haitians a lot of pleasure in lives that contain very little of it. Possessed people are the center of attention; they are applauded. If the congregation approves, they are rewarded. It is very difficult to say whether this kind of possession is voluntary. Some people readily become possessed in the presence of others who already are. In Haiti, possession cannot be explained by individual psychology, as it must be in our society; rather, it must be explained by the religious attitudes toward it. People are convinced that the *loa* are all around them all the time. Possession is something like the arrival of a friend. Messages from the gods are received any time of the day, and the world becomes a mixture of the ordinary and the divine.

Drugs as Windows on the Divine. The use of drugs in communicating with the divine is worldwide. For example, when the Spanish conquistadors reached Mexico, they found in the religions of the Native Americans, and especially of the Aztecs, a highly sophisticated use of mind-altering drugs that were a vital part in religious ritual. The drugs (sometimes said to be gods themselves) provided a pathway of communication between the gods and the priests, who also performed cures. One of the most important of those drugs was the cactus known as *peyotl* in Aztec (peyote). The Spanish priests, of course, claimed that the Indians used the drug to get in touch with the devil; they tried for centuries,

unsuccessfully, to stamp out its use. Manuscripts from the 1500s that reported information from the Indians correctly state that peyote has three effects: it changes perception of visual stimuli, it produces hallucinations, and has a tendency to relax its users and even put them to sleep. The Spanish Inquisition, which was a movement within the Roman Catholic church to cast out devils and bring sinners back to the orthodox fold (and, in the process, to achieve political hegemony), was imported into Mexico. By 1620, use of peyote had been declared heresy as well as the work of the devil.

Although there are some descriptions from earlier periods, the best descriptions of the use of peyote are those of Lumholtz who spent several months among the Huichol Indians of northern Mexico near the end of the nineteenth century. By the 1970s, there were about ten thousand of these Indians, living high in the Sierra Madre Occidental (Myerhoff 1974). Huichol religion is a complex symbolization of natural forces. Fire is the main god. Huichol say fire existed even before the sun. Fire is addressed as Grandfather and the sun as Father. The highest of the female gods is Grandmother Growth. Peyote is an integral part of their communication with the supernatural world. The hallucinations brought on by the peyote are said to be evidence of the divine.

Huichol ritual is performed to make rain and give thanks for crops. It centers around a mythic identity of deer, corn, and peyote. Huichol say that corn, their basic food, was once a deer (which was their basic food when they were still hunting and gathering), and that peyote is both the original ear of corn and the original deer antler. Peyote, deer, and corn are, they say, all the same thing.

12-11. Drugs are used in many cultures to get in contact with the divine. The Huichol of Mexico use peyote. Hallucinogenic mushrooms are used in other parts of Middle America. Beer, wine and spirits are all associated with religion in some part of the world or other. This drawing of a sacred mushroom from Mexico is taken from the Florentine Codex, Book 11 of Sahagun. The bird-spirit on top of the mushroom probably represents somebody's idea of the hallucinogenic vision.

and singing their rituals, eating peyote, and drinking beer make the fiesta an enjoyable time as well as a holy time. Indeed, for the Huichol, blessedness, security and joy are all the same thing.

Peyote became an important ingredient in the "Native American Church," which spread to many Indian reservations early in the twentieth century. Peyote is used to maintain the visions of the indigenous Native American religions, all of which emphasize the place of human beings as part of nature. The religion provides both an identity and great comfort. Peyote is considered sacred, to be used only in a religious context and only for sacred purposes (Aberle 1966). Many states have laws allowing the use of peyote. However, in 1990 the Supreme Court of the United States decided that use of peyote was not protected as one of the freedoms of religion. Rather, it was a drug; the laws prohibiting drugs were of greater consequence than this particular manifestation of freedom of religion, the court said. Because the decision was so recent, the impact on the Native American community cannot yet be assessed.

Shamans as Messengers to the Divine. Widespread throughout the world is the role of the **shaman**. His job (occasionally, but rarely, women may be shamans) is to keep open the doorway between the two worlds—to communicate between the world of spirits and the human world. The shaman, it is said, can directly experience the supernatural. He can travel to that realm and can interact with the spirits. Rather than needing a divining apparatus, he goes face-to-face with the spirits to wrest from them the information that is needed. He becomes possessed by spirits. Unlike the vodou practitioners, he can also possess the spirits—he can enter into trance at will. The shaman uses drugs to traverse the boundary between the two worlds. Unlike ordinary human beings, the shaman also has power in the other world. The drug is a tool that can be manipulated to affect a cure, capture a lost soul, or find out why the gods are angry.

Shamans are found in Siberia, throughout indigenous North and South America—indeed, almost every place except Africa. In many places, they were the people who

Every October, the Huichol still send a group of their priests to the state of San Luis Potosi, far to the east, to gather the peyote that will be needed for the rites of their annual ritual cycle. In the old days, the journey was a dangerous one through enemy territory and took some forty days; in the 1970s, when they were accompanied by Furst and Myerhoff, it was done by automobile, but many of its details were unchanged. They still visited the same sites and shrines along the journey; they still had to bring back holy water from certain water holes as well as the peyote cactus itself. They still "hunted" the peyote with arrows, as if it were in fact a deer.

This pilgrimage to gather peyote is one of great responsibility because the supply of holy water and of peyote is essential to the rituals that promote the growth of crops and children. If the journey is successful, food, health and happiness (and cultural continuity) are assured.

The most important Huichol ceremony of the year is the Fiesta of the Peyote, held for three days in January. They prepare elaborate costumes and make great quantities of corn beer. The people who took the pilgrimage in the fall make offerings to the god of Fire; the sacred water gathered during the pilgrimage is also drunk and offered to the gods. Dancing

Creed: Religion and Ideology

preserved indigenous culture in the face of the encroaching modern world, yet they have also been among the first to take advantage of the modern world: to read and write, to go into the new courts to defend their people and their cultures.

Many American preachers assume the role of shaman. They claim to speak directly to the supernatural—God speaks to them, even takes them on journeys. They are charismatic and consummate performers and often become important political figures. They are adroit manipulators of the most profound symbols of Western religions. They use all the means of the shaman to engender belief—healing, faith, catharsis to relieve anxieties of the person and the group. They claim to be able to tap into the divine energy, power, spirit (call it what they will) of the Divine realm. And, most important of all, they hold the power of making that supernatural, chaotic but revitalizing energy available to their congregations. Like any good shaman, the charismatic preacher's direct contact with the supernatural allows his followers to share in this association—they can then speak in tongues and bathe in the Holy Spirit.

WE, THE ALIEN

Some Premises Underlying Religions

At the basis of every religion lie certain philosophical premises. These premises are the bedrock of faith. Under ordinary circumstances, they would never be questioned. If premises are opened to question as a result of colonization, banned by government, or condemned by missionaries, the whole system may come tumbling down. People are left with nothing but despair, as we will see in later chapters.

Ecology as a Religious Premise. Some religions are based on the premise that human beings occupy a place in the environment just like other creatures. Other religions are based on the diametrically opposed premise that human beings are the designated beneficiaries of the environment. The most notable of pro-ecology religions are those of the Australian aborigines and some of the Native Americans.

12-12. Every religion, and every science, has in it some attitude toward the environment. The goal of the Australians is to become part of the environment, not to control it.

In the late 1700s soon after permanent British settlements were formed in Australia, the astonishing statement appeared and reappeared that the aboriginal people had no religion at all. The native Australians were said to lack a high god; therefore, it was concluded that they did not have a religion. Their rituals were fairly short, even though preparing for them often took a long time. Rituals were associated with life crises like initiation or with maintenance of given species of plants and animals in specific places. Europeans of the day decided that such rituals could not be worship. Some of the rituals involved knocking out teeth, circumcision, subincision, and other painful ordeals—could *that* be religion? No prayers could be found. Neither could ideas about heaven or hell. Early observers, hemmed in by their own definitions of religion, could not see what was in fact there: a poetic and deeply felt set of beliefs and practices.

A few decades later, the assessment changed, but no better understanding emerged. Considerable data on Australian myth and ritual had been accumulated, but the nineteenth

12-13. Australian aborigines consider dream time to extend from the original creation into the present and to include themselves. Creation continues every day anew and permeates day-to-day life. In this picture, a novice, blindfolded, is being led by his guardian across symbols of the mythic tracks that stem from the dream time.

century was an era in which all searches were for origins. Scholars of the period fell upon the religion of the Australians as the most primitive religion ever known. They made the mistake of confusing "primitive" with "early." Instead of seeing Australian religion as the result of forty thousand or more years of adjustment, they said it was frozen in time—the religion of early man.

Australian religion is indeed very different from the religions of the Western world, but the secret of understanding it is really very simple: one must start with world-view. How do aborigines see the world and themselves in it? Australian aboriginals postulated that they are an integral part of the world, not master of any of it. They and everything in the world came into being in a time called the dreaming or dream time (Chapter 11). In one sense, the dreaming was long ago; in another sense it is eternal and therefore always present. The dreaming refers to a mythological period that extends into the present and the future; it had a beginning but it will not end. Dream time is not like time as we understand it—it entails the ongoing creation and reshaping of the world, humanizing and culturizing it. The mythic beings of the dream time were shape changing, sometimes taking human form, sometimes animal form. Some of them were self-created. Some had special powers that could affect nature and humanity. Some of these beings are believed to have created human life, including the ancestors of contemporary aborigines. As these beings moved across the land in tracks still known to the aborigines, some of them became anchored to specific sites, but their essential qualities were not changed. These eternal beings are as much alive today as they ever were (Berndt 1974) and they will live forever. For the aborigines, "myth is daily expression of the eternal" (Yengoyan 1979). When the aborigines tell their myths, they never use the past tense, or even the present tense. Rather they use a tense called the imperfective (which they share with Russian and many other languages) which indicates that the action is not completed yet—that it is ongoing (Yengoyan 1990).

The Australian continent is crisscrossed with the tracks or pathways of the people and other creatures of the dream time. Well into the twentieth century, the aborigines thought of themselves as moving along these same tracks as they moved about the land hunting and gathering. They were, in their own view, living and behaving beside the creatures of the dream time, who were still very much there.

There was, thus, a deep association—indeed, an identity—between man and nature. This idea is difficult in English because we so uncompromisingly separate humankind from the rest of nature. What we see as two things—human beings and environment—were one for aborigines. People *were* nature. They did not see nature as something for human beings to exploit, as is the case in worldviews like our own. Because they were an integral part of nature, everything they did had an impact on maintaining it as it was now and had always been. Natural phenomena were interpreted as signs from the dream time for peoples of today. "Anyone who,

understandingly, has moved in the Australian bush with Aboriginal associates . . . moves not in a landscape, but in a humanized realm saturated with significations. . . . Body, spirit, name, shadow, track *and* totem and its sacred place were all within one system. They imply each other" (Stanner 1965).

12-14. *Some peoples fill the entire world with symbolism. For Australian aboriginees, meaning is everywhere, in everything. In the mythic drama being enacted here, the man on the ground represents a kangaroo.*

The goal of the Australians was to maintain the continuity of this thoroughly integrated environment that included themselves. Their attempt gave rise to the feeling that people have their place in a harmoniously ordered universe. Australian rituals emphasize the relationship of a person to his "dreaming," and become the core of his activity—the most important point in his spiritual identity.

The aboriginal world is thus a universe of symbolism—one could almost say of symbolism run rampant. Like symbols everywhere, the relation of symbol to meaning is cultural and arbitrary. Australian religion assumes an unchanging world (all of whose history is still with us daily) and that living people are still an integral part of an ongoing creation.

Some American Indian religions, although their mythologies and rituals are very different, also view their relationship with the environment as one of integration and participation (Ortiz 1969). The environmentalist movement aims to restructure our attitudes toward nature so that we understand and express in our behavior the respect the Australians and American Indians have for the human place in the totality of living things.

Creed: Religion and Ideology

If all the beasts were gone, men would die from great loneliness of spirit. For whatever happens to the beast also happens to man. All things are connected. Whatever befalls the earth, befalls the sons of the earth.

Chief Seathl, Suwanish Tribe, from an address to the President of the United States, 1855. Quoted in *Sequoia Bark*, of Sequoia and Kings Canyon National Parks, July 14-17, 1989.

THEY SAID IT

Religion and Human Evil. Religions based on the premise that human beings contain within themselves all the sources of evil, as well as good, are sometimes confused with the practices that Westerners call **witchcraft**. Africa is a witch-ridden continent (Evans-Pritchard 1937; Bohannan and Bohannan 1953). Here we shall cite only one Native American religion, which makes the points clearly and well.

Navajo religion is based on two premises: the first is the idea of harmony (something like some of the legal systems we studied in Chapter 7). The Navajo postulate that the world was created to be harmonious, in line with immanent powers in the universe that suffuse all nature. Harmony is maintained as long as everyone proceeds in the proper way, which makes everything beautiful. When people deviate from the way, it has bitter consequences for the whole system. The Navajo have rituals that restore the beautiful,

12-15. Evil may stem from human action, from arbitrary or evil spirits, from the nature of the universe. It may be averted or avoided by many means, particularly ritual means. Navajo sand paintings, like the one shown here created for the benefit of a sick child, were created to symbolize good and evil, gods and spirits. Each element of the painting has a symbolic meaning. After the ritual, the sand paintings are destroyed.

harmonious and reciprocal qualities of the correct way.

The second premise underlying Navajo religion—and many other aspects of Navajo life—is the idea of strict reciprocity. A favor must be returned. Injuries are also returned. Thus, gifts and favors compel responses, although the two may not be symmetrical, especially if the two people are of vastly different economic capabilities. Disservices and disfavors are also returned reciprocally.

Navajo postulate the same kind of reciprocal responses from their supernatural forces as from their neighbors. The supernatural forces are likely to harm one—that is, to get even reciprocally—if taboos are broken. One has only to discover which gifts will constrain the powers to respond.

Navajo also postulate that misfortune comes from three sources: (1) from injuring or doing disservices to supernatural forces, especially breaking taboos associated with those forces, (2) by contagion, especially ritual contamination from corpses and ghosts of the dead, and (3) from the witchcraft of people who have not lived up to the harmonious goals and who have hence done disservices to others for that reason or out of hate or spite.

There were twenty-six Navajo ceremonies from which to choose in the 1960s (Aberle 1966)—the number is now about the same. These ceremonies are performed when specialists, called ''singers,'' are called in. The beneficiary of the ceremony may be ill and seeking recovery, or may be perfectly healthy but wishing to prevent misfortune. The patient, knowing which taboo was transgressed, selects which chant-ritual is to be performed. If the patient does not know, a diagnostician will be consulted—a hand-trembler, a stargazer, or someone called a ''listener'' who receives messages from the supernaturals.

The specialists are trained by other specialists—usually kinfolk so that the fees for instruction can be kept low. The neophyte specialist must undergo the ceremony as beneficiary, and then must perform it with the teacher as beneficiary. Because Navajo are convinced that one should never reveal everything one knows, some details of the ceremony are usually held back. As a result, some singers know only parts of the ceremonies, different specialists perform ceremonies somewhat differently, and ceremonies change slightly from generation to generation.

The curing ceremony involves creating a sand painting on the ground, then placing the patient on it. During that period the patient himself or herself becomes a holy personage. The chanting and the fees paid to the specialists are said to create a correct reciprocity with the supernatural powers so that curing can occur. The paintings are destroyed at the end of the ritual. Navajo fear that the patient will actually get worse if the ceremonies are not carried out correctly.

Navajo say that if a misfortune or an illness is not corrected by the ceremony, and certainly after several ceremonies, then the cause is witchcraft. They recognize four different kinds of witchcraft (Kluckhohn 1944), each called a different name, although Navajo say that practitioners of all such evildoings hang together. They are:

(a) *Witchery* caused by witches using what English-speaking Navajo call a ''poison,'' which is a powder said to be prepared from the flesh of corpses. The powder may be dropped into the hogan through the smokehole or put into the nose of the victim when he or she is asleep, or blown into the victim's face when he or she is in a large crowd. Witches are associated with death. They become witches in order to work vengeance on their enemies who have, in their own opinion, done them disservices. In the process of becoming a witch, a person is said to be required to sacrifice a close kinsperson, probably a sibling. Witches are active at night, when they take the form of animals—particularly wolves and coyotes. It is said that a witch who has been in the area the night before can sometimes be tracked by following the tracks of such animals. Sometimes the tracks lead to the house of another Navajo. Sometimes a witch is shot at night—and people learn who it is when someone, perhaps far away, emerges with an unexplainable wound. Masquerading as these were-animals, witches are said to meet at night and sit around in circles eating the flesh of corpses, which may even be stored in the caves where they meet. Some people say that the witches in these meetings make sand paintings like those used in curing, but these paintings represent their intended victims.

(b) *Sorcery* is believed to work in a different way, involving spells that are said over something associated with the victim: clothing, hair, nail parings, feces and the like. These items are said to be buried either with the flesh of corpses or with something stolen from a grave. The sorcerer then sings a song—perhaps a ''good song'' sung backward. Each sorcerer is said to be associated either with a particular supernatural power (represented by the sun, the earth, lightning or darkness) or an animal such as a bear, a snake or an owl. Sorcery can be used to ruin crops, kill livestock, or make an automobile stall.

(c) *Wizardry* is a practice that is said to involve shooting objects into the body of the intended victims—English-speaking Navajo call it ''bean shooting.'' Almost all wizards are said to be old men. The object is to cause illness.

(d) *Frenzy witchcraft* is primarily love magic, using plants such as jimpson weed, datura, or other nightshades to attract a specific person. These potions can be administered in cigarettes, in food, even by kissing.

Navajo religion (including witchcraft) is based on a theory of reciprocity in which people are responsible for reciprocating the good deeds of others and thwarting the misfortunes that occur when others (including the supernatural powers) do not behave justly or well. In contrast, most Christian religions are based on a set of moral obligations laid down by a high god, transgression of which leads to sin and hence to difficulty.

Navajo children learn ideas about religion and witchcraft from their parents, who invoke these ideas when they are unable to deal with practical or social problems in other ways (Kluckhohn 1944)—just as American parents blame the will of God when they can find no other explanation. There are many factors and events that people cannot control, especially illness, long periods of hunger, or want. Witchcraft is regarded as a last-chance means of achieving power if one can't get it any other way or of expressing what is not culturally allowed, including antagonism.

A belief in witchcraft is rational. One of the great insights into witchcraft is that if you accept its premises—that misfortune is caused by the ill will of other people—it is a perfectly logical set of beliefs (Evans-Pritchard 1937). Indeed, it is probably true that if you accept the premises of any religion, its theology and practice follow logically.

Religion and Denunciation. Buddhism is a religion based on a logic that denies any virtue in personal reward. In fact, Buddhism tries to overcome the idea of the personal. It is a calm religion, based on rationality and knowledge of ''the way.'' Buddhism is a magnificently satisfying set of ideas, but it is hard to live up to the goals of the sacrifice of self, pleasures, and comfort. However, there are overt ways for people to ''beat the system'' so that the Buddhist design for living can still offer ample personal rewards in life.

12-16. The complex meanings of Burmese Buddhism are symbolized in their figures of the Buddha and in many icons and elements of the architecture of Buddhist temples. This shrine with its Buddha is in Pegu, north of Rangoon.

Buddhism would seem to be unique in its responses to the eternal questions. There are two sorts of Buddhism: Mahayana Buddhism, practiced in India and Eastern Asia, and Theravada Buddhism, which is practiced in Thailand, Burma, Cambodia and Ceylon. Theravada Buddhism in Burma (Spiro 1970) has no saints or saviors. Its few rituals are simple. It is built around ''five concepts,'' none of which

mean exactly what the English words to describe them ordinarily mean. Those principles are:

(1) *Materialism,* a doctrine that human beings do not have souls. People are an aggregate of factors that disappear at death; the world is made up of atoms, in constant motion. Atoms are recycled in reincarnation to a new life, but neither soul nor body survive to participate in the new life.

(2) *Atheism* comes closer to what the word means in ordinary language. Buddhism is a religion without a god. It has ''no Creator who brought [the world] into being, who guides its course, or who presides over the destiny of man'' (Spiro 1970). There is no god to whom an individual can turn for salvation.

(3) *Pessimism* implies a doctrine of suffering. No matter how pleasurable, when looked at from the standpoint of Buddhist meditation, every action is said to involve suffering. The wheel of life and of reincarnation is a never-ending road of suffering. The word ''suffering'' would appear not to mean precisely what it means in everyday English.

(4) **Nihilism** means that everything in the world is in a state of impermanence. There is no reality—anything that is real one moment is something else the next. The goal should be nirvana, the extinction of existence—to bring an endless cycle of reincarnations to an end.

(5) *Egoism* implies that since there is no god, no savior, no one who watches over—then there is no self. Yet salvation depends on personal actions.

Theravada Buddhism may be the most difficult religion in the world to practice literally. Most adherents do not try. Instead of searching for the nothingness of nirvana, they lead moral lives in an attempt to improve their position on the wheel of life next time around. They may also turn to other religions, because Buddhism is not an exclusive religion. Unlike Christianity or Judaism or Islam, Buddhism has no sanctions against accepting other religions at the same time as one accepts Buddhism. Thus, Buddhism is likely to be associated with at least one other religion. The way Buddhism is practiced more closely resembles religion in most other societies than Buddhist scripture itself would suggest (Spiro 1970).

Buddhism is, in spite of lacking a personalized savior, a salvation religion. Buddhists have to save themselves. In one sense everybody has to save themselves, no matter what the religion; the difference is in the amount of support the person gets. The Buddha himself postponed his own entry into nirvana in order to delineate the path that he had followed to achieve nirvana. He got no extra merits for doing this— he had already earned his nirvana. His concern for fellow human beings was so great that he postponed his reward of nirvana in order to help them. Thus, the path, the way, that he showed is the way to salvation.

Five Main Points of Theravada Buddhism

Materialism Atoms making up the body are continually recycled, but neither soul nor body survive to participate in the next life.

Atheism There is no god to whom one can turn for salvation.

Pessimism All human experience is suffering. Reincarnation is a never-ending wheel of suffering. We should desire nirvana so as to get out of the constant reincarnation and the suffering that goes with it.

Nihilism There is no reality: nirvana will bring the cycle of incarnations to an end.

Egoism Since there is no god, there is no self. Suffering and death are normal—the only thing that makes them regrettable is that they are suffered by an aware self.

12-17. Theravada Buddhism is based on five main points, but they are difficult to live up to, and people have found ways around them.

One of the basic tenets of the Buddha's way is to eliminate suffering by eliminating desire. Wanting what one does not have or being too deeply attached to what one already has leads to nothing but suffering. The way to eliminate such suffering is to get rid of the desire for such things. One must not cling to self; the only reason that aging, illness, and death are suffering is that they are perceived as *my* aging, *my* illness, *my* death. If you can get rid of the "my," these events are neutral events in accordance with the laws of nature.

There is also an idea called karma for adding up the merits and demerits of the journey toward nirvana. Indeed, "the moral universe is government by the law of karma . . . the law of action and retribution" (Spiro 1970). There are morally good acts and morally bad acts. Both lead to retribution that will influence one's rebirth after death.

The Buddhist definition of the good life is to search first for morality and only later to achieve the higher goals through meditation and wisdom. Morality is achieved by overcoming ignorance. That means giving up a self, realizing that all existence is impermanent, and that desire can lead only to suffering. Some Buddhists cannot contemplate the complete nonexistence implied by nirvana. "When religious doctrines are inconsistent with the actors' cognitive and perceptual structures, they will be rejected. . . . Religious doctrines are accepted if they can be used to satisfy various of the needs of the faithful" (Spiro 1970).

As a result, we can understand why most Burmese Buddhists try to assure a better position in their next incarnation rather than to achieve the obliteration of nirvana. What they cannot have in this life, they hope to get in another. In their daily lives, they do not accept the proposition that pleasure is suffering; they do not want to give up the things that provide pleasure. Suffering, they say, results from evil spirits, poverty, and tyrannous governments. Suffering is a result of bad karma which can be undone only by counteracting it with good karma. Some Burmese even reject the search for nirvana. Most are aware, however, that not aiming toward nirvana is heresy—they say they want nirvana but are not yet far enough along to seek it.

In this situation, the idea of merit, or good karma, for good deeds takes on greater significance. There are three ways to get merit: by charity, by moral thoughts and actions, and by meditations.

Ritual in Theravada Buddhism exists in practice, even though it is denigrated in the sacred writings, which are devoted largely to salvation, not to the religion of everyday life. Like other religions, it has instrumental rituals to achieve desired ends such as physical health or favorable weather; commemorative rituals to honor historical or mythical events; rituals of passage to honor a person's trail through the life course; and expressive rituals to permit the expression of emotions.

Religion answers more or less the same questions everywhere, but there is an extraordinarily broad range of symbols and beliefs with which to face those questions. Religion is also universally a source of strength in adversity and a means of maintaining peace and predictability within the community.

Creed: Religion and Ideology

IDEOLOGY AND CULTS

Ideologies are often compared to religions; cults, at least by their members, are said to *be* religions. Both share aspects of religions. Almost surely, no definitions distinguishing them will be commonly acceptable.

Ideology and Science

An ideology is a set of doctrines, assertions and intentions that underlie a social or political movement. Although ideologies may provide answers to the eternal questions, they are also likely to provide answers to additional questions such as the nature of power in human affairs that extend into the political sphere. Communism, conservatism, liberalism, and nazism are all ideologies. Although ideologies often contain visionary speculations about the nature of human beings and human society, their purpose usually has to do with changing the power dimensions of the society. Established religions can become or espouse political ideologies when they are used as blueprints for political action rather than designs for living. Ideology, like religion, calls for faith over inquiry.

12-18. Ideologies like Marxism or conservatism, if followed too slavishly, make inquiry impossible. They resemble some religions in disallowing challenge to the basic premises. Thus they undercut the capacity for reexamination of propositions and insights that might come from looking at old ideas from new angles.

Ideologies can be centered around almost any idea: justice, equality, ethnic purity, social welfare, or many other issues. Ideologists demand that adherents be in complete agreement by accepting all the ideological doctrines, or else be branded wrong or evil. Indeed, some people consider their ideologies to be transcendent over law and organized religion.

Ideologies may be strong for the same reason that religions are strong: they give vital answers to at least some of the eternal questions, and the answer is considered of greater moment than the question. Ideologies provide "maps of problematic social reality" (Geertz 1964).

Ideologies differ from social science (or any other science) in that their propositions are not presented as theory to be criticized, tested, and improved, but rather as premises to be accepted on faith. Science underlies our modern worldview. Scientism, however, is an ideology—that is to say, many nonscientists (and some scientists) are convinced not only that science can explain the universe, but that it can save the world. The difficulty in such a position is easily seen when we examine what people, using technology and ideology, have done to the environment.

The Australian aborigines and the Native Americans sought rewards by disappearing into the totality of Nature. Their beliefs were based on their intimate knowledge of nature and their myths of the way that they, their society and their ancestors fit into the natural world. In contrast, today's industrial and post-industrial people seek rewards by separating themselves from Nature so they can understand it, control it, and exploit it. They make a dualism of the knower and the known instead of a unity of the knower as part of the known. The question resolves into the mode of understanding the universe from the inside and understanding it from the outside. Scientists are outsiders. Aborigines are insiders. Each approach provides its rewards and presents its problems.

Note that I did not say that scientists wanted to control Nature. That is a different issue—not unimportant, but different. It is part of the ideology of scientism, not part of the method or goals of science.

WE, THE ALIEN

If science is misunderstood and turned into an ideology, often called scientism, the genius of science is killed—dead. Scientism may be a tendency to reduce all reality and experience to mathematical descriptions just to make it "look" scientific; it may be putting undue weight on the numbers of SAT tests with no concern for the cultural background of the people taking the test. The morality of science, like the morality of religion, must be kept under close and constant surveillance.

Cults

Differentiating a cult from a sect of an established religion may be impossible. **Cult** has become an uninviting word often used to describe organizations that are discredited by everybody but their members. Cults are almost always minority religious groups (but small, accepted religious orders like Quakers or Mennonites are not cults).

A few cults develop into established religions. Christianity began as a cult of Judaism; Mormonism began as a cult of Christianity. Most, however, do not survive. People who are attracted to cults often find that the cult supplies answers not just to eternal questions but to personal decisions they must make in their lives. A cult hence "frees" them from indecision (Whalen 1981). Many organized religions are torn by cults from time to time—cults form when some small portion of followers focus on a part of the teachings about the eternal questions, either reinterpreting them or setting them into new contexts. Most cult founders and members are convinced there is something deeply wrong with society that can be corrected only by changing the religious and moral practices.

Cults were common in early American society, as they are common in many countries of Europe and Asia. Cults again became widespread in the United States in the 1960s, when many people were convinced that American life abounded in sin and evil. Thousands of young people abandoned their educations, their families, and entered the cults. For some, the cults were a welcome refuge from drugs; for others, they were a refuge from forces they perceived as evil or meaningless in their society. The cults were a way of expressing discomfort—a way of dropping out of the confusion of modern life.

These young people in the 1960s were searching for something. They did not know what it was, but many thought they had found it in the cults. Secret rituals in many cults reinforced the hold on their members. The power of group participation may provide a secure and closed in-group—

outsiders became "the enemy." The members, often uncomfortable with the larger society before they came into the cult, came actually to fear the larger world.

One of the best known cults of the 1970s was that created by the Reverend Sun Myung Moon called the Unification Church. Rev. Moon was born in Korea. Brought up Christian, he set out to create what he called the "new, ultimate, final truth" for his followers. After receiving a Japanese education, he returned to Korea to involve himself with a Christian splinter group that believed the next Messiah would be Korean. He was excommunicated from the Korean Presbyterian Church because of his activities with this group. He began his own church, whose expenses were paid by factories he controlled.

Moon said that Jesus appeared to him in January of 1972, telling him to bring his message to America. When Moon objected that he knew no English, Jesus told him that was

12-19. Cults sometimes offer solace and shelter when the realities of society become overwhelming or distasteful. In the 1960s and early 1970s, thousands of young people joined cults like The Unification Church under the direction of the Rev. Sun Myung Moon. Here Rev. Moon blesses over two thousand couples, all of whom were members of his church and had their spouses selected for them from among other members of the cult.

Creed: Religion and Ideology

not important—that He would care for Moon and see that the message was got out. Moon soon began his American Mission and formed his church. Its members were called Moonies; 35 percent came from Catholic, 45 percent from Protestant and about 7 percent from Jewish households. They worked full time at their religion. Indeed, they worked twelve hours a day every day begging or peddling candy or flowers to increase the wealth of the church to carry on what they defined as the work of God. The entire income was handed over to church officials in return for a place to sleep, plain but adequate diet, the promise of a better world and a set of idealistic goals with which they could identify. Drugs were forbidden. Sex was forbidden to new members. When they had proved themselves for three years by sticking to this regimen, they could be married—their partners were chosen by the church. Mass marriages occurred every year.

Meanwhile, the Unification Church and the Rev. Moon became rich. They bought expensive properties in several parts of the United States, including hotels to house themselves. The Rev. Moon lived in a mansion overlooking the Hudson River. His nine children attended expensive schools. He had several limousines and a cabin cruiser.

The Unification Church was widely accused of brainwashing its members, as were many other cults that became popular at this period of American history. Some parents became frantic. A new service was established: people were paid by the parents of Moonies to kidnap their children and forcibly counter-brainwash them. About half those kidnapped went back into the movement.

American culture, at the time, was in the throes of the Vietnam War which offered few outlets to attract idealistic and committed young people. Many cults of that time and since have used social sciences and psychology to state their platforms. Dianetics and Scientology are a case in point—their founder rewrote Freudian psychology and the confessional part of the Roman Catholic religion into a new amalgam. The Hare Krishna, a Hindu sect organized in the fifteenth century, blossomed in the United States, using chants and begging to achieve peace and salvation.

Most cults are temporary groups that give highly moral and strict regimens to people who lack them. Many of them help such people. They are beset, however, by being out of step with society, by their social position as hangers-on of established religions, and often by corrupt leadership.

A Word on Easy Answers. Ideologies abound in the modern world. When choices are as many and varied as they are in complex cultures, one must find ways to simplify. Ideologies supply simplifications that are sometimes useful. When, in the process, they lull their adherents into stopping all inquiry, they stultify growth. Ideologies (no matter the kernels of truth in them) put dangerous hobbles on science and social science as well as on religion and on public opinion.

Science lacks an important element when it is confronted by powerful ideologies. Science as a worldview does not have a built-in moral system. The business of science is to provide good questions continually—to probe for more questions. In contrast, ideologies and cults seek to dry up the questions. They provide tight moral systems with built-in answers to difficult questions. They claim to provide clear paths through the maze of difficult choices—then, sometimes years later, adherents see that the cost has been imprisonment in a social trap. When you cannot ask questions, you are at the mercy of people who provide answers. Whenever we give up seeking better answers, culture becomes our prison instead of our tool.

CONCLUDING THOUGHTS

Both religion and science offer ways of explaining the unknown. Science focuses on discovering the best questions. Religion focuses on comforting and traditionally workable answers to the eternal questions that perplex people of all societies. The combination of the questions and the answers are the worldview. Exploring worldviews is a major task for anthropologists—and questioning their own is one of the most demanding parts of it.

BUZZWORDS

cult this word has several meanings. On the one hand, it applies to an organization that conducts ritual or religious observations. It may also refer to a religious group that is out of step with the major religions of the society but attracts people searching for security, comfort and predictability. Finally, it may apply to religious movements that emerge to deal with situations of cultural contact.

divination telling the unknown or foretelling the future by omens or by prophecy that taps information beyond that known to ordinary people.

nihilism rejection of belief in religion, laws, government. In Buddhism, it is the idea that there is no reality over time and that everything in the world is in a state of impermanence.

shaman a priest found in many Siberian and North American societies; the priest is said to have direct access to the supernatural powers.

totemism another religion made up by anthropologists. People in many parts of the world do indeed categorize nature so that some people are put into some of the natural categories. They suppose a special relationship among the members of the category, including the people in it. Such beliefs are often the basis of ritual, but they are not organized into "religions" by the people who hold the beliefs or practice the ritual.

vodou (voodoo) an African-based religion in the Caribbean, particularly Haiti, in which spirits are said to be immanent at all times and may possess people. The word has been extended in American English to mean sorcery, magic, and conjuration.

witchcraft an irrational means of associating the misfortunes of some people with antisocial or unaccepted practices by other people, with the usual premise that the misfortune was caused by the unacceptable people.

worldview the combination of ideas, including religious and ritual ideas, about how the world was made, the forces that make it continue to run, and the place of persons and social groups in that world.

CONTEXT

V

We now know something about the biological underpinnings of culture, about what culture is, and how people learn it. We know that people create their own individual persons and constantly recreate their societies in the processes of using culture. We have taken a look at some of the many ways culture can be institutionalized.

Now we can investigate the processes by which culture works—especially the way culture is altered when its context is changed. More than the other social sciences, anthropology is acutely aware of context—consideration of the way environment, technology and social organization are interconnected—and of the impact of several cultures on one another.

We have to learn to use anthropology to look into our present-day world—and into what our future might be.

Concluding Thoughts offers a short summary of the anthropological ideas that can make the life of every educated person more meaningful. Such a summary is a review, but—far more important—it flings out a challenge for the future. How can anthropology help us make our lives and our culture more sensible and more satisfying?

Books to Change Your Life   *Martha C. Ward*

Bodley, John H.

1985   *Anthropology and Contemporary Human Problems, Second Edition*. Mountain View, CA: Mayfield Publishing Co.

1987   *Tribal Peoples and Development Issues*. Mountain View, CA: Mayfield Publishing Co.

1990   *Victims of Progress, Third Edition*. Mountain View, CA: Mayfield Publishing Co.

Bodley's books are standards that illustrate the effects of Westernization, contact, colonialism and "modernization" that have swept through and, in some cases swept away, the tribal cultures of the world.

Fossey, Dian

1984   *Gorillas in the Mist*. Boston: Houghton Mifflin Co. A movie of the same name made Fossey's pioneering research and preservation efforts famous. The book is about falling in love with gorillas, saving them from poachers and telling the rest of us why silverback males are useful, how primate babies grow up with identifiable personalities and what females do in heat.

Harris, Marvin

1974   *Cows, Pigs, Wars and Witches: The Riddles of Culture*. New York: Random House.

1977   *Cannibals and Kings: The Origins of Cultures*. New York: Random House.

1985   *Good to Eat: Riddles of Food and Culture*. New York: Simon & Schuster.

1987   *Why Nothing Works: The Anthropology of Daily Life*. New York: Simon & Schuster.

1989   *Our Kind: Who We Are, Where We Came From, Where We Are Going*. New York: Harper & Row, Publishers, Inc.

You will enjoy reading these books even if you violently disagree with his interpretations. Marvin Harris writes well and simply. He routinely puts a spin to his theory and data that makes good reading and a great starting point for your term papers.

Kehoe, Alice Beck

1989   *The Ghost Dance: Ethnohistory and Revitalization*. New York: Holt, Rinehart and Winston, Inc. Most students want to know what really happened at Wounded Knee, what happened to the Indian warriors who defeated General Custer and what does all this have to do with religious movements and survival under almost intolerable stress. Here you will find out.

Keiser, R. Lincoln

1969   *The Vice Lords: Warriors of the Streets*. New York: Holt, Rinehart and Winston, Inc. Street gangs and urban crime are hot topics. This enduring analysis not only shows you what gangs were like a few years ago (they are deadlier now, but were deadly then) but is a classic of urban anthropology.

Kroeber, Theodora

1961   *Ishi in Two Worlds: A Biography of the Last Wild Indian in North America*. Berkeley, CA: University of California Press. This book, written by the fine writer who was wife to the pioneering anthropologist Alfred Kroeber and mother to leading science fiction writer Ursula LeGuin, will break your heart. The last Yahi Indian, his family, language and culture irretrievably lost, finally gave up and came out of the wilderness where he had been living alone. He was taken to the University Museum of the University of California in Berkeley, where he worked and lived as he adapted to life in early twentieth-century United States.

Mead, Margaret

1956   *New Lives for Old: Cultural Transformation—Manus, 1928-1953*. New York: William Morrow and Co. Reissued 1980 by Greenwood Press, Westport, CT. This book tells you what it feels like to be in an isolated, so-called "primitive" culture when hordes of Americans and other foreigners descend and create monumental changes. It stands alone, but can be read as a continuation of *Growing Up in New Guinea* (1930). Mead tells you here what happened to the characters in her earlier book when the twentieth century landed.

Spradley, James P.

1972   *The Cultural Experience: Ethnography in Complex Society*. Chicago: Science Research Associates. Reissued 1988 by Waveland Press, Inc., Prospect Heights, IL. Students like you designed the projects, conducted the research, and wrote this book. Spradley was a most unusual and gifted anthropologist who thought a lot about how to do fieldwork research in complex societies such as ours. He wrote several good books: *You Owe Yourself a Drunk: An Ethnography of Urban Nomads* (Boston: Little, Brown & Co., 1970. Reissued 1990 by University Press of America, Inc., Lanham, MD) is about homeless men in Seattle before homelessness became a recognized problem. The one that shows his research strategy best is probably *The Cocktail Waitress: Women's Work in a Man's World* (with Brenda J. Mann) [New York: John Wiley & Sons, Inc., 1975. Reissued by McGraw-Hill Publishing Co., Boston]. After reading this one, you will never take waitresses for granted again—and you will understand more about the anthropology of modern life than you ever imagined.

How Culture Works

13

PROPOSITIONS AND PREMISES

- To understand culture change, one has to shift the focus on the idea of culture from the noun aspect to the verb aspect: instead of asking what it is, we have to ask how it works. That means we must now examine processes (the dynamic aspects of culture) as well as institutions (the structural aspects).

- One basic tool for studying cultural process is the action chain.

- Some cultural processes are cyclic, in that they recur. Others are trajectories: there is a beginning, middle and end. The daily round is cyclic; technical processes or running a meeting are trajectories.

- Action chains may become destructive. If people are locked into a destructive action chain—that is, if they can't stop it or change it—it may become a social trap.

- Culture grows. Invention, diffusion (borrowing or taking over cultural items from another group), and recontexting of materials within a culture are part of cultural processes, although the rates at which invention and diffusion occur vary with many factors.

- Small changes in action chains and other cultural processes may occur constantly with comparatively little impact on an entire culture. Then, when those small changes stack up, the culture may seem to change suddenly. These periods can be called culture crests.

- Cultural evolution results when cultural changes mount to the point that it is impossible for people to return to earlier solutions.

- Europe reached a culture crest in the years surrounding 1400. The results were the expansion of European societies against all the others in the world and the spreading of European culture throughout the globe.

It is as important to know how culture works as it is to know how the universe works or how your body works. Knowing how it works is the first requirement for healing and remodeling it. Culture is information, in addition to all the other attributes ascribed to it. Using an analogy to computers, we can see that culture is a bank of information in the sense of data. It is also information in the sense of the program in the software that organizes, manipulates and uses the data. In this chapter, we shall examine how culture is patterned, how it is changed, how it can be replaced.

CULTURE DYNAMICS

When people get frustrated in their efforts to carry on their daily lives, they can do one of two things. They can either inure themselves to the frustration, or they can try to reduce the frustration by looking for better ways to do what they have to do. Few people look for new ways to do things if the old ways are working well enough. Even fewer search for completely new ways to do things before they have exhausted those ways that they or their neighbors already know.

13-1. A culture pool comprises all the culture available to a group of interacting individuals. It is comparable to a gene pool, which comprises all the genes available in an interbreeding population.

All the culture that is available to a group of people can be called its **culture pool.** The culture pool is analogous to the gene pool. A gene pool is the collection of all genes available in an interbreeding population. All newly-born members of the population show a mixture of some of the available genes. A culture pool is the totality of culture within an interacting population. Both gene pools and culture pools expand and contract as individual persons travel or migrate, and so come into contact with other persons and populations.

Gene loss is possible, especially in small gene pools. It is most likely to happen when the presence or absence of a specific gene is irrelevant to the survival of the species. Culture loss also happens; certain aspects may be irrelevant to survival if there is some other, better way to carry out any necessary purposes.

Each of us is a particular concatenation of some of the genes available in the gene pool. Each of us also learns and performs some of the culture that is available in our environment in the culture pool.

To understand the culture pool, we will consider several processes in this chapter. These will include "strips of behavior" (see Chapter 11) and how they form action chains; we will discuss both cycles and trajectories. We will also look at the idea of social traps and how we can get locked into

---

13-2. Loss of some culture is irrelevant if there are other ways to do whatever necessary tasks the lost items did.

---

them. We will, further, ask how and why people make inventions and thus enlarge the culture pool, or how they take something out of one context and put it into another, creating a new cultural pattern. We ask how people get ideas or material items from other cultures and recontext those foreign ideas and objects into their own culture. We want to know how culture as a whole changes as a result of such inventions or recontexting, and how it proceeds, like a wave, to change and swell gradually until it crests. The ultimate question, then, becomes how does culture evolve?

Action Chains

Culture strips are made up of acts or events that follow one another in a preordained order. These acts or events form chains. Once begun, the entire chain of acts must be followed through if any of the actions are to have their intended effect.

Chains or strips of action or events, seen from the standpoint of the actors, are called **action chains** (Hall 1977; Bohannan 1963 called them event sequences). Some action chains can be carried out by a single person. Painting a picture or building a cabinet involves an action chain. Anyone who paints a picture or builds a house must do things in the "right" order. Solitaire card games, too, are action chains.

However, most action chains require at least two people. A two-person action chain is "reminiscent of a dance that is used as a means of reaching a common goal that can be reached only after, and not before, each link in the chain has been forged" (Hall 1977). Hall gives as an example the fifteen steps in the mating procedure of sticklebacks. If one step is omitted or done in the wrong order or if it fails, successful mating cannot result. He then adds that he seriously doubts that human beings do anything of a social nature that is not an action chain. "Indeed, even shaking hands is a short action chain" (Hall 1977). Courtship is a more or less complicated action chain carried out by at least two persons; if more than two get involved, the number of necessary actions in the chain may multiply. Games like checkers or bridge proceed along action chains.

Thus, there is always a "right" way to do things (and then, the old saying goes, there's the army's way). That means that you not only adjudge what you are going to do, but the order in which you are going to do it. The rightness may be determined by the chemical and physical demands of the material world. Carpentry is a case in point: you can't put on the roof before the supports are in place. If the required actions are not followed in the right order, the structure may collapse. At best, the work at later stages is much more difficult.

If the correct order is determined by culture, the governing

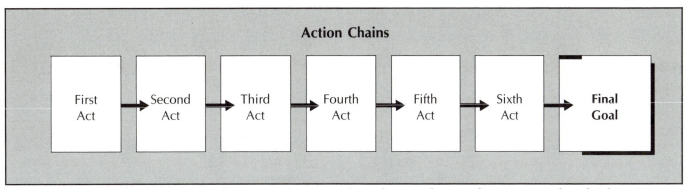

Action Chains

First Act → Second Act → Third Act → Fourth Act → Fifth Act → Sixth Act → **Final Goal**

13-3. *Action chains are social processes. Any series of acts that must be carried out in a preordained order if any of the acts are to be effective is an action chain. Most action chains involve two or more people.*

criteria are expressed in terms of efficiency or "appropriateness." A court process is another example of a pattern of repeating events. The court is called to order; the presentation of the claims, the evidence, calling witnesses, the summing up, the jury report, the sentencing—all must be done in the right order. Procedure in any parliament is of great importance—the rules of protocol must be observed if different views are to be heard and sensible decisions reached.

Cooking offers still another example: there are cultural differences in the action chains of cooking that lead to different resulting tastes, even when the ingredients are the same. For example, you would never know by the taste alone that a Chinese dish called kung-pao chicken (cut up the chicken into small pieces, add whole peanuts, add whole red peppers, and cook on a very hot fire) has approximately the same ingredients as a West African ground-nut stew (leave the chicken ingredients in large chunks, grind the peanuts

into peanut butter, add ground red peppers, then cook a long time on a slow fire).

Two-person chains are social processes. Successful action by two or more people not only demands that the actions of each proceed in a specific order but that the two sets of actions be intermeshed. All social relationships are chains composed of two or more overlapped and interlinked strips performed by individuals.

When two individuals interact, each influences the action of the other. The result is an action chain created by the interlinked feedback of the two actors (see 13-4). Each is in the environment of the other. The relationship so formed takes on a life of its own, not totally determined by either actor, as both react to the environment that includes the other. It is, to paraphrase both Shakespeare and François Villon, a beast with two heads.

Conversation is a complex action chain involving two or more persons. One person at a time is speaking. But the others

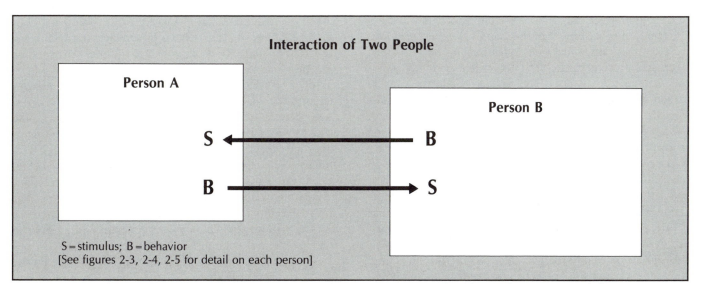

Interaction of Two People

Person A

Person B

S ← B

B → S

S = stimulus; B = behavior
[See figures 2-3, 2-4, 2-5 for detail on each person]

13-4. *The behavior of each participant is part of the environment of the other. When one person behaves in reaction to his or her environment, the other person notes the behavior and takes it into consideration in determining what to do. In this way, a social relationship can be built up like choreography—and we find the social organization in action.*

How Culture Works

are not idle. Listening behavior is noticeable, and it changes from one culture to another.

 American white middle class people indicate that they are listening by maintaining eye contact, blinking when a point is made, and nodding occasionally. Other Americans express quite different behavior. In the 1960s, it was discovered that some black children in inner city schools gave a signal when they initially tuned in to what their teacher was saying. After that, they did not consider it necessary to look at the teacher or to nod. They gave another signal when they tuned out. White middle class teachers were often nonplussed—they admitted that the children who were categorized as not listening did in fact know what had been said. However, their listening behavior did not match the pattern the teachers expected. They assumed that the children were not listening.

WE, THE ALIEN

In Chapter 2, we described the pattern of learning which takes place within the individual. A social dyad exists when each of two people is part of the environment to which the other is reacting.

Each person in a two-person action chain is in the perceptual space of the other. The monitor/comparator of one cannot help being affected by the other (13-4). Under those conditions, "common understandings" appear; common understandings are one of the underpinnings of any culture.

Change of procedure or of the "correct" order of actions in an action chain is analogous to learning in the individual. Because culture is inside both actors (but certainly is not identical in the two) and also outside them, the outside standard becomes something with which each of them must struggle and compromise.

That external standard is a product of interaction among many people. It is the public part of the culture—the culture in the environment. The culture in every person's head must adapt to (which is not the same thing as accepting uncritically) that standard.

An **event chain** is just like an action chain except that it focuses on processes themselves instead of on the actors. An event chain is evident in the specifics of culture, with little attention paid to the particular people who are acting. The necessary sequence of a chain of events—and each one of the events may itself be an event chain at a simpler level—enables social life to proceed. Many of the flowcharts that have been presented in the course of this book are event chains. As we shall see in Chapter 15, event chains show

their real elegance and potential usefulness when social science turns to policy considerations.

As far as I can discover, the first successful description of an event chain was used to explain ritual (Van Gennep [1908] 1960). 13-5 below is a quick synopsis of our detailed discussion in Chapter 11.

13-5. One of the earliest examples of an action (or event) chain was a rite of passage ritual. This trajectory always happens in the same order: first, the individual is removed from his or her position in society and put in a position outside it. While on the outside, the individual learns and behaves without the weight of social requirements. Then he or she is reintroduced into society as the third action of the trajectory. The person thereupon occupies a different social position.

A feud is an unsuccessful action chain. It starts out like any chain of legal actions. One party performs an act—say a killing. The kinsmen of the victim then kill a member of the original killer's group as a counteraction. However, the kinsmen of the new victim interpret the new killing not as a counteraction but as a fresh breach—and so it goes, victim after victim. No point of correction is ever reached. The actors have struck a social trap and do not have sufficient culture to escape from it.

As we saw in Chapter 5, a marriage is an involved event chain. Marriages in all societies follow the pattern illustrated in 13-6.

As our feud example illustrates, grave risks result when people follow event chains and action chains uncritically. We have encountered the danger of **social traps** in earlier chapters. Social traps are "situations in which [people] or organizations or whole societies get themselves started in some direction or some set of relationships that later prove to be unpleasant or lethal and that they see no easy way to back out of or to avoid" (Platt 1973). Only human creativity can detect and ameliorate social traps. Dueling was another example of an action chain which was difficult to stop because it had to do with the ideas of honor—there was no way to save face except to carry on with the duel. The Greek city-states perished because they could not find a way out of the social trap of warfare with one another to settle their inner city problems. Ethnic loyalties are a serious social trap that the Soviet state has not fully solved. A permanent underclass and the agonies of unemployment are manifestations of the social traps in a capitalist system; government action has ameliorated the situation somewhat, but has not altered the action chain that leads to the trap. Even a love affair can be a social trap if you don't know how to get out of it. I have met people who got married so that they could get divorced because they couldn't figure out any better way to end the relationship.

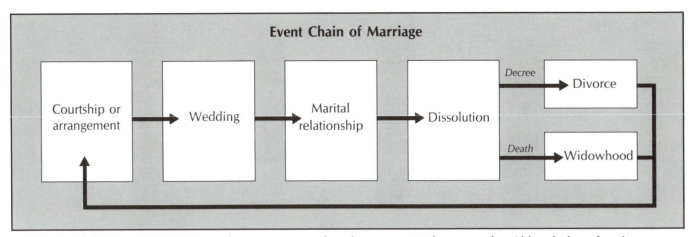

Event Chain of Marriage

Courtship or arrangement → Wedding → Marital relationship → Dissolution

Dissolution → *Decree* → Divorce

Dissolution → *Death* → Widowhood

13-6. Event chains are sets of type-occurrences that always occur in the same order. Although the order of some events may change slightly from one culture to another, that point in itself is instructive. Marriages follow this kind of event chain in all societies. They begin with an arrangement of the marriage (by its principals or others), followed by a wedding. The marriage relationship grows and changes as the partners age. All marriages end, either by death or by divorce. The surviving partners are allowed to remarry in most, but not quite all, societies.

A social trap is a situation in which an action chain leads to unpleasant or lethal outcomes. With a change of context, a beneficial or neutral action chain can become a social trap.

13-7.

Some people in some societies insist that virtues such as honesty and keeping one's word demand that once any action chain is entered, the parties to it must carry it through, no matter what the cost. That mislabeled virtue is the root of many social traps. In other situations, action chains can be broken off, especially if people can save face while ending the chain. We need, but do not have, detailed information on why face-saving devices are not known or used—only then can we understand thoroughly how people get locked in to social traps. These lock-ins are created when people insist on carrying through action chains that they know to be damaging—indeed, to be social traps.

Cycles and Trajectories

Some action chains form **cycles**. The last act in the action chain leads back to another performance of the first act—a sort of social perpetual motion. Our daily round of activities is a cycle. We get up, eat, go to work or school, eat, work some more, go home, watch TV, brush our teeth, go to sleep, and wake up to do it all again the next day. Although each day is obviously a little different—some are better, some worse—we follow routines (another theatrical analogy). Office and factory workers follow weekly routines; students and professors follow semester routines; farmers follow seasonal or annual routines. Such routines are cyclic in that one day leads directly to the next; one week after another, season after season, year in year out.

Other action chains form **trajectories**. They have a beginning and a middle and an end. Trajectories such as the life course may be repeated by many persons, although each person does it a little differently from everyone else and can do it only once. As T.S. Eliot put it, "You'd be bored. Birth, and copulation, and death. That's all the facts when you come to brass tacks: Birth, and copulation, and death." The life

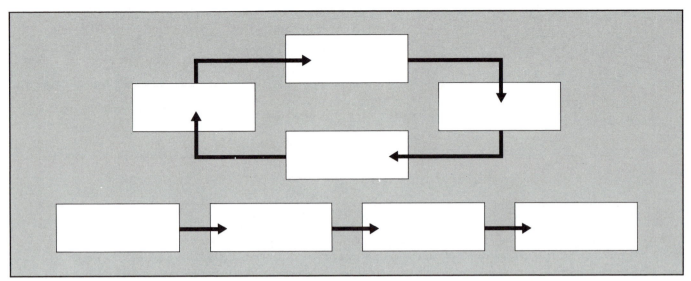

13-8. *The top diagram illustrates a cycle; the bottom diagram illustrates a trajectory. The trajectory can also be called a flowchart.*

course is not a cycle, except in the postulates of some Asian religions.

Cycles and trajectories provide some of the most permanent landmarks of our lives. We know that day follows night, that Monday follows Sunday, that spring follows winter, that baking the bread follows its rising. We know what to expect and, hence, how to deal with cyclical events. Trajectories may be trickier, especially those that you can do only once. We can know about them too, from the experience of our family and our friends.

Invention

Human beings are inventive when they perceive needs that are unfulfilled or when they are convinced that there must be a better way to do something than the ways they are now using.

Invention changes culture—that is, indeed, its point. However, a culture is a system in the sense that its parts fit together and imply one another. Therefore, to change one part puts all the rest under greater or lesser strain. Great changes in the environment also put strains on the cultural system—may even make it unworkable—and, therefore, lead to the perception of new needs. Sudden changes in government, like revolution or conquest, lead to new views and new needs.

Unless the cultural system is in a state of total equilibrium (which is rare and may, in fact, have existed only in the minds of social scientists), there are *always* new needs. The new needs may not be sufficiently urgent for anybody to be driven to do anything about them. Examples of threats to the cultural system are: long-term weather changes, increased population, epidemics, or war. Such monumental events account for a major part of human ingenuity. They are immense challenges to which people respond by inventing new culture.

13-9. *Culture can be changed by invention, reinterpretation, diffusion, recontexting, and probably by many other processes.*

At the beginning of the Industrial Revolution, for example, weaving machinery was invented to bring down the price of cloth, which was scarce and expensive. Soon the machines were able to weave much faster than thread could be made. Thereupon, the need for spinning machines was felt—and the spinning machine was invented to replace hand-operated spinning wheels. The new spinning and weaving machines meant that the bottleneck was now in getting the seeds out of cotton so that the new spinning machines could turn it into thread at their full capacity. By the time the cotton gin was invented to get the seeds out, the original weaving machine had itself become inadequate. New improvements were then made in the weaving machines. These processes created an entire textile industry within a comparatively few years. Cloth became inexpensive. Cheap cloth led, in turn, to vast change in all parts of the culture. People dressed differently—they could now have more than one set of clothes; they did not have to wear the same thing for everything they did. "Appropriate dress" took on new meaning. Their health was affected—plenty of cloth meant they could and did wash their clothes more often. They slept differently because bed linens became available. They draped their houses differently—whereas windows were formerly blocked only by shutters, they could now be "closed" by curtains. All these things had an impact not only on trade but on family life itself.

The steel industry and the automobile industry grew up in the same way—that is, new inventions led to new needs

13-10. *One successful invention leads to the need for a new one, as this series from the textile industry illustrates. Pictured left to right: an early hand loom, the Arkwright spinning frame and the cotton gin invented by Eli Whitney in the late 1700s.*

for further inventions. Soon the petroleum industry followed along as the need for a new fuel to run automobiles increased. Steel eventually suffered when the need for fuel economy led to automobiles with aluminum and plastic bodies.

The computer industry is going through a similar development even as you read this sentence. The early personal computers were slow, in the sense that people had to wait for them to do some of the computations. It was human impatience, not the speed relative to anything that had been available previously, that defined the machine as slow. The next technical goal became to improve the computer to the point that its users were never aware of waiting for it. The changes that the computer has wrought on society are almost unimaginable. They have affected the banking system, which has altered world economies. They have altered manufacturing processes—we cannot imagine how people got it all done without computers. The list seems interminable—computers have changed everything.

There are social inventions as well as technological inventions. The clan was an invention for turning some but not all kinship relationships to totally new purposes, as we saw in Chapter 5. The state was an invention for creating a hierarchy of roles in which power could be lodged, independent of specific individuals, as we saw in Chapter 8. The publicly owned corporation was an invention for financing large undertakings when nobody has enough money to undertake them alone.

The story of social and technological inventions is the story of civilization. In one sense all inventions, even those that concentrate on technology, involve social processes. The production line was as important an invention as the reaper, which harvests grain. The production line altered the work lives of many people almost out of recognition. Weaving machines affected the clothes we wear, and the reaper affected our diet.

The corporation was as important an invention as the steam engine. The shape of the corporation in the coming decades will be somewhat different from what it is now—this social form is still in the maturational processes. Democracy was as important an invention as the plow. It seems to be spreading, but running a democracy requires an educated public and a capacity to include bicentric modes of settling differences and disputes *within* the unicentric governmental forms. Learning how to listen to many different ideas, then selecting those that everybody (well, enough people anyhow) will stick to takes very special training and an institutional structure that can support it.

Inventiveness is, whether technological or social, limited by cultural preconditions. An invention is of no immediate value if the necessary preconditions are not present. Leonardo da Vinci designed an airplane about A.D.1500, but because engines had not been invented to provide the thrust, and for other reasons, it could not be built. Household inventions are closely associated with the position of women in society. In the early days of the Industrial Revolution, the position of servants changed—many servants, especially women, could

How Culture Works

13-11. *Social inventions are as important as technological inventions. The lineage organization (the photograph above shows members of a Tiv lineage with the wives of two members), the state (the United States capitol) and the corporation are all social inventions of immense importance.*

13-12. Public reception of an invention is even more decisive than the invention itself in influencing culture change.

do better in the factories, working for wages. As women were divided into workers and ladies, many household inventions were created to help ladies fill the gap. Then people began to realize they could make money from the manufacture of these inventions. Many household aids were created. Interestingly, the total amount of time that people spend on housework, food preparation, shopping and the like has changed little—more time shopping, less time on housework, different people doing it. People, especially women on the second shift, are still tied closely to maintenance work.

Bathroom inventions offer an example of how preconditions shape results. Bathrooms are closely tied to ideas about cleanliness and privacy. The Romans saw a bath as a public event. Victorians, on the other hand, saw a bathroom as no more than a way to get clean in decent privacy. American hot tubs are somewhere in the middle.

Preconditions affecting inventions of new types of household or office furniture are ideas about comfort (which changed radically in Europe and America in the 1700s and again in the 1900s) as well as ideas about efficiency and privacy, intimacy and social relationships.

The public reception of an invention is just as important as its creation. Thousands of inventions are made each month, many of them even patented, that the public is not interested in. Such inventions merely disappear. My own father invented and patented an inter-step to be attached to a ladder so that you could stand equidistant between two rungs. Nobody cared, so the patent is somewhere in my hoard of family treasures. Some attics are full of such patents.

Some of these rejected inventions may be reinvented once the preconditions are right—that is, once there is a public readiness to accept the other changes that the new invention requires. I know a man who, in the 1960s, invented an ingenious engine based on the mobius strip—a highly fuel-efficient engine that could be made to burn with little emission. But he discovered that, except for his method of sealing the motor, it had been invented in the 1890s. His reinvention was useless in this capitalist society because he could not patent it, and hence the likelihood of making money from manufacturing it was severely reduced. The fact that it is more efficient and cleaner than the piston engine was not, in our system, considered adequate reason for experimenting with switching over to a new kind of engine. It may have been that, had the earlier patent not existed, the whole internal combustion in automobiles would have been altered—and improved.

Thus, acceptance depends in large part on whether or not people are uncomfortable enough with their present way of doing things that they are willing to change their habit patterns—that is, to change their responses. It also depends on who first takes up the new invention. Some inventions may succeed if they are first accepted by an elite group. The car telephone spread quickly from executives in Mercedes-Benzes to salesmen in Ford Escorts. The videophone was effectively rejected by everybody as early as the 1950s. Many styles in clothes and music work the other direction—they begin in the inner city and soon work their way into the suburbs.

The need for new social inventions has never been more urgent than it is today, although people in our society are not as sensitive to this need as they are to technological needs. We need new institutions that can amass enough capital to clean up the environment and deal with problems of poverty and homelessness. We need new institutions for educating people of all ages in a situation in which our traditional methods no longer work well enough. We need new social institutions to provide help for the disabled of all ages.

But creating these new social institutions is a more difficult and gradual process for two reasons: (1) people will have to make immense changes in their basic social values and associations in order to invent the new institutions, and (2) nobody has yet figured out how to profit from creating and using such institutions—after all, we are a capitalist society in which people expect to make money from their inventions.

Diffusion

The second important way to get new culture is to borrow ideas and technology. Meanings can be learned from your neighbors; tools can be borrowed and copied. Some inventions, once made and accepted, spread rapidly. The process by which culture spreads across the geography is called **diffusion**. The idea of agriculture, for example, has been

How Culture Works

invented several times, in several parts of the world, and diffused from those points. The use of new food crops may spread rapidly. Beef, for example, came from the Old World to the New very quickly after the Spanish invasion. Potatoes went from the New World to the Old. Maize, a New World crop, became one of the staple foods of Africa within a very short time. The idea of the wheel, once discovered, quickly became almost universal. The idea of the water wheel to turn gears, and then of the noria to use the water wheel to raise water from low to higher levels spread rapidly. So did the windmill.

In the late 1800s and the early 1900s, anthropologists were arguing heatedly about whether *any* invention could be made more than once. Could the same improvement be invented many times or is every invention diffused from one original source? Today we know that the same inventions are often made in many places—and also that the diffusion both of ideas and technology takes place all the time.

As with invention, the reception of a diffused idea or item is the vital point. Many peoples know about technologies or practices of their neighbors but do not choose to use them—to do so would create unacceptable changes in other parts of their own culture and would lead them to have to change their own habit patterns.

Culture Crests

Cultural changes occur all the time. If a people's culture is efficiently adapted to its environment, the rate of change may be very slow. It may appear that there is little or no change at all for centuries. It is not in the nature of culture, however, to remain static. Environmental forces change. People adapt to new climatic situations, to new population pressures, or to challenges that arise from the actions of their neighbors. Some people have new ideas—it is a human characteristic. These individuals may begin to do things new ways. A few of those new ways may be taken up by others. Eventually, cultures accommodate small changes.

It may take eons, but over time those small changes stack up. At some point the cumulative change will become massive enough that a people's overall pattern of using and adapting to the environment has changed. The old ways no longer work—they may even be forgotten.

A fundamental turning point in the growth and development of a culture is thus reached. Small cultural changes have accumulated to such an extent that suddenly—at least it seems sudden to scholars who study it and sometimes to people who are living it—the old ways are seen to be irrelevant. They may even have become unintelligible. That turning point can be called a **culture crest**. History and prehistory can best be explained as a series of culture crests.

A dramatic example of a culture crest was set in motion by ecological change about twelve thousand years ago at the end of the last Ice Age. The desiccation of the Afro-Asian prairie lands presented a formidable challenge to the peoples of their area. The result was a desert that stretches from Western Africa across the Sahara, the Arabian peninsula

13-13. A culture crest is the point at which the cumulative small changes in culture suddenly add up to a total change in activities and lifestyle. The Agricultural Revolution, the Urban Revolution, and the Industrial Revolution are all culture crests.

and central Asia to the Gobi Desert in northeastern China and Mongolia. People responded with a whole series of cultural readjustments, some of which led to the beginnings of agriculture and eventually to the first civilizations.

Technological changes can also lead to culture crests. In several parts of the world, for example, improvements in sailing ships and navigational instruments resulted from the strong desire to trade with other civilizations and to explore new lands. In Europe after the fourteenth century, these technological improvements led to what Euro-Americans chauvinistically call the voyages of discovery, and hence to a whole new set of challenges. As Europeans responded to the challenges which trade and empire gave rise to, they eventually created the global mercantile empires—a culture crest that changed the entire world.

With every culture crest, whole ranges of peoples' expectations are transformed. The cycles of daily activity are vastly different from those of their ancestors. The trajectories of the social relations that people create and live by are altered.

Contemporary civilization would seem right now to be in the throes of a gigantic culture crest. Our needs for resources and excitement, among other things, are driving us to explore the bottom of the sea and are thrusting us into space. The new technologies, discoveries, and opportunities that result from space exploration are likely to induce social changes as great as those produced by the agricultural or industrial revolutions.

Culture crests are, as we shall see in the second part of this chapter, the dividing points between the major periods of human prehistory and history. None was planned. Each came about because of invention and then the diffusion and gradual acceptance of new ways. Then, as enough change accumulated, it became impossible to ignore the realization that "everything is different."

Evolution

The idea of evolution is an ancient one—Greek philosophers thought about it; Roman poets wrote about it. It is a simple idea: every social or technological situation allows certain possible changes. Forces always gather to prevent such changes. However, if and when those forces of conservatism are overcome and a change actually occurs, the actual results of the change alter the possibilities. Some options that were possible before are no longer possible. New options are opened up for the first time.

Cultural evolution was, when it was first suggested, not in the least threatening to anybody. The controversy began

MR. BERGH TO THE RESCUE.

THE DEFRAUDED GORILLA. "That *Man* wants to claim my Pedigree. He says he is one of my Descendants."

Mr. BERGH. "Now, Mr. DARWIN, how could you insult him so?"

13-14. The idea of evolution was accepted for culture long before it was applied to biology, where it challenged religious ideas about creation, and therefore was found dangerous.

when the old idea of cultural evolution was recontexted into biology. There it contradicted the entrenched religious doctrine, forcing a new look at the accepted answers to the eternal questions. Difficulties emerged that have not been totally solved even in the present day—some people still refuse to accept the idea of evolution applied to biology even as they accept the same idea when it is applied to culture.

Evolution requires an input of new information into a biological or cultural pool. It also requires a way in which the system can get rid of genetic information or cultural traditions.

The processes by which evolution proceeds are of course the results of the very processes by which culture change occurs. One important characteristic defines the evolutionary step: a biological or cultural change that is an evolutionary step makes it impossible to go back to the way things were before the step was taken.

Cycles are the basis of some forms of evolution. In an all-but-flippant illustration of such evolution that is nevertheless enlightening, anthropologist Michael Thompson (1979) has analyzed the chicken and the egg problem. Obviously, neither comes first—rather, there is a cycle in which chickens lay eggs that hatch into chickens that lay eggs . . . and so on. The trouble with too much social science of the past is that it focused on chickens and eggs. It would have done better to focus on the processes of laying of eggs and hatching of chickens, as in 13-15.

When we emphasize the *processes* of hatching and laying, we do not have to wonder about what relationship the chicken has to the egg. As one wiseacre put it, a chicken is an egg's way of making another egg. Chickens and eggs are both temporary stages in the larger cyclical process.

Only one point has to be inserted to get a fundamental explanation of biological evolution: new genetic material must be added, and other genetic material is sometimes lost. 13-16 shows how it works.

The genetic gain usually comes from slight chemical alterations in genetic information that are called mutations. Most mutations are not beneficial and the creature who bears them usually does not live to pass them on. A few mutations are neutral.

A very few mutations may be advantageous. Through such processes, plants and animals adapt; their characteristics change.

Cultural action works in much the same way. Innovation is a process for putting new culture or new cultural interpretations into the system by invention and diffusion. Culture loss occurs either when innovations are not accepted or when some element of culture becomes unnecessary and is forgotten

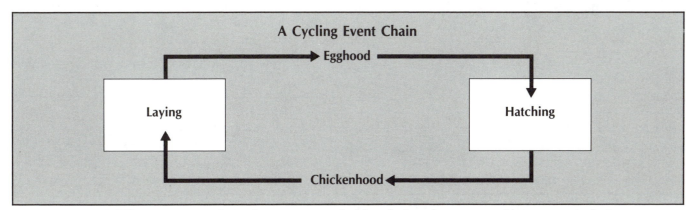

A Cycling Event Chain

Egghood

Laying

Hatching

Chickenhood

13-15. When we examine this cycle, it is more profitable to look at the processes of becoming—the laying of an egg and the hatching of a chicken—than to look at the egg and the chicken as mere things. In the same way, in examining all cultural cycles (action chains that fold back on themselves and begin again) it is more profitable to look at the processes than at the forms.

How Culture Works

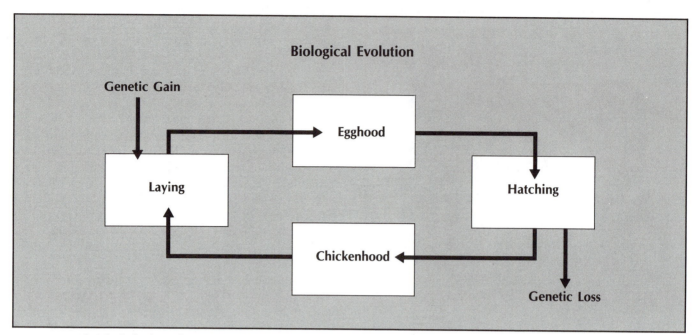

13-16. *In biological evolution, change occurs when new genes are added. The change, particularly genetic alternations, is most often not conducive to health and growth or to successful reproduction. As a result, it disappears. The biological change is made permanent when genes are lost that make it impossible to return to earlier states.*

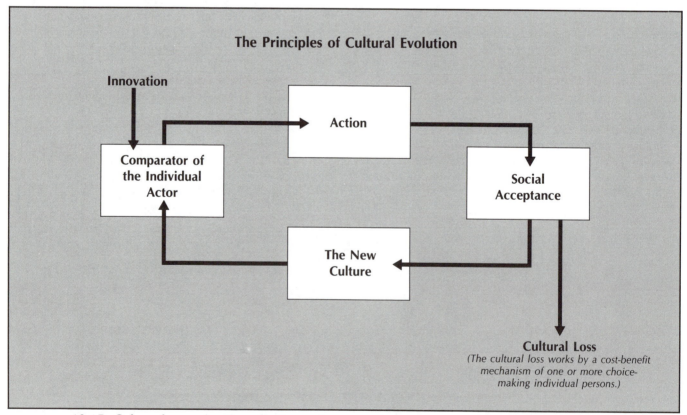

13-17. *Culture change takes place when innovation appears in the comparator of the individual acting person (2-5). If the individual chooses, he or she may change the type of action which used to occur habitually. Only with social acceptance and ultimate loss of earlier ways of behaving and dealing with problems does cultural evolution occur. If an innovative action is greeted with social acceptance, the new culture is apparent to the behaving individual, and the information in that person's comparator is changed permanently.*

or else is replaced with some other cultural element.

Cultural evolution ultimately depends on the type and rate of culture loss. If enough improvements in the efficiency and rewards of culture are made, it becomes unthinkable that people would try to live without them. If, as a result of some catastrophe, our world were to lose agriculture, the ideas of agriculture would be in the heads of any survivors and they would manage to reconstruct it. It is true that any details that were not in the heads of the particular survivors would have to be either foregone or reinvented, but enough is in their heads that agriculture could soon be reestablished. The same is true of something as simple as money: once we understand the way the several functions of money fit together, its simplifying force means that no one would be able to go back to the days before money was invented. Both money and agriculture are simplifying ideas that are essential in societies as large as civilizations. They will be retained unless they are replaced with more efficient means of doing what they do. Today's world society depends on computers. If we were to lose computers, disaster would strike world society. Although it is too early to tell for sure, we could probably not go back to the smaller, slower national forms of economy and polity that preceded the computer. If the right people survive, they could reinvent computers—if they do not, disaster stalks.

To sum up, culture *change* occurs all the time. Culture *crests* occur when the changes more or less suddenly become overwhelming—when totally new patterns seem to appear. Cultural *evolution* occurs whenever sufficient new culture is taken up and old culture is lost so that we cannot go back to earlier ways.

We live in a world in which the processes of culture are going on all around us all the time. The picture of stability— the idea that culture is a "thing" that is just out there— gives way, under study, to the idea that the cultural processes are constantly proceeding. It may even mistakenly seem to the individual observer that the present arrangement of culture is eternal. Understanding the flow and ebb of culture and of its many parts is, in a sense, counterintuitive. It *seems* just to be there. It also seems, when we are participating in culture, that it should work like common sense, which it often does not. Yet we all know that today is not quite like yesterday, and tomorrow will be different from today. The differences may seem trivial and irrelevant—until the culture crests occur to make us realize that we have changed our ways or until cultural evolution makes it impossible for us to go back to earlier ways.

THE EXPLOSION OF EUROPE

The cultural processes discussed in the first half of this chapter worked in Europe just as they work in the rest of the world. European culture arrived at a culture crest in the 1400s that changed the entire world.

The world's two hemispheres were not regularly in touch before the late 1400s, although we know that contacts between them had occurred. Japanese pottery from about A.D.300 has been found on the coast of Ecuador. Norwegian anthropologist and adventurer Thor Heyerdahl journeyed by raft from South America to Polynesia to prove that it could be done. Many anthropologists recognize the validity of his claim (some do not) that art styles and similarities in tools make it likely that there was repeated contact between Polynesia and the western coast of South America.

In the same vein, there are stories of early Irish seamen in leather boats reaching the eastern shores of North America at very early dates. We know for sure, on the basis of both written and archaeological evidence, that Leif Eriksson reached Labrador and Newfoundland about A.D.1000 Columbus himself was in Iceland during his youth, and, with his own eyes, saw ice floes coming from the northwest. One of those floes carried three human corpses—obviously, he reasoned, there were people living in that direction.

Within each hemisphere trade routes had proliferated. People and goods and ideas passed along those routes. Well-traveled trade routes extended from Peking across central Asia to Constantinople and through the Mediterranean to Greece and Venice. Others stretched across the top of north Africa and from there down into and beyond the Sahara. Still others ran from Persia to India to Malaya and back to East Africa. In the New World, trade routes from the civilizations of Middle America reached north into Arizona and New Mexico and northeast into the Mississippi Valley; the civilizations of the Andes spread from Ecuador deep into Chile and north into Colombia. These trade routes served not just for the spread of goods, but for the dispersal of culture of every kind.

Thus, the peoples of the world were interconnected. Even societies that thought of themselves as culturally separated were linked to other groups by kinship or by trade. Throughout the world, states expanded. They captured other peoples and absorbed them into growing political systems. Trade networks and commerce connected each of the two hemispheres; so did repeated conquests. In both hemispheres the social boundaries were permeable, and were constantly permeated— the result was an interwoven social fabric and growing cultural continuity. There were a few isolated societies. In the late 1940s, Australians discovered a huge population— millions of people—in the central highlands of New Guinea whom no outsiders had known were there. It was probably the last such discovery that will ever be made. However, isolated groups are only temporarily isolated. Isolation lasts for only brief periods of time—people keep moving.

Thus, the world before the discoveries of Columbus did not actually accord with the model that many anthropologists had of it—it was not made up of the distinct and separate cultures they imagined. Their misconceptions of a period before European expansion in which there was little or no culture change were understandable. Until 1960 or so, anthropologists, with only a few exceptions, worked either in the colonies of the European powers or else on the

How Culture Works

13-18. *The last large population to feel the impact of European expansionism were the peoples of the interior of New Guinea in the late 1940s. Here an Australian colonial official, looking back at his interpreter, works with groups of New Guinea men, separated by their "administrative groups," that are assigned numbers. Because no unexplored areas of the world's surface are left, no other peoples unknown to the modern West will be found.*

reservations set aside for Native Americans, Australian aborigines, native New Zealanders, and South African Bantu. They were, with good reason, mightily impressed with the amount of culture change that was going on around them. They were moved by the discomfort of colonial and reservation peoples. It was reasonable (but incorrect) for them to accept the premise that before the impact of European colonial powers, little or no change had been occurring in "native" cultures. Today it is necessary to do specific research into the history of ideas to understand how such a notion took root. We now see clearly that it was Europe and America that had been changing at a rapid rate—Europe was, in the midst of this change, experiencing a culture crest that manifested itself by a previously impossible expansion. It made everything else look as if it were standing still.

Expansion

Two kinds of cultural innovations made the expansion of Europe possible—indeed, necessary. One was technological, the other social. Although the innovations were many, we shall concentrate on two: the technical improvements in sailing technology and the social invention that came to be called mercantile capitalism.

The sailing ship was created in Egypt: the idea of sails appeared about 3200 B.C.; the idea of making the hull of a boat from wooden planks arrived a couple of hundred years later. For four and a half millennia after that, no fundamental changes were made in the design of ships, although attempts were made to build bigger ships and to improve the rig, which is the mast and sails.

Great advances in the rig of sailing ships were finally made during the 1400s. Of primary importance was the invention of the triangular sails called lateen sails. Before this time, sails had been square or rectangular and could not be easily manipulated to allow the ship to travel against the wind. The new triangular sails were far more manageable; they made sailing against the wind a simple matter (even though it is immensely hard work).

Other dramatic improvements in sailing technology occurred about the same time: magnetic compasses (invented by the Chinese and used in the Mediterranean by about

For a long time Europe was of little account in the affairs of the wider world. . . . The Portuguese, the first Europeans to reach Asia, became known as *Ferenghi* in Malaya and *Fo-lang-ki* in China. Only gradually did the Chinese learn to distinguish between the Portuguese and the Jesuits from "I-ta-li" who were at Portuguese Macao, and between the Dutch (Ho-lan) and the English. On the other side of the world, the Aztec ruler would wonder whether the arriving Spaniards were gods or men, although an empirically minded Tlaxcaltec war leader solved the problem by holding a Spanish prisoner under water until he died like any other mortal. In the Pacific, the incoming Europeans came to be known as Cookies, after Captain Cook. [With] speed and intensity . . . these 'red-haired, high-nosed external barbarians' imposed themselves on different parts of the world.

Eric R. Wolf (1982)

THEY SAID IT

13-19. *A combination of technological innovations like improved sails and boat design (as shown in this German etching from 1503) and social innovations like the mercantilist empires led to the expansion of Europe, beginning in the 1400s. Mercantilist empires were based on the premises that wealth was limited to precious metals and gems, that wealth by right was the property of the monarch (the state), and that trade therefore should be regulated by the state. The aim of trade and exploration was to enrich the state.*

A.D.1100) and chronometers (first used to determine location at sea about 1500) were improved. Use of maps was very old—perhaps older even than writing. The Alexandrian scholar Ptolemy made maps of the world as early as A.D.150, but those maps were not known in Europe until about 1400. About the same time, the sailor's map called *portolano* came into use in the Mediterranean. Maps and celestial charts were constantly improved in the 1400s; Columbus himself was a mapmaker trained in Holland.

At about the same time—in the 1400s—revolutionary advances were made in metallurgy, particularly in methods of smelting iron, in making alloys, in making wire and rolling steel. The tools of war were improved: on land, mortars and shotguns gave advantages against cavalry, which had ruled warfare all during the feudal period. Cannons could soon be attached to ships, which created a heretofore unknown naval advantage. These advances were part of a more general advance in manufacturing: improvements in the windmill and new gravity-propelled water wheels allowed efficient mechanical use of bellows, hammers, saws and grinders.

All these factors (in combination with many others) were making the social arrangements of European feudalism obsolete. The social traps of the estate system, which disallowed movement of people into new regions and also into the new trades, began to crack. Muslim Arabs had captured Iberia, the Balkans and the lands between the Black and Caspian seas. In the late 1400s, both the Iberians (the Portuguese and Spanish) and the Russians organized efficient armed forces that eventually drove the Muslims back. Columbus got financing from Queen Isabella for his first voyage the same year that her forces drove the Muslims out

of Spain. Both the Western Europeans and the Russians turned their new-found strengths into creating new empires. The Russians drove across continental Siberia, eventually crossing the Bering Strait and taking Alaska. They got as far down the coast as California (you can see the ruins of Russian forts in several places along the Pacific Coast of the United States). The Spanish and the Portuguese expanded by sea, a move the Portuguese began in the early 1400s. The Portuguese established trading posts all around the shores of Africa and into the East Indies and on the east coast of Brazil; the Spanish discovered and colonized the Caribbean and South America. Within a very short time, European culture had been planted in every part of the world.

Mercantilism and Empire. Such rapid expansion and the ensuing sudden increase in trade took place before anything like today's science of economics had been devised. The ideas of those days about what we today call "the economy" are referred to by historians as mercantilism. **Mercantilism** was a system of financing trade and war that made two fundamental assumptions. The first was that the state was the only organization with enough power or resources or information (all maps were top secret) to finance and regulate trade. The second assumption was that gold and silver were the only measure of wealth. States waged war in order to control more and more of that wealth. All the European powers were mercantilist at the time the Spanish and Portuguese discovered the New World. Their search for wealth was (obviously, given such premises) a search for silver and gold.

Mercantilist doctrine held that the store of the world's wealth (that is, gold, silver and jewels) was limited. Every state's struggle to improve itself was what twentieth-century social scientists call a "zero-sum game." That is to say, for every winner, there had to be a loser. The struggle for wealth, therefore, was a struggle to get more wealth by forcefully depriving everybody else of *their* wealth. It was—and is—a social trap.

The aim of trade and exploration was to enrich the treasuries of the state. The cultural premise was that such enrichment had to be done at the expense of other peoples. Any nation that lacked gold and silver mines had to get its wealth either by piracy or by means of a favorable balance of trade—that is, by exporting more than it imported. The wealth from the positive balance flowed into the royal treasury. It was then used to reward loyal followers and to finance the wars against other powers who wanted their wealth, or who had resources that had to be captured. This system became a vicious cycle—a social trap. It followed that the major purpose of overseas colonies was to send wealth back to the royal treasury of the mother country.

The expansion of the Iberian peoples was also underlaid by a set of religious assumptions. Whipped to a fury by their victories over the Moors—which they saw as the victory of Christendom over Islam—they allowed themselves also to give way to immense Messianic movements (of the sort we shall discuss in the next chapter). Their mission was religious expansion—to Christianize the entire world. In Spain and elsewhere, the power of the Catholic church expanded as the church took possession of large tracts of land won back from the Moors. That power grew further as the Pope extended the power of the Inquisition. The Iberians took as their goal not just to corner all the world's wealth, but also, and at the same time, to Christianize all the world's peoples.

Other European cultural ideas also travelled with the Iberians. We saw in Chapter 9 that no civilization in the history of the world had escaped the institution of slavery during the phase of development that saw the growth of urban agglomerations and the state. Iberians had used African slaves, as well as others, for centuries, and had themselves been subject to enslavement in Muslim lands. Slavery was one of their basic assumptions about what constituted a society.

"The basic procedures of domination" (Ribeiro 1968) that the imperial Spanish followed in Latin American colonies thus became:

- getting rid of the rulers of the Native American populations;
- giving grants called *latifundias*—large tracts of land and the people on them—to Spanish conquistadors in return for services to the crown;
- imposing conscriptive labor on the basis of their ideas about the institutions of slavery;
- giving state-controlled bureaucracies the power to collect taxes, report the results, and send most of the collected wealth to the king of Spain.

Within a very short time, these policies led to the collapse of the Native American societies. Hundreds of thousands of people died from European diseases to which they had no immunity and from the conditions of their enforced work as slaves. That fact did not lead the mercantilist empires out of the social trap created by their basic cultural premises: when the American labor supply was exhausted, they turned to Africa and imported slaves. Wholly new kinds of society arose on the ruins of the old ones—in Africa as well as in the New World and in Europe.

Capitalism and Empire. Meanwhile, the other European powers—Holland, England and France—were not idle. As a result of their social innovations such as the capitalized stock corporation, their empires developed into a different sort. They were able to invent a new social form known as capitalism, and with it were far better equipped to take advantage of the cultural innovations of the Industrial Revolution.

Under mercantilism, the central government of a kingdom was the only institution that could accumulate enough capital either to finance the kind of voyages that Columbus undertook or to import large quantities of trade goods. Capitalism was an invention that (among many other things) created new institutions that could afford the immense cost of overseas trade and discovery without the aid of the imperial government.

Most of the ideas that underlay capitalism were ancient. However, the way these ideas were brought together and organized took on a totally new form. Long-term trade in luxury goods—exotic cloth, coffee, tea, sugar, and spices as well as wealth like gold, silver, and gemstones—was very old. Not until capitalism, however, did everyday necessities

13-21. *Capitalism came to replace mercantilism beginning in the 1600s. The primary capitalist empires were English, Dutch, and French. The premises of capitalism were that land, labor, know-how and money itself were all wealth. The purposes of empire were still to increase wealth. The primary institutions of capitalism were (and are) the market mechanism and the joint-stock corporation. This etching shows Dutch colonials watching ships of the Dutch East India Company enter the harbor of Batavia.*

of life enter long-distance trade.

The earliest manifestations of what was to become industrial capitalism were the joint-stock companies, also known as corporations, created in Holland and England. The idea of the corporation goes back at least to Roman times. Corporations had been used in England after the Norman period to enable the central government to control the Anglo-Saxon barons whom they had conquered. Until the Dutch East India Company was organized in 1602, the primary use of the corporation was not for commercial or business purposes, and no corporation had permanent capital. Even when they were used to finance business, those early corporations had to be formed anew for each venture and ended when that venture either failed or paid off.

A joint-stock company is an on-going business organization. It is owned by many people, each of whom holds some shares in the enterprise. The result was that many people could put in relatively small amounts of money to capitalize the venture. They then shared both the risk and the profits. The idea of joint-stock companies had begun in the early 1500s in England and Holland as a mode of financing international trade. A century later, the idea had reached maturity. The most famous of the new joint-stock companies were the British East India Company, the British West Africa Company, and the Hudson's Bay Company (which is still doing business in Canada). We have already mentioned the Dutch East India Company.

The separation of the joint-stock company from the government did not come readily or easily. The companies often carried out legal and warfare functions on contract with the governments. Indeed, conquering, taxing, and establishing new governing bodies appeared in some places to be

an even more important part of company business than the business of trade. Many of the American colonies were founded by chartered corporations that had royal grants of monopoly privileges; their job was to govern as well as to trade.

By 1700, joint-stock companies were common. They were the forerunners of the modern corporation, which is the central institution of modern capitalist economies. Many of the most important characteristics of modern corporations are old—for example, the requirement that stock companies be recognized by the state if they are to do business. Others are new—for example, the government's considering the corporation to be a legal person quite independent of its officers or its shareholders.

Capitalism as we know it today is sometimes said to stem from the mid-1700s, when the French worked diligently to restrict governmental regulation and control—a policy they called *laissez faire*. The origin of capitalism is sometimes dated from the publication of Adam Smith's *Wealth of Nations* in 1776 (the publication of that book also heralded the beginning of the modern science of economics).

By the late 1700s, the British government had removed most of its mercantilist controls. Other trading nations also accepted capitalism. The essence of capitalism is allowing the choices of purchasers and producers—that is, the cost-benefit principle as it is manifest in the market—to set prices and policy. Markets were ancient—they had always been peripheral to householding as a form of economy. But now a "great transformation" began. Land entered the market; so did labor; so did money. Rents, wages, and interest were involved in the same markets as resources, agricultural produce and manufactured goods. None of these was in itself a new idea, but their association with the market principle and hence with one another, was new (Polanyi 1944). Householding as an economic form began to diminish in importance before the steamroller of the market. Businessmen, industry, and commerce had moved center stage. As the governments gave up mercantilism, with its centralized treasury and its heavy import duties, they turned to the taxation of quite different items.

The Industrial Revolution vastly increased the number of high cost business opportunities. Corporations were necessary to finance them. It was at this period that the modern corporation, as the primary organizational tool of capitalism, triumphed. Even today, corporations continue to grow and change with needs and resources of the people they serve as well as the skills and greed of their officers and shareholders.

Radical upheaval confronted the common people as capitalism grew. Householding as the basic form of economy all but disappeared—along with it went the ability of the family to be self-sufficient. Wages were no longer a supplementary form of income—for most people they became the *only* form of income, including subsistence.

The onslaught of a society based almost solely on market exchange, which included the market value of labor and land

How Culture Works

13-22. The onslaught of market capitalism began in England and spread throughout the world. People in many parts of the globe, beginning in Europe, suffered severely as they were forced to depend less on householding and to sell their labor on the market.

in the same market as raw materials and products, began in England and spread slowly throughout Europe and much of the rest of the world. Working for a wage became the only way to get the wherewithal to live—surely one of the most momentous changes that ever occurred in human history. The idea of "the family wage" revolutionized family organization and included a considerable alteration in the position of women in society.

Modern capitalism developed first in England in the late eighteenth century, and came to dominate the world in the nineteenth century. The controlling ideas of capitalism are very different from those of mercantilism:

- self-interest is the servant of society;
- the role of government in business should be minimized; indeed government and business should be entirely separate spheres;
- private property is sacrosanct;
- religious salvation is associated with worldly success—the so-called Protestant ethic.

It was not long before the ills associated with unrestricted capitalism began to erupt:

- economic instability and business cycles of boom and bust that arise from lags in supply and demand;
- gross inequality in the distribution of wealth as labor entered the same market as land, entrepreneurial skill and the products themselves. Early capitalists were able to hire cheap labor—indeed, starvation labor. The working men and women and their children put in six very long days a week. Child labor was extensive and abusive: children were sometimes chained to their machines. Women worked twelve-hour shifts seven days a week. However, to save their souls on Sunday, the capitalists gave money to the parish to make up the shortfall between the

starvation wages and the amount necessary to maintain subsistence (based, in England, on the price of bread and beer). It was situations such as these that inspired Karl Marx in his assault against the capitalist system;
- utter neglect of the public interest, because, at least in those days, capitalists turned out to be interested in personal profit and nothing else.

Seldom in the history of the world has the entire culture of humankind undergone such an immense change. Not only was human inhumanity (if we may call it that) rampant—child labor, inadequate incomes and, hence, inadequate nutrition, the seeds of environmental degradation that have grown into ravening weeds in our own day—but people in this new context had no way to judge the possibilities of a better life. They were trapped in what seemed a desperate situation.

13-23. The difficulties in unrestricted capitalism include business cycles of boom and bust, inequalities in distribution of wealth, sweated labor and child labor, neglect of the public interest. Modern capitalistic systems have addressed all these problems and are concerned with solving them. The photograph shows traders on the Tokyo Stock Exchange.

Alternatives—one might almost say antidotes—to capitalism began to build. Most of those alternatives wanted to give old powers back to the state, and perhaps add some new powers as well. Mercantilism itself could not return—the context in which it thrived was gone. But government controls on capitalism were soon instituted. Indeed, the most powerful new function of the state soon came to be controlling the free market in order to reduce the human misery. There has not been a society in Europe or America since the early 1800s that did not have significant government controls on the free market.

This turn to new forms of government control has been called **socialism**. Today, the best known of the many socialisms are Marxism and Fabian socialism, but there have been many versions of socialism since the middle 1800s. They differed mainly on the basis of people's ideas of the powers that they would choose to give the government in order to reduce human misery. The most obvious of these socialisms is Communism—or, rather, the communisms, for that of Russia was very different from that of China or Yugoslavia or even Cuba. In our own day, communism seems to be breaking down as an economic and political form. More and more people realize that the connection between the idea of a fair society as a worthy goal and communism as a means for achieving that goal, is illusory. Small-scale benevolent and democratic socialist governments like that of Sweden seem to work well, and will undoubtedly continue to do so as long as the people concur that what they get in return for staggeringly high taxes is worth the price. How capitalism will react to the demise of communism and how its own innate excesses may be controlled have yet to be worked out.

Today corporations and governments are the only institutions that control massive resources. The world needs to invent a new kind of institution that can create and control wealth to solve global problems such as the environment, education, and human rights. Governments and business struggle with problems affecting quality of life, but they were not designed to solve such issues.

13-25.

A massive problem remains: big business and government are still the only institutions that have or can get massive resources. Further, massive resources are needed to achieve pro-social and economic ends in mass society. Both business and government have great difficulty with the problem. The common good has been either hopelessly politicized or else left at the mercy of the profit motive in capitalism. I do not mean that there are no concerned and caring politicians and businesspersons. There are. Rather, it is becoming evident that the world is still waiting for a new social invention that will allow people to amass enough capital to clean up the environment and take care of medical costs and other social inequities—in short, to run a complex economy and still assure the welfare of all. The task is to leave in place the immense advantages of capitalism as the central economic system, to leave in place or improve the great advantages of democracy as the political system—and then, in addition, create a system that will deal with what have become the social problems of both systems—welfare, the environment, education, to name but a few.

13-24. The socialisms (of which communism was the most extreme) began as modes of getting rid of the problems created by allowing the market mechanism to dominate society. Socialism as a political form for controlling the excesses of the market rather than replacing it has had some successes. Socialist regimes that tried to banish the market principle have not been successful, as this line of Moscow women shopping for meat shows clearly.

CONCLUDING THOUGHTS

Shifting the focus from the noun aspects of culture (its structural components and how they fit together) to its verb aspects (cultural dynamics and how processes interweave) helps us to understand the implications of the vast culture change that we will examine in the next two chapters. Culture grows by invention, diffusion and recontexting. Changes may be small, but many small changes may add up to the point that culture crests—just as a wave crests before it crashes on the shore. Culture has changed—if the changes are such that it is not possible for people to go back to earlier ways, cultural evolution has occurred.

The people on the other side of the expanding frontiers created by the culture crest in Europe were suddenly confronted with enormous problems. Today they call it "the European problem" (a sort of take-off on their having been called "the native problem" for many years). Societies all over the world have had to stagger out from under the impact. Their struggle continues today. And its solutions are creating still newer problems and challenges. It is the human condition.

BUZZWORDS

action chain   a series of acts that must be performed in the right order if any of the acts are to be effective.

cultural evolution   a series of situations in which changes in cultural activity have become so pronounced that it is impossible to return to earlier cultural or social forms. Seen from this standpoint, all culture grows out of earlier situations. The story of cultural evolution is a series of such steps.

culture crest   the point at which small culture changes suddenly become sufficiently strong to make an immense impact, heading the cultural process in new directions.

culture pool   all the culture available to a group of people.

cycle   an action chain in which the last act leads back to the first so that the whole chain is repeated.

diffusion   spreading of culture over wider geographical areas, especially from the place of invention to new areas, where it may be used in ways very different from those in the places where it was invented.

event chain   a series of events that must occur in the right order.

mercantilism   an economic system based on the ideas that the only true wealth is silver and gold and that prosperity depends on a favorable balance of trade. Mercantilism replaced feudalism, as the focus of political power changed from ownership of land to the control of money and trade.

socialism   a theory or system of government in which the means of production and distribution are owned and controlled by the state.

social trap   an action chain that leads to disaster if it cannot be stopped.

trajectory   an action chain with a beginning, a middle, and an end. Some trajectories may be repeated, but they do not lead to a cycle.

From Colonialism to Global Society

14

PROPOSITIONS AND PREMISES

■ People of a society may be contacted or overrun by others from the outside. When Westerners, responding to their own cultural pressures to search for wealth and power, burst in on and, in many cases, conquered the peoples of the non-Western world, the cultures on "the other side of the frontier" were dealt a blow that led to immense changes.

■ Some societies suffered extinction when they were hit by Western expansion. Others collapsed and had to reorganize their cultures completely. Still others resisted and adapted to the new situation. Some learned to live in a state of cultural dissonance between their indigenous culture and that of colonial powers.

■ The Third World emerged as many societies that had formerly been self-sufficient in all but luxury items entered into extensive trade in necessities. As agricultural and mining production in the Third World rose, their dependency on trade with the Western or communist worlds also increased. The increase in production has not so much improved the situation of Third World people as it has enriched the First and Second worlds.

■ Poverty is an aspect of all societies and, hence, is a global problem.

■ As culture grows at ever faster speeds, it becomes more and more difficult to discover paradigms for examining it that actually reflect the changes as they occur.

■ Both worldwide culture and many microcultures based on common interest or locality are emerging. Human beings at the beginning of the twenty-first century are each living in several cultures, not just one.

In the years after A.D.1400, as Europeans expanded around the world, they ran head-on into all the cultures in their path. The contact and clash of these many cultures led to immense changes in all the cultures of the world.

The discovery of the extraordinary biological and cultural diversity of humankind between the late fifteenth and nineteenth centuries was one of the great intellectual watersheds of Western civilization. . . . The long centuries of Western discovery are a story of confrontation and noncomprehension, of cautious encounters between strangers, of searches for gold and brutal military campaigns, of profitable trading, land grabbing, and missionary endeavor. They are also a weary chronicle of pathos and tragedy, of bitter disillusionment between societies living in totally incomprehensible worlds. The intellectual, moral, and spiritual effects of the clash are with us to this day.

Brian M. Fagan (1984)

THEY SAID IT

Both sides asked the question: were these strange peoples really human? The Spanish asked whether the Native Americans were human or animal or something in between. Did they have souls that could be saved? The Native Americans they confronted asked the same question—are these newcomers really human or were they gods?

The central problem was—and still is—getting observed cultural and physical differences out of the premises (thus *assuming* that the differences are indeed significant) and into the hypotheses (so that you can ask *whether* the differences are significant, and if so in what way).

Two premises blinded the Europeans in refining their definition of "human." On the one hand was "the great chain of being"—a theory that ranked all creatures from inferior to superior. "Naturally," human beings were at the top. If you accepted that premise, the subsequent step of ranking human beings seemed a rational exercise. If the Europeans defined themselves as "civilized" and thus "higher," then obviously the people they contacted were "lower."

The other blinding premise was the concept of the noble savage; it grew out of the idea that civilized human beings had fallen from grace (and, the logic went, the "natural" human being before the fall must have been healthy, fair-minded, and happy). The noble savage image, while attributing some positive aspects, also relegated non-European peoples to a childlike state incapable of mature adult reasoning.

14-1. *When what we ethnocentrically call the "voyages of discovery" occurred in the 1400s and 1500s, Europeans began encroaching on all the societies of the world—a process that still continues. This reconstruction of Columbus' ship "Santa Maria" was made for the Chicago World's Fair in 1893.*

Changing these entrenched premises took centuries.

The peoples who were hit by expanding European powers reacted in several ways. A few peoples simply disappeared—they either died out like the Tasmanians or the Yana Indians of northern California (Kroeber 1961), or they, like the Khoikhoi of South Africa, were absorbed into other populations after their culture was completely annihilated. Many cultural systems collapsed utterly—the meanings they had lived by evaporated; their assumptions ceased to work and they could not find adequate new ways of doing what their lives required. Other peoples struggled to adapt, but constant changes in colonial policy (which, from the standpoint of the colonizers, were improvements) made for constant and alien new demands to which the colonized peoples were expected to adjust. To the colonized, the colonizers were willful and unpredictable.

European empire builders were accompanied by Christian missionaries dedicated to the idea that "natives" were human, that they had souls that must be saved. European adventurers, settlers, planters, traders, and miners often claimed that "natives" were not real people and, hence, could be hunted and killed with impunity. The conflict of these ideas was often sharp.

Today we can see that the power systems of native peoples were attacked by both groups. Their kinship and family kinship systems were undermined by missionaries. Their economic systems were exploded by both traders and governments. Their systems of meaning were rendered meaningless by all the Europeans who appeared among them. Disease besieged the peoples of the Americas and the Pacific

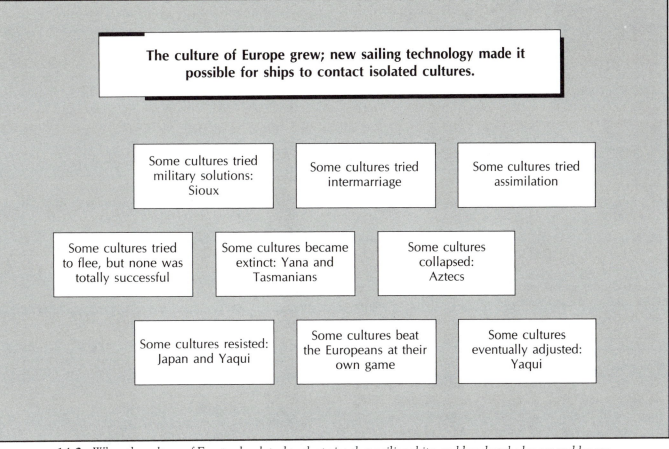

The culture of Europe grew; new sailing technology made it possible for ships to contact isolated cultures.

Some cultures tried military solutions: Sioux

Some cultures tried intermarriage

Some cultures tried assimilation

Some cultures tried to flee, but none was totally successful

Some cultures became extinct: Yana and Tasmanians

Some cultures collapsed: Aztecs

Some cultures resisted: Japan and Yaqui

Some cultures beat the Europeans at their own game

Some cultures eventually adjusted: Yaqui

14-2. When the culture of Europe developed to the point that sailing ships could undertake longer and longer voyages, Europeans came into close touch with all of the cultures of the world. The result was catastrophe for many of those cultures. They reacted in several ways, many of them destructive.

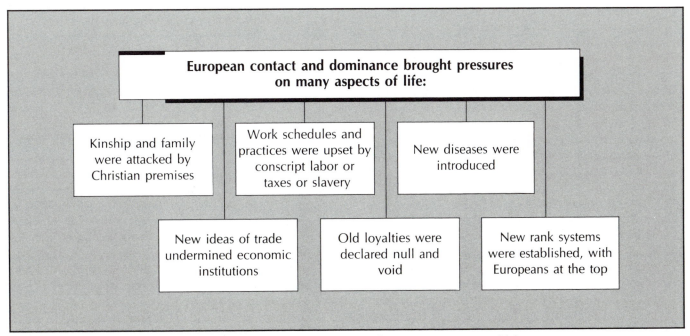

European contact and dominance brought pressures on many aspects of life:

Kinship and family were attacked by Christian premises

Work schedules and practices were upset by conscript labor or taxes or slavery

New diseases were introduced

New ideas of trade undermined economic institutions

Old loyalties were declared null and void

New rank systems were established, with Europeans at the top

14-3. European colonial domination brought pressures to bear on every aspect of life.

From Colonialism to Global Society

(Africans suffered less from disease—they already shared the same disease pool as Europeans). All of the European empires instituted slavery to provide labor for mines or plantations.

Such disasters of culture contact were happening all over the world. The entire continents of North America, South America, and Africa were affected. Most of Asia was also subject to contact. The Russian empire had all of Siberia; the French and English empires fought over India; the Dutch and English empires fought over the East Indies. All of them were involved in annexing the Pacific Islands. The world was caught up in this mass movement and culture struggle.

From the point of view of the native peoples, the expansion of Europe was a cataclysm, a natural disaster.

COLONIALISM

Colonialism is as ancient as empire. A colony is a group of people in a territory that is under the political hegemony of an alien ruler. It is most often formed by conquest. The ancient empires and city-states had colonies, sometimes made up of settlers from the metropolis but more often of conquered peoples.

Colonies were organized and used in many ways. The colonies of the European empires were considered sources of revenue—either of wealth in precious metals for mercantilist empires like Spain or of markets for capitalist empires like England and Holland.

Colonized peoples adhered to cultural ideas that were totally different from the ideas of their colonizers. The most obvious difference in many cases was in their attitudes toward ecology and the environment. Most peoples had lived in a state of balance with nature—had, indeed, structured their lives and their religious beliefs to maintain that balance—before colonization. The Judeo-Christian attitude, on the other hand, was that God had created the world especially for them to exploit to the glory of His name. These incompatible differences led to constant miscommunication. When people do not share cultural premises, they cannot work together. Therefore, colonial culture and society are always marred by opposing values and intentions.

The government of colonies removed great areas of decision from the lives of the colonized peoples, who experienced colonization as a debilitating lack of control over their own lives. Self-reliance no longer worked. Predictability was gone. The imperial forces established either slavery-like systems or else they demanded taxes be paid in cash, thus requiring people who had formerly worked only for subsistence or limited local trade to resort to low wage labor to get the necessary tax money or else to conscript labor which was considered "payment in kind." When people tried to behave in their accustomed ways (as diagrammed in Chapter 2), they found alien forces in their cultural environment that were neither understandable nor predictable in light of their prior experience.

Decisions made by colonial powers are always made on the basis of the needs of the colonizers. Even the most well-intended efforts of the colonizers reflected their own view of what was "best" for the colonized people. The colonized people were thus not allowed to define their own needs. In many areas of life, they could no longer take direct action to satisfy those needs. The feelings and reactions of the colonized are vividly drawn by Aime Cesaire, a poet from the Caribbean island of Martinique who was educated in Paris:

 Colonialization . . . dehumanizes even the most civilized man. . . . I look around and wherever there are colonizers and colonized face to face, I see force, brutality, cruelty, sadism, conflict, and, in a parody of education, the hasty manufacture of a few thousand subordinate functionaries, 'boys,' artisans, office clerks, and interpreters necessary for the smooth operation of business. . . .

They talk to me about progress, about 'achievements,' diseases cured, improved standards of living.

_I_ am talking about societies drained of their essence, cultures trampled underfoot, institutions undermined, lands confiscated, religions smashed, magnificent artistic creations destroyed, extraordinary _possibilities_ wiped out.

They throw facts at my head, statistics, mileages of roads, canals and railroad tracks.

_I_ am talking about thousands of men sacrificed . . . about millions of men torn from their gods, their land, . . . from life, from the dance, from wisdom.

_I_ am talking about millions of men in whom fear has been cunningly instilled, who have been taught to have an inferiority complex, to tremble, kneel, despair, and behave like flunkeys.

Aime Cesaire (1972)

THEY SAID IT

The colonizing powers' own view of their mission contrasts sharply with the results described by Cesaire. Both governors and missionaries saw themselves as bearers of civilization bringing order and God and prosperity to the colonized peoples. In spite of gross ethnocentrism, many of them honestly did have the welfare of native peoples at heart. But it was welfare only to the colonizers who defined it. From the other side of the frontier, "welfare" appeared to be—at best—mere paternalism.

Colonialism is a difficult and ultimately unworkable social system. Most of the world's societies felt its impact between 1500 and 1960. It is an inherently unstable form of govern-

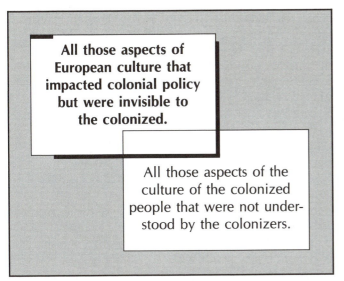

All those aspects of European culture that impacted colonial policy but were invisible to the colonized.

All those aspects of the culture of the colonized people that were not understood by the colonizers.

14-4. The cultures of the colonizers and the colonized overlapped in only a few areas. Even when those areas were understood by both parties, there were vast reaches of European culture the colonized peoples never saw and had no way of divining. There were ideas among the colonized people that the colonizers never understood or valued. As a result, almost all colonized peoples were, in their own eyes, undervalued. As a result of being undervalued (as well as for many other reasons) they hated the colonizers, even when they liked some individuals.

14-5. Colonialism means that one cultural group is under the hegemony of another cultural group. Because the two are likely to begin with different premises and have different goals, the situation is usually beset by cultural dissonance. Miscommunication is common. It is difficult to cooperate, even if the will to do so is there, if you do not know the premises and goals. Moreover, people's decisions about their own lives were curtailed by the presence of the colonial power. Colonial powers give orders and run things in the way they think best, often with no comprehension that the people disagreed or did not understand. This picture shows two colonial officers sitting in a Tiv gathering in 1950. "Tor Tiv," the chief whom the British appointed and set over the Tiv, a chiefless people, is sitting at the table at the left. Kyagba, the most prominent elder of southern Tivland, is sitting in a chair, back to the camera at the right.

From Colonialism to Global Society

ment; communication between the governors and the governed is never adequate. Most countries—from the United States in the late 1700s to Africa in the middle 1900s—had to break free.

Extinction

Many peoples of North and South America, some in the Pacific islands, and a few in Africa perished in the face of the forward push of European colonization.

One of the most searing stories about a now extinct people is that of the aborigines who lived on the island of Tasmania, south of the main island of Australia. In 1772, a small group of Frenchmen landed on the southern shore of Tasmania. A band of aborigines—about thirty people—advanced with pointed sticks and sharp stones. The French worked their way cautiously up the beach; the aborigines at the same time made a huge pile of driftwood. With no common language, they were forced back on smiling to show good will (but it can also mask ill will) and gesture (which may not be interpreted the same way in different cultures). The French tried to give the aborigines trade beads and chickens, but the aborigines refused them adamantly and gestured to the wood pile. The French captain, having no idea what they meant or what they expected him to do, set fire to the wood. The dismayed Tasmanians flung spears and rocks and ran away into the woods (Fagan 1984). The important point here is that there was no cultural communication or understanding between the two groups. To the French, the beads and chickens indicated a desire to trade and the pile of driftwood looked like a bonfire; there is no way to know what either the pile of wood or the beads meant to the aborigines. Miscommunication was complete. We shall see repeatedly that miscommunication of this kind lay behind at least some of the difficulty that occurred between colonists and colonized peoples.

At the time of this first visit, there were about eighty bands of aborigines on the island of Tasmania, each living on two hundred or three hundred square miles of land; each had a stretch of seacoast to exploit for oysters and mussels. These bands were organized into nine groups, each with a distinctive culture and language.

In the next 125 years, nine scientific expeditions and five trading ships met Tasmanians. Whatever records remained were so utterly under the influence of preconceived premises

about the nature of savages that they contain almost no information about Tasmanian culture. We do know, however, that they went naked in all but the coldest weather; that they ate oysters and mussels (but not fish), land animals such as wombats and kangaroos; and gathered vegetable foods. Their technology was simple—they did not use boomerangs as some Australians did; their digging sticks and other tools had no stone points. Yet their way of life was secure, even generous; with it they had survived and prospered for the eight thousand or more years since the sea level had been raised at the end of the last glaciation and isolated them on their island.

In the early 1800s, the British considered the Tasmanians "friendly." At that time, another French scientific expedition arrived for the ostensible purpose of studying Tasmania. The governor of New South Wales in adjoining Australia was, however, afraid that the French would seize that island for Napoleon, so he garrisoned the entire island of Tasmania with settlements of convicts. These newcomers were the first European permanent residents. They clashed head-on with the native Tasmanians. The first of their new settlements was precisely in line with a traditional game-run along which the Tasmanians had annual drives. As the aborigines drove

14-7. *The Tasmanians were extinct in less than a hundred years after colonization of their large island began. This old photograph shows Tucanini, one of the last surviving Tasmanians.*

the herd of kangaroos into the new village, the settlers thought they were being attacked and opened fire. Twenty Tasmanian aborigines were killed.

As the number and size of the settlements increased, the aboriginal people moved inland. The settlers also moved inland. Hostile incidents increased. Outlaws called bush-rangers left the settlements for the mountains and preyed on aborigines. Soon sheep ranches took over more and more territory, squeezing the aboriginal people farther back. The aboriginal peoples themselves began to raid cattle and sheep from the ranches in order to live.

After only thirty years of contact with the settlers, only about 250 aborigines survived. Few colonists cared whether any survived at all. These few survivors were formally placed under the protection of the British crown. They were captured and taken to Flinders Island, off the northeast coast of Tasmania. In their new surroundings, they could not hunt or gather their own food or take care of any other of their needs; they were made to wear European clothes, but nobody told them about keeping them clean. In 1849, the few survivors were again moved, this time to Hobart, the capital city of Tasmania. There they died of drink and influenza. The last Tasmanian aborigine died in 1876, just seventy-three years after colonization had begun (Fagan 1984).

Peoples like the Ona in Tierra del Fuego at the southern tip of South America became extinct. So did some hunting and gathering peoples of Africa, South Asia, and Australia. The process is going on right now among the Amazon peoples of South America.

Cultural Collapse

Literally hundreds—perhaps even thousands—of cultures collapsed as a result of European impact. One of the most dramatic—in part because it had so far to fall—was that of the Aztecs of the Valley of Mexico.

The Aztecs were Johnny-come-latelies in the Valley of Mexico. In A.D. 1150, they had been a nomadic tribe (related

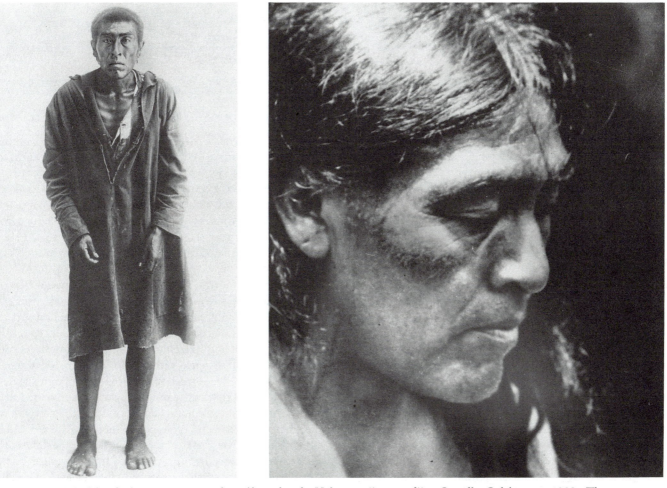

14-8. Ishi, the last surviving member of his tribe, the Yahi, was "captured" in Oroville, California in 1908. The photo on the left was taken just after that event. Because nobody could communicate with him, and nobody knew what else to do with him, he was put into the local jail. He was befriended by anthropologists at the University of California, Berkeley, and brought there, where he spent his last years living in and being custodian of the museum. You can see the whole story in his face.

From Colonialism to Global Society

14-9. *Whole cultures can be destroyed, or made to collapse, by the colonization process. The immense cities of Aztec culture (Tenochtitlan, where Mexico City now stands, is shown here) were destroyed along with the Aztec political system and art. Aztecs live on today as pauperized Mexican Indians.*

to the Comanche and Shoshone in today's United States), but they were aggressive and came under the aegis of a war god named Huitzilopochtli. In the next three hundred years, they out-fought, out-bred and outsmarted all the other tribal groups in the area. Aztec hegemony was consolidated by Moctezuma I, who ruled from 1440-1468 in his capital Tenochtitlan, built on an island in the middle of a shallow lake that in those days filled the Valley of Mexico. The Spanish were amazed at the city of Tenochtitlan. It covered six square miles. One Spanish report estimated sixty thousand houses in the city. At the center of it all were Moctezuma's palace and the pyramids topped with altars where human sacrifices were performed.

All the other kingdoms in the valley—and most of those between the Caribbean and the Pacific Ocean—paid tribute to the Aztecs. The Aztec empire was built around "a superbly efficient tribute-gathering machine" (Fagan 1984). Yet, all the people who paid tribute to them hated the Aztecs. The war god Huitzilopochtli was at the center of the Aztec pantheon. His hunger for human blood was insatiable. Constant warfare had to be maintained to provide enough captives to be sacrificed at the temple of the god.

Aztec myths told of five Worlds of the Sun, each following the other. These worlds, and everything in them, were all destined to oblivion. At the time of the Spanish Conquest, the Aztecs were living in the fifth of the Worlds of the Sun. All the earlier worlds had been ruled by gods who had created

them. These gods constantly quarreled with one another. The Aztec myths said further that the war gods had driven out the great god Quetzalcoatl, the feathered serpent, who had resolved to return one day to claim his kingdoms. Quetzalcoatl had built a raft of serpents and disappeared toward the East into the sea. He was expected to return from the East. The year set for his return was the first Year of the Reed, which occurred every fifty-two years in the Aztec calendrical cycle.

Hernanado Cortes' ships appeared from the East in the first Year of the Reed. Moctezuma thus "knew" from his study of the myths that this strange phenomenon was the returning Quetzalcoatl. He sent important nobles to receive the god. Great misunderstanding began to be played out, similar to what happened with the Tasmanians. Moctezuma's emissaries did the correct thing from their point of view: they offered incense to the supposed gods and presented them with the correct ceremonial capes of magnificently-colored feathers, which Aztec gods were supposed to wear. The Spanish, however, interpreted the situation far differently. To them, this was the beginning of a trading venture. They brushed aside the feather capes and offered glass beads. They made the Aztecs understand that they were looking not for feathered capes but for gold. Gold ornaments were brought. More were requested. Both groups were totally under the influence of their own cultural premises—and the two sets of cultural assumptions overlapped not at all. It was a situation of total misunderstanding.

Cortes marched from the sea near Vera Cruz (which he founded in the image of a proper Spanish city) to the Valley of Mexico. He had fairly good intelligence about the political details of the Aztec empire (but apparently not the religious ones). Cortes had found a mistress who knew both the Maya and Aztec languages and was busily learning Spanish. He had picked up in Yucatan a shipwrecked Spaniard who had learned Maya. Communication of a sort was thus becoming possible. Cortes discovered the hatreds of many of the subordinated societies for the Aztecs. He made powerful alliances with some of these groups, who joined him in marching on the Aztec capital of Tenochtitlan. Obviously, they had their own premises and their own agendas for destroying Aztec power. By using such allies, moreover, Cortes' intelligence was greatly improved.

Throughout his encounter with the Spanish, Moctezuma followed, to the utmost, the protocol of his religion. His emissaries gave Cortes the mask and feathered headdress of Quetzalcoatl. Cortes apparently donned them for a short while in the presence of those emissaries, thus proving that he was indeed the returning god. The Spanish intention was, throughout, to get gold, destroy Aztec religion, and replace it with Christianity. But Cortes was received by Moctezuma as the returning Quetzalcoatl.

The story of the toppling and murder of Moctezuma is long and fascinating. At its end, the Spanish, with the help of Indian allies, destroyed the entire city and everything they could find that in any way reflected the Aztec religion. The inhabitants of the city were reduced to starvation. The myth was brought to life. The Age of the Fifth Sun had ended in disaster as had been foretold. A new era began—one not anticipated in the myth. Mexico City was built on the ruins of Tenochtitlan, and a new civilization was begun.

Resistance and Adaptation

Other cultures struggled over decades and centuries with the colonial situation and its aftermath. Among the best documented is the case of the Yaqui who, when the Spanish first appeared on their horizon in 1533, lived in what is today southern Sonora, in Mexico (Spicer 1961). The Yaqui have undergone four complete changes of culture and of social space during their history of contact first with the Spanish colonizers and later with the Mexican government. Each phase demanded a different culture and a different set of required adaptations.

(1) For almost one hundred years after the conquest of Mexico, Yaqui contacts with the Spanish invaders were sporadic. To the Spanish, the Yaqui lived in a peripheral area far to the northwest. At that time, the Yaqui formed sixteen groups that farmed the river valleys and harvested

14-10a. *Many cultures undergo vast adjustments to European contact. Yaqui had to make major cultural adjustments at least four times as first the Spanish and later the Mexican government replaced Indian customs. This sketch shows some of the changes that were introduced by the Jesuit missionaires in the early 1600s.*

From Colonialism to Global Society

shellfish from the Sea of Cortes. Their settlements ranged from three to four hundred people. Their economy was based on householding; there was no trade in food. They were accomplished warriors; warfare among themselves and with neighboring peoples such as the Mayo to their south, was bitter. In the early 1500s, they fought and won against Spanish troops, thus burnishing their reputation as fierce warriors.

(2) Then, in the 150 years between 1617 and 1767, Yaqui had intensive contact with Jesuit missionaries—few in number, but powerful in influence. When the Jesuits arrived, they assumed that the Yaqui had no religion because they went naked, whole groups got greatly intoxicated together in general orgies, and there were rumors of ritual cannibalism. The missionaries sought to stamp out all of these customs as well as to stop warfare and to spread the word of a benevolent deity. The Jesuits built missions and established the new type of community that centered around the mission church. This kind of community was new to Yaqui, but they willingly moved from their farms and small settlements (called *rancherias* in Spanish) into the new villages. No Spanish soldiers enforced the changes; the Yaqui freely made the decision to move. All this was accomplished in about seven years. For 125 years the Yaqui accepted the Jesuits and the form of community they had introduced—indeed, this kind of community came to be regarded as Yaqui tradition; in later years they even fought to retain it. Yaqui catechists were taught Spanish and were taught to read. During this period, the Yaqui were converted to Christianity, but they did not feel any pressures from the political arm of the Spanish government.

A revolt began in 1739 when a Yaqui in one of the towns was whipped on the orders of a missionary; it became serious only when an anti-Jesuit provincial governor stepped in. The Yaqui were protective of the Jesuits but sought to chase all other Spaniards from their general area. They killed as many as a thousand Spanish settlers in the area around them. Five thousand Yaqui were also killed; their resistance was crushed, and a presidio was built on the edge of their country.

Then, in 1767, for reasons that had no bearing on their activities in Yaqui country, the Jesuits were expelled from New Spain. Yaquis had by then begun to work in the mines that had been discovered in their territory. During most of the Jesuit period, the Yaqui had been kept isolated from much contact with Spanish culture, but their culture had been vastly enriched by Jesuit imports—these were by and large additions to the culture, not replacements.

(3) After the departure of the Jesuits, the Yaqui settlements became autonomous communities and remained so until 1887. During the Mexican Revolution of independence from Spain, Yaqui and several neighboring tribes tried to establish an independent Indian nation. When the Yaqui leader was killed by the Mexican armies, the alliance dissolved.

During this period, Yaquis largely controlled their own affairs, but their culture was immensely different as a result of the experiences first with Spanish colonizers and then with

Mexican government authorities. Yaquis were working in the mines and were migrating to the towns of Hermosillo and Guaymas. In this period, fewer and fewer were willing to live in their old towns, and some began to assimilate into the general Mexican population. There was, however, constant trouble because the Yaquis would not accept a position subordinate to Mexicans, and the Mexicans refused to acknowledge Yaqui autonomy. The Yaqui regarded their churches as separate from the churches of Mexican Catholics; their religion during this period was a series of cults of Jesus and the Virgin derived from Catholicism combined with military societies and deer dancers derived from their ancient religion.

Perhaps the most important thing about the period of autonomous towns was that interest in military matters superseded interest in producing surpluses of food and other goods, which was a value that the Jesuits had carefully instilled.

(4) The Yaqui were not willing, however, to give up their independence. Another war erupted in the 1880s, under the leadership of a Yaqui who had experience in the Mexican army and had been appointed by the Mexican governor of Sonora to be *alcalde major*, the highest Mexican authority, in the Yaqui towns. The Yaqui were crushed by Mexican troops. In the ten years or so following, the Yaqui constantly harassed the Mexican settlers who kept coming into their territory. The government thereupon decided that the only way to get peace in the area was to deport large numbers

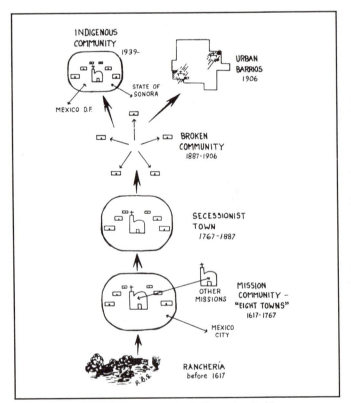

14-10b. *This sketch shows the different kinds of communities that Yaqui have had to adapt to since the early 1600s.*

of Yaquis to Yucatan and Oaxaca in the south of Mexico. At least five thousand were rounded up and shipped south. Several thousand others escaped either into Arizona (where their descendants still live) or into still other parts of Mexico. This period of relocated communities continued until Yaquis lived in most states of Mexico and in at least six states of the United States. When things settled down, during the 1920s and 1930s, many Yaqui returned to their homeland and tried to reestablish at least some of their towns. By the 1950s, they were going to school and dealing constantly with the Mexicans; their identity was still maintained by their religion, but their 350 years of resistance had more or less ceased (Spicer 1961).

The point to be garnered from the Yaqui experience is that they had to change their culture and their social structure four different times. It is, of course, true that all of us change all the time and that there were some continuities from one of these phases of Yaqui culture to the other. However, except for their adoption of the Jesuit missions of their own volition, the changes were made against their will and over great opposition. The Yaqui survived even though their culture was contorted again and again over three and a half centuries of struggle.

This pattern—resistance and ultimate adaptation—is the most common result of peoples confronted with colonialism. Hundreds of examples could be cited.

Cultural Dissonance

Culture grows naturally when people change their options and their habits through invention and borrowing. However, under situations of conquest or colonialism, the adjustment is more difficult. The control mechanism in the feedback underlying behavior is turned on its head. The power systems of the society are thereupon upset, which reflects back on the family and kinship systems. Perhaps most vital of all, traditional explanations and meanings no longer work for current events. It is no surprise that many colonized peoples began to search for meaning in new religions and reinterpretation of old religions to cope with cataclysmic upheaval. It should also come as no surprise that these new religions called either for a return to old power systems or else for an inversion of the new power system that would put the colonized people at the top of the status hierarchy and would strengthen morality, especially in the spheres of kinship and family.

Such religions are reactions to stress, and often take the form of cults. As we saw in Chapter 12, cults are likely to occur when the culture in one's head is out of phase with the culture in the environment. The world doesn't make sense, and the feedback that guides behavior does not work.

This phenomenon can be called **cultural dissonance**. Some degree of cultural dissonance is found in societies that are undergoing rapid cultural change as well as in societies that, like most modern nations, are made up of culturally different ethnic groups. When a force like the mass media, especially television, enters the awareness of foreign or even of poor people, it creates knowledge of culture in the head which does not jibe with the culture they experience around them.

Cults are likely to occur in such situations of cultural dissonance. Because the relationship between ends and means is blurred by cultural dissonance, cults often appear to outsiders to be magical or miraculous or absurd. To insiders, the cults are a serious effort to make sense of a senseless world.

In situations of cultural dissonance, action chains become tenuous. In the best of circumstances, we look at the desired end and then check out what kind of behavior is needed to get us there. When action chains fail to work because of the different understandings among the people involved in them, people look to mythical explanations. Action chains, under the best of circumstances, are subject to the distortion of mythical baggage. Mythical explanations are likely to be especially attractive—indeed, overwhelming—when no practical solution to a problem exists.

Social traps arising from flawed premises are common among people in a miserable state. For their own comfort, they postulate that there must be, somewhere, a society where justice and beauty reign undisturbed. Difficulty arises when they create cults that lead people to expect that utopia is imminent.

Most such cults are found in societies in which the eternal questions discussed in Chapter 12 seem to have become insoluble. That is to say, there is no way of convincing yourself that the traditional religious practice works. However, if a new situation can be created in which illness, misfortune

Cults are a common reaction to the cultural dissonance brought on by colonial occupation. Cults occur when people can no longer count on their culture to provide answers to their difficulties. They are social inventions that help people deny the reality and scope of problems.

14-11.

From Colonialism to Global Society

and death do not exist, then they do not need to be explained. One no longer has to ask about the formation of the world and of society, because the world and society either are or will soon become perfect places. This is, by definition, a kind of utopia or even paradise. The Christian paradise is thrust into the next life, and therefore allows us both the utopian vision and the scientific questions. Cult paradises, on the other hand, tend to be postulated for the near future here on this earth, and hence are ways of denying reality.

The easiest way to get rid of any problem is just to deny that it exists. Denial has long been known to be the simplest defense mechanism; the only trouble is that it doesn't work well for very long because you have to spend so much time and effort maintaining the denial—kidding yourself. However, persuading yourself that an external, stress-inducing problem does not exist, or soon will not exist, can be a great emotional relief. It is, in fact, a magical cure for living.

Cults like these are social inventions—usually called millenarian cults by anthropologists to keep them separate from some of the other cults that we discussed in Chapter 12. Millenarian refers to the millennium—a word that means both a thousand years and a period of righteousness and happiness. As with any other innovations, we have to ask not only how and why millenarian cults were invented, but also why and by whom they were accepted. Here we have space to go into only two examples of these religions of the dispossessed: the so-called cargo cults of Melanesia and the ghost dance of the Native Americans almost a hundred years ago.

The Ghost Dance. The earliest cult among Native Americans for which we have good records is the ghost dance (Mooney 1896). The first phase began about 1870 among the Paiute of Nevada. The second phase, far more widespread,

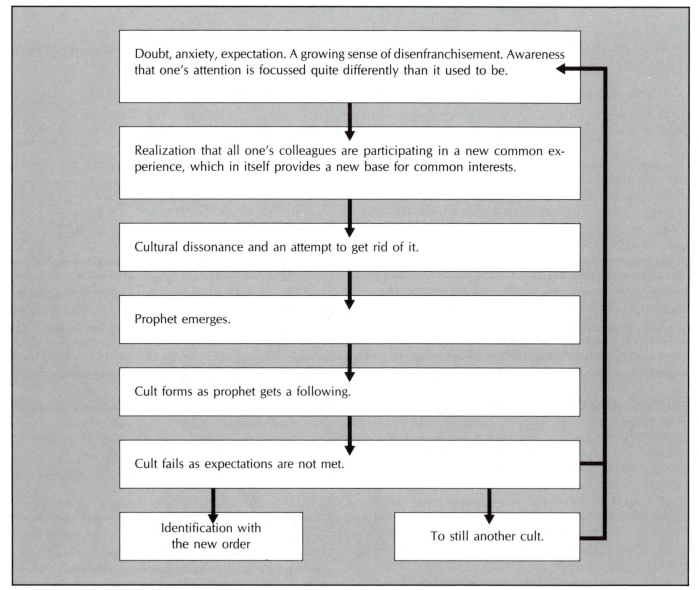

14-12. Action Chain for a Cult.

14-13. *The ghost dance devised by Wovoka (left), a Paiute, on the basis of dreams and visions, spread across the North American continent. Its message was peaceful, but it nevertheless ended in the massacre at Wounded Knee. Its intensity shows the commitment of the Indians to get rid of the American oppressors and find perpetual peace. The photograph at the right records how the bodies of the Native Americans, frozen stiff, were shoveled into a mass grave.*

began when a Paiute prophet named Wovoka experienced visions at the time of an eclipse of the sun, probably the one that occurred on January 1, 1889.

He was about thirty when he announced that he had experienced a great revelation. Wovoka had suffered a serious fever that he associated with that eclipse. He claimed that he had fallen asleep and been spirited away to another world.

Wovoka said not only that he met God, but also that he saw many of his dead friends, now forever young, engaged in traditional Paiute games and activities. He said that God had charged him to return to earth with the message that people should love one another, not quarrel, live in peace with the whites, work hard, and neither lie nor steal. God promised Wovoka that if the people lived this kind of pure life, there would be no further death or illness in the world. All would be reunited with dead relatives and friends. God also gave Wovoka a dance; if people performed the dance, they could hasten the day.

News of Wovoka's vision spread. Representatives of many tribes visited him to learn first hand of his vision and also to learn the dance. When they returned to their own tribal groups, the vision was altered or magnified to fit their specific cultural situations; the dance changed significantly as it spread from one tribal group to another. Each group fitted the vision and the dance to their own set of beliefs, their own religious convictions, and their own needs. New prophets sprang up to reinforce and adapt the vision for local consumption. Wovoka claimed, for example, that there were no trances in the dances of his vision, although trance became an important part of the ghost dance in some tribal groups farther east on the Great Plains.

The ghost dance occurred at the height of frustration among the Native Americans, as they were being settled onto reservations. The United States government had made treaties with most of them, but the land-hungry pioneers who swarmed the frontiers did not feel obliged to keep the treaties, even if they knew of them, which most did not. They claimed that Indian lands were unused and simply moved in and took them. The government did, from time to time, try to stop them but could not. Therefore, government agents had to keep going back to the Indians to revise the treaties—always to the disadvantage of the Indians.

The ghost dance spread far and wide; most, but not quite all, Native American groups were caught up in it. The American Indians had been driven to the wall. Nothing practical that they did had the effect of correcting their situation. The ghost dance was a futile attempt to solve on a supernatural plane the problems that seemed insoluble on the mundane one.

The ghost dance is an excellent example of an attempt to resolve cultural dissonance. Native Americans used their own ideas, their own culture, to create a more comfortable explanation. Like everybody else in the world, they had no culture but their own to use as they created their cults. The ghost dance was not revolutionary. It was not based on new ideas. It was an uprising using cultural principles that no longer worked because they were out of sync with the context of ideas in the larger picture.

From Colonialism to Global Society

Melanesian Cargo Cults. The cargo cults of Melanesia were similar. They occurred in periods of serious frustration, although the frustration itself is not an adequate cause. Just as the ghost dance reflected the culture of the Native Americans who took it up, cargo cults reflected the cultural convictions of the Melanesians who organized and joined them. In both cases, one of the primary factors was lack of specific information about the culture of the colonizers and hence of the larger social picture into which the native culture was thrust (Worsley 1968; Burridge 1969).

Like many other cult movements, cargo cults usually postulated that the ancestors would return and a better day would dawn. The characteristically Melanesian part of the cult is the notion that the ancestors, or somebody, would bring "cargo," which is all the good things of European culture. Melanesians had noted that Europeans did not work directly to produce their food, but rather they imported it as cargo on boats and planes. The trick seemed, then, to lie in finding ways to get the cargo delivered to the Melanesians instead of to the Europeans. The ancestors, or gods, or whoever, would then distribute the cargo to one and all, and in a happy reversal the Melanesians would be on top of the social ranking system with plenty of worldly goods instead of at the bottom with nothing.

Cargo cults varied in the same way that the ghost dance picked up variations as it traveled from one society to another. A common pattern, however, can be found.

We can see that first contact with the more sophisticated culture leads to "a mixture of doubt, anxiety and hopeful expectation" (Burridge 1969). But soon people became aware that they were disenfranchised, that their concerns and worries were vastly different and usually ignored, and that they spent their time at very different tasks than they formerly had. Most especially, they were isolated from the traditional prestige activities. They hence had no way to create a ranking

14-14. *Cargo cults were a series of cultural movements in Melanesia. They sought a formula for having ships and airplanes deliver wealth and food to the Melanesians instead of to the European colonial rulers. Most of these cults postulated the end of, or ruin of, European hegemony. What the colonized peoples saw as the advantages of European culture were to fall into the hands of Melanesians. Among these symbols of a cargo cult, note the Christian cross and the airplane that is to bring the riches.*

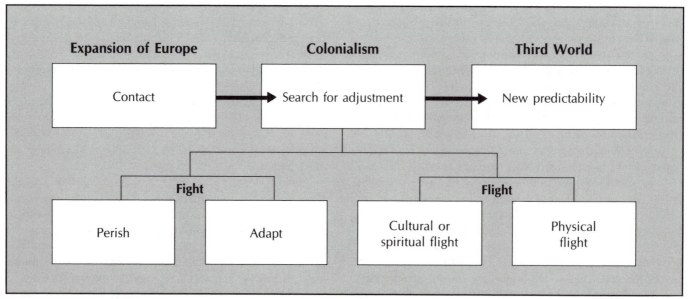

14-15. Cultural Process Resulting from the Expansion of Europe.

system in the new situation. Because the new tasks were defined in terms of reorganized values, individuals were forced back on their own resources which were inadequate to the new culture.

The future became foggy—would these new arrivals go away as suddenly as they came? This insecurity about how things will, or even should, turn out led to general uncertainty. People were terribly aware of not being in charge of their own destinies. Their universe of knowledge was limited to their own culture and what they could observe. When their culture and observations lacked the information necessary to make sense of the current situation, they could go back to earlier times (this attempt is usually called "nativism" by anthropologists) or they could try to understand the principles of the new situation. Necessarily, their understanding of those new principles got mixed up with the traditional principles. The emotional tone of this phase was one of loss.

Being forced into new activities and new experiences did provide a new common experience. People began to associate on the basis of their new common experience of uncertainty instead of on the basis of traditional association. People sought leaders who would explain how to perceive the new situation.

Dissonance results from the clash of old and new cultures, and people try to find ways to get rid of it. The question becomes, what can people do to improve what they are perceiving? Economic issues may be the first to surface, and new organization may evolve around economic issues. How is one to deal with environment and raw materials? What do we do about this new medium called money and the vast inequalities that it introduces? Given this new cultural environment, what does it mean to be human? What are the indicators of virtue and well-being?

At this point, a prophet is likely to emerge to tie all the new ideas together and provide new answers. It is his task to create symbols for the new situation. The cult surfaces as people try to transcend their new and difficult position.

Cults thereupon develop around the teachings of the prophet. If the cult is not well planned—that is to say, if it promises more or less instant relief which it cannot deliver—it will have a short life as people come to see that its premises are inadequate. Sooner or later, that happens to all such cults. Two things can then happen: you can go on to a new level of education and integration into the new situation, or else you go back to square one.

Cults are affected by the ideas people have about the way culture changes. It is astonishing, given how much study anthropologists have lavished on culture change, that there is no systematic comparative study of the ideas various colonized peoples hold or have held on the subject. We can discern that the Aztecs considered all change prescribed by the gods. The people of Melanesia had fateful ideas about the nature of culture change: it was always catastrophic. Therefore, when they anticipated change, they expected it to be catastrophic (McDowell 1988).

In short, there would seem to be a human need for predictability and self-reliance—people need to feel that they can affect their own security and their own activities. Indeed, given the basic way people behave, we can see that there is a terrible cost associated with depriving people of at least a degree of self-reliance.

When infrahuman animals are faced with strangers in their territories, they have two choices: flight or fight. Human animals have, of course, retained those two options. However, the presence of culture has added to those options something that might be called "cultural flight." That is to say, they stay on the ground, but change their cultural definitions in such a way that their perception of the situation is altered.

This idea of cultural flight is one that dominates the reaction of peoples to the incursion of European powers. The Tasmanians perished. The Aztecs' culture perished, although descendants of Aztecs live on. The Yaqui went through a series of tumultuous adaptations. I do not know a people who successfully fled the European invaders. The most common occupants of the culture flight box are religious movements and cults.

THE THIRD WORLD

The term **Third World** was coined shortly after World War II, although its roots are much older. When it was first used, the word had primarily a political meaning—the nations that would not join the Cold War by siding with either the capitalist First World (The Free World) or the communist Second World. In those days, both sides tried to get all countries to line up with one side or the other. Those that held out for their own destiny became known as the Third World. During the 1950s, however, the term took on an economic meaning; it came to mean the underdeveloped portion of the globe (the word "underdeveloped" became popular at the same time). The Third World included over one hundred states and about three quarters of the world's population. The main components of the Third World were former colonies of the European powers: all of Latin America, Africa, the Pacific Islands, and all of Asia except Japan and Israel.

The formation of the Third World was a result of history after 1500. The expansion of Europe created colonial countries. Many of them were turned into producers of raw material for the European market, and later for Anglo-America as well. These countries also entered the world market system as purchasers of European or American goods.

Underdevelopment

The story of underdevelopment in the Third World is so complex and so urgent that it would take another book, another course—and some new and original analysis—to go into it thoroughly. Here we will note only that underdevelopment follows not just on the heels of colonialism but on the continued spread of the market.

From Colonialism to Global Society

| Free World | Communist World | Third World |

14-16. The Third World was first recognized in a political context—those countries which were not part of either the Free World or the Communist World and refused to throw in their lot with either. These countries soon came to be called underdeveloped, as economic criteria became more central than political ones. The Third World is made up primarily of countries that were colonized or (like China) had their culture seriously interfered with by the expansion of Europe. If, however, you have to put each country in one box or the other, it soon becomes evident that this is not a viable classification.

In the fifteenth century the historic mutation occurred when Western Europe's capitalist economy generated for the first time a mass trade in necessities that overshadowed the traditional limited trade in luxuries. The new trade, precisely because it was a mass trade, involved entire populations which, willingly or unwillingly, produced for the new global market economy such necessities as foodstuffs, lumber and metals from Eastern Europe, bullion, sugar, tobacco, indigo and cotton from the Americas, slaves from Africa to work the American plantations, and rubber, tea, coffee, tin and jute from Asia. This trade inevitably led to the integration of entire societies into the new global economic order. . . .

The discrepancy in average per capita income was roughly 3 to 1 in 1500, it had increased to 5 to 1 by 1850, to 6 to 1 by 1900, to 10 to 1 by 1960 and to 14 to 1 by 1970. Far from benefitting all parties concerned, the global market economy is widening the gap between poor and rich countries, and at a constantly accelerating rate.

Lefton S. Stavrianos (1981)

THEY SAID IT

14-17. Many parts of the Third World act as suppliers of resources and products to the developed world. Yet their economic and political institutions are such that poverty continues to spread. Social innovations have not kept up with technological progress anywhere on the globe. This 1989 picture shows a man and his nine-year-old daughter who hire themselves out to pull carts loaded with firewood into the city. For a day's work they take home about $1.50.

When the agricultural practices of the West were extended to the Third World, production increased markedly. This so-called Green Revolution, however, created an additional need for fertilizer, irrigation and labor practices that require large amounts of capital. Peasant farmers could no longer make it on small pieces of land. Many of them gave up and went to the cities. Their fields were either abandoned or bought by capital-intensive agribusiness and consolidated into large farms. In such places as India, Mexico, Pakistan, and the Philippines, most peasant farmers were left out because they had no capital to change to new methods of farming. The few farmers who were successful at agribusiness turned the rest of the farmers into a labor pool. The majority of peasants, having failed at switching to the new kind of farming, went to the cities as laborers where they failed again because they had no marketable skills. Householding gave way totally to market economy, leaving masses of people with nothing to back them up. Production of subsistence crops had languished at the same time that production for the market picked up.

When Vietnam was a French colony, for example, 40 percent of all farms were diverted to export crops like coffee, tea, rubber, and rice. Obviously, that means that 40 percent less food could be produced. The result, throughout the Third World, has been more and more agricultural productivity— but also more and more malnutrition. In 1978 the Food and Agricultural Organization of the United Nations found 450 million malnourished people in the world. Yet, the global production of food was 27 percent higher than it had been in the early 1960s. Ironically, the greatest increase in food production had been in the poorest countries.

Wealthy Mexican farmers use hybrid seeds, machinery, fertilizers and pesticides. They supply 60 percent of the United States market in vegetables at the same time that the number of landless Mexican peasants rose from 1.5 million to 5 million between 1950 and 1980. The same pattern is found in India. Food production rose 100 percent between 1956 and 1978. At the same time, the amount of grain available to the Indian people decreased. Over 315 million Indians ended up below the poverty line (Stavrionos 1981).

14-18. The advance of the Sahara Desert has been going on for ten thousand years and continues today. Today, cultural means of using land—particularly overgrazing— play into the hand of the advancing desert. Yet, much of the serious hunger in Ethiopia (where this picture was taken), as well as other parts of Africa, is a political problem.

The First World has been the major winner—the Third World became not only a source of raw materials for the First World, but also a major market for machinery and chemicals. At the same time, the standard of living of Third World peoples did not improve much, was sometimes lowered, and the effect on the environment has been disastrous. The First World exported their values and practices to the Third World in the name of improvement. Nobody, anywhere, did sufficient examination of the context into which the practices were thrust. Therefore, a kind of neo-colonialism emerged: the Third World was now being used not just for resources and for labor as was true under colonialism. It also became a market for First World goods.

The fact that inventions in social organization have not kept up with advances in technology has created problems. We do not yet know how, socially, to run a world society that has come as far, technologically, as the one we live in. Some of the major problems of the twenty hundreds are at hand: "underdevelopment" is created and currently maintained by the world market system. What do we do with people who are either redundant to—or downright in the way of—the social and economic systems in which they live?

Poverty

The Third World is an integral part of global society. Problems found in the Third World also exist within the national societies of the First and Second worlds. There is less and less room in modern society for people who have no education and no training, or for those who do not have the character structure and cultural know-how to be a cog in the vast production machine.

The situation is simple to understand but difficult to do anything about: to do anything about poverty we must do something about its context. The whole system produces poverty, whether in the Third World or at home. We are heir to a system that depended on a large underclass of exploitable people. As we move beyond that situation, we have not discovered ways to empower the people who, in earlier times, were part of that underclass. In order to do anything about it, the entire system has to be overhauled.

There are at least two reasons that such an overhaul will not be done: the first is simply that the system is too big and complex to be adequately analyzed so that effective programs can be established; the second is that many peoples of the world—and some of the most powerful—do not want their own econiches changed. And you can't change anything without changing everything.

THE GLOBAL SOCIETY

Culture is growing at supersonic speed. Its expansion has accompanied unprecedented population growth. The result is cultural complexity of dazzling, even numbing, proportions. As we have noted before, culture is like a string of beads— picking up one bead disturbs all the rest—every bead is con-

14-19. *Poverty exists in the First and Second worlds as well as in the Third World. Part of the problem is over-population; but part of it is also that no part of techno-logically-developed global society has found adequate places for people who are not educated. This picture was taken in Washington, D.C., on Thanksgiving Day.*

14-20. *World-scale culture, like airport culture or inter-national trade and manufacturing culture, or hotel culture, is growing to be much the same all over the world. If a person knows airport culture, he or she can, with no more than a little language difficulty about details, cope with airports anywhere in the world.*

texted in all the rest. Just so, in today's **global society**, the entire world is the context for all cultural growth and change.

The complexity may, of course, be illusory, arising only because we do not yet have the concepts for fully comprehending it. Finding those concepts is one of the most vital problems in social science.

The Here and Now

Two kinds of new cultures have emerged in this brave new world: new planet-wide culture and new small-scale cultures. The planet-wide culture comes in two forms. On the one hand are institutions that, except for variations in language, are to be found in every corner of the globe. They show a few national or regional variations, but the variations do not interfere with their use by anyone who knows the basic

pattern. The second form results from the interdependencies of all institutions in all parts of the globe.

Airport culture is an example of the first sort. It may have regional "dialects," as it were, but once you have learned airport culture, you can find your way in any airport. International corporations are another example. They do indeed contain some variation, depending largely on the culture and goals of their officers and the needs of the people they serve. However, those differences almost disappear in their overwhelming sameness.

The second form—the interdependencies—are, on the other hand, very different. Far from creating near-identical institutions, they create networks of interdependence. They tie one part of the globe to every other part.

The Earth is indeed one global community—what, in the 1960s when the fact was first discovered, was called a global village. A vivid example of this unity can be found in a report issued by the Tokai Bank in Tokyo about the effects of the next major earthquake in that city. Tokyo is located on the juncture point of four of the Earth's twelve largest tectonic plates. In the past four hundred years, Tokyo has experienced a major earthquake about every seventy years. In its last major quake—the Kanto Quake of 1923—40 percent of Japan's gross national product was destroyed. When the next one hits, there will be immense loss of life—estimates as high as three million people dead. In spite of such losses, Japan will not be the biggest loser when Tokyo's next major quake strikes. Because we now live with a truly global economic system, North and South America will be the gravest losers. Japan will call back her foreign investments in those two continents—they amounted to $1.23 trillion in 1989. The probable $842 billion cost of reconstruction can thus be met. But in Canada and the United States, Brazil and Mexico,

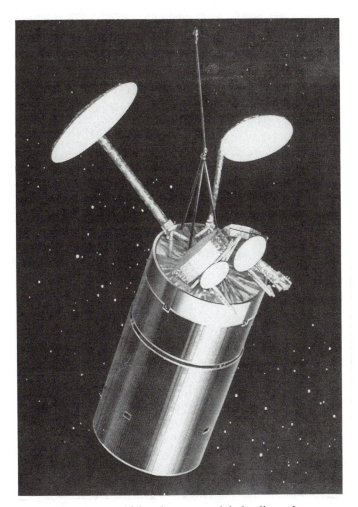

14-21. The world has become a global village. Instant communication, television, and worldwide trade have spread ideas from everywhere to everywhere. This communications satellite was launched in 1990. It joins many others so that all parts of the world can communicate with other parts instantly. Within a few years, many people will have cellular telephones that allow them, using satellites, to talk to anybody in the world who also has a cellular telephone.

communities are self-selected on the basis of common interests—oceanographers, computer programmers, fancy embroiderers, ham radio operators, crossword puzzle addicts. Modern communications technology helps members to keep in touch: telephone, television, computer networks, fax machines.

Think of all the networks, special interest groups, clubs, and organizations you belong to. Are these groups linked together by anything or anybody but you? How are they linked into other such groups and into the outside world? How did you find out about them in the first place? What were the criteria and the steps in joining them? How would you get out of them? For some of us today—at least for some portion of our lives—these cross-cutting ties are of greater importance than our families and of far greater importance than our work groups. These groups influence—sometimes they *are*—your social life. How do they affect your work, your fantasy life, your economic interests?

Each small culture has its own values and its own customs. There are far more of these small, geographically-dispersed cultures to study today than there ever were geographically-separate cultures in the past. The world, taken as a whole, is immensely rich in cultures.

This concomitant growth of worldwide cultures and of small, common-interest cultures means that everybody metaphorically inhabits a two-story building. The lower story is the global culture with its similarities and interdependencies; it is concerned with political and economic dimensions of life—and it tends to be one big room with everybody in it. The top story, on the other hand, is formed on the basis of common personal interests rather than on the basis of kinship or common geography, which was the old basis. There can be many little rooms in it. While people are participating in the global mass-culture, they are simultaneously forming closer personal groups, each with its own culture.

14-22. The number of small-scale cultures has grown at the same time that global cultures have grown. Most of the world's peoples today live in two-story cultures: the world culture of politics and economics, and the smaller cultures that surround kinship and family, religion, and common interests.

the result will be runaway inflation, bankruptcies, and credit failures; the bottom will drop out of their currencies. Within two years, the Tokai Bank estimates, the Japanese economy will be growing again at the rate of as much as 12 percent a year, while the economies of North and South America, and to a lesser extent of Europe, will decline for many years (Terry 1989).

At the same time that global interdependence and a common world culture have grown, the number of small, local cultures has also blossomed. These small-scale cultures are not geographically separated from one another as were different cultures in the years before 1400 or even as late as 1900. Rather, they are intermixed with one another; each is spread out over wide geographical areas and is made up of people of many walks of life. The members of these cultural

Few of us fully grasp the importance of the fact that each of us lives in a two-story culture: a global culture in which we participate from time to time, and an immense number of self-chosen cultures in a few of which each of us participates all the time. It merely seems "normal" for us in the 1990s to juggle the demands and rewards of all of these cultures—and to be the only person in the world who shares precisely all of our cultural contexts. We have each become our own person—which means having our own set of

From Colonialism to Global Society

cultures, each one shared with a different lot of people. We do realize from time to time that the demands on the individual person are great, but few of us can fathom living in a world in which we do not have what we call the freedom to make all the choices we in fact make. That freedom comes at the price of giving up old-fashioned community.

This immense cultural variety, the gargantuan scale of world society, and the demand for political self-determination on the part of absolutely everybody—all these pressures have shoved the principles of social organization into brand new realms. We are proceeding without maps for the simple reason that history has never been here before to map the terrain.

Social scientists have not yet adequately figured out this new complexity. We can, however, look at a few of the attributes of emerging culture and society and suggest some of the directions our thinking and our research must take. These attributes include:

(1) The emergence of "the person." The very definition of humankind has undergone a revolution.

The individual of the industrial era was a separate, identifiable entity, a social atom structured into the social system in the same way that particles of matter were thought to be built into the mechanistic Newtonian universe. This very identity set up a conceptual and therefore an experiential conflict between individual and collective interests. The emergent view of *person as process* [on the other hand] produces an image of self as part of an evolving social process rather than as a building block in a social structure. It is [this] process of self-discovery, self-actualization, that *resolves* the clash between individual and society. [emphasis added]

Virginia H. Hine (1977)

THEY SAID IT

"The individual" in earlier Western, particularly American, society has been enriched by the emergence of the more rounded idea of "the person" (Roszak 1978). Human rights in the 1960s grew out of concern for "civil rights" of the 1950s. Whereas civil rights had to do with *being allowed to do* one thing or another, human rights have to do with *being* a *person* recognized in one's own right.

Human rights are now an important plank in the foreign policy of the United States and most European nations. The idea is spreading throughout the globe—becoming a value in global culture.

(2) New work groups and work activities. The kind of work

people do is changing. It is trite but true to repeat that we are changing from a nation of manufacturers to a nation that provides services. In the process, new demands on the individual have become commonplace. In more and more service industries, people (like flight attendants) are, in effect, selling their imperturbable good humor (Hochschild 1983), often at considerable emotional cost. They are peddling "happiness," in the face of whatever provocation. We have only just begun to understand the pressure that situation creates for workers.

Even more forceful is the conviction that we must "enjoy" (a very Western concept) our work. We think there are certain kinds of jobs that reward us and help us to "grow as a person" and others that cramp us as persons. People who do not find rewarding jobs work just for the money, then spend that money on the areas of their real interests. Two categories of people are emerging: those who have found the calling they enjoy, and those who haven't.

(3) New kinds of family. We no longer have what we call a "traditional" family—a mommy, a daddy, and 2.3 kids living in a detached villa in the suburbs, going "over the river and through the woods to grandmother's house" for Thanksgiving. We no longer see the traditional extended or polygynous families that were formerly common in much of the Third World. Families of divorce with two households and eight or more grandparents, one-parent families with no support at all, step-families struggling through the uncharted reefs of step-relationships—all these combined now outnumber the "traditional" families. Long life, easy divorce, personally fulfilling jobs—indeed, personhood itself—have changed us irreversibly. We are in the middle of a revolution in family form and family functions—we scarcely know what the norms are. At the same time, "home" has become something of a haven in the top story of personal culture to which one can escape from the bottom story, the global culture and its pressures. The contradictions are troublesome.

(4) Bureaucracy is no longer as far-reaching as it formerly was. A new kind of social organization is emerging, based on the principle of network rather than the principle of hierarchy. This new social form is called a SPIN (Hine 1977). (You need not remember that SPIN is an acronym for Segmented, Polycephalous, Idea-based Network. That is, it works on the principle of segmental opposition that we studied in Chapter 9; it has either many heads or none, which is to say that power is decentralized; it is based on values; and it is a network instead of a formal group with a hierarchal structure.) SPINs have no table of organization that can be charted and hung on the wall as corporations have. They have no bosses, but rather are generalized networks of equals (some individuals and some organizations) drawn together by the power of

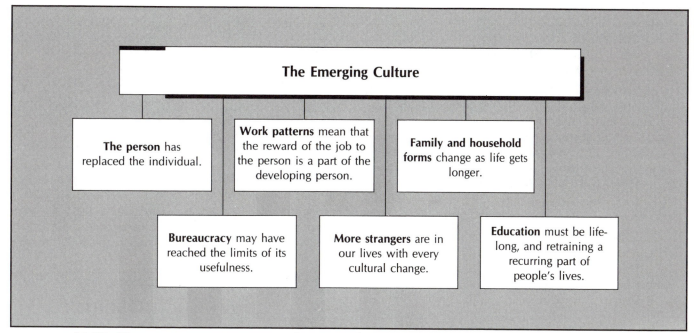

The Emerging Culture

The person has replaced the individual.	**Work patterns** mean that the reward of the job to the person is a part of the developing person.	**Family and household forms** change as life gets longer.
Bureaucracy may have reached the limits of its usefulness.	**More strangers** are in our lives with every cultural change.	**Education** must be life-long, and retraining a recurring part of people's lives.

14-23. We are now seeing an immense change in culture. A few of the demands made by the emerging culture are listed here. By careful observation and analysis, any person can add many others.

conviction. The members—persons and some more or less formal groups or smaller networks—have absolutely nothing in common save that shared conviction. The power of such leaderless, horizontal networks can be broken only by personal fear on the part of members that government bureaucracy will crack down. Even then, the SPIN may simmer for years, to break out again the moment the bureaucracy nods.

14-24. SPINs are emerging everywhere: they are single-interest groups that lack hierarchy or bureaucracy, which use disruption and television to spread their message. They are congeries of small groups that are infiltrating everywhere and having an immense impact worldwide.

SPINs use rallies, television coverage, and the vote to forward their causes and to control bureaucracy. SPINs are *not* mobs. A mob lacks purpose whereas SPINS are built around purposes. Mobs are generally disorderly, even violent. SPINs are generally orderly—at least until the representatives of the hierarchical groups (usually government police forces) try to "control" them, whereupon SPINs may indeed be turned into mobs. In the 1960s and 1970s, rallies of SPINs against the Vietnam War were immensely powerful in altering the political climate of the United States. In the middle 1980s, rallies of anti-nuclear demonstrators in Europe sometimes reached half a million demonstrators, drawn from wide areas and several countries; they got the television coverage that put their position before the entire world—

and made a difference. In the late 1980s and 1990s, SPINs both for and against abortion have dominated American politics. Transnational SPINs like Greenpeace are at least as important as transnational corporations in the totality of global culture.

At a more intimate level, smaller SPINs work much like such informal interest groups, as support groups that bring together people who may have nothing in common except a social conviction or personal problem. They share solutions and offer comfort. There are literally thousands of such support groups in every American city—from Alcoholics Anonymous to rape crisis centers—doing a job that the family never did well, and that the state cannot do at all. Just before Christmas of 1989, a hot line was established to put people in touch with support groups to help reduce the tensions created by the holidays.

(5) To live with large numbers of strangers in our midst was a skill that had to be learned at the time of the Industrial Revolution. Now there are more of them than ever (Lofland 1973). And another new dimension has been added: our lives are full of people whom we know only in a single context, or do not know at all, yet who become important to us as persons. I have several friends to whom I often talk on the telephone, and who are important in my life, whom I have never met face to face.

(6) Constant culture change has created a demand for new kinds of education—lifelong learning and recurring reeducation, professional retraining, and, indeed, the education we missed in college because we were so busy getting a professional training. The schools and universities have not yet faced up to these new forms—they

From Colonialism to Global Society

have not yet considered the facts of the new social context. If schools are poorly organized and anti-person, they can even turn off that most pervasive of primate characteristics, curiosity.

University education today has become a "right"; hence, the universities and colleges have changed immensely from what they traditionally were when they were first and foremost depositories of knowledge and havens for scholars rather than educators of the common man and woman. This change often makes both faculty and students uncomfortable. At the same time, the problems inherent in delivery of education and training throughout the life course have scarcely been faced.

(7) Whole new mythologies are emerging. They deal with the chimera of peace, with the satans who have created world hunger, with the overlooked but emerging value of persons—all matters that are being mythologized as our awareness of them emerges. We can see that the villain of the new mythology is always "the system." Most new mythologies arise because the last one supported a different kind of social system and a far different mesh of values than we have now before our eyes.

Tomorrow and the Next Day

Our need to examine the emerging social and cultural context has never been so urgent. Of course we need secure and predictable economic institutions, but they will not be like those of yesteryear; a new kind of institution must face the fact that we live in a global economy, that we are more than just consumers. This is particularly true in light of the fact that today's jobs are very demanding. The adjustment required on the part of the individual worker can be appreciated and eased, but probably no amount of institutionalization can reduce the increased responsibility on the person.

We also need new political institutions that will guarantee individual freedoms but will also get the social work done. We don't have such institutions at the moment. There must be ways better than socialism or the market to guarantee housing and health care, for example, at the same time that the personal freedom treasured and sought after by people all over the world is safeguarded.

At the moment, the American system does provide such freedom. Many countries are far less successful because they do not yet have in place the infrastructure of freedom. The countries emerging from communism have no traditions of democracy. Their people do not really know, as yet, how democracy works or how they have to educate themselves for it. You can't just "do" democracy—it involves a complex culture that must be learned. So far, these people know only that they want their governments off their backs and the only word they know to describe that image is democracy.

How do you govern and provide basic social services for absolute individualists? In 1989, the Chinese communist troops used force to put down a movement toward democ-racy—maybe because they were bad guys who wanted to stay in power, but more likely because they did not have the social inventions required to deal with the choices that were being demanded. Similarly in 1989, when the communist governments of the Eastern European bloc were falling, they had no ready-built institutions or democratic mythology to fall back on. Some of those societies do have democratic traditions in their histories, but they nevertheless lacked organizations to replace or mend their flailing governments immediately.

Today nobody can live in isolation. All of us must face all the major global problems: peace and war, the world's economy, the environment. There is no "away" to throw anything anymore—maybe there never was and it is just becoming apparent. There is no outsider to blame—"we have met the enemy and he is us."

CONCLUDING THOUGHTS

How do you organize and govern a globeful of persons, families, SPINs, support groups? Will such mechanisms as corporations and political parties and governments as we know them be enough to solve the world's economic, political and environmental problems? Probably not. Are we going to let new social institutions drift into being? Probably. Are we going to get as hardheaded about society and culture as we are about chemistry, granted that chemistry is infinitely simpler? I sincerely hope so.

We can never, as individuals or even as nations, solve these problems on the global scale now required. However, if we are aware that vast social currents are moving around us, if we make peace with the fact that tomorrow will be very different from today, and if we realize that change furthers our struggle to survive—in unprecedented numbers and in peace—we have taken the first step.

BUZZWORDS

colonialism   a policy or practice of any nation that holds colonies, especially when that policy involves economic exploitation of the colonized peoples.

cultural dissonance   a situation in which a person knows enough about two different cultures to experience them as contradictory, but not enough to solve the contradiction.

global society   the emerging society made up of all the peoples of the world, brought together by new communications technology, international business and worldwide environmental problems.

Third World   during the Cold War, this term was first used for countries that would not join either the capitalist or the communist worlds. Its meaning soon changed to indicate insufficient economic development and the status of being poor.

Anthropology in a Global Society

15

PROPOSITIONS AND PREMISES

■ As change is guided, the ethical problems come even more to the front: what is "the good" in another culture? for another people? indeed, for one's own culture?

■ Variation in cultural premises make it difficult for people of one culture to assist or even do business with people of other cultures. As people become aware of the problem of differences, more and more anthropologists act as cultural brokers for governments, for businesses, for schools, and for medical delivery teams.

■ The traps for the practicing anthropologist are the same as those for any other anthropologist: ethnocentric bias, dedication to ideologies, and the need to take control.

■ Visionary anthropology turns more and more to long-term ideas about future possibilities. The knowledge that comprises anthropology *can* be used to help design the future (if one can get rid of ethnocentrism, the ideologies, and the idea that one can or should fully control it). Because all peoples have ideas about the future that partially determine their present actions, we can (in very general terms) detect some of the problems that may be encountered as we postulate different possible future conditions.

■ The bicultural vision that anthropology teaches can be used to help people grasp that institutions, as they play themselves out, may not be the same as institutions of the future *or* the past. For this reason, the present set of institutions must eternally be reinvestigated, rethought, and rediscovered.

■ As we proceed through the culture crest of our own day, and move toward the larger galaxy, the cultural challenge, both technical and social, has never been greater.

An old saw about history says that anyone who does not understand the past is condemned to repeat it. It is equally true that anyone who does not understand the successes and failures of other cultures is doomed to try solutions to life problems that have already failed.

It should be evident to all that the gravest global problems are social and cultural, *not* technological. Technology is always invented and utilized in ways that reflect social and cultural values. Americans, and much of the rest of the world, are good at technology. They are far less good at social problems.

The difficulties that beset our own society—environmental catastrophes, homelessness, the deteriorating educational system—are social problems. The difficulties that beset Eastern Europe and the Soviet Union are social problems—the technological component only reflects the deeper social issues. The Soviets are coming back from decades of experimentation with a social system that did not work. They have had almost to start over in learning social know-how in order to prosper in the emerging global society. Not since the American, French and Russian revolutions has there been such immense opportunity for learning social lessons and trying out new social ideas all over the world.

The gravest danger in the capitalist countries today is that they will comfort themselves that they were right all along and then use that as an excuse for not learning lessons. Both Americans and Soviets—and, indeed, everybody else—are dealing with unprecedented problems that arise from the massive scale of global society. The need to understand this emerging society is pressing—anthropology must not turn its back on that challenge.

A new social science is emerging as its global context becomes more evident. Physical science, which underlies technology, has been able to develop more rapidly than social science, which underlies social policy. The reason is easy to find: in spite of the vast actual change that has derived from physical science and technology, those two are nevertheless far less threatening to established ways of doing things than is social science. It is hard to politicize physical science (although, of course, it can be done). It is even harder *not* to politicize social science. In a television interview some years ago, Senator Daniel Patrick Moynihan of New York (himself an accomplished social scientist) was asked how we could put people on the moon but could not solve our social problems. His response was devastating in its simplicity: "You see, there wasn't anybody who didn't want to go to the moon." Politicizing social science may sometimes be a social trap—and so far nobody knows how to avoid it.

As the vital importance of social science becomes more and more evident, many people—including physical and biological scientists—must grasp what social science can do and what it can never do. Because of the word "science," they seem to think that social science should work the same

15-1. All the gravest global problems—overpopulation, world hunger, the threat of atomic warfare, environmental catastrophe—are social problems, not technological problems. The picture was taken in Calcutta, India, one of the most crowded areas of the world.

15-2. Whereas physical science underlies technology, anthropology and the other social sciences underlie social policy.

15-3. In social science, it is difficult to experiment. It is actually impossible to hold conditions constant. The context of social science is always shifting because the scene to be observed and explained is always shifting. People survive by adapting their culture to the environment. The creativity involved in such adaptation leads to conditions that social scientists cannot anticipate.

as what they call the "hard sciences." It doesn't.

Whereas physical scientists can hold context constant in their experiments, social scientists cannot. Whereas technologists can pretest everything by scientific methods, social scientists cannot. We desperately need a way to test social and cultural theories in a context at least approaching the context that they are meant to subserve without the paroxysms that the Soviet Union has gone through to test communism.

To illustrate this point, I turn to a remark made by Dr. Allen Bromley, the scientific advisor for President Bush.

Many of the outstanding problems we face today—such as the fate of the environment, the danger of nuclear war, the curse of world hunger, and the burgeoning costs of medical care, to name just a few—are often laid at the door of science and technology. Yet in all of these cases, the science and technology needed to solve these problems are effectively in hand. What we do not know are the social, behavioral and economic consequences of the various possible courses of action available to us. Nor do we have an adequate understanding of the value systems underlying the decisions we face.

D. Allen Bromley, in a letter dated November 6, 1989.

THEY SAID IT

Dr. Bromley has noted that much of the science to solve our social problems is at hand. He might have added that much of the social science needed to solve our social problems is also at hand. What, then, is lacking?

What is lacking is not just a knowledge of values and consequences as Bromley suggests (although he is certainly right that we need more of that). What is truly lacking is any understanding—even by scientists—that the context has changed. If you change the context in physics, things change. Physicists have the luxury of controlling context.

Context has changed so much that we are in fact living in a new kind of world. What scientists call the "paradigm" has changed. Not just the paradigm of science, but the paradigm of civilization. We have not yet understood what the new paradigm is, let alone caught up with it.

What both social scientists and statesmen need is an early warning system of changes in the *context* of achieving goals and struggling against chaos. The context is the rest of the string of beads—when you pick up one, you have picked them all up. Changes in context feed back into people's goals and demand the establishment of still newer goals.

There are, surely, two requirements: the first is to learn from experience. We desperately need a good survey of social traps in all the social and cultural systems of which we have any record. It is an immense job, but it can be done—and done repeatedly, as context changes. We have to search history for patterns that can help us to understand social and cultural dynamics. Most historians have never been interested in those patterns—their concerns are equally legitimate but they are different. Anthropologists must take on the job of analyzing culture and society with historical data. It may be for social science what mapping the genome is to biological science.

The second requirement is an adequate system of simulations. Computers are by now sophisticated enough, but we need the ingenuity to devise the programs plus the time and money to carry them out. The job requires far more ingenuity than it does time and money. Perfecting ways of simulating social action in a changing context will certainly cost less than the old-fashioned way of trying out a new policy to see if it works.

In brief, we need:

- the will of scholars to gather the information and devise ways of doing the simulations,
- the courage of leaders to dare to be counterintuitive in guiding policy based on research findings, and
- the support of the people—the citizens—who have to pay the price of implementing solutions that will lead to successful policies.

The cost of reform—of all cultural change—is immense and it is painful. Yet, surely we all agree that it is as irresponsible to use force to implement an untried social policy as it is to blast off a rocket with untested O-rings. If nazism and communism have taught us nothing else, they should have taught us that.

On the other hand, we also have to sharpen our skills so that we can detect and understand the cultural changes that happen when we aren't looking. Before the 1960s, for example, nobody had ever heard of support groups. Nobody objected when they appeared—because they solved some problems. They have now become ubiquitous and powerful. The subtle social change came when one of our basic democratic rights—to demonstrate publicly for what we believe in or against what we do not—was combined with a powerful technological invention, television. Support groups could now play to a worldwide audience through demonstrations. An accepted value (demonstration) was recontexted with a small social invention (support groups) through a major technological invention (television) into an undetected (by most of the people) cultural change. We now not only accept the power of television to provide information and to serve as a forum for public issues, we demand constant input. Think about the coverage in Tiananmen Square and the Gulf War.

Many people are unwilling to make the changes in their daily lives that would be necessary to test and to solve our social problems without at least some good simulation. We could, of course, solve the drug problem by making the use of drugs a capital offense and firmly enforcing it. Obviously, we will not do that because the cost in social disorganization and revolution would be far worse than the problem itself. Maybe we could solve it by legalizing drugs and putting a tax on them to establish free therapy programs for addicts (but that assumes that people would not still choose to be addicts). Would a computer simulation ever be able to predict where such a policy might lead? We could solve the problem of the homeless by creating a guaranteed minimal income to all people. Would a capitalist society be willing to do that? Would a society that values work and self-reliance accept members who did not match those expectations? Again, it is context: what changes can we make that will not wreck the culture and disrupt the entire social fabric?

PRACTICING ANTHROPOLOGY TODAY

There is almost no job that cannot be done more creatively with an anthropological angle. Before the middle 1950s, anthropologists who tried to make a difference in the real world dealt almost exclusively with repairing injustices to colonized peoples (including Native Americans). Then, since the demise of colonialism, they have worked to straighten out misunderstandings across cultural barriers. Today they use the most up-to-date technology—and try to use improved social tools—not only to solve Third World difficulties, but also to ease the workings of our own society. To that we must add trying to understand the emerging global society.

We noted in Chapter 1 that practicing anthropology makes a difference by working with the culture already at hand to solve problems with a deadline. Visionary anthropology, as we will see later, tries to make a difference by recognizing and analyzing the emerging cultural and social developments that are not yet fully understood by helping to recontext cultural ways from other places and times, and by dreaming up new cultural and social tools that have never existed.

Today, anthropologists are finding a place in what used to be called the world of affairs. Many are called upon to be administrators or managers. Anthropology provides one of the best trainings a manager can have—it teaches her or him how entire social and cultural systems fit together, and how they fit with individual behavior. At the level of a corporation or an agency, anthropologists can often understand and pinpoint organizational hang-ups and social traps. Those anthropologists who call themselves medical anthropologists work in hospitals or clinics to assist with delivery of medical services and to improve communication between patients and doctors.

One of the most important dimensions of the job of a practicing anthropologist is that of cultural broker—when two different cultures must cooperate and work together, somebody who understands both cultures is necessary if difficulties are to be surmounted.

I know anthropologists who work in banks, and there are a number in the World Bank. Others call themselves media anthropologists and work in news broadcasting. Anthropologists may be found in many pursuits, working to communicate across cultural differences. Some sit on planning commissions; some set up agencies that offer special services to corporations establishing offices or plants in foreign countries; some work for agencies to improve delivery of social services to people whose culture is different from that of the agents. Anthropologists turn up in many places. Better still, anthropological ideas are turning up everywhere.

Medical Anthropology

Medical anthropology has a very special position because, perhaps more than any other anthropological specialty, it has a prominent place both in theoretical anthropology and an equally prominent place in the world of practicing anthropology.

It is readily understandable that patients must cooperate with the doctors in achieving cures. It is somewhat less apparent that they can do so only in terms of their own perceptions of the causes and progress of their diseases and ailments, and that these ideas may well be at odds with the ideas of scientific medicine. Medical doctors see this as a problem in patient education; anthropologists see it at least in part as a problem in the education of doctors.

Learning about the medical beliefs and practices of other peoples can be most informative and valuable. I began to learn something of Tiv medicine when, a few weeks after I arrived in the field, I was awakened one night because a woman had been stung by a scorpion. I had been told by an Irish doctor in the Nigerian Colonial Service to watch out for scorpions, and that if I was stung, I should remember to make an incision at the point of the sting and rub baking soda on it so as to neutralize the acid of the venom.

I had, at the time that the woman was stung, never cut living human flesh. I was reluctant to do so. I gave the woman's husband a razor blade and told him to make incisions in her skin near the sting and put the soda on it. As I write this, I realize that my knowledge of the situation was as meager as his, in spite of my instruction from that Irish doctor.

What the husband did was to make incisions in her skin not just at the site of the sting on her foot, but also at her

I would be dead twice were it not for modern medicine. We in America are blessed with good dentists, with optometrists and gifted surgeons. Few Americans today lose their teeth in old age; but one Tiv told me in 1950, "Teeth are terrible—they hurt when you get them, they hurt while you have them, they hurt when you lose them."

We Westerners do not have to give up activities and constrict our lives because we can no longer see as we get older—we get glasses. I knew a Tiv whose eyelashes grew back into his eyes instead of out from them. One of his brothers pulled them out, one at a time, every six weeks or so, using a knife and his thumbnail. Western doctors have told me that this condition can be surgically repaired fairly simply. I knew another Tiv whose jaw had been knocked out of place when he was a boy. Tiv can set broken long bones, but they do not know how to reset a dislocated jaw. This man struggled all his adult life trying to chew his food and to speak clearly with the handicap of a dislocated jaw.

American medicine is not without problems. First, our medicine gets more expensive as it gets more technologically developed and more capable. Second, modern medicine's reliance on technology is too often a dehumanizing force in physician/patient interaction—the patient's intuitions and the emotional aspects of illness are too often ignored. Third, our mode of delivering medical service is reserved primarily for those who seek it out. The context of medical practice in the United States makes it difficult to help those who do not take themselves to doctors or those who cannot pay. Fourth, some doctors sometimes make misdiagnoses and sometimes find it hard to admit that they don't know much about the ailments that are presented to them. The medical establishment too often chooses not to weed out or expose poor doctors.

Our primary problem is simple to state: how can everyone take full advantage of our medical system? How can we enhance standards of practice, research and education? Westerners are lucky in their medicine—most of the time. But we still have a way to go in understanding how to pay for it and how to make it available to everyone, and how to soften its cold technological edges.

WE THE ALIEN

knee, part way up her thigh, and at her waist. He then rubbed quantities of the soda in all of them. I was frustrated but could not stop him. I knew from my cultural stance that the

extra incisions would have no effect. The next morning, when I could make detailed inquiries, I learned Tiv theory of these matters: the poison travels up the *igbila* (a word that means both veins and tendons), then falls into the stomach. Only then does any real damage begin. The woman's husband was, sensibly enough, trying to shortstop the poison. His wife shared those perceptions, so what he did made good sense to her, made her calmer, lessened her fear and pain. The cure may even have been effective—she was fine within two days.

15-4. One of the tasks of medical anthropology is to improve communication between doctors and patients, especially when the two do not share the same culture.

Just this sort of misunderstanding is what the applied dimension of medical anthropology sets out to avoid. Medical anthropologists seek to talk to curers in many cultures to uncover the deep cultural beliefs that provide the rationale for their cures. The anthropologists can then assist the curers in discussing their knowledge and information with one another and with healers from other cultures, including Western physicians.

People's ideas about the way the body works and about the way medicine works in the body are in most cases closely tied up with their views of the cosmos and how it works. In other words, they are related to people's ideas about religion and science, especially religion.

The Yoruba of southwestern Nigeria, for example, say that simple illnesses are said to result from an imbalance in the body of substances that normally would contribute to health. One of the most obvious of these is what Yoruba call *atosi*. *Atosi* is said to be an important element of the body of every person, and to be related to reproduction. In men, for example, *atosi* increases the amount of semen. However, *atosi* is also the word for gonorrhea. The theory goes that if a man somehow takes on extra *atosi* from a woman with whom he has had sex, the amount of his *atosi* is increased so that illness results. It is being "too much" or "too powerful" that turns something normal in the body into disease. Yoruba say that it arises when a person eats too much sweet food, has too much sexual intercourse, or drinks too much alcohol. *Atosi*, like other such substances, is said to be stored in bags in the body called *apo*. Too much of any of these normal substances makes the bag overflow. When that happens, illness results.

Yoruba call these normal parts of the body by words that mean worms or insects (but since the insects that cause diseases are too small to be visible, the ethnographer translated the term as "germs"). Specialized worms or germs may cause headache, menstrual difficulties, scrotal hernia, chest pains, toothache, and many other ailments.

There are several other dimensions of the real world that Yoruba hold to be relevant to health and illness. Among

15-5. Medical anthropology is one of the most important fields of practicing anthropology. Western medicine, based on biology and chemistry, is more effective than any other known medicine, but is at the same time beset by cultural and social problems. For example, it is at the mercy of the cultural assumption that the patient should seek out the doctor; cultural practices, such as malpractice suits, affect the work of doctors and make American medicine numbingly expensive. Like many other pursuits, American medicine is organized like a latter-day guild, to protect its members as it claims to set and maintain standards. Such an organization serves most doctors and patients well. However, one of the fall-outs is that poor doctors take shelters behind that protection. The little girl getting the injection is a Masai; she lives in Kenya.

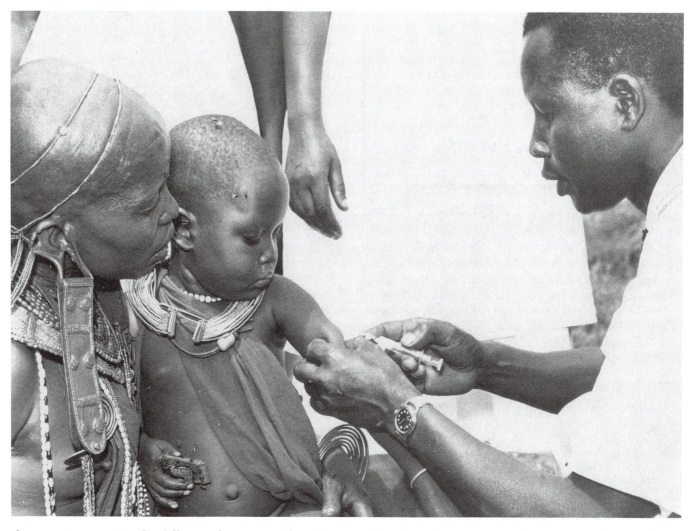

the most important is the difference between moderation and excess. They say that many things are good in moderation that, in excess, lead to disease. Further, in the Yoruba cosmology, some things are meant to be hidden and others revealed. If things that are supposed to be hidden are mistakenly revealed, the result may be illness or social catastrophe. Colors are also of special significance to Yoruba. If the colors are confused, or if one replaces another, illness or disaster may strike—in fact, confusion of colors may be a symptom of illness and disaster (Buckley 1985).

In other words, Yoruba see these common diseases not as invasions of the body (as almost all disease appears to be to Westerners) but as normal parts of the body turned abnormal by excess. In short, disease is part of life. Like everything else, it has to be kept under control by moral living.

In judging these matters, we have to remember two things: first, how recently Western medicine came to be based on science instead of traditional knowledge of herbs and other curing agents. It was only a little over 350 years ago that Harvey discovered the circulation of the blood. His discovery created a revolution in the way people viewed the human body. Only 150 years ago were efficient anesthetics developed; only 125 years ago did adequate antisepsis appear; only a hundred years ago, in 1895, were x-rays developed. The Western medicine that we take for granted is in fact very recent.

Second, we must remember that there remain a lot of people living in Western civilization who are uncomfortable with the separation of medicine from religion. Scientific medicine, no matter its efficacy in curing, does not provide

Anthropology in a Global Society

The Yoruba belief sets our own ideas into relief: we are convinced that without invasions of our bodies by foreign bodies, be they germs or viruses, everything will continue to work well. The germ theory of disease tended to make people obsessive about scrubbing away the germs, about smelly disinfectants. Library book circulation fell because people were afraid they contained germs. Money was considered filthy—since it had passed from hand to hand, there must be lots of exotic germs on it. Only with the discovery of diseases that arise from genetic mutations can we begin to see that some diseases are caused by elements that are already within the body and a natural part of it.

WE, THE ALIEN

the personal comfort or the moral motivation people can get from the spiritual dimension of traditional medicine.

The Western world inherited three primary medical doctrines from ancient times: versions of East Asian medicine, versions of ancient Indian medicine (sometimes called Ayurvedic medicine), and Greek-Arabic medicine (sometimes called European or Hippocratic). All three are based on the idea that the body will cure itself if external and harmful forces are removed. All call on people to eat sensibly (the definition of sensible may change a little from one society

15-6. Americans (at least until the discovery of genetic disorders and the emergence of new branches of medicine to deal with them) believe that illness arises when external organisms (germs or viruses) invade the body. Yoruba, like those pictured here, believe that much illness results from imbalance of the body substances that normally contribute to health. Cultural assumptions about disease are of great importance in the progress of the disease.

to another), to live temperately and morally (the standards for which may also change from one society to another, but not much), and to fit their activities into the social and environmental forces at play in their lives so that tension can be reduced.

All three of these systems of medicine assume that the body is a reflection of the natural energies flowing within it. The

---

All three of these medical traditions assume that the body will heal itself if the context is correct—the social context may be part of the context of health.

East Asian medicine is based on an idea of energy called *chi* (thought of as mystical) and its flow through the body.

Ayurvedic medicine from Ancient India is based on a concept of energies called *prana* organized along certain paths in the body. Disease disrupts the paths.

Greek-Arabic medicine, called Hippocratic, also assumes energies, but largely assumes chemical control of them.

15-7. Three main medicine traditions form the basis of Western medicine today. All, however, have been changed by input from modern science, particularly biology and chemistry.

energy may be called *chi* (as in East Asia) or *prana* (as in India) or something like *elan vital* or aura in Europe. The basic assumptions of all three are that illness is caused by blockages in the energy paths and that a therapy can be effective only if it can correct a flawed energy flow. Massage, acupuncture and other means of manipulating the body can, these medical lores say, correct the energy flow. These medical traditions further assume that every person is a microcosm of the cosmos, although each person is unique. Therefore, to understand an illness, a practitioner must understand both the cosmic principles and the specific condition of the patient.

In such belief systems, an illness will be repeated or will get worse unless the patient alters his or her habits and changes his life so as to remove the cause of the illness, thus allowing a free flow of energies. The goal of treatment is to help the person achieve harmony both within the self and with the social and physical environment.

These ideas are still current in alternative medicines found in Western societies. Within mainstream Euro-American medicine, the energy idiom has been replaced by scientific ideas of anatomy and physiology and chemistry and the metaphor of the body as machine—yet acupuncture, based as it is on energy lines, seems to work in spite of the fact that Western science has difficulty explaining why. Indeed, these time-honored systems have been rejected by such groups as the American Medical Association, although some doctors study and use some aspects of them. Most of the modern medical establishment is uncomfortable with the idea that a social and cultural context can create illness and refuses adamantly to get involved in the relationship between the human individual and the cosmos. Until recently much of the medical establishment refused to admit an association between disease and the mental and spiritual attitudes of patients (English-Lueck 1990).

People cannot "follow the doctor's orders" if their views of what disease is and what medicine should do are at odds with those of the doctor. Among Tiv in the middle twentieth century, a Western doctor could not prescribe medicine with the expectation that any Tiv would follow instructions and take one a day for ten days. The Tiv idea is that any medicine that works will work better if there is more of it. Why wait for ten days? Given their views of anatomy and physiology, that is not an absurd belief.

Medical anthropologists explore not only the relationships between worldview and illness beliefs, but also between disease and nutrition, population growth rates, reproduction and birth control, epidemics such as AIDS and historical plagues. Medical anthropology has an important niche in the cultures of the world and has an assured future. Its recognized contributions to both practicing and visionary anthropology make it a model.

Business Anthropology

There are many broad areas of business to which anthropology is relevant (Baba 1986). The following are only some of them.

Anthropology provides business with a theoretical framework—theories of organization and the theory of culture are as vital to business as is the theory of economics. Although few managers realize it, the so-called science of management depends heavily on anthropological theory applied to the corporation, then given some "how-to" twists.

Probably the single most important anthropological idea for business is the holistic view of culture—everything is connected, and if one element is changed, other contexting elements are likely to change as well. Neither consumers nor employees and employers can change their buying habits or their work habits without changes in the rest of their lives—and therewith great change in the context and organization of the company.

"Company ethnographies" have become a staple—not only in many business schools, but in the companies themselves. Managers are sharply aware of the culture that is projected both within the company and to the outside world. The ideas behind these company cultures are anthropological ideas.

15-8. Anthropologists can, working in business, investigate the organization of work, the needs and wishes of customers, the advantages and disadvantages of certain characteristics of organization and leadership, the nature and tactics of competition, and many other problems of great interest both to theoretical anthropology and to business.

The insights and methods of anthropology have also been useful to corporations in the area of employee relations—work patterns and work groups. Why is the employee turnover rate so high? What qualities do company employees find repellent? They may be fairly easy to change and, from the standpoint of the employees, improve the entire company as a work site.

Anthropologists for over fifty years have been leaders in developing the ideas and tools that are nowadays commonplace in understanding work organizations. They can help explain the complexities of relationships among managers and employees.

Some anthropologists, working as consultants, have even told bosses what they themselves do to upset their employees. I know one anthropologist who specializes in assisting firms in Latin America. In one company doing business all over Latin America, and having extensive networks in Anglo-America as well, she discovered that the employees heard messages quite different from those that the boss thought he had given. When the boss was faced with her statement, "They think you said such and such," his immediate reaction was rage: "I did not say that! Nobody in his right mind could think I did!" Nevertheless, she warned him, that is what they heard. When the boss cooled down, they began a process of figuring out a way for him to say things so that the employees would understand, not misunderstand, what he meant. He and the anthropologist worked together over several months on how to send messages to his employees. Employee problems in his company all but disappeared.

Anyone who tries to determine customer needs and satisfaction would be hard put to improve on anthropological methods for determining how people view their own actions. Anthropology has taught social science both to depend on firsthand contact with a "subject population" (which can be defined as customers just as readily as it can be defined as "natives") and also to maintain that contact over time so they can keep up with changes in ideas and needs and wishes. Anthropology is ready-made to tell business people how their specific products fit into the lives of those who use them, and thus to influence advertising, the direction of research, and even methods of production.

15-9. The holistic view that everything in the culture is connected to everything else may be the most important insight that business persons can get from anthropology: everything they do, every policy, every product, affects the whole culture. The same dictum, of course, applies to government.

The most evident use for anthropologists is in international business. If people have to do business with people from different cultures, they themselves have to learn the other cultures or use cultural brokers to overcome difficulties in intercultural communication.

Anthropologists have been instrumental in training company officers and employees in the cultures they will be encountering and using—both before they go abroad and after they get there. Anthropologists have also helped the families of those employees who must make adjustment to living in foreign countries—sometimes extremely foreign countries.

Anthropologists have helped establish credit institutions in the Third World. Adequate credit is an essential for any developing economy. The introduction of extensive consumer credit in our own society in the late nineteenth and early twentieth centuries expanded business opportunities and improved the lifestyle of ordinary Americans. They could buy a house, furniture and (a little later) a car on credit instead of having first to save up the money. The same kind of revolution is happening today on a modest scale in parts of the Third World. By introducing modest loans of only a few dollars to Bangladesh women, the Grameen bank has been able to help them create small businesses that make them financially independent (Fuglesang and Chandler 1988). In 1990, *Time* magazine celebrated the tenth anniversary of Women's World Banking, which provides small amounts of credit to women in several countries. We may be seeing a new kind of revolution—and a totally new position of women in the developing world.

Anthropologists can, just as importantly, help to make business people aware of their own cultural blinkers. Business people in foreign countries have to learn just how the simplistic stereotypes that some Westerners have of non-Westerners (or that one social class has of another) are often bad for business. By making business people examine their own ethnocentrism (which, if not examined, can lead to their isolation and hence to poor judgments and decisions), they can bring firms into closer association with the views and needs of employees, customers, and competitors.

15-10. Employees of foreign firms, as well as Americans and their families going to work abroad, profit from anthropological training and insight about cultural differences, how to detect them, how to adapt to them and live with them.

Thus, anthropologists are of greatest use to business in doing what they do better than anyone else: qualitative studies of culture and of social groups. But they also add other research techniques and communications skills, including statistics (the more essential when dealing with large societies), computers (new ways of programming qualitative cultural factors are being introduced), and interviewing (a skill that far supersedes just talking to somebody and asking them questions).

Business anthropologists have to work quickly, often with less than perfect data. They have to use their ingenuity and their knowledge of culture to come up with suggestions. Therefore, anthropological generalists are better business anthropologists than are narrow specialists. Exciting careers with good pay, lots of opportunity to travel and live abroad, and wide experience of life in the world can be carved out in business anthropology.

Exciting anthropological careers can also be found in education, in government service or international civil service, and in many other areas. Practicing anthropologists can be found almost any place. Pioneering careers can be built by creative anthropologists who apply anthropology to many areas of modern life where its impact has not yet been felt. The anthropological attitude is a people-centered way of looking at the world. Anthropological ideas illuminate almost every situation.

VISIONARY ANTHROPOLOGY TODAY

Visionary anthropology comprehends at least three major tasks:

• looking at the reality of the here and now by turning the skills and techniques we use for looking at exotic societies onto our own society

- finding ways to anticipate how today's pressures may shape the future
- creating policy for a successful future—how do you get there from here?

For people to perceive changing meanings of social and cultural situations going on around them is almost as difficult as anticipating the society and culture of the future. The boundary between the poorly understood present and the unknowable future is not always clear.

15-11. One major task in anthropology is perceiving the emerging culture and social structure in its own terms rather than in terms of past cultural ideas.

Culture change is sweeping in its breadth and intensity. We are, right now, living on a cusp between the Industrial Age and something else—the next great cultural era. The changes that are brewing are far more elemental than what is tritely called the "postindustrial era." The victories of communication in the immediate past are only curtain raisers for others that are coming. One-way communication—television—covers the world. By the late 1990s, cellular telephones will create efficient and instant two-way communication reaching into every corner of the globe. They will link any two people, from anywhere to anywhere on the globe, using a network of seventy-seven satellites. That means that we will have the possibility not only of a worldwide mass audience but also of total social contact throughout the globe. Just as you cannot get any faster than "instantaneous," you cannot get more inclusive than "everybody."

Moreover, if in the next two or three centuries, we actually succeed in conquering space—conquer in the sense of achievement, not the sense of vanquishment—we will have at our fingertips the immense resources that lie beyond our planet. (And the immense responsibility to avoid raping the universe.) Surely that will be as momentous a change as our animal ancestors emerging from the sea onto dry land. At the moment, the cost of space exploration seems prohibitive to the American taxpayer—but then, the cost of Columbus' voyages seemed prohibitive to Queen Isabella. Americans and Soviets seem to be joining forces to get to Mars. We are living on the cusp of a culture crest.

Prediction and Chaos

Prediction in the human sciences is far more intricate than in the natural sciences. We have noted that if you hold conditions absolutely constant—that is, if there is no change in context—a chemical reaction will run the same way every time. In social science it is utterly impossible to hold conditions constant. The context is slightly different each time an act is repeated. Social science, including anthropology, thus does not have the luxury of repeatable circumstances.

Human beings do indeed repeat cycles and trajectories—until change of context brings us to a point of discomfort, whereupon we change to new cycles and trajectories. Even such apparently simple changes as size of the social group or duration of a process make an immense difference. Take an analogy: a human being twice the size of you and your friends, if all the proportions of the body were kept the same, would collapse because the skeleton could not support the weight (Gleick 1987). The same kind of thing occurs with the scale of social groups. A kinship system that is perfectly adequate for a group of fifty thousand people no longer works if it is applied to a society of five hundred thousand. Hierarchies and bureaucracies allowed for the emergence of the state and the business firm, but today we have to ask whether global society has not reached a scale in which bureaucracies are not useful globally, no matter that they will continue to be useful in business firms and perhaps in local governments. Mass audiences and huge single-interest networks held together by modern media cannot happen in small-scale societies—they are in fact adjustments to size of village factions, and they are emerging as social scale grows more grandiose.

Such facts do not necessarily imply that social sciences are inadequately developed (although that may be the case) but, rather that we are unsure about what prediction in social science *ought* to be in the face of constantly changing contexts. As contexts change, the number of causes behind each effect becomes so immense as to approach chaos. An effect is itself one link in a process that the scientist has picked out of a more inclusive social chain. Physicists have the same problem when they study particles, although particles are neither creative nor stubborn about the way they move. But people are. Human action—based as it is on feedback, creativity, and adaptation to environment—can always find new and original ways to behave in order to resolve persistent problems. That built-in originality will outwit any social or cultural analyst who tries simple prediction.

15-12. The most successful human characteristic in the struggle to adapt to the environment and to new cultural situations is originality of responses. It is the same characteristic that makes prediction in the social sciences almost impossible.

Indeed, originality in adaptation is what human behavior is all about. Creativity, even in the smallest matters, keeps the context of everything in constant change. If people did not invent unpredictable ways of doing things, the species could not prosper. Political systems like dictatorships that attempt to undercut that originality so that human behavior can be made totally predictable always fail.

The chains of cause and effect that social scientists must consider are so complex, and human will (not to say stubbornness) so pervasive, and equifinality (the situation in which different processes lead to the same outcome) so ubiquitous, that to examine prediction in social science means taking a whole new look at just what we mean by prediction.

Prediction and foretelling the future are not the same thing. Scientific prediction works only in specific circumstances, which are precise and limited—that is, in social science terms, when the context doesn't change. But when the number of variables is increased, the many causes begin interacting with one another so that something new and strange happens. Again, analogy is helpful: in the 1950s, it was assumed that weather prediction would soon be a reality—perhaps even weather control. Then scientists learned enough about weather to realize that weather approaches, and then topples into, what is (from a predictive point of view) a state of chaos. Chaos, by definition, is utter unpredictability. Yet, even amid chaos, observable regularities appear, then disappear. Who knows if or when they will reappear? The regularities have no stability. They are there—and then they are gone again. They may reappear; they may not. Although such regular patterns of short-lived stability within chaos have now been mathematically defined (Gleick 1987), our capacity to predict them is not merely limited, it is seriously skewed.

Obviously, then, because so many social and cultural situations are even more complex than the weather, the challenge is daunting. Every time a social scientist changes focus from one culture to another, all the basic assumptions must be reexamined. Generalizations are well and good, and may even be enlightening about the way human beings and human society work. Few generalizations can be used for predicting or even understanding societies other than those for which they were made—subtle differences in the context assure that the total situation is different in the new situation.

To a degree, we *can* predict statistically the outcomes of behavior that lead to gross population growth or consumption patterns—*but* only as long as all the contextual factors are held constant. The moment there is a change in any factors that influence personal behavior, prediction falters and fails. Predicting employment rates or marriage rates or gross national income—all of them are only as good as the premises of people whose behavior influences those rates, and social premises cannot be made to sit still.

It is trite to say that we cannot predict the future. It is nevertheless good for us to know that one reason we cannot is that the adaptive capacity of choice-making has been built into human beings in the course of evolution. It is our glory—and the agony of social science—that, no matter what is predicted, some willful person will insist on doing it *his* way or *her* way. Faced with either new challenges or even with the same old challenges, persons (in their individuality) come up with new and different responses.

Anthropology *can*, however, say something about the future. People, making their choices, are creating the future every day. We can watch them doing it. Individuals set themselves specific goals using some combination of their cultural values and their personal discomforts. They can tell you what is likely to happen if their goals are successful. At

the very least they can tell you what they *want* to happen—what they are trying to achieve. They can make some educated guesses about what their success in one particular cultural dimension might do to the rest of the culture. For example, executives in computer companies give a lot of thought to what their new products are likely to do to society and culture. Sometimes their guesses turn out to be wildly off the mark, but sometimes they are right on. They think about the future and plan for it, no matter how different actual events may turn out to be from what they expected.

15-13. Statistically, some broad assumptions about the future are warranted, especially in the fields of production, distribution and consumption, in demography, and perhaps in other fields as well. However, changes in the context of any of these activities can hopelessly alter what people will do and, hence, instantly falsify the assumed data on which the predictions were made.

Anthropologists, thus, *can* determine what people *think* is going to happen. We can do what Textor (1980) has called "ethnographic futures research." We can gather quite clear ideas about what people think they will have to do to deal with the emerging global situation.

To sum up, the parts of the future that are *not* open to us result from the fact that human ingenuity—and the weather—are eternally bringing something out of left field. People may well not react to future culture the way we determine they might or ought, no matter how impeccable our methods. *That* is the difficult point.

Ethnographic futures research is *not* prediction in the sense of foretelling specific events—that is, it is not fortune-telling. However, we can make postulates about possible futures (Ketudat 1990). We know enough about culture and how it works to be able, sometimes, to point out the places where change is most likely to occur, and perhaps some of the possibilities of new or changed institutions. If we focus on social traps, and try to create ways of recognizing them and avoiding them, we are building a more secure future.

Two social traps lie concealed here, of which we must be constantly wary. First of all, all postulates about possible futures are running postulates: every postulate that is made

---

15-14. Anthropologists can, by techniques known as ethnographic futures research, ask leaders of every field, in any society, what they think their current activities will achieve and what kind of cultural changes may result. Insights about the future gained in this way can often expose social traps or faulty premises, and can suggest questions that allow us to be more perspicacious in our planning.

---

will lead to new arguments and new contexts. Some people will take the postulates of social scientists (or anybody else) about any possible futures and, using that information, work to change the situation so that the social scientist is wrong. The social scientists must stay on their toes, taking the newly created context into consideration and must constantly update their ideas. For example, if social scientists were to postulate that increased private ownership of handguns would result in more needless deaths, people who are in favor of handguns would reach out to counter that argument: they would probably continue to talk about the value of self-reliance, about the constitutional guarantee of the right to bear arms—but would quickly then add new ideas that they had thought of only as a result of the social scientists' postulates. Any postulate based on information can readily and easily be countered with ideology!

The second trap lies in one of our major virtues: being systematically taught that it is part of our democratic heritage to think for ourselves. People cannot, therefore, be blamed for thinking for themselves even on subjects they don't know anything about. The fact that professional musicians know more about music than I do does not deny me the right to opinions about music. My lack of information *would*, however, preclude my formulating good research or reliable policy. In short, all of us, but especially researchers and policymakers, must carefully examine our premises before we do research or formulate policy—or even form our own opinions.

Policy Science

Policy *science* is a means of bringing everything that social scientists, and all other scientists, know about a situation together into an orderly presentation so that policy*makers* can choose among options. It is certainly not a precise science, and probably never will be, any more than diplomacy is a precise art.

In the best of all possible worlds, policy scientists will have brought together knowledge of social processes and social structures, knowledge of cultural values, and knowledge of peoples' goals. They will use simulation to extend the processes they are investigating, showing some of the things that *might* happen if such and such variables were to be inserted into the system. And they will create early-warning systems for social traps.

Policy *scientists* should be scientists. Except for their science values, their ideologies and convictions should be kept at bay. We know that is probably not fully possible, but it may be possible to put together teams in which one member can detect warping caused by the value orientations and ideologies of others. The trick is, of course, to get the ideologist to accept the limitations of his ideology.

The ideology, then, is inserted by the policy*makers*—statesmen. Their convictions and purposes become vital and decisive. Putting both—the policy science and action to create policy—under one skull may be close to impossible. It may be that two roles working together are required, like the two people—visionary and impresario—who so often turn up linked in successful religious movements.

Where Does Science Fiction Start?

The boundary between visionary anthropology that comprehends culture change and process on the one hand and science fiction on the other is a fuzzy one. Yet, settlement in space—until a few years ago, the prerogative of science fiction—is already a fact. Settlements in space may be the turning point of the new culture crest. The first such settlement was built in 1971, when the Soviet Union sent

We *homo sapiens* are by nature wanderers, the inheritors of an exploring and colonizing bent that is deeply embedded in our evolutionary past. . . . We invent tools and devices that enable us to spread into areas for which we are not biologically adapted. . . . The first 'giant leap for mankind' . . . was the descent from the sheltering trees of the tropical forest to the open grassland-woodland environment of the savanna . . . [which were] literally the first steps toward mankind, for they were made on two legs instead of four. This postural revolution left the forelimbs free to make and manipulate tools, to carry babies, food, and other goods and to perform a myriad of tasks. . . . Today, because of continued economic and technological growth, we stand on the threshold of space. . . . Our exploratory bent will be as crucial to our future evolution as it was to our past development. If the technology of space colonization really works, if our descendants do settle throughout the Solar System and then migrate to other star systems, humanity will never be the same again. . . .

Ben R. Finney and Eric M. Jones (1985)

THEY SAID IT

15-15. *As a rule, the best policy decisions are those made on the basis of the best data and the best theories for organizing that data. The most dire traps for policymakers are: (1) ideologies and "isms" to which policymakers have a loyalty, which may create blind spots, (2) incapacity to question cultural axioms and premises, (3) psychic and cultural rigidity, and (4) difficulties in face-saving—of turning back from an intended goal once it has been rendered foolish or futile. You can undoubtedly add other traps.*

aloft the first of seven space stations called Salyut. Two years later, the United States orbited its first space lab.

The crews aboard the Salyut station have included cosmonauts not only from the USSR, but also from East Germany, France, Poland, Czechoslovakia, Bulgaria, Vietnam, Hungary, Cuba, Mongolia, Rumania, and India (Foulkes 1988). This anthropologist cannot help wondering how the cross-cultural communication went.

Cultural growth and change, great as they will be, may not be what astonishes us most about space settlement. Biological evolution may suddenly take a spurt. It is well-known today that biological evolution proceeds not slowly and smoothly through long periods of time, but rather in sudden spurts, as small groups split off from an ancestral stock. Within these small populations, new forms of the species can appear suddenly. Genetic mutations are held in check when they are swamped by huge breeding populations. In isolation, genetic changes can spread rapidly. As such small interbreeding groups scatter first through the solar system and then beyond it to other star systems, new species of human beings will be created.

15-17. *Taking up residence in space has already begun. It will surely continue. Problems of organization in manufactured space environments or environments on the moon or on asteroids or other planets will present what are now unimaginable social problems—undoubtedly even greater problems than the technological ones. These Soviet men were photographed in the Salyut space station in 1978.*

15-16. *These figures summarizing human evolution are almost the anthropological logo. Living in space may create immense and rapid changes in biological evolution, allowing us to put another figure on the right of modern man. Certainly it will create unknowable developments in cultural evolution.*

Although there may be bases on the moon and on Mars, most new space settlements may not be on the surface of other planets, but rather in immense artificially constructed environments created by man—space habitats. The Salyuts and the space labs are to forthcoming living and working environments what the Wright brothers' biplane is to the space shuttle. The environments can be created with landscapes much like those of Earth; they will have gravity created by spinning the structure.

These new space colonies will have to be governed. The people who today are planning space colonies are paying almost no attention to the culture that will be required to do that. Very little planning is given to how families or governments will grow and develop as the colonies are built and as they become a normal part of human life. The planners

are allowing themselves to hide behind such statements as, "Astronauts are professionals; they will do what is expected of them." Perhaps. But what is to be expected of them? This anthropologist doubts that any training is strong enough to withstand the human need to create new kinds of cultural adjustment when it is required. Space pioneers will thus, of necessity, create culture as they go. The planners—insofar as they have considered social problems at all—have fallen into social traps of viewing future society as if it were like the past.

Human beings will carry into space the same kind of prejudices that beset their earthly pursuits. Yet old forms of government will not work in space any more than Old World forms of government worked in the New World. The future governments in space will take off from premises and principles that the people take with them, but they also will adjust to the problems that the new environments and the new societies create.

The impact of space settlements on our life on Earth may well be so great that we cannot even imagine it. Space manufacturing could, in the views of some planetary scientists, clean up the environment and turn Earth into a veritable paradise. We already know how to provide unlimited solar energy for the Earth by deploying the right kind of technology in space. There are technical problems, but today's culture is good at solving technical problems—it is the human social prejudices that create the hard problems.

The impact of space settlement on medicine, recreation, and nationalism will be immense, even if we cannot yet see clearly what it will be. People who are now in school will probably live to see some of the early phases of such change: and they must learn to make whatever adjustments are called for as the emerging situation becomes clearer.

In this process, global culture is likely to expand. But at the same time, small-scale cultures will be turned loose on all those aspects of human life that are irrelevant at the global level. A universal world culture focused on utilization of the unlimited resources of space *could* make the world safe for

15-18. Human beings will carry into space the same disabilities and prejudices that beset their earthly pursuits. These prejudices will affect government family, science, religion—everything. The only way to deal with them is to understand that we have them and to learn to recognize them. We need an early-detection and early-warning system for social traps.

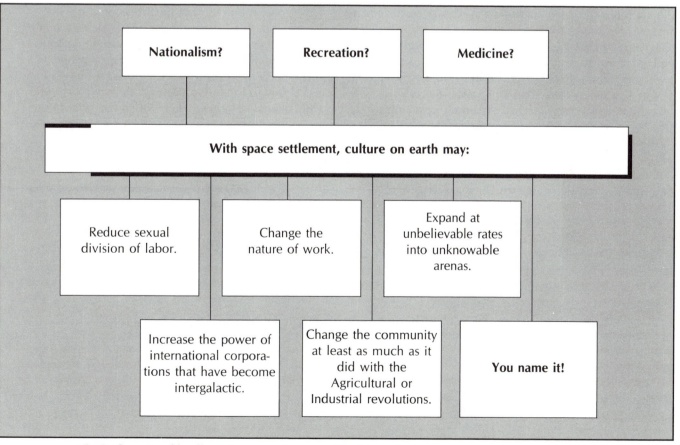

15-19. Some possible effects of space settlement on Earth-bound cultures.

all the specialized cultural differences we would ever be able to think of.

The nature of work will change even more than it already has. The nature of our communities will change, as it did at the time of the Agricultural Revolution and again at the time of the Industrial Revolution. New communities have already been created by telephone and computer. Computer networks are emerging as special-purpose communities. The general-purpose community in which our ancestors—sometimes our grandparents—lived will continue to fade; the people with whom we have most in common and with whom we do most of our business are not our neighbors now. The meaning of "community" and "neighbor" in the space stations can only be guessed.

International—interplanetary, ultimately intergalactic?—corporations and their successors are likely to become more powerful—perhaps as powerful as states (which may or may not survive in the form we know them). This change will speed up as we recognize more and more ecological and cultural problems as global problems.

The division of labor between the sexes may almost disappear, but it may merely change yet again. Families always change and will certainly continue to do so.

Audience, the newly important social form, will almost surely become even more important. Being part of a mass audience will conjoin the people in the new satellite societies and those who are living new kinds of lives on Earth. We now have far more information than people did in the past. Almost surely the communication and personal participation we now have will be child's play compared to what will come. The number of special-purpose cultures sharing world cultures will increase. It may mean that we will get less of our information through social interaction and more as recipients of one-way communications. But worldwide television is being joined by cheap worldwide two-way communication, first by telephone, so it may not mean that at all.

Music and art have already become more and more available to mass audiences. The music of many centuries and many cultures is generally available on compact discs and tapes. Artistic statement has always been social

commentary. What happens in a world in which the statements are based on wide experience of many cultures or in which the audience is a vital part of an intercommunicating global society?

CONCLUDING THOUGHTS

Never has a generation lived at such an exciting time! It is also true, of course, that no former generation has borne the sense of weightlessness that comes from having so many options. Never before have people paid the price of so much freedom. But these options will, if we choose well, lead to a culture so immensely rewarding that we cannot yet contemplate it.

But beware: throughout this book we have seen that humankind can use culture to its own detriment as well as to its benefit. What if culture itself is a social trap?

 Homo sapiens has . . . made of misery itself an evolutionary force; it is the misery man himself creates that urges him up the evolutionary tree. We perceive that *Homo sapiens* has all the capacity to extort new adaptations from his suffering, and that if he does not destroy himself too soon, he may eventually come upon a destiny of great beauty. I say 'may' instead of 'will' because of *Homo sapiens*'s well-known capacity—from bow and arrow to atomic nuclear—to use his discoveries against himself. . . . The capacity to use his culture against himself may yet overtake man and destroy him while he works on his ultimate problem—learning to live with himself.

Jules Henry (1963)

THEY SAID IT

Concluding Thoughts

WHAT EVERY EDUCATED PERSON SHOULD KNOW ABOUT ANTHROPOLOGY

A number of basic anthropological ideas can help us to understand the present human condition and to build the cultural future of humankind. There are many more of these ideas than can be put into any short summary—indeed, forming your own list is probably the best way both to review this course and to plan your future work life. What we give here can only be a start.

Anthropology studies cultures of all sorts. It is just as capable of analyzing modern cultures as primitive ones, being especially apt at ethnography, which is a way of understanding, analyzing, and preserving the way in which a given group of people think about their problems and their lives. Ethnography is achieved by a whole set of methods, of which participant observation is central. It is the anthropological position that ethnography is a preliminary to all other methods in social research.

☐ Anthropology provides us with stereoscopic vision about social and cultural matters. That is to say, it allows us not only to admit that there are many ways to do things, but it can put several of them into focus at once. The "comparative attitude" in anthropology is the best known device for overcoming ethnocentrism.

☐ Anthropology allows us to look at current cultural situations without the blinders that being monocultural puts on a person. It gives us a place to stand while we examine all the options. For this reason, anthropologists are of great help in detecting cultural misunderstandings and miscommunication, and in figuring out what is in fact occurring in our own time.

☐ Anthropology gives us both courage and method to look at alternative futures.

Human beings are mammals who have specialized in culture as their basic mode of adaptation to the environment. This idea has some important consequences:

☐ If we compare social sciences to the biophysical sciences in our quest to be scientific, the analogy should be to biology, not to physics.

☐ Culture is composed fundamentally of technological and social tools (which depend on brainpower and on eye-hand coordination) and meanings (which arise from the human capacity to use symbols, including, but not limited to, language).

☐ All human animal behavior is culturized. When we superadd culture to our behavior, the animal dimension is given expanded options, but does not disappear. People create cultural definitions of efficiency, correctness, and appropriateness to guide the way they carry out their animal behavior.

☐ Changes in the animal dimension of the human species follow the rules of biological evolution, exactly as do biological changes in any other animal species. Changes in the cultural dimension also follow evolutionary rules, although the rate of change can be very much faster. Biological and cultural evolution conjoin to create a single force.

☐ One of the basic distinctions is that between male and female. People may have considerable difficulty distinguishing gender attributes, which are cultural, from biological attributes of the two sexes.

Social organization can be considered a set of tools. Kinship is one fundamental organizational tool. Because we are mammals, the mother-child bond is the most important single relationship in human life. Extension of kinship to include the father is rare to nonexistent among other mammals; investing the father-child relationship with purpose and meaning is an early victory of human culture. Extension of kinfolk recognition to kinfolk beyond the parent-child relationships is the basis of several fundamental social groups.

☐ The human family is a unique organization for mating and rearing the young to the age of reproduction.

☐ The human family can, in very small societies, satisfy all organizational requirements. As the society gets larger, specialist groups occur to take over tasks that the human family cannot adequately perform in large groups. Although the number of tasks that are culturally assigned to a family may be reduced, families remain important social units even in large and highly complex human cultures. For the family to disappear, it would be necessary to find specialist groups for every social task, including the rearing of the young. Because the family is such a highly efficient group, this step seems unlikely to occur.

☐ Specific kinship relationships, especially the descent relationships of mother-child and father-child, can be used to form the basis of specialist groups that still keep the amity and trust of kinship. These specialist groups, such as lineages and clans, can perform economic, political and religious tasks in groups that are too large for the family alone to do them. They disappear when societies reach larger scale.

Another set of tools of social organization center on the use and control of power, which is the capacity to alter environmental conditions or personal behavior of others. The simplest power group is the band—an arrangement for cooperation as well as for control and exploitation of the environment—where it is often conjoined with kinship. The band is an arrangement of power (including equality and sharing) among people. As population size and cultural complexity increase, more specialized institutions appear.

☐ Human beings, like all other animals, must wring a living from the environment in which they live. Technological tools as well as social tools assist in that task. Division of work between the sexes is one of the primary means for organizing society. Other specialist groups, from hunting groups to modern corporations, also perform these tasks.

☐ Human beings, in their quest for adequate resources to maintain life and culture, sometimes fall into disputes. Power must sometimes be used to resolve such disputes. Dispute resolution is an essential dimension of human life; it can take many cultural forms which may, but may not, have something to do with modern ideas of justice. An organization is as good as its mechanisms for resolving disputes.

☐ Government—the maintenance of order and security among the people who live in a specific area—is, among small-scale societies, done by the family or the band. Whenever societies get so large that the family and band can no longer handle these problems, specialized organizations of government like the state appear. The specialized organizations may, however, become social traps.

☐ In the processes of cultural evolution, as power is controlled and used in larger and larger groups, distinctions of rank appear. Indeed, the power distinctions that underlie specialized institutions of government themselves create significant power inequalities. Any idea of inequality can be expanded to the point of absurdity. These distinctions simplify social life, but may also provide the basis for some of the most pervasive of social traps.

Meaning results from the human capacity for symbolizing. We have, using that skill, been able to develop language and art. From that base, we have come to explain the natural world in scientific terms and to postulate a divine world in religious terms. Religion is not only a mode of explanation, but is also an immense reservoir of psychological comfort.

Culture works by means of repetitive cycles, action chains, and trajectories. It (like biological evolutionary forces) is likely to lead us into culture traps. The most important skill we can develop in planning for the future is learning to spot and avoid culture traps.

Go ahead. Prepare your own list of anthropological insights—or any other insights that make life more predictable and more rewarding. It is the human way. If anything seems uncomfortable or inefficient, put your mind to it. Fix it!

Glossary

There were several bases for including definitions in this glossary. First, the names of fields of study are included, as are technical terms in anthropology (a large number of which come from the area of kinship). Words in the general English vocabulary to which anthropologists nevertheless give a special meaning are included. Words that can be found in any good dictionary, to which anthropologists do not give special meaning, are not included.

action chain a series of acts that must be performed in the right order if any of the acts are to be effective.

adjudicate to decide or settle according to the law.

adoption the practice of granting a person (most often a child) a legal kinship position which, by biological descent, is not accurate.

aesthetic a philosophy or point of view about art and the way it is made. In the plural, aesthetics refers to a philosophy of the beautiful (as contrasted with the useful or the scientific).

affine a person to whom one is related through marriage.

aggression a threat of attack by one animal toward another. Aggression is, in ethology, anthropology and psychoanalysis, the response to adrenaline which makes it possible for a creature to press its own demands in order to survive. In the ordinary language it means the first step toward a conflict, and is often confused with conflict.

agnatic pertaining to the male. A parent-child relationship is agnatic if the parent is male.

agonistic behavior the aggression-based behavior among animals that creates social structures.

agriculture the science or art of cultivating the soil. However, anthropologists give additional meanings to the term. When contrasted with horticulture, agriculture means growing crops with the aid of the plow.

animism an attributed form of religion, made up by anthropologists because some people assign characteristics of living persons to animals, nonliving things or phenomena such as rivers and rocks. Animists do indeed hold such beliefs but do not form them into "religions."

anthropology the study of humankind. The word was derived from the Greek words for the study (logos) of human beings (anthropos). It was used before the year 1600 in philosophy and history, but got its present meaning only in about 1870.

Aranda one of the earliest groups of Australian aborigines to be studied.

arbitration settlement of a dispute by a neutral party or group agreed to by the principal of the dispute.

archaeology the study of prehistorical or historical culture by examining the remains of that culture and the people who lived it.

ascendant any person from whom one is descended.

ascription the act of assigning qualities or roles to persons. The opposite is "achieved" to describe qualities or roles that persons earn.

Ashanti a large African kingdom in what is now Ghana. Ashanti had powerful armies in the nineteenth century; the Ashanti War with Great Britain was a difficult victory. We are fortunate that they were studied by one of the finest of early twentieth-century ethnographers, R. S. Rattray. Today the Ashanti like to be called Asante.

avunculocal the couple lives with the groom's mother's brother. This occurs only in matrilineal societies.

Azande live on the boundary between Sudan and Zaire, near Uganda. They are a set of kingdoms to which E. E. Evans-Pritchard devoted much of his working life, beginning study of them in the 1920s, writing about them as late as 1960.

Aztecs the culture of the ruling group in central Mexico at the time of the Spanish invasion. Aztec culture is among the dominant Native American cultures underlying the formation of modern Mexican culture.

band a group of families who live together. In most bands, the families are related by kinship, and in most there is also a hierarchy among the males.

Bedouin Arab of Cyrenaica a set of tribal groups living in the Mediterranean littoral of Libya, near the Egyptian border. Evans-Pritchard began the study of this group just at the end of World War II. Emrys Peters followed him and spent thirty years studying this group.

bicentric a political situation or system in which there are two centers of power. The creative tension between the legislative branch and the executive branch in American government is a case in point. All disputes and all international agreements are bicentric.

bifurcate forked, or divided into two branches. It is used in anthropology only, as far as I know, in describing kinship terminologies, and specifically in "bifurcate merging," where some kin from one fork are amalgamated with some kin of the other fork.

big man a leader whose entire power comes from his or her personal characteristics and charisma.

bilocal the couple lives with the parents of either the bride or the groom.

bridewealth the amount paid by the groom's kinsmen for

rights in a bride—they may include rights to her labor, sexual rights, and rights to filiate her children to the groom's kinship group.

broker   a person who acts as a middleman (or woman) in negotiating bargains, sales; a middleman who knows two cultures and represents persons who know only one of the cultures when they interact with persons of the other culture.

bureaucracy   a hierarchical structure of roles to administer power within a government or a firm.

capitalism   an economic system in which land and resources are owned by individuals, and in which those two as well as labor, risk, and even money itself are controlled by the market mechanism of supply and demand. Another way to put it is that work, resources, land, managerial skill and risk-taking have all been turned into commodities, which means they can be evaluated in terms of money.

caste   a hierarchy of social groups. The most typical example is the caste system of preindependence India, in which the social groups were kinship groups, and the ranking was done on the basis of the principles of purity held by Hindus. Using the word in other contexts almost always results in oversimplification that blurs distinctions that can be otherwise made more effectively.

Cherokee   one of the largest of Native American groups, it was split by government action. Some Cherokee today live in the Carolinas, others in Oklahoma.

clan   a descent group, either agnatic or uterine, whose members do not postulate a known and exact genealogy of descent from the common ancestor or ancestress.

class   hierarchy of cultural items and of the people who have access to or control of them. A class is a group of people who share cultural characteristics and have approximately the same rank in society.

classificatory   anthropological term for the practice of categorizing several types of kin under a single term—especially if the resultant categories include both lineal and nonlineal kin.

cognatic group   a kinship group made up solely of cognatic kinspersons.

collateral   a person with whom one shares ascendant kin, but from whom one is not descended.

colonialism   a policy or practice of any nation that holds colonies, especially when that policy involves economic exploitation of the colonized peoples.

Comanche   the prototype of a warrior society, this Native American group was powerful in the southern Great Plains in the late nineteenth century. Today's Comanches live in Oklahoma.

community   traditionally, a group of people held together by two specific bonds: the bond of common locality and the bond of shared interest. In the Industrial Age, the word is often applied to a group of people who share a common interest, regardless of their residence.

componential   an adjective referring to analysis of a complex situation into its components. A component is any essential part of the complex situation.

conflict   a disagreement, dispute, quarrel, struggle, or fight between two parties. If more parties are involved, they almost always form two sides.

consanguine   literally "common blood" in Latin. Used to refer to all kin except affines.

corporation   a number of persons (individuals or groups) united as one legal person. The most commonly found corporations today are joint-stock companies, in which every person or group who owns shares is a member of the corporation; however, the corporation has a legal identity separate from that of any of its owners.

correction   the result of a successful counteraction—either the original breach of norm is erased by correct behavior or else a price is levied for the incorrect behavior.

counteraction   any action taken at the time a norm is broken. The purpose is to counter the original action.

courtship   an old-fashioned word that means what men do to "win" their brides. When the word was first used, women were not supposed to do anything except resist. Today anthropologists use the word for any traditional way in which women and men find each other.

couvade   the institutionalization of a fiction that a father shares the burdens, symptoms, and rewards of bearing a child.

cross cousin   offspring of opposite sex siblings are cross cousins.

cult   this word has several meanings. On the one hand, it applies to an organization that conducts ritual or religious observations. It may also refer to a religious group that is out of step with the major religions of the society but attracts people searching for security, comfort and predictability. Finally, it may apply to religious movements that emerge to deal with situations of cultural contact.

cultural anthropology   starts from the fact that human beings are tool-using animals who assign meaning to their acts as well as to their bodies. It concerns itself with the toolkits and meanings that peoples have developed.

cultural dissonance   a situation in which a person knows enough about two different cultures to experience them as contradictory, but not enough to solve the contradiction.

cultural evolution   a series of situations in which changes in cultural activity have become so pronounced that it is impossible to return to earlier cultural or social forms. Seen from this standpoint, all culture grows out of earlier situations. The story of cultural evolution is a series of such steps.

culture   the capacity to use tools and symbols.

culture crest   the point at which small culture changes suddenly become sufficiently strong to make an immense impact, heading the cultural process in new directions.

culture pool   all the culture available to a group of people.

cycle   an action chain in which the last act leads back to the first so that the whole chain is repeated.

descent   kinship from ancestors.

Dinka   a Nilotic group in the southern Sudan. They were once an important herding people, but have suffered dismally and their numbers were greatly reduced by the famines that swept the Sahel area and parts of the Horn of Africa in the 1970s and 1980s.

display behavior dominance behavior, specifically the behavior of male animals who are attempting to scare off rivals who are challenging their position in the social hierarchy.

diffusion spreading of culture over wider geographical areas, especially from the place of invention to new areas, where it may be used in ways very different from those in the places where it was invented.

divination telling the unknown or foretelling the future by omens or prophecy that taps information beyond that known to ordinary people.

divorce the undoing of a marriage. It may be done by legal, financial, religious or other means. After a divorce, the marriage no longer exists but is acknowledged once to have existed. It differs from *annulment* which creates a fiction that the marriage never existed in the first place.

dominance refers to positions in a hierarchy. The dominant animal or person is the one at the top: that means he or she can dominate the other animals in the hierarchy.

double descent both the matrilineal group and the patrilineal group are recognized, but are assigned different purposes.

dowry the property that a woman brings with her at the time of marriage. The dowry usually passes to the husband. If the property remains hers, it is called a dot (pronounced doh).

dyad a group of two.

ecology the science that studies the ways in which all living things adapt to one another and to the nonliving part of their environment.

economy a system for managing the production, distribution, and consumption of goods and services.

ego means "I" in Latin. However, in anthropological studies of kinship it refers to the person on whom a genealogy centers. The ego may be a living individual, with ascendants, descendants, and collaterals showing, or it may be an ancestral figure from whom many persons are descended.

enculturation the process by means of which a person learns culture. The word is commonly used in association with "socialization," the process by which a child is, by learning culture, turned into a practicing member of the society.

entrepreneur the person who organizes and manages a business or industrial enterprise, who takes the risk of not making a profit, and who gets the profit when there is one.

environment all of the surrounding conditions and influences that affect the adjustment of living organisms. All of the cultural context into which any specific cultural act is set and by which it is evaluated.

Eskimo the people who inhabit the treeless plain in the very north of the North American and Eurasian continents, and islands such as Greenland. Their numbers had always been only a few thousand. Today most are integrated into the economies and societies of Alaska and Canada.

estate one of the basic ranks in European feudal systems. (The word also has many other meanings, but this is the technical meaning of the term as used in this book.)

ethnic having to do with a particular group of people who share a cultural tradition.

ethnicity identity with or membership in a particular cultural group all of whose members share language, beliefs, customs, values and identity.

ethnocentrism the emotional attitude, whether conscious or unconscious, that regards one's own group and its culture the measure by which all others should be judged.

ethnography the study of a single people and their culture.

ethnoscience a technique of field research that elicits the way in which people themselves picture the organization of their ideas and activities.

ethology the study of characteristic behavior patterns of animals.

event chain a series of events that must occur in the right order.

evolution a process of development or growth through an ongoing accumulation of small changes. Biological evolution deals with changes in the body; cultural evolution deals with changes in tools and meaning.

exogamy the practice forbidding two members of the same kinship group (or, occasionally, some other group) to marry one another. Its opposite is *endogamy*, is the practice that requires that people marry within the kinship group.

extended family a family that includes three or more generations and includes all members of the family back to a single couple (or, in cases of polygyny, a single male), and extends along all lines.

family a woman and her children; most commonly at least one adult male is added. Most commonly that male is the woman's husband, and ideally the father of her children.

femininity the cultural attributes assigned to women. They differ from one society to another, but are almost everywhere associated with maternal behavior and householding.

feud a long, often deadly, conflict between two parties in which there is no way to reach a solution.

feudal system or **feudalism** in Medieval Europe, a system of land and status hierarchies in which the lords "owned" the land, but vassals (yeomen and peasants and some others, depending on the period and the country) also had rights to that land, under the aegis of the lord and owed military service to him.

fictive fictional. Fictive kinship is any use of kinship terms or practices applied to persons who are not biologically related.

flowchart a chart illustrating an action chain or an event chain. The important point in a flowchart is the way in which one act or event in the chain leads to the next.

folklore the traditional beliefs, myths, legends, stories and customs of a people.

fosterage rearing or bringing up a child. The word applies to one's own children, to adoptive children, and to children who are taken in for rearing in foster homes.

fraternal   pertaining to brothers.

gender   the collection of attributes said to be associated with one sex or the other. Gender is a cultural matter, as compared with sex which is a biological matter.

generation   all the people born during a fairly short period of time. Parents and children are of different generations—indeed, lineal kinfolk are necessarily of different generations.

genetics   the branch of biology that studies the principles of heredity and variation in plants and in animals, including human beings.

Gisu   a people who live on the slopes of Mount Elgon, which lies on the boundary between Kenya and Uganda.

global society   the emerging society made up of all the peoples of the world, brought together by new communications technology, international business and worldwide environmental problems.

government   the social organization responsible for settling disputes, maintaining order, and protecting society from external aggressors. Modern governments are loaded with many additional functions.

grammar   the scientific classification of the sounds, forms, and meanings employed in a language, and the way they fit together into a system.

grandfamily   a family of three generations. It is smaller than an extended family because it need not include all descendants of the senior generation.

groom service   the work that a man must do for his wife's father before he may claim her as his wife.

groomwealth   the amount paid by the bride's family in exchange for rights in the groom. Although it is rare, it has been found.

hegemony   dominance of one state or nation over others.

hierarchy   a group of persons or animals or things, arranged one above the other by criteria of class, power, office, authority, or any other criterion that leads to such a ranking system.

Hopi   one of the most studied, but in some senses still least known, groups of Native Americans. Their number is small, but their influence on anthropology has been great. They have lived in northern Arizona for many centuries.

horticulture   growing crops by methods of gardening. No plow is used in horticulture.

household   a group of people who live together in a single dwelling or group of dwellings that is considered a unit by the members of the household and their neighbors in other households.

householding   the economic practice by which a household produces everything, or almost everything, that it consumes. Little exchange or trade enters in.

Huichol   Mexican Indians who live in the far outback country of the states of Chihuahua and Sinaloa.

hypothesis   an assumption about what the truth may be. An hypothesis must be tested to determine whether it is in fact true.

ideology   a set of doctrines or body of opinions.

Idoma   a large group just west of the Tiv along the Benue River in Nigeria. Fieldwork among them was carried out in the late 1940s, but nothing was published.

incest   sexual relations between persons who are closely related by kinship. Except for parents and children and full siblings, the degree of kinship that is defined as incestuous changes from one society to the next.

indenture   a contract by which one is bound to work for someone else. Thus, an indentured servant is one who has signed a contract to work for another until such time as the stipulations of the contract have been achieved.

indigenous   originating in the region of the country or of the world in which it is presently found.

industrialism   a system of social and economic organization in which goods are mass produced by groups of large organizations called industries; especially such a system in which the interests of such large industries prevail in political and economic life.

Inis Beag   is the made up name for a small population living on the islands west of Ireland.

international law   obviously, the original meaning is the law that holds between or among different sovereign nations. It is the most informative type of legal situation in a bicentric political situation. International law differs from law within a state in that no specific body can enforce a decision—putting the decision into effect requires both parties.

institution   a group of people united for a purpose who have adequate organization and technology to carry out that purpose, or at least to make a good try at it.

jural descent   the descent of inheritance of property and titles whether or not it follows biological descent.

Kanuri   one of the large emirates of northern Nigeria. They are a Muslim people with an elaborate state organization.

kinship   a cultural interpretation of the genetic relationships among people.

Kwakiutl   a Canadian-American Indian group living on Vancouver Island. This group is of immense interest to anthropology because Franz Boas studied it so thoroughly beginning late in the nineteenth century and continued through the early decades of the twentieth century. Because of the significance of the ethnographic base, it is a favorite group for continued study.

laissez-faire   French for "let them do" ("what they want" without government interference is implied). It is one of the basic principles followed by most capitalist economies; this principle, and that of the market closely allied with it, is everywhere controlled to a greater or lesser degree by governments.

language   a specific example of a system of human speech that is shared by a group who also share other culture and values.

law   a body of rules recognized by a community as binding on its members. Each law must be a guideline for settling disputes or governing conduct. Although rules are found in all societies, law is usually not highly developed in the absence of a state.

legitimate   rightful, lawful, allowed. When used of kinfolk, it means having a complete set of kin on both the father's and the mother's side. Earlier in this century, it was applied to children whose parents were not married.

Lesu   a group of people on the island of New Ireland in Melanesia. Although the early study of Hortense Powdermaker was important, there have been no return studies.

levirate   the institution in which a man is responsible for the wife or wives of his dead brother (or, occasionally, the wives of his father except for his own mother) or other kinsmen. This resembles inheritance of widows except that subsequent children are filiated to the dead husband. In inheritance of widows, subsequent children are filiated to the living heir.

lineage   a group of people who share descent *either* matrilineally *or* patrilineally from a common ancestor to whom the genealogy of all members is claimed to be known.

lineage system   a hierarchal system of lineages. That is to say, lineages descended from brothers are joined because all are descended from those brothers' father.

linguistics   begins with the human capacity to speak; considers the biology of the vocal apparatus as well as speech, language, and the history and development of languages.

Luo   a Nilotic group that is split into two. Some Luo live in Sudan, a southern group in Kenya. Reports on the Luo are numerous, but scattered.

magic   an irrational association of cause and effect.

mana   a Polynesian word for the sacredness said to be characteristic of chiefs, and dangerous to commoners. (Not to be confused with manna, which the book of Exodus tells us was the food supplied to the Israelites in the wilderness.)

manor   the basic community and production unit in the Medieval European feudal system. Rights in the entire manor are owned by the lord. However, some of the yeomen and peasants have rights in the lands of the estate that the lord cannot abrogate. In modern American English the word is often used to designate only the main house; by extension, any large house.

market   two fundamental meanings must not be confused: market exchange is the exchange of goods or services solely on the basis of price determined by supply and demand. Marketplace is a location where goods are bought and sold. Marketplaces may occur in the absence of market exchange.

market principle   the situation in which the free play of supply and demand create the price of any commodity. It is to be distinguished from the marketplace, which is the location where buyers and sellers meet. In capitalist systems, manufactured goods, produce, labor, capital, land and entrepreneurship all enter the same market.

masculinity   the cultural attributes assigned to men. They differ from one culture to another, but are most often concerned with aggression, protection of family and community, and strength.

matelot   the French word for sailor, to which pirates gave special definition of friend, partner, sexual partner; especially the younger, junior, or economically weaker of the two partners.

matricentric family   a woman and her children. Sometimes called the matrifocal family.

matriliny/matrilineal   descended through a series of uterine relationships (see *uterine*).

matrilocal   the couple lives with the parents of the bride.

maximization   getting the greatest possible benefit from any social or economic transaction.

Mehinaku   one of the most thoroughly studied groups in the Amazon Basin in Brazil.

mercantilism   what follows is the word-for-word definition from *The World Book Dictionary*:

> the economic system prevailing in Europe in the 1500s and 1600s, that favored a balance of exports over imports, preferably in a nation's own ships, and through or to its own trading stations or colonies, receiving in return, whenever possible, precious metals, national wealth being measured by the amount of gold or silver possessed. A nation's agriculture, industry, and trade were regulated with that end in view. Mercantilism became dominant as feudalism waned, and the focus of national power shifted from those who owned land to those who controlled money and trade.

midwife   a woman trained to assist in childbirth.

moiety   each of two comparable groups. The word is especially useful if the entire society is divided into two sections.

monogamy   one husband and one wife.

morpheme   the minimal unit of meaning in a language.

multicentric   describes a legal system or situation in which there are several power structures, none subject to the sovereignty of any others.

nativism   an anthropological term for the movements created among colonized peoples, who attempted to revert to their earlier cultural situation.

Navajo   Native American group living in Arizona, New Mexico and Utah. They have an important place in American history and have been studied by many anthropologists and some historians. The literature on the Navajo is immense.

Ndembu   a society in what is today Zambia, made famous by the elaborate studies of their ritual by Victor Turner.

neolocal   the couple establishes a home of their own and does not live with either parent.

network   a meshing of dyadic social relationships, of which the nodes are individual persons or social groups. Networks form because every person (or group) is involved in many relationships with people who often are not in relationships with one another. Information travels rapidly along networks; individual persons can use them for support.

neuroscience   the science that deals with the brain.

niche a place or position in a system of places or positions.

nihilism rejection of belief in religion, laws, government. In Buddhism, it is the idea that there is no reality over time and that everything in the world is in a state of impermanence.

norm a standard for behavior within a certain group—what it is agreed that people *should* do, a pattern for behavior to be followed. It is often erroneously confused with "average" behavior—that is, what most people do.

nouveau riche French for a person who has newly acquired wealth but does not yet have the manners and other cultural behavior that are assumed to go with wealth.

nuclear family a woman and her children plus her husband. The children were presumably begotten by the husband. In the United States and most other countries, the fact that the children were begotten by someone other than the husband must be determined by a court in order for the husband not to be considered the legal father of the children.

Nuer one of the classic peoples of anthropology, they were studied by Evans-Pritchard in the 1930s, then by Paul Howell in the late 1940s and 1950s. The literature on the Nuer has been much reanalyzed.

omnilateral literally, "all sides." It means counting kin through all links.

omnilineal related in any line—a combination of matrilineal and patrilineal links.

ordeal a legal device for handing the responsibility for judgment to supernatural powers. Accused persons are, in some ordeals, made to undergo dangerous or painful situations so that the opinion of the supernatural power can be determined.

order the state of social activity in which everything is predictable because it is done in accordance with law and custom.

Paiute lived in bands in the northern portions of the Great Basin area of northern Utah and Idaho.

paradigm a pattern of ideas or set of assumptions. Paradigms underlie all our thought but we are often not aware that we arrange our ideas into such paradigms.

parallel cousin offspring of same sex siblings are parallel cousins.

parenting the acts involved in rearing children, giving them sufficient education, physical and moral support, to allow them to grow into adults.

pariah a person (in some cultures, the word is also applied to animals) who is despised and a social outcaste.

participant observation a research technique in which the anthropologist participates in the activities of the people being studied, as far as they will allow. The anthropologist also takes careful notes and makes preliminary analyses that are checked out with the people for correction.

paternity fatherhood. The term is complex. A *sire* is the biological dimension of father; fathers of race horses and other animals are called sires. Paternity is social ascription of fatherhood; it may or may not be the same as the biological paternity.

patriliny/patrilineal descended through a series of agnatic relationships.

patrilocal the couple lives with the parents of the groom.

patron-client a nonkinship relationship in which the low-ranking client depends on the high-ranking patron for welfare and social position. The patron can count on the complete loyalty of the client.

pawn to leave property, or a dependent person, with another as security that a debt will be repaid.

phoneme the minimal unit of sound within a language.

phratry a word of many meanings, but usually implying a group of clans that are associated by nonkinship means.

physical anthropology or **biological anthropology** starts from the biological basis of human beings. It concerns itself with the anatomy and physiology of the human species, with the biology and behavior of those species of apes and monkeys most closely related to human beings, and with the impact of culture on human biology.

polyandry several husbands and one wife.

polygamy plural marriage; both polyandry and polygyny are types of polygamy.

polygyny one husband and several wives.

prejudice an opinion formed without considering all the data or taking time to evaluate other viewpoints. Prejudice is often ethnocentric.

primate an order of mammals that contains monkeys, apes, and human beings.

procreation begetting and conceiving babies.

pseudofamily people who link together and act as if they were a family when, in fact, there is no biological or no legal association among them.

quartering literally, dividing into fourths. In heraldry, it describes a shield divided into four quarters with the coats of arms of one grandparent in each quarter. Genealogists today use the term to mean tracing ancestry back in every line.

race a category of plants or animals (including persons) who share common descent, as marked by common physical characteristics.

ramage a type of organization which branches from a single point, parts of which then branch again at lesser, included points.

reciprocity a type of economy in which services and goods are exchanged between people because of their rank or their relationship. Market principle is not involved. Obviously, reciprocity can be affected by moral values that may demand that specific people help one another regardless of whether the reciprocal service is of equal value.

recontexting taking ideas or things out of one cultural situation, remodeling some of those ideas or things, then setting the remodeled versions into a new cultural situation.

redistribution a type of economy in which goods and services flow into a central point (such as a chiefship or, in the case of taxes, a government), from which other goods and services are handed out to other persons. No reciprocity or market mechanism need be involved.

reproduction is made up of two elements: procreation on the one hand, and rearing children to capable adulthood on the other.

rites of passage rituals held either at specific junctures in the life course or else in the passage of the seasons, for curing or other purposes. A rite of passage is divided into three sections: the first in which a person is separated from his or her previous social position, a second in which the person is in touch with educational and/or mystical forces that provide new capacities, and third, the re-entry into society in a new social position.

ritual carrying out rites so that problems on the earthly plane can be solved symbolically and, hence, a step toward practical solution. Rituals may recur; therefore, the "problems" are not the essential point.

role a part to be played by an individual human being. Roles are marked by rights and obligations, by expected activities, and the moral dimension for judging those activities. Roles are interlinked with one another—one role helps to define others. Persons play roles but are not to be confused with their roles.

romance a Western idea that associates sexuality with love.

sanction a provision of a law that states the penalty for disobeying or the reward for obeying.

schemata (singular, **schema**) conceptual categories, often abstract, for understanding and interrelating what we perceive with what we already know, and for making organized sense of what is in our minds. Schemata are something like a filing system—they give us a place to put new ideas and make it possible to interconnect and find the many different parts of our culture.

segmental opposition a principle in which two equivalent social units that are contrasted to one another, or even in conflict, necessarily join forces when contrasted to another, more inclusive, group.

serf a person of the lowest rank in European feudal systems. These people were sometimes considered to be a part of the land; on those rare occasions when land was sold, the serfs passed to the new owner as part of the land. They are not to be confused with slaves.

settlement a group of dwellings in an area.

sex the biological qualities of being either male or female.

sexuality behavior that involves the sex organs and may stimulate erotic pleasure in other organs as well.

shaman a priest found in many Siberian and North American societies; the priest is said to have direct access to the supernatural powers.

sib in Old English, this word meant "kinsperson." In modern American English, it is sometimes used as an abbreviation for "sibling." The *group* called a sib is made up by counting all kin of a contemporary ego, in any line, to the sixth level (or some other level, depending on the culture). Unfortunately, the word was also used by some anthropologists in the 1940s to mean an agnatic lineal

descent group (the corresponding uterine descent group was called a "clan," also a misnomer).

sibling either a brother or a sister.

sign a thing or action that indicates or conveys a meaning.

Sioux form important elements of American history. Today their homes center in the Dakotas.

slave a person who is the property of another.

socialism a theory or system of government in which the means of production and distribution are owned and controlled by the state.

socialization see *enculturation*.

social trap an action chain that leads to disaster if it cannot be stopped.

society a group of people in interaction who see themselves as a unit, differentiated from other similar units.

Soga a group of African kingdoms, representative of the so-called Interlacustrine Bantu. Studies of the BaGanda and particularly those of the BaNyoro by John Beattie may be used to flesh out the fine ethnography that Lloyd Fallers did not live to complete.

sororal polygyny (sometimes called the **sororate**) polygyny in which a man marries two or more sisters.

speech oral communication by means of language.

state a political organization based on a hierarchy of roles. The hierarchy forms the basis for a bureaucracy.

stepfamily a family in which one of a married pair is parent to the children, but the other spouse is not the parent of the children. Obviously, both spouses may bring children into a stepfamily; children may be born to the stepfamily, whereupon their nuclear family lies within the stepfamily.

stereotype a conventional simplification of a situation that does indeed allow many items to be joined into a class of items, but which nevertheless may leave out some of the most important characteristics of the individual persons or items.

stigma a recognized mark of a rank or office or other special social situation. The word is often associated with disgrace or abnormality.

stratification arranging in layers.

structure anything composed of parts arranged systematically; the relationships among the parts.

subculture this is a made-up word that anthropologists sometimes use to indicate that several varieties of a culture (subcultures) make up an inclusive culture. American culture, for example, is made up of many subcultures. There is difficulty with the word—subcultures are not precise units and they intermingle with one another.

subsistence whatever it is—particularly food—that must be supplied with great regularity in order for life to continue.

succession inheritance or other type of acquisition of rights to office or roles. Succession is to be distinguished from inheritance, which applies to property. One succeeds to the kingship but inherits one's parents' property.

symbol something (a word, a tool, a thing) which stands for an idea, quality, condition, or other abstraction. There is no necessary "natural" association between a symbol and what it stands for; rather, that association is cultural and traditional. The capacity to use symbols is the essential ingredient of living a cultured life.

syntax the patterns within a single language for arranging sounds, words or phrases in order to make sense.

system a set of parts that interlink to form a whole.

tabu (taboo) a Polynesian word for an element so sacred as to be harmful to those not of sufficient rank to deal with it. Taken over into English, it means something that is forbidden—usually having a flavor of sinfulness rather than mere illegality.

taxonomy a classification, particularly of plant or animal species.

Tewa a pueblo group in New Mexico who have the privilege of having their culture explained by one of their own members (Alfonso Ortiz), who totally understands it both as participant and as analyst, and who is dedicated to getting it right.

theocracy a government in which God, or several gods, are recognized as the supreme rulers, and in which divine laws are taken as laws of the state.

Third World during the Cold War, this term was first used for countries that would not join either the capitalist or the communist worlds. Its meaning soon changed to indicate insufficient economic development and the status of being poor.

Tibetan Nepalese a group of Tibetans who have been transplanted to Nepal. They are extremely important in the anthropological literature because it was with studies of these peoples that the mysteries of polyandry were finally analyzed and explained.

Tiv a people in central Nigeria who traditionally had no state organization. It is the largest group of people reported to have run its affairs by the principle of segmental opposition based on a patrilineage system. They are also well known as participants of exchange marriages and for their system of witchcraft.

Tiwi an Australian group living on an island north of the mainland of Australia.

Tonga an African group in present-day Zambia who have had the good fortune to be studied by Elizabeth Colson (later joined by Thayer Scudder) for almost forty years. The ethnographic material on Tonga is rich and the time-sequence is probably unmatched in Africa.

totemism another religion made up by anthropologists. People in many parts of the world do indeed categorize nature so that some people are put into some of the natural categories. They suppose a special relationship among the members of the category, including the people in it. Such beliefs are often the basis of ritual, but they are not organized into "religions" by the people who hold the beliefs or practice the ritual.

trajectory an action chain with a beginning, a middle, and an end. Some trajectories may be repeated, but they do not lead to a cycle.

triad a group or set of three, especially of persons or things. A triad contains three dyads.

Trobriands the people who live on the Trobriand Islands to the northeast of New Guinea. First studied by Bronislaw Malinowski in the early twentieth century, they have been studied by several students since. A long history of study and reanalysis makes them one of the classic anthropological cultures.

unicentric a legal system in which all power is concentrated in one person, one institution or one government. There is no control or no check on the power of that person or group.

unilineal descent descent either through male ancestors or through female ancestors, but never a mixture of the two.

unilocal the couple not only lives with the parents of one or the other, but also lives in the same actual house as the parents.

uterine pertaining to the female. A parent-child relationship is uterine if the parent is female.

uxorilocal the couple lives with the parents of the wife. The word was originally coined to take the place of matrilocal, but both are in common use.

virilocal the couple lives with the parents of the groom. Originally coined to take the place of the term patrilocal, but both are used.

vodou (voodoo) an African-based religion in the Caribbean, particularly Haiti, in which spirits are said to be immanent at all times and may possess people. The word has been extended in American English to mean sorcery, magic, and conjuration.

war a highly organized armed conflict between two highly organized sides.

wedding a social event that creates a marriage. Different societies may celebrate weddings in many different ways.

witchcraft an irrational means of associating the misfortunes of some people with antisocial or unaccepted practices by other people, with the usual premise that the misfortune was caused by the unacceptable people.

Wogeo a people who live on an island to the east of New Guinea.

worldview the combination of ideas, including religious and ritual ideas, about how the world was made, the forces that make it continue to run, and the place of persons and social groups in that world.

Yaqui Native Americans who lived along the rivers of Sonora that flow into the Sea of Cortez. They were strongly influenced by the Spanish missions, and then scattered throughout Mexico by the Mexican government because they were considered troublesome. Some of them fled to, and still live in, the United States. The best studied Yaqui community in the United States is on the outskirts of Tucson, Arizona.

yeoman in the European feudal system, an attendant in a noble household, or a person who has rights to land that are subordinate to those rights in the same land held by the lord.

References Cited

Aberle, David F. 1966. *The Peyote Religion among the Navaho.* Chicago: Aldine Publishing Company. Viking Fund Publications in Anthropology no. 42.

Adam, Leonhard. 1948. "'Virilocal' and 'Uxorilocal.'" *Man*, 48:73.

Akiga (Benjamin Akighirga Sai). 1939. *Akiga's Story.* London: International African Institute.

Anderson, Barbara Gallatin. 1990. *First Fieldwork: The Misadventures of an Anthropologist.* Prospect Heights, IL: Waveland Press.

Ardrey, Robert. 1966. *The Territorial Imperative.* New York: Atheneum Press.

Arendt, Hannah. 1961. *Between Past and Future.* New York: Viking Press.

Armstrong, Robert Plant. 1971. *The Affecting Presence: An Essay in Humanistic Anthropology.* Urbana, Chicago and London: University of Illinois Press.

Axelrod, Robert and William D. Hamilton. 1981. "The Evolution of Cooperation." *Science*, 211:1390-96.

Baba, Marietta L. 1986. *Business and Industrial Anthropology: An Overview.* National Association for the Practice of Anthropology, Washington, DC: NAPA Bulletin no. 2.

Barth, Fredrik, ed. 1969. *Ethnic Groups and Boundaries.* Boston: Little, Brown.

Bateson, Gregory. 1972. *Steps to an Ecology of Mind.* Novato, CA: Chandler Publishing Company.

Benedict, Ruth. 1940. *Race: Science and Politics.* New York: Modern Age.

Berlin, Brent, D. E. Breedlove and P. H. Raven. 1974. *Principles of Tzeltal Plant Classification: An Introduction to the Botanical Ethnography of a Mayan-Speaking People of Highland Chiapas.* New York: Academic.

Berlin, Brent and Paul Kay. 1969. *Basic Color Terms: Their Universality and Evolution.* Berkeley: University of California Press.

Berndt, Ronald. 1974. *Australian Aboriginal Religion.* Leiden, Netherlands: E. J. Brill.

Bohannan, Paul. 1956. "Beauty and Scarification among the Tiv." *Man*, 56: Article 19.

———. 1957 (1989). *Justice and Judgment among the Tiv.* London: Oxford University Press for International African Institute. Reissued with some changes, 1989, Prospect Heights, IL: Waveland Press, 1989.

———. 1963. *Social Anthropology.* New York: Holt, Rinehart and Winston.

———. 1981. "Unseen Community: The Natural History of a Research Project." In Donald A. Messerschmidt, ed., *Anthropologists at Home in North America: Methods and Issues in the Study of One's Own Society.* Cambridge: Cambridge University Press.

———. ed. 1960. *Homicide and Suicide in Africa.* Princeton, NJ: Princeton University Press.

Bohannan, Laura and Paul Bohannan. 1953. *The Tiv of Central Nigeria.* London: International African Institute.

Bright, William. 1968. "Language and Culture," in *Encyclopedia of the Social Sciences.* New York: Macmillan.

Bromley, D. Allen. 1989. Quoted in *Cossa Washington Update*, 3, no. 21 (November 17).

Broude, Gwen J. 1981. "The Cultural Management of Sexuality," in Ruth H. Munroe, Robert L. Munroe and Beatrice B. Whiting, *Handbook of Cross-Cultural Human Development.* New York and London: Garland STPM Press.

Buckley, Anthony D. 1985. *Yoruba Medicine.* Oxford: Clarendon Press.

Buckley, Thomas and Alma Gottlieb, eds. 1988. *Blood Magic: The Anthropology of Menstruation.* Berkeley: University of California Press.

Burch, Ernest S., Jr. 1970. "Marriage and Divorce among the North Alaskan Eskimos," in Paul Bohannan, ed., *Divorce and After.* Garden City, NY: Doubleday.

Burg, B. R. 1983. *Sodomy and the Pirate Tradition: English Sea Rovers in the Seventeenth-Century Caribbean.* New York: New York University Press.

Burridge, Kenelm O. 1969. *New Heaven, New Earth.* New York: Schocken Books.

Casson, Ronald W. 1982. "Schemata in Cognitive Anthropology." *Annual Review of Anthropology*, 12:429-62.

Cesaire, Aime. 1972. *Discourse on Colonialism.* Translated by Joan Pinkham. New York and London: Monthly Review Press. (Original French version published in 1955.)

Cesara, Manda. 1982. *Reflections of a Woman Anthropologist: No Hiding Place.* London and New York: Academic Press.

Cohen, Ronald. 1963. "Brittle Marriage as a Stable System," in Paul Bohannan, ed., *Divorce and After.* New York: Doubleday.

Collier, Jane Fishburne and Sylvia Junko Yanagisako. 1987. *Gender and Kinship: Essays toward a Unified Analysis.* Stanford, CA: Stanford University Press.

Colson, Elizabeth. 1948. "Rain Shrines of the Plateau Tonga of Northern Rhodesia." *Africa*, 18.

———. 1951. "The Plateau Tonga of Northern Rhodesia," in Max Gluckman and Elizabeth Colson, eds., *Seven Tribes of British Central Africa.* Manchester, England: Manchester University Press.

———. 1954. "Ancestral Spirits and Social Structure among the Plateau Tonga." *International Archives of Ethnography*, 47. (Leiden, Netherlands).

———. 1958. *Marriage and the Family among the Plateau Tonga.* Manchester, England: Manchester University Press.

Condor, W. S. and L. W. Sander. 1974. "Neonatal Movement is Synchronized with Adult Speech: Interactional Participation and Language Acquisition." *Science* 183:99-101.

Conley, Frances. 1991. Quoted in "Walking Out on the Boys," *Time*, July 8, 1991:52-53.

Conquest, Robert. 1990. *The Great Terror: A Reassessment.* New York: Oxford University Press.

Darwin, Charles. 1859. *On the Origin of Species.* London: J. Murray.

Dawkins, R. 1976. *The Selfish Gene*. Oxford: Oxford University Press.

DeGobineau, Joseph Arthur, Comte de. (1850) 1915. *The Inequality of the Human Races*. Translated by Adrian Collier. New York: H. Ferbig.

Devereaux, George. 1968. *From Anxiety to Method in the Behavioral Sciences*. Amsterdam: Mouton.

DeVos, George and Hiroshi Wagatsuma. 1967. *Japan's Invisible Race: Caste in Culture and Personality*. Berkeley: University of California Press.

Dunbar, Robin I. M. 1988. *Primate Social Systems*. Ithaca, NY: Comstock Publishing Associates, a division of Cornell University Press.

Dundes, Alan, ed. 1984. *Sacred Narrative: Readings in the Theory of Myth*. Berkeley: University of California Press.

Durkheim, Emile. 1912. *Elementary Forms of the Religious Life*. Paris: F. Alcan.

Eckert, J. Kevin. 1980. *The Unseen Elderly: A Study of Marginally Subsistent Hotel Dwellers*. San Diego, CA: Campanile Press.

Eggan, Fred. 1950. *Social Organization of the Western Pueblos*. Chicago: University of Chicago Press.

Eliade, Mircea. 1984. "Cosmogonic Myth and 'Sacred History,'" in Alan Dundes, *Sacred Narrative: Readings in the Theory of Myth*. Berkeley: University of California Press.

Empson, William. 1951. *The Structure of Complex Words*. London: Chatto and Windus.

English-Lueck, J. A. 1990. *Health in the New Age: A Study in California Holistic Practices*. Albuquerque: University of New Mexico Press.

Evans-Pritchard, E. E. 1937. *Witchcraft, Oracles and Magic among the Azande*. Oxford: Clarendon Press.

———. 1940. *The Nuer: A Description of the Modes of Livelihood and Political Institutions of a Nilotic People*. Oxford: Clarendon Press.

———. 1949. *The Sanusi of Cyrenaica*. Oxford: Clarendon Press.

———. 1965. *Theories of Primitive Religion*. Oxford: Clarendon Press.

Fagan, Brian M. 1984. *Clash of Cultures*. New York: W. H. Freeman and Company.

Fallers, Lloyd A. 1965. *Bantu Bureaucracy: A Century of Political Evolution among the Basoga of Uganda*. Chicago: University of Chicago Press.

Ferguson, Marilyn. 1980. *The Acquirian Conspiracy: Personal and Social Transformation in the 1980s*. Los Angeles: J. P. Tarcher.

Finley, M. I., ed. 1960. *Slavery in Classical Antiquity*. Cambridge: W. Heffer and Sons.

Finney, Ben R. and Eric M. Jones. 1985. *Interstellar Migration and the Human Experience*. Berkeley: University of California Press.

Forde, C. Daryll. 1964. *Yako Studies*. London: Oxford University Press for the International African Institute.

Foulkes, Roland A. 1988. "Anthropology: Its Future on Earth and in Space." Paper read before the 12th International Congress of Anthropological and Ethnological Sciences, Zagreb, Yugoslavia.

Fox, Robin and Lionel Tiger. 1971. *The Imperial Animal*. New York: Holt, Rinehart and Winston.

Frankfort, Henri. 1948. *Kingship and the Gods: A Study of Ancient Near Eastern Religion as the Integration of Society and Nature*. Chicago: University of Chicago Press.

Frazer, James George. 1922. *The Golden Bough: A Study in Magic and Religion*. New York: Macmillan.

Freud, Sigmund. 1930. *Civilization and its Discontents*, in Vol. 21 of *The Standard Edition of the Complete Psychological Works of Sigmund Freud*, pp. 59-145. London: The Hogarth Press.

———. (1905) 1960. *Jokes and their Relation to the Unconscious*, in *The Standard Edition of the Complete Psychological Works of Sigmund Freud*, Vol. 8, translated by James Strachey. London: The Hogarth Press, 1960 (originally published in German as *Der Witz und Seine Beziehung zum Unbewussten*).

Fuglesang, Andreas and Dale Chandler. 1988. *Participation as Process: What we can Learn from Grameen Bank, Bangladesh*. Dhaka, Bangladesh: Grameen Bank.

Furst, Peter. 1975. "Introduction," in Fernando Benitez, *In the Magic Land of Peyote*. Austin: University of Texas Press.

Gearing, Fred. 1962. *Priests and Warriors*. American Anthropological Association Memoir, no. 93. Washington, DC: The Association.

Geertz, Clifford. 1964. "Ideology as a Cultural System," in David E. Apter, ed., *Ideology and Discontent*. New York: The Free Press of Glencoe.

———. 1968. "Religion: Anthropological Study." *Encyclopedia of the Social Sciences*. New York: Macmillan.

Gelles, Richard J. and Murray A. Strauss. 1988. *Intimate Violence*. New York: Simon and Schuster.

Giallombardo, Rose. 1966. *Society of Women: A Study of a Woman's Prison*. New York: John Wiley and Sons.

Glazer, Mark, ed. 1982. *Flour from Another Sack and Other Proverbs: Folk Beliefs, Tales, Riddles and Recipes*. Edinburg, TX: Pan American University Press.

Gleick, James. 1987. *Chaos: Making a New Science*. New York: Viking.

Gluckman, Max. 1955. *The Judicial Process among the Barotse of Northern Rhodesia*. Manchester, England: Manchester University Press.

———. 1965. *The Ideas of Barotse Jurisprudence*. New Haven, CT: Yale University Press.

Godelier, Maurice. 1986. *The Making of Great Men: Male Domination and Power among the New Guinea Baruya*. Translated by Rupert Sawyer. Cambridge: Cambridge University Press (Original French version, *La production des grandes hommes*, Librairie Artheme Fayard, Paris, 1982).

Goffman, Ervin. 1959. *Presentation of Self in Everyday Life*. New York: Doubleday.

Gomme, Laurence. 1880. *Primitive Folk-Moots; or, Open-Air Assemblies in Britain*. London: Sampson Low, Marston, Searle and Rivington.

Goodall, Jane. 1986. *The Chimpanzees of Gombe: Patterns of Behavior*. Cambridge, MA: Belknap Press of Harvard University Press.

Goodenough, Ward. 1955. "A Problem in Malayo-Polynesian Social Organization." *American Anthropologist*, 57:71-83.

Goody, Jack. 1980. "Slavery in Time and Space," in James L. Watson, ed., *Asian and African Systems of Slavery*. Berkeley: University of California Press.

Gould, Richard A. 1969. *Yiwara: Foragers of the Australian Desert*. New York: Charles Scribner's Sons.

Greenhouse, Carol J. 1986. *Praying for Justice: Faith, Order, and Community in an American Town*. Ithaca, NY and London: Cornell University Press.

Gregor, Thomas. 1985. *Anxious Pleasures*. Chicago: University of Chicago Press.

References Cited

Groos, K. 1898. *The Play of Animals*. New York: Appleton.

Hall, Edward T. 1966. *The Hidden Dimension*. New York: Doubleday.

———. 1977. *Beyond Culture*. New York: Doubleday.

Heisel, Marsel A. 1987. "Women and Widows in Turkey: Support Systems," in Helena Znaniecka Lopata, ed., *Widows*, Vol. 1, *The Middle East, Asia and the Pacific*, pp. 79-105. Durham, NC: Duke University Press.

Henry, Jules. 1963. *Culture Against Man*. New York: Random House.

Herdt, Gilbert H. 1984. *Ritualized Homosexuality in Melanesia*. Berkeley: University of California Press.

Hicks, George L. and Philip E. Leis, eds. 1977. *Ethnic Encounters: Identities and Contexts*. North Scituate, MA: Duxbury Press.

Himmelheber, Hans. 1960. *Negerkunst und Negerkunstler*. Braunschweig, East Germany: Klinckhardt and Bierman.

Hine, Virginia H. 1977. "The Basic Paradigm of a Future Socio-Cultural System." *World Issues*, April/May.

Hochschild, Arlie Russell. 1983. *The Managed Heart: Commercialization of Human Feeling*. Berkeley: University of California Press.

Hochschild, Arlie Russell with Anne Machung. 1989. *The Second Shift: Working Parents at the Revolution at Home*. New York: Viking.

Hoebel, E. Adamson. 1954. *The Law of Primitive Man: A Study in Comparative Legal Dynamics*. Cambridge, MA: Harvard University Press.

Honko, Lauri. 1984. "The Problem of Defining Myth," in Alan Dundes, *Sacred Narrative: Readings in the Theory of Myth*. Berkeley: University of California Press.

Howell, Paul Philip. 1954. *A Manual of Nuer Law, being an account of customary law, its evolution and development in the courts established by the Sudan Government*. London: Oxford University Press for International African Institute.

Huizinga, J. 1950. *Homo Ludens*. New York: Roy Publishers.

Isaacs, Harold. 1972. *Idols of the Tribe: Group Identity and Political Change*. New York: Harper & Row.

Jules-Rosette, Bennetta. 1984. *The Messages of Tourist Art: An African Semiotic System in Comparative Perspective*. New York and London: Plenum Press.

Keil, Charles. 1979. *Tiv Song*. Chicago and London: University of Chicago Press.

Keiser, R. Lincoln. 1969. *The Vice Lords, Warriors of the Streets*. New York: Holt, Rinehart and Winston.

Keller, Helen. 1904. *The Story of My Life, and a supplementary account of her education including passages from the reports and letters of her teacher, Anne Mansfield Sullivan*. New York: Grosset and Dunlap.

Ketudat, Sippanondna, with the methodological and editorial collaboration of Robert B. Textor. 1990. *The Middle Path for the Future of Thailand: Technology in Harmony with Culture and Environment*. Honolulu: Institute of Culture and Communication, East-West Center.

Kinsey, Alfred C., Wardell B. Pomeroy and Clyde E. Martin. 1948. *Sexual Behavior in the Human Male*. Philadelphia: W. B. Saunders Company.

Klass, Morton. 1980. *Caste: The Emergence of the South Asian Social System*. Philadelphia: Institute for the Study of Human Issues.

Kluckhohn, Clyde. 1944. *Navaho Witchcraft*. Boston: Beacon Press 1961 (first published by the Peabody Museum of American Archaeology and Ethnology, Harvard University, 1944).

Koo, Jasoon. 1987. "Widows in Seoul, Korea," in Helena Znaniecka Lopata, *Widows*, Vol. 1, *The Middle East, Asia and the Pacific*, pp. 56-78. Durham, NC: Duke University Press.

Kroeber, Theodora. 1961. *Ishi in Two Worlds: A Biography of the Last Wild Indian in North America*. Berkeley and Los Angeles: University of California Press.

LaFontaine, J. S. 1988. *Initiation*. Manchester, England: Manchester University Press.

Langer, Suzanne K. 1953. *Feeling and Form: A Theory of Art, Developed from Philosophy in a New Key*. New York: Charles Scribner's Sons.

Lea, Henry Charles. 1878. *Superstition and Force: Essays on the Wager of Law, the Wager of Battle, the Ordeal, Torture*. Philadelphia: Henry C. Lea.

Lee, Dorothy. 1950. "Codification of Reality: Lineal and Nonlineal." *Psychosomatic Medicine*, no. 12 (May). Reprinted in Dorothy Lee, *Freedom and Culture*. Prospect Heights, IL: Waveland Press, 1987.

Levine, Nancy E. 1988 *The Dynamics of Polyandry: Kinship, Domesticity and Population on the Tibetan Border*. Chicago: University of Chicago Press.

Levine, Robert A. and Donald T. Campbell. 1972 *Ethnocentrism: Theories of Conflict, Ethnic Attitudes and Group Behavior*. New York: John Wiley and Sons.

Levinson, Daniel J. 1978. *The Seasons of a Man's Life*. New York: Alfred A. Knopf.

Lienhardt, Godfrey. 1961. *Divinity and Experience: The Religion of the Dinka*. Oxford: Clarendon Press.

Lindenbaum, Shirley. 1987. "The Mystification of Female Labors," in Jane Fishburne Collier and Sylvia Junko Yanagisako, eds., *Gender and Kinship: Essays toward a Unified Analysis*. Stanford, CA: Stanford University Press.

Loesser, Arthur. 1954. *Men, Women and Pianos: A Social History*. New York: Simon and Schuster.

Lofland, Lynn H. (1973) 1985. *A World of Strangers: Order and Action in Urban Public Space*. Reissue, Prospect Heights, IL: Waveland Press.

Lopata, Helena Znaniecka. 1987. *Widows*. Vol. 1, *The Middle East, Asia and the Pacific*. Durham, NC: Duke University Press.

Lounsbury, Floyd. 1964. "The Formal Analysis of Crow- and Omaha-type Kinship Terminologies," in Ward Goodenough, ed., *Explorations in Cultural Anthropology*. New York: McGraw-Hill.

Lumholtz, Carl. 1900. *Symbolism of the Huichol Indians*. Memoirs of the American Museum of Natural History, Vol. 3. Anthro. Vol. 2, Part 1. New York: The Museum.

Maccoby, Eleanor E. and Carol Nagy Jacklin. 1974. *The Psychology of Sex Differences*. Stanford, CA: Stanford University Press.

Malinowski, Bronislaw. (1922) 1984. *Argonauts of the Western Pacific*. Reissue, Prospect Heights, IL: Waveland Press.

———. 1929. *The Sexual Life of Savages in Northwest Melanesia*. New York: Harvest Books.

———. 1967. *A Diary in the Strict Sense of the Term*. New York: Harcourt Brace.

Marshall, Mac. 1976. "Solidarity or Sterility? Adoption and Fosterage on Namoluk Atoll," in Ivan Brady, ed., *Transactions in Kinship: Adoption and Fosterage in Oceania*. Honolulu: University of Hawaii Press.

Masters, Roger D. 1989. *The Nature of Politics*. New Haven, CT: Yale University Press.

McDowell, Nancy. 1988. "A Note on Cargo Cults and Cultural Constructions of Change." *Pacific Studies*, 11, no. 2:121-134.

Meigs, Anna S. 1984. *Food, Sex and Pollution: A New Guinea Religion*. New Brunswick, NJ: Rutgers University Press.

Messenger, John C. 1971. "Sex and Repression in an Irish Folk Community," in Donald S. Marshall, and Robert C. Suggs, eds., *Human Sexual Behavior: Variations in the Ethnographic Spectrum*. New York: Basic Books.

Metraux, Alfred. 1959. *Voodoo in Haiti*. Translated by Hugo Charteris. London: Andre Deutsch.

Money, John and Anke A. Ehrhardt. 1972. *Man and Woman, Boy and Girl: The Differentiation and Dimorphism of Gender Identity from Conception to Maturity*. Baltimore, MD: Johns Hopkins University Press.

Mooney, James. (1896) 1965. *The Ghost Dance Religion and the Sioux Outbreak of 1890*. Abridged, and with an Introduction by Anthony F. C. Wallace. Chicago: University of Chicago Press.

Munn, Henry. 1973. "The Mushrooms of Language," in Michael J. Harner, ed., *Hallucinogens and Shamanism*, pp. 86-122. New York: Oxford University Press.

Murdock, George Peter. 1949. *Social Structure*. New York: Macmillan.

Myerhoff, Barbara. 1974. *Peyote Hunt: The Sacred Journey of the Huichol Indians*. Ithaca, NY and London: Cornell University Press.

Nader, Laura. 1969. "Styles of Court Procedure: To Make the Balance," in Laura Nader, ed., *Law in Culture and Society*. Hawthorne, NY: Aldine Press.

_____. 1990. *Harmony Ideology and the Construction of Law: Justice and Control in a Zapotec Mountain Village*. Stanford, CA: Stanford University Press.

Nagata, Judith A. 1974. "What is a Malay? Situational Selection of Ethnic Identity in a Plural Society." *American Ethnologist*, 1:331-50.

Netting, Robert McC., Richard R. Wilk and Eric J. Arnould, eds. 1984. *Households: Comparative and Historical Studies of the Domestic Group*. Berkeley: University of California Press.

Nielsen, Joyce McCarl. 1990. *Sex and Gender in Society: Perspectives on Stratification*, 2nd Ed. Prospect Heights, IL: Waveland Press.

Oboler, Regina Smith. 1986. "Nandi Widows," in Betty Potash, *Widows in African Societies: Choices and Constraints*. Stanford, CA: Stanford University Press.

Ortiz, Alfonso, ed. 1972. *New Perspectives on the Pueblos*. A School of American Research Book. Albuquerque: University of New Mexico Press.

_____. 1969. *The Tewa World: Space, Time, Being and Becoming in a Pueblo Society*. Chicago: University of Chicago Press.

Platt, John. 1973. "Social Traps." *American Psychologist*, 28, no. 8:641-51.

Polanyi, Karl. 1957. "The Economy as Instituted Process," in Karl Polanyi, Conrad M. Arensburg and Harry W. Pearson, eds., *Trade and Market in the Early Empires*. Glencoe, IL: The Free Press.

Potash, Betty. 1986. *Widows in African Societies: Choices and Constraints*. Stanford, CA: Stanford University Press.

Powdermaker, Hortense. 1966. *Stranger and Friend: The Way of an Anthropologist*. New York: W. W. Norton and Co.

Powers, William T. 1973. *Behavior: The Control of Perception*.
Chicago: Aldine.

Radcliffe-Brown, A. R. 1950. "Introduction," in A. R. Radcliffe-Brown and Daryll Forde, eds., *African Systems of Kinship and Marriage*. London: Oxford University Press for International African Institute.

Ribeiro, Darcy. 1968. *The Civilizational Process*. Translated by Betty J. Meggers. Washington, DC: Smithsonian Institution Press.

Rivers, W. H. R. 1904. *The Toda*. Cambridge: Cambridge University Press.

Roszak, Theodore. 1978. *Person/Planet: The Creative Disintegration of Industrial Society*. Garden City, NY: Anchor Press/Doubleday.

Rubin, Arnold, Ed. 1988. *Marks of Civilization: Artistic Transformations of the Human Body*. Los Angeles: Museum of Cultural History, University of California, Los Angeles.

Sahlins, Marshall. 1960. "Production, Distribution and Power in a Primitive Society," in A. F. C. Wallace, ed., *Men and Cultures, Selected Papers of the Fifth International Congress of Anthropological and Ethnological Sciences*. Philadelphia: University of Pennsylvania Press.

_____. 1963. "Poor Man, Rich Man, Big-Man, Chief: Political Types in Melanesia and Polynesia." *Comparative Studies in Society and History*, 5:285-303.

Sauer, Norman J. 1988. "If Races Don't Exist, Why Are Forensic Anthropologists so Good at Identifying Them?" Paper read at the 87th Annual Meeting of the American Anthropological Association.

Schaller, George E. 1972. *The Serengeti Lion: A Study of Predator-Prey Relations*. Chicago and London: University of Chicago Press.

Scharer, Hans. 1963. *Ngaju Religion: The Conception of God among a South Borneo People*. Translated by Rodney Needham. The Hague: Martinus Nijhoff (original German, 1946 doctoral dissertation, published that year in Leiden by E. J. Brill).

Schechner, Richard. 1985. *Between Theater and Anthropology*. Philadelphia: University of Pennsylvania Press.

Schwimmer, Eric. 1984. "Male Couples in New Guinea," in Gilbert H. Herdt, ed., *Ritualized Homosexuality in Melanesia*. Berkeley: University of California Press.

Service, Elman R. 1975. *Origins of the State and Civilization: The Process of Cultural Evolution*. New York: W. W. Norton and Co.

Shepherd, Gill. 1987. "Rank, Gender, and Homosexuality: Mombasa as a Key to Understanding Sexual Options," in Pat Caplan, ed., *The Cultural Construction of Sexuality*. London: Tavistock Publications.

Smith, Adam. (1776) 1985. *Wealth of Nations*. New York: McGraw-Hill (several other editions available).

Spicer, Edward H., ed. 1961. *Perspectives in American Indian Culture Change*. Chicago: University of Chicago Press.

Spiro, Melford E. 1970. *Buddhism and Society: A Great Tradition and its Burmese Vicissitudes*. New York: Harper & Row.

Srinivas, M. N. 1962. *Caste in Modern India*. Bombay: Asia Publishing House.

Stanner, W. E. H. 1965. "Religion, Totemism and Symbolism," in Ronald M. Berndt and Catherine H. Berndt, eds., *Aboriginal Man in Australia: Essays in Honour of Emeritus Professor A. P. Elkin*. Sydney: Angus and Robertson.

Stavrionos, Lefton S. 1981. *Global Rift: The Third World Comes of Age*. New York: William Morrow and Co.

References Cited

Strehlow, T. G. H. 1947. *Aranda Traditions*. Melbourne: Melbourne University Press.

Sutherland, E. N. and Donald R. Cressey. 1960. *Criminology*. Philadelphia: Lippincott.

Symons, Donald. 1978. *Play and Aggression: A Study of Rhesus Monkeys*. New York: Columbia University Press.

Terry, Edith. 1989. "When the Big One Hit Tokyo . . . A Scenario for Global Economic Disaster." *World Press*, 36(December):12 (adapted from "Report on Business Magazine" of *Globe and Mail* of Toronto).

Textor, Robert B. 1980. *A Handbook of Ethnographic Futures Research*, 3rd Ed., Version A. Stanford, CA: Stanford University School of Education and Department of Anthropology.

Thomas, Piri. 1967. *Down These Mean Streets*. New York: Alfred A. Knopf.

Thompson, Michael. 1979. *Rubbish Theory*. London: Oxford University Press.

Titiev, Mischa. 1943. "The Influence of Common Residence on the Unilateral Classification of Kindred." *American Anthropologist*, 45:511-30.

Touba, Jacqueline Rudolph. 1987. "The Widows in Iran," in Helena Znaniecka Lopata, *Widows*, Vol. 1: *The Middle East, Asia and the Pacific*, pp. 106-32. Durham, NC: Duke University Press.

Turner, Victor. 1957. *Schism and Continuity in an African Society: A Study of Ndembu Village Life*. Manchester, England: Manchester University Press for Rhodes Livingstone Institute.

Tylor, E. B. (1871) 1958. *Primitive Culture*. Reissue, New York: Harper.

van der Elst, Dirk. 1990. Private conversation on benefits of inequality.

van Gennep, Arnold. (1908) 1960. *The Rites of Passage*. Translated by Monika B. Vizedom and Gabrielle L. Caffee, Introduction by Solon T. Kimball. Chicago: University of Chicago Press.

Wallace, Ernest and E. Adamson Hoebel. 1952. *The Comanches: Lords of the South Plains*. Norman: University of Oklahoma Press.

Wallace, A. F. C. 1970. *Culture and Personality*, 2nd Ed. New York: Random House.

Ward, Martha C. 1989. *Nest in the Wind: Adventures in Anthropology on a Tropical Island*. Prospect Heights, IL: Waveland Press.

Watson, James L., ed. 1980. *Asian and African Systems of Slavery*. Berkeley: University of California Press.

Weiner, Annette B. 1976. *Women of Value, Men of Renown: New Perspectives in Trobriand Exchange*. Austin: University of Texas Press.

Werner, Oswald, K. Y. Begishe, M. A. Austin-Garrison, and June Werner. 1986. "The Anatomical Atlas of the Navajo." Native American Materials Development Center.

Whalen, William Joseph. 1981. *Strange Gods: Contemporary Religious Cults in America*. Huntington, IN: Our Sunday Visitor.

Williams, Walter L. 1986. *The Spirit and the Flesh: Sexual Diversity in American Indian Culture*. Boston, MA: Beacon Press.

Wilson, Godfrey and Monica Wilson. 1954. *The Analysis of Social Change, Based on Observations in Central Africa*. Cambridge, MA: Cambridge University Press.

Witherspoon, Gary. 1975. "Navajo Social Organization," in Vol. 10 of the *Handbook of North American Indians*, pp. 524-35, William G. Surtevant, general editor; Alfonso Ortiz, volume editor. Washington, DC: The Smithsonian Institution.

Wolf, Eric R. 1982. *Europe and the People without History*. Berkeley: University of California Press.

Worsley, Peter. 1968. *The Trumpet Shall Sound: A Study of "Cargo" Cults in Melanesia*, 2nd, Augmented Ed. New York: Schocken Books.

Yengoyan, Aram. 1979. "Economy, Society, and Myth in Aboriginal Australia." *Annual Review of Anthropology*.

_____. In press. "Religion, Morality and the Question of Prophetic Traditions: Christianity and Conversion among the Pitjantjatjara of Central Australia," in Robert Hefner, ed., *Conversion to World Religions: Ethnographic and Historical Interpretations*.

Acknowledgements

Because I am indebted to a lot of people, and so a little hesitant about who to thank for fear of leaving out others just as vital, I have kept this list short. Anybody I inadvertently omitted (and nobody was omitted purposely) is in plenty of good company.

Special mention must go to Martha Ward, who was always at the other end of the telephone when I needed her, and whose fresh viewpoints always helped. She even did a pretty good job of convincing me that I was having fun. Robbie Davis-Floyd taught through the book, went through the manuscript with a fine-tooth comb thus saving me from some real booboos, and did a magnificently sensitive and responsible job on the banks of test questions. Robbie also supplied the data and ideas for "We, The Alien" segments on pages 240 and 244.

Tom Curtin at the Waveland Press has been magnificent — he has guided me through every stage of the book, and his good taste and common sense are evident throughout it. Carol Rowe edited the manuscript ably, and I thank her immensely. Jan Weissman was the photo editor; her good eye is evident — her superb persistence is not. Neil Rowe, bless him, has not only been the boss, but he and Tom have trusted me. Trust is something, I find, that publishers (thinking they already know how to produce books) almost never extend to authors. I have been lucky.

I myself taught through an earlier version of this book at San Diego State University, where I was Visiting Professor for one semester. I am grateful to both graduate and undergraduate students for allowing me to see where their eyes glazed over (and sometimes telling me they were glazing if I missed it), for giving me ideas, and for demanding some changes, most of which they got. Several members of the faculty joined our graduate seminar, to my great benefit — I am especially grateful to Dan Whitney and Phyllis Easland-Whitney, Vivian Rohrl, Phil Greenfeld, Wade Pendleton.

My friend Harvey Wheeler is important in everything I do — after many years, I can still never predict which wall he may come off of. I have been talking with Ned Hall for years; although there are a number of references to his work in this book, my debt to him is much deeper. John Platt has been formative and a good friend, as is evident in the book. Dirk van der Elst twice taught through earlier drafts of the book; we have discussed it interminably, and some of the ideas in it may be his for all I know. Laura Nader straightened me out on some points. Christopher Boehm and Reed Riner have also used earlier drafts of the book. Karl Heider and Tim Asch have made suggestions for the films listed in the Teachers' Guide. Vikram Jayanti has given us permission to use the logo of the anthropologist with a camera observing the processes of human evolution; he got the idea in my office at the University of Southern California, and used it as the logo for his film festivals called "Anthropos." Jim Funaro organized CONTACT and freed me up about "Cultures of the Imagination" — he has also given me permission to use that phrase in the Workbook. The term began in the early meetings of CONTACT and is still used by that organization.

I want also to thank Harriett Prentiss, Ben Kilborn, Denis Bohannan, Simon D'Arcy, Bob Textor, Brian Fagan — and all those people who have helped but who aren't named and to whom I apologize. And special thanks to Lisa who put up with me while I was working on it and pushed me to keep it simple.

Photo Credits

Part I opener: Howell Walker © National Geographic Society

1-1. David A. Medford **1-2.** *top left* Kent Reno/Jeroboam Inc.; *top right* Karen R. Preuss/Jeroboam Inc.; *bottom left* Kit Hedman/Jeroboam Inc.; *bottom right* Kent Reno/Jeroboam Inc. **1-3.** *top left* Ruth and Louis Kirk; *bottom left* Zoological Society of San Diego; *bottom right* Karen Houston Smith **1-9.** Ron Garrison/Zoological Society of San Diego

2-7. © Suzanne Arms-Wimberley **2-8.** Courtesy Laura Gilpin Collection, Amon Carter Museum, Fort Worth, Texas **2-10.** David Seymour—"Chim" © Magnum Photos **2-11.** Bob Clay/Jeroboam Inc. **2-18.** Laura Nader

Part II opener: Malvina Hoffman, Bushman Woman and Baby (South Africa), Field Museum of Natural History, Neg. #MH1C, Chicago

3-1. Craig W. Racicot/Zoological Society of San Diego **3-2.** Pierre L. van den Berghe **3-4.** Betty Coody **3-5.** Henry Moore, *Family Group*, (1948-49). Bronze (cast 1950), 59 1/4 x 46 1/2 x 29 7/8", including base. Collection, The Museum of Modern Art, New York A. Conger Goodyear Fund. **3-7.** *left* Israel Government Tourism Administration; *right* Pierre L. van den Berghe **3-8.** AP/Wide World Photos **3-9.** © 1990 Lamaze Institute for Family Education **3-11.** AP/Wide World Photos **3-12.** AP/Wide World Photos **3-16.** Ken Gaghan/Jeroboam Inc. **3-17.** Jodi Cobb © National Geographic Society

4-1. Novosti from Sovfoto **4-4.** Fredrik Barth **4-6.** Pierre L. van den Berghe **4-8.** The Bettmann Archive **4-9.** The Bettmann Archive **4-11.** Ron Garrison/Zoological Society of San Diego **4-12.** *left* Paul Bohannan; *right* William E. Mitchell **4-14.** Susanne Page **4-17.** Paul Bohannan **4-18.** Nancy Levine

5-1. Pierre L. van den Berghe **5-7.** Beryl Goldberg © 1990 **5-8.** Paul Bohannan **5-16.** William Lee Stokes, *Essentials of Earth History, Third Edition* © 1973, p. 456. Reprinted by permission of Prentice-Hall, Englewood Cliffs, New Jersey **5-17.** *left* U.S. Department of Housing and Urban Development; *right* Courtesy of Milwaukee Public Museum **5-19.** *left* Bill Owens/Jeroboam Inc.; *right* Frieder Sauer/Jeroboam Inc.

Part III opener: Arthur Lavine

6-1. National Anthropological Archives, Smithsonian Institution **6-3.** Paul Bohannan **6-5.** John K. Marshall **6-6.** United Nations/Ida/Pickerelle **6-7.** Paul Bohannan **6-8.** U.S. Department of Agriculture **6-9.** The Bettmann Archive **6-12.** AP/Wide World Photos **6-13.** Dan Manzo of Manzo Brothers Produce, Courtesy of Pike Place Market PDA **6-16.** Carl Mydans, Life Magazine © Time Warner, Inc. **6-21.** Annette Weiner **6-22.** National Anthropological Archives, Smithsonian Institution

7-3. AP/Wide World Photos **7-6.** *top* Ron Garrison/Zoological Society of San Diego; *bottom right* Field Museum of Natural History, Neg. #57554, Chicago **7-7.** National Anthropological Archives, Smithsonian Institution **7-9.** Laura Nader **7-10.** Los Angeles Times Photographic Archive, UCLA Special Collections **7-11.** David Dawley, *A Nation of Lords, Second Edition* © 1992,

Waveland Press, Inc. **7-13.** Pitt Rivers Museum, University of Oxford **7-14.** The Bettmann Archive **7-16.** Pitt Rivers Museum, University of Oxford **7-17.** Paul Bohannan **7-18.** Royal Anthropological Institute Photographic Collection **7-22.** *left* Courtesy Amon Carter Museum, Fort Worth, Texas; *right* AP/Wide World Photos

8-1. Ewing Galloway **8-3.** Courtesy Museum of New Mexico **8-4.** F. Hannah/Arizona State Museum, University of Arizona **8-7.** Bishop Museum **8-8.** AP/Wide World Photos **8-10.** National Anthropological Archives, Smithsonian Institution **8-11.** Bishop Museum **8-12.** Egyptian Expedition, The Metropolitan Museum of Art **8-19.** AP/Wide World Photos

9-2. Laurie Cameron/Jeroboam Inc. **9-3.** The Bettmann Archive **9-6.** *right* U.S. Department of Housing and Urban Development **9-8.** Culver Pictures **9-9.** Courtesy of the New York Historical Society, New York City **9-16.** AP/Wide World Photos **9-20.** UPI/Bettmann

Part IV opener: Pablo Picasso, Spanish, 1881-1973, Sylvette, Bleue-Violette, oil on canvas, 1954, 130.5 x 96.8 cm, Gift of Mary and Leigh Block, 1955.821, photograph © 1991, The Art Institute of Chicago. All rights reserved.

10-2. Kent Reno/Jeroboam Inc. **10-4.** Courtesy American Foundation for the Blind, New York **10-5.** Jose Luis Banus-March/FPG International **10-12.** John F. Kennedy Library **10-13.** Paul Bohannan **10-15.** *left* Paul Bohannan; *right* Jan Yoors **10-16.** Paul Bohannan **10-17.** Courtesy Amon Carter Museum, Fort Worth, Texas **10-18.** *left* AP/Wide World Photos; *right* The Cleveland Museum of Art, Andrew R. and Martha Holden Jennings Fund, 75.101 **10-19.** Smithsonian Institution, Photo No. 56,258 **10-20.** Courtesy of the Trustees of Dartmouth College, Hanover, NH, Jose Clemente Orozco, Mexican, 1883-1949, *The Epic of American Civilization*; Panel #15: *Anglo-American* and Panel #16: *Hispano-America*, Fresco **10-22.** Lowie Museum of Anthropology, The University of California at Berkeley **10-23.** Hirshhorn Museum and Sculpture Garden, Smithsonian Institution, Gift of Joseph H. Hirschhorn, 1966 **10-24.** Karen Houston Smith **10-25.** Deere & Company

11-2. Courtesy of the Indiana University Art Museum, Bloomington **11-5.** G. Lacono/Arizona State Museum, University of Arizona **11-7.** Novosti From Sovfoto **11-9.** Karen Houston Smith **11-10.** Charles M. Keil **11-11.** Charles M. Keil **11-12.** José Cisneros, The Weeping Woman, *Texas Folk and Folklore*, Publications of the Texas Folklore Society, Number XXVI, © 1954 **11-14.** Courtesy of University of Chicago Press **11-16.** Australian Overseas Information Service (AOIS) **11-18.** Edith Turner

12-3. Alinari/Art Resource, New York **12-8.** Paul Bohannan **12-10.** Chantal Regnault **12-11.** From the Florentine Codex, Book 11, by Fray Bernadino de Sahagun **12-13.** "Aboriginal Bora" Crossing the Mystic Figure, Powerhouse, Reproduced courtesy of the Trustees of the Museum of Applied Arts and Sciences, Sydney **12-14.** Mountford-Sheard Collection, Special Collections, State Library of South Australia **12-15.** Courtesy Department of Library

Index

Accent, 198
Acquired culture, 32
Action chains, 258-61
Actor, 218
Adaptation, 309
Adolescence, 32
Adoption, 98
Adult, becoming, 32-33
Adultery, 51, 52, 96, 239
Adulthood
  achieving Hopi, 156
  personal development in, 33
Aesthetics, 204, 210-12
Affect, 204
Affines, 88, 156, 161
Ageism, 71
Aggression, 134-38
  confused with sex, 186
Aggressive drive, 134-35
Aging, 33-34, 41, 169
Agnatic collateral groups, 97-98
Agnatic descent link, 95
Agnatic lineal kinship groups, 94
Agnatic link, 87
Agonistic behavior, 135
Agribusiness, 292-93
Agricultural Revolution, 314
Agriculture, 114
  diffusion, 265-66
  plow, 117-18
  slash and burn, 120-21
  slavery in, 179
  and Third World, 292-93
AIDS, 307
Airport culture, 294
Akiga's Story (Akiga), 37
Alcoholics Anonymous, 297
Allocation, four modes, 125
Alpha male, 136
American Medical Association, 307
American Revolution, 161, 300
Anderson, Barbara Gallatin, 36
Anglo-Saxons, 93, 145, 273
Animals
  communication of, 194-95
  family-like arrangements of, 73-74
Anthropology, 9
  business, 307-8
  and cultural brokerage, 303
  ecological, 119
  economic, 122
  fieldwork in, 4-5
  forensic, 183
  four fields of, 7-9
  and learning, 4
  medical, 303-7
  practicing, 10, 303-8
  and race, 183-84

visionary, 10, 303, 308-14
Aphorism, 221
Applied anthropology, 9
Aranda, 52-53, 228-29
Arbiter and arbitration, 147
Archaeology, 9
Arendt, Hannah, 167
Aristotle, 51, 188
Art
  commercial, 203
  and culture, 201-12
  political, 203
  propagandistic, 203-4
  qualities of, 206-7
  religious, 204
  tourist, 212
Ashanti, 75, 90-91
Assertive behavior, 135
Assumptions, lurking, defined, 80
Atheism, of Buddhism, 248
Atosi, 304
Audience, 218
  of folktales, 222
  mass, 19, 314
  as screen, 212-13
Australian aborigines, 244-45, 270
Authority, 134, 167, 164
Automobile industry, 262
Avunculineal descent line, 96
Avunculocal residence, 76
Ayurvedic medicine, 306-7
Azande, 239, 240
Aztec, 242, 271, 283-85, 291

Baganda, 165
Baltic peoples, 166
Band, 73
Bantu, 270
  bureaucracy of, 164-65
Baptists. *See* Hopewell Baptists
Bateson, Gregory, 208-9
Battle, ordeal by, 146
Baule, 210, 211
Bean shooting, Navajo, 247
Bedouin Arabs, 96, 115
  and clientage, 181-82
Behavior, 14
  agonistic (assertive), 135
  animal, 17
  and kinship terms, 90
  strips of, 218, 258
  violent domestic, 184
Behavior: The Control of Perception (Powers), 27
Being, great chain of, 278
Benedict, Ruth, 184
benge, 239
berdache, 54
Bicentric political action mode, 149, 150

Big men, 157-59
Bilocal residence, 76
Biological anthropology, 7
Biological evolution, 267
Birth control, 307. *See also* Contraception
Brahmins
  Boston, 93
  Indian, 193, 194
Bridewealth, 67-68
British East India Company, 273
British West India Company, 273
Bromley, Allen, 302
Brownsville, Texas, Mexican-American
    legends, 224
Brown vs. Board of Education, 184
Buddhism, 248-49
Bulamogi, 165
Bureaucracy, 163-64
  and global culture, 296-97
  reasons for failure of, 165
Bureau of Indian Affairs, 156
Bush, George, 302
Bushmen. *See* San
Bush-rangers, 283
Business anthropology, 307-8

Cake of custom, 216
Capital
  as production factor, 122, 124-25
Capitalism
  mercantile, 270
  modern, 273-75
  Western, 124-25
Cargo cults, Melanesian, 288, 290-91
Caribbean region, 56, 183, 242, 271
Caste
  and American ranking system, 177-78
  compared with medieval European estate
        system, 175
  Indian, 173-75
Category, social, 22
Centerman. *See* Big men
Ceremonial groups, as government, 155-57
Césaire, Aimé, 280
Cherokee peace and war chiefs, 160-61
Chicamauga, 161
Chiefdoms, Polynesian, 161-63
Child abuse, 184
Child labor, under capitalism, 274
Children, sales of, 180
China
  footbinding, 117-18
  kinship groups in, 92
  political system, 150
  pseudofamilies, 100
  slavery in, 179, 180-81
Chomsky, Noam, 199
Church of England, 72

Industrial Revolution, 118, 262, 263, 272, 273, 297, 314
Industrial society, work types, listed, 111
Inequality, 172
    attitudes creating, 182-88
    beyond, 188
    under capitalism, 274
    and pariahs, 182
    range of
        in slavery, 181
Inis Beag, 49-50
Institutions of rank, 172-73
Insurance, unemployment, 169
Interaction
    and learning of culture, 30-31
    within class
        and American class system, 177
Interest group, and community and settlement, 100-102
International law, 151
Interviewing, in fieldwork, 39, 41
Invention, 262-65
Invocation, 237, 238
Iroquois, 76, 78, 89, 90
Isabella, Queen, 271
Islam, 239. See also Muslims
Isoma ritual, 230-31
Ituri Forest, 114

Japan, 175, 179
Jati, 173
Jesuits, and Yaqui, 286. See also Missionaries
Jews and Jewish religion, 72, 184, 239
John, King, 148
Joint-stock companies, 273
Jokes, 221, 225
Jokes and Their Relation to the Unconscious (Freud), 225
Jones, Eric M., 311
Jukun, 14
Jural descent, 95

Kachina cult, 156
Kalahari Desert, 114
Kanto Quake (1923), 294
Kanuri Muslims, 72
Karma, 249
Kastenbaum, Robert, 34
Keil, Charles, 204, 205, 224
Keller, Helen, 195-96
Kennedy, John F., 202
Khoikhoi, 278
Kin, and homicide incidence, 143
Kinfolk of the head, 93
Kings Canyon National Park, 246
Kinship
    fictive, 98-100
    kinds of, 86-88
    linked with behavior, 90
    metaphoric use of, 99-100
    primate principle of, 17
    removal under slavery, 180, 181
Kinship chains, 95
Kinship groups, 92-100
Kinship terms, 31, 88-92
Korean Presbyterian Church, 251
Kshatriya, 174

Kwakiutl, 129, 130
Kula, 128-29

Labor
    capitalist exploitations of, 274
    division of
        and age, 111
        and bias against women, 184
        domestic, 78
        economist's view of, 113
        by gender or sex, 60, 114-15, 116, 117, 118-19, 145, 314
        in herding societies, 115
        in hunting and gathering societies, 114-15
        in plow agriculture, 117
        as production factor, 122
Labor unions, 118
Land, as production factor, 122-24
Landers, Ann, 186
Landowners and nobility, in medieval Europe, 175
Land rights, 175
Land tenure, 175
Language, 194
    and culture, 198-201
    generative, 199
    and power, 201
    as symbol system, 197
Language communities, 200, 201
Lapps, 115
Latifundia, 272
Law
    and conflict management, 139, 140, 141-43
    ancient Egyptian, 163
Leadership
    of big man, 157-59
    centralized, 159-63
    in lineage systems, 157
    Navajo, 155
    and religion and powers, 155
Learned culture, 32
Learning, 4, 14
    stimulus-response model, 27
Learning deposit, 28
Leewenhoek, Anton van, 51
Legal institutions, basis of, 141
Legend, 221, 224-25
Legitimacy. See Authority
Le Golif, 56
Leif Erikkson, 269
Lenin, Vladimir, 167, 204
Leonardo da Vinci, 263
Leopard-skin chief mediator, Nuer, 146-47, 151
Levine, Nancy, 36, 80-81
levirate, 70-71
Liberia, 145-46, 186
Life
    as changed by culture, 11-14
    journey through a, 29-34
Life course, as trajectory, 261
Life insurance, 70
Life tasks
    human, 19
    primate, 17
Lineages, 95-96
    as government, 157

Lineal kinship, 86-88
Linguistics, 9
Linneaus, 15
Linton, Ralph, 217
Literacy, 19, 32, 220
Loa, 241-42
Loyalty, and bureaucracy, 167
Lozi, 148
Lumholtz, Carl, 242
Luo, 70

Magna Carta, 148
Mahala and Putir myth (Dayak), 228
Mahayana Buddhism, 248
Maintenance, 113
Maintenance work, modern, 265
Malinowski, Bronislaw, 37, 52, 67
Mammals, 15-16, 17, 46
Mana, 161
Maps, 123, 271
Market, 111, 113
    "great transformation" of, 273
Market economy, and Third World, 292-93
Market exchange, 125-26
Marketplace, and market principle, 125-26, 127
Market principle, 125-26, 127, 273
Marriage, 64-72, 78-81
Marx, Karl, 224
Marxism, 275
Masculinity, 56, 58-59, 230, 232
Mass audience, 19, 314
Massachusetts Institute of Technology, 199
Masturbation, 49
Mata Hari, 60
Matelotage, 56
Materialism, of Buddhism, 248
Matricentric family, 64
Matrilineal chains, 87-88
Matrilineal kinship groups, 94
Matrilineal lineages, 96
Matrilocal residence, 75
Matter, as changed by culture, 11-14
Maximization, 124
Mediation, as conflict resolution, 146-47
Medical anthropology, 303-7
Medical doctrines, 306-7
Medicine, and religion, 305-6
Medieval Europe, estate system of, 175, 176, 177
Mehinaku, 50, 53, 54
Melanesia
    big man governments of, 157-59
    cargo cults of, 288, 290-91
Men
    and reproduction, 53-54, 56
    concept of men's work, 118
    and dependent women, 117-18
    Hopi societies of, 156
    and idea of paternity, 80
    and polygyny, 78, 80
    and power-sex confusion, 60
    procreative functions of, 52
    symbolic menstruation, 50, 53
    and violence against women and children, 184
Menes, 163

Index

Taxonomy, 15
Tay-Sachs disease, 183
Technology, and European expansion, 270-71
Television, 209, 221, 287, 295, 302-3, 309, 314
Tenochtitlan, 284, 285
Territoriality, 16, 136
Textor, Robert B., 310
Tewa Pueblo, 150
Theocracies, 162
Theravada Buddhism, 248, 249
Thing, Icelandic, 147-48
Third World, 291-93, 308
Thompson, Michael, 267
Thought, defined, 29
Tiananmen Square, 303
Tibetan Nepalese, 80-81
Time, 308
Tiv, 5, 15, 26, 35, 37-38, 172
  akombo and *tsav*, 240
  art, dance, and music, 204-6
  correction among, 142
  co-wives, 79
  double descent, 96-97
  geographical concepts of, 123-24
  gesturing of, 197
  grammar of, 199
  and government, 159
  as horticulturists, 116
  households of, 76-77
  and incest taboo, 65
  kin terms, 91-92
  language of, 29, 31
  levirate form of, 70-71
  lineage, 164, 264
  marriage rules of, 69
  medicine, 303-4, 307
  and menstruation, 50
  metaphoric kinship, 99
  money system of, 125, 128
  moots of, 148, 157
  pawns among, 181
  scarification, 202
  stories, 222-24
  and truth words, 227
  wife exchange, 127-28
Tiwi, 66, 69
tjurunga, 52
Toda, 81
Tokai Bank, 294-95
Tolstoy, Leo, 220
Tonga, 162
Tools, defined, 7
Totemism, 236
Trade routes, 269
Trajectories, 261-62
Transhumance, 115-16
Transition rites, 237
Trap, social, 252, 258, 260-61
Triad, 22, 98, 99
Tripartitions, Warner's, 176
Trobriand Islands, 37, 50, 51, 52, 67
  reciprocity in, 125, 128-29
Truth, concepts of, 226-27
Tucanini, 282
Turner, Victor, 218

Tyranny
  avoidance by Native Americans, 160-61
  and centralized government, 160
  Soga protection from, 165

Underdevelopment, 291-93
Unemployment, 260
Unemployment insurance, 169
Unicentric political action mode, 149
Unification Church, 251-52
Unilineal descent groups, 95-96
Unilocal residence, 76
Unmarried people, 66
United Nations Food and Agricultural Organization, 293
United States
  adolescence, 32-33
  adoption, 98
  aging, 34, 41
  anticontraceptive prejudice, 54
  Army 14
  big man fascination, 159
  child rearing, 32, 33
  class system variables, 177
  clientage in Northwest, 182
  and couvade, 54
  crime in, 143
  cultural traits ranking system, 175-78
  culture hero stories, 224
  economy of, 122, 127
  ethnicity, 166, 186, 187
  family violence in, 186
  flag symbolism of, 198
  gender determination in, 54
  government responsibility structure, 169
  hierarchy in schools, 136
  household patterns, 76-77, 82
  ideas of art, 201
  killing in, 142
  kinship systems, 93
  life insurance in, 70
  marriage expectations in, 69
  menstrual taboo of, 50
  and monogamous nuclear family, 81-82
  one-parent households of, 76, 82
  political system, 150
  preachers as shamans, 244
  prison homosexuality, 99-100
  racism of, 184
  religious rites and values, 226, 239
  reproductive beliefs, 52
  resource consumption, 110
  as sexuality-negative culture, 49
Untouchables
  Indian, 174
  as useful pariahs, 182
Uterine collateral groups, 97-98
Uterine descent link, 95
Uterine lineal kinship groups, 94
Uterine link, 87
Uxorilocal residence, 75

Vaisha, 174
Values orientation, and American class system, 177
Vancouver Island, 129
Varna, 174

Vietnam War, 252, 297
Villon, François, 259
Violence, male, against women and children, 184
Virilocal residence, 75
Visionary anthropology, 303, 308-14
  and policy science, 311
  prediction and chaos, 309-11
Vodou, 240-42
Voodoo. *See* Vodou

Wager of battle, as conflict resolution, 146
Wallace, A. F. C., 78
Ward, Martha C., 40
Warfare
  Cherokee red chiefs of, 160-61
  and diplomacy, 139-41, 151
  and Greek city-states, 260
  and lineage systems, 157
  and slavery, 180
  technological advances for, 271
Warhol, Andy, 207
Warner, Lloyd, 176
Warrior cultures, 139
Warrior-like professions, 139
Washington, George, 224
Wealth of Nations (Smith), 273
Weddings, 64, 67-68, 100
Weiner, Annette, 52
Weeping woman legend, 224-25
Whitney, Eli, 263
Whorf, Benjamin Lee, 201
Widowers, 64, 66, 69, 71
Widows and widowhood, 64, 66, 69-71
Wilson, Woodrow, 166
Witchcraft, 246-47
Witchery, 247
Witches, 239, 240
Wives
  exchanges of, 127-28
  as universal homicide victims, 143
Wizardry, 247
Wolf, 271
Women
  as backup gender, 60
  under capitalism, 274
  credit institutions, 308
  dependence on men, 117-18
  Gisu, 232
  importance in horticultural societies, 116-17
  and inventions, 263, 265
  Mexican-American weeping legend, 224-25
  Ndembu, 230-31
  nineteenth-century redefinition of, 118
  as political go-betweens in small-scale societies, 151
  and polygyny, 78-80
  procreative rights of, 51
  in Tiv stories, 222-24
  wages of, 119
  and work-related inequality, 188
Women's work, concept of, 111, 118, 184
Women's World Banking, 308
Work, 110-19
  modern service, 296
  nonproductive and productive, 111
Work groups and patterns, 307

About the Author

PAUL BOHANNAN is about as American as you can get. If you draw a line from Seattle to Miami and another from San Diego to Portland, Maine, they cross in Lincoln, Nebraska—that's where he was born. But he didn't stay there long. His father was an engineer who moved a lot, so he doesn't really have a hometown—or didn't until he found Three Rivers, California, just after he retired.

Bohannan gave to the U.S. Army during World War II the five years he would otherwise have given to Greenwich Village (or, in a later era, would have given to Big Sur and Katmandu). He got into anthropology at the University of Arizona because he had to take a required social science course and discovered that he had more talent for anthropology than for chemistry (he tried that) or English literature (he tried that too) or music (he made a living playing piano in a jazz band just after he got out of high school—just long enough to discover that he didn't have any talent).

A Rhodes scholarship to Oxford robbed him of a slot as a graduate student at Harvard, but gave him an opportunity to study with E. E. Evans-Pritchard, Meyer Fortes, and Max Gluckman. Add to that American teachers like Edward Spicer and Emil Haury and you have a pretty broad base.

It took Bohannan four years of classes at the Chicago Institute for Psychoanalysis (1969-1973) to discover that he didn't want to be a psychoanalyst. It took him two years of classes in the Professional Writing Program at the University of Southern California (1986-1988) to find out that he would rather write anthropology than fiction.

Photos by Vikram Jayanti

Field work for three years among the Tiv of Nigeria (1949-1953) is probably the most formative thing that ever happened to him, but he learned a lot from field studies of divorcing people in San Francisco (1963-1964 and again in 1980-1981), stepfamilies in San Diego (1973-1974), and old men living in city-center hotels in San Diego (1974-1976). He taught five years at Oxford, then came home and taught at Princeton, Northwestern, and the University of California/ Santa Barbara. He did five years as Dean of Social Science and Communication at the University of Southern California before he retired to write this book and—with a little luck— several others.